culture

What makes *CULTURE* special?

What's Inside
Engaging pedagogy designed to be eye-catching and visually appealing can be found throughout the text.

As You READ
As You Read introduces the reading with important questions discussed in the chapter.

STUDY TIP
Study Tips call attention to important concepts and suggest effective strategies for learning and studying.

Pop Quiz
Pop Quiz helps students to master key chapter material.

CULTURE THINK
CULTURE Think questions throughout each chapter prompt students to think more deeply about a topic discussed in the text.

POP CULTURE
Pop CULTURE teaches anthropological concepts through popular culture familiar to students.

CULTURE Clips connects students to anthropological videos through a smartphone or any mobile phone with a camera.

Anthropology Works
Anthropology Works explores the impact of anthropology on different professions, such as teaching, counseling, and marketing.

Get Involved sections push students to actively participate in anthropological issues that are relevant to them.

Did You Know provides short, engaging nuggets of information relevant to the chapter.

Did You Know

For REVIEW
For Review summarizes the key points of each chapter in an easy-to-read format.

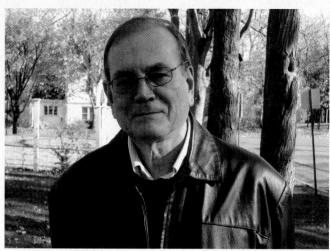

Name: Lisa Gezon

Education: My B.A. in Anthropology is from Albion College in Albion, MI. I got my Ph.D. from the University of Michigan (Conrad Kottak was my advisor).

Occupation: Professor, mother

Hobbies: I like to do yoga with friends, and I sing in a women's chorus. I like to swim, bicycle, take walks, and pet my cats.

Favorite places to travel: As an anthropologist, I enjoy traveling anywhere, but I especially like Madagascar, France, and Costa Rica.

Family: I am the mother of two boys (12 and 13 years old) and aunt to four nephews.

Last books read: The Gift by Hafiz; Little Bee by Chris Cleave; Far From the Madding Crowd by Thomas Hardy

Favorite films: The Color of Paradise, Mississippi Masala, 8 Mile

Latest accomplishment: One month of fieldwork in Madagascar in June, 2010

Favorite quote: "A little learning is a dang'rous thing; Drink deep, or taste not the Pierian spring" —Alexander Pope, 1711, from "An Essay on Criticism"

Name: Conrad Kottak

Education: Columbia College and Columbia University

Occupation: Professor, Anthropologist

Hobbies: Swimming, movies, theater, television

Favorite places to travel: Brazil, New York, San Francisco, London, Paris

Family: Married with two adult children and three grandchildren

Last books read: Person or Persons Unknown by Bruce Alexander

Favorite films: Star Wars (the original one) and Casablanca

Latest accomplishment: Finishing the fourth edition of On Being Different: Diversity and Multiculturalism in the North American Mainstream

Favorite quote: "Never doubt that a small group of concerned citizens can change the world. Indeed, it's the only thing that ever has." —Margaret Mead

Ch. 5
LANGUAGE AND
COMMUNICATION

Brief Contents

^
Ch. 8
FAMILIES, KINSHIP,
AND MARRIAGE

Ch. 12 >
ETHNICITY
AND RACE

Ch. 6 >
MAKING A LIVING

CULTURE

VICE PRESIDENT, EDITORIAL **Michael Ryan**

EDITORIAL DIRECTOR **William R. Glass**

SENIOR SPONSORING EDITOR **Gina Boedeker**

DIRECTOR OF DEVELOPMENT **Rhona Robbin**

DEVELOPMENT EDITOR **Emily Pecora**

EDITORIAL COORDINATOR **Brittany Pogue-Mohammed**

TEXT PERMISSIONS EDITOR **Karyn L. Morrison**

MARKETING MANAGER **Patrick Brown**

MARKETING SPECIALIST **Joyce Chiu**

MEDIA PROJECT MANAGERS **Jennifer Barrick & Bethuel Jabez**

PRODUCTION EDITOR **Leslie Racanelli**

MANUSCRIPT EDITOR **Judith Brown**

DESIGN MANAGER **Jeanne Schreiber**

INTERIOR DESIGNER **Linda Robertson**

COVER DESIGNER **Irene Morris**

ART MANAGER **Robin Mouat**

PHOTO RESEARCH COORDINATOR **Nora Agbayani**

PHOTO RESEARCHERS **Judy Mason & Toni Michaels/PhotoFind, LLC**

BUYER **Louis Swaim**

COMPOSITOR **TBH Typecast, Inc.**

PRINTER **Quad/Graphics**

COVER IMAGE **Front cover: © Colin Anderson/Blend Images/Corbis; back cover: © Comstock Images/Alamy**

This book is printed on acid-free paper.

1 2 3 4 5 6 7 8 9 0 QDB/QDB 9 8 7 6 5 4 3 2 1

ISBN: 978-0-07-803502-9
MHID: 0-07-803502-3

Library of Congress Control Number: 2010942152

The Internet addresses listed in the text were accurate at the time of publication. The inclusion of a Web site does not indicate an endorsement by the authors or McGraw-Hill, and McGraw-Hill does not guarantee the accuracy of the information presented at these sites.

www.mhhe.com

What Is Anthropology?   1

Culture 20

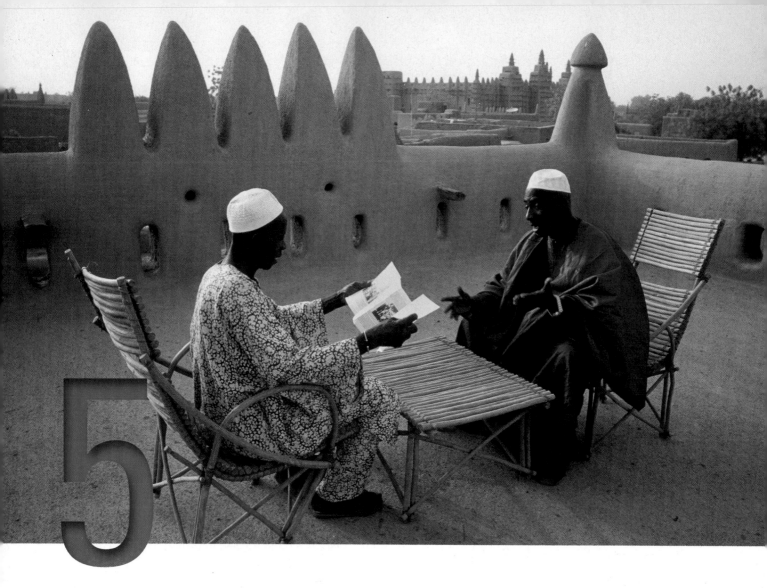

Language and Communication   78

Making a Living   98

Political Systems   118

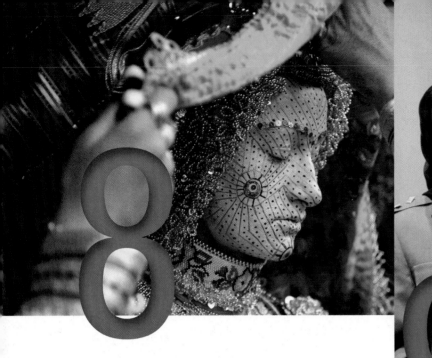

8

Families, Kinship, and Marriage   140

9

Gender   162

10

Religion 184

11

The World System and Colonialism   202

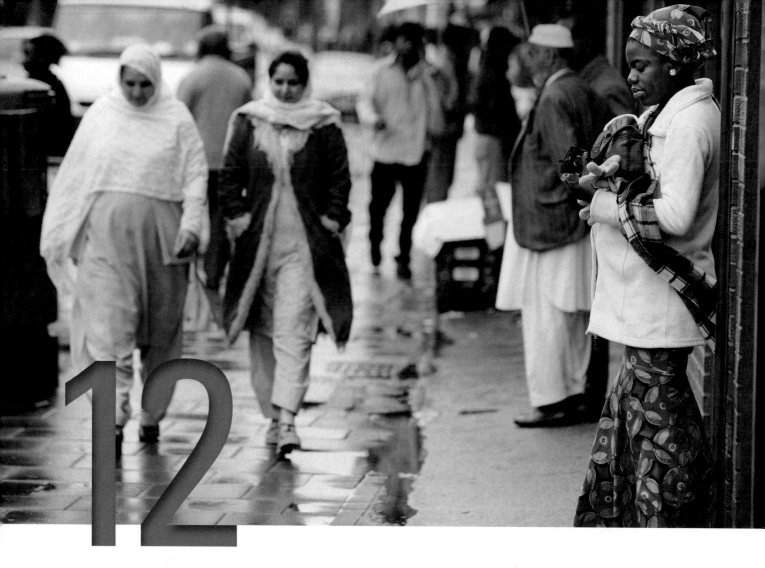

12

Ethnicity and Race   224

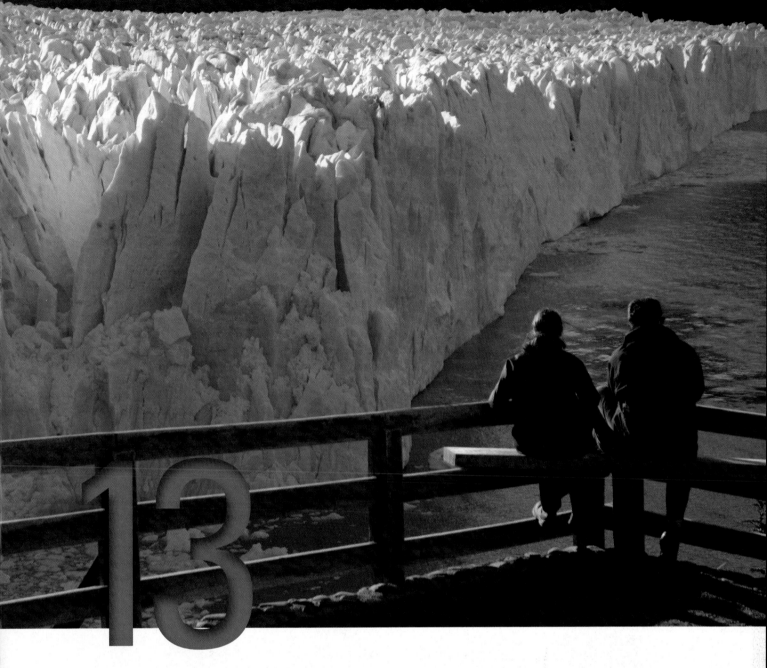

Anthropology's Role in a Globalizing World   245

1

WHAT IS ANTHROPOLOGY?

UNDERSTANDING OURSELVES

When you were young, your parents might have told you that drinking milk and eating vegetables would help you grow up "big and strong." They probably didn't as readily recognize the role that *culture* plays in shaping bodies, personalities, and personal health. If nutrition matters in growth, so, too, do cultural guidelines. Our bodies are affected by the kinds of work we do, the homes we live in, the ways we play and relax, the gender roles of males and females, our religion, and the ways we relate to our family, friends, and neighbors. Culture is an environmental force that affects our development as much as do nutrition, heat, cold, and altitude.

Think about the phrases and sentences you would use to describe yourself in a personal ad or on a networking site—your likes and dislikes, hobbies and habits. How many of these descriptors would be the same if you had been born in a different place or time? We usually think about "who we are" as a collection of set characteristics and tendencies, but this idea is as culturally determined as any of the traits we might put on an "about me" list. In other cultures, people might describe themselves by referencing their relationship to one or more gods, their success as a hunter, or their roles as family members.

Among scholarly disciplines, anthropology stands out as the field that provides the cross-cultural test. How much would we know about human behavior, thought, and feeling if we studied only our own kind? What if our entire understanding of human behavior were based on analysis of questionnaires filled out by college students in Oregon? One culture, age group, or gender can't tell us everything we need to know about what it means to be human. Often culture is "invisible," and thus unexamined, until it is placed in comparison to another culture. For example, to appreciate how watching television affects us as human beings, we need to study not just North America today but some other place—and perhaps also some other time (such as Brazil in the 1980s; see Kottak 1990b). The cross-cultural test is fundamental to the anthropological approach, which orients this textbook.

- What is anthropology, and how does it differ from other fields that study human beings?

- How useful is the race concept in understanding human diversity?

- What are the four subfields of anthropology?

>> The Cross-Cultural Perspective

"That's just human nature." "People are pretty much the same all over the world." Such opinions, which we hear in conversations, in the mass media, and in a dozen scenes in daily life, promote the erroneous idea that people in other countries have the same desires, feelings, values, and aspirations that we do. Such statements proclaim that because people are essentially the same, they are eager to receive the ideas, beliefs, values, institutions, practices, and products of an expansive North American culture. Often this assumption turns out to be wrong.

ethnography Fieldwork in a particular culture.

Anthropology offers a broader view—a distinctive comparative, cross-cultural perspective. Most people think that anthropologists study nonindustrial societies, and they do—but that's not all they do. Although Lisa Gezon has done some research on sustainable agriculture and water use in the state of Georgia, USA, she has spent most of her research time in Madagascar, a large island off the southeast coast of Africa. With Conrad Kottak as her graduate school adviser, she first studied how people in a local chiefdom responded to forest conservation. In her next study, she traced the drug *khat* as it went from farmers' fields, into the hands of traders, and finally into the mouths of urban consumers. Conrad Kottak's research also has taken him to remote villages in Brazil and Madagascar. In Brazil he sailed with fishers in simple sailboats on Atlantic waters. Among Madagascar's Betsileo people he worked in rice fields and took part in ceremonies in which he entered tombs to rewrap the corpses of decaying ancestors.

Anthropology, which originated as the study of nonindustrial peoples, is a comparative science that now extends to all societies, ancient and modern, simple and complex. Most of the other social sciences tend to focus on a single society, usually an industrial nation such as the United States or Canada. Anthropology offers a unique cross-cultural perspective, constantly comparing the customs of one society with those of others.

To become a cultural anthropologist, one normally does **ethnography** (the first-

In Mozambique's Gaza province, the Dutch ethnographer Janine van Vugt (red hair) sits on a mat near reed houses, talking to local women.

hand, personal study of local settings). Ethnographic fieldwork usually entails spending a year or more in another society, living with the local people and learning about their way of life. No matter how much the ethnographer discovers about the society, he or she remains an alien there. That experience of alienation has a profound impact. Having learned to respect other customs and beliefs, anthropologists can never forget that there is a wider world. There are normal ways of thinking and acting other than our own.

>> Human Adaptability

Anthropologists study human beings wherever and whenever they find them—in a Turkish café, a Mesopotamian tomb, or a North American shopping mall. Anthropology is the exploration of human diversity in time and space. Anthropology studies the whole of the human condition: past, present, and future; biology, society, language, and culture. Of particular interest is the diversity that comes through human adaptability.

Humans are among the world's most adaptable animals. In the Andes of South America, people wake up in villages

A culture produces a degree of consistency among members of the same society. Cultural celebrations, such as this Kurdish wedding, are patterned in particular ways based on cultural traditions.

16,000 feet above sea level and then trek 1,500 feet higher to work in tin mines. Tribes in the Australian desert worship animals and discuss philosophy. People survive malaria in the tropics. Men have walked on the moon. The model of the starship *Enterprise* in Washington's Smithsonian Institution symbolizes the desire to "seek out new life and civilizations, to boldly go where no one has gone before." Wishes to know the unknown, control the uncontrollable, and create order out of chaos find expression among all peoples. Creativity, adaptability, and flexibility are basic human attributes, and human diversity is the subject matter of anthropology.

Students often are surprised by the breadth of **anthropology,** which is the study of the human species and its immediate ancestors. Anthropology is a uniquely comparative and **holistic** science. *Holism* refers to the study of the whole of the human condition: past, present, and future; biology, society, language, and culture.

People share *society*—organized life in groups—with other animals, including baboons, wolves, and even ants. Culture, however, is more distinctly human. **Cultures** are traditions and customs, transmitted through learning, that form and guide the beliefs and behavior of the people exposed to them. Children learn such a tradition by growing up in a particular society, through a process called enculturation. Cultural traditions include customs and opinions, developed over the generations, about proper and improper behavior. These traditions answer such questions as: How should we do things? How do we make sense of the world? How do we tell right from wrong? What is right, and what is wrong? A culture produces a degree of consistency in behavior and thought among the people who live in a particular society.

anthropology The study of the human species and its immediate ancestors.

holistic Pertaining to the whole of the human condition, past, present, and future; biology, society, language, and culture.

culture Traditions and customs that govern behavior and beliefs; distinctly human; transmitted through learning.

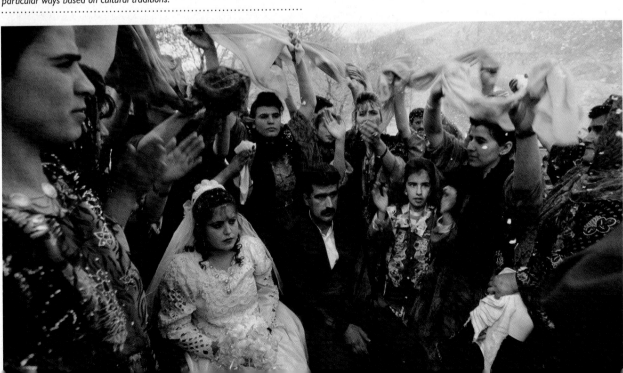

The most critical element of cultural traditions is their transmission through learning rather than through biological inheritance. Culture is not itself biological, but it rests on certain features of human biology. For more than a million years, humans have had at least some of the biological capacities on which culture depends. These abilities are to learn, to think symbolically, to use language, and to employ tools and other products in organizing their lives and adapting to their environments.

Anthropology confronts and ponders major questions of human existence as it explores human biological and cultural diversity in time and space. By examining ancient bones and tools, we unravel the mysteries of human origins. When did our ancestors separate from those remote great-aunts and great-uncles whose descendants are the apes? Where and when did *Homo sapiens* originate? How has our species changed? What are we now, and where are we going? How have changes in culture and society influenced biological change? Our genus, *Homo,* has been changing for more than one million years. Humans continue to adapt and change both biologically and culturally.

adaptation The process by which organisms cope with environmental stresses.

food production Plant cultivation and animal domestication.

general anthropology The field of anthropology as a whole, consisting of cultural, archaeological, biological, and linguistic anthropology.

ADAPTATION, VARIATION, AND CHANGE

Adaptation refers to the processes by which organisms cope with environmental forces and stresses, such as those

CULTURETHINK

How have people adapted to changing economic conditions? Different jobs are available now than were available two generations ago. Talk with people (for example, your grandparents) who sought jobs at an earlier time in history. What kinds of jobs did they see as available? What kind of training did they require? How have things changed for you?

posed by climate and *topography,* or terrains, also called landforms. How do organisms change to fit their environments, such as dry climates or high mountain altitudes? Like other animals, humans use biological means of adaptation. But humans are unique in also having cultural means of adaptation. Table 1.1 summarizes the cultural and biological means that humans use to adapt to high altitudes.

Mountainous terrains pose particular challenges, those associated with high altitude and oxygen deprivation. Consider four ways (one cultural and three biological) in which humans may cope with low oxygen pressure at high altitudes. Illustrating cultural (technological) adaptation would be a pressurized airplane cabin equipped with oxygen masks. There are three ways of adapting biologically to high altitudes: genetic adaptation, long-term physiological adaptation, and short-term physiological adaptation. First, native populations of high-altitude areas, such as the Andes of Peru and the Himalayas of Tibet and Nepal, seem to have acquired certain genetic advantages for life at very high altitudes. The Andean tendency to develop a voluminous chest and lungs probably has a genetic

TABLE 1.1

Forms of Cultural and Biological Adaptation (to High Altitude)

Form of Adaptation	Type of Adaptation	Example
Technology	Cultural	Pressurized airplane cabin with oxygen masks
Genetic adaptation (occurs over generations)	Biological	Larger "barrel chests" of native highlanders
Short-term physiological adaptation (occurs spontaneously when the individual organism enters a new environment)	Biological	Increased heart rate, hyperventilation
Long-term adaptation (occurs during growth and development of the individual organism)	Biological	More efficient respiratory system, to extract oxygen from "thin air"

basis. Second, regardless of their genes, people who grow up at a high altitude become physiologically more efficient there than genetically similar people who have grown up at sea level would be. This illustrates long-term physiological adaptation during the body's growth and development. Third, humans also have the capacity for short-term or immediate physiological adaptation. Thus, when lowlanders arrive in the highlands, they immediately increase their breathing and heart rates. Hyperventilation increases the oxygen in their lungs and arteries. As the pulse also increases, blood reaches their tissues more rapidly. All these varied adaptive responses— cultural and biological— achieve a single goal: maintaining an adequate supply of oxygen to the body.

The Sherpas of Nepal, one of whom is shown here (on the right) with a female trekker, have adapted culturally and biologically to their high altitude environment.

As human history has unfolded, the social and cultural means of adaptation have become increasingly important. In this process, humans have devised diverse ways of coping with the range of environments they have occupied in time and space. The rate of cultural adaptation and change has accelerated, particularly during the past ten thousand years. For millions of years, hunting and gathering of nature's bounty—*foraging*—was the sole basis of human subsistence. It took only a few thousand years, however, for **food production** (the cultivation of plants and domestication of animals), which originated some ten to twelve thousand years ago, to replace foraging in most areas. The first civilizations rose between 6000 and 5000 B.P. ("before the present"—years ago, in this case, five to six thousand years ago). These were large, powerful, and complex societies, such as ancient Egypt, that conquered and governed large geographic areas.

Much more recently, the spread of industrial production has profoundly affected human life. Throughout human history, major innovations have spread at the expense of earlier ones. Each economic revolution has had social and cultural repercussions. Today's global economy and communications link all contemporary people, directly or indirectly, in the modern world system. People must cope with forces generated by progressively larger systems—region, nation, and world. The study of such contemporary adaptations generates new challenges for anthropology: "The cultures of world peoples need to be constantly rediscovered as these people reinvent them in changing historical circumstances" (Marcus and Fischer 1986, p. 24).

>> General Anthropology

The academic discipline of anthropology, also known as **general anthropology,** or "four-field" anthropology, includes four main subdisciplines or subfields. They are sociocultural, archaeological, biological, and linguistic anthropology. (From here on, the shorter term *cultural anthropology* will be used as a synonym for "sociocultural anthropology.") Of the subfields, cultural anthropology has the largest membership. Most departments of anthropology teach courses in all four subfields.

There are historical reasons for the inclusion of four subfields in a single discipline. The origin of anthropol-

CULTURE THINK

What unites the four subdisciplines of anthropology into a single discipline? How might anthropology's diversity—as a discipline that includes biological as well as cultural perspectives, for example—be a strength? How might it be a weakness?

ogy as a scientific field, and of American anthropology in particular, can be traced to the nineteenth century. Early American anthropologists were concerned especially with the history and cultures of the native peoples of North America. Interest in the origins and diversity of Native Americans brought together studies of customs, social life, language, and physical traits. Anthropologists still ponder such questions as: Where did Native Americans come from? How many waves of migration brought them to the New World? What are the linguistic, cultural, and biological links among Native Americans and between them and Asia? (Note that a unified four-field anthropology did not develop in Europe, where the subfields tend to exist separately.)

racial classification The attempt to assign humans to discrete categories (purportedly) based on common ancestry.

There also are logical reasons for the unity of American anthropology. Each subfield considers variation in time and space (that is, in different geographic areas). Cultural and archaeological anthropologists study (among many other topics) changes in social life and customs. Archaeologists use studies of living societies to imagine what life might have been like in the past. Biological anthropologists examine evolutionary changes in physical form, for example, anatomical changes that might have been associated with the origin of tool use or language. Linguistic anthropologists may reconstruct the basics of ancient languages by studying modern ones.

Ely S. Parker, or Ha-sa-no-an-da, was a Seneca Indian who made significant contributions to early anthropology.

The subfields influence each other as anthropologists talk to each other, read books and journals, and meet in professional organizations. Anthropologists share certain key assumptions. Perhaps the most fundamental is the idea that sound conclusions about "human nature" cannot be derived from studying a single population, nation, society, or cultural tradition. A comparative, cross-cultural approach is essential.

General anthropology explores the basics of human biology, society, and culture and considers their interrelations. The four-field approach has been particularly effective in examining the relation between biology (e.g., "race"—see below) and culture. About seventy years ago, the famed anthropologist Ruth Benedict realized, "In World history, those who have helped to build the same

culture are not necessarily of one race, and those of the same race have not all participated in one culture" (Benedict 1940, Ch. 2). This statement is even truer in today's globalizing world. How do contemporary anthropologists deal with issues of human biological diversity and race?

>> Human Biological Diversity and the Race Concept

The photos in this book offer only a glimpse of the range of human biological variation. Additional illustration comes from your own experience. Look around you in your classroom or library, or at the mall or multiplex. Inevitably you'll see people whose ancestors lived in many lands. The first (Native) Americans had to cross a land bridge that once linked Siberia to North America. For later immigrants, perhaps including your own parents or grandparents, the voyage may have been across the sea or overland from nations to the south. They came for many reasons. Some came voluntarily, while others were brought here in chains. The scale of migration in today's world is so vast that millions of people routinely cross national borders or live far from the homelands of their grandparents. Now meeting every day are diverse human beings whose biological features reflect adaptation to a wide range of environments other than the ones they now inhabit. Physical contrasts are evident to anyone. Anthropology's job is to explain them.

Historically, scientists have approached the study of human biological diversity in two main ways: (1) racial classification (now largely abandoned) versus (2) the current explanatory approach, which focuses on understanding specific differences. First we'll consider problems with **racial classification**—the attempt to assign humans to discrete categories (purportedly) based on common ancestry. Then we'll offer some explanations for specific aspects of human biological diversity (in this case, light versus dark skin color). *Biological differences are real, important, and apparent to us all.* Modern scientists find it most productive to seek explanations for this diversity, rather than trying to pigeonhole people into categories called races.

What is race anyway? In theory, a biological race would be a geographically isolated subdivision of a species. (A *species* is a population whose members can interbreed to produce offspring that can live and reproduce.) Such a *subspecies* would be capable of interbreeding with other subspecies of the same species, but it would not actually do so because of its geographic isolation. Some biologists also use "race" to refer to "breeds," as of

Photos, from left to right: an Aymaran woman from Bolivia; a Samburu woman from Kenya; a woman from Guangzhou province, People's Republic of China; a young Norwegian woman with blonde hair and blue eyes.

dogs or roses. Thus, a pit bull and a Chihuahua would be different races of dogs. Such domesticated "races" have been bred by humans for generations. Humanity (*Homo sapiens*) lacks such races because human populations have not been isolated enough from one another to develop into such discrete groups. Nor have humans experienced controlled breeding like that which has created the various kinds of dogs and roses.

A race is supposed to reflect shared *genetic* material (inherited from a common ancestor), but early scholars instead used *phenotypical* traits (usually skin color) for human racial classification. **Phenotype** refers to an organism's evident traits, its "manifest biology"—anatomy and physiology. Humans display hundreds of evident (detectable) physical traits. They range from skin color, hair form, eye color, and facial features (which are visible) to blood groups and enzyme production (which become evident through testing).

Racial classifications based on phenotype raise the problem of deciding which traits are most important. Should races be defined by height, weight, body shape, facial features, teeth, skull form, or skin color? Like their fellow citizens, early European and American scientists gave priority to skin color. Many school books and encyclopedias still proclaim the existence of three great races: the white, the black, and the yellow. This overly simplistic classification was compatible with the political use of race during the colonial period of the late nineteenth and early twentieth centuries. Such a tripartite scheme kept white Europeans neatly separate from their African, Asian, and Native American subjects. Then colonial empires began to break up, and after World War II, scientists began to question established racial categories.

Politics aside, one obvious problem with such racial labels is that they don't accurately describe skin color. "White" people are more pink, beige, or tan than white. "Black" people are various shades of brown, and "yellow" people are tan or beige. These terms also have been dignified by more scientific-*sounding* synonyms—Caucasoid, Negroid, and Mongoloid—which actually have no more of a scientific basis than do white, black, and yellow.

> **phenotype** An organism's evident traits, its "manifest biology"—anatomy and physiology.

It's true also that many human populations don't fit neatly into any one of the three "great races." For example, where does one put the Polynesians? Polynesia is a triangle of South Pacific islands formed by Hawaii to the north, Easter Island to the east, and New Zealand to the southwest. Does the bronze skin color of Polynesians place them with the Caucasoids or the Mongoloids? Some scientists, recognizing this problem, enlarged the original tripartite scheme to include the Polynesian race. Native Americans present an additional problem. Are they red or yellow? Again, some scientists add a fifth race—the red, or Amerindian—to the major racial groups.

Many people in southern India have dark skins, but scientists have been reluctant to classify them with black Africans because of their Caucasoid facial features and hair form. Some, therefore, have created a separate race for these people. What about the Australian aborigines, hunters and gatherers native to the most isolated continent? By skin color, one might place some Native Australians in the same race as tropical Africans. However, similarities to Europeans in hair color (light or reddish) and facial features have led some scientists to classify them as Cauca-

Answers: (left to right): Polynesian, southern Indian, Native Australian, San

soids. But there is no evidence that Australians are closer genetically or historically to either of these groups than they are to Asians. Recognizing this problem, scientists often regard Native Australians as a separate race.

Finally, consider the San ("Bushmen") of the Kalahari Desert in southern Africa. Scientists have perceived their skin color as varying from brown to yellow. Those who regard San skin as yellow have placed them in the same category as Asians. In theory, people of the same race share more recent common ancestry with each other than they do with any others; but there is no evidence for recent common ancestry between San and Asians. More reasonably, the San are classified as members of the Capoid (from the Cape of Good Hope) race, which is seen as being different from other groups inhabiting tropical Africa.

biocultural Referring to the inclusion and combination (to solve a common problem) of both biological and cultural approaches—one of anthropology's hallmarks.

Similar problems arise when any single trait is used as a basis for racial classification. An attempt to use facial features, height, weight, or any other phenotypical trait is fraught with difficulties. For example, consider the Nilotes, natives of the upper Nile region of Uganda and Sudan. Nilotes tend to be tall and to have long, narrow noses. Certain Scandinavians also are tall, with similar noses. Given the distance between their homelands, to classify them as members of the same race makes little sense. There is no reason to assume that Nilotes and Scandinavians are more closely related to each other than either is to shorter (and nearer) populations with different kinds of noses.

Would it be better to base racial classifications on a combination of physical traits? This would avoid some of the problems just discussed, but others would arise. First, skin color, stature, skull form, and facial features (nose form, eye shape, lip thickness) don't go together as a unit. For example, people with dark skin may be tall or short and have hair ranging from straight to very curly. Dark-haired populations may have light or dark skin, along with various skull forms, facial features, and body sizes and shapes. The number of combinations is very

large, and the amount that heredity (versus environment) contributes to such phenotypical traits is often unclear.

There is a final objection to racial classification based on phenotype. The phenotypical characteristics on which races are based supposedly reflect genetic material that is shared and that has stayed the same for long periods. But phenotypical similarities and differences don't necessarily have a genetic basis. Because of changes in the environment that affect individuals during growth and development, the range of phenotypes characteristic of a population may change without any genetic change. There are several examples. In the early twentieth century, the anthropologist Franz Boas (1940/1966) described changes in skull form among the children of Europeans who had migrated to the United States. The reason for this wasn't a change in genes, since the European immigrants tended to marry among themselves. Some of their children had been born in Europe and merely raised in the United States. Something in the new environment, probably in the diet, was producing this change. We know now that changes in average height and weight produced by dietary differences in a few generations are common and have nothing to do with race or genetics.

Anthropology's comparative, biocultural perspective recognizes that environmental factors, including customary diet and other cultural forces, constantly mold human biology. (**Biocultural** refers to the inclusion and combination of both biological and cultural perspectives and approaches to comment on or solve a particular issue or problem.) Culture is a key environmental force in determining how human bodies grow and develop. Cultural traditions promote certain activities and abilities, discourage others, and set standards of physical well-being and attractiveness.

STUDY **TIP**

What's wrong with classifying people by race?

- Human groups haven't been isolated from each other long enough to form genetically separate groups.

- Many individuals, and even whole human populations, don't fit neatly into common racial categories.

- Not all phenotypic differences have a genetic basis.

Bodies—ideal and actual—vary from culture to culture and within one culture over time. Ideal bodies change from generation to generation and, with the influence of the mass media, even from decade to decade. Old movies make it easy for us to study bodies and clothing over time. Such movie stars of the past as Humphrey Bogart and Barbara Stanwyck wore stylish hats and smoked cigarettes. Contemporary American men and women wear baseball caps and lift weights. When asked how he recognized Americans in the street, one European mentioned lifting (of weights, and its effects on the body) and tennis shoes (an item of dress considered inelegant in Europe, but a mainstay of hard-core American touring).

> "The purpose of anthropology is to make the world safe for human differences."
>
> Ruth Benedict

EXPLANATORY APPROACHES TO HUMAN DIVERSITY

Traditional racial classification assumed that biological characteristics were determined by heredity and were stable (immutable) over long periods. We know now that a biological similarity doesn't necessarily indicate recent common ancestry. Dark skin color, for example, can be shared by tropical Africans and Native Australians for reasons other than common ancestry. It is not possible to *define human races* biologically. Still, scientists have made much progress in *explaining* variation in skin color, along with many other expressions of human biological diversity. We shift now from classification to *explanation,* in which natural selection plays a key role.

First recognized by Charles Darwin and Alfred Russel Wallace, **natural selection** is the process by which the forms most fit to survive and reproduce in a given environment—such as the tropics—do so in greater numbers than others in the same population do. Over the years, the less fit organisms die out and the favored types survive by producing more offspring. The role of natural selection

in producing variation in skin color illustrates the explanatory approach to human biological diversity. Comparable explanations have been provided for many other aspects of human biological variation.

Melanin, the primary determinant of human skin color, is a chemical substance manufactured in the epidermis, or outer skin layer. The melanin cells of darker-skinned people produce more and larger granules of melanin than do those of lighter-skinned people. By screening out ultraviolet (uv) radiation from the sun, melanin offers protection against a variety of maladies, including sunburn and skin cancer.

Before the sixteenth century, most of the world's very dark skinned populations lived in the **tropics,** a belt extending about 23 degrees north and south of the equator, between the Tropic of Cancer and the Tropic of Capricorn. The association between dark skin color and a tropical habitat existed throughout the Old World, where humans and their ancestors have lived for millions of years. The darkest populations of Africa evolved not in shady equatorial forests but in sunny open grassland, or savanna, country.

Outside the tropics, skin color tends to be lighter. Moving north in Africa, for example, there is a gradual transition from dark brown to medium brown. Average skin color continues to lighten as one moves through the Middle East, into southern Europe, through central Europe, and to the north. South of the tropics skin color also is lighter. In the Americas, by contrast, tropical populations don't have very dark skin. This is because the settlement of the New World, by light-skinned Asian ancestors of Native Americans, was relatively recent, probably dating back no more than eighteen thousand years.

How, aside from migrations, can we explain the geographic distribution of human skin color? Natural selection provides an answer. In the tropics, intense UV radiation poses a series of threats that make light skin color an adaptive disadvantage. First, UV radiation can cause severe sunburn, which aside from discomfort can lead to vulnerabilities in the body. By damaging sweat glands, sunburn reduces the body's ability to perspire and thus to regulate its own temperature (thermoregulation). Sunburn also can increase susceptibility to disease. Yet another disadvantage of having light skin color in the tropics is that exposure to UV radiation can cause skin cancer (Blum 1961). Melanin, nature's own sunscreen, confers a selective advantage (i.e., a

natural selection Originally formulated by Charles Darwin and Alfred Russel Wallace; the process by which nature selects the forms most fit to survive and reproduce in a given environment, such as the tropics.

tropics Geographic belt extending about 23 degrees north and south of the equator, between the Tropic of Cancer (north) and the Tropic of Capricorn (south).

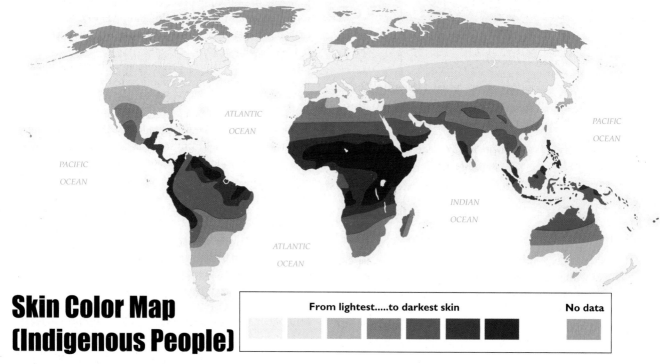

Skin Color Map (Indigenous People)

| From lightest.....to darkest skin | No data |

Before the sixteenth century, most of the world's very dark skinned populations lived in the tropics, a belt extending about 23 degrees north and south of the equator. Outside the tropics, skin color tends to be lighter.

Source: G. Chaplin, "Geographic Distribution of Environmental Factors Influencing Human Skin Coloration," *American Journal of Physical Anthropology* 125:292–302, 2004; map updated in 2007.

better chance to survive and reproduce) on darker-skinned people living in the tropics because it helps protect them from sunburn and skin cancer.

Another selective factor in the geographic distribution of human skin color relates to the manufacture (synthesis) of vitamin D in the body. Years ago, W. F. Loomis (1967) focused on the role of UV radiation in stimulating the manufacture of vitamin D by the human body. The unclothed human body can produce its own vitamin D when exposed to sufficient sunlight. However, in a cloudy environment that also is so cold that people have to dress themselves much of the year (such as northern Europe, where very light skin color evolved), clothing interferes with the body's manufacture of vitamin D. The ensuing shortage of vitamin D diminishes the absorption of calcium in the intestines. A nutritional disease known as rickets, which softens and deforms the bones, may develop. In women, deformation of the pelvic bones from rickets can interfere with childbirth. In cold northern areas, light skin color maximizes the absorption of UV radiation and the synthesis of vitamin D by the

few parts of the body that are exposed to direct sunlight. There has been selection against dark skin color in northern areas because melanin screens out UV radiation.

This natural selection continues today: East Asians who have migrated recently from India and Pakistan to northern areas of the United Kingdom have a higher incidence of rickets and osteoporosis (also related to vitamin D and calcium deficiency) than the general British population. A related illustration involves Eskimos (Inuit) and other indigenous inhabitants of northern Alaska and northern Canada. According to Nina Jablonski (quoted in Iqbal 2002), "Looking at Alaska, one would think that the native people should be pale as ghosts." One reason they aren't is that they haven't inhabited this region very long in terms of geological time. Even more important, their traditional diet, which is rich in seafood, including fish oils, supplies sufficient vitamin D so as to make a reduction in pigmentation unnecessary. However, and again illustrating natural selection at work today, "when these people don't eat their aboriginal diets of fish and marine mammals, they suffer tremendously high rates of vitamin D-deficiency diseases such as rickets in children and osteoporosis in adults" (Jablonski quoted in Iqbal 2002). Far from being immutable, skin color can become an evolutionary liability very quickly.

According to Jablonski and George Chaplin (2000), another key factor explaining the geographic distribution of skin color involves the effects of UV radiation on folate, an essential nutrient that the human body manufactures from folic acid. Folate is needed for cell division and the production of new DNA. Pregnant women require large

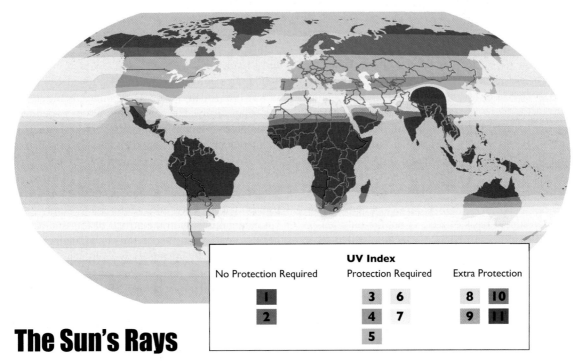

The Sun's Rays

UV Index

No Protection Required	Protection Required		Extra Protection	
1	3	6	8	10
2	4	7	9	11
	5			

This color-coded map of the world shows the mean annual UV radiation level in 2003, with purple designating the lowest radiation levels, and red designating the highest. How does this data fit with the skin color map on page 10?

amounts of folate to support rapid cell division in the embryo, and there is a direct connection between folate and individual reproductive success. Folate deficiency causes neural tube defects (NTDs) in human embryos. NTDs are marked by the incomplete closure of the neural tube, so the spine and spinal cord fail to develop completely. One NTD, anencephaly (with the brain an exposed mass), results in stillbirth or death soon after delivery. With spina bifida, another NTD, survival rates are higher, but babies have severe disabilities, including paralysis. NTDs are the second-most-common human birth defect after cardiac abnormalities. Today, women of reproductive age are advised to take folate supplements to prevent serious birth defects such as spina bifida.

Natural sunlight and UV radiation destroy folate in the human body. Because melanin, as we have seen, protects against UV hazards, such as sunburn and its consequences, dark skin coloration is adaptive in the tropics. Now we see that melanin also is adaptive because it conserves folate in

Rickets, based on a significant vitamin D deficiency, can lead to softening of the bones, which may result in bow legs as illustrated by the child shown in this nineteenth century photo.

the human body and thus protects against NTDs, which are much more common in light-skinned than in darker-skinned populations (Jablonski and Chaplin 2000). Studies confirm that Africans and African Americans have a low incidence of severe folate deficiency, even among individuals with marginal nutritional status. Folate also plays a role in another process that is central to reproduction, spermatogenesis—the production of sperm. In mice and rats, folate deficiency can cause male sterility; it may well play a similar role in humans.

Today, of course, cultural alternatives to biological adaptation permit light-skinned people to survive in the tropics and darker-skinned people to live in the far north. People can clothe themselves and seek shelter from the sun; they can use artificial sunscreens if they lack the natural protection that melanin provides. Dark-skinned people living in the north can, indeed must, get vitamin D from their diet or take supplements. Today, pregnant women are routinely advised to take folic acid or folate supplements as a hedge against NTDs. Even so, light skin color still is correlated with a higher incidence of spina bifida. Jablonski and Chaplin (2000) explain variation in human skin color as resulting from a balancing act between the evolutionary needs to (1) protect against all UV hazards (favoring dark skin in the tropics) and (2) have an adequate supply of vitamin D (favoring lighter skin outside the tropics).

This discussion of skin color shows that common ancestry, the presumed basis of race, is not the only reason for biological similarities. Natural selection, still at work today, makes a major contribution to variations in human skin color, as well as to many other human biological differences and similarities.

cultural anthropology The study of human society and culture; describes, analyzes, interprets, and explains social and cultural similarities and differences.

ethnology The theoretical, comparative study of society and culture; compares cultures in time and space.

>> The Subdisciplines of Anthropology

CULTURAL ANTHROPOLOGY

The study of human society and culture, known as **cultural anthropology,** is the subfield that describes, analyzes, interprets, and explains social and cultural similarities and differences. To study and interpret cultural diversity, cultural anthropologists engage in two kinds of activity: ethnography (based on fieldwork) and ethnology (based on cross-cultural comparison). Ethnography provides an account of a particular community, society, or culture. During ethnographic fieldwork, the ethnographer gathers data that he or she organizes, describes, analyzes, and interprets to build and present that account, which may be in the form of a book, article, or film. Traditionally, ethnographers have lived in small communities and studied local behavior, beliefs, customs, social life, economic activities, politics, and religion (see Wolcott 2008).

The anthropological perspective derived from ethnographic field work often differs radically from that of economics or political science. Those fields focus on national and official organizations and policies and often on elites. The groups that anthropologists traditionally have studied usually have been relatively poor and powerless. Ethnographers often observe discriminatory practices directed toward such people, who experience food shortages, dietary deficien-

President Barack Obama and his mother, Ann Dunham, who was a cultural and applied anthropologist, in an undated photo from the 1960s.

cies, and other aspects of poverty. Political scientists tend to study programs that national planners develop, while anthropologists discover how these programs work on the local level.

Cultures are not isolated. As noted by Franz Boas (1940/1966) many years ago, contact between neighboring tribes always has existed and has extended over enormous areas. Human populations construct their cultures in interaction with one another, and not in isolation (Wolf 1982, p. ix). Villagers increasingly participate in regional, national, and world events. Exposure to external forces comes through the mass media, migration, and modern transportation. City and nation increasingly invade local communities with the arrival of tourists, development agents, government and religious officials, and political candidates. Such linkages are prominent components of regional, national, and international systems of politics, economics, and information. These larger systems increasingly affect the people and places anthropology traditionally has studied. The study of such linkages and systems is part of the subject matter of modern anthropology.

Ethnology examines, interprets, analyzes, and compares the results of ethnography—the data gathered in different societies. It uses such data to compare and contrast and to make generalizations about society and culture. Looking beyond the particular to the more general, ethnologists attempt to identify and explain cultural differences and similarities, to test hypotheses, and to build theory to enhance our understanding of how social and cultural systems work. Ethnology gets its data for comparison not just from ethnography but also from the other subfields, particularly from archaeological anthropology, which reconstructs social systems of the past. (Table 1.2 summarizes the main contrasts between ethnography and ethnology.)

ARCHAEOLOGICAL ANTHROPOLOGY

The subfield **archaeological anthropology** (more simply, "archaeology") reconstructs, describes, and interprets human behavior and cultural patterns through material remains. At sites where people live or have lived, archaeologists find *artifacts*—material items that humans have made, used, or modified, such as tools, weapons, campsites, buildings, and garbage. Plant and animal remains and ancient garbage tell stories about consumption and activities. Wild and domesticated grains have different characteristics, which allow archaeologists to distinguish between gathering and cultivation. Examination of animal bones reveals the ages of slaughtered animals and provides other infor-

TABLE 1.2

Ethnography and Ethnology—Two Dimensions of Cultural Anthropology	
Ethnography	**Ethnology**
Requires field work to collect data	Uses data collected by a series of researchers
Often descriptive	Usually synthetic
Group/community specific	Comparative/cross-cultural

mation useful in determining whether species were wild or domesticated.

Analyzing such data, archaeologists answer several questions about ancient economies. Did the group get its meat from hunting, or did it domesticate and breed animals, killing only those of a certain age and sex? Did plant food come from wild plants or from sowing, tending, and harvesting crops? Did the residents make, trade for, or buy particular items? Were raw materials available locally? If not, where did they come from? From such information, archaeologists reconstruct patterns of production, trade, and consumption.

Archaeologists have spent much time studying potsherds, fragments of earthenware. Potsherds are more durable than many other artifacts, such as textiles and wood. The quantity of pottery fragments allows estimates of population size and density. The discovery that potters used materials that were not available locally suggests systems of trade. Similarities in manufacture and decoration at different sites may be proof of cultural connections. Groups with similar pots may be historically related. Perhaps they shared common cultural ancestors, traded with each other, or belonged to the same political system.

Many archaeologists examine paleoecology. *Ecology* is the study of interrelations among living things in an environment. The organisms and environment together constitute an *ecosystem,* a patterned arrangement of energy flows and exchanges. Human ecology studies ecosystems that include people, focusing on the ways in which human use "of nature influences and is influenced by social organization and cultural values" (Bennett 1969, pp. 10–11). *Paleoecology* looks at the ecosystems of the past.

In addition to reconstructing ecological patterns, archaeologists may infer cultural transformations, for example, by observing changes in the size and type of sites

and the distance between them. A city develops in a region where only towns, villages, and hamlets existed a few centuries earlier. The number of settlement levels (city, town, village, hamlet) in a society is a measure of social complexity. Buildings offer clues about political and religious features. Temples and pyramids suggest that an ancient society had an authority structure capable of marshaling the labor needed to build such monuments. The presence or absence of certain structures, like the pyramids of ancient Egypt and Mexico, reveals differences in function between settlements. For example, some towns were places where people came to

> **archaeological anthropology**
> The branch of anthropology, commonly known as archaeology, that reconstructs, describes, and interprets human behavior and cultural patterns through material remains; best known for the study of prehistory.

PUP CULTURE

Consider any one of the four *Indiana Jones* movies directed by Steven Spielberg. Archaeologists often complain that these movies distort public perceptions of their field by portraying archaeologists as greedy, adventurous, amoral, unscientific looters. How, if at all, has Indiana Jones influenced your views about archaeology? More generally, do media portrayals of archaeologists make you think more favorably or less favorably about the field of archaeology?

An archaeological team works at Harappa, one site from an ancient Indus River civilization dating back some 4,800 years.

attend ceremonies. Others were burial sites; still others were farming communities.

Archaeologists also reconstruct behavior patterns and lifestyles of the past by excavating. This involves digging through a succession of levels at a particular site. In a given area, through time, settlements may change in form and purpose, as may the connections between settlements. Excavation can document changes in economic, social, and political activities.

Although archaeologists are best known for studying prehistory—that is, the period before the invention of writing—they also study the cultures of historical and even living peoples (see Sabloff 2008). Studying sunken ships off the Florida coast, archaeologists have been able to verify the living conditions on the vessels that brought ancestral African Americans to the New World as enslaved people. In a research project begun in 1973 in Tucson, Arizona, archaeologist William Rathje has learned about contemporary life by studying modern garbage. The value of "garbology," as Rathje calls it, is that it provides "evidence of what people did, not what they think they did, what they think they should have done, or what the interviewer thinks they should have done" (Harrison, Rathje, and Hughes 1994, p. 108). What people report may contrast strongly with their real behavior as revealed by garbology. For example, the garbologists discovered that the three Tucson neighborhoods that reported the lowest beer consumption actually had the highest number of discarded beer cans per household (Podolefsky and Brown 1992, p. 100)! Rathje's garbology also exposed misconceptions about how much of different kinds of trash are in landfills: While most people thought that fast-food containers and disposable diapers were major waste problems, in fact they were relatively insignificant compared with paper, including environmentally friendly, recyclable paper (Rathje and Murphy 2001).

BIOLOGICAL, OR PHYSICAL, ANTHROPOLOGY

The subject matter of **biological,** or **physical, anthropology** is human biological diversity in time and space. The focus on biological variation unites five special interests within biological anthropology:

Did You Know?

A 2009 report funded by the U.S. Department of Education has recommended garbology as a way to learn about patterns of drinking on college campuses. It suggests counting beer cans in dorms on different days to learn when students are drinking. What do you think someone would learn by looking through the trash where you live?

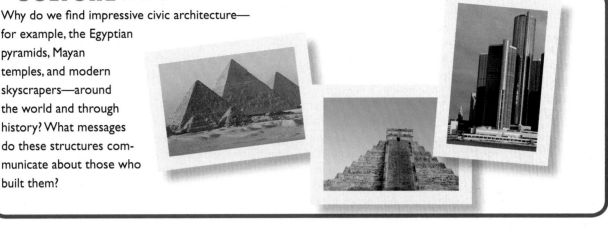

- Human evolution as revealed by the fossil record (paleoanthropology)
- Human genetics
- Human growth and development
- Human biological plasticity (the body's ability to change as it copes with stresses, such as heat, cold, and altitude)
- The biology, evolution, behavior, and social life of monkeys, apes, and other nonhuman primates

These interests link physical anthropology to other fields: biology, zoology, geology, anatomy, physiology, medicine, and public health. *Osteology*—the study of bones—helps paleoanthropologists, who examine skulls, teeth, and bones, to identify human ancestors and to chart changes in anatomy over time. A *paleontologist* is a scientist who studies fossils. A *paleoanthropologist* is one sort of paleontologist, one who studies the fossil record of human evolution. Paleoanthropologists often collaborate with archaeologists, who study artifacts, in reconstructing biological and cultural aspects of human evolution. Fossils and tools often are found together. Different types of tools provide information about the habits, customs, and lifestyles of the ancestral humans who used them.

More than a century ago, Charles Darwin noticed that the variety that exists within any population permits some individuals (those with the favored characteristics) to do better than others at surviving and reproducing. Genetics, which developed later, enlightens us about the causes and transmission of this variety. However, it isn't just genes that cause variety. During any individual's lifetime, the environment works along with heredity to determine biological features. For example, people with a genetic tendency to be tall will be shorter if they are poorly nourished during childhood. Thus, biological anthropology also investigates the influence of environment on the body as it grows and matures. Among the environmental factors that influence the body as it develops are nutrition, altitude, temperature, and disease, as well as cultural factors, such as the standards of attractiveness we considered previously.

Biological anthropology (along with zoology) also includes primatology. The **primates** include our closest relatives—apes and monkeys. Primatologists study their biology, evolution, behavior, and social life, often in the primates' natural environments. Primatology assists paleoanthropology, because primate behavior may shed light on early human behavior and human nature.

biological (physical) anthropology The branch of anthropology that studies human biological diversity in time and space—for instance, hominid evolution, human genetics, human biological adaptation; also includes primatology (behavior and evolution of monkeys and apes).

primates Members of the zoological order that includes humans, apes, monkeys, and prosimians, such as lemurs.

LINGUISTIC ANTHROPOLOGY

We don't know (and probably never will) when our ancestors acquired the ability to speak, although biological anthropologists have looked to the anatomy of the face and the skull to speculate about the origin of language. And primatologists have described the communication systems of mon-

Primatologists study the evolution, biology, behavior, and social life of monkeys and apes, such as these young orangutans.

keys and apes. We do know that well-developed, grammatically complex languages have existed for thousands of years. Linguistic anthropology offers further illustration of anthropology's interest in comparison, variation, and change. **Linguistic anthropology** studies language in its social and cultural context, across space and over time. Some linguistic anthropologists make inferences about universal features of language, linked perhaps to uniformities in the human brain. Others reconstruct ancient languages by comparing their contemporary descendants and in so doing make discoveries about history. Still others study linguistic differences to discover varied perceptions and patterns of thought in different cultures.

Historical linguistics considers variation in time, such as the changes in sounds, grammar, and vocabulary between Middle English (spoken from approximately 1050 to 1550 C.E.) and modern English. **Sociolinguistics** investigates relationships between social and linguistic variation. No language is a homogeneous system in which everyone speaks just like everyone else. How do different speakers use a given language? How do linguistic features correlate with social factors, including class and gender differences (Tannen 1990)? One reason for variation is geography, as in regional dialects and accents. Linguistic variation also is expressed in the bilingualism of ethnic groups. Linguistic and cultural anthropologists collaborate in studying links between language and many other aspects of culture, such as how people reckon kinship and how they perceive and classify colors.

>> Anthropology and Other Academic Fields

As mentioned previously, one of the main differences between anthropology and the other fields that study people is holism, anthropology's unique blend of biological, social, cultural, linguistic, historical, and contemporary perspectives. Paradoxically, while distinguishing anthropology, this breadth is what also links it to many other disciplines. Techniques used to date fossils and artifacts have come to anthropology from physics, chemistry, and geology. Because plant and animal remains often are found with human bones and artifacts, anthropologists collaborate with botanists, zoologists, and paleontologists.

As a discipline that is both scientific and humanistic, anthropology has links with many other academic fields.

Anthropology is a **science**—a "systematic field of study or body of knowledge that aims, through experiment, observation, and deduction, to produce reliable explanations of phenomena, with references to the material and physical world" (*Webster's New World Encyclopedia* 1993, p. 937). The following chapters present anthropology as a humanistic science devoted to discovering, describing, understanding, and explaining similarities and differences in time and space among humans and our ancestors. Clyde Kluckhohn (1944) described anthropology as "the science of human similarities and differences" (p. 9). His statement of the need for such a field still stands: "Anthropology provides a scientific basis for dealing with the crucial dilemma of the world today: how can peoples of different appearance, mutually unintelligible languages, and dissimilar ways of life get along peaceably together?" (p. 9). Anthropology has compiled an impressive body of knowledge that this textbook attempts to encapsulate.

Besides its links to the natural sciences (e.g., geology, zoology), and social sciences (e.g., sociology, psychology), anthropology also has strong links to the humanities. The humanities include English, comparative literature, classics, folklore, philosophy, and the arts. These fields study languages, texts, philosophies, arts, music, performances, and other forms of creative expression. Ethnomusicology, which studies forms of musical expression on a worldwide basis, is especially closely related to anthropology. Also linked is folklore, the systematic study of tales, myths, and legends from a variety of cultures. One might well argue that anthropology is among the most humanistic of all academic fields because of its fundamental respect for human diversity. *Humanism* refers to respect for human diversity and welfare. Anthropologists listen to, record, and represent voices from a multitude of nations and cultures. Anthropology values local knowledge, diverse worldviews, and alternative philosophies. Cultural anthropology and linguistic anthropology in particular bring a comparative and nonelitist perspective to forms of creative expression, including language, art, narratives, music, and dance, viewed in their social and cultural context.

CULTURETHINK

How is anthropology among the most humanistic of all academic disciplines? How does each of the sub-disciplines contribute to its humanism? *Humanism* refers to respect for human diversity and welfare.

>> Applied Anthropology

Anthropology is not a science of the exotic carried on by quaint scholars in ivory towers. Rather, anthropology has a lot to tell the public. Anthropology's foremost professional organization, the American Anthropological Association (AAA), has formally acknowledged a public service role by recognizing that anthropology has two dimensions:

Anthropology Works

People in many different careers can use anthropological insights. For example, a psychologist, nurse, teacher, politician, or even a business executive would benefit from being sensitive to cultural differences.

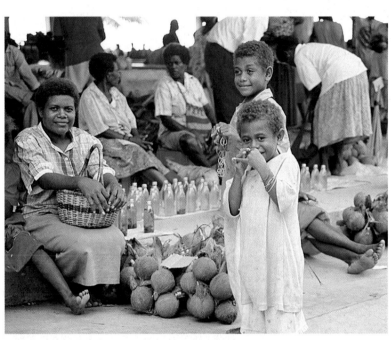

Bronislaw Malinowski is famous for his field work among the matrilineal Trobriand Islanders of the South Pacific. Does this Trobriand market scene suggest anything about the status of Trobriand women?

(1) academic or general anthropology and (2) practicing, or **applied anthropology.** The latter refers to the application of anthropological data, perspectives, theory, and methods to identify, assess, and solve contemporary social problems. As Erve Chambers (1987, p. 309) states it, applied anthropology is the "field of inquiry concerned with the relationships between anthropological knowledge and the uses of that knowledge in the world beyond anthropology." More and more anthropologists from the four subfields now work in such "applied" areas as public health, family planning, business, economic development, and cultural resource management.

Applied anthropology encompasses any use of the knowledge

and/or techniques of the four subfields to identify, assess, and solve practical problems. Because of anthropology's breadth, it has many applications. For example, applied medical anthropologists consider both the sociocultural and the biological contexts and implications of disease and illness. Perceptions of good and bad health, along with actual health threats and problems, differ among societies. Various ethnic groups recognize different illnesses, symptoms, and causes and have developed different health care systems and treatment strategies.

Applied archaeology, usually called *public archaeology,* includes such activities as cultural resource management, contract archaeology, public educational programs, and historic preservation. An important role for public archaeology has been created by legislation requiring evaluation of sites threatened by dams, highways, and other construction activities. To decide what needs saving, and to preserve significant information about the past when sites cannot be saved, is the work of **cultural resource management (CRM).** CRM involves not only preserving sites but also allowing their destruction if they are not significant. The "management" part of the term refers to the evaluation and decision-making process. Cultural resource managers work for federal, state, and county agencies and other clients. Applied cultural anthropologists sometimes work with the public archaeologists, assessing the human problems generated by the proposed change and determining how they can be reduced.

> **applied anthropology** The application of anthropological data, perspectives, theory, and methods to identify, assess, and solve contemporary social problems.
>
> **cultural resource management (CRM)** The branch of applied archaeology aimed at preserving sites threatened by dams, highways, and other projects.

Learn more about the breadth and unity of the four subfields of anthropology at americananthropologicalassociation .org, the website of American anthropologists' foremost professional society. Under "About AAA," click on "What Is Anthropology?" While you're there, also explore "What Do Anthropologists Do?"

get involved!

For REVIEW

I. **What is anthropology, and how does it differ from other fields that study human beings?**

- Anthropology is the holistic, biocultural, and comparative study of humanity. Unlike other fields that study humans, anthropology explores the whole of the human condition: the origins of, and changes in, our biological and cultural adaptations, and the world's vast diversity of societies, languages, customs, and beliefs. Anthropology seeks to explain both the differences and the similarities among peoples everywhere, past, present, and future.

II. **How useful is the race concept in understanding human diversity?**

- Race is a problematic concept because humans do not fit neatly into any racial classifications. Contemporary anthropology's biocultural perspective offers a much more fruitful approach to human biological diversity than pigeonholing humans into racial categories. Anthropologists today focus on specific biological differences, such as skin color, and use the concept of natural selection to explain them.

III. **What are the four subfields of anthropology?**

- The four subfields are cultural, archaeological, biological, and linguistic anthropology. Cultural anthropology explores human society and culture, describing and explaining cultural similarities and differences. Archaeology reconstructs, describes, and interprets cultural patterns, often of prehistoric populations, through material remains. Biological anthropology studies human biological diversity in time and space. Linguistic anthropology studies language in its social and cultural context across time and space. These subfields have a strong academic dimension, but anthropologists from each subfield are increasingly applying their knowledge to identify, assess, and solve contemporary social problems.

CULTURE CLIPS

TO ACCESS THESE VIDEOS ON YOUR COMPUTER, VISIT

www.mhhe.com/gezonqr

I-1

I-2

I-3

Pop Quiz

1. Which of the following statements most completely characterizes anthropology as a unique field of study?

   a. It studies only ancient and nonindustrial societies.

   b. It includes biology.

   c. It deals with crucial world dilemmas.

   d. It is comparative and holistic.

2. What is the most critical element of cultural traditions?

   a. Their stability owing to the unchanging characteristics of human biology.

   b. Their tendency to change radically every generation.

c. Their transmission through learning rather than through biological inheritance.

d. Their tendency to remain unchanged despite changing historical circumstances.

3. How has human reliance on cultural means of adaptation changed?

a. Humans are just beginning to depend on them.

b. Human have become increasingly dependent on them.

c. Humans have become entirely reliant on biological means.

d. Humans no longer use cultural means.

4. Anthropology's focus on both culture and biology:

a. Is not a characteristic of anthropology in America.

b. Means that biological anthropologists do not collaborate with other biological scientists.

c. Allows anthropology to address how culture influences biological traits and vice versa.

d. Is insignificant, since biology is studied by biological anthropologists while culture is studied by cultural anthropologists.

5. Which of the following expresses scientists' preference for explaining biological differences among humans rather than pigeonholing humans into racial classifications?

a. Skin color presents a useful basis for assigning humans to racial classifications.

b. All human populations fit neatly into one or other of the so-called great races.

c. Scientists who have used four to five or so physical traits to classify races find that these traits always go together as a unit in a population.

d. Natural selection, such as that against the concentration of melanin in skin in northern regions, contributes to differences in human skin color.

6. Four-field anthropology:

a. Was shaped largely by early American anthropologists' interests in Native Americans.

b. Lacks unity, since only archaeology and biological anthropology consider variation in time and space.

c. Lacks unity because the four subfields do not share key assumptions.

d. Is weak in examining the relation between biology and culture.

7. Which of the following accurately distinguishes ethnography from ethnology?

a. Ethnology focuses on the study of particular cultures, while ethnography looks at cultures comparatively.

b. Traditionally, ethnography was done in large societies with wealth and power, while ethnology focused on small societies with little wealth.

c. Ethnography studies cultures that are isolated from one another, while ethnology studies nations influenced by globalization.

d. Ethnologists look beyond the particular cultural data that ethnographers describe and interpret to compare and contrast and make generalizations about society and culture.

8. Archaeological anthropology is *not* likely to use which of the following approaches in reconstructing human cultural patterns:

a. Examination of paleoecology.

b. Excavation.

c. Recovery and interpretation of human material remains.

d. Observation of nonhuman primates in their natural settings.

9. Anthropology is a humanistic science most particularly because:

a. The techniques it uses come from a variety of sciences, including those that study humans' relations with other animals.

b. It discovers, describes, and attempts to explain similarities and differences among humans, with concern for the full diversity of worldviews and voices.

c. It is a systematic study that respects experiment, observation, and deduction as applied to both contemporary human life and human evolution.

d. Over the years it has compiled an impressive body of knowledge about human life.

10. All of the following are true about applied anthropology *except* that:

a. It uses the knowledge, perspectives, or methods of the four subfields to identify, assess, and solve practical human problems.

b. It is a growing aspect of anthropology, with increasingly more anthropologists developing applied components of their work.

c. It is less relevant for archaeology, since archaeology concerns the material culture of societies that no longer exist.

d. It has many applications because of anthropology's breadth.

1. (d), 2. (c), 3. (b), 4. (c), 5. (d), 6. (a), 7. (d), 8. (d), 9. (b), 10. (c)

2

CULTURE

UNDERSTANDING OURSELVES

How special are you? To what extent are you "your own person," and to what extent are you a product of your particular culture? Americans may not fully appreciate the power of culture because of the value their culture places on "the *individual*." Yet individualism itself is a distinctive *shared* value, a feature of American culture, transmitted constantly in our daily lives. From the late Mr. (Fred) Rogers of daytime TV to parents, grandparents, and teachers, our enculturative agents insist we are all "someone special." That we are individuals first and members of groups second is the opposite of this chapter's lesson about culture. Certainly we have distinctive features because we are individuals, but we have other distinct attributes because we belong to cultural groups.

For example, a comparison of the United States with Brazil, Italy, or virtually any Latin nation reveals striking contrasts between a national culture (American) that discourages physical affection and national cultures in which the opposite is true. Brazilians approach, touch, and kiss one another much more frequently than North Americans do. In personal encounters, the Brazilian characteristically moves closer, while the North American is apt to retreat. Such movements are products of years of exposure to particular cultural traditions. Middle-class Brazilians teach their kids—both boys and girls—to kiss every adult relative they see. Given the size of Brazilian extended families, this can mean hundreds of people. Women continue kissing all those people throughout their lives, while men typically continue to kiss female relatives and friends, as well as their fathers and uncles.

Do you kiss your father? Your uncle? Your grandfather? How about your mother, aunt, or grandmother? The answer to these questions may differ between men and women, and for male and female relatives. Culture can help us to make sense of these differences.

As You READ

- What is culture, and why do we study it?
- What is the relation between culture and the individual?
- How does culture change?

>> What Is Culture?

Humans share *society,* organized life in groups, with other animals—social animals, such as monkeys, wolves, and ants. Other animals, especially the great apes, have rudimentary cultural abilities, but only humans have fully elaborated cultures—distinctive traditions and customs transmitted over the generations through learning and through language.

The concept of culture has long been basic to anthropology. Well over a century ago, in his book *Primitive Culture,* the British anthropologist Edward Tylor proposed that cultures—systems of human behavior and thought—obey natural laws and therefore can be studied scientifically. Tylor's definition of culture still offers an overview of the subject matter of anthropology and is widely quoted.

"Culture . . . is that complex whole which includes knowledge, belief, arts, morals, law, custom, and any other

People learn and share beliefs and behavior as members of cultural groups, for example, in this Muslim primary school in Marrakesh, Morocco.

capabilities and habits acquired by man as a member of society" (Tylor 1871/1958, p. 1). The crucial phrase here is "acquired . . . as a member of society." Tylor's definition focuses on attributes that people acquire not through biological inheritance but by growing up in a particular society in which they are exposed to a specific cultural tradition. **Enculturation** is the process by which a child *learns* his or her culture.

CULTURE IS LEARNED

The ease with which children absorb any cultural tradition rests on the uniquely elaborated human capacity to learn. Other animals may learn from experience, so that, for example, they avoid fire after discovering that it hurts. Social animals also learn from other members of their group. Wolves, for instance, learn hunting strategies from other pack members. Such social learning is particularly important among monkeys and apes, our closest biological relatives. But our own *cultural learning* depends on the uniquely developed human capacity to use **symbols,** signs that have no necessary or natural connection to the things they stand for or signify.

On the basis of cultural learning, people create, remember, and deal with ideas. They grasp and apply specific systems of symbolic meaning. Anthropologist Clifford Geertz defined culture as ideas based on cultural learning and symbols. Cultures have been characterized as sets of "control mechanisms—plans, recipes, rules, instructions, what computer engineers call programs for the governing of behavior" (Geertz 1973, p. 44). These programs are absorbed by people through enculturation in particular traditions. People gradually internalize a previously established system of meanings and symbols, which helps guide their behavior and perceptions throughout their lives.

Every person begins immediately, through a process of conscious and unconscious learning and interaction with others, to internalize, or incorporate, a cultural tradition through the process of enculturation. Sometimes culture is taught directly, as when parents tell their children to say "thank you" when someone gives them something or does them a favor.

Culture also is transmitted through observation. Children pay attention to the things that go on around them. They modify their behavior not just because other people tell them to do so but as a result of their own observations and growing awareness of what their culture considers right and wrong. Culture also is absorbed unconsciously. North Americans acquire their culture's notions about how far apart people should stand when they talk, not by being told directly to maintain a certain distance, but through a gradual process of observation, experience, and conscious and unconscious behavior modification. No one tells Latins to stand closer together than North Americans do; they learn to do so as part of their cultural tradition.

> **enculturation** The social process by which culture is learned and transmitted across the generations.
>
> **symbol** A verbal or nonverbal sign that arbitrarily and by convention stands for something else, with which it has no necessary or natural connection.

CULTURE IS SYMBOLIC

Symbolic thought is unique and crucial to humans and to cultural learning. A symbol is something verbal or nonverbal, within a particular language or culture, that comes to stand for something else. Anthropologist Leslie White defined culture as

> dependent upon symbolling. . . . Culture consists of tools, implements, utensils, clothing, ornaments, customs, institutions, beliefs, rituals, games, works of art, language, etc. (White 1959, p. 3)

For White, culture originated when our ancestors acquired the ability to use symbols, that is, to originate and bestow meaning on a thing or event and, correspondingly, to grasp and appreciate such meanings (White 1959, p. 3).

There need be no obvious, natural, or necessary connection between the symbol and what it symbolizes. The familiar pet that barks is no more naturally a *dog* than it is a *chien, Hund,* or *mbwa,* the words for "dog" in French, German, and Swahili, respectively. Language is one of the distinctive possessions of *Homo sapiens.* No other animal has developed anything approaching the complexity of language, with its multitude of symbols.

Symbols often are linguistic. There also are myriad nonverbal symbols, such as flags, which stand for various countries, and the arches that symbolize a particular fast-food chain. Holy water is a potent symbol in Roman Catholicism. As is true of all symbols, the association be-

STUDY TIP

Culture is transmitted in three ways: direct teaching, observation, and unconscious absorption.

tween a symbol (water) and what is symbolized (holiness) is arbitrary and conventional. Water probably is not intrinsically holier than milk, blood, or other natural liquids. Nor is holy water chemically different from ordinary water. Holy water is a symbol within Roman Catholicism, which is part of an international cultural system. A natural thing has been associated arbitrarily with a particular meaning for Catholics, who share common beliefs and experiences that are based on learning and transmitted across the generations.

For hundreds of thousands of years, humans have shared the abilities on which culture rests—the abilities to learn, to think symbolically, to manipulate language, and to use tools and other cultural products in organizing their lives and coping with their environments. Every contemporary human population has the ability to use symbols and thus to create and maintain culture. Our nearest relatives—chimpanzees and gorillas—have rudimentary cultural abilities. However, no other animal has elaborated cultural abilities to the extent that *Homo* has.

CULTURE IS SHARED

Culture is an attribute not of individuals per se but of individuals as members of *groups*. Culture is transmitted in society. Don't we learn our culture by observing, listening, talking, and interacting with many other people? Shared beliefs, values, memories, and expectations link people who grow up in the same culture. Enculturation unifies people by providing us with common experiences.

Today's parents were yesterday's children. If they grew up in North America, they absorbed certain values and beliefs transmitted over the generations. People become agents in the enculturation of their children, just as their parents were for them. Although a culture constantly changes, certain fundamental beliefs, values, worldviews, and child-rearing practices endure. Consider a simple American example of enduring shared enculturation. As children, when we didn't finish a meal, our parents may have reminded us to think of starving children in some

foreign country, just as our grandparents might have done a generation earlier. The specific country changes (China, India, Bangladesh, Ethiopia, Somalia, Rwanda—what was it in your home?). Still, American culture goes on transmitting the idea that by eating all our brussels sprouts or broccoli, we can justify our own good fortune, compared to a hungry child in an impoverished or war-ravaged country.

CULTURE AND NATURE

Culture takes the natural biological urges we share with other animals and teaches us how to express them in particular ways. People have to eat, but culture teaches us what, when, and how. In many cultures people have their main meal at noon, but most North Americans prefer a large dinner. English people eat fish for breakfast, but North Americans prefer hotcakes and cold cereals. Brazilians put hot milk into strong coffee, whereas many North Americans pour cold milk into a weaker brew. Midwesterners dine at five or six, Spaniards at ten.

Cultural habits, perceptions, and inventions mold "human nature" into many forms. People have to eliminate wastes from their bodies. But some cultures teach people to defecate standing, while others tell them to do it sitting down. Peasant women in the Andean highlands squat in the streets and urinate, getting all the privacy they need from their massive skirts. All these habits are parts of cultural traditions that have converted natural acts into cultural customs.

Our culture—and cultural changes—affect how we perceive nature, human nature, and "the natural." Through science, invention, and discovery, cultural advances have overcome many "natural" limitations. We prevent and cure diseases such as polio and smallpox, which felled our ancestors. We use Viagra to enhance or restore sexual potency. Through cloning, scientists have challenged the way we think about biological identity and the meaning of life itself. Culture, of course, does not always protect us from natural threats. Hurricanes, floods, earthquakes, and other natural forces regularly overthrow our wishes to modify

Culture is all encompassing. Lady Gaga is part of American culture as well as American popular culture.

the environment through building, development, and expansion. Can you think of other ways in which nature strikes back at culture?

CULTURE IS ALL-ENCOMPASSING

For anthropologists, culture includes much more than refinement, good taste, sophistication, education, and appreciation of the fine arts. Not only college graduates but all people are "cultured." The most interesting and significant cultural forces are those that affect people every day of their lives, particularly those that influence children during enculturation.

Culture, as defined anthropologically, encompasses features that are sometimes regarded as trivial or unworthy of serious study, such as those of "popular" culture. To understand contemporary North American culture, we must consider television, fast-food restaurants, sports, and games. As a cultural manifestation, a rock star may be as interesting as a symphony conductor (or vice versa); a comic book may be as significant as a book-award winner.

CULTURE IS INTEGRATED

Cultures are not haphazard collections of customs and beliefs. Cultures are integrated, patterned systems. If one part of the system (the overall economy, for instance) changes, other parts change as well. For example, during the 1950s most American women planned domestic careers as homemakers and mothers. Most of today's college women, by contrast, expect to get paying jobs when they graduate.

What are some of the social repercussions of this particular economic change? Attitudes and behavior regarding marriage, family, and children have changed. Late marriage, "living together," and divorce have become more common. The average age at first marriage for American women rose from twenty years old in 1955 to twenty-six in 2007. The comparable figures for men were twenty-three and twenty-eight (U.S. Census Bureau 2007). The number of currently divorced Americans quadrupled from four million in 1970 to about twenty-three million in 2007 (U.S. Census Bureau 2008). Work competes with marriage and family responsibilities and reduces the time available to invest in child care.

English people eat fish for breakfast, but North Americans prefer hot cakes and cold cereal.

STUDY **TIP**

Name the seven characteristics of culture described in this chapter (hint: start with "learned").

Anthropology Works

Anthropology teaches people working for disaster relief agencies to be aware of how proposed solutions (change of residence, for example) will affect all aspects of people's lives. How might life be different for people who have to move to a new neighborhood or city, away from their friends, schools, workplace, and family? What if they move from multifamily compounds to single-family residences?

and cultural means of adaptation has increased during human evolution and plays a crucial role.

Sometimes, adaptive behavior that offers short-term benefits to particular subgroups or individuals may harm the environment and threaten the group's long-term survival. Economic growth may benefit some people while it depletes resources needed for society at large or for future generations. Thus, cultural traits, patterns, and inventions can also be *maladaptive,* threatening the group's continued existence (survival and reproduction). Air conditioners help us deal with heat, as fires and furnaces protect us against the cold. Automobiles permit us to make a living by getting us from home to workplace. But the by-products of such "beneficial" technology often create new problems.

>> Culture's Evolutionary Basis

The human capacity for culture has an evolutionary basis that extends back at least two and a half million years to early toolmakers. Evidence for these toolmakers exists in the archeological record. Based on observation of tool use and manufacture by apes, however, scientists believe the evolutionary basis for culture may extend even further back.

Similarities between humans and apes, our closest relatives, are evident in anatomy, brain structure, genetics, and biochemistry. Most closely related to us are the African great apes: chimpanzees and gorillas. *Hominidae* is the zoological family that includes fossil and living humans, as well as chimps and gorillas. We refer to members of this family as **hominids.** We use the term **hominins** for the group that leads to humans but not to chimps and gorillas and that encompasses all the human species that have ever existed.

core values Key, basic, or central values that integrate a culture and help distinguish it from others.

hominids Members of the zoological family that includes fossil and living humans, chimps, and gorillas.

hominins Members of the evolutionary line leading to and including modern humans, as distinct from chimps and gorillas.

Cultures are integrated not simply by their dominant economic activities and related social patterns but also by sets of values, ideas, symbols, and judgments. Cultures train their individual members to share certain personality traits. A set of characteristic **core values** (key, basic, central values) integrates each culture and helps distinguish it from others. For instance, the work ethic and individualism are core values that have integrated American culture for generations. Different sets of dominant values influence the patterns of other cultures.

Many human traits reflect the fact that our primate ancestors lived in the trees. These traits include grasping ability and manual dexterity (especially opposable thumbs), depth and color vision, learning ability based on a large brain, substantial parental investment in a limited number of offspring, and tendencies toward sociality and cooperation. Like other primates, humans have flexible, five-fingered hands and *opposable thumbs:* Each thumb can touch all the other fingers on the same hand. Like monkeys and apes, humans also have excellent depth and color vision. Our eyes are placed forward in the skull and look directly ahead, so that their fields of vision overlap. Depth perception, impossible without overlapping visual fields, proved adaptive—for judging distance, for example—in the trees. Having color and depth vision also facilitates the identification of various food sources, as well as mutual grooming—picking out burrs, insects, and other small ob-

CULTURE CAN BE ADAPTIVE AND MALADAPTIVE

Humans have both biological and cultural ways of coping with environmental stresses. Besides our biological means of adaptation, we also use "cultural adaptive kits," which contain customary activities and tools that aid us. Although humans continue to adapt biologically, reliance on social

CULTURETHINK

Many cultural patterns such as overconsumption and pollution appear to be maladaptive in the long run. Do you agree? Can you think of others?

jects from hair. Such grooming is one way of forming and maintaining social bonds.

The combination of manual dexterity and depth perception allows monkeys, apes, and humans to pick up small objects, hold them in front of their eyes, and appraise them. Our ability to thread a needle reflects an intricate interplay of hands and eyes that took millions of years of primate evolution to achieve. Such dexterity, including the opposable thumb, confers a tremendous advantage in manipulating objects and is essential to a major human adaptive capacity: toolmaking.

In primates, and especially in humans, the ratio of brain size to body size exceeds that of most mammals. Even more important, the brain's outer layer—concerned with memory, association, and integration—is relatively larger. Monkeys, apes, and humans store an array of images in their memories, which permits them to learn more. Such a capacity for learning is another tremendous adaptive advantage. Like most other primates, humans usually give birth to a single offspring. Receiving more parental attention, that one infant has enhanced learning opportunities. The need for longer and more attentive care of offspring places a selective value on support by a social group. Humans have developed considerably the primate tendency to be social animals, living and interacting regularly with other members of their species.

WHAT WE SHARE WITH OTHER PRIMATES

There is a substantial gap between primate *society* (organized life in groups) and fully developed human *culture*, which is based on symbolic thought. Nevertheless, studies of nonhuman primates reveal many similarities with humans, such as the ability to learn from experience and change behavior as a result. Apes and monkeys, like humans, learn throughout their lives. For example, in one group of Japanese macaques (land-dwelling monkeys), a three-year-old female started washing sweet potatoes before she ate them. First her mother, then her age peers, and finally the entire troop began washing sweet potatoes as well. The ability to benefit from experience confers a tremendous adaptive advantage, permitting the avoidance of fatal mistakes. Faced with environmental change, humans and other primates don't have to wait for a genetic or physiologi-

cal response. They can modify learned behavior and social patterns instead.

Although humans employ tools much more than any other animal does, tool use also turns up among several nonhuman species, including birds, beavers, sea otters, and especially apes (see Mayell 2003). Humans are also not the only animals that make tools with a specific purpose in mind. Chimpanzees living in the Tai forest of Ivory Coast make and use stone tools to break open hard, golf-ball-sized nuts (Mercader, Panger, and Boesch 2002). At specific sites, the chimps gather nuts, place them on stumps or flat rocks, which are used as anvils, and pound the nuts with heavy stones. The chimps must select hammer stones suited to smashing the nuts and carry them to where the nut trees grow. Nut cracking is a learned skill, with mothers showing their young how to do it.

In 1960, Jane Goodall (1996) began observing wild chimps—including their tool use and hunting behavior—at Gombe Stream National Park in Tanzania, East Africa. The most studied form of ape toolmaking involves "termiting," in which chimps make tools to probe termite hills. They choose twigs, which they modify by removing leaves and peeling off bark to expose the sticky surface beneath. They carry the twigs to termite hills, dig holes with their fingers, and insert the twigs. Finally, they pull out the twigs and dine on termites that were attracted to the sticky surface. Given what is known about ape tool use and manufacture, it is almost certain that early hominins shared this ability, although the first evidence for hominin stone toolmaking dates back only two and a half million years. In addition, *bipedalism* (moving around upright on two legs) would have permitted the carrying and use of tools and weapons against predators and competitors in an open grassland habitat.

Tool use by chimps. These chimps in Liberia are using stone tools to crack palm nuts, as described in the text.
....

age of twenty-six individuals (almost always adult and adolescent males). Most hunts (78 percent) result in at least one prey item being caught—a much higher success rate than that among lions (26 percent), hyenas (34 percent), or cheetahs (30 percent). Chimps' favored prey in Kibale Park is the red colobus monkey (Mitani and Watts 1999).

Archaeological evidence suggests that humans hunted by at least two and a half million years ago, based on stone meat-cutting tools found at Olduvai Gorge in Tanzania. Given our current understanding of hunting and toolmaking by chimps, we can infer that hominids may have been hunting much earlier than the first archaeological evidence attests. However, because chimps typically devour the monkeys they kill, leaving few remains, we may never find archaeological evidence for the first hominin hunt, especially if it was done without stone tools.

The apes have other abilities essential to culture. Wild chimps and orangs aim and throw objects. Gorillas build nests, and they throw branches, grass, vines, and other objects. Hominins have elaborated the capacity to aim and throw, without which we never would have developed projectile technology and weaponry—or baseball.

Like toolmaking, hunting once was cited as a distinctive human activity not shared with the apes. Again, however, primate research shows that other primates, especially chimpanzees, are habitual hunters. For example, in Uganda's Kibale National Park, chimps form large hunting parties, including an aver-

HOW WE DIFFER FROM OTHER PRIMATES

Although chimps often share meat from a hunt, apes and monkeys (except for nursing infants) tend to feed themselves individually. Cooperation and sharing are much more developed among humans. Until fairly recently (twelve thousand to ten thousand years ago), all humans were hunter-gatherers living in small social groups called bands. In some world areas, the hunter-gatherer way of life

TABLE 2.1

Cultural Features of Chimpanzees (Rudimentary) and Humans (Fully Developed)		
	Chimpanzees	**Humans**
Cultural Learning	Rudimentary	Fully developed
Tool Use	Occasional	Habitual
Tool Manufacture	Occasional: hammer stones, termiting	Habitual and sophisticated
Aimed Throwing	Occasional objects, not tools	Projectile technology
Hunting	Significant, but no tools	Basic hominin subsistence strategy, with tools
Food Sharing	Meat sharing after hunt	Basic to human life
Cooperation	Occasional in hunting	Basic to human life
Mating and Marriage	Female estrus cycle, limited pair bonds	Year-round mating, marriage, and exogamy
Kin Ties	Limited by dispersal at adolescence	Maintained through sons and daughters

persisted into recent times, permitting study by ethnographers. In such societies, men and women bring resources back to the camp and share them. Everyone shares the meat from a large animal. Nourished and protected by younger band members, elders live past reproductive age and are respected for their knowledge and experience. Humans are among the most cooperative of the primates—in the food quest and other social activities. In addition, the amount of information stored in a human band is far greater than that in any other primate group.

Another difference between humans and other primates involves mating. Among baboons and chimps, most mating occurs when females enter estrus, during which they ovulate. In estrus, the vaginal area swells and reddens, and receptive females form temporary bonds with, and mate with, males. Human females, by contrast, lack a visible estrus cycle, and their ovulation is concealed. Not knowing when ovulation is occurring, humans maximize their reproductive success by mating throughout the year. Human pair bonds for mating are more exclusive and more durable than are those of chimps. Related to our more constant sexuality, all human societies have some form of marriage. Marriage gives mating a reliable basis and grants to each spouse special, though not always exclusive, sexual rights in the other.

Marriage creates another major contrast between humans and nonhuman primates: exogamy and kinship systems. Most cultures have rules of *exogamy* requiring marriage outside one's kin or local group. Coupled with the recognition of kinship, exogamy confers adaptive advantages because it creates ties between the spouses' different kin groups. Their children have relatives, and therefore allies, in two kin groups rather than just one. The key point here is that ties of affection and mutual support between members of different local groups tend to be absent among primates other than *Homo*. Other primates tend to disperse at adolescence. Among chimps and gorillas, females tend to migrate, seeking mates in other groups. Humans also choose mates from outside the natal group, and usually at least one spouse moves. However, *humans maintain lifelong ties with sons and daughters.* The systems of kinship and marriage that preserve these links provide a major contrast between humans and other primates. Table 2.1 lists differences in the cultural abilities of humans and chimpanzees, our nearest relatives.

>> Universality, Generality, and Particularity

Anthropologists agree that cultural learning is uniquely elaborated among humans and that all humans have culture. Anthropologists also accept a doctrine termed in the nineteenth century "the psychic unity of man." This means that although *individuals* differ in their emotional and intellectual tendencies and capacities, all human *populations* have equivalent capacities for culture. Regardless of their

genes or their physical appearance, people can learn *any* cultural tradition.

To understand this point, consider that contemporary Americans and Canadians are the genetically mixed descendants of people from all over the world. Our ancestors were biologically varied, lived in different countries and continents, and participated in hundreds of cultural traditions. However, early colonists, later immigrants, and their descendants all have become active participants in American and Canadian life. All now share a common national culture.

To recognize biopsychological equality is not to deny differences among populations. In studying human diversity in time and space, anthropologists distinguish among the universal, the generalized, and the particular. Certain biological, psychological, social, and cultural features are **universal,** found in every culture. Others are merely **generalities,** common to several but not all human groups. Still other traits are **particularities,** unique to certain cultural traditions.

universal Something that exists in every culture.

generality Culture pattern or trait that exists in some but not all societies.

particularity Distinctive or unique culture trait, pattern, or integration.

UNIVERSALS AND GENERALITIES

Biologically based universals include a long period of infant dependency, year-round (rather than seasonal) sexuality, and a complex brain that enables us to use symbols, languages, and tools. Among the social universals is life in groups and in some kind of family (see Brown 1991). Generalities occur in certain times and places but not in all cultures. They may be widespread, but they are not universal. One cultural generality that is present in many but not all societies is the *nuclear family,* a kinship group consisting of parents and children. Although many middle-class Americans ethnocentrically view the nuclear family as a proper and "natural" group, it is not universal. It was absent, for example, among the Nayars, located on India's Malabar Coast. Traditionally, the Nayars lived in female-headed households, and husbands and wives did not live together. In many other societies, the nuclear family is submerged in larger kin groups, such as extended families, lineages, and clans.

Societies can share the same beliefs and customs because of borrowing or through (cultural) inheritance from a common cultural ancestor. Speaking English is a generality shared by North Americans and Australians because both countries had English settlers. Another reason for generalities is domination, as in colonial rule, when a more powerful culture imposes customs and procedures on another one. In many countries, use of the English language reflects colonial history. More recently, English has spread through *diffusion* (cultural borrowing) to many other countries, as it has become the world's foremost language for business and travel.

PARTICULARITY: PATTERNS OF CULTURE

A cultural particularity is a trait or feature of culture that is not generalized or widespread; rather it is confined to a single place, culture, or society. Yet because of cultural borrowing, which has accelerated through modern transportation and communication systems, traits that once were limited in their distribution have become more widespread. Traits that are useful, that have the capacity to please large audiences, and that don't clash with the cultural values of potential adopters are more likely to be borrowed than others are. Still, certain cultural particularities persist. One example is a particular food dish (e.g., pork barbeque with a mustard-based sauce available only in South Carolina,

or the pastie—beef stew baked in pie dough characteristic of Michigan's upper peninsula). McDonald's food outlets, on the other hand, once confined to San Bernardino, California, have spread across the globe through diffusion. But there are other reasons why cultural particularities are increasingly rare. Many cultural traits are shared as cultural universals and as a result of independent invention. When facing similar problems, people in different places have come up with similar solutions. Again and again, similar cultural causes have produced similar cultural results.

At the level of the individual cultural trait or element (e.g., bow and arrow, hot dog, MTV), particularities may be getting rarer. But at a higher level, particularity is more obvious. Different cultures emphasize different things. Cultures are integrated and patterned differently and display tremendous variation and diversity. When cultural traits are borrowed, they are modified to fit the culture that adopts them. They are reintegrated—patterned anew—to fit their new setting. MTV in Germany or Brazil isn't at all the same thing as MTV in the United States. As stated in the earlier section "Culture Is Integrated," patterned beliefs, customs, and practices lend distinctiveness to particular cultural traditions.

Consider universal life-cycle events, such as birth, puberty, marriage, parenthood, and death, that many cultures observe and celebrate. The occasions (e.g., marriage, death) may be the same and universal, but the patterns of ceremonial observance may be dramatically different. Cultures vary in just which events merit special celebration. Americans, for example, regard expensive weddings as more socially appropriate than lavish funerals. The Betsileo of Madagascar take the opposite view. The marriage ceremony is a minor event that brings together just the couple and a few close relatives. A funeral is a measure of the deceased person's social position and lifetime achievement, and it may attract a thousand people. Why use money on a house, the Betsileo say, when one can use it on the tomb where one will spend eternity in the company of dead relatives? How unlike contemporary Americans' dreams of home ownership and preference for quick and inexpensive funerals. Cremation, an increasingly common option in the United States, would horrify the Betsileo, for whom ancestral bones and relics are important ritual objects.

Cultures use rituals to mark such universal life-cycle events as birth, puberty, marriage, parenthood, and death. But particular cultures differ as to which events merit special celebration and in the emotions expressed during their rituals. Compare the wedding party (left) in Bali, Indonesia, with the funeral (right) among the Tanala of eastern Madagascar. How would you describe the emotions suggested by the photos?

Cultures vary tremendously in their beliefs, practices, integration, and patterning. By focusing on and trying to explain alternative customs, anthropology forces us to reappraise our familiar ways of thinking. In a world full of cultural diversity, contemporary American culture is just one cultural variant, more powerful perhaps, but no more natural, than the others.

>> Culture and the Individual: Agency and Practice

Generations of anthropologists have theorized about the relationship between the "system," on one hand, and the "person" or "individual" on the other. The system can refer to various concepts, including culture, society, social relations, or social structure. Individual human beings always make up, or constitute, the system. But, living within that system, humans also are constrained (to some extent, at least) by its rules and by the actions of other individuals. Cultural rules provide guidance about what to do and how to do it, but people don't always do what the rules say should be done. People use their culture actively and creatively, rather than blindly following its dictates. Humans aren't passive beings doomed to follow their cultural traditions like programmed robots. Cultures are dynamic and constantly changing. People learn, interpret, and manipulate the same rule in different ways—or they emphasize different rules that better suit their interests. Culture is *contested:* Different groups in society struggle with one another over whose ideas, values, goals, and beliefs will prevail. Even common symbols may have radically different meanings to different individuals and groups in the same culture. Golden arches may cause one person to salivate while another plots a vegetarian protest. The same flag may be waved to support or oppose a given war.

Even when they agree about what should be done, people don't always do as their culture directs or as other people expect. Many rules are violated, some very often (for example, automobile speed limits). Some anthropologists find it useful to distinguish between ideal and real culture. The *ideal culture* consists of what people say they should do and what they say they do. *Real culture* refers to their actual behavior as observed by the anthropologist.

Culture is both public and individual, both in the world and in people's minds. Anthropologists are interested not only in public and collective behavior but also in how individuals think, feel, and act. The individual and culture are linked because human social life is a process in which individuals internalize the meanings of public (i.e., cultural) messages. Then, alone and in groups, people influence culture by converting their private (and often divergent) understandings into public expressions (D'Andrade 1984).

Conventionally, culture has been seen as social glue transmitted across the generations, binding people through their common past, rather than as something being continually created and reworked in the present. The tendency to view culture as an entity rather than as a process is changing. Contemporary anthropologists now emphasize how day-to-day action, practice, or resistance can make and remake culture (Gupta and Ferguson 1997b). *Agency* refers to the actions that individuals take, both alone and in groups, in forming and transforming cultural identities.

The approach to culture known as *practice theory* (Ortner 1984) recognizes that individuals within a society or culture have diverse motives and intentions and different degrees of power and influence. Such contrasts may be associated with gender, age, ethnicity, class, and other social variables. Practice theory focuses on how such varied individuals—through their ordinary and extraordinary actions and practices—manage to influence, create, and transform the world they live in. Practice theory appropriately recognizes a reciprocal relation between culture (the system—see above) and the individual. The system shapes how individuals experience and respond to external events, but individuals also play an active role in how society functions and changes. Practice theory recognizes both constraints on individuals and the flexibility and changeability of cultures and social systems.

CULTURETHINK

People use their agency to create new meanings. What messages do these variations on the American flag carry? Would some Americans find some of these symbols un-American?

national culture Cultural experiences, beliefs, learned behavior patterns, and values shared by citizens of the same nation.

international culture Cultural traditions that extend beyond national boundaries.

>> Levels of Culture

We distinguish between different levels of culture: national, international, and subcultural. In today's world these distinctions are increasingly important. **National culture** embodies those beliefs, learned behavior patterns, values, and institutions shared by citizens of the same nation. **International culture** extends beyond and across national boundaries. Because culture is transmitted through learning rather than genetically, cultural

Levels of Culture, with Examples from Sports and Food

TABLE 2.2

Levels of Culture	Sports Examples	Food Examples
International	Soccer, basketball	Pizza
National	Monster truck rallies	Apple pie
Subculture	Bocce	Big Joe Pork Barbecue (South Carolina)

traits can spread through borrowing or diffusion from one group to another.

Because of diffusion, migration, colonialism, and globalization, many cultural traits and patterns have acquired international scope. The contemporary United States, Canada, Great Britain, and Australia share cultural traits they have inherited from their common linguistic and cultural ancestors in Great Britain. Roman Catholics in many different countries share beliefs, symbols, experiences, and values transmitted by their church. The World Cup has become an international cultural event, as people in many countries know the rules of, play, and follow soccer.

Cultures also can be smaller than nations (see Jenks 2005). Although people who live in the same country share a national cultural tradition, all cultures also contain diversity. Individuals, families, communities, regions, classes, and other groups within a culture have different learning experiences as well as shared ones. **Subcultures** are different symbol-based patterns and traditions associated with particular groups in the same complex society. In large or diverse nations such as the United States or Canada, a variety of subcultures originate in region, ethnicity, language, class, and religion. The religious backgrounds of Jews, Baptists, and Roman Catholics create subcultural differences between them. While sharing a common national culture, U.S. northerners and southerners also differ in their beliefs, values, and customary behavior as a result of national and regional history. French-speaking Canadians sometimes pointedly contrast with English-speaking people in the same country. Italian Americans have ethnic traditions different from those of Irish, Polish, and African Americans. Table 2.2 lists sports and food examples illustrating levels of culture.

Nowadays, many anthropologists are reluctant to use the term *subculture*. They feel that the prefix *sub-* is offensive because it means "below." Subcultures thus may

subcultures Different cultural symbol-based traditions associated with subgroups in the same complex society.

ethnocentrism The tendency to view one's own culture as best and to judge the behavior and beliefs of culturally different people by one's own standards.

be perceived as "less than" or somehow inferior to a dominant, elite, or national culture. In this discussion of levels of culture, we intend no such implication. Our point is simply that nations may contain many different culturally defined groups. As mentioned earlier, culture is contested. Various groups may strive to promote the correctness and value of their own practices, values, and beliefs in comparison with those of other groups or the nation as a whole.

>> Ethnocentrism, Cultural Relativism, and Human Rights

The tendency to view one's own culture as superior and to apply one's own cultural values in judging the behavior and beliefs of people raised in other cultures is known as **ethnocentrism.** We hear ethnocentric statements all the time. Ethnocentrism contributes to social solidarity, a sense of value and community, among people who share a cultural tradition. People everywhere think that the familiar explanations, opinions, and customs are true, right, proper, and moral. They regard different behavior as strange, immoral, or savage. Often other societies are not considered fully human. Their members may be castigated as cannibals, thieves, or people who do not bury their dead.

CULTURETHINK

Cite one or more examples of ethnocentrism you have encountered.

Among several tribes in the Trans-Fly region of Papua New Guinea, homosexuality was valued over heterosexuality (see Chapter 9). Men who grew up in the Etoro tribe (Kelly 1976) favored oral sex between men, while their neighbors the Marind-anim encouraged men to engage in anal sex. (In both groups heterosexual coitus was stigmatized and allowed only for reproduction.) Etoro men considered Marind-anim

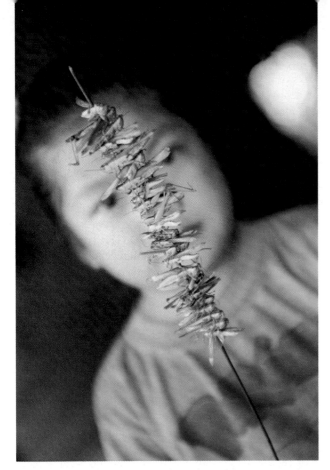

Would you say you have an ethnocentric position on eating grasshoppers?

anal sex to be disgusting, while seeing nothing abnormal about their own oral homosexual practices.

Opposing ethnocentrism is **cultural relativism,** the viewpoint that behavior in one culture should not be judged by the standards of another culture. This position also presents problems. At its most extreme, cultural relativism argues that there is no superior, international, or universal morality, that the moral and ethical rules of all cultures deserve equal respect. In the extreme relativist view, Nazi Germany would be evaluated as nonjudgmentally as Athenian Greece.

In today's world, human rights advocates challenge many tenets of cultural relativism. For example, several societies in Africa and the Middle East have traditions of female genital modification (FGM). *Clitoridectomy* is the removal of a girl's clitoris. Infibulation involves sewing the lips (labia) of the vagina, to constrict the vaginal opening. Both procedures reduce female sexual pleasure, and, it is believed in some cultures, the likelihood of adultery. Human rights advocates, especially women's rights groups, oppose such prac-

tices. The idea is that the tradition infringes on a basic human right—control over one's body and one's sexuality. Some African countries have banned or otherwise discouraged the procedures, as have Western nations that receive immigrants from such cultures. Similar issues arise with circumcision and other male genital operations. Is it right for a baby boy to be circumcised without his permission, as has been done routinely in the United States? Is it proper to require adolescent boys to undergo collective circumcision to fulfill cultural tradition, as has been done in parts of Africa and Australia?

Some argue that the problems with relativism can be solved by distinguishing between methodological and moral relativism. In anthropology, cultural relativism is not a moral position, but a methodological one: To understand another culture fully, you must try to see how the people in that culture see things. What motivates them—what are they thinking—when they do those things? Such an approach does not preclude making moral judgments or taking action. When faced with Nazi atrocities, a methodological relativist would have a moral obligation to stop doing anthropology and take action to intervene. In the FGM example, one can understand the *motivations* for the practice by looking at the situation from the point of view of those who engage in it. Having done this, one then faces the moral question of whether to intervene to stop it. We should recognize as well that different people and groups living in the same society—for example, women and men, old and

> **cultural relativism** The position that the values and standards of cultures differ and deserve respect. Anthropology is characterized by methodological rather than moral relativism: In order to understand another culture fully, anthropologists try to understand its members' beliefs and motivations. Methodological relativism does not preclude making moral judgments or taking action.

Human rights activists in Lafayette Park across from the White House urge action on behalf of the people of Sudan's Darfur region, where a protracted civil war has killed at least 200,000 people and displaced two million others.

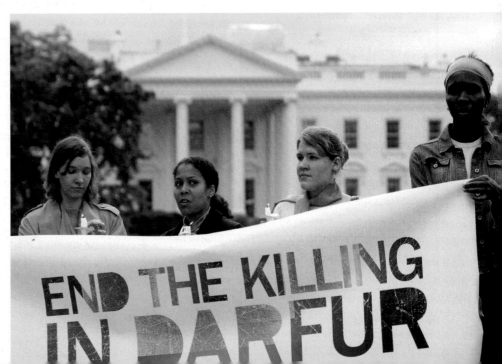

END THE KILLING IN DARFUR

young, the more and less powerful—can have widely different views about what is proper, necessary, and moral (see Hunt 2007).

The idea of **human rights** invokes a realm of justice and morality beyond and superior to the laws and customs of particular countries, cultures, and religions (see R. Wilson 1996). Human rights include the right to speak freely, to hold religious beliefs without persecution, and not to be murdered, injured, or enslaved or imprisoned without charge. Such rights are seen as *inalienable* (nations cannot abridge or terminate them) and international (larger than and superior to individual nations and cultures). Four United Nations documents describe nearly all the human rights that have been internationally recognized. Those documents are the U.N. Charter; the Universal Declaration of Human Rights; the Covenant on Economic, Social and Cultural Rights; and the Covenant on Civil and Political Rights.

Alongside the human rights movement has arisen an awareness of the need to preserve cultural rights. Unlike human rights, **cultural rights** are vested not in individuals but in groups, such as religious and ethnic minorities and indigenous societies. Cultural rights include a group's ability to preserve its culture, to raise its children in the ways of its forebears, to continue its language, and not to be deprived of its economic base by the nation in which it is located (Greaves 1995). The related notion of indigenous **intellectual property rights (IPR)** has arisen in an attempt to conserve each society's cultural base—its core beliefs, knowledge, and practices (see Merry 2006). Much traditional cultural knowledge has commercial value. Examples include ethnomedicine (traditional medical knowledge and techniques), cosmetics, cultivated plants, foods, folklore, arts, crafts, songs, dances, costumes, and rituals (see Nazarea 2006). According to the IPR concept, a particular group may determine how indigenous knowledge and its products may be used and distributed and the level of compensation required.

The notion of cultural rights is related to the idea of cultural relativism, and the problem discussed previously arises again. What does one do about cultural rights that interfere with human rights? We believe that anthropology's main job is to present accurate accounts and explanations of cultural phenomena. The anthropologist doesn't have to approve infanticide, cannibalism, or torture to record their existence and determine their causes and the motivations behind them. However, each anthropologist has a choice about where he or she will do fieldwork. Some anthropologists choose not to study a particular culture because they discover in advance or early in fieldwork that behavior they consider morally repugnant is practiced there. Anthropologists respect human diversity. Most ethnographers try to be objective, accurate, and sensitive in their accounts of other cultures. However, objectivity, sensitivity, and a cross-cultural perspective don't mean that anthropologists have to ignore international standards of justice and morality. What do you think?

human rights Doctrine that invokes a realm of justice and morality beyond and superior to particular countries, cultures, and religions. Human rights, usually seen as vested in individuals, include the right to speak freely, to hold religious beliefs without persecution, and not to be enslaved.

cultural rights Doctrine that certain rights are vested not in individuals but in identifiable groups, such as religious and ethnic minorities and indigenous societies.

intellectual property rights (IPR) Each society's cultural base—its core beliefs and principles. IPR is claimed as a group right—a cultural right, allowing indigenous groups to control who may know and use their collective knowledge and its applications.

CULTURETHINK

Where should we draw the line between acceptance based on cultural relativism and objection based on a violation of human rights? Some examples are easy: The Holocaust was clearly unacceptable. What about some current controversial issues: Is arranged marriage always wrong? Female (or male) circumcision? Drug dealing? Think of other controversial issues that require cultural understanding in order to accurately assess whether they involve unacceptable human rights violations.

>> Mechanisms of Cultural Change

Why and how do cultures change? We gave some examples earlier of **diffusion,** or borrowing of traits between cultures. Such exchange of information and products has gone on throughout human history because cultures have never been truly isolated. Contact between neighboring groups has always existed and has extended over vast areas (Boas 1940/1966). Diffusion is *direct* when two cultures trade with, intermarry among, or wage war on one another. Diffusion is *forced* when one culture subjugates another and imposes its customs on the dominated group. Diffusion is *indirect* when items or traits move from group A to group C via group B without any firsthand contact between A and C. In this case, group B might consist of traders or merchants who take products from a variety of places to new markets. Or group B might be geographically situated between A and C, so that what it gets from A eventually winds up in C, and vice versa. In today's world,

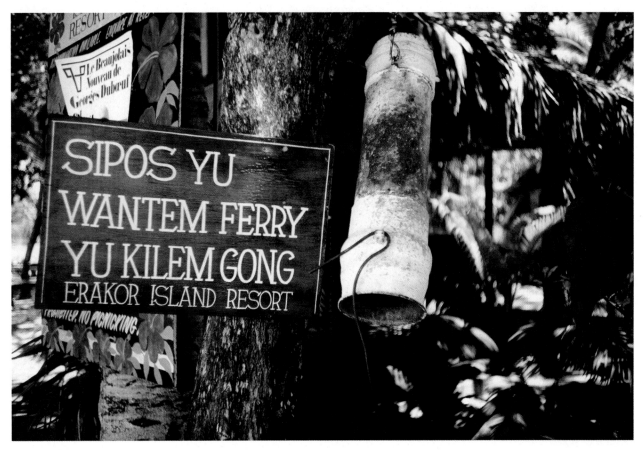

Illustrating acculturation is this sign in pidgin English at a landing on Efate Island, Vanuatu, South Pacific. It reads, "If you want the ferry to come, strike the gong."

much international diffusion is indirect—culture spread by the mass media and advanced information technology.

Acculturation, a second mechanism of cultural change, is the exchange of cultural features that results when groups have continuous firsthand contact. The cultures of either or both groups may be changed by this contact (Redfield, Linton, and Herskovits 1936). With acculturation, parts of the cultures change, but each group remains distinct. One example of acculturation is a *pidgin,* a mixed language that develops to ease communication between members of different cultures in contact. This usually happens in situations of trade or colonialism. Pidgin English, for example, is a simplified form of English. It blends English grammar with the grammar of a native language. Pidgin English was first used for commerce in Chinese ports.

Similar pidgins developed later in Papua New Guinea and West Africa. In situations of continuous contact, cultures have also exchanged and blended foods, recipes, music, dances, clothing, tools, and technologies.

Independent invention—the process by which humans innovate, creatively finding solutions to problems—is a third mechanism of cultural change. Faced with comparable problems and challenges, people in different societies have innovated and changed in similar ways, which is one reason cultural generalities exist.

diffusion Borrowing between cultures either directly or through intermediaries.

acculturation The exchange of cultural features that results when groups come into continuous firsthand contact; the original cultural patterns of either or both groups may be altered, but the groups remain distinct.

independent invention Development of the same culture trait or pattern in separate cultures as a result of comparable needs and circumstances.

CULTURE THINK

White Americans took Native American children from their families and placed them in boarding schools where they were not allowed to speak their own language or wear local clothing and adornments. What mechanism of cultural change did they experience? Think of other examples of cultural change and identify the mechanism at work.

STUDY TIP

Three mechanisms of culture change are diffusion (direct, forced, and indirect), acculturation, and independent invention.

In our interlinked, twenty-first century world, even men in remote villages may have access to computers and the Internet. Shown here, two men with a laptop in the village of Bhaktapur, Nepal.

One example is the independent invention of agriculture in the Middle East and Mexico. Over the course of human history, major innovations have spread at the expense of earlier ones. Often a major invention, such as agriculture, triggers a series of subsequent interrelated changes. These economic revolutions have social and cultural repercussions. Thus in both Mexico and the Middle East, agriculture led to many social, political, and legal changes, including notions of property and distinctions in wealth, class, and power (see Naylor 1996).

>> Globalization

The term **globalization** encompasses a series of processes, including diffusion, migration, and acculturation, working to promote change in a world in which nations and people are increasingly interlinked and mutually dependent. Promoting such linkages are economic and political forces, as well as modern systems of transportation and communication. The forces of globalization include international

globalization A set of processes, including diffusion, migration, and acculturation, that promote change in today's interlinked world.

STUDY **TIP**

Globalization is a complex set of processes. It helps to think of it as having three main characteristics:

- Increasing global political and economic interdependence;
- Increased mobility of people (migration and travel);
- Fast and efficient communications technologies that link people across the globe.

commerce and finance, travel and tourism, transnational migration, the media, and various high-tech information flows (see Appadurai 2001; Friedman and Friedman 2008; Scholte 2000). During the Cold War, which ended with the fall of the Soviet Union, the basis of international alliance was political, ideological, and military. More recent international pacts have shifted toward trade and economic issues. New economic unions (which have met considerable resistance in their member nations) have been created through the North American Free Trade Agreement (NAFTA), the World Trade Organization (WTO), and the European Union (EU).

Communication systems and the media play a significant role in today's process of globalization. Long-distance communication is easier, faster, and cheaper than ever, and extends to remote areas. The mass media help propel a globally spreading culture of consumption. Within nations and across their borders, the media spread information about products, services, rights, institutions, lifestyles, and the perceived costs and benefits of globalization. Emigrants transmit information and resources transnationally, as they maintain their ties with home (phoning, faxing, emailing, making visits, sending money). In a sense, such people live *multilocally*—in different places and cultures at once. They learn to play various social roles and to change behavior and identity depending on the situation (see Cresswell 2006).

The effects of globalization are broad and not always welcome. Local people must cope increasingly with forces generated by progressively larger systems—region, nation, and world. An army of outsiders now intrudes on people everywhere. Tourism has become the world's number one industry (see Holden 2005). Economic development agents and the media promote the idea that work should be for cash rather than mainly for subsistence. Indigenous peoples and traditional societies have devised various strategies to deal with threats to their autonomy, identity, and livelihood (Maybury-Lewis

2002). New forms of political mobilization and cultural expression, including the rights movements discussed previously, are emerging from the interplay of local, regional, national, and international cultural forces (see Ong and Collier 2005).

get involved!

Interview a friend, a classmate, or a relative who is a member of an immigrant group. If no one you know meets this description, perhaps a friend can recommend someone who does. Ask about particular beliefs, traditions, values, or symbols. Which of these views or traditions might other Americans see as strange or improper? Can you determine what the person you interview finds odd in America's national culture? Note any ethnocentric statements you hear from this person and any ethnocentrism you experience yourself during the interview.

> 66 I learned much more about acting from philosophy courses, psychology courses, history and anthropology than I ever learned in acting class. 99

Tim Robbins

For REVIEW

I. What is culture, and why do we study it?

- Culture, which is distinctly human, refers to customary behavior and beliefs that are passed on through learning and symbols. We study culture to understand the human condition: our origins in our primate ancestors' evolving capacity for culture, our shared human capacity for culture, culture's unique and universal forms, how we think and act as members of groups, and how we organize and change our lives and our relations with others. The study of culture also teaches us about our unique relation to nature, the significance of understanding ourselves as biocultural creatures, and our interactions, both adaptive and maladaptive, with our environments.

II. What is the relation between culture and the individual?

- Cultural rules constrain individuals but do not dictate their behavior. People use culture actively and creatively. They interpret and manipulate the rules in different ways, emphasize rules that best suit their needs, and contest the rules. People play an active role in how society functions and changes. Having internalized the meanings of cultural messages, individuals then influence their culture by converting their private (often divergent) understandings into public expressions.

III. How does culture change?

- Culture changes through three chief mechanisms: diffusion, acculturation, and independent invention. Diffusion is the spread of cultural traits as groups borrow from one another. Acculturation involves the exchange of cultural features that results when groups have continuous first-hand contact. Independent invention is the development of the same cultural trait in separate cultures as a result of comparable circumstances. In addition, globalization—a series of processes that includes diffusion, acculturation, and migration—promotes change in our contemporary world, where nations and peoples are increasingly linked and interdependent.

Pop Quiz

1. Which of the following is *not* one of the ways in which individuals acquire culture?
   a. Genetic transmission
   b. Conscious and unconscious learning
   c. Observation
   d. Direct instruction

2. Which of the following statements about culture is false?
   a. Despite increased reliance on cultural means of adaptation, humans still adapt biologically.
   b. Cultural traditions are transmitted through learning.
   c. Cultural patterns might offer short-term benefits to a particular group but nevertheless threaten that group's long-term survival.
   d. If certain cultural patterns offer short-term benefits, they usually are adaptive in the long run as well.

3. The chapter's discussion of the similarities and differences between humans and apes:
   a. States that all hominids have evolved the same capacities for culture.
   b. Emphasizes culture's evolutionary basis, stressing the interaction between biology and culture.
   c. States that genetics has been more important than culture in determining our particular evolutionary path.
   d. Illustrates how human females' lack of a visible estrus cycle determined our unique capacity for culture.

4. The "psychic unity" of humans, a doctrine that most anthropologists accept, means that:
   a. Psychology is the exclusive domain of the academic discipline of psychology.
   b. Genetically mixed descendants of people from around the world will not be capable of acquiring the common national culture of the country they now live in.
   c. Although individuals differ in their emotional and intellectual tendencies, all human populations have equivalent capacities for culture.
   d. Psychological attributes are determined by our genes.

5. Anthropologists have found that certain biological, psychological, social, and cultural features are universal, found in every society. All the following are examples of universal features *except:*
   a. A long period of infant dependency.
   b. Seasonal (rather than year-round) sexuality.
   c. Life in groups and in some kind of family.
   d. Capacity to use symbols, languages, and tools.

6. Which of the following statements about culture is false?
   a. All human groups possess some form of culture.
   b. Culture is the major reason for human adaptability.
   c. Human groups differ in their capacities for culture.
   d. The capacity for culture has its basis in human evolution.

7. Anthropologists have noted that culture is often contested. This means that:
   a. Different groups in a society struggle over whose ideas, values, goals, and beliefs will prevail.
   b. Certain symbols may have different meanings to specific individuals and groups, even though most common symbols are agreed upon by everyone in a culture.
   c. Humans are passive beings who must follow their cultural traditions.
   d. "Real" culture (the actual behavior of individuals in a society) is of primary importance to anthropological study, while "ideal" culture has no significance.

8. In anthropology, cultural relativism:
   a. Is primarily a methodological position rather than a moral one.
   b. Is equally a moral and a methodological stance toward other cultures.
   c. Is synonymous with moral relativism.
   d. Is a political position that argues for the defense of human rights, regardless of culture.

9. Agriculture developed in at least seven different regions of the world. Therefore, agriculture is an example of which mechanism of cultural change?
   a. Acculturation
   b. Enculturation
   c. Independent invention
   d. Diffusion

10. The series of processes that are making nations and people increasingly interlinked and mutually dependent is known as:
    a. Acculturation
    b. Independent invention
    c. Diffusion
    d. Globalization

1. (a), 2. (d), 3. (b), 4. (c), 5. (b), 6. (c), 7. (a), 8. (a), 9. (c), 10. (d)

3

ETHICS
AND METHODS

UNDERSTANDING OURSELVES

"Been on any digs lately?" Ask your instructor if she or he has been asked this question. Then ask how often he or she actually has been on a dig. Remember that anthropology has four subfields, only two of which (archaeology and biological anthropology) require much digging—in the ground at least. To be sure, cultural anthropologists "dig out" information about varied lifestyles. Traditionally cultural anthropologists have done a variant on the *Star Trek* mission of seeking out, if not new, at least different "life" and "civilizations."

Despite globalization, the cultural diversity under anthropological scrutiny right now may be as great as ever, because anthropologists now study modern nations. Today's cultural anthropologists are as likely to be studying artists in Miami or bankers in Beirut as Trobriand sailors in the South Pacific. Still, we can't forget that anthropology did originate in non-Western, nonindustrial societies. Its research techniques were developed to deal with small populations. Even when working in modern nations, anthropologists still consider ethnography with small groups to be an excellent way of learning about how people live their lives and make decisions.

Before this course, did you know the names of any anthropologists? If so, which ones? For the general public, biological anthropologists tend to be better known than cultural anthropologists because of what they study. You're more likely to have seen film of Jane Goodall with chimps or a paleoanthropologist holding a skull than an ethnographer at work. One particularly wise and charismatic cultural anthropologist and an important public figure through her death in 1978 was Margaret Mead. Famed for her work on teen sexuality in Samoa and gender roles in New Guinea, Mead may well be the most famous anthropologist who ever lived. She appeared regularly on NBC's *Tonight Show.* In all her ventures—including teaching, museum work, TV, anthropological films, popular books, and magazines—Mead helped Americans appreciate the relevance of anthropology to understanding their daily lives. Her work is featured here and elsewhere in this book.

As You READ

- What ethical concerns and issues must anthropologists consider?
- Where and how do cultural anthropologists do fieldwork?
- What are some ways of studying complex societies in modern nations?

>> Ethics and Anthropology

As the main organization representing the breadth of anthropology (all four subfields, academic, and applied dimensions), the American Anthropological Association (AAA) believes that generating and using knowledge of the peoples of the world, past and present, is a worthy goal. The mission of the AAA is to advance anthropological research and encourage the spread of anthropological knowledge through publications, teaching, public education, and application. Part of that mission is to help educate AAA members about ethical obligations and challenges (http://www.aaanet.org).

Anthropologists increasingly are mindful of the fact that science exists in society, and in the context of law and ethics. Anthropologists can't study things simply because they happen to be interesting or of value to science. As anthropologists conduct research and engage in other professional activities, ethical issues inevitably arise. Anthropologists typically have worked abroad, outside their own society. In the context of international contacts and cultural diversity, different value systems will meet, and often compete. To guide its members in making decisions

CULTURETHINK

Ethical decisions rarely are easy or obvious. They require thoughtful consideration of whom and what may be harmed—physically, socially, psychologically, or otherwise. What difficult ethical decisions have you had to make? Looking back, do you think you made the right decision?

involving ethics and values, the AAA offers a Code of Ethics.

The most recent revision of the code, adopted in 2009, recognizes that anthropologists have obligations to their scholarly field, to the wider society and culture, and to the human species, other species, and the environment. This code's aim is to offer guidelines and to promote discussion and education, rather than to investigate allegations of misconduct. The AAA code addresses several contexts in which anthropologists work. Its main points may be summarized as follows:

> Anthropologists should be open and honest about . . . their research projects with all parties affected by the research. These parties should be informed about the nature, procedures, purpose(s), potential impacts, and source(s) of support for the research. Researchers should not compromise anthropological ethics in order to conduct research. They should . . . pay attention to proper relations between themselves as guests and the host nations and communities where they work. The AAA does not advise anthropologists to avoid taking stands on issues. Indeed, . . . seeking to shape actions and policies may be as ethically justifiable as inaction.

The full Code of Ethics is available at the AAA website (http://www.aaanet.org/issues/policy-advocacy/Code-of-Ethics.cfm).

Most ethnographers (field-workers in cultural anthropology) work outside their nations of origin. In the host country (the nation where the research takes place), the ethnographer seeks permissions, cooperation, and knowledge from government officials, scholars, and many others, most importantly the people of the community being studied. Cultural sensitivity is paramount when the research subjects are living people into whose lives the anthropologist intrudes. Anthropologists need to establish and maintain appropriate, collaborative, and nonexploit-

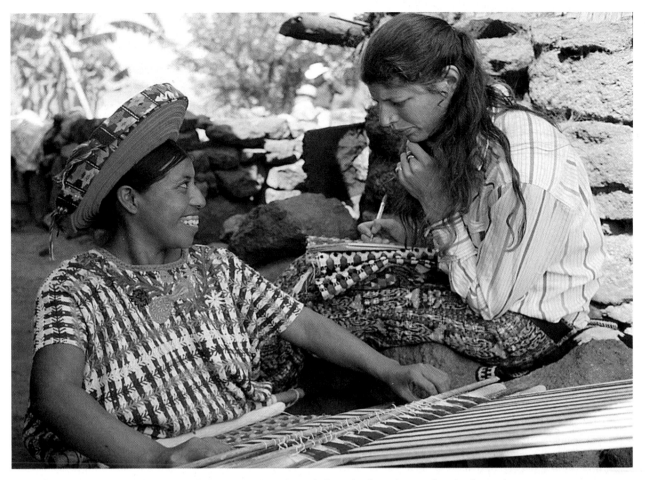

Anthropologists such as Christie Kiefer typically form personal relationships with their cultural consultants, such as this Guatemalan weaver.

CULTURE THINK

During the 1980s, anthropologist Nancy Scheper-Hughes studied survival strategies in a poverty-stricken Brazilian shantytown. Because they lacked the resources needed to ensure the survival of their children, women often neglected sickly babies who seemed doomed to die. Dr. Scheper-Hughes treated and fed one of those babies, who then lived to be a healthy adult. Did she do the right thing? What are the costs and benefits of the decision she made?

ative relationships with colleagues and communities in the host country.

To work in a host country and community, researchers must inform officials and colleagues there about the purpose and funding, and the anticipated results and impacts,

of the research. Researchers have to gain the informed consent of all affected parties—from the authorities who control access to the field site to the members of the community to be studied. Before the research begins, people should be informed about the purpose, nature, and procedures of the research and its potential costs and benefits to them. **Informed consent** (agreement to take part in the research, after having been so informed) should be obtained from anyone who provides information or who might be affected by the research.

> **informed consent** An agreement sought by ethnographers from community members to take part in research.

According to the AAA code, anthropologists have a debt to the people they work with in the field, and they should reciprocate in appropriate ways. For example, it

STUDY TIP

The AAA Code of Ethics recognizes obligations to four major constituents: the scholarly field, the people being studied or related to the study, other species, and the environment.

is highly appropriate for North American anthropologists working in another country to (1) include host country colleagues in their research plans and funding requests, (2) establish collaborative relationships with those colleagues and their institutions, and (3) include host country colleagues in publication of the research results. Of course, in cultural anthropology, as in all the subfields, anthropologists' primary ethical obligation is to the people being studied. Their welfare and interests come first.

>> Research Methods

Cultural anthropology and sociology share an interest in social relations, organization, and behavior. Important differences between these disciplines arose, however, from the kinds of societies each traditionally studied. Initially, sociologists focused on the industrial West; anthropologists, on nonindustrial societies. Different methods of data collection and analysis emerged to deal with those different kinds of societies. To study large-scale, complex nations, sociologists came to rely on questionnaires and

World-famous anthropologist Margaret Mead in the field in Bali, Indonesia, in 1957.

other means of gathering masses of quantifiable data. For many years, sampling and statistical techniques have been basic to sociology, whereas statistical training has been less common in anthropology (although this is changing somewhat as anthropologists work increasingly in modern nations).

Traditional ethnographers studied small, nonliterate (without writing) populations and relied on ethnographic methods appropriate to that context. "Ethnography is a research process in which the anthropologist closely observes, records, and engages in the daily life of another culture—an experience labeled as the fieldwork method—and then writes accounts of this culture, emphasizing descriptive detail" (Marcus and Fischer 1986, p. 18). One key method described in this quote is **participant observation**—taking part in the events one is observing, describing, and analyzing.

Anthropology started to separate from sociology around 1900. Early students of society, such as the French scholar Émile Durkheim, were among the founders of both sociology and anthropology. Comparing the organization of simple and complex societies, Durkheim studied the religions of Native Australians (Durkheim 1912/2001), as well as mass phenomena (such as suicide rates) in modern nations (Durkheim 1897/1951). Eventually, anthropology would specialize in the former, sociology, in the latter.

>> Ethnography: Anthropology's Distinctive Strategy

Anthropology developed into a separate field as early scholars worked on Indian (Native American) reservations and traveled to distant lands to study small groups of foragers (hunters and gatherers) and cultivators. Traditionally, the process of becoming a cultural anthropologist has required a field experience in another society. Early ethnographers lived in small-scale, relatively isolated societies, with simple technologies and economies.

Ethnography thus emerged as a research strategy in societies with greater cultural uniformity and less social differentiation than are found in large, modern, industrial nations. Traditionally, ethnographers have tried to understand the whole of a particular culture (or, more realistically, as much as they can, given limitations of time and perception). To pursue this goal, ethnographers adopt a free-ranging strategy for gathering information. In a given society or community, the ethnographer moves from setting to setting, place to place, and subject to subject to discover the totality and interconnectedness of social life. By expanding our knowledge of the range of human diversity, ethnography provides a foundation for generalizations about human behavior and social life. Ethnographers draw on varied techniques to piece together a picture of otherwise alien lifestyles. Anthropologists usually employ several (but rarely all) of the techniques discussed here (see also Bernard 2006; Wolcott 2008).

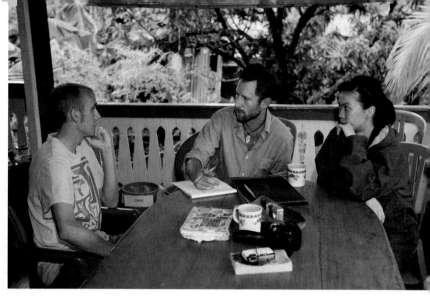

Researchers discuss their work on fishing in Ambuea village, Kaledupa Island, Sulawesi, Indonesia.

>> Ethnographic Techniques

The characteristic *field techniques* of the ethnographer include the following:

- Direct, firsthand observation of behavior, including *participant observation.*

- Conversation with varying degrees of formality, from the daily chitchat, which helps maintain rapport and provides knowledge about what is going on, to prolonged *interviews,* which can be unstructured or structured.

- The *genealogical method.*

- Detailed work with *key consultants,* or *informants,* about particular areas of community life.

- In-depth interviewing, often leading to the collection of *life histories* of particular people (narrators).

- Discovery of local (native) beliefs and perceptions, which may be compared with the ethnographer's own observations and conclusions.

- Problem-oriented research of many sorts.

CULTURETHINK

A conversation with someone can be like an informal interview and a way to get to know more about them. What kinds of information might you learn about someone standing next to you in a long, slow line by engaging in a natural, informal conversation? Try it out, thinking of yourself as an anthropologist.

- Longitudinal research—the continuous long-term study of an area or site.

- Team research—coordinated research by multiple ethnographers.

OBSERVATION AND PARTICIPANT OBSERVATION

Ethnographers must pay attention to hundreds of details of daily life, seasonal events, and unusual happenings. They should record what they see as they see it. Things never will seem quite as strange as they do during the first few weeks in the field. The ethnographer eventually gets used to, and accepts as normal, cultural patterns that initially were alien. Staying a bit more than a year in the field allows the ethnographer to repeat the season of his or her arrival, when certain events and processes may have been missed because of initial unfamiliarity and culture shock.

> **participant observation**
> A characteristic ethnographic technique; taking part in the events one is observing, describing, and analyzing.

Many ethnographers record their impressions in a personal *diary,* which is kept separate from more formal *field notes.* Later, this record of early impressions will help point out some of the most basic aspects of cultural diversity. Such aspects include distinctive smells, noises people make, how they cover their mouths when they eat, and how they gaze at others. These patterns, which are so basic as to seem almost trivial, are part of what Bronislaw Malinowski called "the imponderabilia of native life and of typical behavior" (Malinowski 1922/1961, p. 20). These features of culture are so fundamental that natives take them for granted. They are too basic even to talk about, but the unaccustomed eye of the fledgling ethnographer picks them up. Thereafter, becoming familiar, they fade to the edge of consciousness. Initial impressions are valuable and should be recorded. First and foremost, ethnographers

One ethical requirement of research is that it not harm the people being studied. Usually people provide consent (informed consent, p. 43) by signing a form stating they agree to participate. It's easy to ask for a signature while doing a survey in the United States. What might be the challenges of gaining informed consent while doing ethnography when the topic is sensitive (e.g., drug use) or when the people don't know how to read and write?

should try to be accurate observers, recorders, and reporters of what they see in the field.

As ethnographers, we strive to establish *rapport,* a good, friendly working relationship based on personal contact, with our hosts. One of ethnography's most characteristic procedures is participant observation, which means that we take part in community life as we study it. As human beings living among others, we cannot be totally impartial and detached observers. We take part in many events and processes we are observing and trying to comprehend. By participating, we learn why local people find such events meaningful, as we see how they are organized and conducted.

In Arembepe, Brazil, Conrad Kottak learned about fishing by sailing on the Atlantic with local fishers. He gave Jeep rides to malnourished babies, to pregnant mothers, and once to a teenage girl possessed by a spirit. All of those people needed to consult specialists outside the village. He danced at Arembepe's festive occasions, drank libations commemorating new births, and became a godfather to a village girl. Most anthropologists have similar field experiences. The common humanity of the student and the studied, the ethnographer and the research community, makes participant observation inevitable.

CONVERSATION, INTERVIEWING, AND INTERVIEW SCHEDULES

Participating in local life means that ethnographers constantly talk to people and ask questions. As our knowledge of the native language and culture increases, we understand more. There are several stages in learning a field language. First is the naming phase—asking name after name of the objects around us. Later we are able to pose more complex questions and understand the replies. We begin to understand simple conversations between two villagers. If our language expertise proceeds far enough, we eventually become able to comprehend rapid-fire public discussions and group conversations.

Seated blonde woman (on the right) meets with villagers during field work in Kenya.

One data-gathering technique Kottak has used in both Arembepe and Madagascar involves an ethnographic survey that includes an interview schedule. In 1964, Kottak and his fellow field-workers attempted to complete an interview schedule in each of Arembepe's 160 households. They entered almost every household (fewer than 5 percent refused to participate) to ask a set of questions on a printed form. Their results provided them with a census and basic information about the village. They wrote down the name, age, and gender of each household member. They gathered data on family type, religion, present and previous jobs, income, expenditures, diet, possessions, and many other items on their eight-page form.

Although they were doing a survey, their approach differed from the survey research design routinely used by sociologists and other social scientists working in large, industrial nations. That survey research, discussed below, involves sampling (choosing a small, manageable study group from a larger population). Kottak and his colleagues did not select a partial sample from the total population. Instead, they tried to interview in all households in the community (that is, to have a total sample). They used an interview schedule rather than a questionnaire. With the **interview schedule,** the ethnographer talks face-to-face with people, asks the questions, and writes down the answers. *Questionnaire* procedures tend to be more indirect and impersonal; often the respondent fills in the form.

Kottak's goal of getting a total sample allowed him to meet almost everyone in the village and helped establish rapport. Decades later, Arembepeiros still talk warmly about how these ethnographers were interested enough in them to visit their homes and ask them questions. This stood in sharp contrast to the other outsiders the villagers had known, who considered them too poor and backward to be taken seriously.

Like other survey research, however, Kottak's interview schedule did gather comparable quantifiable information. It gave his group of researchers a basis for assessing patterns and exceptions in village life. Their schedules included a core set of questions that were posed to everyone. Interesting side issues often came up during the interview, which they would pursue then or later.

Kottak and his colleagues followed such leads into many dimensions of village life. One woman, for instance—a midwife—became the key cultural consultant

Anthropology Works

Ethnographic methods help marketing professionals to understand what consumers want and need. Participant observation allows marketers to see for themselves how people use or might use products. Group or individual interviews reveal people's attitudes and perceptions.

they sought out later when they wanted detailed information about local childbirth. Another woman had done an internship in an Afro-Brazilian cult (*candomblé*) in the city. She still went there regularly to study, dance, and get possessed. She became their candomblé expert.

Thus, their interview schedule provided a structure that *directed but did not confine* them as researchers. It enabled their ethnography to be both quantitative and qualitative. The quantitative part consisted of the basic information gathered and later analyzed statistically. The qualitative dimension came from follow-up questions, open-ended discussions, pauses for gossip, and work with key consultants.

interview schedule
Ethnographic tool for structuring a formal interview. A prepared form guides interviews with households or individuals being compared systematically. This contrasts with a questionnaire because the researcher has personal contact and records people's answers.

genealogical method
Procedures by which ethnographers discover and record connections of kinship, descent, and marriage, using diagrams and symbols.

STUDY TIP

An interview schedule uses both qualitative and quantitative methods. It is similar to a *survey* in that it obtains data from many individuals that can be analyzed statistically. It is similar to *ethnographic research* in that the researcher sits with the respondent, asks questions, and writes down the answers.

THE GENEALOGICAL METHOD

As ordinary people, many of us learn about our own ancestry and relatives by tracing our genealogies. Various computer programs now allow us to trace our "family tree" and degrees of relationship. The **genealogical method** is a well-established ethnographic technique. Early ethnographers developed notation and symbols to deal with kinship, descent, and marriage. Genealogy is a prominent building block in the social organization of nonindustrial societies, where people live and work each day with their close kin. Anthropologists need to collect genealogical data to understand current social relations and to reconstruct history. In many nonindustrial societies, kin links are basic to social life. Anthropologists even call such cultures "kin-based societies." Everyone is related, and spends most of his or her time with relatives. Rules of behavior attached to particular kin relations are basic to everyday life (see Carsten 2004). Marriage also is crucial in organizing nonindustrial societies because strategic marriages between villages, tribes, and clans create political alliances.

KEY CULTURAL CONSULTANTS

Every community has people who by accident, experience, talent, or training can provide the most complete or useful information about particular aspects of life. These people are **key cultural consultants,** also called *key informants.* In Ivato, the Betsileo village in Madagascar where Kottak spent most of his time, a man named Rakoto was particularly knowledgeable about village history. When asked to work on a genealogy of the fifty to sixty people buried in the village tomb, however, he called in his cousin Tuesdaysfather, who knew more about that subject. Tuesdaysfather had survived an epidemic of influenza that ravaged Madagascar, along with much of the world, around 1919. Immune to the disease himself, Tuesdaysfather had the grim job of burying his kin as they died. He kept track of everyone buried in the tomb. Tuesdaysfather helped Kottak with the tomb genealogy. Rakoto joined him in providing personal details about the deceased villagers.

key cultural consultant An expert on a particular aspect of local life who helps the ethnographer understand that aspect.

life history Of a cultural consultant; provides a personal cultural portrait of existence or change in a culture.

emic The research strategy that focuses on native explanations and criteria of significance.

etic The research strategy that emphasizes the observer's rather than the natives' explanations, categories, and criteria of significance.

LIFE HISTORIES

In nonindustrial societies as in our own society, individual personalities, interests, and abilities vary. Some villagers prove to be more interested in the ethnographer's work and are more helpful, interesting, and pleasant than others are. Anthropologists develop likes and dislikes in the field as we do at home. Often, when we find someone unusually interesting, we collect his or her **life history.** This recollection of a lifetime of experiences provides a more intimate and personal cultural portrait than would be possible otherwise. Life histories, which may be recorded or videotaped for later review and analysis, reveal how specific people perceive, react to, and contribute to changes that affect their lives. Such accounts can illustrate diversity, which exists within any community, since the focus is on how different people interpret and deal with some of the same problems. Many ethnographers include the collection of life histories as an important part of their research strategy.

LOCAL BELIEFS AND PERCEPTIONS, AND THE ETHNOGRAPHER'S

One goal of ethnography is to discover local (native) views, beliefs, and perceptions, which may be compared with the ethnographer's own observations and conclusions. In the field, ethnographers typically combine two research strategies, the *emic* (native-oriented) and the *etic* (scientist-oriented). These terms, derived from linguistics, have been applied to ethnography by various anthropologists. Marvin Harris (1968/2001) popularized the following meanings of the terms: An **emic** approach investigates how local people think. How do they perceive and categorize the world? What are their rules for behavior? What has meaning for them? How do they imagine and explain things? Operating emically, the ethnographer seeks the "native viewpoint," relying on local people to explain things and to say whether something is significant or not. The term **cultural consultant,** or *informant,* refers to individuals the ethnographer gets to know in the field, the people who teach him or her about their culture, who provide the emic perspective.

The **etic** (scientist-oriented) approach shifts the focus from local observations, categories, explanations, and interpretations to those of the anthropologist. The etic approach recognizes that members of a culture often are too involved in what they are doing to interpret their cultures impartially. Operating etically, the ethnographer emphasizes what he or she (the observer) notices and considers important. As a trained scientist, the ethnographer should try to bring an objective and comprehensive viewpoint to the study of other cultures. Of course, like any other scientist, the ethnographer is also a human being with cultural blinders that prevent complete objectivity. As in other sciences, proper training can reduce, but not totally eliminate, the observer's bias. But anthropologists do have special training to compare behavior between different societies.

What are some examples of emic versus etic perspectives? Consider our holidays. For North Americans, Thanksgiving Day has special significance. In our view (emically), it is a unique cultural celebration that commemorates particular historical themes. But a wider, etic perspective sees Thanksgiving as just one more example of the postharvest festivals held in many societies. Another example: Local people (including many Americans) may believe that chills and drafts cause colds, which scientists know are caused by germs. In cultures that lack the germ theory of disease, illnesses are emically explained by various causes, ranging from spirits to ancestors to witches. *Illness* refers to a culture's (emic) perception and explanation of bad health, whereas *disease* refers to the scientific—etic—explanation of poor health, involving known pathogens.

Ethnographers typically combine emic and etic strategies in their fieldwork. The statements, perceptions, categories, and opinions of local people help ethnographers understand how cultures work. Local beliefs are also interesting and valuable in themselves. However, people often fail to admit, or even recognize, certain causes and consequences of their behavior. This is as true of North Americans as it is of people in other societies.

>> The Evolution of Ethnography

The Polish anthropologist Bronislaw Malinowski (1884–1942), who spent most of his professional life in England, is generally considered the founder of ethnography. Like most anthropologists of his time, Malinowski did *salvage ethnography,* in the belief that the ethnographer's job is to study and record cultural diversity threatened by Westernization. Early ethnographic accounts (ethnographies), such as Malinowski's classic *Argonauts of the Western Pacific* (1922/1961), were similar to earlier traveler and explorer accounts in describing the writer's discovery of unknown people and places. However, the *scientific* aims of ethnographies set them apart from books by explorers and amateurs.

The style that dominated "classic" ethnographies was *ethnographic realism.* The writer's goal was to present an accurate, objective, scientific account of a different way of life, written by someone who knew it firsthand. This knowledge came from an "ethnographic adventure" involving immersion in an alien language and culture. Ethnographers derived their authority—both as scientists and as voices of "the native" or "the other"—from this personal research experience.

> **cultural consultant** Someone the ethnographer gets to know in the field, who teaches him or her about their society and culture (also called *informant*).

Bronislaw Malinowski (1884–1942), who was born in Poland but spent most of his professional life in England, did fieldwork in the Trobriand Islands from 1914 to 1918. Malinowski is generally considered to be the father of ethnography. Does this photo suggest anything about his relationship with Trobriand villagers?

Malinowski's ethnographies were guided by the assumption that aspects of culture are linked and intertwined. Beginning by describing a Trobriand sailing expedition, the ethnographer then follows the links between that entry point and other areas of the culture, such as magic, religion, myths, kinship, and trade. Compared with Malinowski, today's ethnographies tend to be less inclusive and holistic, focusing on particular topics, such as kinship or religion.

According to Malinowski, a primary task of the ethnographer is "to grasp the native's point of view, his relation to life, to realize *his* vision of *his* world" (1922/1961, p. 25—Malinowski's italics). This is a good statement of the need for the emic perspective, as discussed earlier. Since the 1970s, *interpretive anthropology* has considered the task of describing and interpreting that which is meaningful to natives. Interpretivists such as Clifford Geertz (1973) view cultures as meaningful texts that natives constantly "read" and ethnographers must decipher. According to Geertz, anthropologists may choose anything in a culture that interests them, fill in details, and elaborate to inform their readers about meanings in that culture. Meanings are carried by public symbolic forms, including words, rituals, and customs.

A current trend in ethnographic writing is to question traditional goals, methods, and styles, including ethnographic realism and salvage ethnography (Clifford 1982,

STUDY TIP

Malinowski's ethnography is characterized by salvage ethnography, ethnographic realism, use of the ethnographic present, and holism.

1988; Marcus and Cushman 1982). Marcus and Fischer argue that experimentation in ethnographic writing is necessary because all peoples and cultures have already been "discovered" and must now be "rediscovered . . . in changing historical circumstances" (1986, p. 24).

In general, experimental anthropologists see ethnographies as works of art as well as works of science. Ethnographic texts may be viewed as literary creations in which the ethnographer, as mediator, communicates information from the "natives" to readers. Some experimental ethnographies are "dialogic," presenting ethnography as a dialogue between the anthropologist and one or more native informants (e.g., Behar 1993; Dwyer 1982). These works draw attention to ways in which ethnographers, and by extension their readers, communicate with other cultures. Some ethnographies of this type have been criticized for spending too much time talking about the anthropologist and too little time describing the local people and their culture.

The dialogic ethnography is one genre within a larger experimental category—*reflexive ethnography*. Here the ethnographer puts his or her personal feelings and reactions to the field situation right in the text. Experimental writing strategies are prominent in reflexive accounts. The ethnographer may adopt some of the conventions of the novel, including first-person narration, conversations, dialogues, and humor. Experimental ethnographies, using new ways of showing what it means to be a Samoan or a Brazilian, may convey to the reader a richer and more complex understanding of human experience.

CULTURE THINK

Those doing reflexive anthropology have recognized that not even anthropologists can be completely objective. That's why they call for authors to reflect on their own biases and perspectives. Consider yourself: What kinds of biases and perspectives do you think would be found in your own writing?

Linked to salvage ethnography was the idea of the *ethnographic present*—the period before Westernization, when the "true" native culture flourished. This notion often gives classic ethnographies an unrealistic timeless quality. Providing the only jarring note in this idealized picture are occasional comments by the author about traders or missionaries, suggesting that in actuality the natives were already part of the world system.

Anthropologists now recognize that the ethnographic present is a rather unrealistic construct. Cultures have been in contact—and have been changing—throughout history. Most native cultures had at least one major foreign encounter before any anthropologist ever came their way. Most of them already had been incorporated in some fashion into nation-states or colonial systems.

Contemporary ethnographies usually recognize that cultures constantly change and that an ethnographic account applies to a particular moment. A current trend in ethnography is to focus on the ways in which cultural ideas serve political and economic interests. A related trend is the anthropology of globalization, which describes how various particular "natives" participate in broader historical, political, and economic processes (Shostak 1981).

PROBLEM-ORIENTED ETHNOGRAPHY

We see, then, a tendency to move away from holistic accounts toward more problem-focused and experimental ethnographies. Although anthropologists are interested in the whole context of human behavior, it is impossible to study everything. Most ethnographers now enter the field with a specific problem to investigate, and they collect data relevant to that problem (see Chiseri-Strater and Sunstein 2001; Kutsche 1998). Local people's answers to questions are not the only data source. Anthropologists also gather information on factors such as population density, environmental quality, climate, physical geography, diet, and land use. Sometimes this involves direct measurement— of rainfall, temperature, fields, yields, dietary quantities, or time allocation (Bailey 1990; Johnson 1978). Often it means that we consult government records or archives.

The information of interest to ethnographers is not limited to what local people can and do tell us. In an increasingly interconnected and complicated world, local people lack knowledge about many factors that affect their lives. Our local consultants may be as mystified as we are by the exercise of power from regional, national, and international centers.

LONGITUDINAL RESEARCH

Geography limits anthropologists less now than in the past, when it could take months to reach a field site, and return visits were rare. New systems of transportation allow anthropologists to widen the area of their research and to return repeatedly. Ethnographic reports now routinely include data from two or more field stays. **Longitudinal research** is the long-term study of a community, region, society, culture, or other unit, usually based on repeated visits.

One example of such research is the longitudinal study of Gwembe District, Zambia. This study, planned in 1956 as a longitudinal project by Elizabeth Colson and Thayer Scudder, continues with Colson, Scudder, and their associates of various nationalities. Thus, as is often the case with longitudinal research, the Gwembe study also illustrates team research—coordinated research by multiple ethnographers (Colson and Scudder 1975; Scudder and Colson 1980). In this study, four villages in different areas have been followed for five decades. Periodic village censuses provide basic data on population, economy, kinship, and religious behavior. Censused people who have moved are traced and interviewed to see how their lives compare with those of people who have stayed in the villages.

A series of different research questions have emerged, while basic data on communities and individuals continue to be collected. The first focus of study was the impact of a large hydroelectric dam, which subjected the Gwembe people to forced resettlement. The dam also spurred road building and other activities that brought the people of Gwembe more closely in touch with the rest of Zambia. In subsequent research Scudder and Colson (1980) examined how education provided access to new opportunities as it also widened a social gap between people with different educational levels. A third study then examined a change in brewing and drinking patterns, including a rise in alcoholism, in relation to changing markets, transportation, and exposure to town values (Colson and Scudder 1988).

longitudinal research Long-term study of a community, society, culture, or other unit, usually based on repeated visits.

TEAM RESEARCH

As mentioned, longitudinal research often is team research. Kottak's field site of Arembepe, Brazil, for example, first entered the world of anthropology as a field-team village in the 1960s. It was one of four sites for the now defunct Columbia-Cornell-Harvard-Illinois Summer Field Studies Program in Anthropology. For at least three years, that program sent a total of about twenty undergraduates annually,

Conrad Kottak with his Brazilian nephew, Gui Roxo, in the field in Arembepe, Bahia, Brazil.
....

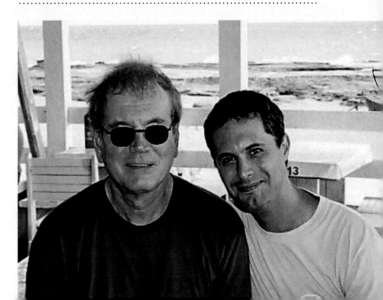

STUDY **TIP**

Approaches that enhance traditional ethnography include study of government and archival documents, longitudinal research, multisited research, and team research.

have studied various topics in Arembepe. In 1990 Doug Jones, a Michigan student doing biocultural research, used Arembepe as a field site to investigate standards of physical attractiveness. In 1996–1997, Janet Dunn studied family planning and changing female reproductive strategies. Chris O'Leary, who first visited Arembepe in summer 1997, investigated a striking aspect of religious change there—the arrival of Protestantism; his dissertation research then examined changing food habits and nutrition in relation to globalization (O'Leary 2002). Arembepe is thus a site where various field-workers have worked as members of a longitudinal team. The more recent researchers have built on prior contacts and findings to increase knowledge about how local people meet and manage new circumstances.

CULTURE, SPACE, AND SCALE

The previous sections on longitudinal and team research illustrate an important shift in cultural anthropology. Traditional ethnographic research focused on a single community or "culture," treated as more or less isolated and unique in time and space. The shift has been toward recognition of ongoing and inescapable flows of people, technology, images, and information. The study of such flows and linkages is now part of the anthropological analysis. In reflecting today's world—in which people, images, and information move about as never before—fieldwork must be more flexible and on a larger scale. Ethnography increasingly is multitimed and multisited. Malinowski could focus on Trobriand culture and spend most of his field time in a particular community. Nowadays we cannot afford to ignore, as Malinowski did, the "outsiders" who increasingly impinge on the places we study (e.g., migrants, refugees, terrorists, warriors, tourists, developers). Integral to our analyses now are the external organizations and forces (e.g., governments, businesses, nongovernmental organizations) now laying claim to land, people, and resources throughout the world. Also important is increased recognition of power differentials and how they affect cultures, and of the importance of diversity within cultures and societies.

Conrad Kottak has been studying Arembepe since 1962. His most recent field trip there was in March 2010. It used to be rare for anthropologists to return to the field, but they do it all the time now because of improved means of transoportation.

the author included, to do brief summer research abroad. They were stationed in rural communities in four countries: Brazil, Ecuador, Mexico, and Peru. Since Kottak's wife, Isabel Wagley Kottak, and he began studying it in 1962, Arembepe has become a longitudinal field site. Three generations of researchers have monitored various aspects of change and development. The community has changed from a village into a town and illustrates the process of globalization at the local level. Its economy, religion, and social life have been transformed (Kottak 2006).

Brazilian and American researchers worked with Kottak on team research projects during the 1980s (on television's impact) and the 1990s (on ecological awareness and environmental risk perception). Graduate students from the University of Michigan have drawn on baseline information from the 1960s as they

Lisa Gezon in Diego Suarez, Madagascar, sitting with her friend (right) who is selling khat, a leafy plant that people chew for a stimulant effect. On the left are Lisa Gezon's Malagasy daughter and sister.

In two volumes of essays edited by Akhil Gupta and James Ferguson (1997a, 1997b), several anthropologists describe problems in trying to locate cultures in bounded spaces. John Durham Peters (1997), for example, notes that, particularly because of the mass media, contemporary people simultaneously experience the local and the global. He describes them as culturally "bifocal"—both "nearsighted" (seeing local events) and "farsighted" (seeing images from far away). Given their bifocality, their interpretations of the local always are influenced by information from outside. Thus, their attitude about a clear blue sky at home is tinged by their knowledge, through weather reports, that a hurricane may be approaching.

The mass media, which anthropologists increasingly study, are oddities in terms of culture and space. Whose image and opinions are these?

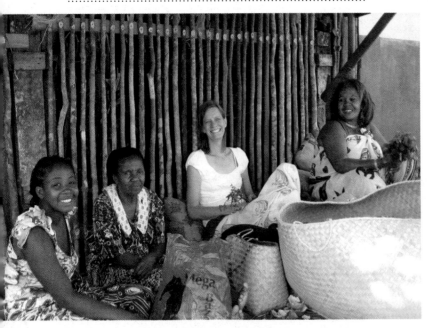

What culture or community do they represent? They certainly aren't local. Media images and messages flow electronically. TV brings them right to you. The Internet lets you discover new cultural possibilities at the click of a mouse. The Internet takes us to virtual places, but in truth the electronic mass media are placeless phenomena, which are transnational in scope and play a role in forming and maintaining cultural identities.

Anthropologists increasingly study people in motion. Examples include people living on or near national borders, nomads, seasonal migrants, homeless and displaced people, immigrants, and refugees. Anthropological research today may take us traveling along with the people we study, as they move from village to city, cross the border, or travel internationally on business. As we'll see in the chapter "Global Issues Today," ethnographers increasingly follow the people and images they study. As fieldwork changes, with less and less of a spatially set field, what can we take from traditional ethnography? Gupta and Ferguson correctly cite the "characteristically anthropological emphasis on daily routine and lived experience" (1997a, p. 5). The treatment of communities as discrete entities may be a thing of the past. However, "anthropology's traditional attention to the close observation of particular lives in particular places" has an enduring importance (Gupta and Ferguson 1997b, p. 25). The method of close observation helps distinguish cultural anthropology from sociology and survey research, to which we now turn.

>> Survey Research

As anthropologists work increasingly in large-scale societies, they have developed innovative ways of blending ethnography and survey research (Fricke 1994). Before examining such combinations of field methods, let's consider survey research and the main differences between survey research and ethnography. Working mainly in large, populous nations, sociologists, political scientists, and economists have developed and refined the **survey research** design, which involves sampling, impersonal data collection, and statistical analysis. Survey research usually draws a **sample** (a manageable study group) from a much larger population. By studying a properly selected and representative sample, social scientists can make accurate inferences about the larger population.

In smaller-scale societies and communities, ethnographers get to know most of the people. Given the greater size and complexity of nations, survey research cannot help being more impersonal. Survey researchers call the people they study *respondents*. These are people who respond to questions during a survey. Sometimes survey researchers personally interview them. Sometimes, after an initial meeting, they ask respondents to fill out a questionnaire. In other cases researchers mail or email printed questionnaires to randomly selected sample members or have paid assistants interview or telephone them. In a **random sample,** all members of the population have an equal statistical chance of being chosen for inclusion. A random sample is selected by randomizing procedures, such as tables of random numbers, which are found in many statistics textbooks.

> **survey research** Characteristic research procedure among social scientists other than anthropologists, which studies society through sampling, statistical analysis, and impersonal data collection.
>
> **sample** A smaller study group chosen to represent a larger population.
>
> **random sample** A sample in which all members of the population have an equal statistical chance of being included.

What kind of social science research is illustrated by exit polling?

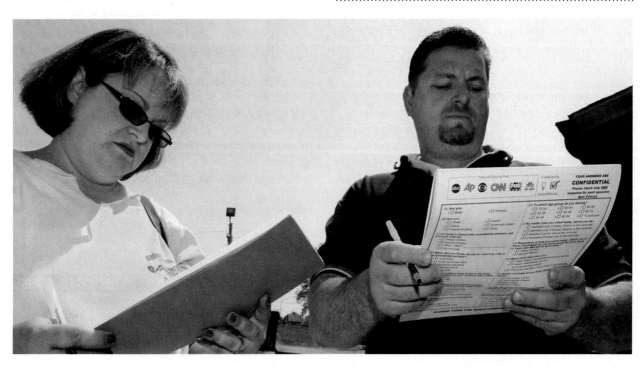

Ethnography and Survey Research Contrasted

Ethnography (Traditional)	Survey Research
Studies whole, functioning communities	Studies a small sample of a larger population
Usually is based on firsthand field work, during which information is collected after rapport, based on personal contact, is established between researcher and hosts	Often is conducted with little or no personal contact between study subjects and researchers, as interviews are frequently conducted by assistants over the phone or in printed form
Traditionally is interested in all aspects of local life (holistic)	Usually focuses on small number of variables (e.g., factors that influence voting) rather than on the totality of people's lives
Traditionally has been conducted in nonindustrial, small-scale societies, where people often do not read and write	Normally is carried out in modern nations, where most people are literate, permitting respondents to fill in their own questionnaires
Makes little use of statistics, because the communities being studied tend to be small, with little diversity besides that based on age, gender, and individual personality variation	Depends heavily on statistical analyses to make inferences regarding a large and diverse population, based on data collected from a small subset of that population

Probably the most familiar example of sampling is the polling used to predict political races. The media hire agencies to estimate outcomes and do exit polls to find out what kinds of people voted for which candidates. During sampling, researchers gather information about age, gender, religion, occupation, income, and political party preference. These characteristics (**variables**—attributes that vary among members of a sample or population) are known to influence political decisions.

Many more variables affect social identities, experiences, and activities in a modern nation than in the small communities where ethnography grew up. In contemporary North America hundreds of factors influence our behavior and attitudes. These social predictors include our religion; the region of the country we grew up in; whether we come from a town, suburb, or city; and our parents' professions, ethnic origins, and income levels.

Ethnography can be used to supplement and fine-tune survey research. Anthropologists can transfer the personal, firsthand techniques of ethnography to virtually any set-

variables Attributes (e.g., sex, age, height, weight) that differ from one person or case to the next.

complex societies Nations; large and populous, with social stratification and central governments.

CULTURETHINK

What are the advantages and disadvantages of doing survey research? What about participant observation and other ethnographic techniques?

ting that includes human beings. A combination of survey research and ethnography can provide new perspectives on life in **complex societies** (large and populous societies with social stratification and central governments). Preliminary ethnography also can help develop culturally appropriate questions for inclusion in surveys.

In any complex society, many predictor variables (*social indicators*) influence behavior and opinions. Because we must be able to detect, measure, and compare the influence of social indicators, many contemporary anthropological studies have a statistical foundation. Even in rural fieldwork, more anthropologists now draw samples, gather quantitative data, and use statistics to interpret them (see Bernard 1998, 2006). Quantifiable information may permit a more precise assessment of similarities and differences among communities. Statistical analysis can support and round out an ethnographic account of local social life.

In the best studies, the hallmark of ethnography remains: Anthropologists enter the community and get to know the people. They participate in local activities, networks, and associations in the city, town, or countryside. They observe and experience social conditions and problems. They watch the effects of national and international policies and programs on local life. The ethnographic method and the emphasis on personal relationships in social research are valuable gifts that cultural anthropology brings to the study of any society.

> "The way to do fieldwork is never to come up for air until it is all over."
>
> Margaret Mead

Join a club or use your classroom to practice participant observation. Your goal as an ethnographer is to take part in the group as you study it. Do you have good enough rapport with group members to take part in their activities? What "imponderabilia" do you observe in the life of the group? Record these. What differences might you see in group members' behavior if they did not know you were an ethnographer observing them rather than being honestly informed, as anthropological ethics demand?

get involved!

For REVIEW

I. What ethical concerns and issues must anthropologists consider?

- Anthropologists need to establish collaborative relationships with colleagues and communities in the host country. Cultural sensitivity is paramount. The AAA Code of Ethics advises researchers to be honest about their research, its purposes, funding, methods, and potential results and impacts. Researchers must obtain the informed consent of all affected parties—from the authorities who control access to the field to the members of the community studied. Ethnographers need not avoid taking stands on community issues; shaping policy may be ethically justifiable.

II. Where and how do cultural anthropologists do fieldwork?

- Early anthropologists worked in small, relatively isolated, societies with a certain cultural uniformity. Ethnographers sought to create a holistic account, revealing a culture's totality and interconnectedness. Ethnographers have developed a variety of techniques. A key method is participant observation, taking part in community life as it is studied. Ethnographers also gather data from conversations and interviews, and by tracing genealogies, working with key cultural consultants, and collecting life histories. Ethnography seeks also to discover the native viewpoint.

- In today's interlinked world, anthropologists increasingly study people on the move. Ethnographers now tend to enter the field with a particular problem to investigate. Enabled by modern systems of transportation, ethnographers often return for multiple stays to monitor change. Such longitudinal research may entail coordinated team research.

III. What are some ways of studying complex societies in modern nations?

- Working in populous, large-scale societies, anthropologists have learned to blend ethnography with survey research. Survey research involves sampling, collecting impersonal data, and statistical analysis. Social scientists make inferences about the larger population by surveying a sample of "respondents." Such quantifiable information allows a more precise assessment of similarities and differences among communities and rounds out the ethnographic account. By providing data acquired by personal, firsthand techniques, ethnography supplements and fine-tunes survey research.

Pop Quiz

1. Which of the following is *not* a part of the AAA Code of Ethics?
   a. The recognition that anthropologists are obligated to their scholarly field, to the wider society and culture, and to the human species.
   b. The recommendation that anthropologists avoid taking stands on issues that arise in their dealings with another culture.
   c. The requirement that all parties involved in doing anthropological research be informed about the nature, procedures, purpose, and potential impacts of the research.
   d. The recommendation that the people anthropologists work with in the field be acknowledged and reciprocated in appropriate ways.

2. Which of the following statements about ethnography is false?
   a. Early ethnographers tried to understand the culture they studied as a whole (that is, sought to make a holistic account).
   b. Ethnographers see little value in collecting quantitative data.
   c. Bronislaw Malinowski, considered the founder of ethnography, sought to grasp the natives' points of view and visions of their world.
   d. Ethnographers today recognize that the culture they study is described only in a moment of time.

3. The friendly working relationship that ethnographers strive to establish with their hosts is known as:
   a. The imponderabilia of native life
   b. Rapport
   c. An interview schedule
   d. Ethnographic realism

4. Which of the following techniques did ethnographers develop as a specific response to the importance of kinship, descent, and marriage in the social organization of nonindustrial societies?
   a. The life history
   b. Participant observation
   c. The interview schedule
   d. The genealogical method

5. All the following are true about ethnography *except:*
   a. It was traditionally used to study whole communities.
   b. It is based on firsthand fieldwork.
   c. It is more personal than survey research.
   d. It privileges ethnographers' observations and conclusions over the local people's views and beliefs.

6. Trends in doing ethnography include the following *except:*
   a. A move away from holistic accounts toward investigations of specific problems.
   b. The inclusion of field-gathered data from two or more stays in the field (longitudinal research).
   c. Doing more work for colonial governments.
   d. Giving increased attention to contacts from outside the communities being studied.

7. Which of the following is not a key difference between an ethnographic survey approach and the survey procedures commonly used by sociologists? An ethnographic survey:
   a. Typically studies a partial sample.
   b. Uses an interview schedule.
   c. Includes face-to-face interviews with subjects.
   d. Encourages researchers to establish rapport.

8. In a modern world in which people, images, and information move around as never before, ethnography:
   a. Is becoming increasingly challenging for those wishing to focus on a spatially set culture.
   b. Is becoming a less useful and less valuable tool for understanding culture.
   c. Has become more traditional.
   d. Now requires that researchers stay in the same site for more than three years.

9. Which of the following statements is *not* true of the survey approach?
   a. It was developed by social scientists working in large populous nations.
   b. It entails less face-to-face interaction than ethnography.
   c. Quantifiable information obtained from the survey approach is useful for assessing similarities and differences between communities.
   d. Surveying's statistical approach does *not* benefit from being combined with ethnography.

10. Which of the following most completely characterizes the ethnographic approach?
    a. It relies on firsthand contact with the community being studied, including participation in its cultural life and observation of its social conditions.
    b. It takes into consideration people in motion and may require the anthropologist to follow the people being studied.
    c. It involves team research projects.
    d. Sources of data for ethnography include local people's answers to the anthropologist's questions, measurement of environmental conditions, and consultation of government records.

1. (b), 2. (b), 3. (b), 4. (d), 5. (d), 6. (c), 7. (a), 8. (a), 9. (d), 10. (a)

APPLYING
ANTHROPOLOGY

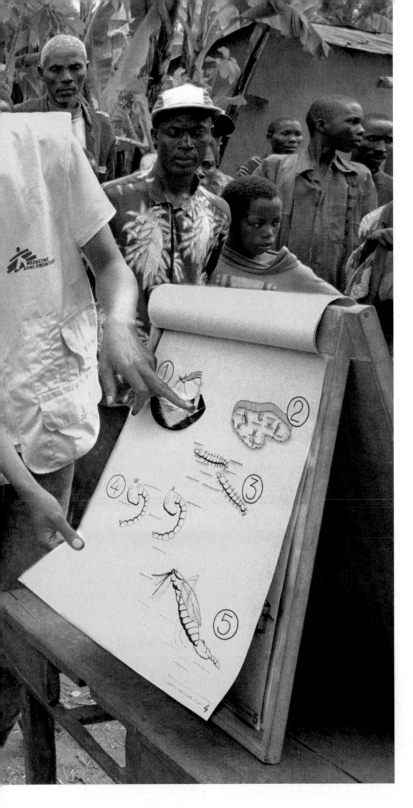

UNDERSTANDING OURSELVES

Is change always good? The idea that innovation is inherently desirable is axiomatic in American culture, especially in advertising. "New and improved" is a slogan we hear all the time—a lot more often than "old reliable." Which do you think is best—change or the status quo? That "new" isn't always "improved" is a painful lesson learned by the Coca-Cola Company (TCCC) in 1985 when it changed the formula of its premier soft drink and introduced "New Coke." After hordes of customers protested, TCCC brought back old, familiar, reliable Coke under the name "Coca-Cola Classic," which thrives today. New Coke, now history, offers a classic case of how not to treat consumers. TCCC tried a *top-down change* (a change initiated at the top of a hierarchy rather than inspired by the people most affected by the change). Customers didn't ask TCCC to change its product; executives made that decision.

The field of market research, which employs a good number of anthropologists, is based on the need to appreciate what actual and potential customers do, think, and want. Smart planners study and listen to people to try to determine *locally based demand.* What changes do the people—and which people—want? How can conflicting wishes and needs be accommodated? Applied anthropologists help answer these questions, which are crucial in understanding whether change is needed and how it will work.

Innovation succeeds best when it is culturally appropriate. This axiom of applied anthropology is a useful guide for international programs aimed at social and economic change as well as for businesses. Each time an organization expands to a new nation, it must devise a culturally appropriate strategy for fitting into the new setting. In their international expansion, companies and organizations have learned that more money, and more progress, can be made by fitting in with, rather than trying to Americanize, local habits.

As You READ

- How can change be bad?
- How can anthropology be applied to education, medicine, and business?
- How does the study of anthropology fit into a career path?

>> What Is Applied Anthropology?

Anthropology has two dimensions: applied anthropology and theoretical/academic anthropology. Applied, or *practical,* anthropology is the use of anthropological data, perspectives, theory, and methods to identify, assess, and solve contemporary problems involving human behavior and social and cultural forces, conditions, and contexts (see Ervin 2005). For example, medical anthropologists have worked as cultural interpreters in public health programs to facilitate their fit into local culture. Many applied anthropol-

ogists have worked for or with international development agencies, such as the World Bank and the U.S. Agency for International Development (USAID). In North America, garbologists help the Environmental Protection Agency, the paper industry, and packaging and trade associations. Archaeology is applied as well in cultural resource management and historic preservation. Biological anthropologists work in public health, nutrition, genetic counseling, substance abuse, epidemiology, aging, and mental illness. Forensic anthropologists work with the police, medical examiners, the courts, and international organizations to identify victims of crimes, accidents, wars, and terrorism. Linguistic anthropologists study physician–patient inter-

TABLE 4.1

The Four Subfields and Two Dimensions of Anthropology

Anthropology's Subfields (Academic Anthropology)	Examples of Application (Applied Anthropology)
Cultural anthropology	Development anthropology
Archaeological anthropology	Cultural resource management (CRM)
Biological or physical anthropology	Forensic anthropology
Linguistic anthropology	Study of linguistic diversity in classrooms

STUDY TIP

Two major differences between anthropologists and many other experts are (1) anthropologists' emphasis on talking with local people, using ethnographic techniques, and (2) anthropologists' holistic approach.

actions and show how dialect differences influence classroom learning. The goal of most applied anthropologists is to find humane and effective ways of helping local people.

One of the most valuable tools in applying anthropology is the ethnographic method. Ethnographers study societies firsthand, living with and learning from ordinary people. Ethnographers are participant observers, taking part in the events they study in order to understand local thought and behavior. Applied anthropologists use ethnographic techniques in both foreign and domestic settings. Other "expert" participants in social-change programs may be content to converse with officials, read reports, and copy statistics. The applied anthropologist's likely early request, however, is some variant of "take me to the local people." We know that people must play an active role in the changes that affect them and that "the people" have information "the experts" lack.

Anthropological theory, the body of findings and generalizations of the four subfields, also guides applied anthropology. Anthropology's holistic perspective—its interest in biology, society, culture, and language—permits the evaluation of many issues that affect people. Theory aids practice, and application fuels theory. As we compare social-change policy and programs, our understanding of cause and effect increases. We add new generalizations about culture change to those discovered in traditional and ancient cultures.

>> The Role of the Applied Anthropologist

EARLY APPLICATIONS

Application was a central concern of early anthropology in Great Britain (in the context of colonialism) and the United States (in the context of Native American policy). Before turning to the new, we should consider some dangers of the old. For the British empire, specifically its African colonies, Malinowski (1929) proposed that "practical anthropology" (his term for colonial applied anthropology) should focus on **Westernization**—the diffusion of European culture into tribal societies. Malinowski questioned

neither the legitimacy of colonialism nor the anthropologist's role in making it work. He saw nothing wrong with aiding colonial regimes by studying land tenure and land use in order to recommend how much of their land local people should be allowed to keep and how much Europeans should get. Malinowski's views exemplify a historical association between early anthropology, particularly in Europe, and colonialism (Maquet 1964).

CULTURE THINK

Malinowski and other early anthropologists have been criticized for supporting the colonial missions of the Western nations that hired them to do ethnographic research. Ethically, whose needs and goals do you think anthropologists should be representing? What would have been the risks and benefits of advocating for local people's rights in Malinowski's day?

During World War II, American anthropologists studied Japanese and German "culture at a distance" in an attempt to predict the behavior of the enemies of the United States. After that war, applied anthropologists worked on Pacific islands to promote local-level cooperation with American policies in various trust territories.

ACADEMIC AND APPLIED ANTHROPOLOGY

Applied anthropology did not disappear during the 1950s and 1960s, but academic anthropology did most of the growing after World War II. The baby boom, which began in 1946 and peaked in 1957, fueled expansion of the American educational system and thus of academic jobs. New junior, community, and four-year colleges opened, and anthropology became a standard part of the college curriculum. During the 1950s and 1960s, most American anthropologists were college professors, although some still worked in agencies and museums.

Westernization The diffusion of European cultures into tribal societies.

This era of academic anthropology continued through the early 1970s. Especially during the Vietnam War, undergraduates flocked to anthropology classes to learn about other cultures. Students were especially interested in Southeast Asia, whose indigenous societies were being disrupted by war. Many anthropologists protested the superpowers' apparent disregard for non-Western lives, values, customs, and social systems.

During the 1970s, and increasingly thereafter, although most anthropologists still worked in academia, others found jobs with international organizations, government, business, hospitals, and schools. This shift toward appli-

During the Vietnam War, many anthropologists protested the superpowers' disregard for the values, customs, social systems, and lives of indigenous peoples. Several anthropologists attended this all-night Columbia University teach-in about the war in 1965.

cation, though only partial, has benefited the profession. It has forced anthropologists to consider the wider social value and implications of their research.

APPLIED ANTHROPOLOGY TODAY

Today, most applied anthropologists see their work as radically removed from the colonial perspective. Modern applied anthropology usually is seen as a helping profession, devoted to assisting local people, as anthropologists speak up for the disenfranchised in the international politi-

cal arena. However, applied anthropologists also solve problems for clients who are neither poor nor powerless. Applied anthropologists working for businesses try to solve the problem of expanding profits for their employer or client. In market research, ethical issues may arise as anthropologists attempt to help companies operate more efficiently and profitably. Ethical ambiguities are present as well in cultural resource management (CRM), in deciding how to preserve significant remains and information when sites are threatened by development or public works. A CRM firm typically is hired by someone seeking to build a road or a factory. In such cases, the client may have a strong interest in an outcome in which no sites are found that need protecting.

Contemporary applied anthropologists still face ethical questions: To whom does the researcher owe loyalty? What problems are involved in holding firm to the truth? What happens when applied anthropologists don't make the policies they are told to implement? How does one criticize programs in which one has participated (see Escobar 1991, 1994)? Anthropology's professional organizations have addressed such questions by establishing codes of ethics and ethics committees. See http://www.aaanet.org for the Code of Ethics of the AAA. As Tice (1997) notes, attention to ethical issues is paramount in the teaching of applied anthropology today.

By instilling an appreciation for human diversity, the entire field of anthropology combats *ethnocentrism*— the tendency to view one's own culture as superior and to use one's own cultural values in judging the behavior

Supervised by archaeologists from India, with funding from the United Nations, these workers are cleaning and restoring the front façade of Cambodia's historical Angkor Wat temple. To decide what needs saving, and to preserve significant information about the past even when sites cannot be saved, is the work of cultural resource management (CRM).

and beliefs of people raised in other societies. Anthropology's broadening, educational role affects the knowledge, values, and attitudes of people exposed to its teachings. This chapter focuses specifically on this question: What specific contributions can anthropology make in identifying and solving problems stirred up by contemporary currents of economic, social, and cultural change, including globalization?

Because anthropologists are experts on human problems and social change and because they study, understand, and respect cultural values, they are highly qualified to suggest, plan, and implement policy affecting people. Proper roles for applied anthropologists include (1) identifying needs for change that local people perceive, (2) working with those people to design culturally appropriate and socially sensitive change, and (3) protecting local people from harmful policies and projects that may threaten them.

Anthropology's systemic perspective recognizes that changes don't occur in a vacuum. A program or project always has multiple effects, some of which are unforeseen. In an American example of unintended consequences, a program aimed at enhancing teachers' appreciation of cultural differences led to ethnic stereotyping (Kleinfield 1975). Specifically, Native American students did not welcome teachers' frequent comments about their Indian heritage. The students felt set apart from their classmates and saw this attention to their ethnicity as patronizing and demeaning. Internationally, dozens of economic development projects intended to increase productivity through irrigation have worsened public health by creating waterways where diseases thrive.

>> Development Anthropology

The branch of applied anthropology that focuses on social issues in, and the cultural dimension of, economic development is called **development anthropology.** Develop-

CULTURE THINK

What's the difference between equity and equality? (*Equality* means that each person or group would be treated the same and receive the same benefits.) What are the challenges in striving for equality as a development goal?

ment anthropologists do not just carry out development policies planned by others; they also plan and guide policy. (For more detailed discussions of issues in development anthropology, see Edelman and Haugerud 2004; Escobar 1995; Ferguson 1995; Nolan 2002; and Robertson 1995.)

Ethical dilemmas often confront development anthropologists (Escobar 1991, 1995). Our respect for cultural diversity often is offended because efforts to extend industry and technology may entail profound cultural changes. Foreign aid usually doesn't go where the need and suffering are greatest. It is spent on political, economic, and strategic priorities as international donors, political leaders and powerful interest groups perceive them. Planners' interests don't always coincide with the best interests of the local people. Although the aim of most development projects is to enhance the quality of life, living standards often decline in the target area (Bodley 1988).

President Barack Obama's mother, Dr. Stanley Ann Dunham Soetoro (1942–1995), was an applied anthropologist. She earned her PhD in 1992 from the University of Hawaii. For her doctoral fieldwork, she studied handicrafts in Java, Indonesia. She became a consultant for the U.S. Agency for International Development and the Ford Foundation.

Did You Know?

EQUITY

A commonly stated goal of recent development policy is to promote equity. **Increased equity** means reduced poverty and a more even distribution of wealth. If projects are to increase equity, however, they must have the support of reform-minded governments. Wealthy and powerful people typically resist projects that threaten their vested interests.

Some types of development projects, particularly irrigation schemes, are more likely than others to widen wealth disparities, that is, to have a negative equity impact. An initial uneven distribution of resources (particularly land) often becomes the basis for greater skewing after the project. The social impact of new technology tends to be more severe, contributing negatively to quality of life and to equity, when inputs are channeled to or through the rich.

Many fisheries projects also have had negative equity results (see Durrenberger and King 2000). In Bahia, Brazil (Kottak 2006), sailboat owners (but not nonowners) received loans to buy motors for their boats. To repay the loans, the owners increased the percentage of the catch they took from the men who fished in their boats. Over the years, they used their rising profits to buy larger and more

development anthropology The branch of applied anthropology that focuses on social issues in, and the cultural dimension of, economic development.

equity, increased A reduction in absolute poverty and a fairer (more even) distribution of wealth.

A mix of boats harbored at Dai-Lanh fishing village in Vietnam. A boat owner receives a loan to buy a motor. To repay the loan, he increases the share of the catch he takes from his crew. Later, he uses his rising profits to buy a more expensive boat and takes even more from his crew. Can a more equitable solution be found?

expensive boats. The result was stratification—the creation of a group of wealthy people within a formerly egalitarian community. These events hampered individual initiative and interfered with further development of the fishing industry. With new boats so expensive, ambitious young men who once would have sought careers in fishing no longer had any way to obtain their own boats. They sought wage labor on land instead. To avoid such results, credit-granting agencies must seek out enterprising young fishers rather than giving loans only to owners and established businesspeople.

overinnovation Characteristic of development projects that require major changes in people's daily lives, especially ones that interfere with customary subsistence pursuits.

>> Strategies for Innovation

Development anthropologists, who are concerned with social issues in, and the cultural dimension of, economic development, must work closely with local people to assess and help them realize their own wishes and needs for change. Development anthropologists can help identify, plan, and implement beneficial projects by consulting with local people and responding to their expressed needs (Cernea 1991).

In a comparative study of sixty-eight rural development projects from around the world, Conrad Kottak found the *culturally compatible* economic development projects to be twice as successful financially as the incompatible ones (Kottak 1990b, 1991). This finding shows that using anthropological expertise in planning to ensure cultural compatibility is cost effective. To maximize social and economic benefits, projects must (1) be culturally compatible, (2) respond to locally perceived needs, (3) involve men and women in planning and carrying out the changes that affect them, (4) harness traditional organizations, and (5) be flexible.

OVERINNOVATION

In Kottak's comparative study, the compatible and successful projects avoided the fallacy of **overinnovation** (too much change). We would expect people to resist development projects that require major changes in their daily lives. People usually want to change just enough to keep what they have. Motives for modifying behavior come from the traditional culture and the small concerns of ordinary life. Peasants' values are not such abstract ones as "learning a better way," "progressing," "increasing technical know-how," "improving efficiency," or "adopting modern techniques." (Those phrases exemplify intervention philosophy.)

Instead, people's objectives are down-to-earth and specific ones. They want to improve yields in a rice field, amass resources for a ceremony, get a child through school, or have enough cash to pay the tax bill. The goals and values of subsistence producers differ from those of people who produce for cash, just as they differ from the intervention philosophy of development planners. Different value systems must be considered during planning.

In Kottak's comparative study, the projects that failed were usually incompatible both economically and culturally. For example, one South Asian project promoted the cultivation of onions and peppers, expecting this practice to fit into a preexisting labor-intensive system of rice growing. Cultivation of these cash crops wasn't traditional in the area. It conflicted with existing crop priorities and other interests of farmers. Also, the labor peaks for pepper and onion production coincided with those for rice, to which the farmers gave priority.

Throughout the world, project problems have arisen from inadequate attention to, and consequent lack of fit with, local culture. Another naive and incompatible project was an overinnovative scheme in Ethiopia. Its major fallacy was to try to convert nomadic herders into sedentary cultivators. It ignored traditional land rights. Outsiders—commercial farmers—were to get much of the herders' territory. The pastoralists were expected to settle down and start farming. This project helped wealthy outsiders instead of the local people. The planners naively expected free-ranging herders to give up a generations-old way of life to work three times harder growing rice and picking cotton for bosses.

STUDY **TIP**

Be able to identify the five criteria for successful projects that maximize social and economic benefits.

UNDERDIFFERENTIATION

The fallacy of **underdifferentiation** is the tendency to view the "less developed countries" as more alike than they are. Development agencies have often ignored cultural diversity (e.g., between Brazil and Burundi) and adopted a uniform approach to deal with very different sets of people. Neglecting cultural diversity, many projects also have tried to impose incompatible property notions and social units. Most often, the faulty social design assumes either (1) individualistic productive units that are privately owned by an individual or couple and worked by a nuclear family or (2) cooperatives that are at least par-tially based on models from the former Eastern bloc and Socialist countries.

One example of faulty Euro-American models (the individual and the nuclear family) was a West African project designed for an area where the extended family was the basic social unit. The project succeeded despite its faulty social design because the participants used their traditional extended family networks to attract additional settlers. Eventually, twice as many people as planned benefited as extended family members flocked to the project area. Here, settlers modified the project design that had been imposed on them by following the principles of their traditional society.

The second dubious foreign social model that is common in development strategy is the cooperative. In the comparative study of rural development projects, new cooperatives fared badly. Cooperatives succeeded only when they harnessed preexisting local-level communal institutions. This is a corollary of a more general rule: Participants' groups are most effective when they are based on traditional social organization or on a socio-economic similarity among members.

Neither foreign social model—the nuclear family farm nor the cooperative—has an unblemished record in development. An alternative is needed: greater use of indigenous social models in economic development. These are traditional social units, such as the clans, lineages, and other extended kin groups

underdifferentiation Planning fallacy of viewing less-developed countries as an undifferentiated group; ignoring cultural diversity and adopting a uniform approach (often ethnocentric) for very different types of project beneficiaries.

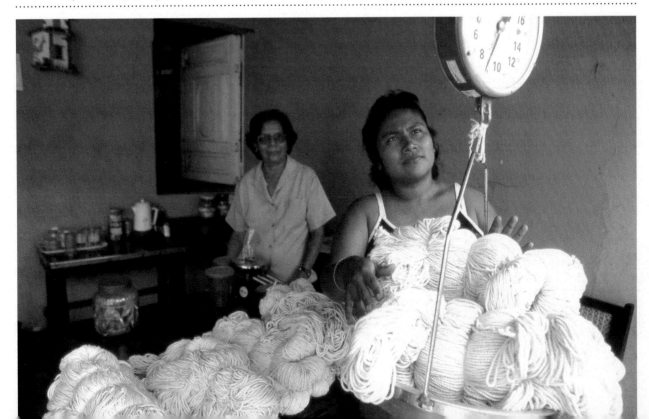

To maximize benefits, development projects should respond to locally perceived needs. Shown here (foreground) is the president of a Nicaraguan cooperative that makes and markets hammocks. This cooperative has been assisted by a nongovernmental organization (NGO) whose goals include increasing the benefits that women derive from economic development.

of Africa, Oceania, and many other nations, with their communally held estates and resources. The most humane and productive strategy for change is to base the social design for innovation on traditional social forms in each target area.

INDIGENOUS MODELS

Many governments are not genuinely, or realistically, committed to improving the lives of their citizens. Interference by major powers also has kept governments from enacting needed reforms. In some nations, however, the government acts more as an agent of the people. Madagascar provides an example. The people of Madagascar, the Malagasy, had been organized into descent groups before the origin of the state. The Merina, creators of the major precolonial state of Madagascar, wove descent groups into its structure, making members of important groups advisers to the king and thus giving them authority in government. The Merina state made provisions for the people it ruled. It collected taxes and organized labor for public works projects. In return, it redistributed resources to peasants in need. It also granted them some protection against war and slave raids and allowed them to cultivate their rice fields in peace. The government maintained the water works for rice cultivation. It opened to ambitious peasant boys the chance of becoming, through hard work and study, state bureaucrats.

Throughout the history of the Merina state—and continuing in modern Madagascar—there have been strong relationships between the individual, the descent group, and the state. Local Malagasy communities, where residence is based on descent, are more cohesive and homogeneous than are communities in Latin America or North America. Madagascar gained political independence from France in 1960. Although it still was economically dependent on France when Conrad Kottak first did research there in 1966–1967, the new government had an economic development policy aimed at increasing the ability of the Malagasy to feed themselves. Government policy emphasized

anthropology and education Anthropological research in classrooms, homes, and neighborhoods, viewing students as total cultural creatures whose enculturation and attitudes toward education belong to a larger context that includes family, peers, and society.

increased production of rice, a subsistence crop, rather than cash crops. Furthermore, local communities, with their traditional cooperative patterns and solidarity based on kinship and descent, were treated as partners in, not obstacles to, the development process.

In a sense, the descent group is preadapted to equitable national development. In Madagascar, members of local descent groups have customarily pooled their resources to educate their ambitious members. Once educated, these men and women gain economically secure positions in the nation. They then share the advantages of their new positions with their kin. For example, they give room and board to rural cousins attending school and help them find jobs.

Malagasy administrations appear generally to have shared a commitment to democratic economic development. Perhaps this is because government officials are of the peasantry or have strong personal ties to it. By contrast, in Latin American countries, the elites and the lower class have different origins and no strong connections through kinship, descent, or marriage.

Furthermore, societies with descent-group organization contradict an assumption that many social scientists and economists seem to make. It is not inevitable that as nations become more tied to the world capitalist economy, indigenous forms of social organization will break down into nuclear family organization, impersonality, and alienation. Descent groups, with their traditional communalism and corporate solidarity, have important roles to play in economic development.

Realistic development promotes change but not over-innovation. Many changes are possible if the aim is to preserve local systems while making them work better. Successful economic development projects respect, or at least don't attack, local cultural patterns. Effective development draws on indigenous cultural practices and social structures.

>> Anthropology and Education

Attention to culture also is fundamental to **anthropology and education,** involving research that extends from classrooms into homes, neighborhoods, and communities (see Spindler 2000, 2005). In classrooms, anthropologists have observed interactions among teachers, students, parents, and visitors. Jules Henry's classic account of the American elementary school classroom (1955) shows how students learn to conform to and compete with their peers. Anthropologists view children as total cultural creatures whose enculturation and

Afghan girls attend a lesson at the secondary school in Sarkani village, Kunar Province, eastern Afghanistan. What do you see here that differs from classrooms in your country?

CULTURETHINK

Based on your own experience and observations, what are some problems in your country's educational system? What stakeholders are involved in this situation? (A *stakeholder* is someone who takes part in and can be affected by a group's actions. Teachers would be one example.) How would you go about finding a solution?

The anthropologists also found that certain practices were preventing Hispanics from being adequately educated. For example, the teachers' union and the board of education had agreed to teach "English as a foreign language." However, they had provided no bilingual teachers to work with Spanish-speaking students. The school was assigning all students (including non-Hispanics) with low reading scores and behavior problems to the English-as-a-foreign-language classroom. This educational disaster brought together in the classroom a teacher who spoke no Spanish, children who barely spoke English, and a group of English-speaking students with reading and behavior problems. The Spanish speakers were falling behind not just in reading but in all subjects. They could at least have kept up in the other subjects if a Spanish speaker had been teaching them science, social studies, and math until they were ready for English-language instruction in those areas.

attitudes toward education belong to a context that includes family and peers.

Sociolinguists and cultural anthropologists work side by side in education research. For example, in a study of Puerto Rican seventh-graders in the urban Midwest (Hill-Burnett 1978), anthropologists uncovered some misconceptions held by teachers. The teachers mistakenly had assumed that Puerto Rican parents valued education less than did non-Hispanics, but in-depth interviews revealed that the Puerto Rican parents valued it more.

>> Urban Anthropology

Alan and Josephine Smart (2003) note that cities have long been influenced by global forces, including world capitalism and colonialism. The roles of cities in the world system have changed recently, however, as a result of the time-space compression made possible by modern transportation and communication systems. That is, everything appears closer today because contact and movement are so much easier.

One-sixth of Earth's population lives in urban slums. Roçinha (shown here) is a populous shantytown within the city of Rio de Janeiro, Brazil. How might anthropologists study slums?

Watch a few episodes of the Fox TV series *Bones*—based on characters created by Kathy Reichs, a physical and forensic anthropologist. *Bones* is one of the very few TV programs featuring a professional anthropologist, the character Temperance Brennan, aka "Bones" to her FBI agent partner, Seely Booth. As you watch the program, pay attention to the following questions: How do Dr. Brennan's attitudes, beliefs, and opinions differ from those of other members of the cast? How do her statements compare and contrast with anthropological perspectives as presented in this textbook? Ask your professor what she or he thinks about some of the statements you write down and quote from Dr. Brennan.

In the context of contemporary globalization, the mass media can become as important as local factors in guiding daily routines, dreams, and aspirations. People live in particular places, but their imaginations and attachments don't have to be locally confined (Appadurai 1996). People migrate to cities partly for economic reasons, but also to be where the action is. Rural Brazilians routinely cite *movimento,* urban movement and excitement, as something to be valued. International migrants tend to settle in the largest cities, where the most is happening. For example, in Canada, which has the second highest percentage of foreign-born population after Australia, 71.2 percent of immigrants settled in Toronto, Vancouver, or Montreal. Nearly half of Toronto's citizens were born outside Canada (Smart and Smart 2003).

urban anthropology The anthropological study of life in and around world cities, including the study of urban social problems, differences between urban and other environments, and adaptation to city life.

The proportion of the world's population living in cities has been increasing ever since the Industrial Revolution. About 3 percent of people were city dwellers in 1800, compared with 13 percent in 1900, over 40 percent in 1980, and about 50 percent today (see Smart and Smart 2003). The More Developed Countries (MDCs) were 76 percent urbanized in 1999, compared with 39 percent for the Less Developed Countries (LDCs). However, the urbanization growth rate is much faster in the LDCs (Smart and Smart 2003). The world had 16 cities with more than a million people in 1900, but there were 314 such cities in 2005. By 2025, 60 percent of the global population will be urban (Butler 2005; Stevens 1992).

About one billion people, one-sixth of Earth's population, live in urban slums, mostly without water, sanitation, public services, and legal security (Vidal 2003). If current trends continue, urban population increase and the concentration of people in slums will be accompanied by rising rates of crime, along with water, air, and noise pollution. These problems will be most severe in the LDCs.

As industrialization and urbanization spread globally, anthropologists increasingly study these processes and the social problems they create. **Urban anthropology,** which has theoretical (basic research) and applied dimensions, is the cross-cultural and ethnographic study of global urbanization and life in cities (see Aoyagi, Nas, and Traphagan 1998; Gmelch and Zenner 2002; Smart and Smart 2003; Stevenson 2003). The United States and Canada have become popular arenas for urban anthropological research on topics such as immigration, ethnicity, poverty, class, and urban violence (Mullings 1987; Vigil 2003).

URBAN VERSUS RURAL

Recognizing that a city is a social context that is very different from a tribal or peasant village, an early student of urbanization, the anthropologist Robert Redfield, focused on contrasts between rural and urban life. He contrasted rural communities, whose social relations are on a face-to-face basis, with cities, where impersonality characterizes many aspects of life. Redfield (1941) proposed that urbanization be studied along a rural–urban continuum. He described differences in values and social relations in four sites that spanned such a continuum. In Mexico's Yucatán peninsula, Redfield compared an isolated Maya-speaking Indian community, a rural peasant village, a small provincial city, and a large capital. Several studies in Africa (Little 1971) and Asia were influenced by Redfield's view that cities are centers through which cultural innovations spread to rural and tribal areas.

In any nation, urban and rural represent different social systems. However, cultural diffusion or borrowing occurs as people, products, images, and messages move from one to the other. Migrants bring rural practices and beliefs to cities and take urban patterns back home. The experiences and social forms of the rural area affect adaptation to city life. City folk also develop new institutions to meet specific urban needs (Mitchell 1966).

An applied anthropology approach to urban planning would start by identifying key social groups in the urban context. After identifying those groups, the anthropologist might elicit their wishes for change, convey those needs to funding agencies, and work with agencies and local people to realize those goals. In Africa relevant groups might include ethnic associations, occupational groups, social clubs, religious groups, and burial societies. Through membership in such groups, urban Africans maintain wide networks of personal contacts and support (Banton 1957; Little 1965). These groups also have links with, and provide cash support and urban lodging for, their rural relatives. Sometimes such groups think of themselves as a gigantic kin group, a clan that includes urban and rural members. Members may call one another "brother" and "sister." As in an extended family, rich members help their poor relatives. A member's improper behavior can lead to expulsion—an unhappy fate for a migrant in a large ethnically heterogeneous city.

> "I must admit that I personally measure success in terms of the contributions an individual makes to her or his fellow human beings."
>
> Margaret Mead

One role for the urban applied anthropologist is to help relevant social groups deal with urban institutions, such as legal and social services, with which recent migrants may be unfamiliar. In certain North American cities, as in Africa, kin-based ethnic associations are relevant urban groups. One example comes from Los Angeles, which has the largest Samoan immigrant community (over twelve thousand people) in the United States. Samoans in Los Angeles draw on their traditional system of *matai* (*matai* means "chief"; the matai system now refers to respect for elders) to deal with modern urban problems. One example: In 1992, a white police officer shot and killed two unarmed Samoan brothers. When a judge dismissed charges against the officer, local leaders used

the matai system to calm angry youths (who have formed gangs, like other ethnic groups in the Los Angeles area). Clan leaders and elders organized a well-attended community meeting, in which they urged young members to be patient. The Samoans then used the American judicial system. They brought a civil case against the officer in question and pressed the U.S. Justice Department to initiate a civil rights case in the matter (Mydans 1992b). Not all conflicts involving gangs and law enforcement end so peacefully.

James Vigil (2003) examines gang violence in the context of large-scale immigrant adaptation to American cities. He notes that before the 1970s most gangs were located in white ethnic enclaves in eastern and midwestern cities. Back then, gang incidents typically were brawls involving fists, sticks, and knives. Today, gangs more often are composed of nonwhite ethnic groups, and handguns have replaced the less lethal weapons of the past. Gangs still consist mostly of male adolescents who have grown up together, usually in a low-income neighborhood, where it's estimated that about 10 percent of young men join gangs. Female gang members are much rarer—from 4 to 15 percent of gang members. With gangs organized hierarchically by age, older members push younger ones (usually fourteen- to eighteen-year-olds) to carry out violent acts against rivals (Vigil 2003).

The populations that include most of today's gang members settled originally in poorer urban areas. On the East Coast these usually were run-down neighborhoods where a criminal lifestyle already was present. Around Los Angeles, urban migrants created squatterlike settlements in previously empty spaces. Immigrants tend to reside in neighborhoods apart from middle-class people, thus limiting their opportunities for integration. Confined in this manner, and facing residential overcrowding, poor people often experience frustration, which can lead to aggressive acts (Vigil 2003). At the same time, industries and jobs have moved from inner cities to distant suburbs and foreign nations. Urban minority youth have limited access to entry-level jobs; often they receive harsh treatment from authorities, especially law enforcement. Frustration and competition over resources can spark aggressive incidents, fueling urban violence. For survival, many residents of abandoned neighborhoods have turned to informal and illegal economic arrangements, of which drug trafficking in particular has heightened gang violence (Vigil 2003). How might an applied anthropologist approach the problem of urban violence? Which groups would need to be involved in the study?

CULTURETHINK

How might an applied anthropologist approach the problem of urban violence? Which groups would need to be involved in the study?

>> Medical Anthropology

The branch of anthropology known as **medical anthropology** is both academic/theoretical and applied/practical and includes anthropologists from all four subfields (see Anderson 1996; Briggs 2005; Brown 1998; Dressler et al. 2005; Joralemon 2006; Singer and Baer 2007; Trevathan, Smith, and McKenna 2007). Medical anthropologists examine such questions as which diseases and health conditions affect particular populations (and why) and how illness is socially constructed, diagnosed, managed, and treated in various societies.

medical anthropology Unites biological and cultural anthropologists in the study of disease, health problems, health care systems, and theories about illness in different cultures and ethnic groups.

disease An etic, or scientifically identified, health threat caused by a bacterium, virus, fungus, parasite, or other pathogen.

illness An emic condition of poor health felt by the individual.

Disease refers to a scientifically identified health threat caused genetically or by a bacterium, virus, fungus, parasite, or other pathogen. **Illness** is a condition of poor health perceived or felt by an individual (Inhorn and Brown 1990). Perceptions of good and bad health, along with health threats and problems, are culturally constructed. Various ethnic groups and cultures recognize different illnesses, symptoms, and causes and have developed different health care systems and treatment strategies.

The incidence and severity of *disease* vary as well (see Baer, Singer, and Susser 2003; Barnes 2005). Group differences are evident in the United States. Keppel, Pearch, and Wagener (2002) examined data between 1990 and 1998 using ten health status indicators in relation to racial and ethnic categories from the U.S. census: non-Hispanic white, non-Hispanic black, Hispanic, American Indian or Alaska Native, and Asian or Pacific Islander. Black Americans' rates for six measures (total mortality, heart disease, lung cancer, breast cancer, stroke, and homicide) exceeded those of other groups by a factor ranging from 2.5 to almost 10. Other ethnic groups had higher rates for suicide (white Americans) and motor vehicle accidents (American Indians and Alaskan Natives). Overall, Asians had the longest life spans (see Dressler et al. 2005).

Hurtado and colleagues (2005) note the prevalence of poor health and unusually high rates of early mortality among indigenous populations in South America. Life expectancy at birth is at least twenty years shorter among indigenous groups compared with other South Americans. In 2000, the life expectancy of indigenous peoples in Brazil and Venezuela was lower than that in Sierra Leone, which had the lowest reported national life expectancy in the world (Hurtado et al. 2005).

How can applied anthropologists help ameliorate the large health disparity between indigenous peoples and other populations? Hurtado and colleagues (2005) suggest three steps: (1) Identify the most pressing health problems that indigenous communities face; (2) gather information on solutions to those problems; and (3) implement solutions in partnership with the agencies and organizations in charge of public health programs for indigenous populations.

In many areas, the world system and colonialism worsened the health of indigenous peoples by spreading diseases, warfare, servitude, and other stressors. Traditionally and in ancient times, hunter-gatherers, because of their small numbers, mobility, and relative isolation from other groups, lacked most of the epidemic infectious diseases that affect agrarian and urban societies (Cohen and Armelagos 1984; Inhorn and Brown 1990). Epidemic diseases such as cholera, typhoid, and bubonic plague thrive in dense populations, and thus among farmers and city dwellers. The spread of malaria has been linked to population growth and deforestation associated with food production.

Certain diseases, and physical conditions such as obesity, have spread with economic development and globalization (Ulijaszek and Lofink 2006). *Schistosomiasis,* or bilharzia (blood and liver flukes), is probably the fastest-spreading and most dangerous parasitic infection now known. It is propagated by snails that live in ponds, lakes, and waterways, usually those created by irrigation projects. A study done in a Nile Delta village in Egypt (Farooq 1966) illustrated the role of culture (religion) in the spread of schistosomiasis. The disease was more common among Muslims than among Christians because of an Islamic practice called *wudu*—ritual ablution (bathing) before prayer. The applied anthropology approach to reducing such diseases is to see if local people perceive a connection between the vector (e.g., snails in the water) and the disease. If not, such information may be provided by enlisting active local groups, schools, and the media.

The highest global rates of HIV infection and AIDS-related deaths are in Africa, especially southern Africa. As it kills productive adults, AIDS leaves behind children and seniors who have difficulty replacing the

STUDY TIP

Three ways of identifying, classifying, and explaining illness, called disease theories, are (1) personalistic, (2) naturalistic, and (3) emotionalistic.

What kind of disease theory does acupuncture—a Chinese healing practice of inserting needles into the body to reduce pain and balance energies—exemplify?

lost labor force (Baro and Deubel 2006). In southern and eastern Africa, AIDS and other sexually transmitted diseases (STDs) have spread along highways, via encounters between male truckers and female prostitutes. STDs also are spread through prostitution, as young men from rural areas seek wage work in cities, labor camps, and mines. When the men return to their natal villages, they infect their wives (Larson 1989; Miller and Rockwell 1988). Cities also are prime sites of STD transmission in Europe, Asia, and North and South America (see Baer, Singer, and Susser 2003; French 2002). Cultural factors also affect the spread of HIV, which is less likely to be transmitted when men are circumcised than when they are not.

The kinds of and incidence of disease vary among societies, and cultures interpret and treat illness differently. Standards for sick and healthy bodies are cultural constructions that vary in time and space (Martin 1992). Still, all societies have what George Foster and Barbara Anderson call "disease-theory systems" to identify, classify, and explain illness. According to Foster and Anderson (1978), there are three basic theories about the causes of illness: personalistic, naturalistic, and emotionalistic. *Personalistic disease theories* blame illness on agents, such as sorcerers, witches, ghosts, or ancestral spirits. *Naturalistic disease theories* explain illness in impersonal terms. One example is Western medicine, or *biomedicine,* which aims to link illness to scientifically demonstrated agents that bear no personal malice toward their victims. Thus Western medicine attributes illness to organisms (e.g., bacteria, viruses, fungi, or parasites), accidents, toxic materials, or genes.

Other naturalistic ethnomedical systems blame poor health on unbalanced body fluids. Many Latin societies classify food, drink, and environmental conditions as "hot" or "cold." People

believe their health suffers when they eat or drink hot or cold substances together or under inappropriate conditions. For example, one shouldn't drink something cold after a hot bath or eat a pineapple (a "cold" fruit) when one is menstruating (a "hot" condition).

Emotionalistic disease theories assume that emotional experiences cause illness. For example, Latin Americans may develop *susto,* an illness caused by anxiety or fright (Bolton 1981; Finkler 1985). Its symptoms (lethargy, vagueness, distraction) are similar to those of "soul loss," a diagnosis of similar symptoms made by people in Madagascar. Modern psychoanalysis also focuses on the role of the emotions in physical and psychological well-being.

All societies have **health care systems** consisting of beliefs, customs, specialists, and techniques aimed at ensuring health and at preventing, diagnosing, and curing illness. A society's illness-causation theory influences treatment. When illness has a personalistic cause, magicoreligious specialists may be good curers. They draw on varied techniques (occult and practical) that are part of their special expertise. A shaman may cure soul loss by enticing the spirit back into the body. Shamans may ease difficult childbirths by asking spirits to travel up the birth canal to guide the baby out (Lévi-Strauss 1967). A shaman may cure a cough by counteracting a curse or removing a substance introduced by a sorcerer.

If there is a "world's oldest profession" besides hunter and gatherer, it is **curer,** often a shaman. The curer's role has some universal features (Foster and Anderson 1978). Thus curers emerge through a culturally defined process of

> **health care systems** Beliefs, customs, and specialists concerned with ensuring health and preventing and curing illness; a cultural universal.
>
> **curer** Specialized role acquired through a culturally appropriate process of selection, training, certification, and acquisition of a professional image; the curer is consulted by patients, who believe in his or her special powers, and receives some form of special consideration; a cultural universal.

A traditional healer at work in Malaysia. Shown here, mugwort, a small, spongy herb, is burned to facilitate healing. The healer lights one end of a moxa stick, roughly the shape and size of a cigar, and attaches it, or holds it close, to the area being treated for several minutes until the area turns red. The purpose of moxibustion is to strengthen the blood, stimulate spiritual energy, and maintain general health.

selection (parental prodding, inheritance, visions, dream instructions) and training (apprentice shamanship, medical school). Eventually, the curer is certified by older practitioners and acquires a professional image. Patients believe in the skills of the curer, whom they consult and compensate.

We should not lose sight, ethnocentrically, of the difference between **scientific medicine** and Western medicine per se. Despite advances in technology, genomics, molecular biology, pathology, surgery, diagnostics, and applications, many Western medical procedures have little justification in logic or fact. Overprescription of drugs, unnecessary surgery, and the impersonality and inequality of the physician–patient relationship are questionable features of Western medical systems (see Briggs 2005 for linguistic aspects of this inequality). Also, overuse of antibiotics, not just for people but also in animal feed, seems to be triggering an explosion of resistant microorganisms, which may pose a long-term global public health hazard.

scientific medicine As distinguished from Western medicine, a health care system based on scientific knowledge and procedures, encompassing such fields as pathology, microbiology, biochemistry, surgery, diagnostic technology, and applications.

Still, biomedicine surpasses tribal treatment in many ways. Although medicines such as quinine, coca, opium, ephedrine, and rauwolfia were discovered in nonindustrial societies, thousands of effective drugs are available today to treat myriad diseases. Preventive health care improved during the twentieth century. Today's surgical procedures are much safer and more effective than those of traditional societies.

But industrialization and globalization have spawned their own health problems. Modern stressors include poor nutrition, dangerous machinery, impersonal work, isolation, poverty, homelessness, substance abuse, and noise, air, and water pollution (see McElroy and Townsend 2003). Health problems in industrial nations are caused as much by economic, social, political, and cultural factors as by pathogens. In modern North America, for example, poverty contributes to many illnesses, including arthritis, heart conditions, back problems, and hearing and vision impairment (see Bailey 2000). Poverty also is a factor in the differential spread of infectious diseases.

In the United States and other developed countries today, good health has become something of an ethical imperative (Foucault 1990). Individuals are expected to regulate their behavior and shape themselves in keeping with new medical knowledge. Those who do so acquire the status of sanitary citizens—people with modern understanding of the body, health, and illness, who practice hygiene and depend on doctors and nurses when they are sick. People who act differently (e.g., smokers, overeaters, those who avoid doctors) are stigmatized as unsanitary and blamed for their own health problems (Briggs 2005; Foucault 1990).

Even getting an epidemic disease such as cholera or living in an infected neighborhood may be interpreted today as a moral failure. It's assumed that people who are properly informed and act rationally can avoid such "preventable" diseases. Individuals are expected to follow scientifically based imperatives (e.g., "boil water," "don't smoke"). People (e.g., gay men, Haitians, smokers, veterans) can become objects of avoidance and discrimination simply by belonging to a group seen as having a greater risk of getting a particular disease (Briggs 2005).

Medical anthropologists have served as cultural interpreters in public health programs, which must pay attention to local theories about the nature, causes, and treatment of illness. Health interventions cannot simply be forced on communities. They must fit into local cultures and be accepted by local people. When Western medicine is introduced, people usually retain many of their old methods while also accepting new ones (see Green 1987/1992). Native curers may go on treating certain conditions (spirit possession), whereas doctors may deal with others. If both modern and traditional specialists are consulted and the patient is cured, the native curer may get as much or more credit than the physician.

A more personal treatment of illness that emulates the non-Western curer-patient-community relationship could probably benefit Western systems. Western medicine tends to draw a rigid line between biological and psychological causation. Non-Western theories usually lack this sharp distinction, recognizing that poor health has intertwined physical, emotional, and social causes. The mind-body opposition is part of Western folk taxonomy, not of science (see also Brown 1998; Helman 2001; Joralemon 2006; Strathern and Stewart 1999).

Medical anthropologists increasingly are examining the impact of new scientific and medical techniques on ideas about life, death, and *personhood* (what is and is not a person). For decades, disagreements about personhood—about when life begins and ends—have been part of political and religious discussions of contraception, abortion, assisted suicide, and euthanasia (mercy killing). More recent additions to such discussions include stem cell research, frozen embryos, assisted reproduction, genetic screening, cloning, and life-prolonging medical treatments. Ideas about what it means to be human and to be alive or dead are being reformulated.

In the United States, the controversy surrounding the death of Terri Schiavo in 2005 brought such questions into public debate. Kaufman and Morgan (2005) emphasize the contrast between what they call low-tech and high-tech births and deaths in today's world. A desperately poor young mother dies of AIDS in Africa while half a world away an American child of privilege is born as the result of a $50,000 in-vitro fertilization procedure. Medical anthropologists increasingly are concerned with new and contrasting conditions that allow humans to enter, live, and depart life, and with how the boundaries of life and death are being questioned and negotiated in the twenty-first century.

┌─**CULTURE**THINK─────────────

Consider one of the controversial health issues listed on pp. 72–73. What do you think, for example, of life-prolonging medical treatments and assisted suicide for terminal patients?

>> Anthropology and Business

Carol Taylor (1987) discusses the value of an "anthropologist-in-residence" in a large, complex organization, such as a hospital or a business. When information and decisions usually move through a rigid hierarchy, a free-ranging ethnographer can be a perceptive oddball. If allowed to observe and converse freely with all types and levels of personnel, the anthropologist may acquire a unique perspective on organizational conditions and problems. Also, high-tech companies, such as Xerox, IBM, and Apple, have employed anthropologists in various roles. Closely observing how people actually use computer products, anthropologists work with engineers to design products that are more user-friendly.

For many years anthropologists have used ethnography to study business settings (Arensberg 1987; Jordan 2003). For example, ethnographic research in an auto factory may view workers, managers, and executives as different social categories participating in a common social system. Each group has characteristic attitudes, values, and behavior patterns. These are transmitted through *microenculturation,* the process by which people learn particular roles in a limited social system. The free-ranging nature of ethnography takes the anthropologist back and forth from worker to executive. Each is an individual with a personal viewpoint and a cultural creature whose perspective is, to some extent, shared with other members of a group. Applied anthropologists have acted as "cultural brokers," translating managers' goals or workers' concerns to the other group (see Ferraro 2006).

For business, key features of anthropology include (1) ethnography and observation as ways of gathering data, (2) cross-cultural expertise, and (3) focus on cultural diversity. A primary business application of anthropology has to do with knowledge of how consumers use products.

By studying social interactions in factories such as this one, applied anthropologists have acted as "cultural brokers," translating managers' goals or workers' concerns to the other.

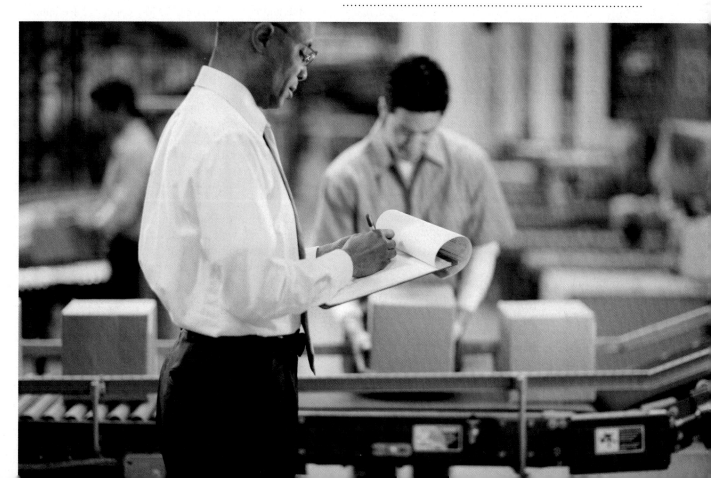

Businesses hire anthropologists because of the usefulness of observation in natural settings and the focus on cultural diversity. Thus, Hallmark Cards has hired anthropologists to observe parties, holidays, and celebrations of ethnic groups to improve its ability to design cards for targeted audiences. Anthropologists go into people's homes to see how they actually use products (see Sunderland and Denny 2007).

>> Careers and Anthropology

Many college students find anthropology interesting and consider majoring in it. However, their parents or friends may discourage them by asking, "What kind of job are you going to get with an anthropology major?" The first step in answering this question is to consider the more general question, "What do you do with any college major?" The answer is, "Not much, without a good bit of effort, thought, and planning." A survey of graduates of the University of Michigan's literary college showed that few had jobs that were clearly linked to their majors. Medicine, law, and many other professions require advanced degrees. Although many colleges offer bachelor's degrees in engineering, business, accounting, and social work, master's degrees often are needed to get the best jobs in those fields. Anthropologists, too, need an advanced degree, almost always a PhD, to find gainful employment in academic, museum, or applied anthropology.

A broad college education, and even a major in anthropology, can be an excellent foundation for success in many fields. A recent survey of women executives showed that most had not majored in business but in the social sciences or humanities. Only after graduating did they study business, obtaining a master's degree in business administration. These executives felt that the breadth of their college educations had contributed to their business careers. Anthropology majors go on to medical, law, and business schools and find success in many professions that often have little explicit connection to anthropology.

CULTURETHINK

What job(s) are you interested in having someday? How would anthropology be useful to you?

Anthropology's breadth provides knowledge and an outlook on the world that are useful in many kinds of work. For example, an anthropology major combined with a master's degree in business is excellent preparation for work in international business. Breadth is anthropology's hallmark. Anthropologists study people biologically, culturally, socially, and linguistically, across time

Anthropology Works

Employees of governmental social service agencies, such as family and children's services or departments of corrections, use anthropological sensitivities to understand cultural diversity and find solutions to problems. In one case, state employees assumed a young mother was neglecting her newborn and were about to put the child into foster care. An anthropologically trained caseworker realized that where the woman came from in Central America, mothers spent one month lying in while their extended family cared for the infant.

and space, in developed and underdeveloped nations, in simple and complex settings. Most colleges have anthropology courses that compare cultures and others that focus on particular world areas, such as Latin America, Asia, and Native North America. The knowledge of foreign areas acquired in such courses can be useful in many jobs. Anthropology's comparative outlook, its longstanding Third World focus, and its appreciation of diverse lifestyles combine to provide an excellent foundation for overseas employment (see Omohundro 2001).

Even for work in North America, the focus on culture is valuable. Every day we hear about cultural differences and about social problems whose solutions require a multicultural viewpoint—an ability to recognize and reconcile ethnic differences. Government, schools, and private firms constantly deal with people from different social classes, ethnic groups, and tribal backgrounds. Physicians, attorneys, social workers, police officers, judges, teachers, and students can all do a better job if they understand social differences in a part of the world such as ours that is one of the most ethnically diverse in history.

Planning and carrying out programs that affect the many social groups within a modern nation requires knowledge about the traditions and beliefs of those groups. Attention to social background and cultural categories helps ensure the welfare of affected ethnic groups, communities, and neighborhoods. Experience in planned social change—whether community organization in North America or economic development overseas—shows that a proper social study should be done before a project or policy is implemented. When local people want the change and it fits their lifestyle and traditions, it will be more successful, beneficial, and cost effective. There will be not only a more humane but also a more economical solution to a real social problem.

People with anthropology backgrounds are doing well in many fields. Even if one's job has little or nothing to do with anthropology in a formal or obvious sense, a background in anthropology provides a useful orientation when we work with our fellow human beings. For most of us, this means every day of our lives.

get involved!

Talk with three fellow students of various cultural backgrounds (different ethnicity, religion, or region). Explain that you are investigating how different groups perceive and respond to illness and its treatment. Ask each student the following questions about their last illness:

- What symptoms did you note?
- What causes did you suspect?
- Does your group have any specific beliefs about the illness, its causes, and its treatment?
- Did you consult a physician or other health care practitioner? If so, what was the diagnosis and the recommended treatment? Did you find the diagnosis acceptable and the treatment, if you tried it, effective? (If you did not consult a practitioner, explain how you attempted to manage your illness.)
- Describe your level of comfort with the setting in which you received diagnosis and treatment.

From these cases, what conclusions can you draw about how cultural background influences our experience of illness, disease, and treatment?

For
REVIEW

CULTURECLIPS

TO ACCESS THESE VIDEOS ON
YOUR COMPUTER, VISIT
www.mhhe.com/gezonqr

4-1

4-2

4-3

I. How can change be bad?

- Applied anthropology recognizes that designs for social or economic change may have unforeseen negative consequences. When foreign aid goes to the developmental priorities as seen by powerful interests rather than to where the need is greatest, the living standards of the needy may actually decline. Channeling inputs through the rich may severely widen economic disparities. Development projects that begin with an uneven distribution of resources often create greater skewing after the project. Projects not implemented by culturally compatible means, failing to use indigenous social models, are less likely to benefit the targeted area.

II. How can anthropology be applied to education, medicine, and business?

- Anthropology and education researchers study the various settings relevant to education. Researchers may identify problematic school practices, misconceptions held by teachers, and problems in interaction among teachers, students, and parents. Researchers then make policy recommendations. Medical anthropologists consider different societies' divergent health care systems and the cultural construction of health and illness. Medical anthropologists serve as cultural interpreters in public health programs and help ensure that interventions fit into local cultures. In businesses and other organizations, ethnographers develop a unique perspective on organizational conditions. They help resolve issues of cultural diversity, study how consumers use products, and translate managers' goals and workers' concerns to the other group.

III. How does the study of anthropology fit into a career path?

- Anthropology's comparative perspective, four-field breadth, and multicultural outlook provide a basis for working in international business and in careers in government, schools, medicine, private firms, or with interest groups that require the ability to recognize and reconcile ethnic differences and understand social problems. Anthropologists with advanced degrees can find employment in academic, museum, or applied anthropology. A background in anthropology can aid and enrich our work with people regardless of the type of employment.

Pop Quiz

1. The use of anthropological data, perspectives, theory, and methods to identify, assess, and solve contemporary problems is known most generally as:
   a. Scientific anthropology
   b. Urban anthropology
   c. Applied anthropology
   d. Development anthropology

2. According to the text, what is the most valuable and distinctive tool of the applied anthropologist?
   a. Knowledge of genetics.
   b. Familiarity with environmental problems.
   c. Statistical expertise.
   d. The ethnographic method.

3. An applied anthropologist today would most likely do which of the following?
   a. Supply information to help colonial regimes.
   b. Offer assistance to local people who lack a voice in the international political arena.
   c. Use survey research to solve economic problems for clients able to pay them.
   d. Supervise the controlled flooding of archaeological sites for underwater archaeology.

4. What situation or event does this chapter use to illustrate some dangers of the old applied anthropology?
   a. The drafting of the American Anthropological Association's ethics guidelines.
   b. Robert Redfield's work contrasting urban and rural communities.
   c. Malinowski's focus on Westernization and his aid of colonial expansion.
   d. The increase in undergraduate anthropology enrollments during the Vietnam War.

5. Which of the following would *not* be a goal of an applied anthropological approach to urban programs?
   a. Work with the target community to ensure that a proposed change is implemented effectively.
   b. Create a universal policy to be applied to all urban communities.
   c. Identify key social groups in the urban context.
   d. Elicit needs and desires from the target community and translate them to funding agencies.

6. In 1992 a white Los Angeles policeman shot and killed two unarmed Samoan brothers. Local Samoan leaders used the traditional *matai* ("chief") system to calm angry youths. This example illustrates:
   a. How an immigrant community can draw on its cultural traditions to adapt to urban life.

   b. That judicial anthropology has little application in urban settings.
   c. The tension between adjustment to a new environment and cultural traditions.
   d. That traditional "clan mentality" often results in excessive violence in urban settings.

7. Most generally, medical anthropology studies:
   a. How indigenous peoples maintain their traditional treatments in societies that offer technologically advanced health care.
   b. The application of traditional health knowledge to the Western medical system.
   c. The academic study and application of Western medicine to solve health problems around the world.
   d. How illness and its diagnosis and treatment are socially constructed and managed in different societies.

8. Which term refers most generally to beliefs, customs, specialists, and techniques aimed at ensuring health and diagnosing and curing illness?
   a. Disease theory
   b. Medical anthropology
   c. Health care system
   d. Shamanism

9. Why would a business or other complex organization hire an anthropologist?
   a. To gain access to the unique, ethnographic perspective on organizational problems.
   b. To learn about the Code of Ethics of the American Anthropological Association.
   c. To ensure that workers' concerns remain those of the workers, and are not translated to managers.
   d. Because anthropologists are cheaper than sociologists and tend to be more presentable.

10. Which of the following points about anthropology and careers is false?
    a. Anthropology offers broad knowledge about human life that is useful in many kinds of work.
    b. The knowledge of foreign cultures acquired in anthropology courses can serve as preparation for work in international business.
    c. Anthropology's focus on culture and its diversity is valuable to any career in which solutions require a multicultural viewpoint.
    d. To gain employment in academic, applied, or museum anthropology, students of anthropology rarely need an advanced degree.

1. (c), 2. (d), 3. (b), 4. (c), 5. (b), 6. (a), 7. (d), 8. (c), 9. (a), 10. (d)

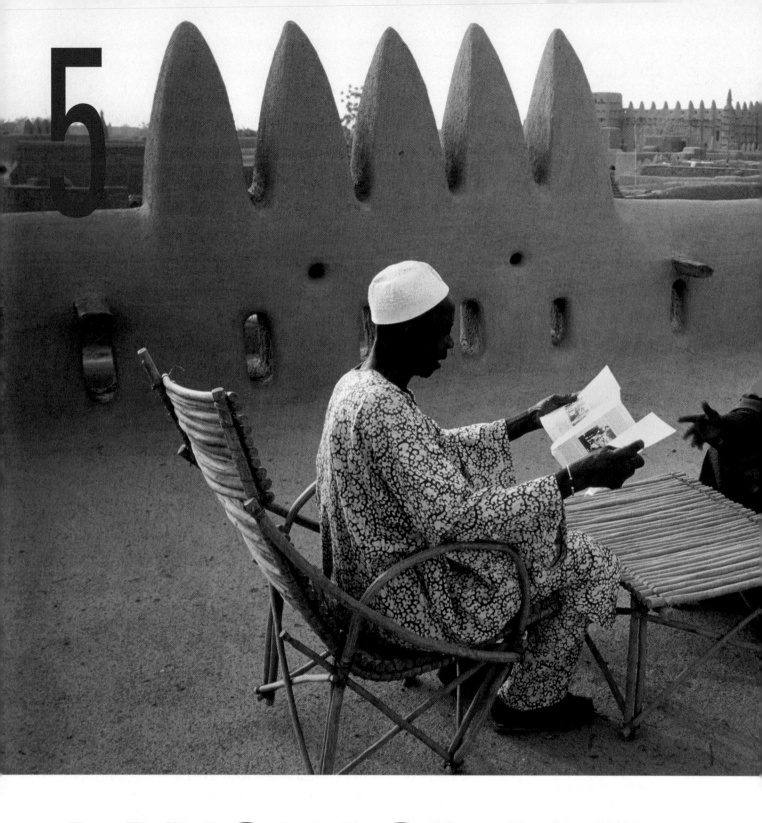

5

LANGUAGE AND
COMMUNICATION

UNDERSTANDING OURSELVES

Can you identify anything distinctive or unusual about the way you talk? If you're from Canada, Virginia, or Savannah, you may say "oot" instead of "out." A southerner may request a "soft drink" rather than the New Yorker's "soda." How might a "Valley Girl" or "surfer dude" talk? Usually when we pay attention to the way we talk, it's because someone else comments on our speech. It may be only when you move from one state or region to another that you realize how much of a regional accent you have.

Unlike grammarians, linguistic anthropologists are interested in what people do say, rather than what they should say. Speech differences are associated with, and tell us a lot about, social variation, such as region, education, ethnic background, and gender. Men and women talk differently. We're sure you can think of examples based on your own experience, although you probably never realized that women tend to peripheralize their vowels (think of the sounds in "weasel" and "whee"), whereas men tend to centralize them (think of "rough" and "ugh"). Men are more likely to speak "ungrammatically" than women are.

Men and women also show differences in their sports and color terminologies. Men typically know more terms related to sports, make more distinctions among them (e.g., *runs* versus *points*), and try to use the terms more precisely than women do. Correspondingly, influenced more by the fashion and cosmetics industries, women use more color terms and attempt to use them more precisely than men do. For example, women are much more likely than men to distinguish between various shades of purple, such as mauve, lilac, lavender, and wisteria. Rare is the man who on the spur of the moment can imagine the difference between fuchsia and magenta or grape and aubergine.

As You READ

- What makes language different from other forms of communication?
- How do anthropologists and linguists study language in general, and specific languages in particular?
- How does language change over short and long periods?

>> Language

Linguistic anthropology illustrates anthropology's characteristic interests in diversity, comparison, and change—but here the focus is on language. Language, spoken (*speech*) and written (*writing*, which has existed for about six thousand years), is our primary means of communication. Like culture in general, of which language is a part, language is transmitted through learning. Language is based on arbitrary, learned associations between words and the things they stand for. Unlike the communication systems of other animals, language allows us to discuss the past and future, share our experiences with others, and benefit from their experiences.

call systems *Systems of communication among nonhuman primates, composed of a limited number of sounds that vary in intensity and duration; tied to environmental stimuli.*

Anthropologists study language in its social and cultural context (see Bonvillain 2008; Salzmann 2007). Some linguistic anthropologists reconstruct ancient languages by comparing their contemporary descendants and, in doing so, make discoveries about history. Others study linguistic differences to discover the varied worldviews and patterns of thought in a multitude of cultures. Sociolinguists examine dialects and styles in a single language to show how speech reflects social differences, as in the above discussion of regional speech contrasts. Linguistic anthropol-

ogists also explore the role of language in colonization and globalization (Geis 1987; Thomas 1999).

>> Nonhuman Primate Communication

CALL SYSTEMS

Only humans speak. No other animal has anything approaching the complexity of language. The natural communication systems of other primates (monkeys and apes) are **call systems.** These vocal systems consist of a limited number of sounds—*calls*—that are produced only when particular environmental stimuli are encountered. Such calls may be varied in intensity and duration, but they are much less flexible than language because they are automatic and can't be combined. When primates encounter food and danger simultaneously, they can make only one call. They can't combine the calls for food and danger into a single utterance, indicating that both are present. At some point in human evolution, however, our ancestors began to combine calls and to understand the combinations. The number of calls also expanded, eventually becoming too great to be transmitted even partly through the genes. Communication came to rely almost totally on learning.

Although wild primates use call systems, the vocal tract of apes is not suitable for speech. Until the 1960s, attempts to teach spoken language to apes suggested that they lack linguistic abilities. In the 1950s, a couple raised a chimpanzee, Viki, as a member of their family and systematically tried to teach her to speak. Viki learned only four words: "mama," "papa," "up," and "cup."

Apes, such as these Congo chimpanzees, use call systems to communicate in the wild. Their vocal systems consist of a limited number of sounds—calls—that are produced only when they encounter particular environmental stimuli.

Hearing-impaired dancers in China's Disabled People's Performing Art Troupe communicate through sign language while undergoing physical conditioning.

SIGN LANGUAGE

More recent experiments have shown that apes can learn to use language, if not speak it (Fouts 1997; Miles 1983). Several apes have learned to converse with people through means other than speech. One such communication system is American Sign Language (ASL), which is widely used by hearing-impaired people in the United States, Canada, and several other nations. British Sign Language (BSL), used in the United Kingdom, differs significantly from ASL, and the two are not mutually intelligible. Sign languages employ a limited number of basic gesture units that are analogous to sounds in spoken language. These units combine to form words and larger units of meaning.

The first chimpanzee to learn ASL was Washoe, a female, who died in 2007 at the age of forty-two. Captured in West Africa, R. Allen Gardner and Beatrice Gardner, scientists at the University of Nevada in Reno, acquired Washoe in 1966, when she was a year old. Four years later, she moved to Norman, Oklahoma, to a converted farm that had become the Institute for Primate Studies. Washoe revolutionized the discussion of the language-learning abilities of apes (Carey 2007). At first she lived in a trailer and heard no spoken language. The researchers always used ASL to communicate with each other in her presence. The chimp gradually acquired a vocabulary of more than one hundred signs representing English words (Gardner, Gardner, and

Did You Know?

Kanzi is a bonobo, a great ape similar to a chimpanzee but genetically and behaviorally closer to humans. He learned to communicate using symbols, or lexigrams, when he was very young. His primary mentor, Sue Savage-Rumbaugh, reported that eight-year-old Kanzi could communicate with grammatical complexity similar to that of a two-year-old child.

Van Cantfort 1989). At the age of two, Washoe began to combine as many as five signs into rudimentary sentences, such as "You, me, go out, hurry."

The second chimp to learn ASL was Lucy, Washoe's junior by one year. Lucy died, or was murdered by poachers, in 1986, after having been introduced to "the wild" in Africa in 1979 (Carter 1988). From her second day of life until her move to Africa, Lucy lived with a family in Norman, Oklahoma. Roger Fouts, a researcher from the nearby Institute for Primate Studies, came two days a week to test and improve Lucy's knowledge of ASL. During the rest of the week, Lucy used ASL to converse with her foster parents. After acquiring language, Washoe and Lucy exhibited several human traits: swearing, joking, telling lies, and trying to teach language to others (Fouts 1997).

When irritated, Washoe called her monkey neighbors at the institute "dirty monkeys." Lucy insulted her "dirty cat." On arrival at Lucy's place, Fouts once found a pile of excrement on the floor. When he asked the chimp what it was, she replied, "dirty, dirty," her expression for feces. Asked whose "dirty, dirty" it was, Lucy named Fouts's coworker, Sue. When Fouts refused to believe her about Sue, the chimp blamed the excrement on Fouts himself.

Cultural transmission of a communication system through learning is a fundamental attribute of language. Washoe, Lucy, and other chimps have tried to teach ASL to other animals, including their own offspring. Washoe taught gestures to other institute chimps, including

cultural transmission A basic feature of language; transmission through learning.

productivity The ability to use the rules of one's language to create new expressions comprehensible to other speakers; a basic feature of language.

her son Sequoia, who died in infancy (Fouts, Fouts, and Van Cantfort 1989).

Because of their size and strength as adults, gorillas are less likely subjects than chimps for such experiments. Lean adult male gorillas in the wild weigh 400 pounds (180 kilograms), and full-grown females can easily reach 250 pounds (110 kilograms). Because of this, psychologist Penny Patterson's work with gorillas at Stanford University seems more daring than the chimp experiments. Patterson raised her now full-grown female gorilla, Koko, in a trailer next to a Stanford museum. Koko's vocabulary surpasses that of any chimp. She regularly employs four hundred ASL signs and has used about seven hundred at least once.

Koko and the chimps also show that apes share still another linguistic ability with humans: **productivity.** Speakers routinely use the rules of their language to produce entirely new expressions that are comprehensible to other native speakers. A human speaker could, for example, create "baboonlet" to refer to a baboon infant. This is done through analogy with English words in which the suffix *-let* designates the young of a species. Anyone who speaks English immediately understands the meaning of the new word. Koko, Washoe, Lucy, and others have shown that apes also are able to use language productively. Lucy used gestures she already knew to create "drinkfruit" for watermelon. Washoe, seeing a swan for the first time, coined "waterbird." Koko, who knew the gestures for "finger" and "bracelet," formed "finger bracelet" when she was given a ring.

Chimps and gorillas have a rudimentary capacity for language. They may never have invented a meaningful gesture system in the wild. Given such a system, however, they show many humanlike abilities in learning and using it. Of course, language use by apes is a product of human intervention and teaching. The experiments mentioned here do not suggest that apes can invent language (nor are human children ever faced with that task). However, young apes have managed to learn the basics of gestural language. They can employ it productively and creatively, although not with the sophistication of human ASL users.

Apes also have demonstrated linguistic **displacement.** Absent in call systems, this is a key ingredient in language. Normally, each call is tied to an environmental stimulus, such as food. Calls are uttered only when that stimulus is present. Displacement means

"He says he wants a lawyer."

Language Contrasted with Call Systems

Human Language	Primate Call Systems
Has the capacity to speak of things and events that are not present (displacement).	Are stimuli-dependent; the food call will be made in the presence of food; it cannot be faked.
Has the capacity to generate new expressions by combining other expressions (productivity).	Consist of a limited number of calls that cannot be combined to produce new calls.
Is group specific in that all humans have the capacity for language, but each linguistic community has its own language, which is culturally transmitted.	Tend to be species specific, with little variation among communities of the same species for each call.

TABLE 5.1

that humans can talk about things that are not present. We don't have to see the objects before we say the words. Human conversations are not limited by place. We can discuss the past and future, share our experiences with others, and benefit from theirs.

Patterson has described several examples of Koko's capacity for displacement (Patterson 1978). The gorilla once expressed sorrow about having bitten Penny three days earlier. Koko has used the sign "later" to postpone doing things she doesn't want to do. Table 5.1 summarizes the contrasts between language, whether sign or spoken, and call systems.

Certain scholars doubt the linguistic abilities of chimps and gorillas (Sebeok and Umiker-Sebeok 1980; Terrace 1979). They contend that Koko and the chimps are comparable to trained circus animals and don't really have linguistic ability. In defense of Patterson and the other researchers (Hill 1978; Van Cantfort and Rimpau 1982), only one of their critics has worked with an ape. This was Herbert Terrace, whose experience teaching a chimp sign language lacked the continuity and personal involvement that have contributed so much to Patterson's success with Koko.

No one denies the huge difference between human language and gorilla signs. There is a major gap between the ability to write a book or say a prayer and the few hundred gestures employed by a well-trained chimp. Apes aren't people, but they aren't just animals either. Let Koko express it: When asked by a reporter whether she was a person or an animal, Koko chose neither. Instead, she signed "fine animal gorilla" (Patterson 1978). For the latest on Koko, see http://koko.org.

Hieroglyphics from an Egyptian tomb illustrate this early form of writing. Language has been around a lot longer than writing. How much longer, do you think?

THE ORIGIN OF LANGUAGE

Although the capacity to remember and combine linguistic symbols may be latent in the apes (Miles 1983), human evolution was needed for this seed to flower into language. A mutated gene known as FOXP2 helps explain why humans speak and chimps don't (Paulson 2005). The key role of FOXP2 in speech came to light in a study of a British family, identified only as KE, half of whose members had an inherited, severe deficit in speech (Trivedi 2001). The same variant form of FOXP2 that is found in chimpanzees causes this disorder. Those who have the nonspeech version of the gene cannot make the fine tongue and lip movements necessary for clear speech, and their speech is unintelligible—even to other members of the KE family (Trivedi 2001). Chimps have the same (genetic) sequence as the KE family members with the speech deficit. Comparing chimp and human genomes, it appears that the speech-friendly form of FOXP2 took hold in humans around 150,000 years ago. This mutation conferred selec-

displacement A linguistic capacity that allows humans to talk about things and events that are not present.

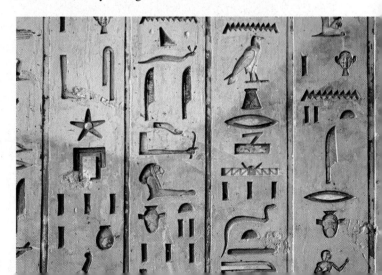

tive advantages (linguistic and cultural abilities) that allowed those who had it to spread at the expense of those who did not (Paulson 2005).

Language offered a tremendous adaptive advantage to *Homo sapiens.* Language permits the information stored by a human society to exceed by far that of any nonhuman group. Language is a uniquely effective vehicle for learning. Because we can speak of things we have never experienced, we can anticipate responses before we encounter the stimuli. Adaptation can occur more rapidly in *Homo* than in the other primates because our adaptive means are more flexible.

CULTURETHINK

How does language provide an adaptive advantage? In other words, how do you think it has helped humans survive?

>> Nonverbal Communication

Language is our principal means of communicating, but it isn't the only one we use. We *communicate* when we transmit information about ourselves to others and receive such information from them. Our expressions, stances, gestures, and movements, even if unconscious, convey information and are part of our

kinesics The study of communication through body movements, stances, gestures, and facial expressions.

communication styles. Deborah Tannen (1990) discusses differences in the communication styles of American men and women, and her comments go beyond language. She notes that American girls and women tend to look directly at each other when they talk, whereas American boys and men do not. Males are more likely to look straight ahead rather than turn and make eye contact with someone, especially another man, seated beside them. Also, in conversational groups, American men tend to relax and sprawl out. American women may adopt a similar relaxed posture in all-female groups, but when they are with men, they tend to draw in their limbs and adopt a tighter stance.

Kinesics is the study of communication through body movements, stances, gestures, and expressions. Linguists pay attention not only to what is said but to how it is said, and to features besides language itself that convey meaning. A speaker's enthusiasm is conveyed not only through words, but also through facial expressions, gestures, and other signs of animation. We use gestures, such as a jab of the hand, for emphasis. We vary our intonation and the pitch or loudness of our voices. We communicate through strategic pauses, and even by being silent. An effective communication strategy may be to alter pitch, voice level, and grammatical forms, such as declaratives ("I am . . ."), imperatives ("Go forth . . ."), and questions ("Are you . . . ?"). Culture teaches us that certain manners and styles should accompany certain kinds of speech. Our demeanor, verbal and nonverbal, when our favorite team is winning would be out of place at a funeral or when a somber subject is being discussed.

Culture always plays a role in shaping the "natural." Cross-culturally, nodding does not always mean affirmative, nor does head shaking from side to side always mean negative. Brazilians wag a finger to mean no. Americans say "uh huh" to affirm, whereas in Madagascar a similar

Men and women have different communication styles, as illustrated in these two photos. Men, for example, are less likely to engage in face-to-face conversation than women are. What differences do you notice in the gender-based communication styles shown here?

sound is made to deny. Americans point with their fingers; the people of Madagascar point with their lips.

Body movements communicate social differences. In Japan, bowing is a regular part of social interaction, but different bows are used depending on the social status of the people who are interacting. In Madagascar and Polynesia, people of lower status should not hold their heads above those of people of higher status. When one approaches someone older or of higher status, one bends one's knees and lowers one's head as a sign of respect. In Madagascar, one always does this, for politeness, when passing between two people. Although our gestures, facial expressions, and body stances have roots in our primate heritage, and can be seen in the monkeys and the apes, they have not escaped cultural shaping. Language, which is so highly dependent on the use of symbols, is the domain of communication in which culture plays the strongest role.

>> The Structure of Language

The scientific study of a spoken language, called **descriptive linguistics,** involves several interrelated areas of analysis: phonology, morphology, lexicon, and syntax. **Phonology,** the study of speech sounds, considers which sounds are present and significant in a given language. **Morphology** studies the way sounds combine to form *morphemes*—words and their meaningful parts. Thus, the word *cats* would be analyzed as containing two morphemes—*cat,* the name for a kind of animal, and *-s,* a morpheme indicating plurality. A language's **lexicon** is a dictionary containing all its morphemes and their meanings. **Syntax** refers to the arrangement and order of words in phrases and sentences. For example, do nouns usually come before or after verbs? Do adjectives normally precede or follow the nouns they modify?

SPEECH SOUNDS

From the movies and TV, and from meeting foreigners, we know something about foreign accents and mispronunciations. We know that someone with a marked French accent doesn't pronounce *r* like an American does. But at least someone from France can distinguish between "craw" and "claw," which someone from Japan may not be able to do. The difference between *r* and *l* makes a difference in English and in French, but it doesn't in Japanese. In linguistics we say that the difference between *r* and *l* is *phonemic* in English and French but not in Japanese. In English and French, *r* and *l* are phonemes but not in Japanese. A **phoneme** is a sound contrast that makes a difference, that differentiates meaning.

We find the phonemes in a given language by comparing *minimal pairs*—words that resemble each other in all but one sound. The words have different meanings, but they differ in just one sound. The contrasting sounds are therefore phonemes in that language. An example in English is the minimal pair *pit/bit.* These two words are distinguished by a single sound contrast between /p/ and /b/ (we enclose phonemes in slashes). Thus /p/ and /b/ are phonemes in English. Another example

descriptive linguistics The scientific study of a spoken language, including its phonology, morphology, lexicon, and syntax.

phonology The study of sounds used in speech.

morphology The study of form; used in linguistics (the study of morphemes and word construction) and for form in general—for example, biomorphology relates to physical form.

lexicon Vocabulary; a dictionary containing all the morphemes in a language and their meaning.

syntax The arrangement and order of words in phrases and sentences.

phoneme Significant sound contrast in a language that serves to distinguish meaning, as in minimal pairs.

Vowel Phonemes in Standard American English

Source: From Aspects of Language, 3rd ed. by Bolinger, Fig. 2.1. Copyright © 1981 Heinle/Arts & Sciences, a part of Cengage Learning, Inc. Reprinted by permission.

High front (spread)	[i]	as in *beat*
Lower high front (spread)	[ɪ]	as in *bit*
Mid front (spread)	[e]	as in *bait*
Lower mid front (spread)	[ɛ]	as in *bet*
Low front	[æ]	as in *bat*
Central	[ə]	as in *butt*
Low back	[a]	as in *pot*
Lower mid back (rounded)	[ɔ]	as in *bought*
Mid back (rounded)	[o]	as in *boat*
Lower high back (rounded)	[ʊ]	as in *put*
High back (rounded)	[u]	as in *boot*

Vocal phonemes are shown according to height of tongue and tongue position at front, center, or back of mouth. Phonetic symbols are identified by English words that include them; note that most are minimal pairs.

normally use the [b] sound to pronounce words spelled with either *b* or *v*.

In any language, a given phoneme extends over a phonetic range. In English the phoneme /p/ ignores the phonetic contrast between the [pʰ] in *pin* and the [p] in *spin*. Most English speakers don't even notice that there is a phonetic difference. The [pʰ] is aspirated, so that a puff of air follows the [p]. The [p] in *spin* is not. (To see the difference, light a match, hold it in front of your mouth, and watch the flame as you pronounce the two words.) The contrast between [pʰ] and [p] is phonemic in some languages, such as Hindi (spoken in India). That is, there are words whose meaning is distinguished only by the contrast between an aspirated and an unaspirated [p].

Native speakers vary in their pronunciation of certain phonemes, such as the /e/ phoneme in the midwestern United States. This variation is important in the evolution of language. Without shifts in pronunciation, there could be no linguistic change. The section on sociolinguistics later in the chapter considers phonetic variation and its relationship to social divisions and the evolution of language.

CULTURETHINK

Say the following words casually, with an informal but acceptable pronunciation: top, stop, little, kitten, Atlanta. Are the *t*'s all pronounced the same? How many variants can you count? (Note: One of them is aspirated.) The sound we think of as *t* can be pronounced in several ways.

is the different vowel sound of *bit* and *beat* (see "Vowel Phonemes in Standard American English," above). This contrast serves to distinguish these two words and the two vowel phonemes written /ɪ/ and /i/ in English.

Standard (American) English (SE), the "region-free" dialect of TV network newscasters, has about thirty-five phonemes—at least eleven vowels and twenty-four consonants. The number of phonemes varies from language to language—from fifteen to sixty, averaging between thirty and forty. The number of phonemes also varies between dialects of a given language. In North American English, for example, vowel phonemes vary noticeably from dialect to dialect. Try pronouncing the words in the figure above, paying attention to (or asking someone else) whether you (or your partner) can distinguish each of the vowel sounds. Most North Americans don't pronounce them all.

Phonetics is the study of speech sounds in general, what people actually say in various languages. **Phonemics** studies only the *significant* sound contrasts (phonemes) of a given language. In English, like /r/ and /l/ (remember *craw* and *claw*), /b/ and /v/ also are phonemes, occurring in minimal pairs like *bat* and *vat*. In Spanish, however, the contrast between [b] and [v] doesn't distinguish meaning, and they therefore are not phonemes (we enclose sounds that are not phonemic in brackets). Spanish speakers

phonetics The study of speech sounds in general; what people actually say in various languages.

phonemics The study of significant sound contrasts (phonemes) of a particular language.

>> Language, Thought, and Culture

The well-known linguist Noam Chomsky (1957) has argued that the human brain contains a limited set of rules for organizing language, so that all languages have a common structural basis. (Chomsky calls this set of rules *universal grammar.*) The fact that people can learn foreign languages and that words and ideas translate from one language to another supports Chomsky's position that all humans have similar linguistic abilities and thought processes. Another line of support comes from creole languages. Such languages develop from pidgins—languages that form in situations of acculturation, when different societies come into contact and must devise a system of communication. Pidgins based on English and native languages developed through trade and colonialism in many world areas, including China, Papua New Guinea, and West Af-

Imagine life without Twitter, Facebook, and texting—means of communication that allow people to stay in almost constant contact with others. Facebook, created in 2004, allows people to send public posts and private messages, share photos, organize events, and remember birthdays. Twitter, launched in 2006, was developed as a way of sending text messages to multiple people. People now use it to keep track of their friends and celebrity favorites (e.g., Ashton Kutcher, Sarah Palin). People emit "tweets" to update people who "follow" them. According to Mashable: The Social Media Guide (mashable.com), Twitter helps people get to know new sides of other people. How does cybercommunication change the quality and quantity of friendships and family ties? How does it affect our awareness of world, national, and local events? Try going a day or even a week without any form of communication that is not absolutely necessary.

the **Sapir-Whorf hypothesis,** after Edward Sapir (1931) and his student Benjamin Lee Whorf (1956), its prominent early advocates. Sapir and Whorf argued that the grammatical categories of particular languages lead their speakers to think about things in different ways. For example, English divides time into past, present,

> **Sapir-Whorf hypothesis**
> Theory that different languages produce different ways of thinking.

and future. Hopi, a language of the Pueblo region of the Native American Southwest, does not. Rather, Hopi distinguishes between events that exist or have existed (what we use present and past to discuss) and those that don't or don't yet (our future events, along with imaginary and hypothetical events). Whorf argued that this difference leads Hopi speakers to think about time and reality in different ways than English speakers do.

A similar example comes from Portuguese, which employs a future subjunctive verb form, introducing a degree of uncertainty into discussions of the future. In English we routinely use the future tense to talk about something we think will happen. We don't feel the need to qualify "The sun'll come out tomorrow," by adding "if it doesn't go supernova." We don't hesitate to proclaim, "I'll see you next year," even when we can't be absolutely sure we will. The Portuguese future subjunctive qualifies the future

rica. Eventually, after generations of being spoken, pidgins may develop into *creole languages.* These are more mature languages, with developed grammatical rules and native speakers (people who learn the language as their primary one during enculturation).

Creoles are spoken in several Caribbean societies. Gullah, which is spoken by African Americans on coastal islands in South Carolina and Georgia, is a creole language. Supporting the idea that creoles are based on universal grammar is the fact that such languages all share certain features. Syntactically, all use particles (e.g., will, was) to form future and past tenses and multiple negation to deny or negate (e.g., he don't got none). Also, all form questions by changing inflection rather than by changing word order. For example, "You're going home for the holidays?" (with a rising tone at the end) rather than "Are you going home for the holidays?"

THE SAPIR-WHORF HYPOTHESIS

Other linguists and anthropologists take a different approach to the relation between language and thought. Rather than seeking universal linguistic structures and processes, they believe that different languages produce different ways of thinking. This position sometimes is known as

Shown here (in 1995) is Leigh Jenkins, who was or is director of cultural preservation for the Hopi council. The Hopi language would not distinguish between was and is in the previous sentence. For the Hopi, present and past are real and are expressed grammatically in the same way, while the future remains hypothetical and has a different grammatical expression.

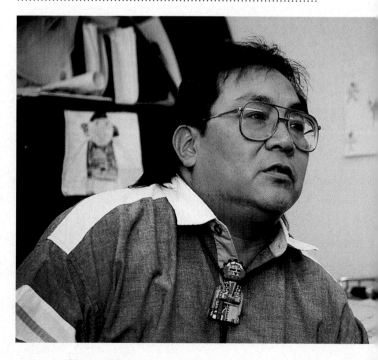

event, recognizing that the future can't be certain. Our way of expressing the future as certain is so ingrained that we don't even think about it, just as the Hopi don't see the need to distinguish between present and past, both of which are real, while the future remains hypothetical. It seems, however, that language does not tightly restrict thought, because cultural changes can produce changes in thought and in language, as we'll see in the next section (see also Gumperz and Levinson 1996).

FOCAL VOCABULARY

As mentioned earlier, a lexicon (or vocabulary) is a language's dictionary, its set of names for things, events, and ideas. Lexicon influences perception. Thus, Eskimos (or Inuit) have several distinct words for different types of snow that in English are all called *snow*. Most English speakers never notice the differences between these types of snow and might have trouble seeing them even if someone pointed them out. Eskimos recognize and think about differences in snow that English speakers don't see because our language gives us just one word.

focal vocabulary A set of words and distinctions that are particularly important to certain groups (those with particular foci of experience or activity), such as types of snow to Eskimos or skiers.

Illustrating focal vocabulary, Eskimos, or Inuit, have several distinct words for different types of snow that in English are all called "snow."

CULTURETHINK

Much of what we communicate is nonverbal and refers to our emotional states and intentions. This leads to frequent miscommunication in texting and online messaging. People use emoticons (☺, ☹, :~/ [confused], :~0 ['hah!' no way!]) and abbreviations (lol—laugh out loud; lmao—laugh my a** off; wtf—what the f**; omg—oh my god) to fill in what would otherwise be communicated by tone of voice, laughter, and facial expression. Have you ever had any miscommunications when texting or emailing? What strategies do you use to communicate more clearly?

Similarly, the Nuer of Sudan have an elaborate vocabulary to describe cattle. Eskimos have several words for snow, and Nuer have dozens for cattle because of their particular histories, economies, and environments (Brown 1958; Eastman 1975). When the need arises, English speakers can also elaborate their snow and cattle vocabularies. For example, skiers name varieties of snow with words that are missing from the lexicons of Florida retirees. Similarly, the cattle vocabulary of a Texas rancher is much more ample than that of a salesperson in a New York City department store. Such specialized sets of terms and distinctions that are particularly important to certain groups (those with particular *foci* of experience or activity) are known as **focal vocabulary.**

Vocabulary is the area of language that changes most readily. New words and distinctions, when needed, appear and spread. For example, who would have "texted" or sent a "tweet" a generation ago? Names for items get simpler as they become common and important. A television has become a *TV,* an automobile a *car,* a digital video disc a *DVD,* and cell phone applications *apps.*

Language, culture, and thought are interrelated. Opposing the Sapir-Whorf hypothesis, however, it might be more accurate to say that changes in culture produce changes in language and thought than to say the reverse. Consider differences between female and male Americans

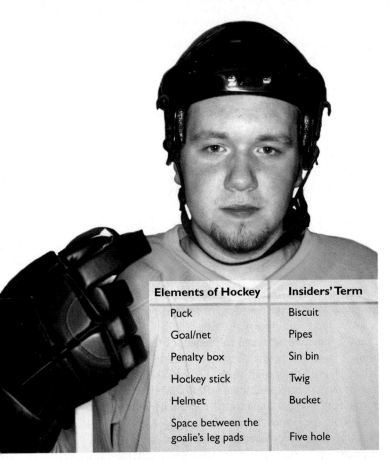

Elements of Hockey	Insiders' Term
Puck	Biscuit
Goal/net	Pipes
Penalty box	Sin bin
Hockey stick	Twig
Helmet	Bucket
Space between the goalie's leg pads	Five hole

Focal Vocabulary for Hockey

red, *yellow, blue, green, brown, pink, orange,* and *purple* (they evolved in more or less that order). The number of terms varied with cultural complexity. Representing one extreme were Papua New Guinea cultivators and Australian hunters and gatherers, who used only two basic terms, which translate as *black* and *white* or *dark* and *light*. At the other end of the continuum were European and Asian languages with all the color terms. Color terminology was most developed in areas with a history of using dyes and artificial coloring.

>> Sociolinguistics

No language is a uniform system in which everyone talks just like everyone else. The field of **sociolinguistics** investigates relationships between social and linguistic variation (Romaine 2000; Trudgill 2000). How do different speakers use a given language? How do linguistic features correlate with social diversity and stratification, including class, ethnic, and gender differences (Tannen 1990, 1993)? How is language used to express, reinforce, or resist power (Geis 1987; Lakoff 2000)?

Sociolinguists focus on features that vary systematically with social position and situation. To study variation, sociolinguists observe, define, and measure variable use of language in real-world situations. To show that linguistic features correlate with social, economic, and political differences, social attributes of speakers must be measured and related to speech (Fasold 1990; Labov 1972a).

> **semantics** A language's meaning system.
>
> **sociolinguistics** Study of relationships between social and linguistic variation; study of language in its social context.

regarding the color terms they use (Lakoff 2004). Distinctions implied by such terms as *salmon, rust, peach, beige, teal, mauve, cranberry,* and *dusky orange* aren't in the vocabularies of most American men. Many of them weren't even in American women's lexicons fifty years ago. These changes reflect changes in American economy, society, and culture. Color terms and distinctions have increased with the growth of the fashion and cosmetic industries. A similar contrast (and growth) in Americans' lexicons shows up in football, basketball, and hockey vocabularies. Sports fans, more often males than females, use more terms concerning, and make more elaborate distinctions between, the games they watch, such as hockey. Thus, cultural contrasts and changes affect lexical distinctions (for instance, *peach* versus *salmon*) within semantic domains (for instance, color terminology). **Semantics** refers to a language's meaning system.

The ways in which people divide the world—the lexical contrasts they perceive as meaningful or significant—reflect their experiences (see Bicker, Sillitoe, and Pottier 2004). Anthropologists have discovered that certain sets of vocabulary items evolve in a determined order. For example, after studying more than a hundred languages, Berlin and Kay (1969/1992) discovered ten basic color terms: *white, black,*

How might social variation show up in texting?

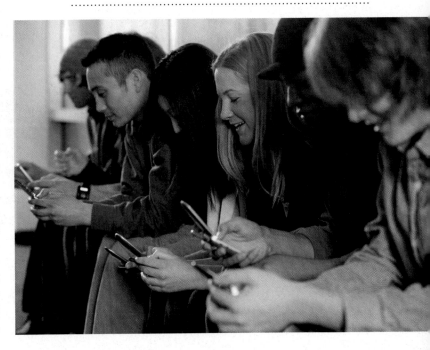

Anthropology Works

Understanding language variation can help educators identify the difference between genuine speech disabilities and dialect differences. Anthropological training shows that different ways of pronouncing words are not necessarily due to individual deficiencies.

Variation within a language at a given time is historical change in progress. The same forces that, working gradually, have produced large-scale linguistic change over the centuries are still at work today. Linguistic change doesn't occur in a vacuum but in society. When new ways of speaking are associated with social factors, they are imitated, and they spread. In this way, a language changes.

LINGUISTIC DIVERSITY WITHIN NATIONS

As an illustration of the linguistic variation encountered in all nations, consider the contemporary United States. Ethnic diversity is revealed by the fact that millions of Americans learn first languages other than English. Spanish is the most common. Most of those people eventually become bilinguals, adding English as a second language. In many multilingual (including colonized) nations, people use two languages on different occasions—one in the home, for example, and the other on the job or in public.

style shifts Variations in speech in different contexts.

diglossia The existence of "high" (formal) and "low" (familial) dialects of a single language, such as German.

Whether bilingual or not, we all vary our speech in different contexts; we engage in **style shifts.** In certain parts of Europe, people regularly switch dialects. This phenomenon, known as **diglossia,** applies to "high" and "low" variants of the same language, for example, in German and Flemish (spoken in Belgium). People employ the high variant at universities and in writing, professions, and the mass media. They use the low variant for ordinary conversation with family members and friends.

Just as social situations influence our speech, so do geographical, cultural, and socioeconomic differences. Many dialects coexist in the United States with Standard (American) English (SE). SE itself is a dialect that differs, say, from "BBC English," which is the preferred dialect in Great Britain. Different dialects are equally effective as systems of communication, which is language's main job. Our tendency to think of particular dialects as cruder or more sophisticated than others is a social rather than a linguistic judgment. We rank certain speech patterns as better or worse because we recognize that they are used by groups that we also rank. People who say *dese, dem,* and *dere* instead of *these, them,* and *there* communicate perfectly well with anyone who recognizes that the *d* sound systematically replaces the *th* sound in their speech. However, this form of speech has become an indicator of low social rank. We call it, like the use of *ain't,* "uneducated speech." The use of *dem, dese,* and *dere* is one of many phonological differences that Americans recognize and look down on.

GENDER SPEECH CONTRASTS

Comparing men and women, there are differences in phonology, grammar, and vocabulary, and in the body stances and movements that accompany speech (Eckert and McConnell-Ginet 2003; Lakoff 2004; Tannen 1990). In phonology, American women tend to pronounce their vowels more peripherally ("rant," "rint" when saying "rent"), whereas men tend to pronounce theirs more centrally ("runt"). In public contexts, Japanese women tend to adopt an artificially high voice, for the sake of politeness, according to their traditional culture. Women tend to be more careful about uneducated speech. This trend shows up in both the United States and England. Men may adopt working-class speech because they associate it with masculinity. Perhaps women pay more attention to the media, in which standard dialects are employed.

According to Robin Lakoff (2004), the use of certain types of words and expressions has been associated with women's traditional lesser power in American society (see also Coates 1986; Romaine 1999; Tannen 1990, 1993). For example, "Oh dear," "Oh fudge," and "Goodness!" are less forceful than "Hell" and "Damn." Watch the lips of a disgruntled male athlete in a televised competition, such as a football game. What's the likelihood he's saying "Phooey on you"? Women also are more likely to use such adjec-

CULTURETHINK

The text identifies several factors that make the speech of men and women different, including pronunciation, types of words and expressions, and overall linguistic styles. Pay attention to the conversations around you: Do you notice these differences? Do you agree with Tannen that men tend to value hierarchy, while women focus on building relationships?

tives as *adorable, charming, sweet, cute, lovely,* and *divine* than men are.

Differences in the linguistic strategies and behavior of men and women are examined in several books by the well-known sociolinguist Deborah Tannen (1990, 1993). Tannen uses the terms "rapport" and "report" to contrast women's and men's overall linguistic styles. Women, says Tannen, typically use language and the body movements that accompany it to build rapport—social connections with others. Men, on the other hand, tend to make reports, reciting information that serves to establish a place for themselves in a hierarchy, as they also attempt to determine the relative ranks of their conversation mates.

STRATIFICATION AND SYMBOLIC DOMINATION

We use and evaluate speech in the context of *extralinguistic* forces—social, political, and economic. Mainstream Americans evaluate the speech of low-status groups negatively, calling it "uneducated." This is not because these ways of speaking are bad in themselves but because they have come to symbolize low status. Consider variation in the pronunciation of *r*. In some parts of the United States, *r* is regularly pronounced, and in other (*r*less) areas, it is not. Originally, American *r*less speech was modeled on the fashionable speech of England. Because of its prestige, *r*lessness was adopted in many areas and continues as the norm around Boston and in the South.

New Yorkers sought prestige by dropping their *r*'s in the nineteenth century, after having pronounced them in the eighteenth. Contemporary New Yorkers are going back to the eighteenth-century pattern of pronouncing *r*'s. What matters, and what governs linguistic change, is not the reverberation of a strong midwestern *r* but social evaluation, whether *r*'s happen to be "in" or "out."

Studies of *r* pronunciation in New York City have clarified the mechanisms of phonological change. William Labov (1972b) focused on whether *r* was pronounced after vowels in such words as *car, floor, card,* and *fourth.* To get data on how this linguistic variation correlated with social class, he used a series of rapid encounters with employees in three New York City department stores, each of whose prices and locations attracted a different socioeconomic group. Saks Fifth Avenue (68 encounters) catered to the upper middle class, Macy's (125) attracted middle-class shoppers, and S. Klein's (71) had predominantly lower-middle-class and working-class customers. The class origins of store personnel reflected those of their customers.

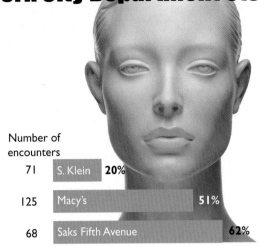

Pronunciation of *r* in New York City Department Stores

Number of encounters		
71	S. Klein	20%
125	Macy's	51%
68	Saks Fifth Avenue	62%

Percentage *r* pronunciation

Having already determined that a certain department was on the fourth floor, Labov approached ground-floor salespeople and asked where that department was. After the salesperson had answered, "Fourth floor," Labov repeated his "Where?" in order to get a second response. The second reply was more formal and emphatic, the salesperson presumably thinking that Labov hadn't heard or understood the first answer. For each salesperson, therefore, Labov had two samples of /r/ pronunciation in two words.

Labov calculated the percentages of workers who pronounced /r/ at least once during the interview. These were 62 percent at Saks, 51 percent at Macy's, but only 20 percent at S. Klein's. He also found that on upper floors, where he asked, "What floor is this?" (and where more expensive items were sold), personnel pronounced *r* more often than ground-floor salespeople did.

In Labov's study, *r* pronunciation was clearly associated with prestige. Certainly the job interviewers who had hired the salespeople never counted *r*'s before offering employment. However, they did use speech evaluations to make judgments about how effective certain people would be in selling particular kinds of merchandise. In other words, they practiced sociolinguistic discrimination, using linguistic features in deciding who got certain jobs.

Our speech habits help determine our access to employment and other material resources. Because of this, "proper language" itself becomes a strategic resource—and a path to wealth, prestige, and power (Gal 1989; Thomas and Wareing 2004). Illustrating this, many ethnographers have described the importance of verbal skill and oratory in politics (Beeman 1986; Bloch 1975; Brenneis 1988; Geis 1987; Lakoff 2000). Ronald Reagan, known as a "great communicator," dominated American society in the 1980s as a two-term president. Another twice-elected president, Bill Clinton, despite his southern accent, was known for his verbal skills in certain contexts (e.g., televised debates

STUDY TIP

Sociolinguistics investigates language variation within a population. Language differences correlate with such factors as dialect, gender, class, and ethnicity.

CULTURETHINK

How should schools treat children who speak different languages and dialects? Should they require them to use the standard, prestigious speech pattern?

and town-hall meetings). Communications flaws may have helped doom the presidencies of Gerald Ford, Jimmy Carter, and George Bush the elder. Does his use of language affect your perception of Barack Obama?

The French anthropologist Pierre Bourdieu views linguistic practices as *symbolic capital* that properly trained people may convert into economic and social capital. The value of a dialect—its standing in a "linguistic market"—depends on the extent to which it provides access to desired positions in the labor market. In turn, this reflects its legitimacy by formal institutions—educational institutions, state, church, and prestige media. Even people who don't use the prestige dialect accept its authority and correctness, its "symbolic domination" (Bourdieu 1982, 1984). Thus, linguistic forms, which lack power in themselves, take on the power of the groups they symbolize. The education system, however (defending its own worth), denies linguistic relativity. It misrepresents prestige speech as being inherently better. The linguistic insecurity often felt by lower-class and minority speakers is a result of this symbolic domination.

Black English Vernacular (BEV) A rule-governed dialect of American English (sometimes called ebonics) with roots in southern English. African American youth and many adults speak BEV in their casual, intimate speech.

BLACK ENGLISH VERNACULAR (BEV)

The sociolinguist William Labov and several associates, both white and black, have conducted detailed studies of what they call **Black English Vernacular (BEV).** (*Vernacular* means ordinary, casual speech.) BEV is the "relatively uniform dialect spoken by the majority of black youth in most parts of the United States today, especially in the inner-city areas of New York, Boston, Detroit, Philadelphia, Washington,

Although never a native speaker of BEV, President Barack Obama, speaking here in 2009 to the National Academy of Sciences, exemplifies an upwardly mobile person with an unusually effective mastery of SE.

Cleveland, . . . and other urban centers. It is also spoken in most rural areas and used in the casual, intimate speech of many adults" (Labov 1972a, p. xiii). This does not imply that all, or even most, African Americans speak BEV.

BEV is a complex linguistic system with its own rules, which linguists have described. Consider some of the phonological and grammatical differences between BEV and SE. One phonological difference is that BEV speakers are less likely to pronounce *r* than SE speakers are. Actually, many SE speakers don't pronounce *r*'s that come right before a consonant (card) or at the end of a word (car). But SE speakers usually do pronounce an *r* that comes right before a vowel, either at the end of a word (four o'clock) or within a word (Carol). BEV speakers, by contrast, are much more likely to omit such intervocalic (between vowels) *r*'s. The result is that speakers of the two dialects have different *homonyms* (words that sound the same but have different meanings). BEV speakers who don't pronounce intervocalic *r*'s have the following homonyms: Carol/Cal; Paris/pass.

Observing different phonological rules, BEV speakers pronounce certain words differently than SE speakers do. Particularly in the elementary school context, the homonyms of BEV-speaking students typically differ from those of their SE-speaking teachers. To evaluate reading accuracy, teachers should determine whether students are recognizing the different meanings of such BEV homonyms as *passed, past,* and *pass.* Teachers need to make sure students understand what they are reading, which is probably more important than whether they are pronouncing words correctly according to the SE norm.

Phonological rules may lead BEV speakers to omit *-ed* as a past-tense marker and *-s* as a marker of plurality. However, other speech contexts demonstrate that BEV speakers do understand the difference between past and present verbs, and between singular and plural nouns. Confirming this are irregular verbs (e.g., *tell, told*) and irregular plurals (e.g., *child, children*), in which BEV works the same as SE.

SE is not superior to BEV as a linguistic system, but it does happen to be the prestige dialect—the one used in the mass media, in writing, and in most public and professional contexts. SE is the dialect that has the most "symbolic capital." In areas of Germany where there is diglossia, speakers of Plattdeusch (Low German) learn the High German dialect to communicate appropriately in the national context. Similarly, upwardly mobile BEV-speaking students learn SE.

Rap and hip-hop weave BEV into musical expression. Here we see Common performing with Pharrell Williams, Shay Haley and Chad Hugo of N.E.R.D during the 2008 BET Hip Hop Awards.

>> Historical Linguistics

Sociolinguists study contemporary variation in speech, which is language change in progress. **Historical linguistics** deals with longer-term change. Historical linguists can reconstruct many features of past languages by studying contemporary **daughter languages.** These are languages that descend from the same parent language and that have been changing separately for hundreds or even thousands of years. We call the original language from which they diverge the **protolanguage.** Romance languages such as French and Spanish, for example, are daughter languages of Latin, their common protolanguage. German, English, Dutch, and the Scandinavian languages are daughter languages of proto-Germanic. The Romance languages and the Germanic languages all belong to the Indo-European language family. Their common protolanguage is called Proto-Indo-European (PIE). Historical linguists classify languages according to their degree of relationship (see "PIE Family Tree" on page 94).

Language changes over time. It evolves—varies, spreads, divides into **language subgroups** (those within a taxonomy of related languages that are most closely related). Dialects of a single parent language become distinct daughter languages, especially if they are isolated from one another. Some of them split, and new "granddaughter" languages develop. If people remain in the ancestral homeland, their speech patterns also change. The evolving speech in the ancestral homeland should be considered a daughter language like the others.

A close relationship between languages doesn't necessarily mean that their speakers are closely related biologically or culturally, because people can adopt new languages. In the equatorial forests of Africa, "pygmy" hunters have discarded their ancestral languages and now speak those of the cultivators who have migrated to the area. Immigrants to the United States spoke many different languages on arrival, but their descendants now speak fluent English.

historical linguistics Subdivision of linguistics that studies languages over time.

daughter languages Languages developing out of the same parent language; for example, French and Spanish are daughter languages of Latin.

protolanguage Language ancestral to several daughter languages.

language subgroups Languages within a taxonomy of related languages that are most closely related.

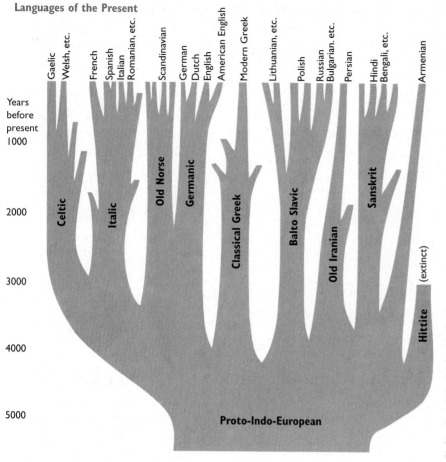

Languages of the Present

Years before present
1000
2000
3000
4000
5000

Gaelic
Welsh, etc.
French
Spanish
Italian
Romanian, etc.
Scandinavian
German
Dutch
English
American English
Modern Greek
Lithuanian, etc.
Polish
Russian
Bulgarian. etc.
Persian
Hindi
Bengali, etc.
Armenian

Celtic
Italic
Old Norse
Germanic
Classical Greek
Balto Slavic
Old Iranian
Sanskrit
Hittite (extinct)

Proto-Indo-European

PIE Family Tree

Main languages and subgroups of the Indo-European language stock, showing approximate time to their divergence.

Knowledge of linguistic relationships often is valuable to anthropologists interested in history, particularly events during the past five thousand years. Cultural features may (or may not) correlate with the distribution of language families. Groups that speak related languages may (or may not) be more culturally similar to each other than they are to groups whose speech derives from different linguistic ancestors. Of course, cultural similarities aren't limited to speakers of related languages. Even groups whose members speak unrelated languages have contact through trade, intermarriage, and warfare. Ideas and inventions diffuse widely among human groups. Many items of vocabulary in contemporary English, particularly food items, such as "beef" and "pork," come from French. Even without written documentation of France's influence after the Norman Conquest of England in 1066, linguistic evidence in contemporary English

Did You Know?

Papua New Guinea, an island with just over six million people, once had at least 841 spoken languages. Many of those languages are endangered, and some have no living speakers.

would reveal a long period of important firsthand contact with France. Similarly, linguistic evidence may confirm cultural contact and borrowing when written history is lacking. By considering which words have been borrowed, we also can make inferences about the nature of the contact.

LANGUAGE LOSS

One aspect of linguistic history is language loss. When languages disappear, cultural diversity is reduced as well. According to linguist K. David Harrison, "When we lose a language, we lose centuries of thinking about time, seasons, sea creatures, reindeer, edible flowers, mathematics, landscapes, myths, music, the unknown and the everyday" (quoted in Maugh 2007). Harrison's recent book, *When Languages Die* (2007), notes that an indigenous language goes extinct every two weeks, as its last speakers die. The world's linguistic diversity has been cut in half (measured by number of distinct languages) in the past five hundred years, and half of the remaining languages are predicted to disappear during this century. Colonial languages (e.g., English, Spanish, Portuguese, French, Dutch, Russian) have expanded at the expense of indigenous ones. Of approximately seven thousand remaining languages, about 20 percent are endangered, compared with 18 percent of mammals, 8 percent of plants, and 5 percent of birds (Maugh 2007).

Harrison, who teaches at Swarthmore College in Pennsylvania, is director of research for the Living Tongues Institute for Endangered Languages (http://www .livingtongues.org), which works to maintain, preserve, and revitalize endangered languages through multimedia documentation projects. Researchers from the institute use digital audio and video equipment to record the last speakers of the most endangered languages. *National Geographic*'s Enduring Voices Project (http://www.nationalgeographic .com/mission/enduringvoices/) strives to preserve endangered languages by identifying the geographic areas with unique, poorly understood, or threatened languages and by documenting those languages and cultures.

The website shows various language hot spots where the endangerment rate ranges from low to severe. In the United States, the rate is high in an area encompassing Oklahoma, Texas, and New Mexico, where 40 Native American languages are at risk. The top hot spot is northern Australia, where 153 Aboriginal languages are endangered (Maugh 2007). Other hot spots are in central South America, the

Internet Top 10 Languages

Millions of users

Language	Users
English	464
Chinese	321
Spanish	131
Japanese	94
French	74
Portuguese	73
German	65
Arabic	41
Russian	38
Korean	37
Rest of world languages	258

Pacific Northwest of North America, and eastern Siberia. In all these areas, indigenous tongues have yielded, either voluntarily or through coercion, to a colonial language.

Despite language loss, linguistic diversity is alive and well in many countries, including India. Despite that nation's colonial history, only about a tenth of the Indian population speaks English. Even many of those English speakers prefer to read, and to seek Internet content, in their own regional languages. Local entrepreneurs and international companies such as Google, Yahoo, and Microsoft are rushing to meet the demand for Web content in local languages. This example illustrates one of the main lessons of applied anthropology, that external inputs fit in best when they are tailored properly to local settings.

get involved!

Sociolinguists have studied the ways that speech patterns differ between American men and American women. Save emails from your male and female friends and family members to see if there are comparable differences in electronic communication styles. Are there different ratios of what sociolinguist Deborah Tannen calls "rapport" (building social connections) and "report" (reciting information)? How about differences in kinds of words used, size and completeness of sentences, and typography? Does the use of emoticons vary, both in type (joking or serious, reassuring or negative) and in number? Keep a table of your findings: women's style on one side, men's on the other.

For REVIEW

I. What makes language different from other forms of communication?

- The communication systems used by other animals lack the complexity and adaptive advantages characteristic of language. Wild primates use calls—sounds limited in number and produced only when particular environmental stimuli are encountered. Calls are automatic and cannot be combined. Language, by contrast, is based on arbitrary, learned associations between words and the things they represent. The fundamental attributes of language are (1) cultural transmission through learning; (2) productivity—the ability to produce new expressions by combining other expressions; and (3) displacement—the ability to talk about things not present.

II. How do anthropologists and linguists study language in general and specific languages in particular?

- Anthropologists and linguists study a specific spoken language by describing its significant sounds and how they combine to form words and their meaningful parts. These scientists also compile a lexicon of the language's morphemes and their meanings, and they study syntax, the order and arrangement of words in phrases and sentences. Phonetics is the study of speech sounds in general. Some linguists seek universal linguistic structures and processes. Still others examine how different linguistic structures produce varied ways of thinking.

III. How does language change over short and long periods?

- Sociolinguists study relationships between social and linguistic variation in a society, including linguistic diversity within nations, gender speech contrasts, and the stratification of language. Such contemporary variation within a language is language change in progress. When new ways of speaking are associated with social factors, these ways spread, and language changes. Dealing with long-term change, historical linguists reconstruct features of past languages by studying contemporary daughter languages, descendants of the same parent language that have been changing separately for hundreds or even thousands of years. Language evolves, spreads, and divides into subgroups. Another area of language change is language loss. The past five hundred years have seen the world's linguistic diversity reduced by half. Colonial languages have expanded at the expense of indigenous languages.

Pop Quiz

1. Studies of communication among nonhuman primates reveal that:
    a. Like humans, though to a lesser degree, apes possess the linguistic ability of productivity.
    b. Nonhuman primates can create flexible call systems, so that, for example, a call for food may be combined with a call indicating that danger is also present.
    c. Nonhuman primate call systems vary greatly among communities of the same species.
    d. Primates other than humans can speak.

2. Washoe and Lucy's effort to teach sign language to other chimpanzees is an example of:
    a. A call system
    b. Displacement
    c. Productivity
    d. Cultural transmission

3. Recent research on the origin of language suggests that:
    a. The capacity to remember and combine linguistic symbols is latent in all mammals.
    b. A mutation in humans that occurred around 150,000 years ago may have conferred selective advantages (linguistic and cultural abilities) to those who had it.
    c. Fine tongue and lip movements that are necessary for clear speech are passed on through enculturation.
    d. The earliest forms of language slowed human adaptation because they were less effective for information storage and learning than were call systems.

4. The study of communication through body movements, stances, gestures, and facial expressions is called:
    a. Semantics
    b. Kinesics
    c. Protolanguage
    d. Diglossia

5. The area of analysis of a spoken language that refers to all of a language's morphemes and their meanings is:
    a. Syntax
    b. Semantics
    c. Phonology
    d. Lexicon

6. The Sapir-Whorf hypothesis states that:
    a. The Hopi do not divide time into past, present, and future; the Hopi have no concept of time.
    b. Different languages produce different ways of thinking.
    c. Changes in culture produce changes in language and thought.
    d. All languages share the same grammatical categories.

7. Studies of the differences in the use of color terms between female and male Americans suggest that:
    a. Changes in culture produce changes in language and thought.
    b. Changes in the American economy, society, and culture have no impact on the use of color terms.
    c. Women and men are equally susceptible to the marketing tactics of the cosmetic industry.
    d. Different languages produce different ways of thinking.

8. Which of the following statements about sociolinguistics is false:
    a. It investigates the relationships between social and linguistic variation.
    b. It has found that speakers retain their speech patterns even as the social context changes.
    c. It has found that men and women's speech varies in all these ways: phonology, grammar, vocabulary, body stances, and movements accompanying speech.
    d. It considers the different social standings of a society's dialects, which include a prestige language that provides greater access to desirable jobs and is legitimized by the society's formal institutions.

9. Which of the following statements about Black English Vernacular (BEV) is true?
    a. BEV is a simple linguistic system with its own rules.
    b. All African Americans speak BEV.
    c. As a linguistic system, Standard English is superior to BEV.
    d. Upwardly mobile BEV-speaking students typically consider Standard English to be society's prestige dialect and learn it.

10. Historical linguistics studies all of the following except:
    a. Features of past languages reconstructed from the study of contemporary, or daughter, languages.
    b. The nature of contact between groups by way of linguistic evidence.
    c. Short-term language change.
    d. The loss of indigenous languages as colonial languages have expanded.

1. (a), 2. (d), 3. (b), 4. (b), 5. (d), 6. (b), 7. (a), 8. (b), 9. (d), 10. (c)

6

MAKING A LIVING

UNDERSTANDING OURSELVES

In the non-Western societies where ethnography originated, the need to balance work (making a living) and family wasn't as stark as it is for us. In traditional societies, one's workmates usually were also one's kin. There was no need for a "take your child to work" day because most women did that every day. People didn't work with strangers. Home and office, society and economy, were intertwined.

The fact that subsistence and sociality are both basic human needs creates conflicts in modern society. People have to make choices about allocating their time and energy between work and family. Think about the choices your parents have made in terms of economic versus social goals. Have their decisions maximized their incomes, their lifestyles, their individual happiness, family benefits, or what? What about you? What factors motivated you when you chose to apply to and attend college? Did you want to stay close to home, to attend college with friends, or to maintain a romantic attachment (all social reasons)? Did you seek the lowest tuition and college costs—or get a generous scholarship (economic decisions)? Did you choose prestige, or perhaps the likelihood that one day you would earn more money because of the reputation of your alma mater (maximizing prestige and future wealth)? Economists tend to assume that the profit motive rules in contemporary society. However, different individuals, like different cultures, may choose to pursue goals other than monetary gain.

Studies show that most American women now expect to join the paid labor force, just as men do. But the family remains attractive. Most young women and some men also plan to stay home with small children and return to work once their children enter school. How about you? If you have definite career plans, how do you imagine your work will fit in with your future family life—if you have one planned? What do your parents want most for you—a successful career or a happy family life, with children? Probably both. Will it be easy to fulfill such expectations?

- What are the major adaptive strategies found in nonindustrial societies?

- What is an economy, and what is economizing behavior?

- What principles regulate the exchange of goods and services in various societies?

>> Adaptive Strategies

In today's globalizing world, communities and societies are being incorporated, at an accelerating rate, into larger systems. The origin (around ten thousand years ago) and spread of food production (plant cultivation and animal domestication) led to the formation of larger and more powerful social and political systems. Food production led to major changes in human life. The pace of cultural transformation increased enormously. This chapter provides a framework for understanding a variety of human adaptive strategies and economic systems.

The anthropologist Yehudi Cohen (1974) used the term *adaptive strategy* to describe a society's system of economic production. Cohen argued that the most important reason for similarities between two (or more) unrelated societies is their possession of a similar adaptive strategy. In other words, similar economic causes have similar sociocultural effects. For example, there are clear similarities among societies that have a foraging (hunting and gathering) strategy. Cohen developed a typology of societies based on correlations between their economies and their social features. His typology includes these five adaptive strategies: foraging, horticulture, agriculture, pastoralism, and industrialism. Industrialism is discussed in the chapter, "The World System and Colonialism." This chapter focuses on the first four adaptive strategies.

Drag net fishing at China Beach (aka My Khe Beach) Danang, Vietnam. Fishing is a form of foraging.

FORAGING

Until ten thousand years ago all humans were foragers. However, environmental differences created substantial contrasts among the world's foragers. Some, like the people who lived in Europe during the ice ages, were big-game hunters. Today, hunters in the Arctic still focus on large animals and herd animals; they have much less vegetation and variety in their diets than do tropical foragers. Moving from colder to hotter areas, the number of species increases. The tropics contain tremendous biodiversity, and tropical foragers typically hunt and gather a wide range of plant and animal species. The same may be true in temperate areas. For example, on the North Pacific Coast of North America, foragers could draw on varied sea, river, and land species, such as salmon and other fish, sea mammals, berries, and mountain goats. Despite differences caused by such environmental variation, all foraging economies have shared one essential feature: People rely on nature to make their living.

Animal domestication (initially of sheep and goats) and plant cultivation (of wheat and barley) began ten to twelve

STUDY TIP

Foraging has several characteristics:

- People rely on nature to make a living, with little management of natural resources;

  - It requires less work than farming;

  - Foraging traditionally correlates with the band social unit and with a mobile lifestyle;

- Modern foragers live on marginal lands (lands not good for agricultural production) and do not survive solely by foraging.

thousand years ago in the Middle East. Cultivation based on different crops, such as corn (maize), manioc (cassava), and potatoes, arose independently in the Americas. In both hemispheres most foragers eventually turned to food production. Today most foragers have at least some dependence on food production or on food producers (Kent 1992).

The foraging way of life survived into modern times in certain forests, deserts, islands, and very cold areas—places where food production was not practicable with simple technology (see Lee and Daly 1999). In many areas, foragers were exposed to the "idea" of food production but never adopted it because their own economies provided a perfectly adequate and nutritious diet—with a lot less work. In some places, people reverted to foraging after trying food production and abandoning it. In most areas where hunter-gatherers did survive, foraging should be described as "recent" rather than "contemporary." *All modern foragers live in nation-states and depend to some extent on government assistance.* They are in contact with food-producing neighbors as well as with missionaries and other outsiders. We should not view contemporary foragers as isolated or pristine survivors of the Stone Age. Modern foragers are influenced by national and international policies and political and economic events in the world system.

Although foraging is disappearing rapidly as a way of life, we can trace the outlines of Africa's two broad belts of recent foraging. One is the Kalahari Desert of southern Africa. This is the home of the San ("Bushmen"), who include the Ju/'hoansi (see Kent 1996; Lee 2003). The other main African foraging area is the equatorial forest of central and eastern Africa, home of the Mbuti, Efe, and other "pygmies" (Bailey et al. 1989; Turnbull 1965).

People still do, or until recently did, subsistence foraging in certain remote forests in Madagascar, Southeast Asia, Malaysia, the Philippines, and on certain islands off the Indian coast. Some of the best-known recent foragers are the aborigines of Australia. Those Native Australians lived on their island continent for more than sixty thousand years without developing food production.

The Western Hemisphere also had recent foragers. The Eskimos, or Inuit, of Alaska and Canada are well-known hunters. These (and other) northern foragers now use modern technology, including rifles and snowmobiles, in their subsistence activities (Pelto 1973). The native populations of California, Oregon, Washington, and British Columbia all were foragers, as were those of inland subarctic Canada and the Great Lakes. For many Native Americans, fishing, hunting, and gathering remain important subsistence (and sometimes commercial) activities.

Coastal foragers also lived near the southern tip of South America, in Patagonia. On the grassy plains of Argentina, southern Brazil, Uruguay, and Paraguay, there were other hunter-gatherers. The contemporary Aché of Paraguay usually are called hunter-gatherers, although they now get just a third of their livelihood from foraging. The Aché also grow crops, have domesticated animals, and live in or near mission posts, where they receive food from missionaries (Hawkes, O'Connell, and Hill 1982; Hill et al. 1987).

Throughout the world, foraging survived in environments that posed major obstacles to food production. (Some foragers took refuge in such areas after the rise of food production, the state, colonialism, or the modern world system.) The difficulties of cultivating at the North Pole are obvious. In southern Africa, the Dobe Ju/'hoansi San area studied by Richard Lee and others is surrounded by a waterless belt 43 to 124 miles (70 to 200 kilometers) in breadth (Solway and Lee 1990).

Environmental obstacles to food production aren't the only reason foragers survived. As shown in "Worldwide Distribution of Recent Hunter-Gatherers," their niches had one thing in common—their marginality. Their environments were not of immediate interest to farmers, herders, or colonialists. The foraging way of life persisted in a few areas that could be cultivated, even after contact with farmers. Those tenacious foragers, like the indigenous peoples of what is now California and the Pacific Northwest, did not adopt food production, because they were supporting themselves adequately by hunting and gathering. As the modern world system spreads, the number of foragers continues to decline.

Most of the estimated one hundred thousand San who survive today live in poverty on society's fringes. Each year more and more foragers come under the control of nation-states and are influenced by forces of globalization. As described by Motseta (2006), between 1997 and 2002, the government of Botswana in southern Africa relocated about three thousand Basarwa San Bushmen outside their ancestral territory, which was converted into a reserve for wildlife protection. The Basarwa received some compensation for their land, along with access to schools, medical facilities, and job training in resettlement centers. Critics claim this resettlement turned a society of free hunter-gatherers into communities dependent on food aid and government handouts (Motseta 2006).

In 2006 Botswana's High Court ruled that the Basarwa had been wrongly evicted from the "Central Kalahari Game Reserve." In the context of global political action for cultural rights, this verdict was hailed as a victory for

Historically Known Foragers (Hunter-gatherers)

1 Eskimos or Inuit	16 Native Australians
2 Subarctic Indians	
3 Northwest Coast Indians	17 Maori
4 Plateau Indians	18 Toala
5 California Indians	19 Agta
6 Great Basin Indians	20 Punan
7 Plains Indians	21 Kubu
8 Amazon Basin Hunter-gatherers	22 Semang
	23 Andaman Islanders
9 Gran Chaco Indians	24 Mlabri
10 Tehuelche	25 Vedda
11 Fuegians	26 Kadar
12 "Pygmies"	27 Chenchu
13 Okiek	28 Birhor
14 Hadza	29 Ainu
15 San	30 Chukchi

Worldwide Distribution of Recent Hunter-Gatherers

Souce: Adaptation from map by Ray Sim, in Göran Burenhult, ed. *Encyclopedia of Humankind: People of the Stone Age*, p. 193. © 1933. Reprinted by permission of Weldon Owen Pty. Ltd.

correlation An association between two or more variables such that when one changes (varies), the other(s) also change(s) (covaries); for example, temperature and sweating.

band Basic unit of social organization among foragers. A band includes fewer than 100 people; it often splits up seasonally.

indigenous peoples around the world (Motseta 2006). In December 2006, Botswana's attorney general recognized the court order to allow the Basarwa to return to their ancestral lands, while imposing conditions likely to prevent most of them from doing so. Only the 189 people who filed the lawsuit would have automatic right of return with their children, compared with some 2,000 Basarwa wishing to return. The others would have to apply for special permits. Returning Basarwa would be allowed to build only temporary structures and to use enough water for subsistence needs. Water would be a major obstacle because the government shut the main well in 2002, and water is scarce in the Kalahari. Furthermore, anyone wishing to hunt would have to apply for a permit. So goes the foraging way of life in the world today.

CULTURETHINK

The case of the Botswana Basarwa San is typical of global indigenous rights issues. Why do you think the government of Botswana removed the San from their ancestral territory? What were the costs and potential benefits for the San people of moving out? After they won the lawsuit in 2006, was moving back to the territory an attractive option for the San? Why or why not?

Correlates of Foraging Typologies, such as Cohen's adaptive strategies, are useful because they suggest **correlations**—association or covariation between two or more variables. (Correlated variables are factors that are linked and interrelated, such as food intake and body weight, such that when one increases or decreases, the other changes too.) Ethnographic studies in hundreds of societies have revealed many correlations between the economy and social life. Associated (correlated) with each adaptive strategy is a bundle of particular sociocultural features. Correlations, however, rarely are perfect. Some foragers lack cultural features usually associated with foraging, and some of those features are found in groups with other adaptive strategies.

What, then, are some correlates of foraging? People who subsisted by hunting and gathering often, but not always (see the section "Potlatching" at the end of the chapter), lived in band-organized societies. Their basic social unit, the **band,** was a small group of fewer than a hundred people, all related by kinship or marriage. Among some foragers, band size stayed about the same year-round. In others, the band split up for part of the year. Families left to gather resources that were better exploited by just a few people. Later, they regrouped for cooperative work and ceremonies.

One typical characteristic of the foraging life was mobility. In many San groups, as among the Mbuti of Congo, people shifted band membership several times in a lifetime. One might be born, for example, in a band in which one's mother had kin. Later, one's family might move to a band in which the father had relatives. Because bands were exogamous (people married outside their own band) one's parents came from two different bands, and one's grandparents might have come from four. People could join any band to which they had kin or marital links. A couple could live in, or shift between, the husband's and the wife's band.

All human societies have some kind of division of labor based on gender. (See the chapter "Gender" for more on this.) Among foragers, men typically hunt and fish while women gather and collect, but the specific nature of the work varies among cultures. Sometimes women's work contributes most to the diet. Sometimes male hunting and fishing predominate. Among foragers in tropical and semitropical areas, gathering tends to contribute more to the diet than hunting and fishing do.

All foragers make social distinctions based on age. Old people often receive great respect as guardians of myths, legends, stories, and traditions. Younger people value the elders' special knowledge of ritual and practical matters. Most foraging societies are *egalitarian*. This means that contrasts in prestige are minor and are based on age and gender.

When considering issues of "human nature," we should remember that the egalitarian band was a basic form of human social life for most of our history. Food production has existed less than 1 percent of the time *Homo* has spent on Earth. However, it has produced huge social differences. We now consider the main economic features of food-producing strategies.

>> Adaptive Strategies Based on Food Production

In Cohen's typology, the three adaptive strategies based on food production in nonindustrial societies are horticulture, agriculture, and pastoralism. Just as they do in the United States and Canada, people in nonindustrial societies carry out a variety of economic activities. Each adaptive strategy refers to the main economic activity. Pastoralists (herders), for example, consume milk, butter, blood, and meat from their animals as mainstays of their diet. However, they also add grain to their diet by doing some cultivating or by trading with neighbors.

HORTICULTURE

Two types of cultivation found in nonindustrial societies are horticulture and agriculture. Both differ from the farming systems of industrial nations such as the United States and Canada, which use large land areas, machinery, and petrochemicals. According to Cohen, **horticulture** is cul-

Horticulture systems typically use simple technology. Here, after the land has been cleared using slash-and-burn techniques, a woman uses a digging stick to plant mountain rice in Madagascar.

CULTURETHINK

In slash-and-burn horticulture, the land is cleared by cutting down (slashing) and burning trees and bush, using simple technology. What are the likely environmental effects of this kind of cultivation with low population numbers? What if the population increases?

tivation that makes intensive use of *none* of the factors of production: land, labor, capital, and machinery. Horticulturalists use simple tools

horticulture Nonindustrial system of plant cultivation in which plots lie fallow for varying lengths of time.

such as hoes and digging sticks to grow their crops. Their fields lie fallow for varying lengths of time. Horticulture often involves *slash-and-burn* techniques. Here, horticulturalists clear land by cutting down (slashing) and burning forest or bush or by setting fire to the grass covering the plot. The vegetation is broken down, pests are killed, and the ashes remain to fertilize the soil. Crops then are sown, tended, and harvested. Use of the plot is not continuous. Often it is cultivated only for a year or two.

When horticulturalists abandon a plot because of soil exhaustion or a thick weed cover, they clear another piece of land, and the original plot reverts to forest. After several

Agriculture requires more labor than horticulture does and uses land intensively and continuously. Labor demands associated with agriculture reflect its use of domesticated animals, irrigation, and terracing. Shown here, rice farmers in Saramsa, Sikkim, India, work in flooded terraces.

years of fallowing, the cultivator returns to farm the original plot again. Because the relationship between people and land is not permanent, horticulture also is called *shifting cultivation*. Shifting cultivation does not mean that whole villages must move when plots are abandoned. Among the Kuikuru of the South American tropical forest, one village of 150 people remained in the same place for ninety years (Carneiro 1956). Kuikuru houses were large and well made. Because the work involved in building them was substantial, the Kuikuru preferred to walk farther to their fields than to construct a new village. They shifted their plots rather than their settlements. On the other hand, horticulturalists in the montaña (Andean foothills) of Peru lived in small villages of about thirty people (Carneiro 1961/1968). Their houses were small and simple. After a few years in one place, these people built new villages near virgin land. Because their houses were so simple, they preferred rebuilding to walking even a half mile to their fields.

agriculture Nonindustrial system of plant cultivation characterized by continuous and intensive use of land and labor.

AGRICULTURE

The intensive and continuous use of land in **agriculture** requires more labor than horticulture does. The greater labor demands associated with agriculture reflect its use of domesticated animals, irrigation, or terracing.

Domesticated Animals Many agriculturists use animals as means of production—for transport, as cultivating machines, and for their manure. Asian farmers typically incorporate cattle and/or water buffalo into their agricultural economies. Those rice farmers may use cattle to trample pre-tilled flooded fields, thus mixing soil and water, before

transplanting. Many agriculturists attach animals to plows and harrows for field preparation before planting or transplanting. Also, agriculturists typically collect manure from their animals, using it to fertilize their plots, thus increasing yields. Animals are attached to carts for transport and also to implements of cultivation.

Irrigation While horticulturalists must await the rainy season, agriculturists can schedule their planting in advance because they control water. Like other irrigation experts in the Philippines, the Ifugao water their fields with canals from rivers, streams, springs, and ponds. Irrigation makes it possible to cultivate a plot year after year. Irrigation enriches the soil because the irrigated field is a unique ecosystem with several species of plants and animals, many of them minute organisms, whose wastes fertilize the land.

An irrigated field is a capital investment that usually increases in value. It takes time for a field to start yielding; it reaches full productivity only after several years of cultivation. The Ifugao, like other irrigators, have farmed the same fields for generations. In some agricultural areas, including the Middle East, however, salts carried in the irrigation water can make fields unusable after fifty or sixty years.

Terracing The Ifugao also have mastered the agricultural technique of terracing. Their homeland has small valleys separated by steep hillsides. Because the population is dense, people need to farm the hills. If they simply planted on the steep hillsides, fertile soil and crops would be washed away during the rainy season. To prevent this, the Ifugao cut into the hillside and build stage after stage of terraced fields rising above the valley floor. Springs located above the terraces supply their irrigation water. The labor necessary to build and maintain a system of terraces is great. Terrace walls crumble each year and must be partially rebuilt. The canals that bring water down through the terraces also demand attention.

Costs and Benefits of Agriculture Agriculture requires human labor to build and maintain irrigation systems, terraces, and other works. People must feed, water, and care for their animals. But agricultural land can yield one or two crops annually for years, or even generations. An agricultural field does not necessarily produce a higher single-year yield than does a horticultural plot. The first crop grown by horticulturalists on long-idle land may be larger than that from an agricultural plot of the same size. Furthermore, because agriculturists work harder than horticulturalists do, agriculture's yield relative to the labor invested also is lower. Agriculture's main advantage is that the long-term yield per area is far greater and more dependable. Because a single field sustains its owners year after year, there is no need to maintain a reserve of uncultivated land as horticulturalists do. This is why agricultural societies tend to be more densely populated than horticultural ones.

AGRICULTURAL INTENSIFICATION: PEOPLE AND THE ENVIRONMENT

The range of environments available for food production has widened as people have increased their control over nature. For example, in arid areas of California, where Native Americans once foraged, modern irrigation technology now sustains rich agricultural estates. Agriculturists live in many areas that are too arid for nonirrigators or too hilly for non-terracers. Increasing labor intensity and permanent land use have major demographic, social, political, and environmental consequences.

Thus, because of their permanent fields, agriculturists are sedentary. People live in larger and more permanent communities located closer to other settlements. Growth in population size and density increases contact between individuals and groups. There is more need to regulate interpersonal relations, including conflicts of interest. Economies that support more people usually require more coordination in the use of land, labor, and other resources (see the next chapter).

Intensive agriculture has significant environmental effects. Irrigation ditches and paddies (fields with irrigated rice) become repositories for organic wastes, chemicals (such as salts), and disease microorganisms. Intensive agriculture typically spreads at the expense of trees and forests, which are cut down to be replaced by fields. Accompanying such deforestation is loss of environmental diversity (see Srivastava, Smith, and Forno 1999). Agricultural economies grow increasingly specialized. They focus on one or a few caloric staples, such as rice, and on the animals that aid the agricultural economy. Because tropical horticulturalists typically cultivate dozens of plant species simultaneously, a horticultural plot mirrors the botanical diversity found in a tropical forest. Agricultural plots, by contrast, reduce ecological diversity by cutting down trees and concentrating on a few staple foods. Such crop specialization is true of agriculturists both in the tropics (e.g., Indonesian paddy farmers) and outside the tropics (e.g., Middle Eastern irrigation farmers).

Agriculturists attempt to reduce risk in production by favoring stability in the form of a reliable annual harvest and long-term production. Tropical foragers and horticulturalists, by contrast, attempt to reduce risk by relying on multiple species and benefiting from ecological diversity. The agricultural strategy is to put all one's eggs in one big and very dependable basket. The strategy of tropical foragers and horticulturalists is to have several smaller baskets, a few of which may fail without endangering subsistence.

The agricultural strategy makes sense when there are lots of children to raise and adults to be fed. Foraging and horticulture, of course, are associated with smaller, sparser, and more mobile populations.

Agricultural economies also pose a series of regulatory problems. How is water to be managed? How are disputes about access to and distribution of water to be resolved? With more people living closer together on more valuable land, agriculturists are more likely to come into conflict than are foragers and horticulturalists. The social and political implications of food production and intensification are examined more fully in the next chapter.

pastoralists People who use a food-producing strategy of adaptation based on caring for herds of domesticated animals.

nomadism, pastoral Movement throughout the year by the whole pastoral group (men, women, and children) with their animals. More generally, such constant movement in pursuit of strategic resources.

transhumance One of two variants of pastoralism in which part of the population moves seasonally with the herds while the other part remains in home villages.

PASTORALISM

Herders, or **pastoralists,** are people whose activities focus on such domesticated animals as cattle, sheep, goats, camels, yak, and reindeer. They live in North and sub-Saharan Africa, the Middle East, Europe, and Asia. East African pastoralists, like many others, live in symbiosis with their herds. (*Symbiosis* is an obligatory interaction between groups—here, humans and animals—that is beneficial to each.) Herders attempt to protect their animals and to ensure their reproduction in return for food and other products, such as leather. Herds provide dairy products and meat.

People use livestock in various ways. Natives of North America's Great Plains, for example, didn't eat, but only rode, their horses. (Europeans reintroduced horses to the Western Hemisphere; the native American horse had become extinct thousands of years earlier.) For Plains Indians, horses served as "tools of the trade," means of production used to *hunt* buffalo, a main target of their economies. So the Plains Indians were not true pastoralists but hunters who used horses—as many agriculturists use animals—as means of production.

Pastoralists, by contrast, typically use their herds for food. They consume their meat, blood, and milk, from which they make yogurt, butter, and cheese. Although some pastoralists rely on their herds more completely than others do, it is impossible to base subsistence solely on animals. Most pastoralists therefore supplement their diet by hunting, gathering, fishing, cultivating, or trading.

In the sixteenth century, the Samis (also known as Lapps or Laplanders) of Norway, Sweden, and Finland domesticated the reindeer, which their ancestors used to hunt. Like other herders, they follow their animals as they make an annual trek, in this case from coast to interior. Today's Samis use modern technology, such as snowmobiles and four-wheel-drive vehicles, to accompany their herds on their annual nomadic trek. Although their environment is harsher, the Samis, like other herders, live in nation-states and must deal with outsiders, including government officials, as they follow their herds and make their living through animal husbandry, trade, and sales (Hoge 2001).

Unlike foraging and cultivation, which existed throughout the world before the Industrial Revolution, pastoralism was confined almost totally to the Old World. Before European conquest, the only pastoralists in the Americas lived in the Andean region of South America. They used their llamas and alpacas for food and wool and in agriculture and transport. Much more recently, Navajo of the southwestern United States developed a pastoral economy based on sheep, which were brought to North America by Europeans. The populous Navajo became the major pastoral population in the Western Hemisphere.

Two patterns of movement occur with pastoralism: *nomadism* and *transhumance*. Both are based on the fact that herds must move to use pasture available in particular places in different seasons. In pastoral **nomadism,** the entire group—women, men, and children—moves with the animals throughout the year. The Middle East and North Africa provide numerous examples of pastoral nomads. In Iran, for example, the Basseri and the Qashqai ethnic groups traditionally followed a nomadic route more than 300 miles (480 kilometers) long (see Salzman 2004).

CULTURE THINK

Many agree that pastoral nomadism could only have emerged after the rise of agriculture. Why would this be true?

With **transhumance,** part of the group moves with the herds, but most people stay in the home village. There are examples from Europe and Africa. In Europe's Alps only the shepherds and goatherds—not the whole village—accompany the flocks to highland meadows in summer. Among the Turkana of Uganda, men and boys accompany the herds to distant pastures, while much of the village stays put and does some horticultural farming. During their annual trek, pastoral nomads trade for crops and other products with more sedentary people. Transhumants don't have to trade for crops. Because only part of the population accompanies the herds, transhumants can maintain year-round villages and grow their own crops. Table 6.1 summarizes Cohen's adaptive strategies discussed in this chapter.

Did You Know?

One underlying cause of the conflict in Darfur, Sudan, is rivalry between agriculturalists and pastoralist groups due to drought-related land and water scarcity. The involvement of the Sudanese military exacerbated tensions and escalated violence between local populations.

Yehudi Cohen's Adaptive Strategies (Economic Typology) Summarized

Adaptive Strategy	Also Known As	Key Features/Varieties
Foraging	Hunting-gathering	Mobility, use of nature's resources
Horticulture	Slash-and-burn, shifting cultivation, swiddening, dry farming	Fallow period
Agriculture	Intensive farming	Continuous use of land, intensive use of labor
Pastoralism	Herding	Nomadism and transhumance
Industrialism	Industrial production	Factory production, capitalism, socialist production

TABLE 6.1

STUDY TIP

The four adaptive strategies discussed in this chapter are

- Foraging
- Horticulture
- Agriculture
- Pastoralism

>> Economic Systems

An **economy** is a system of production, distribution, and consumption of resources; *economics* is the study of such systems. Economists focus on modern nations and capitalist systems. Anthropologists have broadened understanding of economic principles by gathering data on nonindustrial economies. Economic anthropology studies economics from a comparative perspective (see Gudeman 1999; Plattner 1989; Sahlins 2004; Wilk 1996).

A **mode of production** is a way of organizing production—"a set of social relations through which labor is deployed to wrest energy from nature by means of tools, skills, organization, and knowledge" (Wolf 1982, p. 75). In the capitalist mode of production, money buys labor power, and a social gap between the people (bosses and workers) is involved in the production process. By contrast, in nonindustrial societies, labor usually is not bought but is given

as a social obligation. In such a *kin-based* mode of production, mutual aid in production is one among many expressions of a larger web of social relations.

Societies representing each of the adaptive strategies just discussed (e.g., foraging) tend to have similar modes of production. Differences in the mode of production within a given strategy may reflect differences in environments, target resources, or cultural traditions (Kelly 1995). Thus a foraging mode of production may be based on individual hunters or teams, depending on whether the game is a solitary or a herd animal. Gathering usually is more individualistic than hunting, although teams of collectors may assemble when abundant resources ripen and must be harvested quickly. Fishing may be done alone (as in ice or spear fishing) or in crews (as with open-sea fishing and hunting of sea mammals).

> **economy** A population's system of production, distribution, and consumption of resources.
>
> **mode of production** Way of organizing production—a set of social relations through which labor is deployed to wrest energy from nature by means of tools, skills, and knowledge.

DIVISION OF LABOR

Although some kind of division of economic labor related to age and gender is a cultural universal, the specific tasks assigned to each sex and to people of different ages vary (see the chapter "Gender"). Many horticultural societies assign a major productive role to women, but some make men's work primary. Similarly, among pastoralists, men generally tend large animals, but in some societies women

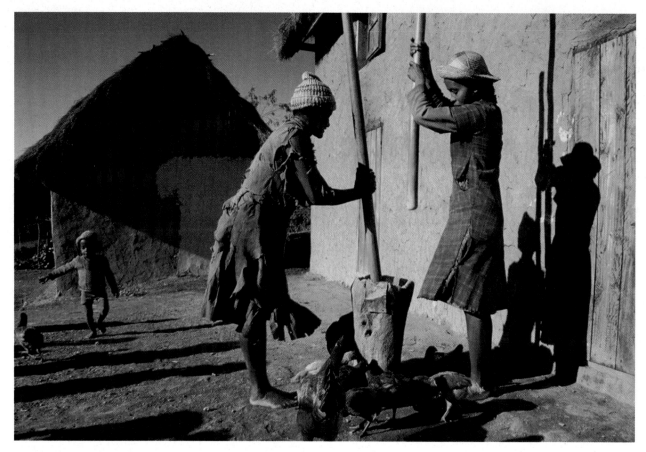

Women hull rice in a Betsileo village. In the village of Ivato, farmers who traditionally grew only rice in their fields now use the same land for commercial crops, such as carrots, after the annual rice harvest.

do the milking. Jobs accomplished through teamwork in some cultivating societies are done in other societies by smaller groups or by individuals working over a longer period.

The Betsileo of Madagascar have two stages of teamwork in rice cultivation: transplanting and harvesting. Both feature a traditional division of labor by age and gender that is well known and repeated across the generations. The first job in transplanting is the trampling of a flooded, previously tilled field by young men driving cattle in order to mix earth and water. They bring cattle to the fields just before transplanting. The young men yell at and beat the cattle, striving to drive them into a frenzy so they will trample the fields properly. Trampling breaks up clumps of earth and mixes irrigation water with soil to form a smooth mud. Once the tramplers leave the field, older men arrive. With their spades they break up the clumps the cattle missed. Meanwhile, the owner and other adults uproot rice seedlings and bring them to the field. Women plant the seedlings.

At harvest time, four or five months later, young men cut the rice off the stalks. Young women carry it to the clearing above the field. Older women arrange and stack it. The oldest men and women then stand on the stack,

means (or factors) of production Land, labor, technology, and capital—major productive resources.

stomping and compacting it. Three days later, young men thresh the rice, beating the stalks against a rock to remove the grain. Older men then beat the stalks with sticks to make sure all the grains have fallen off.

MEANS OF PRODUCTION

In nonindustrial societies the relationship between the worker and the means of production is more intimate than it is in industrial nations. **Means, or factors, of production** include land (territory), labor, and technology.

Land as a Means of Production Among foragers, ties between people and land were less permanent than among food producers. Although many bands had territories, the boundaries usually were not marked, and there

STUDY TIP

Mode of production refers to the way of organizing production: capitalist or kin-based. Means of production refers to the materials or factors with which production is carried out: land, labor, and technology.

was no way they could be enforced. The hunter's stake in an animal was more important than where the animal finally died. A person acquired the rights to use a band's territory by being born in the band or by joining it through a tie of kinship or marriage. In Botswana in southern Africa, Ju/'hoansi San women habitually used specific tracts of berry-bearing trees. When a woman changed bands, she immediately acquired a new gathering area.

Among food producers, rights to the means of production also come through kinship and marriage. Descent groups (groups whose members claim common ancestry) are common among nonindustrial food producers. Those who descend from the founder share the group's territory and resources. If the adaptive strategy is horticulture, the estate includes gardens and fallow land for shifting cultivation. As members of a descent group, pastoralists have access to animals to start their own herds, to grazing land, to garden land, and to other means of production.

Labor, Tools, and Specialization

Like land, labor is a means of production. In nonindustrial societies, access to both land and labor comes through social links such as kinship, marriage, and descent. Mutual aid in production is merely one aspect of ongoing social relations that are expressed on many other occasions.

Nonindustrial societies contrast with industrial nations regarding another means of production—technology. Manufacturing often is linked to age and gender. Women may weave and men may make pottery, or vice versa. Most people of a particular age and gender share the technical knowledge associated with that age and gender. If married women customarily make baskets, most married women know how to make baskets. Neither technology nor technical knowledge is very specialized.

Some tribal societies, however, do promote specialization. Among the Yanomami of Venezuela and Brazil, for instance, certain villages manufacture clay pots and others make hammocks. They don't specialize, as one might suppose, because certain raw materials happen to be available near particular villages. Clay suitable for pots is widely available. Everyone knows how to make pots, but not everybody does so. Craft specialization reflects the social and political environment rather than the natural environment. Such specialization promotes trade, which is the first step in creating an alliance with enemy villages (Chagnon 1997).

ALIENATION IN INDUSTRIAL ECONOMIES

There are significant contrasts between industrial and nonindustrial economies. When factory workers produce for their employer's profit, they may be *alienated* from the items they make: They don't feel strong pride in or personal identification with their products. They see their product as belonging to someone other than the man or woman whose labor actually produced it. In nonindustrial societies, by contrast, people usually see their work through from start to finish and feel a sense of accomplishment.

CULTURETHINK

Think of a job you have had. How did you and your coworkers feel alienated from, or attached to, the products you made or the services you provided? Did that affect the quality of your performance?

In nonindustrial societies the economic relation between coworkers is just one aspect of a more general social relation. They aren't just coworkers but kin or in-laws. In industrial nations, people usually don't work with relatives and neighbors. If coworkers are friends, the personal relationship often develops out of their common employment rather than being based on a previous association.

Thus, industrial workers have impersonal relations with their products, coworkers, and employers. People sell their labor for cash, and work stands apart from family life. In nonindustrial societies, the relations of production, distribution, and consumption are *social relations with economic aspects*. Economy is not a separate entity but is *embedded* in the society.

A Case of Industrial Alienation For decades, the government of Malaysia has promoted export-oriented industry, allowing transnational companies to install manufacturing operations in rural Malaysia. In search of cheaper labor, corporations headquartered in Japan, Western Europe, and the United States have moved labor-intensive factories to developing countries. Malaysia has hundreds of Japanese and American subsidiaries, which produce garments, foodstuffs, and electronics components. Thousands of young Malaysian women from peasant families now assemble microchips and microcomponents for transistors and capacitors. Aihwa Ong (1987) studied electronics assembly workers in an area where 85 percent of the workers were young unmarried females from nearby villages.

Ong found that, unlike village women, female factory workers had to cope with a rigid work routine and constant supervision by men. The discipline that factories value was being taught in local schools, where uniforms helped prepare girls for the factory dress code. Village women wear loose, flowing tunics, sarongs, and sandals, but factory workers had to don tight overalls and heavy rubber gloves, in which they felt constrained. Assembling electronics components requires precise, concentrated labor. Labor in these factories illustrates the separation of intellectual and manual activity—the alienation that Karl Marx considered the defining feature of industrial work. One woman said about her bosses, "They exhaust us very much, as if they

How might factory work, as shown here in this Chinese garment factory, create alienation?

do not think that we too are human beings" (Ong 1987, p. 202). Nor does factory work bring women a substantial financial reward, given low wages, job uncertainty, and family claims on wages. Although young women typically work just a few years, production quotas, three daily shifts, overtime, and surveillance take their toll in mental and physical exhaustion.

One response to factory relations of production has been spirit possession (factory women are possessed by spirits). Ong interprets this phenomenon as the women's unconscious protest against labor discipline and male control of the industrial setting. Sometimes possession takes the form of mass hysteria. Spirits have simultaneously invaded as many as 120 factory workers. *Weretigers* (the Malay equivalent of the werewolf) arrive to avenge the construction of a factory on aboriginal burial grounds. Disturbed earth and grave spirits swarm on the shop floor. First the women see the spirits; then their bodies are invaded. The weretigers send the women into sobbing, laughing, and shrieking fits. To deal with possession, factories employ local medicine men, who sacrifice chickens and goats to fend off the spirits. This solution works only some of the time; possession still goes on. Ong argues that spirit possession expresses anguish at, and resistance to, capitalist relations of production. By engaging in this form of rebellion, however, factory women avoid a direct confrontation with the source of their distress. Ong concludes that spirit possession, while expressing repressed resentment, doesn't do much to modify factory conditions. (Other tactics, such as union-

ization, would do more.) Spirit possession may even help maintain the current system by operating as a safety valve for accumulated tensions.

>> Economizing and Maximization

Economic anthropologists have been concerned with two main questions:

- How are production, distribution, and consumption organized in different societies? This question focuses on *systems* of human behavior and their organization.

- What motivates people in different societies to produce, distribute or exchange, and consume? Here the focus is not on systems of behavior but on the *individuals* who participate in those systems.

Anthropologists view economic systems and motivations in a cross-cultural perspective. Motivation is a concern of psychologists, but it also has been a concern of economists and anthropologists. American economists assume that producers and distributors make decisions rationally, using the *profit motive,* as do consumers when they shop around for the best value. Although anthropologists know that the profit motive is not universal, the assumption that individuals try to maximize profits is basic to capitalism and to Western economic theory. In fact, the subject matter of economics often is defined as *economizing,* or

Anthropology Works

the rational allocation of scarce means (or resources) to alternative ends (or uses).

What does that mean? Classical economic theory assumes that our wants are infinite, while our means are limited. People must make choices about how to use their scarce resources—their time, labor, money, and capital. Western economists assume that when confronted with choices and decisions, people tend to make the one that maximizes profit. This is assumed to be the most rational choice.

The idea that individuals choose to maximize profits was a basic assumption of the classical economists of the nineteenth century and one held by many contemporary economists. Certain economists now recognize that individuals may be motivated by many other goals. Depending on the society and the situation, people may try to maximize profit, wealth, prestige, pleasure, comfort, or social harmony. Individuals may want to realize their personal or family ambitions or those of another group to which they belong (see Sahlins 2004).

ALTERNATIVE ENDS

To what uses do people put their scarce resources? Throughout the world, people devote some of their time and energy to building up a *subsistence fund* (Wolf 1966). In other words, they have to work to eat, to replace the calories they use in daily activity. People also must invest in a *replacement fund*. They must maintain their technology and other items essential to production. If a hoe or plow breaks, they must repair or replace it. They also must obtain and replace items that are essential not to production but to everyday life, such as clothing and shelter.

People everywhere also have to invest in a *social fund*. They must help their friends, relatives, in-laws, and neighbors. It is useful to distinguish between a social fund and a *ceremonial fund*. The latter term refers to expenditures on ceremonies or rituals. To prepare a festival honoring one's ancestors, for example, requires time and the outlay of wealth.

Citizens of nonindustrial states also must allocate scarce resources to a *rent fund*. We think of rent as payment for the use of property. Rent fund, however, has a wider meaning. It refers to resources that people must render to an individual or agency that is superior politically or economically. Tenant farmers and sharecroppers, for example, either pay rent or give some of their produce to their landlords, as peasants did under feudalism.

Peasants are small-scale agriculturists who live in nonindustrial states and have rent fund obligations (see Kearney 1996). They produce to feed themselves, to sell their produce, and to pay rent. All peasants have two things in common:

- They live in state-organized societies;
- They produce food without the elaborate technology—chemical fertilizers, tractors, airplanes to spray crops, and so on—of modern farming or agribusiness.

Besides paying rent to landlords, peasants must satisfy government obligations, paying taxes in the form of money, produce, or labor. The rent fund is not simply an *additional* obligation for peasants. Often it becomes their foremost and unavoidable duty. Sometimes their own diets suffer as a result. The demands of social superiors may divert resources from subsistence, replacement, social, and ceremonial funds.

> **peasant** Small-scale agriculturist living in a state, with rent fund obligations.

CULTURETHINK

Think of examples of how you and your family set money aside for various purposes in subsistence, replacement, social, ceremonial, and rent funds.

Motivations vary from society to society, and people often lack freedom of choice in allocating their resources. Because of obligations to pay rent, peasants may allocate their scarce means toward ends that are not their own but those of government officials. Thus, even in societies in which there is a profit motive, people often are prevented from rationally maximizing self-interest by factors beyond their control.

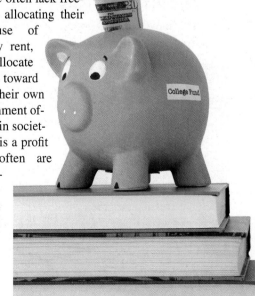

>> Distribution, Exchange

The economist Karl Polanyi (1968) stimulated the comparative study of exchange, and several anthropologists followed his lead. Polanyi defined three principles that guide exchanges: the market principle, redistribution, and reciprocity. These principles all can be present in the same society, but in that case they govern different kinds of transactions. In any society, one of them usually dominates. The principle of exchange that dominates in a given society is the one that allocates the means of production.

THE MARKET PRINCIPLE

In today's world capitalist economy, the **market principle** dominates. It governs the distribution of the means of production—land, labor, natural resources, technology, and capital. With market exchange, items are bought and sold, using money, with an eye to maximizing profit, and value is determined by the *law of supply and demand* (things cost more the scarcer they are and the more people want them). Bargaining is characteristic of market-principle exchanges. The buyer and seller strive to maximize—to get their "money's worth." Bargaining doesn't require that the buyer and seller meet. Consumers bargain whenever they shop around or use advertisements or the Internet in their decision making (see Madra 2004).

market principle Profit-oriented principle of exchange that dominates in states, particularly industrial states. Goods and services are bought and sold, and values are determined by supply and demand.

redistribution Major exchange mode of chiefdoms, many archaic states, and some states with managed economies.

reciprocity One of the three principles of exchange. Governs exchange between social equals; major exchange mode in band and tribal societies.

REDISTRIBUTION

The movement of goods, services, or their equivalent from the local level to a center is known as **redistribution.** The center may be a capital, a regional collection point, or a storehouse near a chief's residence. Products often move through a hierarchy of officials for storage at the center. Along the way, officials and their dependents may consume some of the products, but the exchange principle here is *re*distribution. The flow of goods eventually reverses direction—out from the center, down through the hierarchy, and back to the common people.

One example of a redistributive system comes from the Cherokee (the original owners of the Tennessee Valley), productive farmers who subsisted on maize, beans, and squash, supplemented by hunting and fishing. The Cherokee had chiefs, and each of their main villages had a central plaza, where meetings of the chief's council took place and where redistributive feasts were held. According to Cherokee custom, each family farm had an area where the family could set aside part of their annual harvest for the chief. This supply of corn was used to feed the needy, as well as travelers and warriors journeying through friendly territory. This store of food was available to all who needed it, with the understanding that it "belonged" to the chief and was available through his generosity. The chief also hosted the redistributive feasts held in the main settlements (Harris 1978).

RECIPROCITY

The exchange between social equals, who normally are related by kinship, marriage, or another close personal tie, is known as **reciprocity.** Because it occurs between social equals, it is dominant in the more egalitarian societies—among foragers, cultivators, and pastoralists. There are three degrees of reciprocity: *generalized, balanced,* and *negative* (Sahlins 1968, 2004; Service 1966). These may be imagined as areas of a continuum defined by these questions:

- How closely related are the parties to the exchange?
- How quickly and unselfishly are gifts reciprocated?

Generalized reciprocity, the purest form of reciprocity, is characteristic of exchanges between closely related people. In *balanced reciprocity,* social distance increases, as does the need to reciprocate. In *negative reciprocity,* social distance is greatest and reciprocation is most calculated. This range, from generalized to negative, is called the **reciprocity continuum.**

With generalized reciprocity, someone gives to another person and expects nothing immediate in return. Such exchanges are not primarily economic transactions but expressions of personal relationships. Most parents don't

STUDY **TIP**

Three principles of exchange are

- The market principle
- Redistribution
- Reciprocity

try to get the best possible immediate return for their investment.

Generalized reciprocity and balanced reciprocity are based on trust and a social tie. Negative reciprocity involves the attempt to get something for as little as possible, even if it means being cagey or deceitful or cheating. Among the most extreme and "negative" examples of negative reciprocity was nineteenth-century horse thievery by North American Plains Indians. Men would sneak into camps and villages of neighboring tribes to steal horses. A similar pattern of livestock (cattle) raiding continues today in East Africa, among tribes such as the Kuria (Fleisher 2000). In these cases, the party that starts the raiding can expect reciprocity—a raid on their own village—or worse. The Kuria hunt down cattle thieves and kill them. It's still reciprocity, governed by "Do unto others as they have done unto you."

One way of reducing the tension in situations of potential negative reciprocity is to engage in "silent trade." One example was the silent trade of the Mbuti pygmy foragers of the African equatorial forest and their neighboring horticultural villagers. There was no personal contact during their exchanges. A Mbuti hunter left game, honey, or another forest product at a customary site. Villagers collected it and left crops in exchange. Often the parties bargained silently. If one felt the return was insufficient, he or she simply left it at the trading site. If the other party wanted to continue trade, it was increased.

> **reciprocity continuum**
> Regarding exchanges, a range running from generalized reciprocity (closely related/deferred return) through balanced reciprocity, to negative reciprocity (strangers/immediate return).

keep accounts of every penny they spend on their children. They merely hope their children will respect their culture's customs involving obligations to parents.

Among foragers, generalized reciprocity usually has governed exchanges. People routinely have shared with other band members (Bird-David 1992; Kent 1992). So strong is the ethic of sharing that most foragers have lacked an expression for "thank you." To offer thanks would be impolite because it would imply that a particular act of sharing, which is the keystone of egalitarian society, was unusual. Among the Semai, foragers of central Malaysia (Dentan 1979), to express gratitude would suggest surprise at the hunter's success (Harris 1974).

Balanced reciprocity applies to exchanges between people who are more distantly related than are members of the same band or household. In a horticultural society, for example, a man presents a gift to someone in another village. The recipient may be a cousin, a trading partner, or a brother's fictive kinsman. The giver expects something in return. This may not come immediately, but the social relationship will be strained if there is no reciprocation.

Exchanges in nonindustrial societies also may illustrate negative reciprocity, mainly in dealing with people on the fringes of or outside their social systems. To people who live in a world of close personal relations, exchanges with outsiders are full of ambiguity and distrust. Exchange is one way of establishing friendly relations, but when trade begins, the relationship is still tentative. Often the initial exchange is close to being purely economic; people want to get something back immediately. Just as in market economies, but without using money, they

Sharing the fruits of production, a keystone of many nonindustrial societies, also has been a goal of socialist nations, such as China. These workers in Yunnan province strive for an equal distribution of meat.

COEXISTENCE
OF EXCHANGE PRINCIPLES

In today's North America, the market principle governs most exchanges, from the sale of the means of production to the sale of consumer goods. We also have redistribution. Some of our tax money goes to support the government, but some of it also comes back to us in the form of social services, education, health care, and road building. We also have reciprocal exchanges. Generalized reciprocity characterizes the relationship between parents and children.

potlatch Competitive feast among Indians on the North Pacific Coast of North America.

However, even here the dominant market mentality surfaces in comments about the high cost of raising children and in the stereotypical statement of the disappointed parent: "We gave you everything money could buy."

Exchanges of gifts, cards, and invitations exemplify reciprocity, usually balanced. Everyone has heard remarks like "They invited us to their daughter's wedding, so when ours gets married, we'll have to invite them" and "They've been here for dinner three times and haven't invited us yet. I don't think we should ask them back until they do." Such precise balancing of reciprocity would be out of place in a foraging band, where resources are communal (common to all) and daily sharing based on generalized reciprocity is an essential ingredient of social life and survival.

Location of Potlatching Groups

Indians of the Northwest Coast
■ Ethnic groups
Groups of Salish speech appear in lower case.

Many hip-hop lyrics center around how much money the artist has in comparison to others, how much more money the artist has now than before his or her music career took off, and how this money often leads to problems. Locate and read the lyrics to these songs: "Beamer, Benz, or Bentley," "Mo Money Mo Problems," and "It's All about the Benjamins." What do they say about the music industry and the artist? Do you believe that these musicians have as much money as they say they have, or is their bragging a technique to place themselves above others, a lesson in bravado? Might these lyrics entice you into beginning a seemingly lucrative music career? Why or why not? What does this say about our culture?

POTLATCHING

One of the most famous cultural practices studied by ethnographers is the **potlatch.** This is a festive event within a regional exchange system among tribes of the North Pacific Coast of North America, including the Salish and Kwakiutl of Washington and British Columbia. Some tribes still practice the potlatch, sometimes as a memorial to the dead (Kan 1986, 1989). At each such event, assisted by members of their communities, potlatch sponsors traditionally gave away food, blankets, pieces of copper, or other items. In return for this, they got prestige. To give a potlatch enhanced one's reputation. Prestige increased with the lavishness of the potlatch—the value of the goods given away in it.

The potlatching tribes were foragers, but atypical ones for relatively recent times. They were sedentary and had chiefs. They had access to a wide variety of land and sea resources. Among their most important foods were salmon, herring, candlefish, berries, mountain goats, seals, and porpoises (Piddocke 1969).

According to classical economic theory, the profit motive is universal, with the goal of maximizing material benefits. How then does one explain the potlatch, in which substantial wealth is given away? In his influential book *Theory of the Leisure Class* (1899/1992), economist and social commentator Thorstein Veblen cited potlatching as an example of conspicuous consumption, claiming that potlatching was based on an economically irrational drive for prestige. This interpretation stressed the lavishness and supposed wastefulness, especially of the Kwakiutl displays, to support the contention that in some societies people strive to maximize prestige at the expense of their material well-being. This interpretation has been challenged.

Ecological anthropology, also known as *cultural ecology,* is a theoretical school that attempts to interpret cultural practices, such as the potlatch, in terms of their long-term role in helping humans adapt to their environments. Wayne Suttles (1960) and Andrew Vayda (1961/1968) saw potlatching not in terms of its immediate wastefulness, but in terms of its long-term role as a cultural adaptive mechanism. This view also helps us understand similar patterns of lavish feasting throughout the world. Here is the ecological interpretation: *Customs such as the potlatch are cultural adaptations to alternating periods of local abundance and shortage.*

How does this work? Although the natural environment of the North Pacific Coast is favorable, resources do fluctuate from year to year and place to place. Salmon and herring aren't equally abundant every year in a given locality. One village can have a good year while another is experiencing a bad one. Later their fortunes reverse. In this context, the potlatch cycle had adaptive value, and the potlatch was not a competitive display that brought no material benefit.

A village enjoying an especially good year had a surplus of subsistence items, which it could trade for more durable wealth items, such as blankets, canoes, or pieces of copper. Wealth, in turn, by being distributed, could be converted into prestige. Members of several villages were invited to any potlatch and took home the resources that were given away. In this way, potlatching linked villages together in a regional economy—an exchange system that distributed food and wealth from wealthy to needy communities. In return, the potlatch sponsors and their villages got prestige. The decision to potlatch was determined by the health of the local economy. If there had been subsistence surpluses, and thus a buildup of wealth over several good years, a village could afford a potlatch to convert its surplus food and wealth into prestige.

The long-term adaptive value of intercommunity feasting becomes clear when a formerly prosperous village had a run of bad luck. Its people started accepting invitations to potlatches in villages that were doing better. The tables were turned as the temporarily rich became temporarily poor and vice versa.

The newly needy accepted food and wealth items. They were willing to receive rather than bestow gifts and thus to relinquish some of their stored-up prestige. They hoped their luck would eventually improve so that resources could be recouped and prestige regained.

The potlatch linked local groups along the North Pacific Coast into a regional alliance and exchange network. Potlatching and intervillage exchange had adaptive functions, regardless of the motivations of the individual participants. The anthropologists who stressed rivalry for prestige were not wrong. They were merely emphasizing *motivations* at the expense of an analysis of economic and ecological *systems.*

The use of feasts to enhance individual and community reputations and to redistribute wealth is not peculiar to populations of the North Pacific Coast. Competitive feasting is widely characteristic of nonindustrial food producers. But among most surviving foragers, who live in marginal areas, resources are too meager to support feasting on such a level. In such societies, sharing rather than competition prevails.

How do aspects of modern economic life compare to tribal North Pacific Coast potlatching? Talk with friends from wealthy families or go into an affluent neighborhood and observe its inhabitants' lifestyles and consumption behavior. What roles might huge mansions, lavish parties, and private jets, for example, have other than flaunting wealth? Can you think of ways in which they might help connect people (within or between families, social clubs, or large political or economic networks)? Stoke the larger economy? Help distribute wealth to the needy? Do any of the practices you see suggest that Americans may favor competition and social prestige at the expense of society's overall social and environmental well-being?

get involved!

For REVIEW

CULTURE CLIPS

TO ACCESS THESE VIDEOS ON YOUR COMPUTER, VISIT

www.mhhe.com/gezonqr

6-1

6-2

6-3

I. What are the major adaptive strategies found in non-industrial societies?

- Foraging, or hunting and gathering, was the only human adaptive strategy until the advent of food production. Modern foragers depend in part on food production or food producers. Horticulture is cultivation that does not make intensive use of land, labor, capital, or machinery. After cultivating a plot for one or two years, horticulturalists abandon it, seek other land to cultivate, then return to the original plot after a fallow period. Agriculture is cultivation characterized by continuous, intensive use of land and labor. Agriculturalists may use irrigation, terracing, or domesticated animals for production. Pastoralism is the herding of domesticated animals used for food and other products. In pastoral nomadism, the entire group moves with the animals to pasturage throughout the year, often trading for crops with sedentary people. With transhumance, part of the group moves with the herds; the other part stays in the village and grows crops.

II. What is an economy, and what is economizing behavior?

- An economy is a system of production, distribution, and consumption of resources. Western economists assume that when confronted with choices, people tend to make the one that maximizes profit. These theorists focus on economizing, the rational allocation of scarce resources to alternative uses. However, in nonindustrial societies, indeed even in our own society, people often maximize alternative values, such as pleasure or social harmony. Even in societies where there is a profit motive, factors beyond their control may prevent people from rationally maximizing self-interest.

III. What principles regulate the exchange of goods and services in various societies?

- The market principle dominates in the world capitalist economy. It involves buying and selling items, using money, with the goal of maximizing profit; the law of supply and demand determines value. The redistribution principle operates when goods or services move from the local level to a center. The flow of goods eventually moves out of the center and back to the people. In reciprocity, exchange occurs between social equals related by kinship, marriage, or other close ties. With generalized reciprocity, someone gives to another person and expects nothing immediate in return. As social distance increases, reciprocity becomes balanced and, finally, negative. The potlatch was a North Pacific Coast tribal feast in which sponsors gave away goods in return for prestige. The exchange served to distribute wealth from wealthy to needy communities.

Pop Quiz

1. The concept of an adaptive strategy:
   a. Establishes random causal connections rather than associations or correlations between economic and cultural variables.
   b. Was designed to analyze the economic activities associated with food production in nonindustrial societies engaged in the cultivation of food.
   c. Is used to describe any society's system of economic production.
   d. Has become incorporated into anthropologists' approach to categorizing societies, replacing the use of cultural patterns.

2. Which of the following statements about foraging is false?
   a. All modern foragers have contacts with nonforaging societies.
   b. Some foragers have incorporated modern technology, such as rifles and snowmobiles, into their subsistence activities.
   c. All modern foragers live in nation-states and are influenced by national and international policies and by events in the world system.
   d. Foraging societies have all changed in similar ways because they have faced similar circumstances that encourage their adoption of food production.

3. Which of the following is associated with horticulture?
   a. Intensive use of land and human labor.
   b. Use of irrigation and terracing.
   c. Use of draft animals.
   d. Periodic cycles of cultivation and fallowing.

4. Which of the following statements about horticulture is true?
   a. It typically supports life in dense populations, including cities.
   b. It may lead to soil exhaustion or thick weed cover after many years of having cultivated a plot.
   c. It makes use of simple tools for growing crops.
   d. It requires more labor than does agriculture.

5. The key factor that distinguishes agriculturists from horticulturalists is that agriculturalists:
   a. Can produce one or two crops annually but only for a very few years.
   b. Clear a tract of land they wish to use by cutting down trees and setting fire to the forest or bush.
   c. Use land intensively and continuously.
   d. Generally have much more leisure time at their disposal than do horticulturalists.

6. Which of the following is *not* a consequence of agriculture?

   a. Agriculture promotes nomadism to allow farmers to take full advantage of their land.
   b. Agriculture often spreads at the expense of trees and forests, which are cut down to make room for fields, thus reducing ecological diversity.
   c. By favoring dependability and size of the long-term yield, agricultural societies tend to be more densely populated than horticultural societies.
   d. Agriculture poses regulatory problems, such as resolving disputes about access to water and coordinating the use of land, labor, and other resources.

7. Which of the following is found in all adaptive strategies?
   a. The use of domesticated animals as a means of production.
   b. Transhumance.
   c. Some kind of division of labor based on gender.
   d. Intensive use of land.

8. Most generally, economic alienation in industrial societies comes about as a result of:
   a. Separation of workers from the products they make.
   b. Loss of land.
   c. Negative reciprocity.
   d. Discontent due to low pay.

9. Which of these statements about generalized reciprocity is true?
   a. It involves the immediate return of the object exchanged.
   b. It usually develops after the evolution of redistribution but before the market principle.
   c. It is the characteristic form of exchange in egalitarian societies.
   d. It disappears with the origin of the state.

10. All of the following are true about potlatching *except:*
    a. It is a festive event among North Pacific Coast tribes that involves potlatch sponsors, assisted by their communities, giving away valuable goods.
    b. The prestige of the potlatch sponsor increases with the lavishness of the potlatch and the value of the goods given away.
    c. Potlatching links villages in a regional exchange system that distributes food and wealth from wealthy to needy communities.
    d. The giving away of substantial wealth in the potlatch indicates that it is a classic case of economically wasteful behavior.

1. (c), 2. (d), 3. (d), 4. (c), 5. (c), 6. (a), 7. (c), 8. (a), 9. (c), 10. (d)

7

POLITICAL SYSTEMS

UNDERSTANDING OURSELVES

A "big man on campus" is a collegian who is very well known and/or popular. Useful in becoming a BMOC (see http://www.ehow.com/how_2112834_be-big-man-campus.html) are lots of friends, a cool car, a hip wardrobe, a nice smile, a sports connection, and a sense of humor. "Big man" has a related meaning in anthropology. Many indigenous cultures had a political figure that anthropologists call the "big man." Such a leader achieved his status through hard work, amassing wealth in the form of pigs and other native riches. The personality characteristics that enabled the big man to attract loyal supporters (aka lots of friends), included wealth, generosity, eloquence, physical fitness, bravery, and supernatural powers.

Do any of these factors contribute to political success today? Although contemporary politicians may use their own wealth to finance their campaigns, they also solicit labor and money (rather than pigs) from supporters. And, like big men, successful American politicians try to be generous with their supporters. Payback may take the form of largesse (e.g., earmarks) to a particular area. Tribal big men amass wealth and then give away pigs. Successful American politicians dish out "pork."

As with the big man, eloquence and communication skills contribute to political success (e.g., Barack Obama, Bill Clinton, and Ronald Reagan), although lack of such skills isn't necessarily fatal (e.g., either President Bush). What about physical fitness? Hair, height, health (and even a nice smile) are certainly political advantages. Bravery, as demonstrated through military service, can help political careers, but it certainly isn't required. Nor does it guarantee success. Just ask John McCain or John Kerry. Supernatural powers? Candidates who proclaim themselves atheists are as rare as self-identified witches.

Contemporary politics isn't just about personality, however, as it is in big man systems. We live in a state-organized, stratified society with inherited wealth, power, and privilege, all of which have political implications. As is typical of states, inheritance and kin connections play a role in political success. Just think of Kennedys, Bushes, Gores, and Clintons.

As You READ

- What kinds of political systems have existed worldwide, and what are their social and economic correlates?
- What is social status, and how does it relate to political systems?
- How does the state differ from other forms of political organization?

>> What Is "The Political"?

Anthropologists and political scientists share an interest in political systems and organization, but the anthropological approach is global and comparative and includes nonstates as well as the states and nation-states usually studied by

Through public action, citizens can influence government policy. Shown here is a 2008 student rally in Rome. They are protesting educational reforms proposed by the government.

political scientists. Anthropological studies have revealed substantial variation in power, authority, and legal systems in different societies. (*Power* is the ability to exercise one's will over others; *authority* is the socially approved use of power.) (See Gledhill 2000; Kurtz 2001; Lewellen 2003; Nugent and Vincent 2004; Wolf with Silverman 2001.)

Morton Fried offered this definition of political organization:

> Political organization comprises those portions of social organization that specifically relate to the individuals or groups that manage the affairs of public policy or seek to

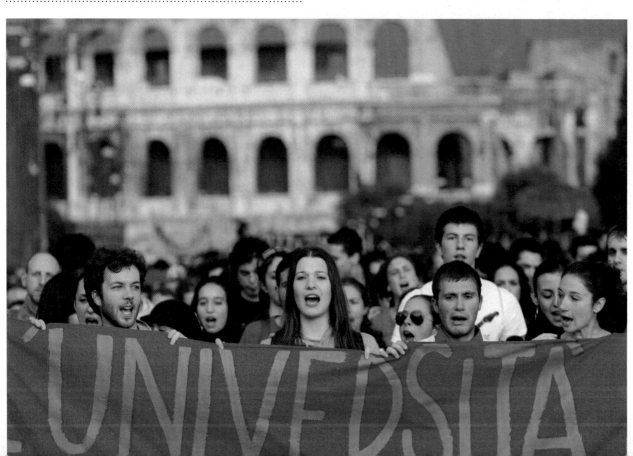

control the appointment or activities of those individuals or groups. (Fried 1967, pp. 20–21)

This definition certainly fits contemporary North America. Under "individuals or groups that manage the affairs of public policy" come federal, state (provincial), and local (municipal) governments. Those who seek to influence public policy include such interest groups as political parties, unions, corporations, consumers, activists, action committees, religious groups, and nongovernmental organizations (NGOs).

Fried's definition is much less applicable to nonstates, where it often was difficult to detect any "public policy." For this reason, we prefer to speak of *socio*political organization in discussing the regulation or management of relations among groups and their representatives. Political regulation includes such processes as decision making, social control, and conflict resolution. The study of political regulation draws our attention to those who make decisions and resolve conflicts—whether or not there are formal leaders.

Ethnographic and archaeological studies in hundreds of places have revealed many correlations between economy and social and political organization.

>> Types and Trends in Political Organization

Decades ago, the anthropologist Elman Service (1962) listed four types, or levels, of political organization: band, tribe, chiefdom, and state. Today, none of the first three types can be studied as a self-contained form of political organization, since all exist within the context of nation-states and are subject to state control (see Ferguson 2002). There is archaeological evidence for early bands, tribes, and chiefdoms that existed before the first states appeared. But because anthropology came into being long after the origin of the state, anthropologists never have been able to observe "in the flesh" a band, tribe, or chiefdom outside the influence of some state. There still may be local political leaders (e.g., village heads) and regional figures (e.g., chiefs) of the sort discussed in this chapter,

but all now exist and function within the context of state organization.

We saw earlier that a *band* refers to a small *kin-based* group (all its members are related by kinship or marriage) found among foragers. **Tribes** had economies based on nonintensive food production (horticulture and pastoralism). Living in villages and organized into kin groups based on common descent (clans and lineages—see the next chapter), tribes lacked a formal government and had no reliable means of enforcing political decisions. **Chiefdom** refers to a form of sociopolitical organization intermediate between the tribe and the state. In chiefdoms, social relations were based mainly on kinship, marriage, descent, age, generation, and gender—just as they were in bands and tribes. Although chiefdoms were kin-based, they featured differential access to resources (some people had more wealth, prestige, and power than others did) and a permanent political structure. The **state** is a form of sociopolitical organization based on a formal government structure and socioeconomic stratification.

The four labels in Service's typology are much too simple to account for the full range of political diversity and complexity known to archaeology and ethnography. We'll see, for instance, that tribes have varied widely in their political systems and institutions. Nevertheless, Service's typology does highlight some significant contrasts in political organization, especially those between states and nonstates. For example, in bands and tribes—unlike states, which have clearly visible governments—political organization did not stand out as separate and distinct from the total social order. In bands and tribes, it was difficult to characterize an act or event as political rather than merely social.

Service's labels "band," "tribe," "chiefdom," and "state" are categories or types within a **sociopolitical typology.** These types are correlated with the adaptive strategies (economic typology) discussed in the chapter "Making a

tribe Form of sociopolitical organization usually based on horticulture or pastoralism. Socioeconomic stratification and centralized rule are absent in tribes, and there is no means of enforcing political decisions.

chiefdom Form of sociopolitical organization intermediate between the tribe and the state; kin-based with differential access to resources and a permanent political structure.

state (nation-state) Complex sociopolitical system that administers a territory and populace with substantial contrasts in occupation, wealth, prestige, and power. An independent, centrally organized political unit, a government.

sociopolitical typology Classification scheme based on the scale and complexity of social organization and the effectiveness of political regulation; includes band, tribe, chiefdom, and state.

STUDY **TIP**

Service's four levels of political organization include

- Bands (foraging; small, kin-based)
- Tribes (based on nonintensive food production)
- Chiefdoms (intermediate between tribe and state)
- State (formal government with stratification)

Living." Thus, foragers (an economic type) tended to have band organization (a sociopolitical type). Similarly, many horticulturalists and pastoralists lived in tribes. Although most chiefdoms had farming economies, herding was important in some Middle Eastern chiefdoms. Nonindustrial states usually had an agricultural base.

With food production came larger, denser populations and more complex economies than was the case among foragers. These features posed new regulatory problems, which gave rise to more complex relations and linkages. Many sociopolitical trends reflect the increased regulatory demands associated with food production. Archaeologists have studied these trends through time, and cultural anthropologists have observed them among more contemporary groups.

This chapter examines a series of societies with different political systems. We address a common set of questions for each one: What kinds of social groups does the society have? How do the groups link with larger ones? How do the groups represent themselves to each other? How are their internal and external relations regulated? To answer these questions, we begin with bands and tribes and then consider chiefdoms and states.

>> Band Organization

Modern hunter-gatherers represent today's remnants of foraging band societies. The strong ties they maintain with sociopolitical groups outside the band make them markedly different from Stone Age hunter-gatherers. Modern foragers live in nation-states and an interlinked world. The pygmies of Congo, for example, have for generations shared a social world and economic exchanges with their neighbors who are cultivators. All foragers now trade with food producers. In addition, most contemporary hunter-gatherers rely on governments and on missionaries for at least part of what they consume.

THE SAN

The Basarwa San are an example of foraging bands whose lives have been impacted significantly by outside groups. In the previous chapter, "Making a Living," we saw how the Basarwa San are affected by policies of the government of Botswana, which relocated them after converting their ancestral lands into a

wildlife reserve (Motseta 2006). The government of Botswana is not the first to implement policies and systems that affect the Basarwa San. San speakers ("Bushmen") of southern Africa have been influenced by Bantu speakers (farmers and herders) for two thousand years and by Europeans for centuries. Edwin Wilmsen (1989) argues that many San descend from herders who were pushed into the desert by poverty or oppression. He sees the San today as a rural underclass in a larger political and economic system dominated by Europeans and Bantu food producers. As a result of this system, many San now tend cattle for wealthier Bantu rather than foraging independently. They also have domesticated animals, indicating their movement away from their foraging lifestyle.

Susan Kent (1992, 1996) notes a tendency to stereotype foragers, to treat them all as alike. They used to be stereotyped as isolated, primitive survivors of the Stone Age. A new stereotype sees them as culturally deprived people forced by states, colonialism, or world events into marginal environments. Although this view often is exaggerated, it probably is more accurate than the former one.

Kent (1996) stresses variation among foragers, focusing on diversity in time and space among the San. The nature of San life has changed considerably since the 1950s and 1960s, when a series of anthropologists from Harvard University, including Richard Lee, embarked on a systematic study of life in the Kalahari. Lee and others have documented many of the changes in various publications (Lee 1979, 1984, 2003; Silberbauer 1981; Tanaka 1980). Such longitudinal research monitors variation in time, while fieldwork in many San areas has revealed variation in space. One of the most important contrasts was found to be that between settled (sedentary) and nomadic groups (Kent and Vierich 1989). Although sedentary lifestyles have increased substantially in recent years, some San groups (along rivers) have been sedentary for generations. Others, including the Dobe Ju/'hoansi San studied by Lee (1984, 2003) and the Kutse San that Kent studied, have retained more of the hunter-gatherer lifestyle.

Among tropical foragers, women make an important economic contribution through gathering, as is true among the San shown here in Namibia. What evidence do you see in this photo that contemporary foragers participate in the modern world system?

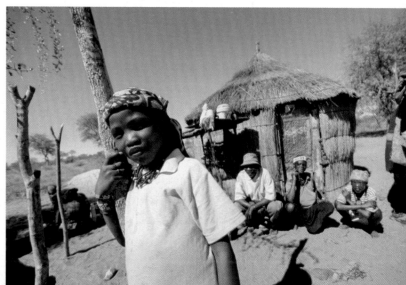

To the extent that foraging has been the basis of subsistence for bands, however, contemporary and recent hunter-gatherers like the San can illustrate links between a foraging economy and other aspects of band society and culture. For example, San groups that still are mobile, or that were so until recently, emphasize social, political, and gender equality, which are traditional band characteristics. A social system based on kinship, reciprocity, and sharing is appropriate for an economy with few people and limited resources. The nomadic pursuit of wild plants and animals tends to discourage permanent settlement, wealth accumulation, and status distinctions. In this context, families and bands have been adaptive social units. People have to share meat when they get it; otherwise it rots.

CULTURETHINK

What were some characteristics of traditional bands—ones that had foraging as the basis of the economy? What has changed for foraging bands in contemporary times?

In the past, foraging bands—small, nomadic or semi-nomadic social units—formed seasonally when component nuclear families got together. The particular families in a band varied from year to year. Marriage and kinship created ties between members of different bands. Trade and visiting also linked them. Band leaders were leaders in name only. In such an egalitarian society, they were first among equals. Sometimes they gave advice or made decisions, but they had no way to enforce their decisions. Given the spread of states and the modern world system, it is increasingly difficult for ethnographers to find and observe such patterns of band organization.

THE INUIT

The aboriginal Inuit (Hoebel 1954, 1954/1968), another group of foragers, provide a good example of methods of settling disputes—**conflict resolution**—in stateless societies. All societies have ways of settling disputes (of variable effectiveness) along with cultural rules or norms about proper and improper behavior. *Norms* are cultural standards or guidelines that enable individuals to distinguish between appropriate and inappropriate behavior in a given society (N. Kottak 2002). Rules and norms are cultural universals, but only state societies, those with established governments, have formal laws that are formulated, proclaimed, and enforced.

Foragers lacked formal **law** in the sense of a legal code with trial and enforcement, but they did have methods of social control and dispute settlement. The absence of law did not mean total anarchy. As described by E. A. Hoebel (1954) in a classic ethnographic study of conflict resolution, a sparse population of some twenty thousand Inuit spanned 6,000 miles (9,500 kilometers) of the Arctic region (see "Location of the Inuit"). The most significant social groups were the nuclear family and the band. Personal re-

conflict resolution The means by which disputes are socially regulated and settled; found in all societies, but the resolution methods tend to be more formal and effective in states than in nonstates.

law A legal code, including trial and enforcement; characteristic of state-organized societies.

Location of the Inuit

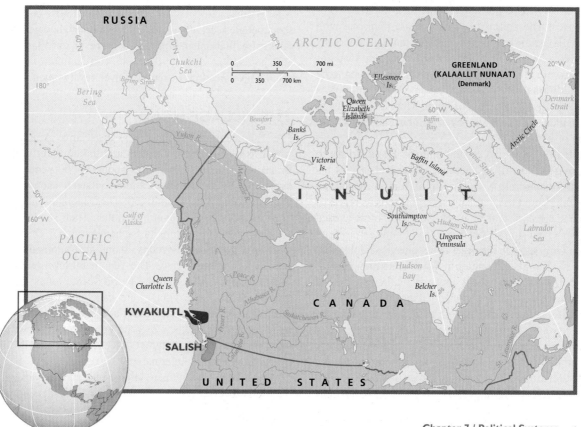

Anthropology Works

Conflict-resolution professionals, such as lawyers, counselors, and mediators, find it useful to be aware of informal as well as formal ways of resolving conflict. *Mediators*— people trained to be a neutral third party—draw on cultural norms in finding ways to help disputing parties reach an agreement peacefully.

necessary for subsistence. Every woman could obtain the materials needed to make clothing, prepare food, and do domestic work. Inuit men could even hunt and fish in the territories of other local groups. There was no notion of private ownership of territory or animals.

>> Tribal Societies

As is true of foraging bands, there are no totally autonomous tribes in today's world. Still, there are societies, for example, in Papua New Guinea and in South America's tropical forests, in which tribal principles continue to operate. Tribes typically have a horticultural or pastoral economy and are organized by village life or membership in *descent groups* (kin groups whose members trace descent from a common ancestor). Tribes lack socioeconomic stratification (i.e., a class structure) and a formal government of their own. A few tribes still conduct small-scale warfare, in the form of intervillage raiding. Tribes have more effective regulatory mechanisms than foragers do, but tribal societies have no sure means of enforcing political decisions. The main regulatory officials are village heads, big men, descent-group leaders, village councils, and leaders of pantribal associations (discussed later in the chapter). All these figures and groups have limited authority.

Like foragers, horticulturalists tend to be egalitarian, although some have marked *gender stratification:* an unequal distribution of resources, power, prestige, and personal freedom between men and women (see the chapter "Gender"). Horticultural villages usually are small, with low population density and open access to strategic resources. Age, gender, and personal traits determine how much respect people receive and how much support they get from others. Egalitarianism diminishes, however, as village size and population density increase. Horticultural villages usually have headmen—rarely, if ever, headwomen.

THE VILLAGE HEAD

The Yanomami (Chagnon 1997) are Native Americans who live in southern Venezuela and the adjacent part of Brazil. Their tribal society has about 26,000 people living in 200 to 250 widely scattered villages, each with a population between 40 and 250. The Yanomami are horticulturalists who also hunt and gather. Their staple crops are bananas and plantains (a bananalike crop). There are more significant social groups among the Yanomami than exist in a foraging society. The Yanomami have families, villages, and descent groups. Their descent groups, which span more than one village, are patrilineal (ancestry is traced back through males only) and exogamous (people must marry outside their own descent group). However, local branches of two different descent groups may live in the same village and intermarry.

As has been true in many village-based tribal societies, traditionally among the Yanomami the only leadership po-

lationships linked the families and bands. Some bands had headmen. There were also shamans (part-time religious specialists). However, these positions conferred little power on those who occupied them.

Hunting and fishing by men were the primary Inuit subsistence activities. The diverse and abundant plant foods available in warmer areas, where female labor in gathering is important, were absent in the Arctic. Traveling on land and sea in a bitter environment, Inuit men faced more dangers than women did. The traditional male role took its toll in lives, so that adult women outnumbered men. This permitted some men to have two or three wives. The ability to support more than one wife conferred a certain amount of prestige, but it also encouraged envy. (*Prestige* is esteem, respect, or approval for culturally valued acts or qualities.) If a man seemed to be taking additional wives just to enhance his reputation, a rival was likely to steal one of them. Most disputes were between men and originated over women, caused by wife stealing or adultery.

A jilted husband had several options. He could try to kill the wife stealer. If he succeeded, however, one of his rival's kinsmen surely would try to kill him in retaliation. One dispute could escalate into several deaths as relatives avenged a succession of murders. No government existed to intervene and stop such a *blood feud* (a murderous feud between families). On the other hand, one also could challenge a rival to a song battle. In a public setting, contestants made up insulting songs about each other. At the end of the match, the audience proclaimed the winner. If a man whose wife had been stolen won, there was no guarantee she would return. Often she stayed with her abductor.

Thefts are common in societies with marked property differentials, like our own, but thefts are uncommon among foragers. Each Inuit had access to the resources needed to sustain life. Every man could hunt, fish, and make the tools sition has been that of **village head** (always a man). His authority, like that of a foraging band's leader, is severely limited. If a headman wants something done, he must lead by example and persuasion. The headman lacks the right to issue orders. He can only persuade, harangue, and try to influence public opinion. For example, if he wants people to clean up the central plaza in preparation for a feast, he must start sweeping it himself, hoping his covillagers will take the hint and relieve him.

When conflict erupts within the village, the headman may be called on as a mediator who listens to both sides. He will give an opinion and advice. If a disputant is unsatisfied, the headman has no power to back his decisions and no way to impose punishments. Like the band leader, he is first among equals.

A Yanomami village headman also must lead in generosity. Because he must be more generous than any other villager, he cultivates more land. His garden provides much of the food consumed when his village holds a feast for another village. The headman represents the village in its dealings with outsiders, including agents of the governments of Venezuela and Brazil.

The way a person acts as headman depends on his personal traits and the number of supporters he can muster. One village headman, Kaobawa, intervened in a dispute between a husband and a wife and kept him from killing her (Chagnon 1983/1992). He also guaranteed safety to a delegation from a village with which a covillager of his wanted to start a war. Kaobawa was a particularly effective headman. He had demonstrated his fierceness in battle, but he also knew how to use diplomacy to avoid offending other villagers. No one in the village had a better personality for the headmanship. Nor (because Kaobawa had many brothers) did anyone have more sup-

porters. Among the Yanomami, when a group is dissatisfied with a village headman, its members can leave and found a new village; this is done from time to time.

Yanomami society, with its many villages and descent groups, is more complex than a band-organized society. The Yanomami also face more regulatory problems. A headman sometimes can prevent a specific violent act, but intervillage raiding has been a feature of some areas of Yanomami territory, particularly those studied by Chagnon (1997).

We also must stress that the Yanomami are not isolated from outside events, including missionization. They live in two nation-states, Venezuela and Brazil, and external warfare waged by Brazilian ranchers and miners increasingly has threatened them (Chagnon 1997; *Cultural Survival Quarterly* 1989; Ferguson 1995). During a Brazilian gold rush between 1987 and 1991, one Yanomami died each day, on average, from external attacks. By 1991, there were some forty thousand Brazilian miners in the Brazilian Yanomami homeland. Some Indians were killed outright. The miners introduced new diseases, and the swollen population ensured that old diseases became epidemic. In 1991, a commission of the American Anthropological Association reported on the plight of the Yanomami (*Anthropology Newsletter,* September 1991). Brazilian Yanomami were dying at a rate of 10 percent annually, and their fertility rate had dropped to zero. Since then, both the Brazilian and Venezuelan governments have intervened to protect the Yanomami. One Brazilian president declared a huge Yanomami territory off-limits to outsiders. Unfortunately, local politicians, miners, and ranchers have increasingly evaded the ban. The future of the Yanomami remains uncertain.

> **village head** Leadership position in a village (as among the Yanomami, where the head is always a man); has limited authority; leads by example and persuasion.
>
> **big man** Figure often found among tribal horticulturalists and pastoralists. The big man occupies no office but creates his reputation through entrepreneurship and generosity to others. Neither his wealth nor his position passes to his heirs.

THE "BIG MAN"

Many societies of the South Pacific, particularly in the Melanesian Islands and Papua New Guinea, had a kind of political leader that we call the big man. The **big man** (almost always a male) was an elaborate version of the village head, but with one significant difference. The village head's leadership is within one village; the big man had supporters in several villages. The big man therefore was a regulator of *regional* political organization.

The Kapauku Papuans live in Irian Jaya, Indonesia (which is on the island of New Guinea). Anthropologist Leopold Pospisil (1963) studied the Kapauku (then

A Yanomami leader today—no longer just a village head. Kopenawa Yanomami, claiming to represent his people, holds a letter for German Chancellor Angela Merkel.

Frau Bundeskanzlerin
Angela Merkel

The big man persuades people to organize feasts, which distribute pork and wealth. Shown here is such a regional event, drawing on several villages, in Papua New Guinea. Big men owe their status to their individual personalities rather than to inherited wealth or position. Does our society have equivalents of big men?

forty-five thousand people), who grow crops (with the sweet potato as their staple) and raise pigs. Their economy is too complex to be described as simple horticulture. Kapauku cultivation has used varied techniques for specific kinds of land. Labor-intensive cultivation in valleys involves mutual aid in turning the soil before planting. The digging of long drainage ditches, which a big man often helped organize, is even more complex. Kapauku plant cultivation supports a larger and denser population than does the simpler horticulture of the Yanomami. Kapauku society could not survive in its current form without collective cultivation and political regulation of the more complex economic tasks.

The key political figure among the Kapauku was the big man, known as a *tonowi*. A tonowi achieved his status through hard work, amassing wealth in the form of pigs and other native riches.

The term *status* often is used as a synonym for prestige. In that context, "She's got a lot of status" means she's got a lot of prestige; people look up to her. Among social scientists, that's not the primary meaning of status. Social scientists use *status* more neutrally—for any social position, no matter what the prestige. In this sense, **status** encompasses the various positions that people occupy in society, such as spouse, parent, trading partner, teacher, student, salesperson, big man, and many others. People always occupy multiple statuses (e.g., son, brother, father, big man). Among the statuses we occupy, particular ones dominate in particular settings, such as son or daughter at home and student in the classroom (see "Social Statuses").

Some statuses are **ascribed:** People have little or no choice about occupying them. Age is an ascribed status; we can't choose not to age. One's status as a member of the nobility, or as a male or a female, usually is ascribed; people are born members of a certain social category and remain so all their lives. **Achieved statuses,** by contrast, aren't automatic; they come through

High School Popularity

What makes high school girls popular?

According to college women:		According to college men:
1	Grades/intelligence	2
2	Participation in sports	3
3	General sociability	4
4	Physical attractiveness	1
	Popularity with boys	5
5	Clothes	

What makes high school boys popular?

According to college women:		According to college men:
1	Participation in sports	1
2	Grades/intelligence	2
	Popularity with girls	3
3	General sociability	4
4	Physical attractiveness	
5	School clubs/government	
	Car	5

How does this big man on campus compare with the Melanesian big man?

Note: Students at the following universities were asked in which ways adolescents in their high schools had gained prestige with their peers: Cornell University, Louisiana State University, Southeastern Louisiana University, State University of New York at Albany, State University of New York at Stony Brook, the University of Georgia, and the University of New Hampshire.

Source: Suitor et al. 2001:445.

Social Statuses

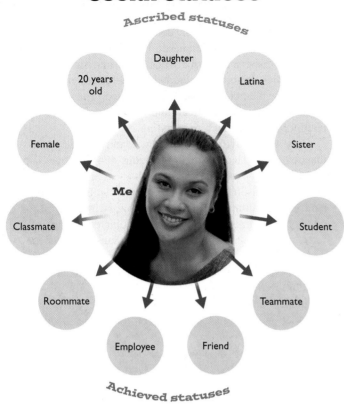

Ascribed statuses

- Daughter
- Latina
- 20 years old
- Female
- Sister
- Me
- Classmate
- Student
- Roommate
- Teammate
- Employee
- Friend

Achieved statuses

porters. He sponsored ceremonial pig feasts in which pigs were slaughtered and their meat distributed to guests.

Unlike the Yanomami village head, a big man's wealth exceeded that of his fellows. His supporters, recognizing his past favors and anticipating future rewards, recognized him as a leader and accepted his decisions as binding. The big man was an important regulator of regional events in Kapauku life. He helped determine the dates for feasts and markets. He persuaded people to sponsor feasts, which distributed pork and wealth. He initiated economic projects requiring the cooperation of a regional community.

The Kapauku big man again exemplifies a generalization about leadership in tribal societies: If someone achieves wealth and widespread respect and support, he or she must be generous. The big man worked hard not to hoard wealth but to give away the fruits of his labor, to convert wealth into prestige and gratitude. A stingy big man would lose his support, his reputation plummeting. Selfish and greedy big men sometimes were murdered by their fellows (Zimmer-Tamakoshi 1997).

> **status** Any position that determines where someone fits in society; may be ascribed or achieved.
>
> **ascribed status** Social status that people have little or no choice about occupying (e.g., race or gender).
>
> **achieved status** Social status that comes through talents, actions, efforts, activities, and accomplishments (e.g., big man or convicted felon).

choices, actions, efforts, talents, or accomplishments, and may be positive or negative. Examples of achieved statuses include big man, healer, senator, convicted felon, terrorist, salesperson, union member, father, and college student.

The achieved status of big men rested on certain characteristics that distinguished the big man from his fellows: wealth, generosity, eloquence, physical fitness, bravery, and supernatural powers. Men became big men because they had certain personalities. They amassed resources during their own lifetime; they did not inherit their wealth or position. A determined man could become a big man, creating wealth through hard work and good judgment. Wealth resulted from successful pig breeding and trading. As a man's pig herd and prestige grew, he attracted sup-

PANTRIBAL SODALITIES AND AGE GRADES

Big men could forge regional political organization, albeit temporarily, by mobilizing people from several villages. Other social and political mechanisms in tribal societies—such as a belief in common ancestry, kinship, or descent—could be used to link local groups within a region. The same descent group might span several villages, and its dispersed members might follow a descent group leader.

To what extent has the political success of the Kennedys family been achieved, or ascribed?

POPCULTURE

Superhero films celebrate differences in power between those heroes and ordinary people. Power differentials also are key interests in political anthropology. Some superheroes (e.g., the X-Men) are born with their special powers. Others (e.g., Iron Man and Batman) use technology to become superhuman. Still others (e.g., Spiderman and the Fantastic Four) get their powers accidentally. In each case, is superherodom an ascribed status or an achieved status? How about Superman?

Principles other than kinship also can link local groups. In a modern nation, a labor union, national sorority or fraternity, political party, or religious denomination may provide such a nonkin-based link. In tribes, nonkin groups called *associations,* or *sodalities,* may serve the same linking function. Often, sodalities are based on common age or gender, with all-male sodalities more common than all-female ones.

Pantribal sodalities (those that extend across the whole tribe, spanning several villages) sometimes arose in areas where two or more different cultures came into regular contact. Such sodalities were especially likely to develop in the presence of warfare between tribes. Drawing their membership from different villages of the same tribe, pantribal sodalities could mobilize men in many local groups for attack or retaliation against another tribe.

CULTURETHINK

Do you or your family belong to any kind of sodality, or nonkin group?

In the cross-cultural study of nonkin groups, we must distinguish between those that are confined to a single village and those that span several local groups. Only the latter, the pantribal groups, are important in general military mobilization and regional political organization. Localized men's houses and clubs, limited to particular villages, are found in many horticultural societies in tropical South America, Melanesia, and Papua New Guinea. These groups may organize village activities and even intervillage raiding. However, their leaders are similar to village heads, and their political scope is mainly local. The following discussion concerns pantribal groups.

pantribal sodality A nonkin-based group that exists throughout a tribe, spanning several villages.

age set Group uniting all men or women (usually men) born during a certain time span; this group controls property and often has political and military functions.

The best examples of pantribal sodalities come from the Central Plains of North America and from tropical Africa. During the eighteenth and nineteenth centuries, Native American societies of the Great Plains of the United States and Canada experienced a rapid growth of pantribal sodalities. This development reflected an economic change that followed the spread of horses, which had been reintroduced to the Americas by the Spanish, to the states between the Rocky Mountains and the Mississippi River. Many Plains Indian societies changed their adaptive strategies because of the horse. At first they had been foragers who hunted bison (buffalo) on foot. Later they adopted a mixed economy based on hunting, gathering, and horticulture. Finally they changed to a much more specialized economy based on horseback hunting of bison (eventually with rifles).

As the Plains tribes were undergoing these changes, other Indians also adopted horseback hunting and moved into the Plains. Attempting to occupy the same area, groups came into conflict. A pattern of warfare developed in which the members of one tribe raided another, usually for horses. The new economy demanded that people follow the movement of the bison herds. During the winter, when the bison dispersed, a tribe fragmented into small bands and families. In the summer, as huge herds assembled on the Plains, members of the tribe reunited. They camped together for social, political, and religious activities, but mainly for communal bison hunting.

Only two activities in the new adaptive strategy demanded strong leadership: organizing and carrying out raids on enemy camps (to capture horses) and managing the summer bison hunt. All the Plains societies developed pantribal sodalities, and leadership roles within them, to police the summer hunt. Leaders coordinated hunting efforts, making sure that people did not cause a stampede with an early shot or an ill-advised action. Leaders imposed severe penalties, including seizure of a culprit's wealth, for disobedience.

Some Plains sodalities were **age sets** of increasing rank. Each set included all the men—from that tribe's component bands—born during a certain time span. Each set had its distinctive dances, songs, possessions, and privileges. Members of each set had to pool their wealth to buy admission to the next higher level as they moved up the age hierarchy. Most Plains societies had pantribal warrior associations whose rituals celebrated militarism. As noted previously, the leaders of these associations organized bison hunting and raiding. They also arbitrated disputes during the summer, when many people came together.

Many tribes that adopted this Plains strategy of adaptation had once been foragers for whom hunting and gathering had been individual or small-group affairs. They never had come together previously as a single social unit. Age and gender were available as social principles that could quickly and efficiently forge unrelated people into pantribal groups.

Raiding of one tribe by another, this time for cattle rather than horses, also was common in eastern and southeastern Africa, where pantribal sodalities, including age sets, also developed. Among the pastoral Masai of Kenya, men born during the same four-year period were circumcised together and belonged to the same named group, an age set, throughout their lives. The sets moved through age grades, the most important of which was the warrior grade. Members of a set felt a strong allegiance to one another.

CULTURETHINK

The text describes three forms of tribal leadership: village heads, big men, and pantribal sodalities. What characteristics do they have in common? How are they different? Think, for example, about the amount of authority each has and the size of the group governed.

Here we see the Masai warrior (ilmurran) age grade dancing with a group of girls of a lower age grade (intoyie). Do we have any equivalents of age sets or grades in our own society?

Masai women lacked comparable set organization, but they also passed through culturally recognized age grades: the initiate, the married woman, and the postmenopausal woman.

To understand the difference between an age set and an age grade, think of a college class, the Class of 2014, for example, and its progress through the university. The age set would be the group of people constituting the Class of 2014, while the first ("freshman"), sophomore, junior, and senior years would represent the age grades.

Not all societies with age grades also have age sets. When there are no sets, men can enter or leave a particular grade individually or collectively, often by going through a predetermined ritual. The grades most commonly recognized in Africa are these:

- Recently initiated youths
- Warriors
- One or more grades of mature men who play important roles in pantribal government
- Elders, who may have special ritual responsibilities

In certain parts of West and Central Africa, the pantribal sodalities are *secret societies,* made up exclusively of men or women. Like our college fraternities and sororities, these associations have secret initiation ceremonies. Among the Mende of Sierra Leone, men's and women's secret societies were very influential. The men's group, the Poro, trained boys in social conduct, ethics, and religion and supervised political and economic activities.

Leadership roles in the Poro often overshadowed village headship and played an important part in social control, dispute management, and tribal political regulation. Age, gender, and ritual can link members of different local groups into a single social collectivity in a tribe and thus create a sense of ethnic identity, of belonging to the same cultural tradition.

NOMADIC POLITICS

Although many pastoralists, such as the Masai, live in tribes, a range of demographic and sociopolitical diversity occurs with pastoralism. A comparison of pastoralists shows that as regulatory problems increase, political hierarchies are more complex. Political organization is less personal, more formal, and less kinship-oriented. The pastoral strategy of adaptation does not dictate any particular political organization. Unlike the Masai and other tribal herders, some pastoralists have chiefs and live in nation-states.

The scope of political authority among pastoralists expands considerably as regulatory problems increase in densely populated regions. Consider two Iranian pastoral nomadic tribes—the Basseri and the Qashqai (Salzman 1974). Starting each year from a plateau near the coast, these groups took their animals to grazing land 17,000 feet (5,400 meters) above sea level. The Basseri and the Qashqai shared this route with one another and with several other ethnic groups (see "Location of the Basseri and Qashqai" on page 130).

Location of the Basseri and Qashqai

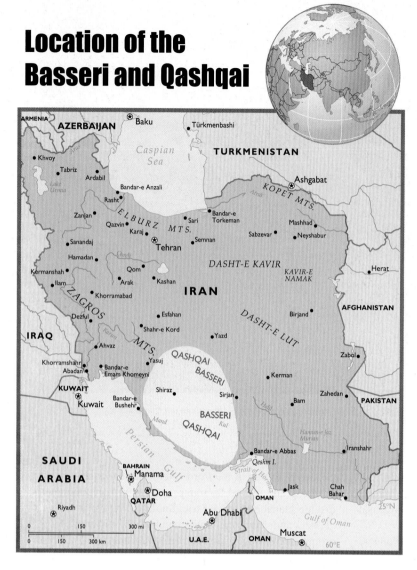

In Qashqai society, allegiance shifted from the person to the office. The Qashqai had multiple levels of authority and more powerful chiefs, or khans. Managing four hundred thousand people required a complex hierarchy. Heading it was the il-khan, helped by a deputy, under whom were the heads of constituent tribes, under each of whom were descent-group heads.

A case illustrates just how developed the Qashqai authority structure was. A hailstorm prevented some nomads from joining the annual migration at the appointed time. Although everyone recognized that they were not responsible for their delay, the il-khan assigned them less favorable grazing land, for that year only, in place of their usual pasture. The tardy herders and other Qashqai considered the judgment fair and didn't question it. Thus, Qashqai authorities regulated the annual migration. They also adjudicated disputes between people, tribes, and descent groups.

These Iranian cases illustrate the fact that pastoralism often is just one among many specialized economic activities within complex nation-states and regional systems. As part of a larger whole, pastoral tribes are constantly pitted against other ethnic groups. In these nations, the state becomes a final authority, a higher-level regulator that attempts to limit conflict between ethnic groups. State organization arose not just to manage agricultural economies but also to regulate the activities of ethnic groups within expanding social and economic systems (see Das and Poole 2004).

>> Chiefdoms

Having looked at bands and tribes, we turn to more complex forms of sociopolitical organization—chiefdoms and states. The first states emerged in the Old World about fifty-five hundred years ago. The first chiefdoms developed perhaps a thousand years earlier, but few survive today. In many parts of the world, the chiefdom was a transitional form of organization that emerged during the evolution of tribes into states. State formation began in Mesopotamia (currently Iran and Iraq). It next occurred in Egypt, the Indus Valley of Pakistan and India, and northern China. A few thousand years later states arose in two parts of the Western Hemisphere—Mesoamerica (Mexico, Guatemala, Belize) and the central Andes (Peru and Bolivia). Early states are known as *archaic states,* or nonindustrial states, in contrast to modern industrial nation-states. Robert Carneiro defines the state as "an autonomous political unit encompassing many communities within its territory, having a centralized government with the power to collect

Use of the same pasture land at different times was carefully scheduled. Ethnic-group movements were tightly coordinated. Expressing this schedule is *il-rah,* a concept common to all Iranian nomads. A group's il-rah is its customary path in time and space. It is the schedule, different for each group, of when specific areas can be used in the annual trek.

Each tribe had its own leader, known as the *khan* or *il-khan.* The Basseri khan, because he dealt with a smaller population, faced fewer problems in coordinating its movements than did the leaders of the Qashqai. Correspondingly, his rights, privileges, duties, and authority were weaker. Nevertheless, his authority exceeded that of any political figure discussed so far. The khan's authority still came from his personal traits rather than from his office. That is, the Basseri followed a particular khan not because of a political position he happened to fill but because of their personal allegiance and loyalty to him as a man. The khan relied on the support of the heads of the descent groups into which Basseri society was divided.

office Permanent political position.

taxes, draft men for work or war, and decree and enforce laws" (Carneiro 1970, p. 733).

The chiefdom and the state, like many categories used by social scientists, are *ideal types*. That is, they are labels that make social contrasts seem sharper than they really are. In reality there is a continuum from tribe to chiefdom to state. Some societies had many attributes of chiefdoms but retained tribal features. Some advanced chiefdoms had many attributes of archaic states and thus are difficult to assign to either category. Recognizing this "continuous change" (Johnson and Earle 2000), some anthropologists speak of "complex chiefdoms" (Earle 1987, 1997), which are almost states.

CULTURETHINK

Consider the pros and cons of ideal types. Is such a typology a valuable way of presenting information, or is it misleading? Do the categories of band, tribe, chiefdom, and state help you understand cross-cultural politics?

POLITICAL AND ECONOMIC SYSTEMS IN CHIEFDOMS

Areas with chiefdoms included the circum-Caribbean (e.g., Caribbean islands, Panama, Colombia), lowland Amazonia, what is now the southeastern United States, and Polynesia. Between the emergence and spread of food production and the expansion of the Roman empire, much of Europe was organized at the chiefdom level. Europe reverted to this level for centuries after the fall of Rome in the fifth century c.e. Chiefdoms created the megalithic cultures of Europe, such as the one that built Stonehenge. Bear in mind that chiefdoms and states can fall (disintegrate) as well as rise.

Chiefdoms created the megalithic cultures of Europe, such as the one that built Stonehenge more than five thousand years ago. Between the emergence and spread of food production and the expansion of the Roman empire, much of Europe was organized at the chiefdom level, to which it reverted after the fall of Rome.

Much of our ethnographic knowledge about chiefdoms comes from Polynesia, where they were common at the time of European exploration. In chiefdoms, social relations are based mainly on kinship, marriage, descent, age, generation, and gender—just as they are in bands and tribes. This is a fundamental difference between chiefdoms and states. States bring nonrelatives together and oblige them all to pledge allegiance to a government.

Unlike bands and tribes, however, chiefdoms are characterized by *permanent political regulation* of the territory they administer. They have a clear-cut and enduring regional political system. Chiefdoms may include thousands of people living in many villages or hamlets. Regulation is carried out by the chief and his or her assistants, who occupy political offices. An **office** is a permanent position, which must be refilled when it is vacated by death or retirement. Because offices are refilled systematically, the structure of a chiefdom endures across the generations, ensuring permanent political regulation.

In the Polynesian chiefdoms, the chiefs were full-time political specialists in charge of regulating the economy—production, distribution, and consumption. Polynesian chiefs relied on religion to buttress their authority. They regulated production by commanding or prohibiting (using religious taboos) the cultivation of certain lands and crops. Chiefs also regulated distribution and consumption. At certain seasons—often on a ritual occasion such as a first-fruit ceremony—people would offer part of their harvest to the chief through his or her representatives. Products moved up the hierarchy, eventually reaching the chief. Conversely, illustrating obligatory sharing with kin, chiefs sponsored feasts at which they gave back much of what they had received.

Such a flow of resources to and then from a central office is known as *chiefly redistribution*. Redistribution offers economic advantages. If the different areas specialized in particular crops, goods, or services, chiefly redistribution made those products available to the entire society. Chiefly redistribution also played a role in risk management. It stimulated production beyond the immediate subsistence level and provided a central storehouse for goods that might become scarce at times of famine (Earle 1987, 1997).

Neither band nor tribal leaders have permanent positions or can enforce decisions, unlike chiefs and state leaders, who hold offices and have clear-cut authority.

SOCIAL STATUS IN CHIEFDOMS

Social status in chiefdoms was based on seniority of descent. Because rank, power, prestige, and resources came through kinship and descent, Polynesian chiefs kept extremely long genealogies. Some chiefs (without writing) managed to trace their ancestry back fifty generations. All the people in the chiefdom were thought to be related to each other. Presumably, all were descended from a group of founding ancestors.

The status of chief was ascribed, based on seniority of descent. The chief would be the oldest child (usually son) of the oldest child of the oldest child, and so on. Degrees of seniority were calculated so intricately on some islands that there were as many ranks as people. For example, the third son would rank below the second, who in turn would rank below the first. The children of an eldest brother, however, would all rank above the children of the next brother, whose children would in turn outrank those of younger brothers. However, even the lowest-ranking person in a chiefdom was still the chief's relative. In such a kin-based context, everyone, even a chief, had to share with his or her relatives.

Because everyone had a slightly different status, it was difficult to draw a line between elites and common people. Other chiefdoms calculated seniority differently and had shorter genealogies than did those in Polynesia. Still, the concern

Did You Know?

Indigenous leaders remain politically relevant. In Madagascar, for example, national presidents have routinely consulted local chiefs, realizing that the chiefs have a strong influence on their followers.

differential access Unequal access to resources; basic attribute of chiefdoms and states. Superordinates have favored access to such resources, while the access of subordinates is limited by superordinates.

This photo, taken in 1981 in Neiafu, Savaii, Western Samoa, shows an orator chief, or tulafale. His speaking staff and the fly whisk over his shoulder symbolize his status as a tulafale. Traditional Samoa provides one example of a Polynesian chiefdom. How do chiefs differ from ordinary people?

for seniority and the lack of sharp gaps between elites and commoners are features of all chiefdoms.

STATUS SYSTEMS IN CHIEFDOMS AND STATES

The status systems of chiefdoms and states are similar in that both are based on **differential access** to resources. This means that some men and women had privileged access to power, prestige, and wealth. They controlled strategic resources such as land and water. Earle characterizes chiefs as "an incipient aristocracy with advantages in wealth and lifestyle" (1987, p. 290). Nevertheless, differential access in chiefdoms was tied very much to kinship. The people with privileged access were generally chiefs and their nearest relatives and assistants.

Compared with chiefdoms, archaic states drew a much firmer line between elites and masses, distinguishing at least between nobles and commoners. Kinship ties did not extend from the nobles to the commoners because of *stratum endogamy*—marriage within one's own group. Commoners married commoners; elites married elites.

Such a division of society into socioeconomic strata contrasts strongly with bands and tribes, whose status systems are based on prestige, rather than on differential access to resources. The prestige differentials that do exist in bands reflect special qualities and abilities. Successful hunters get respect from their fellows if they are generous. So does a skilled curer, dancer, storyteller—or anyone else with a talent or skill that others appreciate.

In tribes, some prestige goes to descent-group leaders, to village heads, and especially to the big man. All these figures must be generous, however. If they accumulate more resources—such as property or food—than others in the village, they must share them with the others. Since strategic resources are available to everyone, social classes based on the possession of unequal amounts of resources can never exist.

In many tribes, particularly those with patrilineal descent (descent traced through males only), men have much greater prestige and power than women do. The gender contrast in rights may diminish in chiefdoms, where prestige and access to resources are based on seniority of descent, so that some women are senior to some men. Unlike big men, chiefs are exempt from ordinary work and have rights and privileges that are unavailable to the masses. Like big men, however, they still return much of the wealth they take in.

THE EMERGENCE OF STRATIFICATION

The status system in chiefdoms, although based on differential access, differed from the status system in states because the privileged few were always relatives and assistants of the chief. However, this type of status sys-

Max Weber's Three Dimensions of Stratification

Wealth = Economic status   Power = Political status   Prestige = Social status

tem didn't last very long. Chiefs would start acting like kings and try to erode the kinship basis of the chiefdom. In Madagascar they would do this by demoting their more distant relatives to commoner status and banning marriage between nobles and commoners (Kottak 1980). Such moves, if accepted by the society, created separate social strata—*unrelated* groups that differ in their access to wealth, prestige, and power. (A *stratum* is one of two or more groups that contrast in social status and access to strategic resources. Each stratum includes people of both sexes and all ages.) The creation of separate social strata is called **stratification,** and its emergence signified the transition from chiefdom to state. *The presence of stratification is one of the key distinguishing features of a state.*

The influential sociologist Max Weber (1922/1968) defined three related dimensions of social stratification: (1) Economic status, or **wealth,** encompasses all a person's material assets, including income, land, and other types of property; (2) **power,** the ability to exercise one's will over others—to do what one wants—is the basis of political status; (3) **prestige**—the basis of social status—refers to esteem, respect, or approval for acts, deeds, or qualities considered exemplary. Prestige involves worth, respect, and "cultural capital" (Bourdieu 1984), which often bring economic benefits as well.

In archaic states—for the first time in human evolution—there were contrasts in wealth, power, and prestige between entire groups (social strata) of men and women. Each stratum included people of both sexes and all ages. The **superordinate** (the higher, or elite) stratum had privileged access to wealth, power, and other valued resources. Access to resources by members of the **subordinate** (lower, or underprivileged) stratum was limited by the privileged group.

OPEN- AND CLOSED-CLASS SYSTEMS

Inequalities, which are built into the structure of state-organized societies, tend to persist across the genera-

tions. The extent to which they do or don't is a measure of the openness of the stratification system—the ease of social mobility it permits. **Vertical mobility** is an upward or downward change in a person's social status. A truly **open-class system** would facilitate mobility. Individual achievement and personal merit would determine social rank. Hierarchical social statuses would be achieved on the basis of people's efforts. Ascribed statuses (family background, ethnicity, gender, religion) would be less important.

Stratification has taken many forms, including caste, slavery, and class systems. **Caste systems** are closed, hereditary systems of stratification that often are dictated by religion. Hierarchical social status is ascribed at birth, so that people are locked into their parents' social position. Caste lines are clearly defined, and legal and religious sanctions are applied against those who seek to cross them.

In **slavery,** the most inhumane, coercive, and degrading form of legal stratification, people who are conquered or stolen from their homelands become

stratification Characteristic of a system with socioeconomic strata.

wealth All a person's material assets, including income, land, and other types of property; the basis of economic status.

power The ability to exercise one's will over others—to do what one wants; the basis of political status.

prestige Esteem, respect, or approval for acts, deeds, or qualities considered exemplary.

superordinate The higher, or privileged, group in a stratified system.

subordinate The lower, or underprivileged, group in a stratified system.

vertical mobility Upward or downward change in a person's social status.

open-class system Stratification system that facilitates social mobility, with individual achievement and personal merit determining social rank.

caste system Closed, hereditary system of stratification, often dictated by religion; hierarchical social status is ascribed at birth, so that people are locked into their parents' social position.

slavery The most extreme, coercive, abusive, and inhumane form of legalized inequality; people are treated as property.

Dalit ("untouchable") women work with cow dung on the outskirts of the northern Indian city of Lucknow.

someone's property. In the Atlantic slave trade, millions of human beings were treated as commodities. The plantation systems of the Caribbean, the southeastern United States, and Brazil were based on forced slave labor. Lacking control over the means of production as well as their own destinies, slaves were forced to live and work at their master's whim. Defined as lesser—or less than—human beings, slaves lacked legal rights. They could be sold and resold; their families were split apart. Unlike the poorest nonslaves, enslaved people had nothing to sell—not even their own labor (Mintz 1985).

Modern class structures, featuring forms of stratification more open than slavery, caste systems, or the status systems of ancient states, have developed in recent times. Still, socioeconomic stratification continues as a defining feature of all states, archaic or industrial. The elites control a significant part of the means of production—for example, land, herds, water, capital, farms, or factories. Those born at the bottom of the hierarchy have reduced chances of so-

CULTURETHINK

Is there an open-class system in your country? To what extent is there vertical mobility? What factors make it difficult for people to move up or down from their family's status?

cial mobility. Because of elite ownership rights, ordinary people lack free access to resources. Only in states do the elites get to keep their differential wealth. Unlike big men and chiefs, they don't have to give it back to the people whose labor has built and increased it.

>> States

Table 7.1 summarizes the information presented so far on bands, tribes, chiefdoms, and states. States, remember, are autonomous political units with social classes and a formal government, based on law. States tend to be large and populous, as compared to bands, tribes, and chiefdoms. Certain statuses, systems, and subsystems with specialized functions are found in all states (see Sharma and Gupta 2006). They include the following:

- *Population control:* fixing of boundaries, establishment of citizenship categories, and the taking of a census.
- *Judiciary:* laws, legal procedure, and judges.
- *Enforcement:* permanent military and police forces.
- *Fiscal:* taxation.

In archaic states, these subsystems were integrated by a ruling system or government composed of civil, military, and religious officials (Fried 1960).

POPULATION CONTROL

To know whom they govern, states typically conduct censuses. States demarcate boundaries that separate them from other societies. Customs agents, immigration officers, navies, and coast guards patrol frontiers. Even nonindustrial states have boundary-maintenance forces. In Buganda, an archaic state on the shores of Lake Victoria in Uganda, the king rewarded military officers with estates in outlying provinces. They became his guardians against foreign intrusion.

States also control population through administrative subdivision: provinces, districts, "states," counties, subcounties, and parishes. Lower-level officials manage the populations and territories of the subdivisions.

In nonstates, people work and relax with their relatives, in-laws, and agemates—people with whom they have a personal relationship. Such a personal social life existed throughout most of human history, but food production spelled its eventual decline. After millions of years of human evolution, it took only a few thousand years for the population increase and regulatory problems spawned by food production to lead from tribe to chiefdom to state. With state organization, kinship's pervasive role diminished. Descent groups may continue as kin groups within archaic states, but their importance in political organization declines.

Economic Basis of and Political Regulation in Bands, Tribes, Chiefdoms, and States

Sociopolitical Type	Economic Type	Examples	Type of Regulation
Band	Foraging	Inuit, San	Local
Tribe	Horticulture, pastoralism	Yanomami, Kapauku, Masai	Local, temporary regional
Chiefdom	Productive horticulture, pastoral nomadism, agriculture	Qashqai, Polynesia, Cherokee	Permanent regional
State	Agriculture, industrialism	Ancient Mesopotamia, contemporary U.S., Canada	Permanent regional

TABLE 7.1

States foster geographic mobility and resettlement, severing long-standing ties among people, land, and kin (Smith 2003). Population displacements have increased in the modern world and with globalization. War, famine, and job seeking across national boundaries churn up migratory currents. People in states come to identify themselves by new statuses, both ascribed and achieved—including ethnicity, residence, occupation, party, religion, and team or club affiliation—rather than only as members of a descent group or extended family.

States also manage their populations by granting different rights and obligations to citizens and noncitizens. Status distinctions among citizens are also common. Many archaic states granted different rights to nobles, commoners, and slaves. Unequal rights within state-organized societies persist in today's world. In recent American history, before the Emancipation Proclamation, there were different laws for enslaved and free people. In European colonies, separate courts judged cases involving only natives and cases involving Europeans. In contemporary America, a military code of justice and court system continue to coexist alongside the civil judiciary.

JUDICIARY SYSTEMS

States have *laws* based on precedent and legislative proclamations. Without writing, laws may be preserved in oral tradition, with justices, elders, and other specialists responsible for remembering them. Oral traditions as repositories of legal wisdom have continued in some nations with writing, such as Great Britain. Laws regulate relations between individuals and groups.

Crimes are violations of the legal code, with specified types of punishment. However, a given act, such as killing someone, may be legally defined in different ways (e.g., as manslaughter, justifiable homicide, or first-degree murder). Furthermore, even in contemporary North America, where justice is supposed to be "blind" to social distinctions, the poor are prosecuted more often and more severely than are the rich.

CULTURE THINK

Compare and contrast leadership characteristics among bands, tribes, chiefdoms, and states. Are they permanent or temporary positions? Do they have the authority to enforce decisions? How much territory or how many people do they govern? Try drawing a chart or some other visual representation of this information.

To handle disputes and crimes, all states have courts and judges. Precolonial African states had subcounty, county, and district courts, plus a high court formed by the king or queen and his or her advisers. Most states allow appeals to higher courts, although people are encouraged to solve problems locally.

A striking contrast between states and nonstates is intervention in family affairs. In states, aspects of parenting and marriage enter the domain of public law. Governments step in to halt blood feuds and regulate previously private disputes. States attempt to curb *internal* conflict, but they aren't always successful. About 85 percent of the world's armed conflicts since 1945 have begun within states—in efforts to overthrow a ruling regime or as disputes over tribal, religious, and ethnic minority issues (see Chatterjee 2004). Only 15 percent have been fights across national borders (Barnaby 1984). Rebellion, resistance, repression, terrorism, and warfare continue (see Nordstrom 2004; Tishkov 2004). Indeed, recent states have perpetrated some of history's bloodiest deeds.

> "Treat all men alike. Give them the same law. Give them an even chance to live and grow."
>
> Chief Joseph

ENFORCEMENT SYSTEMS

All states have agents to enforce judicial decisions. Confinement requires jailers. If there is a death penalty, it requires executioners. Agents of the state have the power to collect fines and confiscate property.

As a relatively new form of sociopolitical organization, states have competed successfully with nonstates throughout the world. A government suppresses internal disorder (with police) and guards the nation against external threats (with the military). Military organization helps states subdue neighboring nonstates, but this is not the only reason for the spread of state organization. Although states impose hardships, they also offer advantages. They provide protection from outsiders and preserve internal order. By promoting internal peace, states enhance production. Their economies support massive, dense populations, which supply armies and colonists to promote expansion. A major concern of government is to defend hierarchy, property, and the power of the law.

FISCAL SYSTEMS

A financial, or **fiscal,** system is needed in states to support rulers, nobles, officials, judges, military personnel,

All states have law enforcement officials, such as this U.S. Marshal.

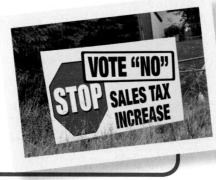

Many argue that taxes are necessary to the functioning of a state. Do you agree? What kinds of goods and services do taxes pay for in your community?

into or through the state. Taxes support government and the ruling class, which is clearly separated from the common people in regard to activities, privileges, rights, and obligations. Taxes also support the many specialists—administrators, tax collectors, judges, lawmakers, generals, scholars, and priests. As the state matures, the segment of the population freed from direct concern with subsistence grows.

The elites of archaic states reveled in the consumption of *sumptuary goods*—jewelry, exotic food and drink, and stylish clothing reserved for, or affordable only by, the rich. Peasants' diets suffered as they struggled to meet government demands. Commoners perished in territorial wars that had little relevance to their own needs. Are any of these observations true of contemporary states?

fiscal Pertaining to finances and taxation.

and thousands of other specialists. As in the chiefdom, the state intervenes in production, distribution, and consumption. The state may decree that a certain area will produce certain things or forbid certain activities in particular places. Although, like chiefdoms, states also have redistribution (through taxation), generosity and sharing are played down. Less of what comes in flows back to the people.

In nonstates, people customarily share with relatives, but residents of states face added obligations to bureaucrats and officials. Citizens must turn over a substantial portion of what they produce to the state. Of the resources that the state collects, it reallocates part for the general good and uses another part (often larger) for the elite.

The state does not bring more freedom or leisure to the common people, who usually work harder than do people in nonstates. They may be called on to build monumental public works. Some of these projects, such as dams and irrigation systems, may be economically necessary. People also build temples, palaces, and tombs for the elites.

Markets and trade usually are under at least some state control, with officials overseeing distribution and exchange, standardizing weights and measures, and collecting taxes on goods passing

Can you find parallels to the Melanesian "big man" on your campus? Talk with dorm residents or members of Greek houses or other social circles to see which students tend to take charge and acquire prestige. Or think back to high school. Who were the big men and women in your graduating class? How did their achievements compare with those described for big men in the text? Typically such individuals are self-made, gaining respect through efforts and personal qualities. But ask what effect family privilege, race, or ethnicity might have on their status. Consider too what values or actions might serve to level that status, bringing it in line with campus norms. Think of a campus big man or woman you know. Would you want to level or support his or her status? Why?

get involved!

For REVIEW

CULTURECLIPS

TO ACCESS THESE VIDEOS ON
YOUR COMPUTER, VISIT

www.mhhe.com/gezonqr

7-1

7-2

7-3

I. What kinds of political systems have existed world-wide, and what are their social and economic correlates?

- Bands are small groups of foragers related by kinship or marriage. Foraging encourages equality, reciprocity, and sharing as well as mobility. Band leaders are first among equals; they lack sure ways to enforce decisions and have only local influence. Tribes, which have horticultural or pastoral economies, are organized around village life and descent groups. The village headman and the "big man," a regional leader, have limited authority. Chiefdoms have horticultural, pastoral nomadic, or agricultural economies. While kin-based, they feature differential access to resources and permanent political regulation of a territory. Chiefs, whose status is based on seniority of descent, receive products that come upward through the hierarchy, then redistribute them to the people. The state is an independent, centrally organized political unit with marked socioeconomic stratification. The economy is typically agricultural or industrial. Political regulation is permanent and regional.

II. What is social status, and how does it relate to political systems?

- *Status* refers to social position. Ascribed status is automatic; achieved status comes through choice, personality, talent, or accomplishment. In bands, successful hunters or talented curers earn respect but do not inherit positions nor enjoy differential access to resources. In tribes, descent group leaders, village heads, and, especially, the big man must be generous. The big man amasses resources through effort; his achieved status gives him authority to regulate events and persuade people. In chiefdoms, chiefs and their assistants occupy political offices, which are permanent positions. States emerged when chiefs started to erode the kinship basis of the chiefdom and create separate strata—unrelated groups differing in economic, political, and social status. New kinds of statuses arise in states, such as ethnic, party, and occupational.

III. How does the state differ from other forms of political organization?

- Marked social stratification distinguishes states from other forms of political organization. Whereas chiefdoms allowed differential access to resources, it was closely tied to kinship seniority; in states, each social stratum comprises unrelated groups. Inequalities are built into states and tend to persist across generations. Also distinctive of states is formal government. Government fixes boundaries, establishes citizenship, and conducts censuses; decrees and enforces laws; handles disputes through courts; guards the nation and promotes expansion with a military; and collects taxes. States tend to be large and populous and to foster geographic mobility, severing long-standing ties among people, land, and kin.

Pop Quiz

1. The text argues that the term *sociopolitical* is preferable to Morton Fried's *political organization* because:
   a. Both anthropologists and political scientists prefer *sociopolitical*.
   b. Fried spoke of the management of "public policy" in his definition of *political organization,* making this term less applicable to nonstates.
   c. Nonstate societies show more correlations between social and political organization than do state societies.
   d. The term *political* refers only to contemporary Western states.

2. Band societies:
   a. Lack develop political systems that encourage equality.
   b. Are isolated survivors of the Stone Age.
   c. Have cultural rules that help members to distinguish between proper and improper behavior.
   d. Lack means for conflict resolution since bands do not have established governments or formal laws.

3. All the following statements about the San of southern African are true *except:*
   a. The San live within nation-states and are affected by world events.
   b. San society and economy vary in time and space, with settled ways of life on the increase among many San while others have retained more of their hunter-gatherer lifestyle.
   c. One researcher sees the San today as a rural underclass in a larger political and economic system.
   d. No San today retain their foraging lifestyle.

4. Which of the following factors is responsible for the recent changes in Yanomami tribal society?
   a. Big men have amassed so much wealth that the Yanomami have begun to regard them as chiefs.
   b. The Brazilian and Venezuelan governments have relocated Yanomami to other territories to protect them from big business enterprises.
   c. Intervillage trade and cooperation have led to the expansion of Yanomami tribal society.
   d. Gold miners and cattle ranchers have encroached on Yanomami territory and attacked its people; the miners have introduced new diseases.

5. Why are pantribal sodalities and age grades described in a chapter on political systems?
   a. They are organizing principles used to mobilize and link local groups to form alliances.
   b. They are among the statuses and systems with specialized functions that are found in all states.
   c. They are organizing principles that stress the importance of kinship ties.
   d. The leadership roles within them are important factors in the evolution of states.

6. The comparison between the Basseri and the Qashqai, two Iranian nomadic tribes, illustrates that:
   a. Among tribal sociopolitical organizations, pastoralists are the least likely to interact with other populations in the same space and time.
   b. As regulatory problems increase, political hierarchies become more complex.
   c. As regulatory problems decrease, political hierarchies become more complex.
   d. State organization arises to manage agricultural economies.

7. In foraging and tribal societies, what is the basis for the degree of respect or status attached to an individual?
   a. Prestige inherited from parents.
   b. Personal attributes, such as wisdom, leadership skills, and generosity.
   c. The amount of possessions one owns and the ability to convert them into cash.
   d. The amount of territory a person owns.

8. In what kind of society does differential access to strategic resources based on social stratification occur?
   a. Chiefdoms
   b. Bands
   c. States
   d. Tribes

9. All the following are interrelated dimensions of social stratification as defined by the sociologist Max Weber *except:*
   a. Power over others.
   b. Prestige, the basis of social status.
   c. The permanence of social position.
   d. Wealth, or economic status.

10. Which of the following would not constitute a status or specialized function that is found in all states?
    a. Control of populations.
    b. Agents to enforce judicial decisions, police the society, and guard the nation against external threats.
    c. Elimination of different rights granted to different social classes.
    d. Taxation.

1. (b), 2. (c), 3. (d), 4. (d), 5. (a), 6. (b), 7. (b), 8. (c), 9. (c), 10. (c)

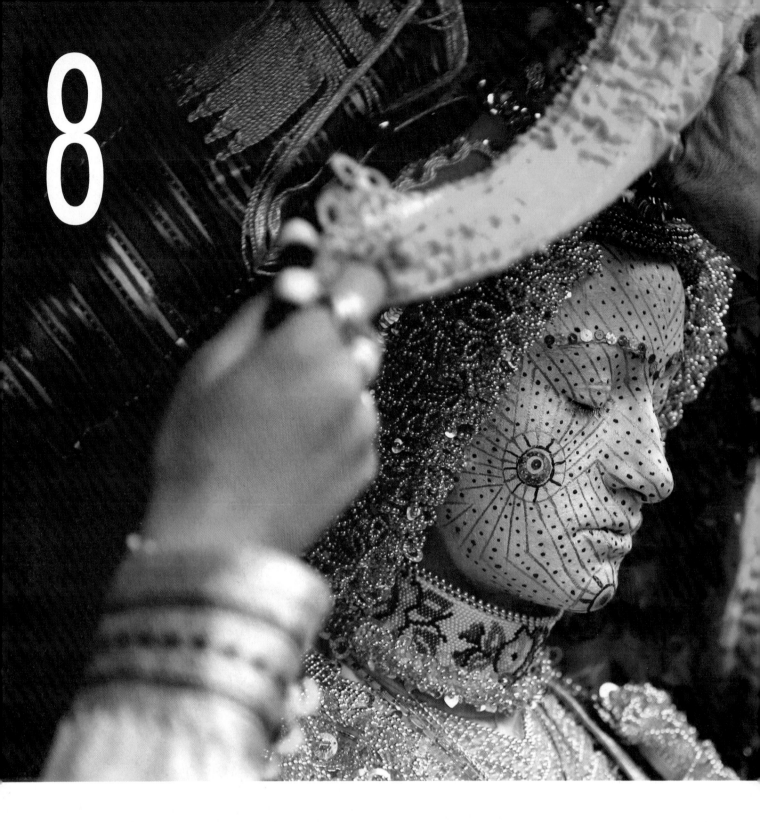

8

FAMILIES, KINSHIP, AND MARRIAGE

UNDERSTANDING OURSELVES

Although it remains something of an ideal in our culture, the nuclear family (mom, dad, and kids) now accounts for fewer than one-fourth of all American households. What kind of family raised you? According to the radio talk show psychologist (and undergraduate anthropology major) Dr. Joy Browne, the dual job of parents or caretakers is to give their kids "roots and wings." Roots, she says, are the easier part. In other words, it's easier to raise children than to let them go. Has that been true of those who raised you? We've heard comments about today's "helicopter parents" hovering over even their college-aged kids, using cell phones, email, and texting to follow their progeny more closely than in previous generations.

It can be difficult to make the transition between the family that raised us (our family of orientation) and the family we create when (or if) we form a long-term romantic partnership and have children (our family of procreation). Contemporary Americans usually get a head start by "leaving home" long before we marry. We go off to college or find a job that enables us to support ourselves so that we can live independently, or with roommates. In nonindustrial societies a woman often must leave her home village and her own kin and move in with her husband and his relatives. Many such women complain about feeling isolated in their husband's village, where they may be mistreated by their husband or in-laws.

Even in contemporary North America, conflicts with in-laws aren't at all uncommon. Just read "Dear Abby" or listen to Dr. Joy Browne (cited above) for a week. Even more of a challenge is learning to live with our spouse or domestic partner. Cohabitation always raises issues of accommodation and adjustment. Initially the couple is just that, unless there are children from a previous marriage. If there are, adjustment issues will involve stepparent-hood and likely a prior spouse or partner. Once a couple has its own child, family loyalty shifts, but not completely, from the family of orientation to the family that includes spouse and child(ren). The cycle of "marriage and the family" begins anew.

As You READ

- What forms of kinship exist cross-culturally, and what are their social correlates?
- How do families and descent groups differ?
- How is marriage defined and regulated, and what rights does it convey?

>> Families

The societies anthropologists traditionally have studied have stimulated a strong interest in families, along with larger systems of kinship and marriage. The wide web of kinship—as vital in daily life in nonindustrial societies as work outside the home is in our own—has become an essential part of anthropology because of its importance to the people we study. We are ready to take a closer look at the systems of kinship and marriage that have organized human life for much of our history.

Ethnographers quickly recognize social divisions, or groups, within any society they study. They learn about significant groups by observing their activities and membership. Often people live in the same village or neighborhood or work, socialize, or celebrate together because they are related in some way. A significant kin group might consist of descendants of the same grandfather. These people live in neighboring houses, farm adjoining fields, and help each other in daily tasks. Groups based on other kin links get together less often in that society.

This polygynous family (a man with multiple wives) in Mali, West Africa, displays their normal weekly diet on the roof of their mud-brick home. Ethnographers have studied many family types besides the nuclear family—the traditional American ideal.

The nuclear family (parents and children) is one kind of kin group that is widespread in human societies. Other kin groups include extended families (families consisting of three or more generations) and descent groups—lineages and clans.

Much of kinship is *culturally constructed,* that is, based on learning and variable from culture to culture (McKinnon 2005; Schneider 1967). Different societies have different kinds of families, households, kin groups, marriage customs, and living arrangements. Consider the term *family,* which is basic, *familiar* (so much so it even shares its root with *familiar*), and difficult to define in a way that applies to all cultures. A **family** is a group of people (e.g., parents, children, siblings, grandparents, grandchildren, uncles, aunts, nephews, nieces, cousins, spouses, siblings-in-law, parents-in-law, children-in-law) who are considered to be related in some way, such as by "blood" (common ancestry or descent) or marriage. Some families, such as the nuclear family, are residentially based; its members live together. Others are not; they live apart but come together for family reunions of various sorts from time to time.

Consider a striking contrast between the United States and Brazil, the two most populous countries of the Western Hemisphere, in the meaning and role of family. American adults usually define their family as consisting of their spouse and children. When middle-class Brazilians talk about their family (*família*), they mean their parents, siblings, aunts, uncles, grandparents, and cousins. Later they add their children, but rarely the husband or wife, who has his or her own family. The children are shared by the two families. Because middle-class Americans typically lack an extended family support system, marriage assumes more importance. The husband–wife relationship is supposed to take precedence over either spouse's relationship with his or her own parents. This places a significant strain on North American marriages.

Living in a less mobile society, Brazilians stay in closer face-to-face contact with their relatives, including members of the extended family, than North Americans do. Residents of Rio de Janeiro and São Paulo, two of South America's largest cities, are reluctant to leave those urban centers to live away from family and friends. Brazilians find it hard to imagine, and unpleasant to live in, social worlds without relatives. Contrast this with a characteristic American theme: learning to live with strangers.

NUCLEAR AND EXTENDED FAMILIES

A nuclear family is *impermanent;* it lasts only as long as the parents and children remain together. Most people belong to at least two nuclear families at different times in their lives. They are born into a family consisting of their parents and siblings. When they reach adulthood, they may marry and establish a nuclear family that includes the spouse and eventually children. Since most societies permit divorce, some people establish more than one family through marriage.

Anthropologists distinguish between the **family of orientation** (the family in which one is born and grows up) and the **family of procreation** (formed when one marries and has children). From the individual's point of view, the critical relationships are with parents and siblings in the family of orientation and with spouse and children in the family of procreation. In Brazil, as we just saw, the family of orientation predominates, whereas in the United States it is the family of procreation.

In most societies, relations with nuclear family members (parents, siblings, and children) take precedence over

family A group of people (e.g., parents, children, siblings, grandparents, grandchildren, uncles, aunts, nephews, nieces, cousins, spouses, siblings-in-law, parents-in-law, children-in-law) who are considered to be related in some way, such as by "blood" (common ancestry or descent) or marriage.

family of orientation Nuclear family in which one is born and grows up.

family of procreation Nuclear family established when one marries and has children.

relations with other kin. Nuclear family organization is very widespread but not universal, and its significance in society differs greatly from one place to another. In a few societies, such as the classic Nayar case described a little later in the chapter, nuclear families are rare or nonexistent.

neolocality Postmarital residence pattern in which a couple establishes a new place of residence rather than living with or near either set of parents.

extended family household Expanded household including three or more generations.

In others, the nuclear family plays no special role in social life. Other social units—most notably descent groups and extended families—can assume many of the functions otherwise associated with the nuclear family.

Consider an example from the former Yugoslavia. Traditionally, among the Muslims of western Bosnia, nuclear families lacked autonomy (Lockwood 1975). Several such families lived in an extended family household called a *zadruga*. The zadruga was headed by a male household head and his wife, the senior woman. It included married sons and their wives and children, and unmarried sons and daughters. Each nuclear family had a sleeping room, decorated and partly furnished from the bride's trousseau. Zadruga members shared possessions, however—even clothing and trousseau items. Such a residential unit is known as a *patrilocal* extended family because each couple resides in the husband's father's household after marriage.

The zadruga took precedence over its component units. There were three successive meal settings—for men, women, and children, respectively. Traditionally, all children over the age of twelve slept together in boys' or girls' rooms. When a woman wished to visit another village, she sought the permission of the male zadruga head. Although men usually felt closer to their own children than to those of their brothers, they were obliged to treat them equally. Children were disciplined by any adult in the household. When a nuclear family broke up, children under age seven went with the mother. Older children could choose between their parents. Children were considered part of the household where they were born even if their mother left. One widow who remarried had to leave her five children, all over the age of seven, in their father's zadruga, now headed by his brother.

Another example of an alternative to the nuclear family is provided by the Nayar (or Nair), a large and powerful caste on the Malabar Coast of southern India (Gough 1959; Shivaram 1996). Their traditional kinship system was matrilineal (descent traced only through females). Nayar lived in matrilineal extended family compounds called *tarawads*—a residential complex with several buildings, its own temple, granary, water well, orchards, gardens, and land holdings. Headed by a senior woman, assisted by her brother, the tarawad housed her siblings, sisters' children, and other *matrikin*—matrilineal relatives.

Traditional Nayar marriage seems to have been hardly more than a formality: a kind of coming-of-age ritual. A young woman would go through a marriage ceremony with a man, after which they might spend a few days together at her tarawad. Then the man would return to his own tarawad, where he lived with his sisters, aunts, and other matrikin. Nayar men belonged to a warrior class, who left home regularly for military expeditions, returning permanently to their tarawad on retirement. Nayar women could have multiple sexual partners. Children became members of the mother's tarawad; they were not considered to be relatives of their biological father. Indeed, many Nayar children didn't even know who their biological father (genitor) was. Child care was the responsibility of the tarawad. Nayar society therefore reproduced itself biologically without the nuclear family.

INDUSTRIALISM AND FAMILY ORGANIZATION

For many Americans and Canadians, the nuclear family is the only well-defined kin group. Family isolation arises from geographic mobility, which is associated with industrialism, so that a nuclear family focus is characteristic of many modern nations. Born into a family of orientation, North Americans leave home for college or work, and the break with parents is under way. Selling our labor on the market, we often move to places where jobs are available. Eventually most North Americans marry and start a family of procreation.

Many married couples live hundreds of miles from their parents. Their jobs have determined where they live. Such a postmarital residence pattern is **neolocality:** Married couples are expected to establish a new place of residence—a "home of their own." Among middle-class North Americans, neolocal residence is both a cultural preference

Unable to survive economically as nuclear family units, relatives may band together in an expanded family household and pool their resources. This photo, taken in 2002 in Munich, Germany, shows German Roma, or Gypsies. Together with her children and grandchildren, this grandmother resides in an expanded family household.

In their 2009 book *Media and Middle-Class Moms: Images and Realities of Work and Family,* Lara Descartes and Conrad Kottak point out that, contrary to popular belief, it is the 1980s—not the 1950s—that best qualifies as the golden decade of the TV family. Not only did such family-oriented programs as *The Cosby Show* and *Family Ties* dominate Nielsen's top ten, there also was a revival of interest in earlier family shows. The now iconic series *Leave It to Beaver,* for example, never made it into even the Nielsen top thirty shows during its original broadcast years, 1957–1963. In the mid-1980s, *Beaver* reappeared in syndication, in a reunion telemovie, and in a sequel series. Idealized media representations of traditional nuclear families increased in tandem with the subversion of that structure by socioeconomic fact, as the divorce rate rose and more and more women joined the workforce. To be sure, 1980s shows featured working women like Claire Huxtable and Elyze Keaton. And they, too, were idealized in their ability to blend professional success with exemplary motherhood. Watch a few episodes, and evaluate Claire or Elyze as role models compared with the reality of your own family life.

and a statistical norm. Most middle-class Americans eventually establish households and nuclear families of their own.

There are significant differences between middle-class and poorer North Americans. For example, in the lower class, the incidence of expanded family households (those that include nonnuclear relatives) is greater than it is in the

middle class. When an *expanded family household* includes three or more generations, it is an **extended family household,** such as the zadruga. Another type of expanded family is the *collateral household,* which includes siblings and their spouses and children.

The higher proportion of expanded family households among poorer Americans has been explained as an adaptation to poverty (Stack 1975). Unable to survive economically as nuclear family units, relatives band together in an expanded household and pool their resources. Adaptation to poverty causes kinship values and attitudes to diverge from middle-class norms. Thus, when North Americans raised in poverty achieve financial success, they often feel obligated to provide financial help to a wide circle of less fortunate relatives (see Willie 2003).

CHANGES IN NORTH AMERICAN KINSHIP

Although the nuclear family remains a cultural ideal for many Americans, the "Changes in Organization" chart on page 146 shows that nuclear families accounted for 23 percent of American households in 2007 (see "Households by Type" also on page 146). Other domestic arrangements now outnumber the "traditional" American household more than four to one. There are several reasons for this changing household composition. Women increasingly are joining men in the cash workforce. This often removes them from their family of orientation while making it economically feasible to

CULTURETHINK

The average age of first marriage in 2009 was almost twenty-six for women and twenty-eight for men. Consider the people you know: How much (if at all) do they vary from this national norm?

Changes in Family and Household Organization in the United States, 1970 vs. 2007

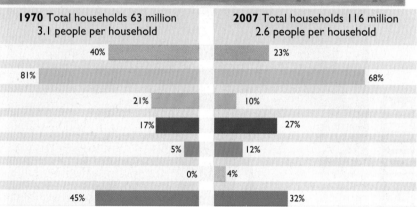

	1970 Total households 63 million — 3.1 people per household	**2007** Total households 116 million — 2.6 people per household
Married couples living with children	40%	23%
Family households	81%	68%
Households with five or more people	21%	10%
People living alone	17%	27%
Percentage of single-mother families	5%	12%
Percentage of single-father families	0%	4%
Households with own children under 18	45%	32%

Sources: From U.S. Census data in J. M. Fields, "America's Families and Living Arrangements: 2003," *Current Population Reports,* P20–553, November 2004, http://ww.census .gov/prod/2004pubs/p20-553.pdf, p. 4; J. M. Fields and L. M. Casper, "America's Families and Living Arrangements: Population Characteristics 2000," *Current Population Reports,* P20–537, June 2001, http://www.census.gov/prod/2001pubs/p20-537.pdf; U.S. Census Bureau, *Statistical Abstract of the United States 2009,* Tables 58, 60, 63, http://www.census.gov/compendia/statab/2009edition.html.

Households by Type: Selected Years, 1970–2007

Nonfamily households

Year	Other nonfamily households	Women living alone	Men living alone	Other family households	Married couples without children	Married couples with children
1970	1.7%	11.5%	5.6%	10.6%	30.3%	40.3%
1980	3.6%	14.0%	8.6%	12.9%	29.9%	30.9%
1990	4.6%	14.9%	9.7%	14.8%	29.8%	26.3%
1995	5.0%	14.7%	10.2%	15.6%	28.9%	25.5%
2000	5.7%	14.8%	10.7%	16.0%	28.7%	24.1%
2007	5.6%	15.2%	11.7%	16.8%	28.3%	22.5%

Family households

Sources: J. M. Fields, "America's Families and Living Arrangements: 2003," *Current Population Reports,* P20–553. November 2004, http://www.census.gov/prod2004pubs/p20-553.pdf, p. 4; *Statistical Abstract of the United States* 2009, Table 58, p. 52, and Table 60, p. 53, http://www.census.gov/compendia/statab/2009edition.html.

Ratio of Divorces to Marriages per 1,000 U.S. Population, Selected Years, 1950–2006

Ratio of divorces to marriages per 1,000 U.S. population

Source: Statistical Abstract of the United States 2009, Table 77, p. 63, http://www.census.gov/compendia/statab/2009edition.html.

delay marriage. Furthermore, job demands compete with romantic attachments. The median age at first marriage for American women rose from twenty-one years in 1970 to twenty-six in 2009. For men the comparable ages were twenty-three and twenty-eight (U.S. Census Bureau 2010).

The U.S. divorce rate also has risen, making divorced Americans much more common today than they were in 1970. U.S. Census Bureau figures show that between 1970 and 2007 the number of divorced Americans quintupled—some 23 million in 2007 versus 4.3 million in 1970. (Note, however, that each divorce creates two divorced people.) The figure above shows the ratio of divorces to marriages in the United States for selected years between 1950 and 2006. The major jump in the American divorce rate took place between 1960 and 1980. During that period the ratio of divorces to marriage doubled. Since 1980 the ratio has stayed the same, slightly below 50 percent. That is, each year there are about half as many new divorces as there are new marriages.

The rate of growth in single-parent families also has outstripped population growth, quintupling from fewer

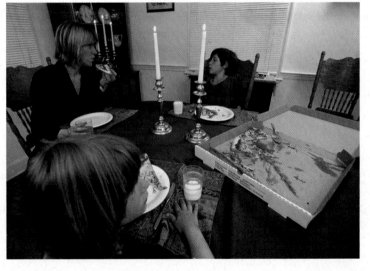

In contemporary North America, single-parent families have increased at a rapid rate. In 1960, 88 percent of American children lived with both parents, compared with 68 percent today. This divorced mom, Valerie Jones, enjoys a candlelight dinner with her kids. What do you see as the main differences between nuclear families and single-parent families?

than 4 million in 1970 to 19 million in 2007. (The overall American population in 2007 was 1.5 times its size in 1970.) The percentage (22.6 percent) of children living in fatherless (mother-headed, no resident dad) households in 2007 was more than twice the 1970 rate, while the percentage (3.2 percent) in motherless (father-headed, no resident mom) homes increased fourfold. About 57 percent of American women and 60 percent of American men were currently married in 2006, versus 60 and 65 percent, respectively, in 1970 (Fields 2004; Fields and Casper 2001; Statistical Abstract of the United States 2009). Recent census data also reveal that more American women are now living without a husband than with one. In 2005, 51 percent of women said they were living without a spouse, compared with 35 percent in 1950 and 49 percent in 2000 (Roberts et al. 2007).

To be sure, contemporary Americans maintain social lives through work, friendship, sports, clubs, religion, and organized social activities. But the growing isolation from kin that these figures suggest may well be unprecedented in human history.

Rise of Single-Parent Families in the United States, 1970–2004

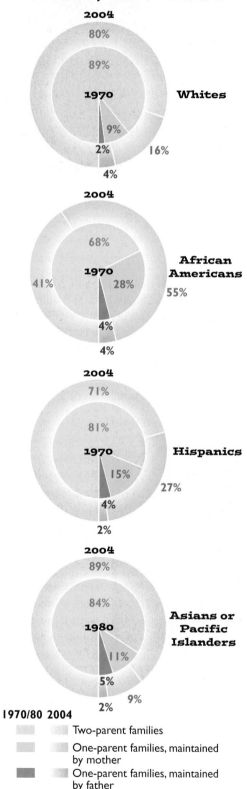

2004
80%
89%
1970
Whites
9%
2%
16%
4%

2004
68%
1970
African Americans
41%
28%
55%
4%
4%

2004
71%
81%
1970
Hispanics
15%
27%
4%
2%

2004
89%
84%
1980
Asians or Pacific Islanders
11%
5%
9%
2%

1970/80 2004
- Two-parent families
- One-parent families, maintained by mother
- One-parent families, maintained by father

Note: "Children" refers to children under 18. Early data for Asian Americans are for 1980. Hispanics can be of any race. Not included are unrelated people living together with no children present. All data exclude the 4 percent of children in nonparental households.

Source: Bureau of the Census 1994:63; Kreider 2008.

The "Households and Family Size" chart documents similar changes in family and household size in the United States and Canada between 1980 and 2007. Those figures confirm a general trend toward smaller families and living units in North America. This trend is also detectable in Western Europe and other industrial nations.

Immigrants often are shocked by what they perceive as weak kinship bonds and lack of proper respect for family in contemporary North America. In fact, most of the people whom middle-class North Americans see every day are either nonrelatives or members of the nuclear family. On the other hand, Stack's (1975) study of welfare-dependent families in a ghetto area of a midwestern city shows that regular sharing with nonnuclear relatives is an important strategy that the urban poor use to adapt to poverty.

THE FAMILY AMONG FORAGERS

Foraging societies are far removed from industrial nations in terms of social complexity, but they feature geographic mobility, which is associated with nomadic or seminomadic hunting and gathering. Here again, the nuclear family often is the most significant kin group, although in no foraging society is it the only group based on kinship. The two basic social units of traditional foraging societies are the nuclear family and the band.

Unlike middle-class couples in industrial nations, foragers don't usually reside neolocally. Instead, they join a band in which either the husband or the wife has relatives. However, couples and families may move from one band to another several times. Although nuclear families are ultimately as impermanent among foragers as they are in any other society, they usually are more stable than bands are.

Many foraging societies lacked year-round band organization. The Native American Shoshone of Utah and Nevada provide an example. The resources available to the Shoshone were so meager that for most of the year families traveled alone through the countryside hunting and gathering. In certain seasons families assembled to hunt cooperatively as a band, but after just a few months together they dispersed.

In neither industrial nor foraging economies are people permanently tied to the land. The mobility and the emphasis on small, economically self-sufficient family units promote the nuclear family as a basic kin group in both types of societies.

CULTURE THINK

Think of the nuclear family as an economic adaptation. What features do foragers and people living in industrial nations have in common that make the nuclear family practical? How is this different from nonindustrial food-producing societies?

Household and Family Size in the United States and Canada, 1980 vs. 2007

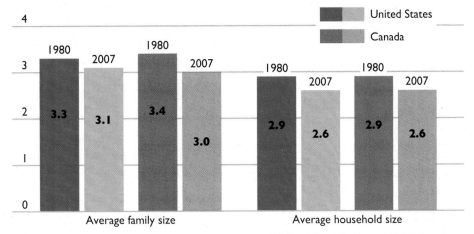

| | United States |
| | Canada |

4

1980 **3.3** — 2007 **3.1** | 1980 **3.4** — 2007 **3.0** — Average family size

1980 **2.9** — 2007 **2.6** | 1980 **2.9** — 2007 **2.6** — Average household size

Sources: J. M. Fields, "America's Families and Living Arrangements: 2003," *Current Population Reports,* P20–553. November 2004, http://www.census.gov/prod2004pubs/p20-553.pdf, pp. 3–4; U.S. Census Bureau, *Statistical Abstract of the United States,* 2009, Table 58, p. 52; *Statistics Canada,* 2006 Census, http://www12.statcan.ca/english/census06/data/topics/, http://www40.statcan.ca/101/cst01/famil532.

>> Descent

We've seen that the nuclear family is important in industrial nations and among foragers. The analogous group among nonindustrial food producers is the descent group. A **descent group** is a *permanent* social unit whose members claim common ancestry. Descent group members believe they all descend from those common ancestors. The group endures even though its membership changes, as members are born and die, move in and move out. Often, descent-group membership is determined at birth and is lifelong. In this case, it is an ascribed status.

CHARACTERISTICS OF DESCENT GROUPS

Descent groups frequently are exogamous (members seek their mates from other descent groups). Two common rules serve to admit certain people as descent-group members while excluding others. With a rule of **patrilineal descent,** people automatically have lifetime membership in their father's group. The children of the group's men join the group, but the children of the group's women are excluded. With **matrilineal descent,** people join the mother's group automatically at birth and stay members throughout life. Matrilineal descent groups therefore include only the children of the group's women.

Matrilineal and patrilineal descent are types of **unilineal descent.** This means the descent rule uses one line only, either the male or the female line. Patrilineal descent is much more common than matrilineal descent. In a sample of 564 societies (Murdock 1957), about three times as many were found to be patrilineal (247 to 84).

> **descent group** A permanent social unit whose members claim common ancestry; fundamental to tribal society.
>
> **patrilineal descent** Unilineal descent rule in which people join the father's group automatically at birth and stay members throughout life.
>
> **matrilineal descent** Unilineal descent rule in which people join the mother's group automatically at birth and stay members throughout life.
>
> **unilineal descent** Matrilineal or patrilineal descent.

A Patrilineage Five Generations Deep

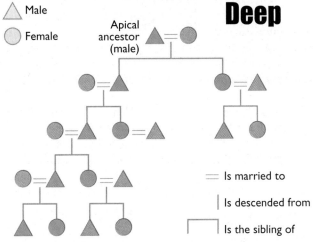

△ Male
○ Female

Apical ancestor (male)

═ Is married to

│ Is descended from

⊓ Is the sibling of

Lineages are based on demonstrated descent from an apical ancestor. With patrilineal descent, children of the group's men (blue) are included as descent-group members. Children of the group's women are excluded; they belong to their father's patrilineage.

A Matrilineage Five Generations Deep

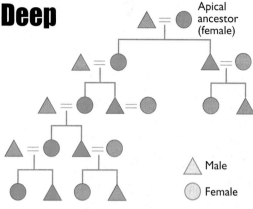

Apical ancestor (female)

△ Male

○ Female

Matrilineages are based on demonstrated descent from a female ancestor. Only the children of the group's women (blue) belong to the matrilineage. The children of the group's men are excluded; they belong to their mother's matrilineage.

Descent groups may be **lineages** or **clans.** Common to both is the belief that members descend from the same *apical ancestor,* the person who stands at the apex, or top, of the common genealogy. For example, Adam and Eve are the apical ancestors of the biblical Jews, and, according to the Bible, of all humanity. Since Eve is said to have come from Adam's rib, Adam stands as the original apical ancestor for the patrilineal genealogy laid out in the Bible.

lineage Unilineal descent group based on demonstrated descent.

clan Unilineal descent group based on stipulated descent.

patrilocality Customary residence with the husband's relatives after marriage, so that children grow up in their father's community.

matrilocality Customary residence with the wife's relatives after marriage, so that children grow up in their mother's community.

How do lineages and clans differ? A lineage uses *demonstrated descent.* Members recite the names of their forebears from the apical ancestor through the present. (This doesn't mean their recitations are accurate, only that lineage members think they are.) In the Bible the litany of men who "begat" other men is a demonstration of genealogical descent for a large patrilineage that ultimately includes Jews and Arabs (who share Abraham as their last common apical ancestor).

Unlike lineages, clans use *stipulated descent.* Clan members merely say they descend from the apical ancestor, without trying to trace the actual genealogical links. The Betsileo of Madagascar have both clans and lineages. Descent may be demonstrated for the most recent eight to ten generations, then stipulated for the more remote past—sometimes with mermaids and vaguely defined foreign royalty mentioned among the founders (Kottak 1980). Like the Betsileo, many societies have both lineages and clans. In such a case, clans have more members and cover a larger geographical area than lineages do. Sometimes a clan's apical ancestor is not a human at all but an animal or plant (called a *totem*).

The economic types that usually have descent group organization are horticulture, pastoralism, and agriculture. Such societies tend to have several descent groups. Any one of them may be confined to a single village, but usually they span more than one village. Two or more local branches of different descent groups may live in the same village. Descent groups in the same village or different villages may establish alliances through frequent intermarriage.

LINEAGES, CLANS, AND RESIDENCE RULES

As we've seen, descent groups, unlike families, are permanent and enduring units, with new members added in every generation. Members have access to the lineage estate, where some of them must live, in order to benefit from and manage that estate across the generations. An easy way to keep members at home is to have a rule about who belongs to the descent group and where they should live after they get married. Patrilineal and matrilineal descent, and the postmarital residence rules that usually accompany them, ensure that about half the people born in each generation will spend their lives on the ancestral estate.

Patrilocality is the rule that when a couple marries, it moves to the husband's community, so that their children will grow up in their father's village. Patrilocality is associated with patrilineal descent. This makes sense. If the group's male members are expected to exercise their rights in the ancestral estate, it's a good idea to raise them on that estate and to keep them there after they marry. This can be done by having wives move to the husband's village, rather than vice versa.

A less common postmarital residence rule, often associated with matrilineal descent, is **matrilocality:** Married couples live in the wife's community, and their children grow up in their mother's village. This rule keeps related women together. Together, patrilocality and matrilocality are known as *unilocal* rules of postmarital residence.

>> Marriage

"Love and marriage," "marriage and the family": These familiar phrases show how we link the romantic love of two individuals to marriage, and how we link marriage to reproduction and family creation. But marriage is an institution with significant roles and functions in addition to reproduction. What is marriage, anyway?

No definition of marriage is broad enough to apply easily to all societies and situations. A commonly quoted definition comes from *Notes and Queries on Anthropology:*

> Marriage is a union between a man and a woman such that the children born to the woman are recognized as legitimate offspring of both partners. (Royal Anthropological Institute 1951, p. 111)

This definition isn't valid universally for several reasons. In many societies, marriages unite more than two spouses. Here we speak of *plural marriages,* as when a man weds two (or more) women, or a woman weds a group of brothers—an arrangement called *fraternal polyandry* that is characteristic of certain Himalayan cultures. In the Brazilian community of Arembepe, people can choose among various forms of marital union. Most people live in long-term "common-law" domestic partnerships that are not legally sanctioned. Some have civil marriages, which are licensed and legalized by a justice of the peace. Still others go through religious ceremonies, so they are united in "holy matrimony," although not legally. And some have both civil and religious ties. The different forms of union permit someone to have multiple spouses (e.g., one common-law, one civil, one religious) without ever getting divorced.

Some societies recognize various kinds of same-sex marriages. In Sudan, a Nuer woman could marry a woman if her father had only daughters but no male heirs, who are necessary if his patrilineage is to survive. He might ask his daughter to stand as a son in order to take a bride. This daughter would become the socially recognized husband of another woman (the wife). This was a symbolic and social relationship rather than a sexual one. The "wife" had sex with a man or men (whom her female "husband" had to approve) until she got pregnant. The children born to the wife were accepted as the offspring of both the female husband and the wife. Although the female husband was not the actual *genitor* (the biological father) of the children, she was their *pater,* or socially recognized father. What's important in this Nuer case is *social* rather than *biological paternity.* We see again how kinship is socially constructed. The bride's children were considered the legitimate offspring of her female husband, who was biologically a woman but socially a man, and the descent line continued.

INCEST AND EXOGAMY

In nonindustrial societies, a person's social world includes two main categories—friends and strangers. Strangers are potential or actual enemies. Marriage is one of the primary ways of converting strangers into friends, of creating and maintaining personal and political alliances, relationships of affinity. **Exogamy,** the practice of seeking a mate outside one's own group, has adaptive value because it links people into a wider social network that nurtures, helps, and protects them in times of need.

exogamy Mating or marriage outside one's kin group; a cultural universal.

incest Sexual relations with a close relative.

Incest refers to sexual relations with a relative. All cultures have taboos against it. Although the taboo is a cultural universal, cultures define their kin, and thus incest, differently. When unilineal descent is very strongly developed, the parent who belongs to a different descent group than your own isn't considered a relative. Thus, with strict patrilineality, the mother is not a relative but a kind of in-law who has married a member of your own group—your father. With strict matrilineality, the father isn't a relative because he belongs to a different descent group.

The Lakher of Southeast Asia are strictly patrilineal (Leach 1961). Using the male ego (the reference point, the person in question) in the figure below, let's suppose that ego's father and mother get divorced. Each remarries and has a daughter by a second marriage. A Lakher always belongs to his or her father's group, all the members of which (one's *agnates,* or patrikin) are considered too closely related to marry because they are members of the same patrilineal descent group. Therefore, ego can't marry his father's daughter by the second marriage, just as in contemporary North America it's illegal for half-siblings to marry.

In contrast to our society, where all half-siblings are tabooed in marriage, the Lakher would permit ego to marry his mother's daughter by a different father. She is not ego's relative because she belongs to her own father's descent group rather than ego's. The Lakher illustrate very well that definitions of relatives, and therefore of incest, vary from culture to culture.

On February 15, 1946, in Tokyo, American sailor Charles D. Seabolt and his Japanese girlfriend Kaneko are photographed in a park. International marriages are a form of exogamy.

Patrilineal Descent-Group Identity and Incest among the Lakher

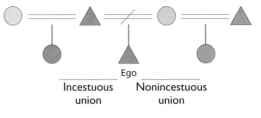

Ego

Incestuous union   Nonincestuous union

●, ▲ : Ego's patrilineage

●, ▲ : Ego's mother's second husband's patrilineage

● : Ego's mother's patrilineage

○ : Ego's father's second wife's patrilineage

⧣ : Separation or divorce.

FD : by second marriage is a comember of ego's descent group and is included within the incest taboo.

MD : by second marriage is not a comember of ego's descent group and is not tabooed.

Although Tabooed, Incest Does Happen There is no simple or universally accepted explanation for the fact that all cultures ban incest. Do primate studies offer any clues? Research with primates shows that adolescent males (among monkeys) or females (among apes) often move away from the group in which they were born (Rodseth et al. 1991). This emigration reduces the frequency of incestuous unions, but it doesn't eliminate them. DNA testing of wild chimps has confirmed incestuous unions between adult sons and their mothers, who reside in the same group. Human behavior with respect to mating with close relatives may express a generalized primate tendency, in which we see both urges and avoidance.

A cross-cultural study of eighty-seven societies (Meigs and Barlow 2002) revealed that incest occurred in several of them. For example, among the Yanomami, Chagnon reported that "incest, far from being feared, is widely practiced" (1967, p. 66). Meyer Fortes observed about the Ashanti: "In the old days it [incest] was punished by death. Nowadays the culprits are heavily fined" (Fortes 1950, p. 257). Among twenty-four Ojibwa individuals from whom he obtained information about incest, A. Irving Hallowell found eight cases of parent–child incest and ten cases of brother–sister incest (Hallowell 1955, pp. 294–295).

In ancient Egypt, sibling marriage apparently was allowed not just for royalty but for commoners as well, in at least some districts. Based on official census records from Roman Egypt (first to third centuries C.E.) preserved on papyrus, 24 percent of all documented marriages in the Arsinoites district were between brothers and sisters. In the second century C.E., the rates were 37 percent for the city of Arsinoe and 19 percent for the surrounding villages. These figures are much higher than any other documented levels of inbreeding among humans (Scheidel 1997).

> "An ounce of blood is worth more than a pound of friendship."
>
> Spanish proverb

CULTURE THINK

We tend to think of incest as wrong because of the potential for genetic defects due to inbreeding. Many states, however, consider it incestuous to have sexual relations with categories of relatives who are not biologically related, such as stepparents and siblings by adoption. Why are these considered wrong?

According to Anna Meigs and Kathleen Barlow (2002), for Western societies with nuclear family organization, father–daughter incest is most common with stepfathers, but it also happens with biological fathers, especially those who were absent or did little caretaking of their daughters in childhood (Williams and Finkelhor 1995). In a carefully designed study, Linda M. Williams and David Finkelhor (1995) found father–daughter incest to be least likely when there was substantial paternal parenting of daughters who were four to five years old. This experience enhanced the father's parenting skills and his feelings of nurturance, protectiveness, and identification with his daughter, thus reducing the risk of incest.

It has been argued (Hobhouse 1915; Lowie 1920/1961) that the incest taboo is universal because incest horror is instinctive: Humans have a genetically programmed disgust toward incest. Because of this feeling, early humans banned it. However, cultural universality doesn't necessarily entail an instinctual basis. Fire making, for example, is a cultural universal, but it certainly isn't an ability transmitted by the genes. Furthermore, if people really did have an instinctive horror of mating with blood relatives, a formal incest taboo would be unnecessary. No one would do it. As we have just seen, and as social workers, judges, psychiatrists, and psychologists know, incest is more common than we might suppose.

ENDOGAMY

The practice of exogamy pushes social organization outward, establishing and preserving alliances among groups. In contrast, rules of **endogamy** dictate mating or marriage within a group to which one belongs. Endogamic rules are less common but are still familiar to anthropologists. Indeed, most cultures *are* endogamous units, although they usually do not need a formal rule requiring people to marry someone from their own society. In our own society, classes and ethnic groups are quasi-endogamous groups. Members of an ethnic or religious group often want

> **endogamy** Marriage between people of the same social group.

their children to marry within that group, although many of them do not do so. The outmarriage rate varies among such groups, with some more committed to endogamy than others.

Caste An extreme example of endogamy is India's caste system, which was formally abolished in 1949, although its structure and effects linger. Castes are stratified groups in which membership is ascribed at birth and is lifelong. Indian castes are grouped into five major categories, or *varna*. Each is ranked relative to the other four, and these categories extend throughout India. Each varna includes a large number of castes (*jati*), each of which includes people within a region who may intermarry. All the jati in a single varna in a given region are ranked, just as the varna themselves are ranked.

Occupational specialization often sets off one caste from another. A community may include castes of agricultural workers, merchants, artisans, priests, and sweepers. The untouchable varna, found throughout India, includes castes whose ancestry, ritual status, and occupations are considered so impure that higher-caste people hold even casual contact with untouchables to be defiling.

The belief that intercaste sexual unions lead to ritual impurity for the higher-caste partner has been important in maintaining endogamy. A man who has sex with a lower-caste woman can restore his purity with a bath and a prayer. A woman who has intercourse with a man of a lower caste has no such recourse. Her defilement cannot be undone. Because the women have the babies, these differences protect the purity of the caste line, ensuring the pure ancestry of high-caste children. Although Indian castes are endogamous groups, many of them are internally subdivided into exogamous lineages. Traditionally this meant that Indians had to marry a member of another descent group from the same caste. This shows that rules of exogamy and endogamy can coexist in the same society.

Couple getting married in San Francisco after a state supreme court ruling to allow same-sex marriage and before Proposition 8, a state constitutional amendment, banned the practice, and before Proposition 8 was voided by an Appeals Court judge in 2010.

>> Marital Rights and Same-Sex Marriage

The British anthropologist Edmund Leach (1955) observed that, depending on the society, several kinds of rights are allocated by marriage. According to Leach, marriage can, but doesn't always, accomplish the following:

- Establish the legal father of a woman's children and the legal mother of a man's.
- Give either or both spouses a monopoly in the sexuality of the other.
- Give either or both spouses rights to the labor of the other.
- Give either or both spouses rights over the other's property.
- Establish a joint fund of property—a partnership—for the benefit of the children.
- Establish a socially significant "relationship of affinity" between spouses and their relatives.

The discussion of same-sex marriage that follows will serve to illustrate the six rights just listed by seeing what happens in their absence (see also Stone 2004). What if same-sex marriages, which by and large remain illegal in the United States, were legal? Could a same-sex marriage establish legal parentage of children born to one or both partners after the partnership is formed? In the case of a different-sex marriage, children born to the wife after the marriage takes place usually are defined legally as her husband's regardless of whether he is the genitor.

Nowadays, DNA testing makes it possible to establish paternity, just as modern reproductive technology makes it possible for a lesbian couple to have one or both partners artificially inseminated (see Levine 2008). When same-sex marriage is legal, the social construction of kinship easily can make both partners parents. If a Nuer woman married to a woman can be the pater of a child she did not father, why can't two lesbians be the *maters* (socially recognized mothers) of a child one of them did not father? And if a married different-sex couple can adopt a child and have it be theirs through the social and legal construction of kinship, the same logic could be applied to a gay male or lesbian couple.

Continuing with Leach's list of the rights transmitted by marriage, same-sex marriage certainly could give each spouse rights to the sexuality of the other. Same-sex marriages, as forms of monogamous commitment, have been endorsed by representatives of many religions, including Unitarians, Quakers (the Society of Friends), and re-form Jewish synagogues (Eskridge 1996). In June 2003 a court ruling established same-sex marriages as legal in the province of Ontario, Canada. On June 28, 2005, Canada's House of Commons voted to guarantee full marriage rights to same-sex couples throughout that nation. In the United States six states—Massachusetts, Connecticut, Iowa, Vermont, Maine, and New Hampshire—allowed same-sex marriage as of 2009 (see "Same-Sex Marriage Laws"). California rejoined that list in 2010. Civil unions for same-sex couples are legal in New Jersey. In reaction to same-sex marriage, voters in at least eighteen U.S. states have approved measures in their state constitutions defining marriage as an exclusively heterosexual union. On November 4, 2008, Californians voted 52 percent to 48 percent for Proposition 8, overturning the right to same-sex marriage, which the courts had approved earlier that year. An appeals court judge ruled Proposition 8 unconstitutional in 2010 and allowed same-sex marriages in California to resume.

Legal same-sex marriages can easily give each spouse rights to the other spouse's labor and its products. Some societies allow marriage between members of the same biological sex. Several Native American groups had figures known as *berdaches*. These were biological men who assumed many of the manner-

> "Of all the peoples whom I have studied, from city dwellers to cliff dwellers, I always find that at least 50 percent would prefer to have at least one jungle between themselves and their mothers-in-law."
>
> Margaret Mead

isms, behavior patterns, and tasks of women. Sometimes berdaches married men, who shared the products of their labor from hunting and traditional male roles, as the berdache fulfilled the traditional wifely role. Also, in some Native American cultures, a marriage of a "manly-hearted woman" to another woman brought the traditional male–female division of labor to their household. The manly woman hunted and did other male tasks, while the wife played the traditional female role.

There's no logical reason why same-sex marriage cannot give spouses rights over the other's property. But in the United States, the same inheritance rights that apply to male–female couples usually do not apply to same-sex couples. For instance, even in the absence of a will, property can pass to a widow or a widower without going through probate. The wife or husband pays no inheritance tax. This benefit is not available to gay men and lesbians. When a same-sex partner is in a nursing home, prison, or hospital, the other partner may not have the same visiting rights as would a husband, wife, or biological relative (Weston 1991).

What about Leach's fifth right—to establish a joint fund of property—to benefit the children? Here again, gay and lesbian couples are at a disadvantage. If there are children, property is separately, rather than jointly, transmitted. Some organizations do make staff benefits, such as health and dental insurance, available to same-sex domestic partners.

Finally, there is the matter of establishing a socially significant "relationship of affinity" between spouses and their relatives. In many societies, one of the main roles of marriage is to establish an alliance between groups, in addition to the individual bond. *Affinals* are relatives through

CULTURETHINK

Imagine you are an anthropologist on an expert panel debating same-sex marriage. Would you argue for or against it? For what reasons? (Make reference to material in the text.)

marriage, such as a brother-in-law or mother-in-law. For same-sex couples in contemporary North America, affinal relations are problematic. In an unofficial union, terms like "daughter-in-law" and "mother-in-law" may sound strange. Many parents are suspicious of their children's sexuality and lifestyle choices and may not recognize a relationship of affinity with a child's partner of the same sex.

This discussion of same-sex marriage is intended to illustrate the different kinds of rights that typically accompany marriage, by seeing what may happen when there is a permanent pair bond without legal sanction. In just six of the United States are such unions fully legal. As we have seen, same-sex unions have been recognized in different historical and cultural settings. In certain African cultures, including the Igbo of Nigeria and the Lovedu of South Africa, women could marry other women. In situations in which women, such as prominent market women in West Africa, are able to amass property and other forms of wealth, they may take a wife. Such marriage allows the prominent woman to strengthen her social status and the economic importance of her household (Amadiume 1987).

bridewealth A customary gift before, at, or after marriage from the husband and his kin to the wife and her kin.

progeny price A gift from the husband and his kin to the wife and her kin before, at, or after marriage; legitimizes children born to the woman as members of the husband's descent group.

dowry A marital exchange in which the wife's group provides substantial gifts to the husband's family.

>> Marriage across Cultures

Outside industrial societies, marriage often is more a relationship between groups than one between individuals. We think of marriage as an individual matter. Although the bride and groom usually seek their parents' approval, the final choice (to live together, to marry, to divorce) lies with the couple. The idea of romantic love symbolizes this individual relationship.

In nonindustrial societies, although there can be romantic love (Goleman 1992), marriage is a group concern. People don't just take a spouse; they assume obligations to a group of in-laws. When residence is patrilocal, for example, a woman must leave the community where she was born. She faces the prospect of spending the rest of her life in her husband's village, with his relatives. She may even have to transfer her major allegiance from her own group to her husband's.

BRIDEWEALTH AND DOWRY

In societies with descent groups, people enter marriage not alone but with the help of the descent group. Descent-group members often contribute to the **bridewealth,** a customary gift before, at, or after the marriage from the husband and his kin to the wife and her kin. Another word for bridewealth is *brideprice,* but this term is inaccurate because people with the custom don't usually think of marriage as a commercial relationship between a man and an object to be bought and sold.

Bridewealth compensates the bride's group for the loss of her companionship and labor. More important, it makes the children born to the woman full members of her husband's descent group. For this reason, the institution also is called **progeny price.** Rather than the woman herself, it is her children who are permanently transferred to the husband's group. Whatever we call it, such a transfer of wealth at marriage is common in patrilineal groups. In matrilineal societies, children are members of the mother's group, and there is no reason to pay a progeny price.

Dowry is a marital exchange in which the wife's group provides substantial gifts to the husband's family. Dowry, best known from India but also practiced in Europe, correlates with low female status. Women are perceived as burdens. When husbands and their families take a wife, they expect to be compensated for the added responsibility.

Bridewealth exists in many more cultures than dowry does, but the nature and quantity of transferred items differ. In many African societies, cattle constitute bridewealth, but the number of cattle given varies from society to society. As the value of bridewealth increases, marriages become more stable. Bridewealth is insurance against divorce.

Imagine a patrilineal society in which a marriage requires the transfer of about twenty-five cattle from the groom's descent group to the bride's. Michael, a member of descent group A, marries Sarah from group B. His relatives help him assemble the bridewealth. He gets the most help from his close agnates—his older brother, father, father's brother, and closest patrilineal cousins.

The distribution of the cattle once they reach Sarah's group mirrors the manner in which they were assembled. Sarah's father, or her oldest brother if the father is dead, receives her bridewealth. He keeps most of the cattle to use as bridewealth for his sons' marriages. How-

Anthropology Works

Counselors or clinical psychologists would find it helpful to know about cross-cultural patterns of marriage and divorce to better understand the pressures their clients face.

ever, a share also goes to everyone who will be expected to help when Sarah's brothers marry.

When Sarah's brother David gets married, many of the cattle go to a third group—C, which is David's wife's group. Thereafter, they may serve as bridewealth to still other groups. Men constantly use their sisters' bridewealth cattle to acquire their own wives. In a decade, the cattle given when Michael married Sarah will have been exchanged widely.

In such societies marriage entails an agreement between descent groups. If Sarah and Michael try to make their marriage succeed but fail to do so, both groups may conclude that the marriage can't last. Here it becomes especially obvious that marriages are relationships between groups as well as between individuals. If Sarah has a younger sister or niece (her older brother's daughter, for example), the concerned parties may agree to Sarah's replacement by a kinswoman.

However, incompatibility isn't the main problem that threatens marriage in societies with bridewealth. Infertility is a more important concern. If Sarah has no children, she and her group have not fulfilled their part of the marriage agreement. If the relationship is to endure, Sarah's group must furnish another woman, perhaps her younger sister, who can have children. If this happens, Sarah may choose to stay in her husband's village. Perhaps she will someday have a child. If she does stay on, her husband will have established a plural marriage.

Most nonindustrial food-producing societies, unlike most industrial nations, allow **plural marriages,** or *polygamy.* There are two varieties; one is common and the other is very rare. The more common variant is **polygyny,** in which a man has more than one wife. The rare variant is **polyandry,** in which a woman has more than one husband. If the infertile wife remains married to her husband after he has taken a substitute wife provided by her descent group, this is polygyny.

DURABLE ALLIANCES

It is possible to exemplify the group-alliance nature of marriage by examining still another common practice—continuation of marital alliances when one spouse dies.

Sororate What happens if Sarah dies young? Michael's group will ask Sarah's group for a substitute, often her sister. This custom is known as the **sororate.** If Sarah has no sister, or if all her sisters already are married, another woman from her group may be available. Michael marries her, there is no need to return the bridewealth, and the alliance continues.

The sororate exists in both matrilineal and patrilineal societies. In a matrilineal society with matrilocal postmarital residence, a widower may remain with his wife's group by marrying her sister or another female member of her matrilineage.

Levirate What happens if the husband dies? In many

societies, the widow may marry his brother. This custom is known as the **levirate.** Like the sororate, it is a continuation marriage that maintains the alliance between descent groups, in this case by replacing the husband with another member of his group. The implications of the levirate vary with age. One study found that in African societies the levirate, although widely permitted, rarely involves cohabitation of the widow and her new husband. Furthermore, widows don't automatically marry the husband's brother just because they are allowed to. Often they prefer to make other arrangements (Potash 1986).

>> Divorce

In some societies marriages may seem to go on forever, but in our own they are fairly brittle. Ease of divorce varies across cultures. What factors work for and against divorce? As we've seen, marriages that are political alliances between groups are more difficult to dissolve than are marriages that are more individual affairs, of concern mainly to the married couple and their children. Substantial bridewealth may decrease the divorce rate for individuals; replacement marriages (levirate and sororate)

> **plural marriage** Marriage of a man to two or more women (polygyny) or marriage of a woman to two or more men (polyandry)—at the same time.
>
> **sororate** Custom by which a widower marries the sister of the deceased wife.
>
> **levirate** Custom by which a widow marries the brother of her deceased husband.

CULTURETHINK

Consider how each of the following illustrates the importance of marriage as an alliance between groups: arranged marriage, bridewealth, sororate and levirate.

Examples of the sororate and levirate

Sororate

Levirate

● : Sarah's descent group

▲ : Michael's descent group

Did You Know

One sociologist has found what he calls a "divorce divide": People with college degrees are less likely to get a divorce than those without degrees. The divorce rate among college graduates actually decreased between the 1970s and the 1990s.

---

also work to preserve group alliances. Divorce tends to be more common in matrilineal than in patrilineal societies. When residence is matrilocal (in the wife's home village), the wife may simply send off a man with whom she's incompatible.

Among the Hopi of the American Southwest, houses were owned by matrilineal clans, with matrilocal postmarital residence. The household head was the senior woman of that household, which also included her daughters and their husbands and children. A son-in-law had no important role there; he returned to his own mother's home for his clan's social and religious activities. In this matrilineal society, women were socially and economically secure, and the divorce rate was high. Consider the Hopi of Oraibi (Orayvi) pueblo, northeastern Arizona (Levy 1992; Titiev 1992). In a study of the marital histories of 423 Oraibi women, Mischa Titiev found 35 percent to have been divorced at least once. Jerome Levy found that 31 percent of 147 adult women had been divorced and remarried at least once. For comparison, of all ever-married women in the United States, only 4 percent had been divorced in 1960, 10.7 percent in 1980, and 11.5 percent in 2004. Titiev characterizes Hopi marriages as unstable. Part of this brittleness was due to conflicting loyal-

ties to matrikin versus spouse. Most Hopi divorces appear to have been matters of personal choice. Levy generalizes that, cross-culturally, high divorce rates are correlated with a secure female economic position. In Hopi society women were secure in their home and land ownership and in the custody of their children. In addition, there were no formal barriers to divorce.

Divorce is harder in a patrilineal society, especially when substantial bridewealth would have to be reassembled and repaid if the marriage failed. A woman residing patrilocally (in her husband's household and community) might be reluctant to leave him. Unlike the Hopi, where the kids stay with the mother, in patrilineal, patrilocal societies the children of divorce would be expected to remain with their father, as members of his patrilineage. From the women's perspective this is a strong impediment to divorce.

Among foragers, different factors favor or oppose divorce. What factors work against durable marriages? Since foragers tend to lack descent groups, the political alliance functions of marriage are less important to them than they are to food producers. Foragers also tend to have minimal material possessions. The process of dissolving a joint fund of property is less complicated when spouses do not hold substantial resources in common. What factors work in opposition to divorce among foragers? In societies in which

the family is an important year-round unit with a gender-based division of labor, ties between spouses tend to be durable. Also, sparse populations mean few alternative spouses if a marriage doesn't work out.

In contemporary Western societies, we have the idea that romantic love is necessary for a good marriage (see Ingraham 2008). When romance fails, so may the marriage (see "Trends in Marriage and Divorce in the United States"). Or it may not fail, if the other rights associated with marriage, as discussed previously in this chapter, are compelling. Economic ties and obligations to children, along with other factors, such as concern about public opinion, or simple inertia, may keep marriages intact after sex, romance, or companionship fade.

STUDY TIP

Divorce is less common (1) when marriage involves political alliances; (2) where there is brideprice; (3) in patrilineal societies; (4) when women have a low economic position.

Trends in Marriage and Divorce in the United States, 1920–2008

Rate per 1,000 total population

Marriage

Divorce

16 14 12 10 8 6 4 2 0

1920 1930 1940 1950 1960 1970 1980 1990 2000 2008

>> Plural Marriages

In contemporary North America, where divorce is fairly easy and common, **polygamy** (marriage to more than one spouse at the same time) is against the law. Marriage in industrial nations joins individuals, and relationships between individuals can be severed more easily than can those between groups. North Americans are allowed to practice *serial monogamy:* Individuals may have more than one spouse but never, legally, more than one at the same time. As stated earlier, the two forms of polygamy are polygyny and polyandry. Polyandry is practiced in only a few societies, notably among certain groups in Tibet, Nepal, and India. Polygyny is much more common.

Shown here in Mali is an Islamic marabout (religious teacher) with his two wives and children. Would you expect most marriages to be polygynous in a society that allows polygyny?

POLYGYNY

We must distinguish between the social approval of plural marriage and its actual frequency in a particular society. Many cultures approve of a man's having more than one wife. But even when polygyny is encouraged, most people are monogamous, and polygyny characterizes only a fraction of the marriages. Why?

One reason is equal sex ratios. In the United States, about 105 males are born for every 100 females. In adulthood the ratio of men to women equalizes, and eventually it reverses. The average North American woman outlives the average man. In many nonindustrial societies as well, the male-biased sex ratio among children reverses in adulthood.

The custom of men marrying later than women also promotes polygyny. Among Nigeria's Kanuri people (Cohen 1967), men got married between the ages of eighteen and thirty; women, between twelve and fourteen. The age difference between spouses meant there were more widows than widowers. Most of the widows remarried, some in polygynous unions. Among the Kanuri and in other polygynous societies, such as the Tiwi of northern Australia, widows made up a large number of the women involved in plural marriages (Hart, Pilling, and Goodale 1988).

In certain societies, the first wife requests a second wife to help with household chores. The second wife's status is lower than that of the first; they are senior and junior wives. The senior wife sometimes chooses the junior one from among her close kinswomen. Among the Betsileo of Madagascar, the different wives always lived in different villages. A man's first and senior wife, called "Big Wife," lived in the village where he cultivated his best rice field and spent most of his time. High-status men with several rice fields and multiple wives had households near each field. They spent most of their time with the senior wife but visited the others throughout the year.

Plural wives can play important political roles in nonindustrial states. The king of the Merina, a populous society in the highlands of Madagascar, had palaces for each of his twelve wives in different provinces. He stayed with them when he traveled through the kingdom. They were his local agents, overseeing and reporting on provincial matters. The king of Buganda, the major precolonial state of Uganda, took hundreds of wives, representing all the clans in his nation. Everyone in the kingdom became the king's in-law, and all the clans had a chance to provide the next ruler. This was a way of giving the common people a stake in the government.

> **polygamy** Marriage with three or more spouses, at the same time.

These examples show there is no single explanation for polygyny. Its context and function vary from society to society and even within the same society. Some men are

get involved!

Explore your family's history like an anthropologist. Search on one of the free genealogy websites, such as familysearch.org or the family history or public archives sites of a particular state or country. On either (or both) your mother's or your father's side, look for changes across generations: Who got married to whom (from which towns, of which nationalities) and at what ages? Where did the couple reside relative to their parents? Were there divorces? Obtaining this information online may be difficult, but look at any kinship data you do uncover with an eye for investigating social change. If you can't trace your own family history online, choose some well-known person and investigate his or her family history.

polygynous because they have inherited a widow from a brother. Others have plural wives because they seek prestige or want to increase household productivity. Men and women with political and economic ambitions cultivate marital alliances that serve their aims. In many societies, including the Betsileo of Madagascar and the Igbo of Nigeria, women arrange the marriages.

POLYANDRY

Most of the world's polyandrous peoples live in South Asia—Tibet, Nepal, India, and Sri Lanka. Polyandry is rare and practiced under very specific conditions. In some of these areas, polyandry seems to be a cultural adaptation to mobility associated with customary male travel for trade, commerce, and military operations. Polyandry ensures there will be at least one man at home to accomplish male activities within a gender-based division of labor. Fraternal polyandry is also an effective strategy when resources are scarce. Brothers with limited resources (in land) pool their resources in expanded (polyandrous) households. They take just one wife. Polyandry restricts the number of wives and heirs. Less competition among heirs means that land can be transmitted with minimal fragmentation.

For REVIEW

CULTURECLIPS

TO ACCESS THESE VIDEOS ON YOUR COMPUTER, VISIT

www.mhhe.com/gezonqr

8-1

8-2

8-3

I. What forms of kinship exist cross-culturally, and what are their social correlates?

- The nuclear family consists of a married couple and their children. It assumes importance in societies with geographic mobility, which promotes small, economically self-sufficient family units. In industrial societies, a couple typically starts its own nuclear family in a new home. The forager family usually joins a band in which either the husband or the wife has relatives. Extended families include three or more generations. Extended family households occur more frequently where kinspeople need to pool resources. The descent group is a basic kin group among nonindustrial food producers. This perpetual kin group manages an estate across generations.

II. How do families and descent groups differ?

- The descent group is a larger system of kinship and marriage than the family. It is important in nonindustrial food-producing societies. The descent group endures even though its membership changes. Descent group members are admitted into their group based on whether they belong to the father's (patrilineal) or the mother's (matrilineal) side. Descent groups take the form of a lineage or a clan. Members of lineages trace genealogical links, while clan members merely say they descend from the same ancestor. The rule of descent and postmarital residence ensure that at least some members spend their lives on the descent group's estate.

III. How is marriage defined and regulated, and what rights does it convey?

- Worldwide, marriage has various forms, roles, and functions. In many societies, marriage unites more than two spouses: A man may wed two or more women; a woman may wed a group of brothers. Some societies also recognize same-sex marriage. Generally, marriage establishes the legal parents of children, gives spouses the rights to the sexuality, labor, and property of the other, and establishes a socially significant "relationship of affinity." In societies with descent groups, the transfer of wealth from the groom and his kin to the bride and her kin creates and maintains group alliances. Marital alliances can continue when a man marries the sister of his deceased wife or a woman marries the brother of her deceased husband.

Pop Quiz

1. Which of the following explains the reasons for the primacy of the nuclear family in modern North America?
   a. The nuclear family is prefered by North Americans of all ethnicities and social classes.
   b. Geographic mobility separates North Americans from their extended families.
   c. Households tend to be smaller among the urban poor.
   d. The North American family life has evolved parallel with families worldwide, where the nuclear family has become the most developed form of domestic arrangement.

2. Which of the following is *not* true about the nuclear family?
   a. It is universally present in human societies.
   b. Functions associated with nuclear families may be assumed by other social units.
   c. Nuclear families have no special adaptive advantage in conditions associated with poverty.
   d. The geographic mobility of foraging societies encourages the development of the nuclear family.

3. A lineage is distinguished from a clan by this particular characteristic:
   a. The lineage uses stipulated descent.
   b. The lineage believes all its members descend from the same apical ancestor.
   c. Lineage members can name their forebears from the apical ancestor through the present.
   d. Lineages establish alliances with other descent groups.

4. The following is generally true about incest:
   a. All cultures define incest in more or less the same way.
   b. Human behavior with respect to mating with close relatives may express a generalized primate tendency, including both urges and avoidance.
   c. The horror of incest is instinctive.
   d. Incestuous behavior is extremely rare.

5. The rule of endogamy in India's caste system is an extreme example of that practice. All of the following are true of endogamy in India *except:*
   a. The untouchable *varna* is considered so impure by higher-caste people that even casual contact with untouchables is believed to be defiling.
   b. Although the caste system was formally abolished in 1949, its endogamous practices continue to affect Indian society.
   c. Castes are never subdivided into exogamous lineages.

   d. A woman cannot undo the attribution of defilement she suffers by having sexual intercourse with a man of a lower caste.

6. In societies where same-sex marriage is legal, Edmund Leach's rules about the allocation of rights by marriage apply in all of the following ways, *except:*
   a. Both marital partners can be made parents.
   b. Spouses each have rights to the sexuality of the other.
   c. Native American societies that allowed legal same-sex marriages gave each spouse rights to the other spouse's labor and its products.
   d. In contemporary North American society, parents typically recognize affinity, or relation through marriage, with a child's partner of the same sex.

7. The practice by which the husband's group makes a substantial gift to the wife and her kin is called:
   a. Dowry
   b. Bridewealth
   c. Polygyny
   d. Levirate

8. Which of the following statements about divorce is false?
   a. Divorce is less common in matrilineal societies than in patrilineal societies.
   b. Marriage is harder to dissolve when it creates political alliances.
   c. Divorce is rarer in societies in which the husband and his kin group provide substantial bridewealth.
   d. The Western idea of romantic love is not necessarily a strong cement between spouses.

9. Polygamy includes all of these cases *except:*
   a. A man who has three unrelated wives.
   b. A woman who has three husbands, all of whom are brothers.
   c. A man who marries, then divorces, then marries again, then divorces again.
   d. A man who has three related wives.

10. Which of the following statements about marriage is true?
    a. Marriage must involve at least one biological male and at least one biological female.
    b. Marriage involves a woman and the genitor of her children.
    c. Outside industrial societies, marriage is often more a relationship between groups than one between individuals.
    d. Rings must be exchanged.

1. (b), 2. (a), 3. (c), 4. (b), 5. (c), 6. (d), 7. (b), 8. (a), 9. (c), 10. (c)

9

GENDER

UNDERSTANDING OURSELVES

Did you have chores when you were growing up? Was there any gender bias in what you were asked to do compared with your siblings? If you were raised by two parents, did any tension arise over their division of labor? Based on cross-cultural data from societies worldwide, a table in this chapter lists activities that are generally male, generally female, or swing (either male or female). Before you look at that table, see if you can assign the following to one gender or the other (M or F):

hunting large animals ____   cooking ____
gathering wild vegetable foods ____   fetching water ____
tending crops ____   making baskets ____
fishing ____   making drinks ____

Now consult Table 9.1 on page 166 and see how you did. Reflect on your results.

Ideas about gender have changed along with the employment patterns of men and women. Still, the lingering American expectation that proper female behavior should be polite, restrained, and/or meek poses a challenge for women, because American culture also values decisiveness. A man's assertiveness may be admired, but a woman's similar behavior may be labeled "aggressive"—or worse.

Both men and women are constrained by their cultural training. For example, American culture stigmatizes male crying. Becoming a man typically means stifling this natural expression of joy and sadness. American men also are trained to make decisions and stick to them. Our stereotypes associate changing one's mind more with women than with men. What a strange idea—that people shouldn't change their positions if they find a better way. Males, females, and humanity may be equally victimized by aspects of cultural training.

As You READ

- How are biology and culture expressed in human sex/gender systems?
- How do gender, gender roles, and gender stratification correlate with other social, economic, and political variables?
- What is sexual orientation, and how do sexual practices vary cross-culturally?

>> Nature and Nurture

Because anthropologists study biology, society, and culture, they are in a unique position to comment on nature (biological predispositions) and nurture (environment) as determinants of human behavior. Human attitudes, values, and behavior are limited not only by our genetic predispositions—which often are difficult to identify—but also by our experiences during enculturation. Our attributes as adults are determined both by our genes and by our environment during growth and development.

Questions about nature and nurture emerge in the discussion of human sex/gender roles and sexuality. Men and women differ genetically. Women have two X chromosomes, and men have an X and a Y. The father determines a baby's sex because only he has the Y chromosome to transmit. The mother always provides an X chromosome.

The chromosomal difference is expressed in hormonal and physiological contrasts. Humans are sexually dimorphic, more so than some primates, such as gibbons (small tree-living Asiatic apes) and less so than others, such as gorillas and orangutans. **Sexual dimorphism** refers to differences in male and female biology besides the contrasts in breasts and genitals. Women and men differ not just in primary (genitalia and reproductive organs) and secondary (breasts, voice, hair distribution) sexual characteristics, but in average weight, height, strength, and longevity. Women tend to live longer than men and have excellent endurance capabilities. In a given population, men tend to be taller

sexual dimorphism Marked differences, such as in height and weight, in male and female biology besides the contrasts in breasts and genitals.

gender roles The tasks and activities that a culture assigns to each sex.

gender stereotypes Oversimplified but strongly held ideas about the characteristics of males and females.

and to weigh more than women do. Of course, there is a considerable overlap between the sexes in terms of height, weight, and physical strength, and there has been a pronounced reduction in sexual dimorphism during human biological evolution.

Just how far, however, do such genetically and physiologically determined differences go? What effects do they have on the way men and women act and are treated in different societies? Anthropologists have discovered both similarities and differences in the roles of men and women in different cultures. The predominant anthropological position on sex–gender roles and biology may be stated as follows:

> The biological nature of men and women [should be seen] not as a narrow enclosure limiting the human organism, but rather as a broad base upon which a variety of structures can be built. (Friedl 1975, p. 6)

Although in most societies men tend to be somewhat more aggressive than women are, many behavioral and attitudinal differences between the sexes emerge from culture rather than biology. Sex differences are biological, but gender encompasses all the traits that a culture assigns to and inculcates in males and females. *Gender,* in other words, refers to the cultural construction of whether one is female, male, or something else.

STUDY TIP

Sex refers to biological differences, and *gender* to cultural constructions of sex differences. There may be more than two recognized genders in a given society.

Given the "rich and various constructions of gender within the realm of cultural diversity," Susan Bourque and Kay Warren (1987) note that the same images of masculinity and femininity do not always apply. Anthropologists have gathered systematic ethnographic data about similarities and differences involving gender in many cultural settings (Bonvillain 2008; Brettell and Sargent 2005; Gilmore 2001; Kimmel 2007; Mascia-Lees and Black 2000; Nanda 2000; Ward and Edelstein 2008). Anthropologists can detect recurrent themes and patterns involving gender differences. They also can observe that gender roles vary with environment, economy, adaptive strategy, and type of political system. Before we examine the cross-cultural data, some definitions are in order.

Gender roles are the tasks and activities a culture assigns to the sexes. Related to gender roles are **gender stereotypes,** which are oversimplified but strongly held ideas about the characteristics of males and females. **Gender stratification** describes an unequal distribution of rewards (socially valued resources, power, prestige, human rights, and personal freedom) between men and women, reflecting their different positions in a social hierarchy. According to Ann Stoler (1977), the economic determinants of gender status include freedom or autonomy (in disposing of one's labor and

In an episode of *The Simpsons* titled "Lisa vs. Malibu Stacy," eight-year-old Lisa is outraged when her talking doll (Stacy) says things like, "Let's buy makeup so boys will like us." The doll's statement, and Lisa's reaction to it, expose American cultural values reflecting consumerism, gender roles, and gender stereotypes. Watch a few episodes of *The Simpsons, South Park,* or *Family Guy.* What can we learn about gender roles and stereotypes (and about culture and society more generally) by analyzing such popular culture products?

CULTURE THINK

Advertisements communicate gender stereotypes. Focusing on different kinds of products (e.g., cars, cleaning products, clothing, beer), analyze three to five TV ads for the messages they send about what it means to be a man or a woman.

their knowledge, adventures, and feelings in public oratory. They received acclaim as a result. Ilongot women had inferior prestige because they lacked external experiences on which to base knowledge and dramatic expression. On the basis of Rosaldo's study and findings in other stateless societies, Ong (1989) argues that we must distinguish between prestige systems and actual power in a given society. High male prestige may not entail economic or political power held by men over their families.

> **gender stratification** Unequal distribution of rewards (socially valued resources, power, prestige, and personal freedom) between men and women, reflecting their different positions in a social hierarchy.

its fruits) and social power (control over the lives, labor, and produce of others).

In stateless societies, gender stratification often is more obvious in regard to prestige than it is in regard to wealth. In her study of the Ilongots of northern Luzon in the Philippines, Michelle Rosaldo (1980a) described gender differences related to the positive cultural value placed on adventure, travel, and knowledge of the external world. More often than women, Ilongot men, as headhunters, visited distant places. They acquired knowledge of the external world, amassed experiences there, and returned to express

>> Recurrent Gender Patterns

Ethnologists compare ethnographic data from several cultures (i.e., cross-cultural data) to discover and explain differences and similarities. Data relevant to the cross-cultural study of gender can be drawn from the domains of economics, politics, domestic activity, kinship, and marriage. Table 9.1 shows cross-cultural data from 185 randomly selected societies on the division of labor by gender.

Remembering the discussion of universals, generalities, and particularities in the chapter "Culture," the findings in

TABLE 9.1 Generalities in the Division of Labor by Gender, Based on Data from 185 Societies

Generally Male Activities	Swing (Male or Female) Activities	Generally Female Activities
Hunting of large aquatic animals (e.g., whales, walrus)	Making fire	Gathering fuel (e.g., firewood)
Smelting of ores	Body mutilation	Making drinks
Metalworking	Preparing skins	Gathering wild vegetal foods
Lumbering	Gathering small land animals	Dairy production (e.g., churning)
Hunting large land animals	Planting crops	Spinning
Working wood	Making leather products	Doing the laundry
Hunting fowl	Harvesting	Fetching water
Making musical instruments	Tending crops	Cooking
Trapping	Milking	Preparing vegetal foods (e.g., processing cereal grains)
Building boats	Making baskets	
Working stone	Carrying burdens	
Working bone, horn, and shell	Making mats	
Mining and quarrying	Caring for small animals	
Setting bones	Preserving meat and fish	
Butchering*	Loom weaving	
Collecting wild honey	Gathering small aquatic animals	
Clearing land	Clothing manufacture	
Fishing	Making pottery	
Tending large herd animals		
Building houses		
Preparing the soil		
Making nets		
Making rope		

*All the activities above "butchering" are almost always done by men; those from "butchering" through "making rope" usually are done by men.

Table 9.1 about the division of labor by gender illustrate generalities rather than universals. That is, among the societies known to ethnography, there is a very strong tendency for men to build boats, but there are exceptions. One was the Hidatsa, a Native American group in which the women made the boats used to cross the Missouri River. (Traditionally, the Hidatsa were village farmers and bison hunters on the North American Plains; they now live in North Dakota.) Another exception: Pawnee women worked wood; this is the only Native American group that assigned this activity to women. (The Pawnee, also traditionally Plains farmers and bison hunters, originally lived in what is now central Nebraska and central Kansas; they now live on a reservation in north central Oklahoma.)

Exceptions to cross-cultural generalizations may involve societies or individuals. A society like the Hidatsa can contradict the cross-cultural generalization that men build boats by assigning that task to women. Or, in a society where the cultural expectation is that only men build boats, a particular woman or women can contradict that expectation by doing the male activity. Table 9.1 shows that in a sample of 185 societies, certain activities ("swing activities") are assigned to either or both men and women. Among the most important of such activities are planting, tending, and harvesting crops. We'll see below that some societies customarily assign more farming chores to women, whereas others call on men to be the main farm laborers. Among the tasks almost always assigned to men (Table 9.1), some (e.g., hunting large animals on land and sea) seem clearly related to the greater average size and strength of males. Others, such as working wood and making musical instruments, seem more culturally arbitrary. And women, of course, are not exempt from arduous and time-consuming physical labor, such as gathering firewood and fetching water. In Arembepe, Bahia, Brazil, women routinely transported water in five-gallon tins, balanced on their heads, from wells and lagoons located long distances from their homes.

Time and Effort Expended on Subsistence Activities by Men and Women*

More by men	16%
Roughly equal	61%
More by women	23%

* Percentage of 88 randomly selected societies for which information was available on this variable.

Who Does the Domestic Work?*

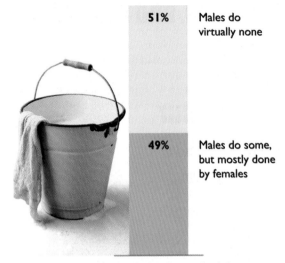

| 51% | Males do virtually none |
| 49% | Males do some, but mostly done by females |

* Percentage of 92 randomly selected societies for which information was available on this variable.

Both women and men have to fit their activities into twenty-four-hour days. Based on cross-cultural data, the figure at left shows that the time and effort spent in subsistence activities by men and women tend to be about equal. If anything, men do slightly less subsistence work than women do. Think about how female domestic activities could have been specified in greater detail in Table 9.1. The original coding of the data in Table 9.1 probably illustrates a male bias, because extradomestic activities received much more prominence than domestic activities did. For example, is collecting wild honey (listed in Table 9.1) more necessary or time-consuming than cleaning a baby's bottom (absent from Table 9.1)? Also, notice that Table 9.1 does not mention trade and market activity, in which either or both men and women are active.

Cross-culturally the subsistence contributions of men and women are roughly equal. But in domestic activities and child care, female labor predominates. "Who Does the Domestic Work?" shows that in about half the societies studied, men did virtually no domestic work. Even in societies where men did some domestic chores, the bulk of such work was done by women. Adding together their subsistence activities and their domestic work, women tend to work more hours than men do. Has this changed in the contemporary world?

What about child care? Women tend to be the main caregivers in most societies, but men often play a role. Cross-cultural data is used to answer the question, "Who—men or women—has final authority over the care, handling, and discipline of children younger than four years?" in a figure on page 168. Women have primary authority over infants in two-thirds of the societies. Given the critical role of breast-feeding in ensuring infant survival, it makes

Who Has the Final Authority over the Care, Handling, and Discipline of Infant Children (under Four Years Old)?*

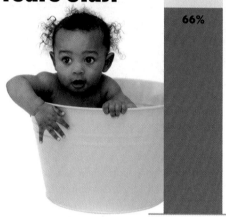

18%	Males have more say
16%	Roughly equal
66%	Females have more say

* Percentage of 67 randomly selected societies for which information was available on this variable.

Does the Society Allow Multiple Spouses?*

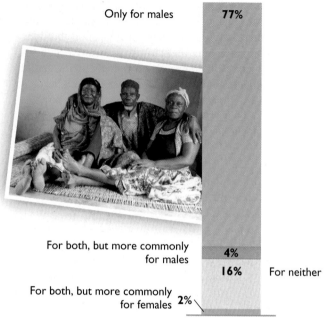

Only for males — 77%

For both, but more commonly for males — 4%

For neither — 16%

For both, but more commonly for females — 2%

* Percentage of 92 randomly selected societies for which information was available on this variable.

sense, for infants especially, for the mother to be the primary caregiver.

There are differences in male and female reproductive strategies. Women work to ensure their progeny will survive by establishing a close bond with each baby. It's also advantageous for a woman to have a reliable mate to ease the child-rearing process and ensure the survival of her children. (Again, there are exceptions, such as the matrilineal Nayar discussed in the previous chapter.) Women can have only so many babies during their reproductive years, which begin after menarche (the advent of first menstruation) and end with menopause (cessation of menstruation). Men, in contrast, have a longer reproductive period, which can last into the elder years. If they choose to do so, men can enhance their reproductive success by impregnating several women over a longer time. Although men do not always have multiple mates, they have a greater tendency to do so than women do, as the next three figures show. Among the societies known to

domestic–public dichotomy Contrast between women's role in the home and men's role in public life, with a corresponding social devaluation of women's work and worth.

ethnography, polygyny is much more common than polyandry, as shown above.

Men mate, within and outside marriage, more than women do. The "Double Standard" figure on the next page shows cross-cultural data on premarital sex, and the

bottom one summarizes the data on extramarital sex. In both cases men are less restricted than women are, although the restrictions are equal in about half the societies studied.

Double standards that restrict women more than men illustrate gender stratification. Several studies have shown that economic roles affect gender stratification. In one cross-cultural study, Sanday (1974) found that gender stratification decreased when men and women made roughly equal contributions to subsistence. She found that gender stratification was greatest when the women contrib-

Is There a Double Standard with Respect to Premarital Sex?*

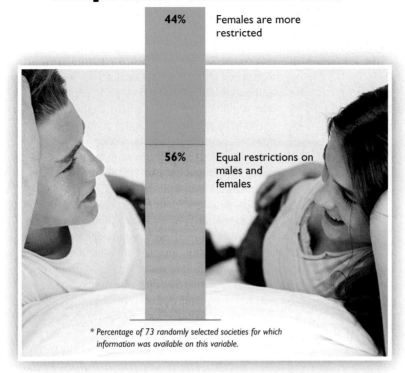

44% Females are more restricted

56% Equal restrictions on males and females

Percentage of 73 randomly selected societies for which information was available on this variable.

Is There a Double Standard with Respect to Extramarital Sex?*

43% Females are more restricted

55% Equal restrictions on males and females

3% Males punished more severely for transgressions

Percentage of 75 randomly selected societies for which information was available on this variable.

uted either much more or much less than the men did.

>> Gender among Foragers

In foraging societies gender stratification was most marked when men contributed much *more* to the diet than women did. This was true among the Inuit and other northern hunters and fishers. Among tropical and semitropical foragers, by contrast, gathering usually supplies more food than hunting and fishing do. Gathering generally is women's work. Men usually hunt and fish, but women also do some fishing and may hunt small animals. When gathering is prominent, gender status tends to be more equal than it is when hunting and fishing are the main subsistence activities.

Gender status also is more equal when the domestic and public spheres aren't sharply separated. (*Domestic* means within or pertaining to the home.) Strong differentiation between the home and the outside world is called the **domestic–public dichotomy** or the *private–public contrast.* The outside world can include politics, trade, warfare, or work. Often when domestic and public spheres are clearly separated, public activities have greater prestige than domestic ones do. This can promote gender stratification, because men are more likely to be active in the public domain than women are. Cross-culturally, women's activities tend to be closer to home than men's are. Thus, another reason hunter-gatherers have less gender stratification than food producers do is that the domestic–public dichotomy is less developed among foragers.

CULTURETHINK

Consider the domestic–public dichotomy in your society. Are domestic (home) and public (the outside world) spheres clearly separated, or do they overlap? Think, for example, about where religious, political, economic, and educational activities tend to take place.

In many societies women routinely do hard physical labor, as illustrated by these women working together to move logs at a sawmill in Langziang, China. Anthropologists have described both commonalities and differences in gender roles and activities among the world's societies.

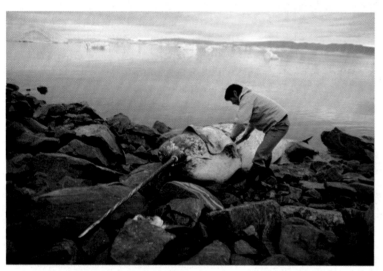

Among foragers, gender stratification tends to increase when men contribute much more to the diet than women do—as has been true among the Inuit and other northern hunters and fishers. Shown here, Mikile, an Inuit hunter, opens up a narwhal he hunted and killed near Qeqertat in northwestern Greenland.

STUDY TIP

Gender status tends to be more equal (in other words, there is less gender stratification) when (1) men and women have similar freedom over their labor and control over the products and labor of others; (2) women and men make roughly equal economic contributions; (3) the domestic and public spheres are not sharply separated; (4) men and women have access to equal prestige.

Certain roles tend to be more sex-linked than others. Men are the usual hunters and warriors. Given such weapons as spears, knives, and bows, men make better fighters because they are bigger and stronger on average than are women in the same population (Divale and Harris 1976). The male hunter–fighter role also reflects a tendency toward greater male mobility. In foraging societies, women are either pregnant or lactating during much of their childbearing years. Late in pregnancy and after childbirth, carrying a baby limits a woman's movements. Among the Agta of the Philippines, however, women not only gather, but they also hunt with dogs while carrying their babies with them (Griffin and Estioko-Griffin 1985). Still, considering cross-cultural data, women rarely are the primary hunters (Friedl 1975). Warfare, which also requires mobility, is not found in most foraging societies, nor is interregional trade well developed. Warfare and trade are two public arenas that contribute to status inequality of males and females among food producers.

The Ju/'hoansi San illustrate the extent to which the activities and spheres of influence of men and women may overlap among foragers (Draper 1975). Traditional Ju/'hoansi gender roles were interdependent. During gathering, women discovered information about game animals, which they passed on to the men. Men and women spent about the same amount of time away from the camp, but neither worked more than three days a week. The Ju/'hoansi saw nothing wrong in doing the work of the other gender. Men often gathered food and collected water. A general sharing ethos dictated that men distribute meat and that women share the fruits of gathering.

It is among foragers that the public and private spheres are least separate, hierarchy is least marked, aggression and competition are most discouraged, and the rights, activities, and spheres of influence of men and women overlap the most. Our ancestors lived entirely by foraging until ten thousand years ago. Despite the popular stereotype of the club-wielding caveman dragging his mate by the hair, relative gender equality is a much more likely ancestral pattern.

>> Gender among Horticulturalists

Gender roles and stratification among cultivators vary widely, depending on specific features of the economy and social structure. Demonstrating this, Martin and Voorhies (1975) studied a sample of 515 horticultural societies, representing all parts of the world. They looked at several factors, including descent and postmarital residence, the percentage of the diet derived from cultivation, and the relative productivity of men and women.

Women are the main producers in horticultural societies. Women like these South American corn farmers do most of the cultivating in such societies. What kinds of roles do women play in contemporary North American farming?

Women turned out to be the main producers in horticultural societies. In 50 percent of those societies, women did most of the cultivating. In 33 percent, contributions to cultivation by men and women were equal (see the figure below). In only 17 percent did men do most of the work. Women tended to do a bit more cultivating in matrilineal compared with patrilineal societies. They dominated horticulture in 64 percent of the matrilineal societies versus 50 percent of the patrilineal ones.

REDUCED GENDER STRATIFICATION— MATRILINEAL– MATRILOCAL SOCIETIES

Cross-cultural variation in gender status is related to rules of descent and postmarital residence (Friedl 1975; Martin and Voorhies 1975). Among horticulturalists with matrilineal descent and *matrilocality* (residence after marriage with the wife's relatives), female status tends to be high. Matriliny and matrilocality disperse related males, rather than consolidating them. By contrast, patriliny and *patrilocality* (residence after marriage with the husband's kin) keep male relatives together—an advantage given warfare. Matrilineal–matrilocal systems tend to occur in societies where population pressure on strategic resources is minimal and warfare is infrequent.

Women tend to have high status in matrilineal, matrilocal societies for several reasons. Descent-group membership, succession to political positions, allocation of land, and overall social identity all come through female links. Among the matrilineal Malays of Negeri Sembilan, Malaysia (Peletz 1988), matriliny gave women sole inheritance of ancestral rice fields. Matrilocality created solidary clusters of female kin. These Malay women had considerable influence beyond the household (Swift 1963). In such matrilineal contexts, women are the basis of the entire social structure. Although public authority nominally may be assigned to the men, much of the power and decision making actually may belong to the senior women.

Male and Female Contributions to Production in Cultivating Societies

Horticulture

17%

50%

33%

(percentage of 104 societies)

Agriculture

81%

15%

3%

(percentage of 93 societies)

Women are primary cultivators

Men are primary cultivators

Equal contributions to cultivation

MATRIARCHY

Cross-culturally, anthropologists have described tremendous variation in the roles of men and women, and the power differentials between them. If a patriarchy is a political system ruled by men, what would a matriarchy be? Would a **matriarchy** be a political system ruled by women, or a political system in which women play a much more prominent role than men do in social and political organization? Anthropologist Peggy Sanday (2002) has concluded that matriarchies exist, but not as mirror images of patriarchies. The superior power that men typically have in a patriarchy isn't matched by women's equally disproportionate power in a matriarchy. Many societies, including the Minangkabau of West Sumatra, Indonesia, whom Sanday has studied for decades, lack the substantial power differentials that typify patriarchal systems. Minangkabau women play a central role in social, economic, and ceremonial life and as key symbols. The primacy of matriliny

> **matriarchy** A political system in which women play a much more prominent role than men do in social and political organization.

A Minangkabau bride and groom in West Sumatra, Indonesia, where anthropologist Peggy Reeves Sanday has conducted several years of ethnographic fieldwork.

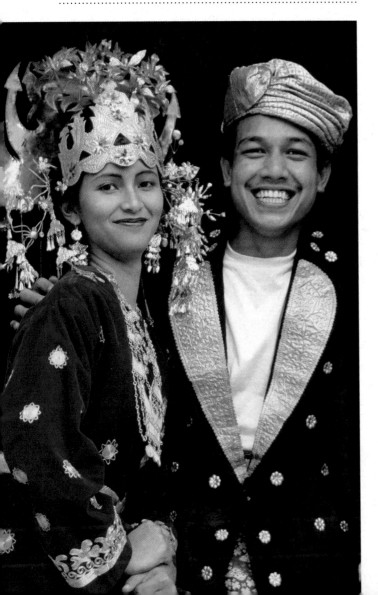

Anthropology Works

People working on international development projects need to be aware of the role women play in family households and economy. Assuming that men are in charge of household budgets or agricultural decision making, for example, would be a mistake in many places.

and matriarchy is evident at the village level, as well as regionally, where seniority of matrilineal descent serves as a way to rank villages.

The four million Minangkabau constitute one of Indonesia's largest ethnic groups. Located in the highlands of West Sumatra, their culture is based on the coexistence of matrilineal custom and a nature-based philosophy called *adat,* complemented by Islam, a more recent (sixteenth-century) arrival. The Minangkabau view men and women as cooperative partners for the common good rather than competitors ruled by self-interest. People gain prestige when they promote social harmony rather than by vying for power.

Sanday considers the Minangkabau a matriarchy because women are the center, origin, and foundation of the social order. Senior women are associated with the central pillar of the traditional house, the oldest one in the village. The oldest village in a cluster is called the "mother village." In ceremonies, women are addressed by the term used for their mythical Queen Mother. Women control land inheritance, and couples reside matrilocally. In the wedding ceremony, the wife collects her husband from his household and, with her female kin, escorts him to hers. If there is a divorce, the husband simply takes his things and leaves. Yet despite the special position of women, the Minangkabau matriarchy is not the equivalent of female rule, given the Minangkabau belief that all decision making should be by consensus.

INCREASED GENDER STRATIFICATION—PATRILINEAL– PATRILOCAL SOCIETIES

Martin and Voorhies (1975) link the decline of matriliny and the spread of the **patrilineal–patrilocal complex** (consisting of patrilineality, patrilocality, warfare, and male supremacy) to pressure on resources. Faced with scarce resources, patrilineal–patrilocal cultivators such as the Yanomami often wage warfare against other villages. This favors patrilocality and patriliny, customs that keep related men together in the same village, where they make strong allies in battle. Such societies tend to have a sharp domestic–public dichotomy, and men tend to dominate the prestige hierarchy. Men may use their public roles in warfare and trade and their greater prestige to

STUDY TIP

Matrilineal and *matrilocal* societies occur where little pressure on resources and low population densities exist. Pressure on resources leads to warfare and intensified production, which favors *patrilocality* and *patrilineality*.

symbolize and reinforce the devaluation or oppression of women.

The patrilineal–patrilocal complex characterizes many societies in highland Papua New Guinea. Women work hard growing and processing subsistence crops, raising and tending pigs (the main domesticated animal and a favorite food), and doing domestic cooking, but they are isolated from the public domain, which men control. Men grow and distribute prestige crops, prepare food for feasts, and arrange marriages. The men even get to trade the pigs and control their use in ritual.

In densely populated areas of the Papua New Guinea highlands, male–female avoidance is associated with strong pressure on resources (Lindenbaum 1972). Men fear all female contacts, including sex. They think that sexual contact with women will weaken them. Indeed, men see

In some parts of Papua New Guinea, the patrilineal–patrilocal complex has extreme social repercussions. Regarding females as dangerous and polluting, men may segregate themselves in men's houses (such as this one, located near the Sepik River), where they hide their precious ritual objects from women. Are there places like this in your society?

everything female as dangerous and polluting. They segregate themselves in men's houses and hide their precious ritual objects from women. They delay marriage, and some never marry.

By contrast, the sparsely populated areas of Papua New Guinea, such as recently settled areas, lack taboos on male–female contacts. The image of woman as polluter fades, heterosexual intercourse is valued, men and women live together, and reproductive rates are high.

> **patrilineal–patrilocal complex** An interrelated constellation of patrilineality, patrilocality, warfare, and male supremacy.

> **extradomestic** Outside the home; within or pertaining to the public domain.

>> Gender among Agriculturists

When the economy is based on agriculture, women typically lose their role as primary cultivators. Certain agricultural techniques, particularly plowing, have been assigned to men because of their greater average size and strength (Martin and Voorhies 1975). Except when irrigation is used, plowing eliminates the need for constant weeding, an activity usually done by women.

Cross-cultural data illustrate these contrasts in productive roles between agricultural and horticultural economies. Women were the main workers in 50 percent of the horticultural societies surveyed but in only 15 percent of the agricultural groups. As shown in the figure on page 171, male subsistence labor dominated 81 percent of the agricultural societies but only 17 percent of the horticultural ones (Martin and Voorhies 1975).

With the advent of agriculture, women were cut off from production for the first time. Belief systems started contrasting men's valuable extradomestic labor with women's domestic role, now viewed as inferior. (**Extradomestic** means outside the home; within or pertaining to the public domain.) Changes in kinship and postmarital residence patterns also hurt women. Descent groups and polygyny declined with agriculture, and the nuclear family became more common. Living with her husband and children, a woman was isolated from her kinswomen and cowives. Female sexuality is carefully supervised in agricultural economies; men have easier access to divorce and extramarital sex, reflecting a "double standard."

Still, female status in agricultural societies is not inevitably bleak. Gender stratification is associated with plow agriculture rather than with intensive cultivation per se. Studies of peasant gender roles and stratification in France and Spain (Harding 1975; Reiter 1975), which have plow agriculture, show that people think of the house as the female sphere and the fields as the male domain. Such a dichotomy is not inevitable, though, as Conrad Kottak's own research among Betsileo agriculturists in Madagascar shows.

Betsileo women play a prominent role in agriculture, contributing a third of the hours invested in rice production. They have their customary tasks in the division of labor, but their work is more seasonal than men's is. No one has much to do during the ceremonial season, between mid-June and mid-September. Men work in the rice fields almost daily the rest of the year. Women's cooperative work occurs during transplanting (mid-September through November) and harvesting (mid-March through early May). Along with other members of the household, women do daily weeding in December and January. After the harvest, all family members work together winnowing the rice and then transporting it to the granary.

patriarchy Political system ruled by men in which women have inferior social and political status, including fewer basic human rights.

If we consider the strenuous daily task of husking rice by pounding (a part of food preparation rather than production per se), women actually contribute slightly more than 50 percent of the labor devoted to producing and preparing rice before cooking.

Not just women's prominent economic role but also their traditional social organization enhances female status among the Betsileo. Although postmarital residence is mainly patrilocal, descent rules permit married women to keep membership in and a strong allegiance to their own descent groups. Kinship is broadly and bilaterally (on both sides—as in contemporary North America) calculated. The Betsileo exemplify Aihwa Ong's (1989) generalization that bilateral (and matrilineal) kinship systems, combined with subsistence economies in which the sexes have complementary roles in food production and distribution, are characterized by reduced gender stratification. Such societies are common among South Asian peasants (Ong 1989).

Traditionally, Betsileo men participate more in politics, but the women also hold political office. Women sell their produce and products in markets, invest in cattle, sponsor ceremonies, and are mentioned during offerings to ancestors. Arranging marriages, an important extradomestic activity, is more women's concern than men's. Sometimes Betsileo women seek their own kinswomen as wives for their sons, reinforcing their own prominence in village life and continuing kin-based female solidarity in the village.

The Betsileo illustrate the idea that intensive cultivation does not necessarily entail sharp gender stratification. We can see that gender roles and stratification reflect not just the type of adaptive strategy but also specific cultural attributes. Betsileo women continue to play a significant role in their society's major economic activity, rice production.

>> Patriarchy and Violence

A political system ruled by men in which women have inferior social and political status, including fewer basic human rights, is known as **patriarchy.** Barbara Miller (1997), in a study of systematic neglect of females, describes women in rural northern India as "the endangered sex." Societies that feature a full-fledged patrilineal–patrilocal complex, replete with warfare and intervillage raiding, also typify

India has been described as a patriarchal culture, in which women routinely are harassed when they move from private (domestic) to public space. The women shown here enjoy their ride, unmolested, on the "Ladies Special" train from Palwal to Delhi.

patriarchy. Such practices as dowry murders, female infanticide, and clitoridectomy exemplify patriarchy, which extends from tribal societies such as the Yanomami to state societies such as India and Pakistan.

Although more prevalent in certain social settings than in others, family violence and domestic abuse of women are worldwide problems. Domestic violence certainly occurs in nuclear family settings, such as Canada and the United States. Cities, with their impersonality and isolation from extended kin networks, are breeding grounds for domestic violence.

We've seen that gender stratification typically is reduced in matrilineal, matrifocal, and bilateral societies in which women have prominent roles in the economy and social life. When a woman lives in her own village, she has kin nearby to look after and protect her interests. Even in patrilocal polygynous settings, women often count on the support of their cowives and sons in disputes with potentially abusive husbands. Such settings, which tend to provide a safe haven for women, are retracting rather than expanding in today's world, however. Isolated families and patrilineal social forms have spread at the expense of matrilineality. Many nations have declared polygyny illegal. More and more women, and men, find themselves cut off from extended kin and families of orientation.

With the spread of the women's rights movement and the human rights movement, attention to domestic violence and abuse of women has increased. Laws have been passed and mediating institutions established. Brazil's female-run police stations for battered women provide an example, as do shelters for victims of domestic abuse in the United States and Canada. But patriarchal institutions do persist in what should be a more enlightened world.

Domestic violence isn't limited to tribal societies. It also occurs in nuclear family settings including the United States, Canada, and the United Kingdom. Shown here, women rally in London, England, on International Women's Day, March 8, 2008.

>> Gender and Industrialism

The domestic–public dichotomy, which is developed most fully among patrilineal–patrilocal food producers and plow agriculturists, also has affected gender stratification in industrial societies, including the United States and Canada. Gender roles have been changing rapidly in North America. The "traditional" idea that "a woman's place is in the home" actually emerged in the United States as industrialism spread after 1900. Earlier, pioneer women in the Midwest and West had been recognized as fully productive workers in farming and home industry. Under industrialism, attitudes about gendered work came to vary with class and region. In early industrial Europe, men, women, and children had flocked to factories as wage laborers. Enslaved Americans of both sexes had done grueling work in cotton fields. With abolition, southern African American women continued working as field hands and domestics. Poor white women labored in the South's early cotton mills. In the 1890s more than one million American women held menial and repetitive unskilled factory positions (Margolis 1984; Martin and Voorhies 1975).

After 1900, European immigration produced a male labor force willing to work for wages lower than those of American-born men. Those immigrant men moved into factory jobs that previously had gone to women. As machine tools and mass production further reduced the need for female labor, the notion that women were biologically unfit for factory work began to gain ground (Martin and Voorhies 1975).

Maxine Margolis (1984, 2000) has shown how gendered work, attitudes, and beliefs have varied in response to American economic needs. For example, wartime shortages of men have promoted the idea that work outside the home is women's patriotic duty. During the world wars the notion that women are unfit for hard

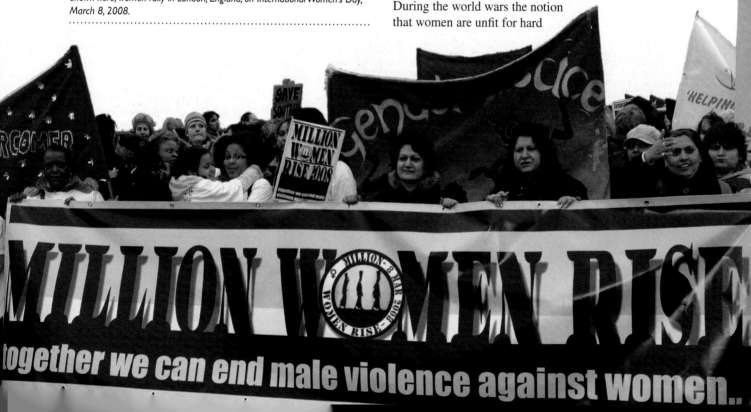

physical labor faded. Inflation and the culture of consumption also have spurred female employment. When prices or demand rise, multiple paychecks help maintain family living standards.

The steady increase in female paid employment since World War II also reflects the baby boom and industrial expansion. American culture traditionally has defined clerical work, teaching, and nursing as female occupations. With rapid population growth and business expansion after World War II, the demand for women to fill such jobs grew steadily. Employers also found they could increase their profits by paying women lower wages than they would have to pay returning male war veterans.

Margolis (1984, 2000) contends that changes in the economy lead to changes in attitudes toward and about

During the world wars the notion that women were biologically unfit for hard physical labor faded. Shown here is World War II's famous Rosie the Riveter. Is there a comparable poster woman today? What does her image say about modern gender roles?

women. Economic changes paved the way for the contemporary women's movement, which also was spurred by the publication of Betty Friedan's book *The Feminine Mystique* in 1963 and the founding of the National Organization of Women (NOW), in 1966. The movement in turn promoted expanded work opportunities for women, including the goal of equal pay for equal work. Between 1970 and 2007, the female percentage of the American workforce rose from 38 percent to 46 percent. In other words, almost half of all Americans who work outside the home are women. Over 71 million women now have paid jobs, compared with 82 million men. Women fill more than half (56 percent) of all professional jobs (*Statistical Abstract of the United States 2009,* p. 384). And it's not mainly single women working, as once was the case. The ever-increasing cash employment of American wives and mothers, including those with children under six years old, is shown in the top figure on the next page.

Note in the top figure that the cash employment of American married men has been falling while that of American married women has been rising. There has been a dramatic change in behavior and attitudes since 1960, when 89 percent of all married men worked, compared with just 32 percent of married women. The comparable figures in 2007 were 77 percent and 62 percent. Ideas about the gender roles of males and females have changed. Compare your grandparents and your parents. Chances are you have a working mother, but your grandmother was more likely a stay-at-home mom. Your grandfather is more likely than your father to have worked in manufacturing and to have belonged to a union. Your father is more likely than your grandfather to have shared child care and domestic responsibilities. Age at marriage has been delayed for both men and women. College educations and professional degrees have increased.

CULTURETHINK

What circumstances shape public attitudes toward women working outside the home, according to the text? Ask around: Is it acceptable, or desirable, for women to work for wages? What reasoning do people use to explain their answers?

Cash Employment of American Mothers, Wives, and Husbands, 1960–2007*

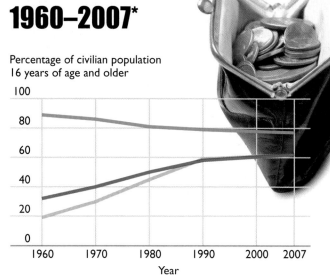

Percentage of civilian population 16 years of age and older

—— Percentage of all married men (wife present)

—— Percentage of all married women (husband present)

—— Percentage of all married women (husband present, with children under six)

Trends in U.S. Women's Participation in the Paid Labor Force, 1890–2008

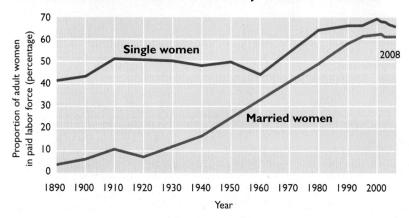

What other changes do you associate with the increase in female employment outside the home?

THE FEMINIZATION OF POVERTY

Alongside the economic gains of many American women stands an opposite extreme: the feminization of poverty, or the increasing representation of women (and their children) among America's poorest people. Women head over half of U.S. households with incomes below the pov-erty line, more than double the number in 1959. Married couples are much more secure economically than single mothers are. The median one-earner family maintained by a single woman had an annual income of $28,829 in 2006, less than half the median income ($69,404) of a married-couple household (*Statistical Abstract of the United States, 2009,* p. 446).

The feminization of poverty isn't just a North American trend. The percentage of female-headed households has been increasing worldwide. In Western Europe, for example, female-headed households rose from 24 percent in 1980 to 31 percent in 1990. The figure ranges from below 20 percent in certain South Asian and Southeast Asian countries to almost 50 percent in certain African countries and the Caribbean (Buvinic 1995).

CULTURE THINK

Although many women are now earning more than men, the feminization of poverty shows that others are earning increasingly less. What are the problems with making general statements about "women" without considering differences among them? What differences besides income would you need to consider?

Why must so many women be solo household heads? Where are the men going, and why are they leaving? Among the causes are male migration, civil strife (men off fighting), divorce, abandonment, widow-hood, unwed adolescent parenthood, and, more generally, the idea that children are women's responsibility. Globally, house-holds headed by women tend to be poorer than those headed by men. In one study, the percentage of single-parent families consid-ered poor was 18 percent in Britain, 20 per-cent in Italy, 25 percent in Switzerland, 40 percent in Ireland, 52 percent in Canada, and 63 percent in the United States.

It is widely believed that one way to improve the situation of poor women is to encourage them to organize. New women's groups can in some cases revive or replace traditional forms of social organization that have been dis-rupted. Membership in a group can help women mobilize resources, enhance production, and reduce the risks and costs associated with credit. By organizing, women also develop self-confidence and decrease dependence on oth-ers. Through such organization, poor women throughout the world are working to determine their own needs and priorities and to change things so as to improve their social and economic situation (Buvinic 1995).

>> What Determines Gender Variation?

We see that gender roles and stratification have varied widely across cultures and through history. Among many foragers and matrilineal cultivators, there is little gender stratification. Competition for resources leads to warfare and the intensification of production, which favor patriliny and patrilocality. To the extent that women lose their productive roles in agricultural societies, the domestic–public dichotomy is accentuated and gender stratification is sharpened. With industrialism, attitudes about gender vary in the context of female extradomestic employment. Gender is flexible and varies with cultural, social, political, and economic factors. The variability of gender in time and space suggests that it will continue to change. The biology of the sexes is not a narrow enclosure limiting humans but a broad base upon which a variety of structures can be built (Friedl 1975).

>> Sexual Orientation

A person's habitual sexual attraction to, and sexual activities with, persons of the opposite sex (*heterosexuality*), the same sex (*homosexuality*), or both sexes (*bisexuality*) is termed their **sexual orientation.** *Asexuality*—indifference toward, or lack of attraction to either sex—also is a sexual orientation. All four of these forms are found in contemporary North America and throughout the world. But each type of desire and experience holds different meanings for individuals and groups. For example, an asexual disposition may be acceptable in some places but perceived as a character flaw in others. Male–male sexual activity may be a private affair in Mexico, rather than public, socially sanctioned, and encouraged as among the Etoro (see below) of Papua New Guinea (see also Blackwood and Wieringa 1999; Boellstorff 2007; Kimmel and Plante 2004; Kottak and Kozaitis 2008; Nanda 2000).

Neither man nor woman, hijras *constitute India's third gender. Many hijras get their income from performing at ceremonies, begging, or prostitution. The beauty contest shown here was organized by an AIDS prevention and relief organization that works with the local hijra community.*

Recently in the United States the tendency has been to see sexual orientation as fixed and biologically based. There is not enough information at this time to determine the exact extent to which sexual orientation is based on biology. What we can say is that all human activities and preferences, including erotic expression, are at least partially culturally constructed.

In any society, individuals will differ in the nature, range, and intensity of their sexual interests and urges. No one knows for sure why such individual sexual differences exist. Part of the answer probably is biological, reflecting genes or hormones (Wade 2005). Another part may have to do with experiences during growth and development. But whatever the reasons for individual variation, culture always plays a role in molding individual sexual urges toward a collective norm. And such sexual norms vary from culture to culture.

twenty—left their families and shared quarters with adult fighting men, who paid bridewealth for them and had sex with them. During this apprenticeship, the young men performed the domestic duties of women. Upon reaching warrior status, these young men took their own younger male brides. Later, retiring from the warrior role, Azande men married women. Flexible in their sexual expression, Azande males had no difficulty shifting from sex with older men (as male brides), to sex with younger men (as warriors), to sex with women (as husbands) (see Murray and Roscoe 1998).

Consider also the Etoro (Kelly 1976), a group of four hundred people who subsist by hunting and horticulture

> **sexual orientation** A person's habitual sexual attraction to, and activities with persons of the opposite sex (heterosexuality), the same sex (homosexuality), or both sexes (bisexuality); also, the lack of attraction (asexuality).

"As far as I'm concerned, being any gender is a drag."

Patti Smith

What do we know about variation in sexual norms from society to society, and over time? A classic cross-cultural study (Ford and Beach 1951) found wide variation in attitudes about masturbation, bestiality (sex with animals), and homosexuality. In a single society, such as the United States, attitudes about sex differ over time and with socioeconomic status, region, and rural versus urban residence. However, even in the 1950s, prior to the "age of sexual permissiveness" (the pre-HIV period from the mid-1960s through the 1970s), research showed that almost all American men (92 percent) and more than half of American women (54 percent) admitted to masturbation. In the famous Kinsey report (Kinsey, Pomeroy, and Martin 1948), 37 percent of the men surveyed admitted having had at least one sexual experience leading to orgasm with another male. In a later study of twelve hundred unmarried women, 26 percent reported same-sex sexual activities. (Because Kinsey's research relied on nonrandom samples, it should be considered merely illustrative, rather than a statistically accurate representation, of sexual behavior at the time.)

Sex acts with people of the same sex were absent, rare, or secret in 37 percent of seventy-six societies for which data were available in the Ford and Beach study (1951). In the other societies, various forms of same-sex sexual activity were acceptable. Sometimes sexual relations between people of the same sex involved transvestism on the part of one of the partners (see Kulick 1998). Transvestism did not characterize male–male sex among the Sudanese Azande, who valued the warrior role (Evans-Pritchard 1970). Prospective warriors—young men aged twelve to

in the Trans-Fly region of Papua New Guinea. The Etoro illustrate the power of culture in molding human sexuality. The following account, based on ethnographic fieldwork by Raymond C. Kelly in the late 1960s, applies only to Etoro males and their beliefs. Etoro cultural norms prevented the male anthropologist who studied them from gathering comparable information about female attitudes. Note, also, that the activities described have been discouraged by missionaries. Since there has been no restudy of the Etoro specifically focusing on these activities, the extent to which these practices continue today is unknown. For this reason, we'll use the past tense in describing them.

Etoro opinions about sexuality were linked to their beliefs about the cycle of birth, physical growth, maturity, old age, and death. Etoro men believed that semen was necessary to give life force to a fetus, which was, they believed, implanted in a woman by an ancestral spirit. Sexual intercourse during pregnancy nourished the growing fetus. The Etoro believed that men had a limited lifetime supply of semen. Any sex act leading to ejaculation was seen as draining that supply, and as sapping a man's virility and vitality. The birth of children, nurtured by semen, symbolized a necessary

Did You Know?

For the first time in U.S. history, the 2010 census counted gay couples as married, even if they were not legally married. In 2000, they could only designate themselves as "unmarried partners" living in the same household.

sacrifice that would lead to the husband's eventual death. Heterosexual intercourse—required only for reproduction—was otherwise discouraged. Women who wanted too much sex were viewed as witches, hazardous to their husbands' health. Etoro culture allowed heterosexual intercourse only about one hundred days a year. The rest of the time it was tabooed. Seasonal birth clustering shows the taboo was respected.

So objectionable was male–female sex that it was removed from community life. It could occur neither in sleeping quarters nor in the fields. Coitus could happen only in the woods, where it was risky because poisonous snakes, the Etoro claimed, were attracted by the sounds and smells of male–female sex.

Although coitus was discouraged, sex acts between men were viewed as essential. Etoro believed that boys could not produce semen on their own. To grow into men and eventually give life force to their children, boys had to acquire semen orally from older men. From the age of ten until adulthood, boys were inseminated by older men. No taboos were attached to this. Such oral insemination could proceed in the sleeping area or garden. Every three years, a group of boys around the age of twenty were formally initiated into manhood. They went to a secluded mountain lodge, where they were visited and inseminated by several older men.

> "Society as a whole benefits immeasurably from a climate in which all persons, regardless of race or gender, may have the opportunity to earn respect, responsibility, advancement and remuneration based on ability."
>
> Sandra Day O'Connor

Male–male sex among the Etoro was governed by a code of propriety. Although sexual relations between older and younger males were considered culturally essential, those between boys of the same age were discouraged. A boy who took semen from other youths was believed to be sapping their life force and stunting their growth. A boy's rapid physical development might suggest he was getting semen from other boys. Like a sex-hungry wife, he might be shunned as a witch.

These sexual practices among the Etoro rested not on hormones or genes but on cultural beliefs and traditions. The Etoro shared a cultural pattern, which Gilbert Herdt (1984) calls "ritualized homosexuality," with some fifty other tribes in Papua New Guinea, especially in that country's Trans-Fly region. These societies illustrate one extreme of a male–female avoidance pattern that is widespread in Papua New Guinea and indeed in many patrilineal–patrilocal societies.

Flexibility in sexual expression seems to be an aspect of our primate heritage. Both masturbation and same-sex sexual activity exist among chimpanzees and other primates. Male bonobos (pygmy chimps) regularly engage in a form of mutual masturbation known as "penis fencing." Females get sexual pleasure from rubbing their genitals against those of other females (de Waal 1997). Our primate sexual potential is molded by culture, the environment, and reproductive necessity. Heterosexual coitus is practiced in all human societies—which, after all, must reproduce themselves—but alternatives also are widespread (Rathus, Nevid, and Fichner-Rathus 2008). Like gender roles and attitudes more generally, the sexual component of human personality and identity—just how we express our "natural" sexual urges—is a matter that culture and environment determine and limit.

CULTURETHINK

People in the United States tend to think of sexual orientation as fixed and unchanging. How does this contrast with sexual practices and identities in other cultures, such as the Azande and the Etoro?

get involved!

You may have known or heard about a woman in a violent marital or dating relationship. To learn about how a woman and her children might find temporary refuge from violent situations, visit the website of Safe Horizon (http://www.safehorizon.org), a New York City support agency. Take the "Domestic Violence Shelter Tour." Listen to the stories of women who have been battered by spouses or boyfriends. Although the women come from different situations, what common circumstances do you find running throughout their lives? How can urban life or immigrant status in a big city weaken women's position? How might the varied services the shelter provides help free women from their economic dependence on the men who batter them and from the feelings these women often have that *they* are to blame for the abuse?

For REVIEW

I. How are biology and culture expressed in human sex/gender systems?

- Although sexual dimorphism decreased during human evolution, males and females still differ physiologically and anatomically.

  Anthropologists have shown that culture is the source of many differences between the sexes and that the roles of men and women both differ and resemble one another in different cultures. "The biological nature of men and women [should be seen] not as a narrow enclosure limiting the human organism, but rather as a broad base upon which a variety of structures can be built." This statement sums up the predominant anthropological position today. Sex differences are biological, but gender encompasses the traits that a culture assigns to males and females. Gender refers to the cultural construction of whether one is female, male, or something else.

II. How do gender, gender roles, and gender stratification correlate with other social, economic, and political variables?

- In foraging societies both the domestic–public dichotomy and gender stratification are limited, and male and female activities tend to overlap. Female status is high among horticulturalists with matrilineal descent and matrilocality. With the advent of plow agriculture, women lost their role as primary cultivators and became more homebound; gender stratification sharpened. Competition for resources favors the patrilineal-patrilocal complex. The superior power that men typically have in a patriarchy isn't matched by women's power in a matriarchy. Industrialization in the United States initially contributed to the notion that women were unfit for factory work, but industrial expansion after World War II increased female paid employment. The rise in poverty of women is a global phenomenon.

III. What is sexual orientation, and how do sexual practices vary cross-culturally?

- Sexual orientation refers to a person's habitual sexual attraction to, and sexual activities with, persons of the opposite sex (heterosexuality), the same sex (homosexuality), or both sexes (bisexuality). Asexuality is indifference toward, or lack of attraction to, either sex. All four forms of orientation occur worldwide but hold different meanings for individuals and groups. Anthropologists generally see sexual orientation as at least partially culturally constructed. In the United States, attitudes about sex have differed over time and with socioeconomic status, region, and rural versus urban residence. Flexibility in sexual expression seems to be an aspect of our primate heritage.

CULTURE CLIPS

TO ACCESS THESE VIDEOS ON YOUR COMPUTER, VISIT

www.mhhe.com/gezonqr

9-1

9-2

9-3

Pop Quiz

1. Consider this quote: "The biological nature of men and women [should be seen] not as a narrow enclosure limiting the human organism, but rather as a broad base upon which a variety of structures can be built." Which of the following best describes this quote's significance?
   a. The quote reflects a cultural generality, rather than a cultural universal.
   b. The quote reflects the predominant anthropological position on sex/gender roles and biology.
   c. This quote summarizes how biological determinists think.
   d. This quote ignores considerable evidence.

2. Hidatsa women made boats, and Pawnee women worked wood. These two cases suggest that:
   a. Biology has nothing to do with gender roles.
   b. Anthropologists are too optimistic about finding a society with gender equality.
   c. There are exceptions to cross-cultural generalizations about the kinds of work men and women usually do in different societies.
   d. A Hidatsa or Pawnee man would never do the female task.

3. Among foragers:
   a. Warfare and trade make men dominant over women.
   b. Female status falls when gathering is more important than hunting.
   c. The lack of a clear domestic–public dichotomy is related to relatively weak gender stratification.
   d. Men and women are completely equal.

4. Which of the following statements about gender status and power in horticultural societies is false?
   a. Where matriliny and matrilocality disperse related males, female status tends to be high.
   b. Matriarchy describes systems in which the women hold superior power to, and rule, the men.
   c. Pressure on resources encourages the spread of the patrilineal–patrilocal complex.
   d. Men may use their public roles to reinforce the devaluation of women.

5. Which of the following is false about gender roles and statuses among agriculturalists?
   a. With agriculture, women tend to lose their role as primary cultivators.
   b. The advent of agriculture in horticultural societies gave women a further advantage in the prestige hierarchy.
   c. With agriculture, polygyny and descent groups declined.
   d. Reduced gender stratification is found in bilateral and matrilineal kinship systems with complementary gender roles in food production.

6. In which kind of society do anthropologists most typically find female genital operations, warfare, female infanticide, and dowry murders?
   a. Patrilineal–patrilocal
   b. Matrilineal–patrilocal
   c. Matrilineal–matrilocal
   d. Patrilineal–matrilocal

7. The idea that "a woman's place is in the home":
   a. Emerged in the United States as industrialism spread after 1900.
   b. Is found in virtually all societies.
   c. Reflects the weakening of a domestic–public dichotomy.
   d. Fuels the contemporary women's movement.

8. In comparing gender roles and status in different societies, we can say that the following is true:
   a. Generally, women's status is relatively high among horticulturalists with matrilineal descent and matrilocal residence.
   b. In a large number of societies women control the strategic resources and carry out the most prestigious activities.
   c. The more women contribute to the domestic sphere, the more power they hold.
   d. The less women contribute to the public sphere, the more power they achieve.

9. "The feminization of poverty" means that:
   a. Poverty has been dressed up to seem more bearable.
   b. Single mothers are more secure economically than are married couples.
   c. Women and their children are increasingly represented among the world's poorest people.
   d. An increasing percentage of female-headed households shows the growing power and independence of women.

10. All the following are key ideas to take away from this chapter's discussion of sexual orientation *except*:
    a. Different types of sexual desires and experiences hold different meanings for individuals and groups.
    b. In any society, individuals will differ in the nature, range, and intensity of sexual interests and urges.
    c. Culture always plays a role in molding individual sexual urges toward a collective norm.
    d. There is conclusive scientific evidence that sexual orientation is genetically determined.

1. (b), 2. (c), 3. (c), 4. (b), 5. (b), 6. (a), 7. (a), 8. (a), 9. (c), 10. (d)

10

RELIGION

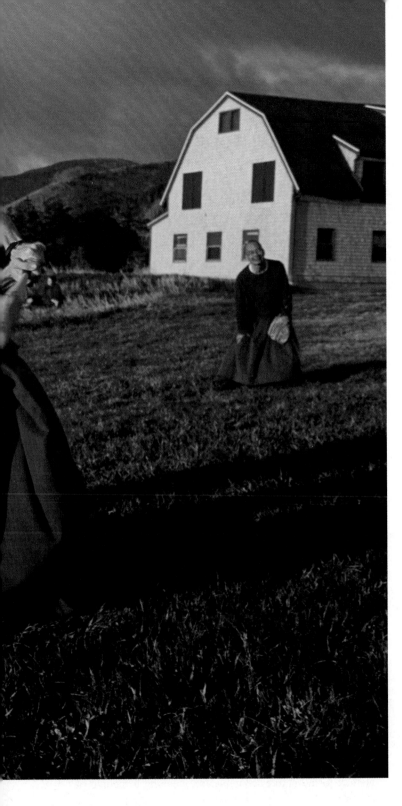

UNDERSTANDING OURSELVES

Ever notice how much baseball players spit? Football players, with their customary headgear, don't spit, nor do basketball players, who might slip on the court. No spitting by tennis players, golfers, gymnasts, or swimmers. But watch any baseball game, and you'll see spitting galore. The custom likely originated on the mound and continues today as a carryover from the days when pitchers routinely chewed tobacco, believing that nicotine enhanced their concentration. The spitting custom spread to other players, who unabashedly spew saliva from the outfield to the dugout steps.

For the student of custom, ritual, and magic, baseball is an especially interesting game, to which lessons from anthropology are easily applied. The pioneering anthropologist Bronislaw Malinowski, writing about Pacific islanders, noted their use of all sorts of magic in sailing, a hazardous activity. He proposed that people turn to magic when they face uncertainty and conditions they can't control (e.g., wind and weather). Like sailing magic, baseball magic, in the form of rituals, taboos, and sacred objects, serves to reduce psychological stress, creating an illusion of control when real control is lacking.

All sorts of magical behaviors surround pitching and batting, which are full of uncertainty. There are fewer rituals for fielding, over which players have more control. Especially obvious are the rituals (like the spitting) of pitchers, who may: tug their cap between pitches, spit in a particular direction, magically manipulate the resin bag, talk to the ball, or wash their hands after giving up a run. Batters have their rituals, too. One major leaguer routinely would spit, then ritually touch his gob with his bat to enhance his success at the plate.

To keep hope alive in situations of uncertainty, and for outcomes we can't control, all societies draw on magic and religion as sources of nonmaterial comfort, explanation, and control. What are your rituals?

As You READ

- What is religion, and what are its various forms, social correlates, and functions?

- What is ritual, and what are its various forms and expressions?

- What role does religion play in maintaining and changing societies?

>> Defining Religion

The anthropologist Anthony F. C. Wallace defined **religion** as "belief and ritual concerned with supernatural beings, powers, and forces" (1966, p. 5). The supernatural is the extraordinary realm outside (but believed to impinge on) the observable world. It is nonempirical and inexplicable in ordinary terms. It must be accepted "on faith."

> **religion** Beliefs and rituals concerned with supernatural beings, powers, and forces.

Supernatural beings—gods and goddesses, ghosts, and souls—are not of the material world. Nor are supernatural forces, some of which may be wielded by beings. Other sacred forces are impersonal; they simply exist. In many societies, however, people believe they can benefit from, become imbued with, or manipulate supernatural forces (see Bowen 2008; Bowie 2006; Crapo 2006; Lambek 2008; Stein and Stein 2008; Warms, Garber, and McGee 2009).

Another definition of religion (Reese 1999) focuses on bodies of people who gather together regularly for worship. These congregants or adherents subscribe to and internalize a common system of meaning. They accept (adhere to or believe in) a set of doctrines involving the relationship between the individual and divinity, the supernatural, or whatever is taken to be the ultimate nature of reality. Anthropologists have stressed the collective, shared, and enacted nature of religion, the emotions it generates, and the meanings it embodies. Emile Durkheim (1912/2001), an early scholar of religion, stressed religious *effervescence,* the bubbling up of collective emotional intensity generated by worship. Victor Turner (1969/1995) updated Durkheim's notion, using the term *communitas,* an intense community spirit, a feeling of great social solidarity, equality, and togetherness. The word *religion* derives from the Latin *religare*—"to tie, to bind," but it is not necessary for all members of a given religion to meet together as a common body. Subgroups meet regularly at local congregation sites. They may attend occasional meetings with adherents representing a wider region. And they may form an imagined community with people of similar faith throughout the world.

CULTURE THINK

Have you ever felt the intense community spirit of *communitas?* What are some secular settings where people might experience *communitas,* or collective effervescence?

Like ethnicity and language, religion also is associated with social divisions within and between societies and nations. Religion both unites and divides. Participation in common rites may affirm, and thus maintain, the social solidarity of a religion's adherents. However, as we know from daily headlines, religious difference also may be associated with bitter enmity.

In studying religion cross-culturally, anthropologists pay attention to the social nature and roles of religion as well as to the nature, content, and meaning to people of religious doctrines, acts, events, settings, practitioners, and organizations. We also consider such verbal manifestations of religious beliefs as prayers, chants, myths, texts, and statements about ethics and morality (see Cunningham 1999; Klass 2003; Lehmann, Meyers, and Moro 2005; Stein and Stein 2005). Religion, by either definition offered here, exists in all human societies. It is a cultural universal. However, we'll see that distinguishing the supernatural from the natural isn't always easy and that different societies conceptualize divinity, supernatural entities, and ultimate realities very differently.

STUDY TIP

Religion has several characteristics:
(1) It is concerned with the supernatural;
(2) it serves emotional needs; (3) it is a collective system of meaning;
(4) it explains the unexplainable;
(5) it is social in nature, based on religious roles.

>> Expressions of Religion

When did religion begin? No one knows for sure. There are suggestions of religion in Neandertal burials and on European cave walls, where painted stick figures may represent shamans—early religious specialists. Nevertheless, any statement about when, where, why, and how religion arose, or any description of its original nature, can be only speculative. Although inconclusive, many such speculations have revealed important functions and effects of religious behavior. Several theories will be examined now.

SPIRITUAL BEINGS

The founder of the anthropology of religion was the Englishman Sir Edward Burnett Tylor (1871/1958). Religion was born, Tylor thought, as people tried to understand conditions and events they could not explain by reference to daily experience. Tylor believed that our ancestors—and contemporary nonindustrial peoples—were particularly intrigued with death, dreaming, and trance. People see images they may remember when they wake up or come out of the trance state. Tylor concluded that attempts to explain dreams and trances led early humans to believe that two entities inhabit the body, one active during the day and the other—a double or soul—active during sleep and trance states. Although they never meet, they are vital to each other. When the double permanently leaves the body, the person dies. Death is departure of the soul. From the Latin for soul, *anima,* Tylor named this belief animism. The soul was one sort of spiritual entity; people remembered various images from their dreams and trances—other spirits. For Tylor, **animism,** the earliest form of religion, was a belief in spiritual beings.

Tylor proposed that religion evolved through stages, beginning with animism. *Polytheism* (the belief in multiple gods) and then *monotheism* (the belief in a single, all-powerful deity) devel-

oped later. Because religion originated to explain things people didn't understand, Tylor thought it would decline as science offered better explanations. To an extent, he was right. We now have scientific explanations for many things that religion once explained. Nevertheless, because religion persists, it must do something more than explain the mysterious. It must, and does, have other functions and meanings.

CULTURETHINK

What kinds of questions does religion answer that science cannot? Do you think, like Tylor did, that religion declines as science provides better answers?

POWERS AND FORCES

Besides animism—and sometimes coexisting with it in the same society—is a view of the supernatural as a domain of impersonal power, or *force,* which people can control under certain conditions. (You'd be right to think of *Star Wars.*) Such a conception of the supernatural is particularly prominent in Melanesia, the area of the South Pacific that includes Papua New Guinea and adjacent islands. Melanesians believed in **mana,** a sacred impersonal force existing in the universe. Mana can reside in people, animals, plants, and objects.

animism Belief in souls or doubles.

mana Sacred impersonal force in Melanesian and Polynesian religions.

Melanesian mana was similar to our notion of efficacy or luck. Melanesians attributed success to mana, which people could acquire or manipulate in different ways, such as through magic. Objects with mana could change someone's luck. For example, a charm or amulet belonging to

This image of Apollo, with a lyre, and Artemis, sacrificing over an alter fire, illustrates ancient Greek polytheism. The red-figured terra-cotta vessel dates from ca. 2500 B.P.

a successful hunter might transmit the hunter's mana to the next person who held or wore it. A woman might put a rock in her garden, see her yields improve dramatically, and attribute the change to the force contained in the rock.

Beliefs in manalike forces are widespread, although the specifics of the religious doctrines vary. Consider the contrast between mana in Melanesia and Polynesia (the islands included in a triangular area marked by Hawaii to the north, Easter Island to the east, and New Zealand to the southwest). In Melanesia, one could acquire mana by chance, or by working hard to get it. In Polynesia, mana wasn't potentially available to everyone but was attached to political offices. Chiefs and nobles had more mana than ordinary people did.

So charged with mana were the highest chiefs that contact with them was dangerous to the commoners. The mana of chiefs flowed out of their bodies wherever they went. It could infect the ground, making it dangerous for others to walk in the chief's footsteps. It could permeate the containers and utensils chiefs used in eating. Contact between chief and commoners was dangerous because mana could have an effect like an electric shock. Because high chiefs had so much mana, their bodies and possessions were **taboo** (set apart as sacred and off-limits to ordinary people). Contact between a high chief and commoners was forbidden. Because ordinary people couldn't bear as much sacred current as royalty could, when commoners were accidentally exposed, purification rites were necessary.

taboo Prohibition backed by supernatural sanctions.

magic Use of supernatural techniques to accomplish specific aims.

One function of religion is to explain. A belief in souls explains what happens in sleep, trance, and death. Melanesian mana explains differential success that people can't understand in ordinary, natural terms. People fail at hunting, war, or gardening not because they are lazy, stupid, or inept but because success comes—or doesn't come—from the supernatural world.

The beliefs in spiritual beings (e.g., animism) and supernatural forces (e.g., mana) fit within the definition of religion given at the beginning of this chapter. Most religions include both spirits and impersonal forces. Likewise the supernatural beliefs of contemporary North Americans include beings (gods, saints, souls, demons) and forces (charms, talismans, crystals, and sacred objects).

MAGIC

Magic refers to supernatural techniques intended to accomplish specific aims. These techniques include spells, formulas, and incantations used with deities or with impersonal forces. Magicians use *imitative magic* to produce a desired effect by imitating it. If magicians wish to injure or kill someone, they may imitate that effect on an image of the victim. Sticking pins in "voodoo dolls" is an example. With *contagious magic,* whatever is done to an object is believed to affect a person who once had contact with it. Sometimes practitioners of contagious magic use body products from prospective victims—their nails or hair, for example. The spell performed on the body product is believed to reach the person eventually and work the desired result (see Stein and Stein 2008).

We find magic in societies with diverse religious beliefs. It can be associated with animism, mana, polytheism, or monotheism. Magic is neither simpler nor more primitive than animism or the belief in mana.

UNCERTAINTY, ANXIETY, SOLACE

Religion and magic don't just explain things. They serve emotional needs as well as cognitive (e.g., explanatory) ones. For example, supernatural beliefs and practices can help reduce anxiety. Religion helps people face death and endure life crises. Magical techniques can dispel doubts that arise when outcomes are beyond human control.

Although all societies have techniques to deal with everyday matters, there are certain aspects of people's lives over which they lack control. When people face uncertainty and danger, according to Malinowski, they turn to magic. As mentioned in "Understanding Ourselves" at the beginning of this chapter, Malinowski found that the Trobriand Islanders used magic when sailing, a hazardous activity. He proposed that because people can't control matters such as wind, weather, and the fish supply, they turn to magic (Malinowski 1931/1978). Gmelch's research on baseball and magic, also discussed in "Understanding Ourselves," confirms Malinowski's conclusion that magic is most prevalent in situations of chance or uncertainty, especially pitching and batting.

Malinowski noted that it was only when confronted by situations they could not control that Trobrianders, out of psychological stress, turned from technology to magic. Despite our improving technical skills, we still can't con-

Trobriand Islanders prepare a traditional trading canoe for use in the Kula, a regional exchange system. The woman brings trade goods in a basket, while the men prepare the long boat to set sail. Magic is often associated with uncertainty, such as sailing in unpredictable waters.

....

CULTURE THINK

Think about superstitions, such as knocking on wood to prevent an unwanted outcome. Think of three additional superstitious behaviors. How many of them are used, like magic, to produce an illusion of control in an uncertain situation?

special (sacred) places and at set times. Rituals include *liturgical orders*—sequences of words and actions invented prior to the current performance of the ritual in which they occur.

These features link rituals to plays, but there are important differences. Plays have audiences rather than participants. Actors merely *portray* something, but ritual performers—who make up congregations—are in *earnest*. Rituals convey information about the participants and their traditions. Repeated year after year, generation after generation, rituals translate enduring messages, values, and sentiments into action.

Rituals are *social* acts. Inevitably, some participants are more committed than others to the beliefs that lie behind the rites. However, just by taking part in a joint public act, the performers signal that they accept a com-

> **ritual** Behavior that is formal, stylized, repetitive, and stereotyped, performed earnestly as a social act; rituals are held at set times and places and have liturgical orders.

trol every outcome, and magic persists in contemporary societies.

RITUALS

Several features distinguish **rituals** from other kinds of behavior (Rappaport 1974, 1999). Rituals are formal—stylized, repetitive, and stereotyped. People perform them in

STUDY TIP

Rituals serve two purposes:

- They convey messages, values, and sentiments;

  - They encourage a common social order.

Did You Know

Mardi Gras exemplifies a ritual of rebellion, in which people are temporarily allowed to reject the dominant social order. Pre-Civil War Mardi Gras clubs originated in Alabama's wealthy, white, Catholic plantation society and eventually moved to Louisiana. The clubs' activities formed part of their winter festivities. The first ball held by a black Mardi Gras club was in 1894.

mon social and moral order, one that transcends their status as individuals.

RITES OF PASSAGE

Magic and religion, as Malinowski noted, can reduce anxiety and allay fears. Ironically, beliefs and rituals also can *create* anxiety and a sense of insecurity and danger (Radcliffe-Brown 1962/1965). Anxiety may arise *because* a rite exists. Indeed, participation in a collective ritual may build up stress, whose common reduction, through the completion of the ritual, enhances the solidarity of the participants.

Rites of passage, such as the collective circumcision of teenagers, can be very stressful. The traditional vision quests of Native Americans, particularly the Plains Indians, illustrate **rites of passage** (customs associated with the transition from one place or stage of life to another), which are found throughout the world. Among the Plains Indians, to move from boyhood to manhood, a youth temporarily separated from his community. After a period of isolation in the wilderness, often featuring fasting and

rites of passage Culturally defined activities associated with the transition from one place or stage of life to another.

liminality The critically important marginal or in-between phase of a rite of passage.

drug consumption, the young man would see a vision, which would become his guardian spirit. He would then return to his community as an adult.

The rites of passage of contemporary societies include confirmations, baptisms, bar and bat mitzvahs, and fraternity hazing. Passage rites involve changes in social status, such as from boyhood to manhood and from nonmember to sorority sister. More generally, a rite of passage may mark any change in place, condition, social position, or age.

All rites of passage have three phases: separation, liminality, and incorporation. In the first phase, people withdraw from the group and begin moving from one place or status to another. In the third phase, they reenter society, having completed the rite. The *liminal* phase is the most interesting. It is the period between states, the limbo during which people have left one place or state but haven't yet entered or joined the next (Turner 1967/1974).

Liminality always has certain characteristics. Liminal people occupy ambiguous social positions. They exist apart from ordinary distinctions and expectations, living in a time out of time. They are cut off from normal social contacts. A variety of contrasts may demarcate liminality from regular social life. For example, among the Ndembu of Zambia, a chief underwent a rite of passage before taking office. During the liminal period, his past and future positions in society were ignored, even reversed. He was subjected to a variety of insults, orders, and humiliations.

Passage rites often are collective. Several individuals—boys being circumcised, fraternity or sorority initiates, men at military boot camps, football players in summer training camps, women becoming nuns—pass through the rites together as a group. Table 10.1 summarizes the contrasts, or oppositions, between liminality and normal social life. Most notable is a social aspect of *collective*

Passage rites are often collective. A group—such as these initiates in Togo or these Navy trainees in San Diego—passes through the rites as a unit. Such liminal people experience the same treatment and conditions and must act alike. They share communitas, an intense community spirit, a feeling of great social solidarity or togetherness.

Oppositions Between Liminality and Normal Social Life

Liminality	Normal Social Structure
Transition	State
Homogeneity	Heterogeneity
Communitas	Structure
Equality	Inequality
Anonymity	Names
Absence of property	Property
Absence of status	Status
Absence of rank	Rank
Humility	Pride
Nakedness or uniform dress	Dress distinctions
Sexual continence or excess	Sexuality
Minimization of sex distinctions	Maximization of sex distinctions
Disregard of personal appearance	Care for personal appearance
Unselfishness	Selfishness
Total obedience	Obedience only to superior rank
Sacredness	Secularity
Sacred instruction	Technical Knowledge
Silence	Speech
Simplicity	Complexity
Acceptance of pain and suffering	Avoidance of pain and suffering

Source: From *The Ritual Process* by Victor Turner. Copyright © 1969 by Aldine Publishers. Reprinted by permission of Aldine Transaction, a division of Transaction Publishers.

TABLE 10.1

liminality called **communitas** (Turner 1967/1974), an intense community spirit, a feeling of great social solidarity, equality, and togetherness. People experiencing liminality together form a community of equals. The social distinctions that have existed before or will exist afterward are forgotten temporarily. Liminal people experience the same treatment and conditions and must act alike. Liminality may be marked ritually and symbolically by *reversals* of ordinary behavior. For example, sexual taboos may be intensified, or conversely, sexual excess may be encouraged. Liminal symbols mark entities and circumstances as extraordinary—outside and beyond ordinary social space and routine social events.

Liminality is basic to every passage rite. Furthermore, in certain societies, including our own, liminal symbols may be used to set off one (religious) group from another, and from society as a whole. Such "permanent liminal groups" (e.g., sects, brotherhoods, and cults) are found most characteristically in nation-states. Such liminal features as humility, poverty, equality, obedience, sexual abstinence, and silence may be required for all sect or cult members. Those who join such a group agree to its rules. As if they were undergoing a passage rite—but in this case a never-ending one—they may rid themselves of their previous possessions and cut themselves off from former social links, including those with family members.

Identity as a group member is expected to transcend individuality. Cult members often wear uniform clothing.

communitas Intense community spirit, a feeling of great social solidarity, equality, and togetherness; characteristic of people experiencing liminality together.

They may try to reduce distinctions based on age and gender by using a common hairstyle (shaved head, short hair, or long hair). With such cults, the individual, so important in American culture, is submerged in the collective. This is one reason Americans are so fearful and suspicious of "cults."

Not all collective rites are rites of passage. Most societies observe occasions on which people come together to worship and, in doing so, affirm and reinforce their solidarity. Rituals such as the totemic ceremonies described below are *rites of intensification:* They demand collective adherence to the rules of ritual behavior and create emotions (the collective spiritual effervescence described by Durkheim 1912/2001) that enhance and intensify social solidarity.

TOTEMISM

The religions of the Native Australians included totemism. *Totems* could be animals, plants, or geographical features. In each tribe, groups of people had particular totems. Members of each totemic group believed themselves to be descendants of their totem. They customarily neither killed nor ate it, but this taboo was lifted once a year, when people assembled for ceremonies dedicated to the totem. These annual rites were believed to be necessary for the totem's survival and reproduction.

Totemism uses nature as a model for society. The totems are usually animals and plants, which are part of nature. People relate to nature through their totemic association with natural species. Because each group has a different totem, social differences mirror natural contrasts. Diversity in the natural order becomes a model for diversity in the social order. However, although totemic plants and animals occupy different niches in nature, on another level they are united because they all are part of nature. The unity of the human social order is enhanced by symbolic association with and imitation of the natural order (Durkheim 1912/2001; Lévi-Strauss 1963; Radcliffe-Brown 1962/1965).

In contemporary nations, too, totems continue to mark groups, such as states and universities (e.g., Badgers, Buckeyes, and Wolverines), professional teams (Lions, Tigers, and Bears), and political parties (donkeys and elephants). Although the modern context is more secular, one can still witness, in intense college football rivalries, some of the effervescence Durkheim noted in Australian totemic religion and other rites of intensification.

Totems are sacred emblems symbolizing common identity. This is true not just among Native Australians, but also among Native American groups of the North Pacific Coast of North America, whose totem poles are well known. Their totemic carvings, which commemorated, and told visual stories about, ancestors, animals, and spirits, were also associated with ceremonies. In totemic rites, people gather together to honor their totem. In so doing, they use ritual to maintain the social oneness that the totem symbolizes.

>> Religion and Social Control

Religion has meaning for people. It helps them cope with adversity and tragedy. It offers hope that things will get better. Lives can be transformed through spiritual healing. Sinners can repent and be saved—or they can go on sinning and be damned. If the faithful truly internalize a system of religious rewards and punishments, their religion becomes a powerful influence on their beliefs, behavior, and what they teach their children.

Many people engage in religious activity because it seems to work. Prayers get answered. Faith healers heal. Sometimes it doesn't take much to convince the faithful that religious actions are effective. Many American Indian people in southwestern Oklahoma use faith healers at high monetary costs, not just because it makes them feel better

Religion can work by getting inside people and mobilizing their emotions—their joy, their wrath, their righteousness. People feel a deep sense of shared joy, meaning, experience, communion, belonging, and commitment to their religion. The power of religion affects action. When religions meet, they can coexist peacefully, or their differences can be a basis for enmity and disharmony, even battle. Religious fervor has inspired Christians on crusades against the infidel and has led Muslims to wage holy wars against non-Islamic peoples. Throughout history, political leaders have used religion to promote and justify their views and policies.

By late September 1996, the Taliban Movement had firmly imposed an extreme form of social control through religious repression on Afghanistan and its people. Led by Muslim clerics, the Taliban aimed to create their version of an Islamic society modeled on the teachings of the Koran (Burns 1997). Various repressive measures were instituted. The Taliban barred women from work and girls from school. Females past puberty were prohibited from talking to men unrelated to them. Women needed an approved reason, such as shopping for food, to leave their homes. Men, who were required to grow bushy beards, also faced an array of bans—against playing cards, listening to music, keeping pigeons, and flying kites.

To enforce their decrees, the Taliban sent armed enforcers throughout the country. These agents took charge

A wandering cow does not perturb these shoppers in Udaipur, Rajasthan. India's zebu cattle are protected by the doctrine of asimsa, a principle of nonviolence that forbids the killing of animals generally. This Hindu doctrine puts the full power of organized religion behind the command not to destroy a valuable resource even in times of extreme need.

about the uncertain, but because it works (Lassiter 1998). Each year legions of Brazilians visit a church, Nosso Senhor do Bomfim, in the city of Salvador, Bahia. They vow to repay "Our Lord" (Nosso Senhor) if healing happens. Showing that the vows work, and are repaid, are the thousands of *ex votos,* plastic impressions of every conceivable body part, that adorn the church, along with photos of people who have been cured.

Near a royal tomb in Kabul, a young boy prepares to launch a kite, illustrating Afghanistan's national (amateur) sport for boys. Banned by the Taliban, kite flying is once again popular.

Witchcraft accusations often are directed at socially marginal or anomalous individuals. Among the Betsileo of Madagascar, for example, who prefer patrilocal postmarital residence, men living in their wife's or their mother's village violate a cultural norm. Linked to their anomalous social position, just a bit of unusual behavior (e.g., staying up late at night) on their part is sufficient for them to be called witches and avoided as a result. In tribes and peasant communities, people who stand out economically, especially if they seem to be benefiting at the expense of others, often face witchcraft accusations, leading to social ostracism or punishment. In this case witchcraft accusation becomes a **leveling mechanism,** a custom or social action that operates to reduce status differences and thus to bring standouts in line with community norms—another form of social control.

To ensure proper behavior, religions offer rewards (e.g., the fellowship of the religious community) and punishments (e.g., the threat of being cast out or excommunicated). Religions, especially the formal organized ones typically found in state societies, often prescribe a code of ethics and morality to guide behavior. The Judaic Ten Commandments laid down a set of prohibitions against killing, stealing, adultery, and other misdeeds. Crimes are breaches of secular laws, as sins are breaches of religious strictures. Some rules (e.g., the Ten Commandments) proscribe or prohibit behavior; others prescribe behavior. The Golden Rule, for instance, is a religious guide to do unto others as you would have them do unto you. Moral codes are ways of maintaining order and stability. Codes of morality and ethics are constantly repeated in religious sermons, catechisms, and the like. They become internalized psychologically. They guide behavior and produce regret, guilt, shame, and the need for forgiveness, expiation, and absolution when they are not followed.

of "beard checks" and other forms of scrutiny on behalf of a religious police force known as the General Department for the Preservation of Virtue and the Elimination of Vice (Burns 1997). By late fall 2001 the Taliban had been overthrown, with a new interim government established in Kabul, the Afghan capital, on December 22. The collapse of the Taliban followed American bombing of Afghanistan in response to the September 11, 2001, attacks on New York's World Trade Center and Washington's Pentagon. As the Taliban yielded Kabul to victorious northern alliance forces, local men flocked to barbershops to have their beards trimmed or shaved. They were using a key Taliban symbol to celebrate the end of religious repression.

"God has no religion."

Mahatma Gandhi

Note that in the case of the Taliban, forms of social control were used to support a strict religious orthodoxy. This wasn't repression in religion's name, but repressive religion. In other countries, secular leaders seeking power may use religious rhetoric to get it.

How may leaders mobilize communities and, in so doing, gain support for their own policies? One way is by persuasion; another is by instilling hatred or fear. Consider witchcraft accusations. Witch hunts can be powerful means of social control by creating a climate of danger and insecurity that affects everyone, not just the people who are likely targets. No one wants to seem deviant, to be accused of being a witch. Witch hunts often take aim at people who can be accused and punished with least chance of retaliation. During the great European witch craze of the fifteenth, sixteenth, and seventeenth centuries (Harris 1974), most accusations and convictions were against poor women with little social support.

leveling mechanisms Customs and social actions that operate to reduce differences in wealth and thus to bring standouts in line with community norms.

shaman A part-time religious practitioner who mediates between ordinary people and supernatural beings and forces.

>> Kinds of Religion

Religion is a cultural universal. But religions exist in particular societies, and cultural differences show up systematically in religious beliefs and practices. For example, the religions of stratified, state societies differ from those of societies with less marked social contrasts and power differentials.

Considering several societies, Wallace (1966) identified four types of religion: shamanic, communal, Olympian, and monotheistic (Table 10.2). The simplest type is shamanic religion. Unlike priests, **shamans** aren't full-time religious officials but part-time religious figures who mediate between people and supernatural beings and forces. All societies have medico-magico-religious specialists. *Shaman* is the general term encompassing curers ("witch doctors"), mediums, spiritualists, astrologers, palm read-

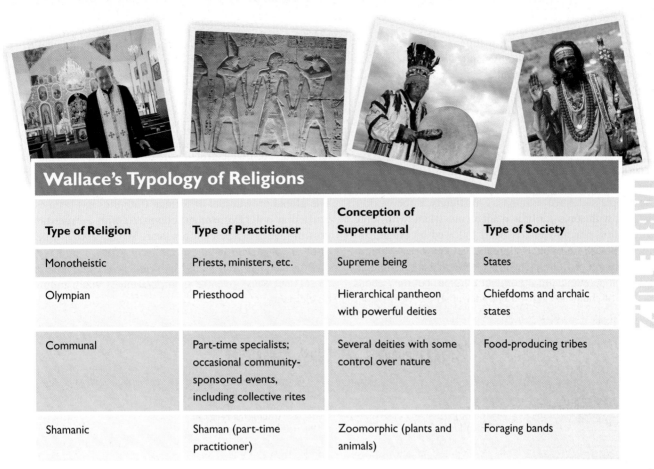

Wallace's Typology of Religions

TABLE 10.2

Type of Religion	Type of Practitioner	Conception of Supernatural	Type of Society
Monotheistic	Priests, ministers, etc.	Supreme being	States
Olympian	Priesthood	Hierarchical pantheon with powerful deities	Chiefdoms and archaic states
Communal	Part-time specialists; occasional community-sponsored events, including collective rites	Several deities with some control over nature	Food-producing tribes
Shamanic	Shaman (part-time practitioner)	Zoomorphic (plants and animals)	Foraging bands

ers, and other diviners. Wallace found shamanic religions to be most characteristic of foraging societies.

Shamans sometimes set themselves off symbolically from ordinary people by assuming a different or ambiguous sex or gender role. (In nation-states, priests, nuns, and vestal virgins do something similar by taking vows of celibacy and chastity.) Among the Chukchee of Siberia (Bogoras 1904), male shamans copied the dress, speech, hair arrangements, and lifestyles of women. These shamans took other men as husbands and sex partners and received respect for their supernatural and curative expertise. Female shamans could join a fourth gender, copying men and taking wives.

Communal religions have, in addition to shamans, community rituals such as harvest ceremonies and collective rites of passage. Although communal religions lack *full-time* religious specialists, they believe in several deities (**polytheism**) who control aspects of nature. Although some hunter-gatherers, including Australian totemites, have communal religions, these religions are more typical of farming societies.

Olympian religions, which arose with state organization and marked social stratification, add full-time religious specialists—professional *priesthoods*. Like the state itself, the priesthood is hierarchically and bureaucratically organized. The term *Olympian* comes from Mount Olympus, home of the classical Greek gods. Olympian religions are polytheistic. They include powerful anthropomorphic

gods with specialized functions, for example, gods of love, war, the sea, and death. Olympian *pantheons* (collections of supernatural beings) were prominent in the religions of many nonindustrial nation-states, including the Aztecs of Mexico, several African and Asian kingdoms, and classical Greece and Rome. Wallace's fourth type—**monotheism**—also has priesthoods and notions of divine power, but it views the supernatural differently. In monotheism, all supernatural phenomena are manifestations of, or are under the control of, a single eternal, omniscient, omnipotent, and omnipresent supreme being.

Robert Bellah (1978) coined the term "world-rejecting religion" to describe most forms of Christianity. The first world-rejecting religions arose in ancient civilizations, along with literacy and a specialized priesthood. These religions are so-named because of their tendency to reject the natural (mundane, ordinary, material, secular) world and to focus instead on a higher (sacred, transcendent)

communal religions In Wallace's typology, these religions have—in addition to shamanic cults—communal cults in which people organize community rituals such as harvest ceremonies and rites of passage.

polytheism Belief in several deities who control aspects of nature.

Olympian religions In Wallace's typology, religions that develop with state organization; have full-time religious specialists—professional priesthoods.

monotheism Worship of an eternal, omniscient, omnipotent, and omnipresent supreme being.

realm of reality. The divine is a domain of exalted morality to which humans can only aspire. Salvation through fusion with the supernatural is the main goal of such religions.

>> World Religions

The number of adherents of the world's major religions today is shown below in "Major World Religions." Based on people's claimed religions, Christianity is the world's largest, with some 2.1 billion adherents. Islam, with some 1.5 billion practitioners, is next, followed by Hinduism, then Chinese traditional religion (also known as Chinese folk religion or Confucianism), and Buddhism. More than a billion people claim no official religion, but only about a fifth of them are self-proclaimed atheists. Worldwide,

Islam is growing at a rate of about 2.9 percent annually, versus 2.3 percent for Christianity, whose overall growth rate is the same as the rate of world population increase (Adherents.com 2002; Ontario Consultants 2001).

Within Christianity, the growth rate varies. There were an estimated 680 million "born-again" Christians (e.g., Pentecostals and Evangelicals) in the world in 2001, with an annual worldwide growth rate of 7 percent, versus just 2.3 percent for Christianity overall. (This would translate into 1.2 billion Pentecostals/Evangelicals by 2010.) The global growth rate of Roman Catholics has been estimated at only 1.3 percent, compared with a Protestant growth rate of 3.3 percent per year (Winter 2001). Much of this explosive growth, especially in Africa, is of a type of Protestantism that would be scarcely recognizable to most Americans, given its incorporation of many animistic elements.

Religions of the World*

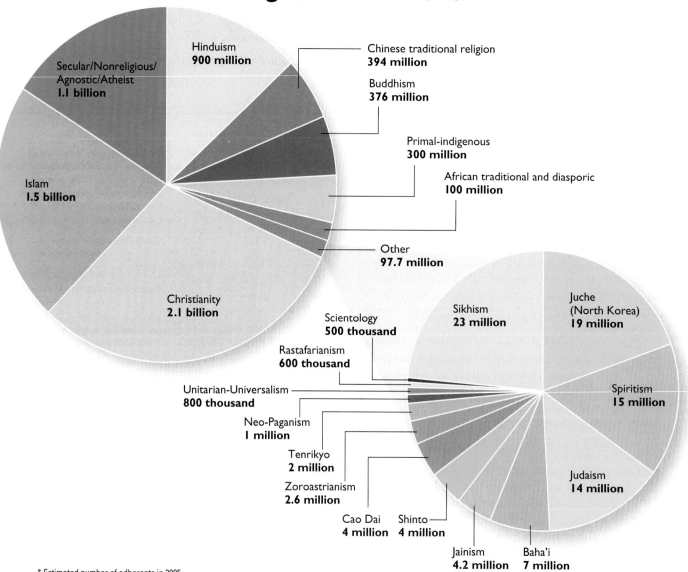

* Estimated number of adherents in 2005

Source: B.A. Robinson, "Religions of the World," Ontario Consultants on Religious Tolerance, www.religioustolerance.org/worldrel.html. Reprinted by permission.

In an analysis of more than a thousand films, Jack Shaheen (2006, 2009) found that only 5 percent of Arab and Muslim characters were presented in a positive light. Arabs repeatedly were caricatured as villains, buffoons, lechers, incompetents, and terrorists. Watch a film or TV show featuring Arab or Islamic characters (e.g., *Babel*, *Syriana*, *24*). How are those characters portrayed? Is religion an important part of the portrayal? Do characters with other ethnic backgrounds (e.g., Latinos, African Americans, non-Hispanic whites) have as many religious markers? How do you account for the differences you note in these portrayals?

>> Religion and Change

Religious fundamentalists seek order based on strict adherence to purportedly traditional standards, beliefs, rules, and customs. Christian and Islamic fundamentalists recognize, decry, and attempt to redress change, yet they also contribute to change (Antoun 2008). In a worldwide process, new religions challenge established churches. In the United States, for example, conservative Christian TV hosts have become influential broadcasters and opinion shapers. In Latin America, evangelical Protestantism is winning millions of converts from Roman Catholicism.

Like political organization, religion helps maintain social order. And like political mobilization, religious energy can be harnessed not just for change but also for revolution. Reacting to conquest or to actual or perceived foreign domination, for instance, religious leaders may seek to al-

Anthropology Works

A politician or a diplomat dealing with foreign affairs would benefit from anthropological perspectives on religious responses to social change. What appear to be struggles over religion often have much deeper roots in unequal access to social and economic goods.

ter or revitalize their society. In an "Islamic Revolution," for example, Iranian ayatollahs marshaled religious fervor to create national solidarity and radical change. We call such movements *nativistic movements* (Linton 1943) or *revitalization movements* (Wallace 1956).

REVITALIZATION MOVEMENTS

Social movements that occur in times of change, in which religious leaders emerge and undertake to alter or revitalize a society, are termed **revitalization movements.** Christianity originated as a revitalization movement. Jesus was one of several prophets who preached new religious doctrines while the Middle East was under Roman rule. It was a time of social unrest, when a foreign power ruled the land. Jesus inspired a new, enduring, and major religion. His contemporaries were not so successful.

The Handsome Lake religion arose around 1800 among the Iroquois of New York State (Wallace 1969). Handsome Lake, the founder of this revitalization movement, was a leader of one of the Iroquois tribes. The Iroquois had suffered because of their support of the British against the American colonials. After the colonial victory and a wave of immigration to their homeland, the Iroquois were dispersed on small reservations. Unable to pursue traditional horticulture and hunting in their homeland, the Iroquois became heavy drinkers and quarreled among themselves.

> **revitalization movements** Movements that occur in times of change, in which religious leaders emerge and undertake to alter or revitalize a society.

Handsome Lake was a heavy drinker who started having visions from heavenly messengers. The spirits warned him that unless the Iroquois changed their ways, they would be destroyed. His visions offered a plan for coping with the new order. Witchcraft, quarreling, and drinking would end. The Iroquois would copy European farming techniques, which, unlike traditional Iroquois horticulture, stressed male rather than female labor. Handsome Lake preached that the Iroquois should also abandon their communal long houses and matrilineal descent groups for more permanent marriages and individual family households. The teachings of Handsome Lake produced a new church and religion, one that still has members in New York and Ontario. This revitalization movement helped the Iroquois adapt to and survive in a modified environment. They eventually

STUDY TIP

Two religious responses to the expansion of the world capitalist economy are fundamentalisms (Christian and Islamic) and revitalization movements (Handsome Lake religion and cargo cults).

gained a reputation among their non-Indian neighbors as sober family farmers.

CARGO CULTS

Like the Handsome Lake religion just discussed, **cargo cults** are revitalization movements. Such movements may emerge when natives have regular contact with industrial societies but lack their wealth, technology, and living standards. Some cargo cults attempt to *explain* European domination and wealth and to achieve similar success magically by mimicking European behavior and manipulating symbols of the desired life style. The cargo cults of Melanesia and Papua New Guinea weave Christian doctrine with aboriginal beliefs. They take their name from their focus on cargo—European goods of the sort natives have seen unloaded from the cargo holds of ships and airplanes.

cargo cults Postcolonial, acculturative, religious movements common in Melanesia that attempt to explain European domination and wealth and to achieve similar success magically by mimicking European behavior.

In one early cult, members believed that the spirits of the dead would arrive in a ship. These ghosts would bring manufactured goods for the natives and would kill all the whites. More recent cults replaced ships with airplanes (Worsley 1959/1985). Many cults have used elements of European culture as sacred objects. The rationale is that Europeans use these objects, have wealth, and therefore must know the "secret of cargo." By mimicking how Europeans use or treat objects, natives hope also to come upon the secret knowledge needed to gain cargo.

Having seen Europeans' reverent treatment of flags and flagpoles, for example, the members of one cult began to worship flagpoles. They believed the flagpoles were sacred towers that could transmit messages between the living and the dead. Other natives built airstrips to entice planes bearing canned goods, portable radios, clothing, wristwatches, and motorcycles. Near the airstrips they made effigies of towers, airplanes, and radios. They talked into the cans in a magical attempt to establish radio contact with the gods. Can you think of anything in your own society (including the media) that features similar behavior?

Some cargo cult prophets proclaimed that success would come through a reversal of European domination and native subjugation. The day was near, they preached, when natives, aided by God, Jesus, or native ancestors, would turn the tables. Native skins would turn white, and those of Europeans would turn brown; Europeans would die or be killed.

Cargo cults blend aboriginal and Christian beliefs. Melanesian myths told of ancestors shedding their skins and changing into powerful beings and of dead people returning to life. Christian missionaries, who had been in Melanesia since the late nineteenth century, also spoke of resurrection. The cults' preoccupation with cargo is related to traditional Melanesian big man systems. In the chapter "Political Systems," we saw that a Melanesian big man had to be generous. People worked for the big man, helping him amass wealth, but eventually he had to give a feast and give away all that wealth.

Because of their experience with big man systems, Melanesians believed that all wealthy people eventually had to give away their wealth. For decades they had attended Christian missions and worked on plantations. All the while they expected Europeans to return the fruits of their labor as their own big men did. When the Europeans refused to distribute the wealth or even to let natives know the secret of its production and distribution, cargo cults developed.

Like arrogant big men, Europeans would be leveled, by death if necessary. However, natives lacked the physical means of doing what their traditions said they should do. Thwarted by well-armed colonial forces, natives resorted to magical leveling. They called on supernatural beings to intercede, to kill or otherwise deflate the European big men and redistribute their wealth.

Cargo cults are religious responses to the expansion of the world capitalist economy. However, this religious mobilization had political and economic results. Cult participation gave

A cargo cult in Vanuatu, a country in Melanesia. Boys and men march with spears, imitating British colonial soldiers. Does anything in your own society remind you of a cargo cult?

Melanesians a basis for common interests and activities and thus helped pave the way for political parties and economic interest organizations. Previously separated by geography, language, and customs, Melanesians started forming larger groups as members of the same cults and followers of the same prophets. The cargo cults paved the way for political action through which the indigenous peoples eventually regained their autonomy.

>> Secular Rituals

In concluding this discussion of religion, we may recognize some problems with the definition of religion given at the beginning of this chapter. The first problem: If we define religion with reference to supernatural beings, powers, and forces, how do we classify ritual-like behaviors that occur in secular contexts? Some anthropologists believe there are both sacred and secular rituals. Secular rituals include formal, invariant, stereotyped, earnest, repetitive

Find a group on campus or in town that might be considered a "permanent liminal group." If you can't find one, read about cults and sects and choose one in the United States or another society you may know well. Learn something about the group's practices and beliefs. Using Table 10.1, list liminal features that seem to fit this group. For example, do you see an absence of rank and a sharing of communitas? Note how such features are revealed in behavior patterns. How would the contrasts between liminality and "normal" social life help explain why outsiders might consider this group strange or even threatening?

get involved!

behavior and rites of passage that take place in nonreligious settings.

A second problem: If the distinction between the supernatural and the natural is not consistently made in a society, how can we tell what is religion and what isn't? The Betsileo of Madagascar, for example, view witches and dead ancestors as real people who play roles in ordinary life. However, their occult powers are not empirically demonstrable.

A third problem: The behavior considered appropriate for religious occasions varies tremendously from culture to culture. One society may consider drunken frenzy the surest sign of faith, whereas another may inculcate quiet reverence. Who is to say which is "more religious"?

For REVIEW

CULTURECLIPS

TO ACCESS THESE VIDEOS ON
YOUR COMPUTER, VISIT

www.mhhe.com/gezonqr

10-1

10-2

10-3

I.   What is religion, and what are its various forms, social correlates, and functions?

• Wallace defined religion as "belief and behavior concerned with supernatural beings, powers, and forces." Religion also encompasses the feelings, meanings, and congregations associated with such belief and behavior. Wallace defined three types of religion: shamanic, which is common in foraging societies; communal, which is typical of farming societies; and Olympian, which is associated with states. Tylor proposed three stages in the evolution of religion: animism, polytheism, and monotheism. Expressions of religion include mana, a sacred impersonal force, and totemism, which uses nature as a model for society. Magic employs supernatural techniques to accomplish specific aims. Magic and religion help to explain the world and serve emotional needs, such as helping people cope with adversity and reducing anxiety, although rites also can create anxiety. Religion can divide as well as unite.

II. What is ritual, and what are its various forms and expressions?

• Rituals consist of behavior that is formal—stylized, repetitive, and stereotyped. People perform rituals in sacred places and at set times. Rituals convey information about the participants and translate enduring messages and values into action. Through ritual people subordinate their particular beliefs to a social collectivity. Rites of passage mark changes in place, condition, age, or social position. These rites have three stages: separation, liminality, and incorporation. In separation, people withdraw from the group; incorporation involves reentering it. Liminality is the limbo in between. In communitas, a liminal characteristic, participants experience social solidarity and equality. Rituals may be secular as well as religious.

III. What role does religion play in maintaining and changing societies?

• Religion establishes and maintains social control through moral and ethical beliefs and real and imagined rewards and punishments. Religion also can mobilize communities for collective action; leaders may use religious rhetoric to gain support for their policies. Some orthodox groups may institute repressive measures to control people's behavior and exclude them from certain activities. Leveling actions bring standouts in line with social norms. Religion can promote change through revitalization movements led by religious figures trying to alter a society and help its people adapt to change. Cargo cults blend aboriginal and Christian beliefs to explain European domination and wealth and achieve similar success magically.

Pop Quiz

1. According to Tylor, through what sequence did religion evolve?
   a. Animism, polytheism, monotheism.
   b. Imitative magic, polytheism, monotheism.
   c. Mana, polytheism, monotheism.
   d. Olympianism, animism, monotheism.

2. Which of the following describes the concept of mana in Polynesian and Melanesian cultures?
   a. Things charged with mana were taboo.
   b. In Melanesia, mana was similar to the notion of luck, anyone could get it; in Polynesia, mana was attached to political elites.
   c. Most anthropologists agree that mana was the most primitive religious doctrine in both areas.
   d. In both Polynesia and Melanesia, mana was concerned with supernatural beings rather than with powers or forces.

3. What is an irony this chapter highlights when describing rites of passage?
   a. Participants in rites of passage often are tricked into believing there is a big change in their status.
   b. The main goal of such rites is to worsen the anxieties caused by other aspects of religion.
   c. Beliefs and rituals can both diminish and create anxiety and a sense of danger.
   d. Rites of passage would be more effective if they did not include the third phase of the rite.

4. What is typically observed during the liminal phase of a rite of passage?
   a. Intensification of social hierarchy.
   b. Symbolic reversals of ordinary behavior.
   c. Formation of a ranking system.
   d. No change in the social norms.

5. This chapter describes how Afghanistan's Taliban movement imposed an extreme form of social control through repressive religion. However:
   a. Secular leaders also use religion for social control.
   b. Religion is used this way only by Muslim clerical leaders.
   c. The Taliban movement had no interest in women's lives; it focused only on men.
   d. The Taliban's extreme forms of social control did not influence people's actions.

6. Which of the following statements does *not* completely apply to Wallace's typology of religions?
   a. Olympian religions arose with state organization and added full-time religious specialists in the form of professional priesthoods.
   b. Communal religions, typical of farming societies, lack full-time religious specialists.
   c. Shamans are full-time religious officials who mediate between people and the supernatural.
   d. In monotheism, supernatural phenomena are manifestations of a single eternal, omnipotent supreme being.

7. Which of the following points is *not* consistent with the chapter's discussion of world religions?
   a. Christianity is the world's largest major religion.
   b. Islam is growing at a faster rate than Christianity.
   c. There is no variation in the growth rate of different groups of Christians.
   d. More than a billion people claim no religion.

8. Which statement most accurately defines a revitalization movement?
   a. It seeks to maintain order through strict adherence to purportedly traditional standards, customs, and beliefs.
   b. More correctly known as a nativistic movement, a revitalization movement seeks to maintain the old native ways of life.
   c. It is a colonial religious movement that lacked adaptive value for the people involved.
   d. It is a social movement that occurs in times of change in which religious leaders undertake to revitalize a society.

9. Cargo cults, which mix Melanesian and Christian beliefs, are:
   a. Religious responses to the expansion of the world capitalistic economy, often with political and economic consequences.
   b. Cultural acts that mock the widespread but erroneous belief of European cultural supremacy.
   c. Movements that arise when natives begin to acquire and benefit from the wealth, technology, and living standards of industrial societies.
   d. Attempts to explain European domination without actually trying to achieve similar successes.

10. Which one of the following would *not* represent a problem with Wallace's definition of religion?
    a. The definition excludes ritual-like behaviors that occur in nonreligious settings.
    b. His concept of the supernatural does not fit with the idea of this realm being outside the observable world.
    c. It fails to consider societies in which the distinction between the supernatural and the natural is not consistently made.
    d. It fails to consider behavior that may be considered appropriate for religious occasions in one culture but not in another.

1. (a), 2. (b), 3. (c), 4. (b), 5. (a), 6. (c), 7. (c), 8. (d), 9. (a), 10. (b)

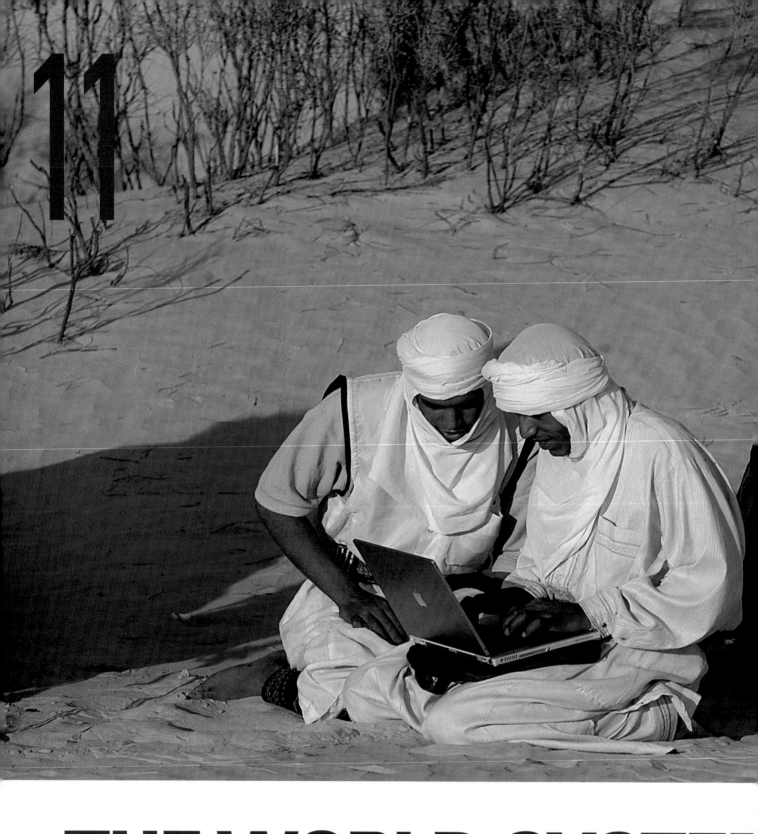

11

THE WORLD SYSTEM
AND COLONIALISM

UNDERSTANDING OURSELVES

In today's world system, people are linked as never before, and descendants of villagers who hosted ethnographers a generation ago now live transnational lives. Conrad Kottak (2010) reports on how transnationalism has affected a village in Madagascar, Ivato, that he first studied in 1966 and 1967.

When Kottak was not "in the field" in Ivato, he rented a small house in Ambalavao, a town whose residents included Indian cloth merchants, Chinese grocers, and a few French people, including two young men in the French equivalent of the Peace Corps. (Madagascar had been a French colony.) One of them, Noel, was courting Lenore, a young woman from a prominent local family originally from Ivato.

On Kottak's next trip to Madagascar, in 1981, he discovered that an active exchange program, including study abroad, had been established between Madagascar and the Soviet Union. One result of this program was that Kottak missed one of his best friends from Ivato who was spending three months studying in Moscow.

When Kottak next visited Madagascar, in 1990, he met Emily, the twenty-two-year-old daughter of Noel and Lenore, whose courtship he had witnessed in 1967. Emily was about to travel to the United States to study marketing. When Kottak saw her again a few months later in Gainesville, Florida, she inquired about her father, whom she had never met. She had sent several letters to France, but Noel never responded.

Descendants of Ambalavao now live all over the world. Emily, a child of colonialism, has two aunts in France and another in Germany. Members of her family, which is not especially wealthy, have traveled to Russia, Canada, the United States, France, Germany, and West Africa. How many of your classmates, including perhaps you, yourself, have recent transnational roots? The son of a man from a rural Kenyan village has even been elected president of the United States.

As You READ

- When and why did the world system develop, and what is it like today?

- When and how did European colonialism develop, and how is its legacy expressed in postcolonial studies?

- How do colonialism, development, industrialization, neoliberalism, and Communism exemplify intervention philosophies?

>> The World System

Although fieldwork in small communities has been anthropology's hallmark, isolated groups are impossible to find today. Truly isolated societies probably never have existed. For thousands of years, human groups have been in contact with one another. Local societies always have participated in a larger system, which today has global dimensions—we call it the *modern world system,* by which we mean a world in which nations are economically and politically interdependent.

The world system and the relations among the countries within it are shaped by the capitalist world economy. A huge increase in international trade during and after the fifteenth century led to the **capitalist world economy** (Wallerstein 1982, 2004b), a single world system committed to production for sale or exchange, with the object of maximizing profits, rather than supplying domestic needs. **Capital** refers to wealth or resources invested in business, with the intent of using the means of production to make a profit.

World-system theory can be traced to the French social historian Fernand Braudel. In his three-volume work *Civi-lization and Capitalism, 15th–18th Century* (1981, 1982, 1992), Braudel argued that society consists of interrelated parts assembled into a system. Societies are subsystems of larger systems, with the world system the largest. The key claim of **world-system theory** is that an identifiable social system, based on wealth and power differentials, extends beyond individual countries. That system is formed by a set of economic and political relations that has characterized much of the globe since the sixteenth century, when the Old World established regular contact with the New World (see Bodley 2008).

According to Wallerstein (1982, 2004b), countries within the world system occupy three different positions of economic and political power: core, semiperiphery, and periphery. The geographic center, or **core,** which is the dominant position in the world system, includes the strongest and most powerful nations, such as the United States, Germany, and Japan. In core nations, "the complexity of economic activities and the level of capital accumulation is the greatest" (Thompson 1983, p. 12). With its sophisticated technologies and mechanized production, the core churns out products that flow mainly to other core countries. Some also go to the periphery and semiperiphery. According to Arrighi (1994), the core monopolizes the most profitable activities, especially the control of world finance.

Semiperiphery and periphery countries have less power, wealth, and influence than the core does. The **semiperiphery** is intermediate between the core and the periphery. Contemporary nations of the semiperiphery, including Brazil, India, and China, are industrialized. Like core nations, they export both industrial goods and commodities, but they lack the power and economic dominance of core nations, although their power and influence are growing rapidly. Brazil, a semiperiphery nation, exports automobiles to Nigeria (a periphery nation) and auto engines, or-

capitalist world economy The single world system, which emerged in the sixteenth century, committed to production for sale, with the object of maximizing profits, rather than supplying domestic needs.

capital Wealth or resources invested in business, with the intent of producing a profit.

Did You Know?

According to the International Labor Organization, 211 million children under the age of fourteen are working around the world to help support their impoverished families. Much of what they produce is imported to the United States and other developed countries.

STUDY TIP

There are three positions in the world system:

- Core (most powerful nations, largest capital accumulation, sophisticated technologies, control over finance).

- Semiperiphery (intermediate between core and periphery, industrialized, exports to core and periphery nations, source of cheap labor).

- Periphery (least powerful nations, less mechanized industries, exports raw materials and agricultural commodities, source of cheap labor).

ange juice extract, coffee, and shrimp to the United States (a core nation). The **periphery** includes the world's least privileged and powerful countries, including Bangladesh, Guatemala, Haiti, and Madagascar, among many others. Economic activities there are less mechanized than are those in the semiperiphery, although some degree of industrialization has reached even peripheral nations. The periphery produces raw materials, agricultural commodities, and, increasingly, human labor for export to the core and the semiperiphery (Shannon 1996).

In the United States and Western Europe today, immigration—legal and illegal—from the periphery and semiperiphery supplies cheap labor for agriculture in core countries. U.S. states as distant as California, Michigan, and South Carolina make significant use of farm labor from Mexico. The availability of relatively cheap workers from noncore nations such as Mexico (in the United States) and Turkey (in Germany) benefits farmers and business owners in core countries, while also supplying remittances to families in the semiperiphery and periphery. As a result of twenty-first-century telecommunications technology, cheap labor doesn't even need to migrate to the United States. Thousands of families in India are being

CULTURE THINK

Look at the labels on your clothing: Where was it made? Where do those nations fit into the world system? (See p. 218 for a map.)

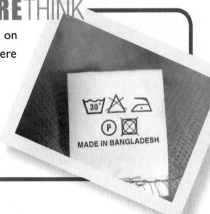

MADE IN BANGLADESH

supported as American companies outsource jobs—from telephone assistance to software engineering—to nations outside the core.

THE EMERGENCE OF THE WORLD SYSTEM

As Europeans took to ships, developing a transoceanic trade-oriented economy, people throughout the world entered Europe's sphere of influence. In the fifteenth century, Europe established regular contact with Asia, Africa, and eventually the New World (the Caribbean and the Americas). Christopher Columbus's first voyage from Spain to the Bahamas and the Caribbean in 1492 was soon followed by additional voyages. These journeys opened the way for a major exchange of people, resources, products, ideas, and diseases, as the Old and New Worlds were forever linked (Crosby 2003; Diamond 1997; Fagan 1998; Viola and Margolis 1991). Led by Spain and Portugal, Europeans extracted silver and gold, conquered the natives (taking some as slaves), and colonized their lands.

Previously in Europe as throughout the world, rural people had produced mainly for their own needs, growing their own food and making clothing, furniture, and tools from local products. Production beyond immediate needs was undertaken to pay taxes and to purchase trade items such as salt and iron. As late as 1650 the English diet was based on locally grown starches (Mintz 1985). In the two hundred years that followed, however, the English became extraordinary consumers of imported goods. One of the earliest and most popular of those goods was sugar (Mintz 1985).

Sugarcane originally was domesticated in Papua New Guinea, and sugar was first processed in India. Reaching Europe via the Middle East and the eastern Mediterranean, it was carried to the New World by Columbus (Mintz 1985). The climate of Brazil and the Caribbean proved ideal for growing sugarcane, and Europeans built plantations there to supply the growing demand for sugar. This led to the development in the seventeenth century of a plantation economy based on a single cash crop—a system known as *monocrop* production.

The demand for sugar in a growing international market spurred the development of the transatlantic slave trade and New World plantation economies based on slave labor. By the eighteenth century, an increased English demand for raw cotton led to rapid settlement of

world-system theory Argument for the historic and contemporary social, political, and economic significance of an identifiable global system, based on wealth and power differentials, that extends beyond individual countries.

core Dominant structural position in the world system; consists of the strongest and most powerful states with advanced systems of production.

semiperiphery Structural position in the world system intermediate between core and periphery; exporters of goods and commodities, but lacking the power of core nations.

periphery Weakest structural position in the world system; less mechanized producers of raw materials, agricultural commodities, and human labor.

From producer to consumer, in the modern world system. The top photo, taken in the Caribbean nation of Dominica, shows the hard labor required to extract sugar using a manual press. In the bottom photo, consumers thousands of miles from the Caribbean take afternoon tea, sweetened with imported sugar. Which of the ingredients in your breakfast today were imported?

what is now the southeastern United States and the emergence there of another slave-based mono-crop production system. Like sugar, cotton was a key trade item that fueled the growth of the world system.

>> Industrialization

By the eighteenth century the stage had been set for the **Industrial Revolution**—the historical transformation (in Europe, after 1750) of "traditional" into "modern" societies through industrialization of the economy. Industrialization required capital for investment. The established system of transoceanic trade and commerce supplied this capital from the enormous profits it generated. Wealthy people sought investment opportunities and eventually found them in machines and engines to drive machines. Capital and scientific innovation fueled invention. Industrialization increased production in both farming and manufacturing.

European industrialization developed from (and eventually replaced) the *domestic system* of manufacture (or home-handicraft system). In this system, an organizer-entrepreneur supplied the raw materials to workers in their homes and collected the finished products from them. The entrepreneur, whose sphere of operations might span several villages, owned the materials, paid for the work, and arranged the marketing.

CAUSES OF THE INDUSTRIAL REVOLUTION

The Industrial Revolution began with cotton products, iron, and pottery. These were widely used goods whose

POPCULTURE

McDonald's is a global chain, and the ingredients in its products illustrate the historical world system in miniature. Consider just the Big Mac. Its two all-beef patties come from cattle, an Old World domesticate. Its special sauce is similar to mayonnaise, invented in France. Lettuce comes from Egypt; cheese from cow's milk (Old World), pickles from India, onions from Iran and West Pakistan. It comes on a sesame seed (India) bun (wheat—Middle East). The Egg McMuffin includes eggs, from chickens (Southeast Asia), and Canadian bacon, from pork (western Asia). The breakfast burrito is based on maize, or corn, a New World product—like the chocolate you might have in your milk or shake. Keep a food diary for two days. Then Google "food origins" or consult a site like http://www.foodtimeline.org/ to see how your own diet illustrates the diverse origins of the foods we eat every day.

STUDY **TIP**

Industrialism draws labor to a central location of production (say, a factory), while people work in their homes in the *domestic system* of manufacture.

manufacture could be broken into simple routine motions that machines could perform. When manufacturing moved from homes to factories, where machinery replaced handwork, agrarian societies evolved into industrial ones. As factories produced cheap staple goods, the Industrial Revolution led to a dramatic increase in production. Industrialization fueled urban growth and created a new kind of city, with factories crowded together in places where coal and labor were cheap.

The Industrial Revolution began in England rather than in France. Why? Unlike the English, the French didn't have to transform their domestic manufacturing system by industrializing. Faced with an increased need for products, with a late eighteenth-century population at least twice that of Great Britain, France could simply augment its domestic system of production by drawing in new homes. Thus, the French increased production *without innovating*—they could enlarge the existing system rather than adopt a new

In the home-handicraft, or domestic, system of production, an organizer supplied raw materials to workers in their homes and collected their products. Family life and work were intertwined, as in this English scene. Is there a modern equivalent to the domestic system of production?

The ART of STOCKING-FRAME-WORK-KNITTING.

Engrav'd for the Universal Magazine 1750 for I. Hinton at the Kings Arms in S.t Pauls Church Yard LONDON.

one. To meet mounting demand for staples—at home and in the colonies—England had to industrialize.

As its industrialization proceeded, Britain's population began to increase dramatically. It doubled during the eighteenth century (especially after 1750) and did so again between 1800 and 1850. This demographic explosion fueled consumption, but British entrepreneurs couldn't meet the increased demand with the traditional production methods. This spurred further experimentation, innovation, and rapid technological change.

English industrialization drew on national advantages in natural resources. Britain was rich in coal and iron ore, and had navigable waterways and easily negotiated coasts. It was a seafaring island-nation located at the crossroads of international trade. These features gave Britain a favored position for importing raw materials and exporting manufactured goods. Another factor in England's industrial growth was the fact that much of its eighteenth-century colonial empire was occupied by English settler families who looked to the mother country as they tried to replicate European civilization in the New World. These colonies bought large quantities of English staples.

> **Industrial Revolution** The historical transformation (in Europe, after 1750) of "traditional" into "modern" societies through industrialization of the economy.

STUDY **TIP**

The Industrial Revolution began in England for several reasons: (1) a dramatic population increase (within England and its colonies) fueled demand for goods; (2) it was rich in raw materials (coal and iron ore) essential to production; (3) expertise in navigation facilitated importing and exporting; (4) the growth of Protestantism among the middle class encouraged a work ethic.

It also has been argued that particular cultural values and religion contributed to industrialization. Many members of the emerging English middle class were Protestant nonconformists. Their beliefs and values encouraged industry, thrift, the dissemination of new knowledge, inventiveness, and willingness to accept change (Weber 1904/1958).

>> Socioeconomic Effects of Industrialization

The socioeconomic effects of industrialization were mixed. English national income tripled between 1700 and 1815 and increased thirty times more by 1939.

Standards of comfort rose, but prosperity was uneven. At first, factory workers' wages were higher than those available in the domestic system. Later, owners started recruiting labor in places where living standards were low and labor (including that of women and children) was cheap.

Social ills worsened with the growth of factory towns and industrial cities, amid conditions like those Charles Dickens described in *Hard Times*. Filth and smoke polluted the nineteenth-century cities. Housing was crowded and unsanitary, with insufficient water and sewage disposal facilities. People experienced rampant disease and rising death rates. This was the world of Ebenezer Scrooge, Bob Cratchit, Tiny Tim—and Karl Marx.

bourgeoisie One of Karl Marx's opposed classes; owners of the means of production (factories, mines, large farms, and other sources of subsistence).

working class (proletariat) Those who must sell their labor to survive; the antithesis of the bourgeoisie in Marx's class analysis.

INDUSTRIAL STRATIFICATION

Social theorists Karl Marx and Max Weber focused on the stratification systems associated with industrialization. From his observations in England and his analysis of nineteenth-century industrial capitalism, Marx (Marx and Engels 1848/1976) saw socioeconomic stratification as a sharp and simple division between two opposed classes: the bourgeoisie (capitalists) and the proletariat (propertyless workers). The bourgeoisie traced its origins to overseas ventures and the world capitalist economy, which had created a wealthy commercial class.

Industrialization shifted production from farms and cottages to mills and factories, where mechanical power was available and where workers could be assembled to operate heavy machinery. The **bourgeoisie** were the owners of the factories, mines, large farms, and other means of production. The **working class,** or **proletariat,** were people who had to sell their labor to survive. With the decline of subsistence production and the rise of urban migration and the possibility of unemployment, the bourgeoisie came to stand between workers and the means of production.

Industrialization hastened the process of *proletarianization*—the separation of workers from the means of production. The bourgeoisie also came to dominate the means of communication, the schools, and other key institutions. *Class consciousness* (recognition of collective interests and personal identification with one's economic group) was a vital part of Marx's view of class. He saw bourgeoisie and proletariat as socioeconomic divisions with radically opposed interests. Marx viewed classes as powerful collective forces that could mobilize human energies to influence the course of history. On the basis of their common experience, workers would develop class consciousness, which could lead to revolutionary change. Although no proletarian revolution was to occur in England, workers did develop organizations to protect their interests and increase their share of industrial profits. During the nineteenth century, trade unions and socialist parties emerged to express a rising anticapitalist spirit. The concerns of the English labor movement were to remove young children from factories and limit the hours during which women and children could work. The profile of stratification in industrial core nations gradually took shape. Capitalists controlled production, but labor was organizing for better wages and working conditions. By 1900 many governments had factory legislation and social-welfare programs. Mass living standards in core nations rose as population grew.

In today's capitalist world system the class division between owners and workers is now worldwide. However, publicly traded companies complicate the division between capitalists and workers in industrial nations. Through pension plans and personal investments, some American workers now have a proprietary interest in the means of production. They are part owners rather than propertyless workers. The key difference is that the wealthy have *control* over these means. The key capitalist now is not the factory owner, who may have been replaced by thousands of stockholders, but the CEO or the chair of the board of directors, neither of whom may actually own the corporation.

Modern stratification systems aren't simple and dichotomous. They include (particularly in core and semiperiphery nations) a middle

Karl Marx observed and analyzed nineteenth-century industrial capitalism. He saw socioeconomic stratification in terms of two opposed classes: bourgeoisie and proletariat.

During the nineteenth and early twentieth centuries, women and children often worked long hours in factories, as in this Macon, Georgia textile mill in 1909.

class of skilled and professional workers. Gerhard Lenski (1966) argues that social equality tends to increase in advanced industrial societies. The masses improve their access to economic benefits and political power. In Lenski's scheme, the shift of political power to the masses reflects the growth of the middle class, which reduces the polarization between owning and working classes. The proliferation of middle-class occupations creates opportunities for social mobility. The stratification system grows more complex (Giddens 1973).

CULTURETHINK

Ask some of the people you know what social class they think they belong to. How about you—what's your class? Why do you think so many Americans identify with the middle class? What are some cultural values associated with being middle class?

In the United States this complex stratification system has gone largely unnoticed by many Americans. Most contemporary Americans, for example, think they belong

to, and claim identity with, the middle class, which they tend to perceive as a vast undifferentiated group. However, there are substantial differences in income and wealth between the richest and the poorest Americans, and the gap is widening. According to U.S. Census data from 1967 to 2000, the top (richest) fifth, or quintile, of American households increased their share of national income by 13.5 percent, while all other quintiles fell. The percentage share of the lowest fifth fell most dramatically—by 17.6 percent. The divergence continues: In 2006 the highest quintile of households received 50.5 percent (versus 49.7 percent in 2000) of all national income, while the lowest fifth received 3.4 percent (versus 3.6 in 2000). Comparable figures in 1967 were 43.8 percent and 4.0 percent. The 2006 ratio was 15:1, versus 14:1 in 2000 and 11:1 in 1967. In other words, the richest fifth of American households, with a mean annual income of $168,170, is now 15 times wealthier than the poorest fifth, with a mean annual income of $11,352 (DeNavas-Walt, Proctor, and Lee; U. S. Census Bureau 2006, http://www.census.gov/hhes/www/income/histinc/h03ar.html). When we consider wealth (investments, property, possessions, etc.) rather than income, the contrast is even more striking: 1 percent of American families hold just over one-third of the nation's wealth (Council on International and Public Affairs 2006). As the chart on page 210 ("Percentage of Wealth Owned, by Percentile") shows, the top 1 percent owns 33.4 percent of all wealth in the United States. By contrast, the bottom 50 percent owns

United States Wealth Owned, 2004

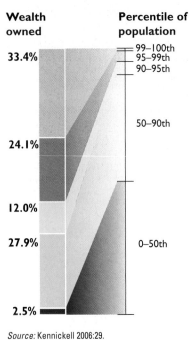

Wealth owned	Percentile of population
33.4%	99–100th / 95–99th / 90–95th
24.1%	50–90th
12.0%	
27.9%	0–50th
2.5%	

Source: Kennickell 2006:29.

just 2.5 percent. In fact, the top 1 percent owns more than the bottom 90 percent combined.

Weber faulted Marx for an overly simple and exclusively economic view of stratification. As we saw in the chapter "Political Systems," Weber (1922/1968) defined three dimensions of social stratification: wealth, power, and prestige. Although, as Weber showed, wealth, power, and prestige are separate components of social ranking, they tend to be correlated. Weber also believed that social identities based on ethnicity, religion, race, nationality, and other attributes could take priority over class (social identity based on economic status). In addition to class contrasts, the modern world system is cross-cut by collective identities based on ethnicity, religion, and nationality (Shannon 1996). Class conflicts tend to occur within nations, and nationalism has prevented global class solidarity, particularly of proletarians.

Although the capitalist class dominates politically in most countries, growing wealth has made it easier for core nations to grant higher wages (Hopkins and Wallerstein 1982). However, the improvement in core workers' living standards wouldn't have occurred without the world system. Without the periphery, core capitalists would have trouble maintaining their profits and also satisfying the demands of core workers. In the periphery, wages and living standards are much lower. The current *world stratification system* features a substantial contrast between both

Max Weber (1864–1920). Did Weber improve on Marx's view of stratification?

capitalists and workers in the core nations and workers on the periphery (see Kerbo 2006).

>> Colonialism

World-system theory stresses the existence of a global culture and economy. It emphasizes historical contacts, linkages, and power differentials between local people and international forces. The major forces influencing cultural interaction during the past five hundred years have been commercial expansion, industrial capitalism, and the dominance of colonial and core nations (Wallerstein 1982, 2004b; Wolf 1982). As state formation had done previously, industrialization accelerated local participation in larger networks. According to Bodley (2007), perpetual expansion is a distinguishing feature of industrial economic systems. Bands and tribes were small, self-sufficient, subsistence-based systems. Industrial economies, by contrast, are large, highly specialized systems in which market exchanges occur with profit as the primary motive (Bodley 2007).

During the nineteenth century, European business interests initiated a concerted search for markets. This process led to European imperialism in Africa, Asia, and Oceania. **Imperialism** refers to a policy of extending the rule of a country or empire over foreign nations and of taking and holding foreign colonies. Imperialism goes back to early states, including Egypt in the Old World and the Incas in the New. Alexander the Great forged a Greek empire, and Julius Caesar and his successors spread the Roman empire. More recent examples include the British, French, and Soviet empires (Scheinman 1980).

After 1850, European imperial expansion was aided by improved transportation, which facilitated the colonization of vast areas of sparsely settled lands in the interior of North and South America and Australia. The new colonies purchased masses of goods from the industrial centers and shipped back wheat, cotton, wool, mutton, beef, and leather. The first phase of European colonialism had been the exploration and exploitation of the Americas and the Caribbean after Columbus. A new second phase began as European nations competed for colonies between 1875 and 1914, setting the stage for World War I.

Colonialism is the political, social, economic, and cultural domination of a territory and its people by a foreign power for an extended time (see Bremen and Shimizu 1999; Cooper and Stoler 1997). If imperialism is almost as old as the state, colonialism can be traced back to the Phoenicians, who established colo-

STUDY **TIP**

Three dimensions of social stratification, according to Weber, are power, prestige, and wealth.

On January 1, 1900, a British officer in India receives a pedicure from a servant. What does this photo say to you about colonialism? Who gives pedicures in your society?

nies along the eastern Mediterranean three thousand years ago. The ancient Greeks and Romans were avid colonizers, as well as empire builders.

The first phase of modern colonialism began with the European "Age of Discovery"—of the Americas and of a sea route to the Far East. After 1492, the Spanish, the original conquerors of the Aztecs and Incas, explored and colonized widely in the New World—the Caribbean, Mexico, the southern portions of what was to become the United States, and Central and South America. In South America, Portugal ruled over Brazil. Rebellions and wars aimed at independence ended the first phase of European colonialism by the early nineteenth century. Brazil declared independence from Portugal in 1822. By 1825 most of Spain's colonies were politically independent. Spain

held onto Cuba and the Philippines until 1898, but otherwise withdrew from the colonial field. During the first phase of colonialism, Spain and Portugal, along with Britain and France, were major colonizing nations. Britain and France dominated the second phase.

BRITISH COLONIALISM

At its peak about 1914, the British empire covered a fifth of the world's land surface and ruled a fourth of its population (see "Map of British Empire in 1765 and 1914" on page 212). Like several other European nations, Britain had two stages of colonialism. The first began with the Elizabethan voyages of the sixteenth century. During the seventeenth century, Britain acquired most of the eastern coast of North America, Canada's St. Lawrence basin, islands in the Caribbean, slave stations in Africa, and interests in India.

> **imperialism** A policy of extending the rule of a nation or empire over foreign nations and of taking and holding foreign colonies.
>
> **colonialism** The political, social, economic, and cultural domination of a territory and its people by a foreign power for an extended time.

The British shared the exploration of the New World with the Spanish, Portuguese, French, and Dutch. The British by and large left Mexico, along with Central and South America, to the Spanish and the Portuguese. The end of the Seven Years' War in 1763 forced a French retreat

STUDY TIP

The two phases of European colonialism include first, the exploration and exploitation of the New World after Columbus; and second, the competition for colonies, ending with World War I.

Map of British Empire in 1765 and 1914

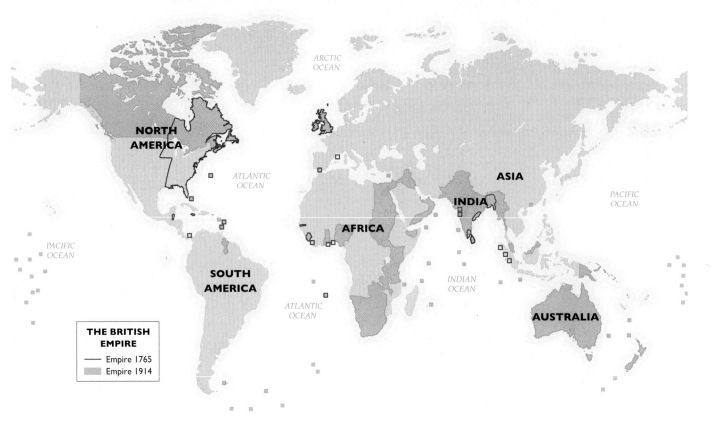

Source: From the *Academic American Encyclopedia,* Vol. 3, p. 496. 1998 Edition. Copyright 1998 by Grolier Incorporated. Reprinted with permission.

from most of Canada and India, where France previously had competed with Britain (Cody 1998; Farr 1980).

The American Revolution ended the first stage of British colonialism. A second colonial empire, on which the "sun never set," rose from the ashes of the first. Beginning in 1788, but intensifying after 1815, the British settled Australia. Britain had acquired Dutch South Africa by 1815. The establishment of Singapore in 1819 provided a base for a British trade network that extended to much of South Asia and along the coast of China. By this time, the empires of Britain's traditional rivals, particularly Spain, had been severely diminished in scope. Britain's position as imperial power and the world's leading industrial nation was unchallenged (Cody 1998; Farr 1980).

During the Victorian Era (1837–1901), as Britain's acquisition of territory and of further trading concessions continued, Prime Minister Benjamin Disraeli implemented a foreign policy justified by a view of imperialism as shouldering "the white man's burden"—a phrase coined by the

CULTURETHINK

The idea of the "white man's burden" was a world-view that made colonialism seem legitimate. Does anything like the "white man's burden" shape current events in politics?

poet Rudyard Kipling. People in the empire were seen as unable to govern themselves, so that British guidance was needed to civilize and Christianize them. This paternalistic and racist doctrine served to legitimize Britain's acquisition and control of parts of central Africa and Asia (Cody 1998).

After World War II, the British empire began to fall apart, with nationalist movements for independence. India became independent in 1947, as did Ireland in 1949. Decolonization in Africa and Asia accelerated during the late 1950s. Today, the ties that remain between Britain and its former colonies are mainly linguistic or cultural rather than political (Cody 1998).

FRENCH COLONIALISM

Two phases also characterized French colonialism. The first began with the explorations of the early 1600s. Before the French revolution in 1789, missionaries, explorers, and traders had carved out niches for France in Canada, the Louisiana territory, several Caribbean islands, and parts of India (Harvey 1980). The Treaty of Paris of 1763 ended the Seven Years' War, the American counterpart of which was the French and Indian War. That treaty awarded Canada to Great Britain, while France retained the prosperous West Indian sugar islands of Guadeloupe and Martinique.

The foundations of the second French empire were established between 1830 and 1870. In Great Britain the

Map of the French Empire at Its Height around 1914

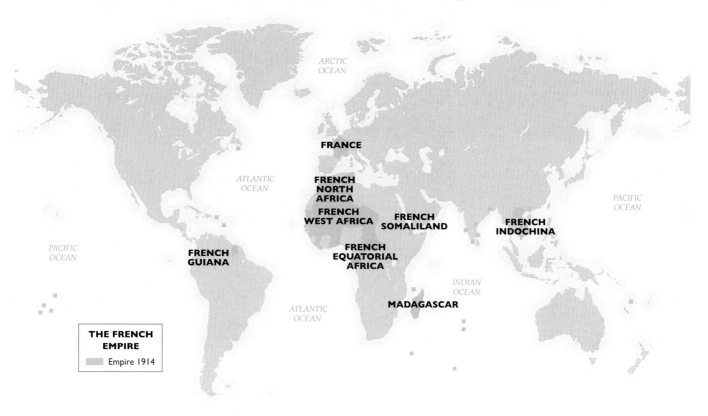

Source: From the *Academic American Encyclopedia,* Vol 3, p. 309. 1998 Edition. Copyright 1998 by Grolier Incorporated. Reprinted with permission.

sheer drive for profit led expansion, but French colonialism was spurred more by the state, church, and armed forces than by pure business interests. France acquired Algeria and part of what eventually became Indochina (Cambodia, Laos, and Vietnam). By 1914 the French empire covered four million square miles and included some sixty million people (see "Map of the French Empire at Its Height"). By 1893 French rule had been fully established in Indochina. Tunisia and Morocco became French protectorates in 1883 and 1912, respectively (Harvey 1980).

To be sure, the French, like the British, had substantial business interests in their colonies, but they also sought, again like the British, international glory and prestige. The French promulgated a *mission civilisatrice,* their equivalent of Britain's "white man's burden." The goal was to implant French culture, language, and religion, Roman Catholicism, throughout the colonies (Harvey 1980).

The French used two forms of colonial rule: *indirect rule,* governing through native leaders and established political structures, in areas with long histories of state organization, such as Morocco and Tunisia; and *direct rule* by French officials in many areas of Africa, where the French imposed new government structures to control diverse societies, many of them previously stateless. Like the British empire, the French empire began to disintegrate after World War II. France fought long—and ultimately futile—wars to keep its empire intact in Indochina and Algeria (Harvey 1980).

COLONIALISM AND IDENTITY

Many geopolitical labels in the news today had no equivalent meaning before colonialism. Whole countries, along with social groups and divisions within them, were colonial inventions. In West Africa, for example, by geographic logic, several adjacent countries could be one (Togo, Ghana, Ivory Coast, Guinea, Guinea-Bissau, Sierra Leone, Liberia). Instead, they are separated by linguistic, political, and economic contrasts promoted under colonialism.

Hundreds of ethnic groups and "tribes" are colonial constructions (see Ranger 1996). The Sukuma of Tanzania, for instance, were first registered as a single tribe by the colonial administration. Then missionaries standardized a series of dialects into a single Sukuma language into which they translated the Bible and other religious texts. Thereafter, those texts were taught in missionary schools and to European foreigners and other non-Sukuma speakers. Over time this standardized the Sukuma language and ethnicity (Finnstrom 1997).

As in most of East Africa, in Rwanda and Burundi farmers and herders live in the same areas and speak the same language. Historically they have shared the same social world, although their social organization is "extremely hierarchical," almost "castelike" (Malkki 1995, p. 24). There has been a tendency to see the pastoral Tutsis as superior to the agricultural Hutus. Tutsis have been presented as nobles, Hutus as commoners. Yet when distributing identity

Tutsi and Hutu originated as arbitrary colonial categories. They became "ethnic" groups subject to mass killings (genocide) in Rwanda in 1994, as portrayed in the film Hotel Rwanda, *shown here.*

postcolonial Referring to interactions between European nations and the societies they colonized (mainly after 1800); more generally, it may be used to signify a position against imperialism and Eurocentrism.

cards in Rwanda, the Belgian colonizers simply identified all people with more than ten head of cattle as Tutsi. Owners of fewer cattle were registered as Hutus (Bjuremalm 1997). Years later, these arbitrary colonial registers were used systematically for "ethnic" identification during the mass killings (genocide) that took place in Rwanda in 1994 (as portrayed vividly in the film *Hotel Rwanda*).

POSTCOLONIAL STUDIES

In anthropology, history, and literature, the field of postcolonial studies has gained prominence since the 1970s (see Ashcroft, Griffiths, and Tiffin 1989; Cooper and Stoler 1997). **Postcolonial** refers to the interactions between European nations and the societies they colonized (mainly after 1800). In 1914, European empires, which

broke up after World War II, ruled more than 85 percent of the world (Petraglia-Bahri 1996). The term *postcolonial* also has been used to describe the second half of the twentieth century in general, the period succeeding colonialism. Even more generically, *postcolonial* may be used to signify a position against imperialism and Eurocentrism (Petraglia-Bahri 1996).

The former colonies (*postcolonies*) can be divided into settler, nonsettler, and mixed (Petraglia-Bahri 1996). The settler countries, with large numbers of European colonists and sparser native populations, include Australia and Canada. Examples of nonsettler countries include India, Pakistan, Bangladesh, Sri Lanka, Malaysia, Indonesia, Nigeria, Senegal, Madagascar, and Jamaica. All these had substantial native populations and relatively few European settlers. Mixed countries include South Africa, Zimbabwe, Kenya, and Algeria. Such countries had significant European settlement despite having sizable native populations.

Given the varied experiences of such countries, postcolonial has to be a loose term. The United States, for instance, was colonized by Europeans and fought a war for independence from Britain. Is the United States a postcolony? It usually isn't perceived as such, given its current world power position, its treatment of native Americans (sometimes called internal colonization), and its annexation of other parts of the world (Petraglia-Bahri 1996). Research in postcolonial studies is growing, permitting a wide-ranging investigation of power relations in varied contexts. Broad topics in the field include the formation of an empire, the impact of colonization, and the state of the postcolony today (Petraglia-Bahri 1996).

CULTURETHINK

Do you think the critique of Eurocentrism is legitimate? Does the perspective of white Europeans (or their descendants) dominate thinking about history and culture? What perspectives do you think a non-Eurocentric point of view would consider?

Anthropology Works

A social studies educator can use insights from anthropology to make connections between historical events and contemporary conditions. Economic expansion during and before European colonialism helped shape the current world system, shedding light on why some nations are poorer than others today.

>> The Role of Development in the World System

During the Industrial Revolution, a strong current of thought viewed industrialization as a beneficial process of organic development and progress. Many economists still assume that industrialization increases production and income. They seek to create in Third World ("developing") countries a process like the one that first occurred spontaneously in eighteenth-century Great Britain.

We have seen that Britain used the notion of a white man's burden to justify its imperialist expansion and that France claimed to be engaged in a *mission civilisatrice*—a civilizing mission—in its colonies. Both these ideas illustrate an **intervention philosophy,** an ideological justification for outsiders to guide native peoples in specific directions. Economic development plans also have intervention philosophies. John Bodley (2008) argues that the basic belief behind interventions—whether by colonialists, missionaries, governments, or development planners—has been the same for more than a hundred years. This belief is that industrialization, modernization, Westernization, and individualism are desirable evolutionary advances and that development schemes that promote them will bring long-term benefits to local people. In a more extreme form, intervention philosophy may pit the assumed wisdom of enlightened colonial or other First World planners against the purported conservatism, ignorance, or "obsolescence" of "inferior" or "backward" local people.

NEOLIBERALISM

One currently influential intervention philosophy, neoliberalism, encompasses a set of assumptions that have become widespread during the last thirty years. Neoliberal policies are being implemented in developing nations, including postsocialist societies (e.g., those of the former Soviet Union). **Neoliberalism** is the current form of the classic economic liberalism laid out in Adam Smith's famous capitalist manifesto, *The Wealth of Nations,* published in 1776, soon after the Industrial Revolution. Smith advocated laissez-faire (hands-off) economics as the basis of capitalism: The government should stay out of its nation's economic affairs. Free trade, Smith thought, was the best way for a nation's economy to develop. There should be no restrictions on manufacturing, no barriers to commerce, and no tariffs. This philosophy is called liberalism because it aimed at liberating, or freeing, the economy from government controls. Economic liberalism encouraged "free" enterprise and competition, with the goal of generating profits. (Note the difference between this meaning of *liberal* and the one that has been popularized on American talk radio, in which people use "liberal"—usually as a derogatory term—as the opposite of "conservative." Ironically, Adam Smith's liberalism is today's capitalist conservatism.)

Economic liberalism prevailed in the United States until President Franklin Roosevelt's New Deal during the 1930s. The Great Depression produced a turn to Keynesian economics, which challenged liberalism. John Maynard Keynes (1927, 1936) insisted that full employment was necessary for capitalism to grow, that governments and central banks should intervene to increase employment, and that government should promote the common good.

> **intervention philosophy** Guiding principle of colonialism, conquest, missionization, or development; an ideological justification for outsiders to guide native peoples in specific directions.
>
> **neoliberalism** Revival of Adam Smith's classic economic liberalism, the idea that governments should not regulate private enterprise and that free market forces should rule; a currently dominant intervention philosophy.

 STUDY TIP

Three phases in the economics of capitalism have been (1) Adam Smith's liberalism (government stays out of the economy); (2) Keynesian economics (the government stimulates the economy); (3) neoliberalism (government promotes free trade).

Especially since the fall of Communism (1989–1991), there has been a revival of economic liberalism, now known as neoliberalism, which has been spreading globally. Around the world, powerful financial institutions, such as the International Monetary Fund (IMF), the World Bank, and the Inter-American Development Bank, have imposed neoliberal policies (see Edelman and Haugerud 2004). Neoliberalism entails open (tariff- and barrier-free) international trade and investment. Profits are sought through lowering of costs, whether through improving productivity, laying off workers, or seeking workers who accept lower wages. In exchange for loans, the governments of postsocialist and developing nations

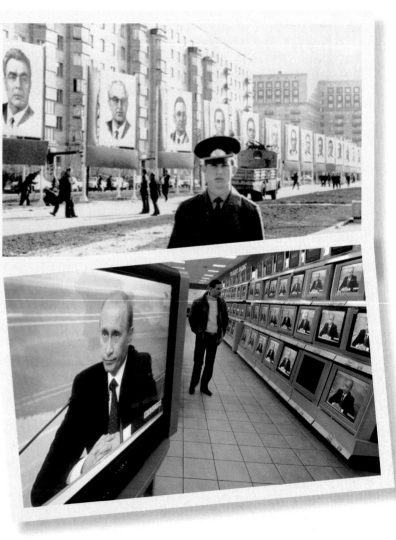

have been required to accept the neoliberal premise that deregulation leads to economic growth, which will eventually benefit everyone through a process sometimes called "trickle down." Accompanying the belief in free markets and the idea of cutting costs is a tendency to impose austerity measures that cut government expenses. This can entail reduced public spending on education, health care, and other social services (Martinez and Garcia 2000).

>> The Second World

The labels "First World," "Second World," and "Third World" represent a common, although ethnocentric, way of categorizing nations. The *First World* refers to the "democratic West"—traditionally conceived in opposition to a "Second World" ruled by "Communism." The *Second World* refers to the former Soviet Union and the socialist and once-socialist countries of Eastern Europe and Asia. Proceeding with this classification, the "less-developed countries" or "developing nations" make up the *Third World*.

communism Spelled with a lowercase c, describes a social system in which the community owns property and people work for the common good.

Communism Spelled with an uppercase C, describes a political movement and doctrine seeking to overthrow capitalism and to establish a form of communism such as that which prevailed in the Soviet Union (USSR) from 1917 to 1991.

COMMUNISM

The two meanings of communism involve how it is written, whether with a lowercase (small) or an uppercase (large) *c*. Small-*c* **communism** describes a social system in which the community owns property and people work for the common good. Large-*C* **Communism** was a political movement and doctrine seeking to overthrow capitalism and establish a form of communism such as that which prevailed in the Soviet Union (USSR) from 1917 to 1991. The heyday of Communism was a forty-year period from 1949 to 1989, when more Communist regimes existed than at any time before or after. Today only five Communist states remain—China, Cuba, Laos, North Korea, and Vietnam—compared with twenty-three in 1985.

Communism, which originated with Russia's Bolshevik Revolution in 1917, and took its inspiration from Karl Marx and Friedrich Engels, was not uniform

over time or among countries. All Communist systems were *authoritarian* (promoting obedience to authority rather than individual freedom). Many were *totalitarian* (banning rival parties and demanding total submission of the individual to the state). Several features distinguished Communist societies from other authoritarian regimes (e.g., Spain under Franco) and from socialism of a social democratic type. First, the Communist Party monopolized power in every Communist state. Second, relations within the party were highly centralized and strictly disciplined. Third, Communist nations had state ownership, rather than private ownership, of the means of production. Finally, all Communist regimes, with the goal of advancing communism, cultivated a sense of belonging to an international movement (Brown 2001).

Social scientists have tended to refer to such societies as socialist rather than Communist. Today research by anthropologists is thriving in *postsocialist* societies—those that once emphasized bureaucratic redistribution of wealth according to a central plan (Verdery 2001). In the postsocialist period, states that once had planned economies

Before and after Communism. Top: on May Day (May 1, 1975), large photos of Politburo members (Communist Party leaders) adorn buildings in Moscow. Bottom: on January 31, 2006, in a Moscow electronics store, a potential customer considers a display of TV sets, broadcasting the annual press conference of Russian then-president, now prime minister Vladimir Putin.

have been following the neoliberal agenda, by divesting themselves of state-owned resources in favor of privatization. Some of them have moved toward formal liberal democracy, with political parties, elections, and a balance of powers (Grekova 2001).

POSTSOCIALIST TRANSITIONS

Neoliberal economists assumed that dismantling the Soviet Union's planned economy would raise gross domestic product (GDP) and living standards. The goal was to enhance production by substituting a decentralized market system and providing incentives through privatization. In October 1991, Boris Yeltsin, who had been elected president of Russia that June, announced a program of radical market-oriented reform, pursuing a changeover to capitalism. Yeltsin's program of "shock therapy" cut subsidies to farms and industries and ended price controls. Since then, postsocialist Russia has faced many problems. The anticipated gains in productivity did not materialize. After the fall of the Soviet Union, Russia's GDP fell by half. Poverty increased, with a quarter of the population now living below the poverty line. Life expectancy and the birth rate declined. Another problem to emerge in the postsocialist transition is corruption. In response, the World Bank and other international organizations have launched anticorruption programs worldwide. *Corruption* is defined as the abuse of public office for private gain.

The World Bank's approach to corruption assumes a clear and sharp distinction between the state (the public or official domain) and the private sphere, and that the two should be kept separate. The idea that the public sphere can be separated neatly from the private sphere is ethnocentric. According to Janine Wedel (2002), postsocialist states provide rich contexts in which to explore variability in relations between public and private domains. Alexei Yurchak (2002, 2005) describes two spheres that operate in Russia today; these spheres do not mesh neatly with the assumption of a public–private split. He calls them the official–public sphere and the personal–public sphere, referring to domains that coexist and sometimes overlap. State officials may respect the law (official–public), while also working with informal or even criminal groups (personal–public). Officials switch from official–public to personal–public behavior all the time, in order to accomplish specific tasks.

>> The World System Today

The process of industrialization continues today, although nations have shifted their positions within the world system (Table 11.1). By 1900, the United States had become a core nation within the world system and had overtaken Great Britain in iron, coal, and cotton production. In a few decades (1868–1900), Japan had changed from a medieval handicraft economy to an industrial one, joining the semiperiphery by 1900 and moving to the core between 1945 and 1970. "The World System in 2000" map on page 218 shows the modern world system.

Twentieth-century industrialization added hundreds of new industries and millions of new jobs. Production increased, often beyond immediate demand, spurring strategies, such as advertising, to sell everything industry could churn out. Mass production gave rise to a culture of consumption, which valued acquisitiveness and conspicuous consumption (Veblen 1934). Industrialization entailed a shift from reliance on renewable resources to the use of fossil fuels. Fossil fuel energy, stored over millions of years, is being depleted rapidly to support a previously unknown and probably unsustainable level of consumption. (See also Chapter 13.)

Ascent and Decline of Nations within the World System

Periphery to Semiperiphery	Semiperiphery to Core	Core to Semiperiphery
United States (1800–1860)	United States (1860–1900)	Spain (1620–1700)
Japan (1868–1900)	Japan (1945–1970)	
Taiwan (1949–1980)	Germany (1870–1900)	
S. Korea (1953–1980)		

Source: Copyright © 1996 Thomas R. Shannon. Reprinted by permission of Westview Press, a member of Perseus Book Group.

TABLE 11.1

The World System Today

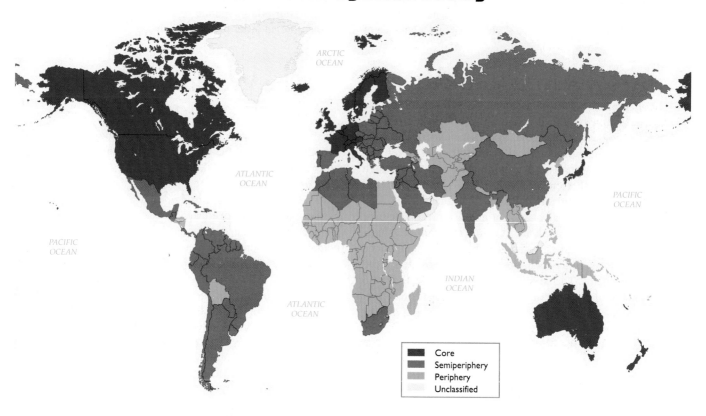

Energy Consumption in Various Contexts

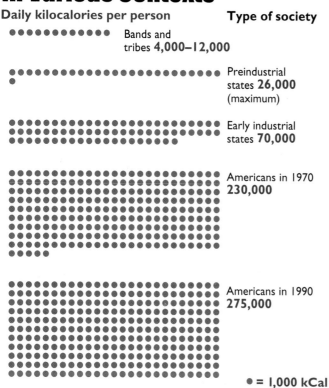

Daily kilocalories per person   **Type of society**

Bands and tribes **4,000–12,000**

Preindustrial states **26,000** (maximum)

Early industrial states **70,000**

Americans in 1970 **230,000**

Americans in 1990 **275,000**

● = 1,000 kCal

Americans are the world's foremost consumers of non-renewable resources as shown in "Energy Consumption in Various Contexts." In terms of energy consumption, the average American is about thirty-five times more expensive than the average forager or tribesperson. Since 1900, the United States has tripled its per capita energy use. It also has increased its total energy consumption thirtyfold.

"Energy Consumption in Selected Countries" compares energy use, per capita and total, in the United States and selected other countries. The United States represents 21.1 percent of the world's annual energy consumption, com-

CULTURETHINK

The amount of energy an individual consumes is sometimes called her or his "ecological footprint." How big is your footprint? What kinds of things do you use energy for each day? How much of that comes from fossil fuels?

Energy Consumption in Selected Countries, 2006

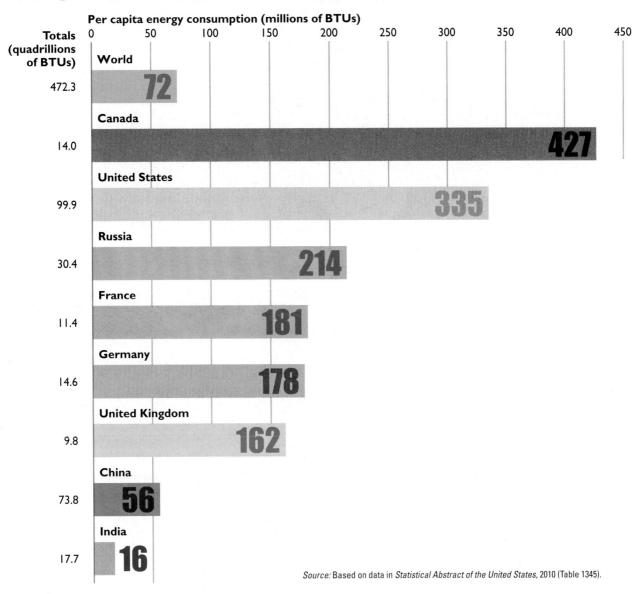

Totals (quadrillions of BTUs)

Per capita energy consumption (millions of BTUs)

World	472.3 — 72
Canada	14.0 — 427
United States	99.9 — 335
Russia	30.4 — 214
France	11.4 — 181
Germany	14.6 — 178
United Kingdom	9.8 — 162
China	73.8 — 56
India	17.7 — 16

Source: Based on data in *Statistical Abstract of the United States,* 2010 (Table 1345).

pared with China's 15.6 percent, but the average American consumes six times the energy used by the average Chinese and twenty-one times the energy used by the average inhabitant of India.

INDUSTRIAL DEGRADATION

Industrialization and factory labor now characterize many societies in Latin America, Africa, the Pacific, and Asia. One effect of the spread of industrialization has been the destruction of indigenous economies, ecologies, and populations. Two centuries ago, as industrialization was developing, fifty million people still lived in politically independent bands, tribes, and chiefdoms. Occupying vast areas, those nonstate societies, although not totally isolated, were only marginally affected by nation-states and the world capitalist economy. In 1800, bands, tribes, and chiefdoms controlled half the globe and 20 percent of its population (Bodley 2008). Industrialization tipped the balance in favor of states (see Hornborg and Crumley 2007).

As industrial states have conquered, annexed, and "developed" nonstates, there has been genocide on a grand scale. *Genocide* refers to a deliberate policy of exterminating a group through warfare or murder. Examples include the Holocaust, Rwanda in 1994, and Bosnia in the early 1990s. Bodley (2008) estimates that an average of 250,000 indigenous people perished annually between 1800 and 1950. Besides warfare, the causes included foreign diseases (to which natives lacked resistance), slavery, land grabbing, and other forms of dispossession and impoverishment.

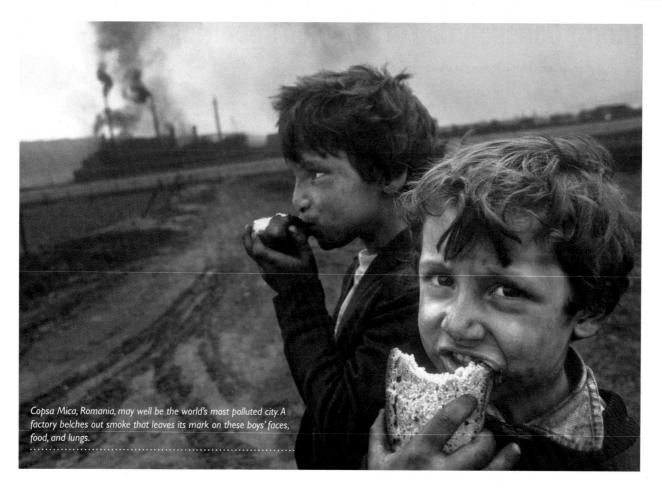

Copsa Mica, Romania, may well be the world's most polluted city. A factory belches out smoke that leaves its mark on these boys' faces, food, and lungs.

"Such is the Old Town of Manchester, and on re-reading my description, I am forced to admit that instead of being exaggerated, it is far from black enough to convey a true impression of the filth, ruin and uninhabitableness, the defiance of all consideration of cleanliness, ventilation, and health which characterise the construction of this single district. . . . Everything which here arouses horror and indignation is of recent origin, belongs to the industrial epoch."

Friedrich Engels, *The Condition of the Working-Class in England*

Many native groups have been incorporated within nation-states, in which they have become ethnic minorities. Some such groups have been able to recoup their population. Many **indigenous peoples** survive and maintain their ethnic identity despite having lost their ancestral cultures to varying degrees (partial ethnocide). And many descendants of tribespeople live on as culturally distinct and self-conscious colonized peoples, many of whom aspire to autonomy. As the original inhabitants of their territories, they are called indigenous peoples (see Maybury-Lewis 2002).

Around the world contemporary nations are repeating—at an accelerated rate—the process of resource depletion that started in Europe and the United States during the Industrial Revolution. Fortunately, today's world has some environmental watchdogs that did not exist during the first centuries of the Industrial Revolution. Given national and international cooperation and sanctions, the modern world may benefit from the lessons of the past (see Hornborg, McNeill, and Martinez-Alier 2007).

indigenous peoples The original inhabitants of particular territories; often descendants of tribespeople who live on as culturally distinct colonized peoples, many of whom aspire to autonomy.

get involved!

Learn to read your dinner plate like a map of the world system. The American diet relies heavily on imports of both goods and labor. Supplementing information on the source of a particular food item (packaging often identifies sources) with Internet research, use the food you eat to gain information on global capitalism and global inequality. For example, let's say your cauliflower came from California. Hondurans who migrated across Mexico to work on farms in California may have harvested your cauliflower. Although working for extremely low wages, Honduran migrant workers manage collectively to send huge remittances in U.S. dollars back to Honduras. Who in the United States might benefit from this and how? Who in Honduras might benefit? Given these facts, what would you suspect is Honduras's position of economic power in the world system?

For REVIEW

I. When and why did the world system develop, and what is it like today?

- A global system of economic and political relations emerged in the fifteenth century, as Europeans established transoceanic trade with other peoples, who then entered Europe's sphere of influence. Over the next several hundred years, an exchange of people, resources, products, ideas, and diseases linked the Old and the New Worlds. By the eighteenth century, European industrialization, fed by capital from transoceanic trade, hastened the separation of workers from the means of production. Today's capitalistic world economy maintains the contrast between owners and workers, but a partial shift in power to the masses has reduced the polarization. Currently, world stratification features a contrast between both capitalists and workers in the core nations and workers on the periphery. Industrialization is implicated in the destruction of indigenous economies, ecologies, and populations and an accelerated rate of resource depletion.

II. When and how did European colonialism develop, and how is its legacy expressed in postcolonial studies?

- The first phase of European colonialism began with the exploration and exploitation of the Americas after Columbus. In the nineteenth century, the search for new markets led European nations to take and hold foreign colonies. During this new phase of colonialism (1875–1914), Britain and France promoted their commercial interests in their respective colonies and sought to "civilize" native peoples. Colonizers constructed whole countries and divisions within them. *Postcolonial* refers to the lasting effects of European colonization and the study of the period after it. The settler, nonsettler, and mixed countries that were former colonies had different colonial experiences. The United States, although colonized, usually isn't perceived as postcolonial because of its current world power position, its treatment of Native Americans, and its annexation of foreign territories.

III. How do colonialism, development, industrialization, neoliberalism, and Communism exemplify intervention philosophies?

- These ideologies and historical developments have been shaped by justifications for guiding native peoples in specific directions. Colonial powers have engaged in political, social, economic, and cultural domination. Paternalistic views of non-Western peoples' "backwardness" helped colonial powers to legitimize imperialist expansion. Development plans assume that retracing the "First World's" path among "developing" countries will promote long-term benefits for them. Powerful financial institutions impose neoliberal policies, entailing open trade and investment, cost control, and austerity measures that cut government aid for social services. Communism has promoted obedience to authority and often demanded total submission of individuals to the state.

Pop Quiz

1. The modern world system is best understood as:
   a. A system in which ethnic groups are increasingly isolated from nation-states.
   b. A system of social class stratification mirroring Karl Marx's theory of class conflict.
   c. A global system in which nations are economically and politically interdependent.
   d. A system whose major contrast pits capitalists against workers in core nations.

2. Which of the following statements about world-system theory is false?
   a. The three different positions of economic and political power are core, semiperiphery, and periphery.
   b. The theory sees society as consisting of inter-related parts.
   c. The theory claims that a set of economic and political relations has characterized much of the globe since the Old World and New World established regular contact.
   d. The theory applies mainly to economic and political relations among Western nations.

3. European development of a transoceanic trade-oriented economy, led to all of the following except:
   a. Peoples of Asia, Africa, and the Americas entered Europe's sphere of influence.
   b. Europeans' consumption of imports spurred the rise of plantation economies in the Americas.
   c. Contact led to a major exchange of people, resources, ideas, and diseases.
   d. Demand for fossil fuels spurred development of slave-based production in the New World.

4. Marx argued that class consciousness results from:
   a. The intersection of ethnic and national identities with social class identity.
   b. Recognizing collective economic interests and identifying with a group sharing those interests.
   c. A growing distinction among religions.
   d. The extension of notions of kinship beyond the boundaries of actual biological relations.

5. Imperialism refers to extending rule of a country or empire over foreign nations and holding foreign colonies, while colonialism refers specifically to:
   a. The political, social, economic, and cultural domination of a territory and its people by a foreign power for an extended time.
   b. Imperial influence that disappears when former colonies gain independence.
   c. European domination of a territory.
   d. Efforts to civilize the world by implanting European languages.

6. Colonial administrators registered the Sukuma of Tanzania as a single tribe. In Rwanda and Burundi, the distribution of colonial identity cards created arbitrary ethnic divisions. These two cases:
   a. Suggest that strong ethnic identities are a key ingredient of development.
   b. Illustrate that ethnic groups and tribes may be colonial constructions.
   c. Show how well-informed administrators were about local cultures.
   d. Show the importance of making clear tribal and ethnic distinctions to reduce conflict.

7. Since the fall of Communism, neoliberalism:
   a. Is no longer seen as a viable economic policy.
   b. Has been associated with open international trade and investment.
   c. Has rejected attempts to lower costs with layoffs.
   d. Has favored increased public spending on education and other social services.

8. Although Communism was not uniform over time or among countries that adopted it:
   a. All Communist systems have been authoritarian.
   b. Few Communist systems have been totalitarian.
   c. All Communist nations mix state ownership with private ownership of means of production.
   d. Few Communist regimes have stressed identification with the international movement.

9. All the following statements about postsocialist societies are supported by research, except:
   a. They typically experience gains in productivity and a higher living standard.
   b. Such societies have promoted privatization to enhance production.
   c. The World Bank's approach to corruption assumes that the public (state) domain should be kept separate from the private domain.
   d. Postsocialist states provide rich contexts in which to explore variability in relations between public and private domains.

10. Which of the following statements does not characterize the modern world system?
    a. Twentieth-century industrialization added hundreds of new industries and millions of new jobs.
    b. Mass production has given rise to a culture of consumption.
    c. The U.S. lags behind India and China in total energy consumption.
    d. Industrialization has caused the destruction of indigenous economies, ecologies, and populations.

1. (c), 2. (d), 3. (d), 4. (b), 5. (a), 6. (b), 7. (b), 8. (a), 9. (a), 10. (c)

12

ETHNICITY AND RACE

WHAT'S TO COME

UNDERSTANDING OURSELVES

How do you imagine human "diversity"? Maybe you associate that word with "race" or "ethnicity." Perhaps you think of differences—like skin or eye color, hair form, or height—that can be observed by the naked eye. In fact, human biological diversity encompasses much more than observable physical differences. It includes, for example, our variable abilities to digest various foods and our innate resistance or susceptibility to particular diseases.

Meeting every day in contemporary North America are people whose ancestors lived in many lands. The first (Native) Americans had to cross a land bridge that once linked Siberia to North America. For later immigrants, perhaps including your own parents or grandparents, the voyage may have been across the sea, or overland from nations to the south. They came for many reasons; some came voluntarily, while others were brought in chains. The scale of migration in today's world is so vast that millions of people routinely cross national borders or live far from the homelands of their grandparents. The American population includes millions of people whose biological features reflect adaptations to environments other than the ones they now inhabit.

Diversity also includes the various identities that the same person may hold in different situations. Part of human adaptive flexibility is our ability to consciously (and sometimes subconsciously) shift self presentation in response to context. Italians, for example, maintain separate sets of clothing to be worn inside and outside the home. They invest much more in their outside wardrobe—thus supporting a vibrant Italian fashion industry—and what it says about their public persona than in indoor garb, which is for family and intimates to see. Both behavior and identities can change with context. One person can be both black and Hispanic, or a father and a ballplayer. One identity is claimed or perceived in certain settings, another in different ones. Among African Americans a "Hispanic" baseball player might be black; among Hispanics, Hispanic. When asked "who are you?" what first comes to mind? How might that vary according to situation?

As You READ

- How are race and ethnicity socially constructed?
- How does contemporary racial classification differ in three contemporary nations: the United States, Japan, and Brazil?
- What are the positive and negative aspects of ethnicity?

>> Ethnic Groups and Ethnicity

As with any culture, members of an **ethnic group** *share* certain beliefs, values, habits, customs, and norms because of their common background. They define themselves as different and special because of cultural features. This distinction may arise from language, religion, historical experience, geographic placement, kinship, or "race" (see

Spickard 2004). Markers of an ethnic group may include a collective name, belief in common descent, a sense of solidarity, and an association with a specific territory, which the group may or may not hold (Ryan 1990, pp. xiii, xiv). Table 12.1 lists American ethnic groups, based on 2008 figures.

According to Fredrik Barth (1969), ethnicity can be said to exist when people claim a certain ethnic identity for themselves and are defined by others as having that identity. **Ethnicity** means identification with, and feeling part of, an ethnic group and exclusion from certain other groups because of this affiliation. Ethnic feelings and associated behavior vary in intensity within ethnic groups and countries and over time. A change in the degree of importance attached to an ethnic identity may reflect political changes (Soviet rule ends—ethnic feeling rises) or individual life-cycle changes (young people relinquish, or old people reclaim, an ethnic background).

Cultural differences may be associated with ethnicity, class, region, or religion. Individuals often have more than one group identity. People may be loyal (depending on circumstances) to their neighborhood, school, town, state or province, region, nation, continent, religion, ethnic group, or interest group (Ryan 1990, p. xxii). In a complex society such as the United States or Canada, people constantly negotiate their social identities. All of us "wear dif-

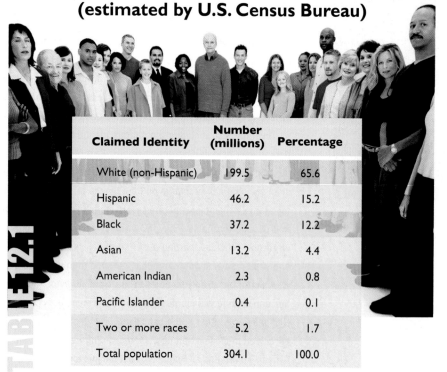

Racial/Ethnic Identification in the United States, 2008 (estimated by U.S. Census Bureau)

Claimed Identity	Number (millions)	Percentage
White (non-Hispanic)	199.5	65.6
Hispanic	46.2	15.2
Black	37.2	12.2
Asian	13.2	4.4
American Indian	2.3	0.8
Pacific Islander	0.4	0.1
Two or more races	5.2	1.7
Total population	304.1	100.0

TABLE 12.1

Source: Statistical Abstract of the United States, 2010, Table 6.

ferent hats," presenting ourselves sometimes as one thing, sometimes as another.

CULTURE THINK

What identities other than ethnicity do people negotiate depending on the situation they are in?

STATUS SHIFTING

Sometimes our identities (aka social statuses) are mutually exclusive. It's hard to be both black and white or male and female. Sometimes, assuming an identity or joining a group requires a conversion experience, acquiring a new and overwhelming primary identity, such as becoming a born-again Christian.

Some statuses aren't mutually exclusive, but contextual. People can be both black and Hispanic or both a mother and a senator. One identity is used in certain settings, another in different ones. We call this the *situational negotiation of social identity* (Leman 2001). Hispanics, for example, may shift ethnic affiliations as they negotiate their identities. "Hispanic" is a category based mainly on language. It includes whites, blacks, and "racially" mixed Spanish speakers and their ethnically conscious descendants. (There also are Native American and even Asian Hispanics.) "Hispanics," the fastest-growing ethnic group in the United States, lumps together people of diverse geographic origin—Puerto Rico, Mexico, Cuba, El Salvador, Guatemala, the Dominican Republic, and other Spanish-speaking countries of Central and South America and the Caribbean. "Latino" is a broader category, which also can include Brazilians (who speak Portuguese). The national origins of American Hispanics/Latinos (excluding Brazilians) in 2008 are shown in the graph below.

Mexican Americans (Chicanos), Cuban Americans, and Puerto Ricans may mobilize to promote general Hispanic issues (e.g., opposition to English-only laws) but act as three separate interest groups in other contexts. Cuban Americans are richer on average than Chicanos and Puerto Ricans are, and their class interests and voting patterns differ. Cubans often vote Republican, but Puerto Ricans and Chicanos are more likely to favor Democrats. Some Mexican Americans whose families have lived in the United States for generations have little in common with new Hispanic immigrants, such as those from Central America. Many Americans (especially those fluent in English) claim Hispanic ethnicity in some contexts but shift to a general "American" identity in others.

In many societies a racial, ethnic, or caste status is associated with a position in the social–political hierarchy. Certain groups, called **minority groups,** are subordinate. They have inferior power and less secure access to resources than do **majority groups** (which are superordinate, dominant, or controlling). Often ethnic groups are minorities. When an ethnic group is assumed to have a biological basis (distinctively shared "blood" or genes), it is called a **race.** Discrimination against such a group is called **racism** (Cohen 1998; Montagu 1997; Scupin 2003; Shanklin 1995; Wade 2002).

> **ethnic group** Group distinguished by cultural similarities (shared among members of that group) and differences (between that group and others); ethnic group members share beliefs, values, habits, customs, and norms, and a common language, religion, history, geography, kinship, and/or race.
>
> **ethnicity** Identification with, and feeling part of, an ethnic group and exclusion from certain other groups because of this affiliation.
>
> **minority groups** Subordinate groups in a social–political hierarchy, with inferior power and less secure access to resources than majority groups have.
>
> **majority groups** Superordinate, dominant, or controlling groups in a social–political hierarchy.
>
> **race** An ethnic group assumed to have a biological basis.
>
> **racism** Discrimination against an ethnic group assumed to have a biological basis.

American Hispanics/ Latinos, 2008

Puerto Rican
8.8%

Cuban
3.5%

Central and South American
16.5%

Mexican
65.8%

Other Hispanic/Latino origin
5.4%

Source: Statistical Abstract of the United States, 2010, Table 6.

STUDY **TIP**

Identity consists both of how people define themselves and how others define them.

After Barack Obama's election to the presidency in 2008, some claimed this as evidence that we live in a "postracial" world, where race is no longer a barrier to success. Do you agree?

>> Race and Ethnicity

Race, like ethnicity in general, is a cultural category rather than a biological reality. That is, ethnic groups, including "races," derive from contrasts perceived and perpetuated in particular societies, rather than from scientific classifications based on common genes (see Wade 2002).

Human races cannot be defined biologically. Only cultural constructions of race are possible—even though the

"Hispanic" and "Latino" are ethnic categories that cross-cut "racial" contrasts such as between "black" and "white." Note the physical diversity among these multiracial schoolchildren in Havana, Cuba.

average person conceptualizes "race" in biological terms (see Mukhopadhyay, Heuze, and Moses 2007). The belief that human races exist and are important is much more common among the public than it is among scientists. Most Americans, for example, believe that their population includes biologically based races to which various labels have been applied. These labels include "white," "black," "yellow," "red," "Caucasoid," "Negroid," "Mongoloid," "Amerindian," "Euro-American," "African American," "Asian American," and "Native American."

We hear the words *ethnicity* and *race* frequently, but American culture doesn't draw a clear line between them. As illustration, consider two articles in the *New York Times* of May 29, 1992. One, discussing the changing ethnic composition of the United States, explains (correctly) that Hispanics "can be of any race" (Barringer 1992, p. A12). In other words, "Hispanic" is an ethnic category that cross-cuts racial contrasts such as that between "black" and "white." The other article reports that during the Los Angeles riots of spring 1992, "hundreds of Hispanic residents were interrogated about their immigration status on the basis of their *race* alone [emphasis added]" (Mydans 1992a, p. A8). Use of "race" here seems inappropriate because "Hispanic" usually is perceived as referring to a linguistically based (Spanish-speaking) ethnic group, rather than a biologically based race. Since these Los Angeles residents were being interrogated because they were Hispanic, the article is actually reporting on ethnic, not racial, discrimination. Given the lack of a precise distinction between

Despite the increasing diversity of American society, some recently popular TV shows (e.g., *Seinfeld, Sex and the City, Entourage, Curb Your Enthusiasm*) have principal characters who are ethnically homogeneous. Other programs, from *Glee,* which is fictional, to MTV's *The Real World* and CBS's *Survivor,* which are classified as "reality shows," make diversity a key part of their cast of characters. What kinds of diversity are shown on *Glee* and *The Real World?* How might you explain the presence or absence of diversity in these seven shows?

race and ethnicity, the term "ethnic group" is preferable to "race" to describe *any* such social group—for example, African Americans, Asian Americans, Irish Americans, Anglo Americans, or Hispanics.

>> The Social Construction of Race

Races are ethnic groups assumed (by members of a particular culture) to have a biological basis, but actually race is socially constructed. The "races" we hear about every day are cultural, or social, rather than biological categories. Many Americans mistakenly assume that whites and blacks, for example, are biologically distinct and that these terms stand for discrete races. But these labels, like racial terms used in other societies, really designate culturally perceived rather than biologically based groups.

CULTURETHINK

Based on your own experiences, think of several ways in which skin color and ethnicity affect judgments and evaluations of people.

HYPODESCENT: RACE IN THE UNITED STATES

How is race culturally constructed in the United States? In American culture, one acquires his or her racial identity at birth, as an ascribed status, but race isn't based on biology or on simple ancestry. Take the case of the child of a "racially mixed" marriage involving one black and one white parent. We know that 50 percent of the child's genes come from one parent and 50 percent from the other. Still, American culture overlooks heredity and classifies this child as black. This rule is arbitrary. On the basis of genotype (genetic composition), it would be just as logical to classify the child as white.

American rules for assigning racial status can be even more arbitrary. In some states, anyone known to have any black ancestor, no matter how remote, is classified as a member of the black race. This is a rule of **descent** (it assigns social identity on the basis of ancestry), but of a sort that is rare outside the contemporary United States. It is called **hypodescent** (Harris and Kottak 1963) because it automatically places the children of a union between members of different groups in the minority group (*hypo* means "lower"). Hypodescent divides American society into groups that have been unequal in their access to wealth, power, and prestige.

The following case from Louisiana is an excellent illustration of the arbitrariness of the hypodescent rule and of the role that governments (federal or, in this case, state) play in legalizing, inventing, or eradicating race and ethnicity (B. Williams 1989). Susie Guillory Phipps, a light-skinned woman with Caucasian features and straight black hair, discovered as an adult that she was black. When Phipps ordered a copy of her birth certificate, she found her race listed as "colored." Since she had been "brought up white and married white twice," Phipps challenged a 1970 Louisiana law declaring anyone with at least one-thirty-second "Negro blood" to be legally black. Although the state's lawyer admitted that Phipps "looks like a white person," the state of Louisiana insisted that her racial classification was proper (Yetman 1991, pp. 3–4).

descent Rule assigning social identity on the basis of some aspect of one's ancestry.

hypodescent A rule that automatically places the children of a union or mating between members of different socioeconomic groups in the less privileged group.

Cases like Phipps's are rare because racial identity usually is ascribed at birth and doesn't change. The rule of hypodescent affects blacks, Asians, Native Americans, and Hispanics differently (see Hunter 2005). Native American or Hispanic identity is easier to negotiate than black identity. The ascription rule isn't as definite, and the assumption of a biological basis isn't as strong.

To be considered Native American, one ancestor out of eight (great-grandparents) or out of four (grandparents) may suffice. This depends on whether the assignment is by federal or state law or by an Indian tribal council. The child of a Hispanic may (or may not, depending on context) claim Hispanic identity. Many Americans with an Indian or Latino grandparent consider themselves white and lay no claim to minority group status.

RACE IN THE U.S. CENSUS

The U.S. Census Bureau has gathered data by race since 1790. Initially this was done because the Constitution specified that a slave counted as three-fifths of a white person, and because Indians were not taxed. The racial categories

A biracial American, Halle Berry, with her mother. What is Halle Berry's race?

included in the 1990 census were "White," "Black or Negro," "Indian (American)," "Eskimo," "Aleut or Pacific Islander," and "Other." A separate question was asked about Spanish–Hispanic heritage. Check out the reproduction of the questionnaire on racial categories in the 2010 census.

Attempts by social scientists and interested citizens to add a "multiracial" census category have been opposed by the National Association for the Advancement of Colored People (NAACP) and the National Council of La Raza (a Hispanic advocacy group). Racial classification is a political issue (Goldberg 2002) involving access to resources, including jobs, voting districts, and federal funding of programs aimed at minorities. The hypodescent rule results in all the population growth being attributed to the minority category. Minorities fear their political clout will decline if their numbers go down.

But things are changing. Choice of "some other race" in the U.S. Census more than doubled from 1980 (6.8 million) to 2000 (over 15 million)—suggesting imprecision in and dissatisfaction with the existing categories (Mar 1997). In the 2000 census, 2.4 percent of Americans, or 6.8 million people, chose a first-ever option of identifying themselves as belonging to more than one race. The number of interracial marriages and children is increasing, with implications for the traditional system of American racial classification. "Interracial," "biracial,"

Questions on Race and Hispanic Origin from Census 2010

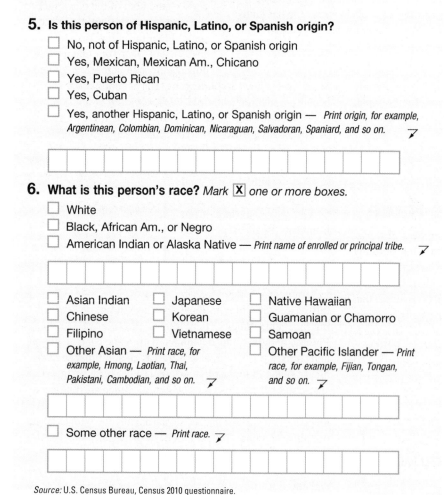

5. Is this person of Hispanic, Latino, or Spanish origin?

☐ No, not of Hispanic, Latino, or Spanish origin
☐ Yes, Mexican, Mexican Am., Chicano
☐ Yes, Puerto Rican
☐ Yes, Cuban
☐ Yes, another Hispanic, Latino, or Spanish origin — *Print origin, for example, Argentinean, Colombian, Dominican, Nicaraguan, Salvadoran, Spaniard, and so on.* ⤢

6. What is this person's race? *Mark* ☒ *one or more boxes.*

☐ White
☐ Black, African Am., or Negro
☐ American Indian or Alaska Native — *Print name of enrolled or principal tribe.* ⤢

☐ Asian Indian   ☐ Japanese   ☐ Native Hawaiian
☐ Chinese   ☐ Korean   ☐ Guamanian or Chamorro
☐ Filipino   ☐ Vietnamese   ☐ Samoan
☐ Other Asian — *Print race, for example, Hmong, Laotian, Thai, Pakistani, Cambodian, and so on.* ⤢   ☐ Other Pacific Islander — *Print race, for example, Fijian, Tongan, and so on.* ⤢

☐ Some other race — *Print race.* ⤢

Source: U.S. Census Bureau, Census 2010 questionnaire.

Visible Minority Population of Canada, 2006 Census

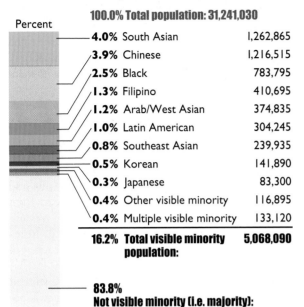

100.0% Total population: 31,241,030

Percent

4.0%	South Asian	1,262,865
3.9%	Chinese	1,216,515
2.5%	Black	783,795
1.3%	Filipino	410,695
1.2%	Arab/West Asian	374,835
1.0%	Latin American	304,245
0.8%	Southeast Asian	239,935
0.5%	Korean	141,890
0.3%	Japanese	83,300
0.4%	Other visible minority	116,895
0.4%	Multiple visible minority	133,120
16.2%	**Total visible minority population:**	**5,068,090**

83.8%
Not visible minority (i.e. majority):
26,172,940

Source: From Statistics Canada, 2006 Census, http://www12
.statcan.ca/english/census06/data/highlights/ethnic.

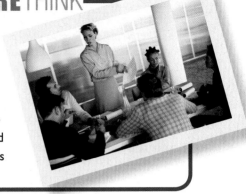
or "multiracial" children who grow up with both parents undoubtedly identify with particular qualities of either parent. To have so important an identity as race dictated by the arbitrary rule of hypodescent is troubling for many of them. It may be especially discordant when racial identity doesn't parallel gender identity, for instance, a boy with a white father and a black mother, or a girl with a white mother and a black father.

How does the Canadian census compare with the American census in its treatment of race? Rather than race, the Canadian census asks about "visible minorities." That country's Employment Equity Act defines such groups as "persons, other than Aboriginal peoples [aka First Nations in Canada, Native Americans in the United States], who are non-Caucasian in race or non-white in colour" (Statistics Canada 2001a). The "Visible Minority Population" figure shows that "South Asian" and "Chinese" are Canada's largest visible minorities. Note that Canada's total visible minority population of 16.2 percent (up from 11.2 percent in 1996) contrasts with a figure of about 25 percent for the United States in the 2000 census and over 33 percent in 2007. In particular, Canada's black population of 2.5 percent contrasts with the American figure

of 12.9 percent (2007) for African Americans, while Canada's Asian population is significantly higher than the U.S. figure of 4.5 percent (2007) on a percentage basis. Only a tiny fraction of the Canadian population (0.4 percent) claimed multiple visible minority affiliation, compared with 2.4 percent claiming "more than one race" in the United States in 2000.

Canada's visible minority population has been increasing steadily. In 1981, 1.1 million visible minorities accounted for 4.7 percent of the total population, versus 16.2 percent today. Visible minorities are growing much faster than is Canada's total population. Between 2001 and 2006, the total population increased 5 percent, while visible minorities rose 27 percent. If recent immigration trends continue, by 2016, visible minorities will account for 20 percent of the Canadian population.

"NOT US": RACE IN JAPAN

American culture ignores considerable diversity in biology, language, and geographic origin as it socially constructs race in the United States. North Americans also overlook diversity by seeing Japan as a nation that is homogeneous in race, ethnicity, language, and culture—an image the Japanese themselves cultivate. Thus in 1986 former Prime Minister Nakasone created an international furor by contrasting his country's supposed homogeneity (responsible, he suggested, for Japan's success at that time in international business) with the ethnically mixed United States.

Japan is hardly the uniform entity Nakasone described. Scholars estimate that 10 percent of Japan's national population are minorities of various sorts. These include aboriginal Ainu, annexed Okinawans, outcast *burakumin,* children of mixed marriages, and immigrant nationalities, especially Koreans, who number more than seven hundred thousand (De Vos, Wetherall, and Stearman 1983; Lie 2001).

To describe racial attitudes in Japan, Jennifer Robertson (1992) uses Kwame Anthony Appiah's (1990) term "intrinsic racism"—the belief that a (perceived) racial difference is a sufficient reason to value one person less than another. In Japan the valued group is majority ("pure") Japanese, who are believed to share "the same blood." Thus, the caption to a printed photo of a Japanese American model reads: "She was born in Japan but raised in Hawaii. Her nationality is American but no foreign blood flows in her veins" (Robertson 1992, p. 5). Something like hypodescent also operates in Japan, but less precisely than in the United States, where mixed offspring automatically become members of the minority group. The children of mixed marriages between majority Japanese and others (including Euro-Americans) may not get the same "racial" label as their minority parent, but they are still stigmatized for their non-Japanese ancestry (De Vos and Wagatsuma 1966).

How is race culturally constructed in Japan? The (majority) Japanese define themselves by opposition to others, whether minority groups in their own nation or outsiders—anyone who is "not us." The "not us" should stay that way; assimilation generally is discouraged. Cultural mechanisms, especially residential segregation and taboos on "interracial" marriage, work to keep minorities "in their place."

In its construction of race, Japanese culture regards certain ethnic groups as having a biological basis, when there is no evidence that they do. The best example is the *burakumin,* a stigmatized group of at least four million outcasts, sometimes compared to India's untouchables. The burakumin are physically and genetically indistinguishable from other Japanese. Many of them "pass" as (and marry) majority Japanese, but a deceptive marriage can end in divorce if burakumin identity is discovered (Aoki and Dardess 1981).

Burakumin are perceived as standing apart from majority Japanese. Through ancestry, descent (and thus, it is

Japan's stigmatized burakumin are physically and genetically indistinguishable from other Japanese. In response to burakumin political mobilization, Japan has dismantled the legal structure of discrimination against burakumin. This Sports Day for burakumin children is one kind of mobilization.

assumed, "blood," or genetics) burakumin are "not us." Majority Japanese try to keep their lineage pure by discouraging mixing. The burakumin are residentially segregated in neighborhoods (rural or urban) called *buraku,* from which the racial label is derived. Compared with majority Japanese, the burakumin are less likely to attend high school and college. When burakumin attend the same schools as majority Japanese, they face discrimination. Majority children and teachers may refuse to eat with them because burakumin are considered unclean.

In applying for university admission or a job and in dealing with the government, Japanese must list their address, which becomes part of a household or family registry. This list makes residence in a buraku, and likely burakumin social status, evident. Schools and companies use this information to discriminate. (The best way to pass is to move so often that the buraku address eventually disappears from the registry.) Majority Japanese also limit "race" mixture by hiring marriage mediators to check out the family histories of prospective spouses. They are especially careful to check for burakumin ancestry (De Vos et al. 1983).

The origin of the burakumin lies in a historical tiered system of stratification (from the Tokugawa period—1603–1868). The top four ranked categories were warrior-administrators (*samurai*), farmers, artisans, and merchants. The ancestors of the burakumin were below this hierarchy, an outcast group who did unclean jobs such as animal slaughter and disposal of the dead. Burakumin still do similar jobs, including work with leather and other animal products. The burakumin are more likely than majority Japanese to do manual labor (including farm work) and to belong to the national lower class. Burakumin and other Japanese minorities also are more likely to have careers in crime, prostitution, entertainment, and sports (De Vos et al. 1983).

Like blacks in the United States, the burakumin are class-stratified. Because certain jobs are reserved for the burakumin, people who are successful in those occupations (e.g., shoe factory owners) can be wealthy. Burakumin also have found jobs as government bureaucrats. Financially successful burakumin can temporarily escape their stigmatized status by travel, including foreign travel.

Discrimination against the burakumin is strikingly like the discrimination that blacks have experienced in the United States. The burakumin often live in villages and neighborhoods with poor housing and sanitation. They have limited access to education, jobs, amenities, and health facilities. In response to burakumin political mobilization, Japan has dismantled the legal structure of discrimination against burakumin and has worked to improve conditions in the buraku. (The website http://blhrri.org/index_e.htm is sponsored by the Buraku Liberation and Human Rights Research Institute and includes the most recent information about the Buraku liberation movement.) Still Japan has yet to institute American-style affirmative action programs for education and jobs. Discrimination against nonmajority Japanese is still the rule in companies. Some employers say that hiring burakumin would give their company an unclean image and thus create a disadvantage in competing with other businesses (De Vos et al. 1983).

PHENOTYPE AND FLUIDITY: RACE IN BRAZIL

There are more flexible, less exclusionary ways of constructing social race than those used in the United States and Japan. Along with the rest of Latin America, Brazil has less exclusionary categories, which permit individuals to change their racial classification. Brazil shares a history of slavery with the United States, but it lacks the hypodescent rule. Nor does Brazil have racial aversion of the sort found in Japan.

Brazilians use many more racial labels—over five hundred were once reported (Harris 1970)—than Americans or Japanese do. In northeastern Brazil, Conrad Kottak found forty different racial terms in use in Arembepe, a village of only seven hundred and fifty people (Kottak 2006). Through their traditional classification system Brazilians recognize and attempt to describe the physical variation that exists in their population. The system used in the United States, by recognizing only three or four races, blinds Americans to an equivalent range of evident physical contrasts. The system Brazilians use to construct social race has other special features. In the United States one's race is an ascribed status; it is assigned automatically by hypodescent and usually doesn't change. In Brazil racial identity is more flexible, more of an achieved status. Brazilian racial classification pays attention to phenotype. As discussed in the chapter "What Is Anthropology," **phenotype** refers to an organism's evident traits, its "manifest biology"—physiology and anatomy, including skin color, hair form, facial features, and eye color. A Brazilian's phenotype and racial label may change because of environmental factors, such as the tanning rays of the sun or the effects of humidity on the hair.

> **phenotype** An organism's evident traits, its "manifest biology"—anatomy and physiology.

These photos, taken in Brazil by Conrad Kottak in 2003 and 2004, give just a glimpse of the spectrum of phenotypical diversity encountered among contemporary Brazilians.

As physical characteristics change (sunlight alters skin color, humidity affects hair form), so do racial terms. Furthermore, racial differences may be so insignificant in structuring community life that people may forget the terms they have applied to others. Sometimes they even forget the ones they've used for themselves. In Arembepe, Kottak made it a habit to ask the same person on different days to tell him the races of others in the village (and his own). In the United States he is "white" or "Euro-American," but in Arembepe he was given several terms besides *branco* ("white"). He could be *claro* ("light"), *louro* ("blond"), *sarará* ("light-skinned redhead"), *mulato claro* ("light mulatto"), or *mulato* ("mulatto"). The racial term used to describe Kottak or anyone else varied from person to person, week to week, even day to day. His best informant, a man with very dark skin color, changed the term he used for himself all the time—from *escuro* ("dark") to *preto* ("black") to *moreno escuro* ("dark brunet").

The American and Japanese racial systems are creations of particular cultures, rather than scientific—or even accurate—descriptions of human biological differences. Brazilian racial classification also is a cultural construction, but Brazilians have developed a way of describing human biological diversity that is more detailed, fluid, and flexible than the systems used in most cultures. Brazil lacks Japan's racial aversion, and it also lacks a rule of descent like that which ascribes racial status in the United States (Degler 1970; Harris 1964).

For centuries the United States and Brazil have had mixed populations, with ancestors from Native America, Europe, Africa, and Asia. Although races have mixed in both countries, Brazilian and American cultures have constructed the results differently.

nation-state An autonomous political entity, a country, such as the United States or Canada.

The historical reasons for this contrast lie mainly in the different characteristics of the settlers of the two countries. The mainly English early settlers of the United States came as women, men, and families, but Brazil's Portuguese colonizers were mainly men—merchants and adventurers. Many of these Portuguese men married Native American women and recog-

nized their racially mixed children as their heirs. Like their North American counterparts, Brazilian plantation owners had sexual relations with their slaves. But the Brazilian landlords more often freed the children that resulted—for demographic and economic reasons. (Sometimes these were their only children.) Freed offspring of master and slave became plantation overseers and foremen and filled many intermediate positions in the emerging Brazilian economy. They were not classed with the slaves, but were allowed to join a new intermediate category. No hypodescent rule developed in Brazil to ensure that whites and blacks remained separate (see Degler 1970; Harris 1964).

>> Ethnic Groups, Nations, and Nationalities

The term *nation* once was synonymous with *tribe* or *ethnic group*. All three of these terms have been used to refer to a single culture sharing a single language, religion, history, territory, ancestry, and kinship. Thus one could speak interchangeably of the Seneca (American Indian) nation, tribe, or ethnic group. Now *nation* has come to mean *state*—an independent, centrally organized political unit, or a government. *Nation* and *state* have become synonymous. Combined in **nation-state** they refer to an autonomous political entity, a country—like the United States, "one nation, indivisible" (see Farner 2004; Gellner 1997; Hastings 1997).

Because of migration, conquest, and colonialism, most nation-states are not ethnically homogeneous. A 2003 study by Fearon found that about 70 percent of all countries have an ethnic group that forms an absolute majority of the population, and the average population share of such groups is 65 percent. The average size of the *second* largest group, or largest ethnic minority, is 17 percent. Only 18 percent of all countries have a single ethnic group that accounts for 90 percent or more of its population.

NATIONALITIES AND IMAGINED COMMUNITIES

Ethnic groups that once had, or wish to have or regain, autonomous political status (their own country) are called **nationalities.** In the words of Benedict Anderson (1991), they are "imagined communities." Even when they be-

CULTURETHINK

How are the Brazilian and Japanese racial labels similar to and different from those of the United States?

come nation-states, they remain imagined communities because most of their members, though feeling comradeship, will never meet (Anderson 1991, pp. 6–10). They can only imagine they all participate in the same unit.

CULTURETHINK

In what ways is the United States an imagined community? What role does the media play in this community creation?

Anderson traces Western European nationalism, which arose in imperial powers such as England, France, and Spain, back to the eighteenth century. He stresses that language and print played a crucial role in the growth of European national consciousness. The novel and the newspaper were "two forms of imagining" communities (consisting of all the people who read the same sources and thus witnessed the same events) that flowered in the eighteenth century (Anderson 1991, pp. 24–25).

Over time, political upheavals, wars, and migration have divided many imagined national communities that arose in the eighteenth and nineteenth centuries. The German and Korean homelands were artificially divided after wars, according to communist and capitalist ideologies. World War I split the Kurds, who remain an imagined community, forming a majority in no state. Kurds are a minority group in Turkey, Iran, Iraq, and Syria.

In creating multitribal and multiethnic states, colonialism often erected boundaries that corresponded poorly with preexisting cultural divisions. But colonial institutions also helped create new "imagined communities" beyond nations. An example is the idea of *négritude* ("Black identity") developed by African intellectuals in Francophone (French-speaking) West Africa. Négritude can be traced to the association and common experience in colonial times of youths from Guinea, Mali, the Ivory Coast, and Senegal at the William Ponty school in Dakar, Senegal (Anderson 1991, pp. 123–124).

> **nationalities** Ethnic groups that once had, or wish to have or regain, autonomous political status (their own country).
>
> **assimilation** The process of change that a minority group may experience when it moves to a country where another culture dominates; the minority is incorporated into the dominant culture to the point that it no longer exists as a separate cultural unit.

>> Ethnic Tolerance and Accommodation

Ethnic diversity may be associated with positive group interaction and coexistence or with conflict (discussed shortly). There are nation-states, including some less developed countries, in which multiple cultural groups live together in reasonable harmony.

ASSIMILATION

The process of change that a minority ethnic group may experience when its members move to a country where another culture dominates is known as **assimilation.** By assimilating, the minority adopts the patterns and norms of its host culture. It is incorporated into the dominant culture to the point that it no longer exists as a separate cultural unit. Some countries, such as Brazil, are more assimilationist than others. Germans, Italians, Japanese, Middle Easterners, and East Europeans started migrating

The United States is increasingly a multicultural society. It features growing ethnic enclaves such as New York's Chinatown, shown here, often located right next to others, such as Little Italy in the same city.

to Brazil late in the nineteenth century. These immigrants have assimilated to a common Brazilian culture, which has Portuguese, African, and Native American roots. The descendants of these immigrants speak the national language (Portuguese) and participate in the national culture. (During World War II, Brazil, which was on the Allied side, forced assimilation by banning instruction in any language other than Portuguese—especially in German.)

THE PLURAL SOCIETY

Assimilation isn't inevitable, and ethnic harmony can exist without it. Ethnic distinctions can persist despite generations of interethnic contact. Through a study of three ethnic groups in Swat, Pakistan, Fredrik Barth (1958/1968) challenged an old idea that interaction always leads to assimilation. He showed that ethnic groups can be in contact for generations without assimilating and can live in peaceful coexistence.

plural society A society that combines ethnic contrasts, ecological specialization (i.e., use of different environmental resources by each ethnic group), and the economic interdependence of those groups.

multiculturalism The view of cultural diversity in a country as something good and desirable; a multicultural society socializes individuals not only into the dominant (national) culture, but also into an ethnic culture.

Barth (1958/1968, p. 324) defines **plural society** (an idea he extended from Pakistan to the entire Middle East) as a society combining ethnic contrasts, ecological specialization (i.e., use of different environmental resources by each ethnic group), and the economic interdependence of those groups. Consider his description of the Middle East (in the 1950s): "The 'environment' of any one ethnic group is not only defined by natural conditions, but also by the presence and activities of the other ethnic groups on which it depends. Each group exploits only part of the total environment, and leaves large parts of it open for other groups to exploit." The ecological interdependence (or, at least, the lack of competition) between ethnic groups may be based on different activities in the same region or on long-term occupation of different regions in the same nation-state.

In Barth's view, ethnic boundaries are most stable and enduring when the groups occupy different ecological niches. That is, they make their living in different ways and don't compete. Ideally, they should depend on each other's activities and exchange with one another. When different ethnic groups exploit the *same* ecological niche, the militarily more powerful group will normally replace the weaker one. If they exploit more or less the same niche, but the weaker group is better able to use marginal environments, they also may coexist (Barth 1958/1968, p. 331). Given niche specialization, ethnic boundaries and interdependence can be maintained, although the specific cultural features of each group may change. By shifting the analytic focus from individual cultures or ethnic groups to *relationships* between cultures or ethnic groups, Barth (1958/1968, 1969) has made important contributions to ethnic studies.

MULTICULTURALISM AND ETHNIC IDENTITY

The view of cultural diversity in a country as something good and desirable is called **multiculturalism** (see Kottak and Kozaitis 2008). The multicultural model is the opposite of the assimilationist model, in which minorities are expected to abandon their cultural traditions and values, replacing them with those of the majority population. The multicultural view encourages the practice of cultural–ethnic traditions. A multicultural society socializes individuals not only into the dominant (national) culture but also into an ethnic culture. Thus in the United States millions of people speak both English and another language, eat both "American" (apple pie, steak, hamburgers) and "ethnic" foods, and celebrate both national (July 4, Thanksgiving) and ethnic–religious holidays.

In the United States and Canada multiculturalism is of growing importance. This reflects an awareness that the number and size of ethnic groups have grown dramatically in recent years. If this trend continues, the ethnic composition of the United States will change dramatically (see "Ethnic Composition of the United States").

Even now, because of immigration and differential population growth, minorities outnumber whites in many urban areas. For example, of the 8,274,527 people living in New York City in 2007, 25 percent were black, 27 per-

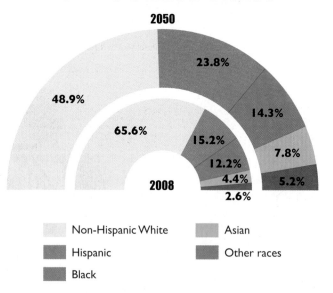

Ethnic Composition of the United States

2050

23.8%

48.9%

14.3%

65.6%

15.2%

7.8%

12.2%

4.4%

5.2%

2008

2.6%

Non-Hispanic White

Asian

Hispanic

Other races

Black

The proportion of the American population that is white and non-Hispanic is declining. The projection for 2050 shown here comes from a U.S. Census Bureau report issued in March 2004. Note especially the dramatic rise in the Hispanic portion of the American population between 2008 and 2050.

Source: Based on data from U.S. Census Bureau, International Data Base, Table 094, http://www.census.gov/ipc/www.idbprint.html; Files 2005 and http://www .census.gov/Press-Release/www/releases/archives/population/010048.html, and Table 12.1 on p. 226.

cent Hispanic, 12 percent Asian, and 36 percent other—including non-Hispanic whites. The comparable figures for Los Angeles (which had 3,770,590 people in 2007) were 10 percent black, 48 percent Hispanic, 11 percent Asian, and 31 percent other, including non-Hispanic whites (U.S. Census Bureau 2008, 2009).

In October 2006, the population of the United States reached 300 million people, just thirty-nine years after reaching 200 million and ninety-one years after reaching the 100 million mark (in 1915). The country's ethnic composition has changed dramatically in the past forty years. The 1970 census, the first to attempt an official count of Hispanics, found they represented no more than 4.7 percent of the American population, compared with 15.2 percent in 2008. The number of African Americans increased from 11.1 percent in 1967 to 12.2 percent in 2008, while (non-Hispanic) whites ("Anglos") declined from 83 percent to 65.6 percent. In 1967 less than 10 million people in the United States (5 percent of the population) had been born elsewhere, compared with more than 36 million immigrants (12 percent) today (Ohlemacher 2006).

In 1973, 78 percent of the students in American public schools were white, and 22 percent were minorities: blacks, Hispanics, Asians, Pacific Islanders, and "others." By 2004, 57 percent of public school students were white, and 43 percent were minorities. If current trends continue, minority students will outnumber (non-Hispanic) white students by 2015. They already do in California, Hawaii, Mississippi, New Mexico, and Texas (Dillon 2006).

Immigration, mainly from southern and eastern Europe, had a similar effect on classroom diversity, at least in the largest American cities, a century ago. A study of American public schools in 1908–1909 found that 42 percent of those urban students were native-born, while 58 percent were immigrants. In a very different (multicultural now versus assimilationist then) context, today's American classrooms have regained the ethnic diversity they demonstrated in the early 1900s, when author Conrad Kottak's German-speaking Austro-Hungarian-born father and grandparents immigrated to the United States.

One response to ethnic diversification and awareness has been for many whites to reclaim ethnic identities (Italian, Albanian, Serbian, Lithuanian, etc.) and to join ethnic associations (clubs, gangs). Some such groups are new. Others have existed for decades, although they lost members during the assimilationist years of the 1920s through the 1950s.

Multiculturalism seeks ways for people to understand and interact that don't depend on sameness but rather on respect for differences. Multiculturalism stresses the interaction of ethnic groups and their contribution to the country. It assumes that each group has something to offer to and learn from the others. Several forces have propelled North America away from the assimilationist model toward multiculturalism. First, multiculturalism reflects the fact of recent large-scale migration, particularly from the "less developed countries" to the "developed" nations of North America and Western Europe. The global scale of modern migration introduces unparalleled ethnic variety to host nations. Multiculturalism is related to globalization: People use modern means of transportation to migrate to nations whose lifestyles they learn about through the media and from tourists who increasingly visit their own countries (see Inda and Rosaldo 2008).

Migration also is fueled by rapid population growth, coupled with insufficient jobs (both for educated and uneducated people), in the less developed countries. As traditional rural economies decline or mechanize, displaced farmers move to cities, where they and their children often are unable to find jobs. As people in the less developed countries get better educations, they seek more skilled employment. They hope to partake of an international culture of consumption that includes such modern amenities as refrigerators, televisions, and automobiles (Ahmed 2004).

In a world with growing rural–urban and transnational migration, ethnic identities are used increasingly to form self-help organizations focused mainly on enhancing the group's economic competitiveness (Williams 1989). People claim and express ethnic identities for political and economic reasons. Michel Laguerre's (1984, 1998) studies of Haitian immigrants in the United States show that they mobilize to deal with the discriminatory structure (racist in this case, since Haitians tend to be black) of American society. Ethnicity (their common Haitian creole language and cultural background) is a basis for their mobilization. Haitian ethnicity helps distinguish them from African Americans and other ethnic groups.

Did You Know?

The American Anthropological Association (AAA) passed a resolution challenging Arizona's 2010 law giving law enforcement agents the right to require people to provide evidence of their citizenship status whether or not they are suspected of committing a crime. The AAA and other groups such as the American Civil Liberties Union (ACLU) believe that the law will make Latinos and other minorities targets of harassment and racial profiling.

STUDY TIP

The United States has moved toward the multicultural model for two primary reasons:

- Ethnic variety has increased with globalization, as people migrate for opportunities in education and skilled employment;

- Ethnic self-help organizations increasingly keep ethnic groups united and mobilized politically.

In the face of globalization, much of the world, including Europe and North America, is experiencing an ethnic revival. The new assertiveness of long-resident ethnic groups extends to the Basques and Catalans in Spain, the Bretons and Corsicans in France, and the Welsh and Scots in the United Kingdom. The United States and Canada are becoming increasingly multicultural, focusing on their internal diversity (see Laguerre 1999). "Melting pots" no longer, they are better described as ethnic "salads" (each ingredient remains distinct, although in the same bowl, with the same dressing).

>> Roots of Ethnic Conflict

Ethnicity, based on perceived cultural similarities and differences in a society or nation, can be expressed in peaceful multiculturalism or in discrimination or violent inter-ethnic confrontation. The roots of ethnic differentiation—and therefore, potentially, of ethnic conflict—can be political, economic, religious, linguistic, cultural, or racial (see Kuper 2006). Why do ethnic differences often lead to conflict and violence? The causes include a sense of injustice because of resource distribution, economic or political competition, and reaction to discrimination, prejudice, and other expressions of devalued identity (see Friedman 2003; Ryan 1990, p. xxvii).

prejudice Devaluing (looking down on) a group because of its assumed behavior, values, capabilities, or attributes.

stereotypes Fixed ideas—often unfavorable—about what members of a group are like.

discrimination Policies and practices that harm a group and its members.

In Iraq, under the dictator Saddam Hussein, one Muslim group (Sunnis) discriminated against others (Shiites and Kurds). Sunnis, although a numeric minority within Iraq's population, enjoyed privileged access to power, prestige, and position. After the 2005 elections, which many Sunnis chose to boycott, Shiites gained political control. A civil war developed out of *sectarian violence* (conflicts among sects of the same religion) as Sunnis (and their foreign supporters) fueled an insurgency against the new government and its foreign supporters, including the United States. Shiites retaliated against Sunni attacks and a history of Sunni privilege and perceived discrimination against Shiites, as Shiite militias engaged in ethnic (sectarian) cleansing of their own.

PREJUDICE AND DISCRIMINATION

Ethnic conflict often arises in reaction to prejudice (attitudes and judgments) or discrimination (action). **Prejudice** means devaluing (looking down on) a group because of its assumed behavior, values, capabilities, or attributes. People are prejudiced when they hold stereotypes about groups and apply them to individuals. (**Stereotypes** are fixed ideas—often unfavorable—about what the members of a group are like.) Prejudiced people assume that members of the group will act as they are "supposed to act" (according to the stereotype) and interpret a wide range of individual behaviors as evidence of the stereotype. They use this behavior to confirm their stereotype (and low opinion) of the group.

Discrimination refers to policies and practices that harm a group and its members. Discrimination may be *de facto* (practiced, but not legally sanctioned) or *de jure* (part of the law). An example of de facto discrimination is the harsher treatment that American minorities (compared with other Americans) tend to get from the police and the judicial system. This unequal treatment isn't legal, but it happens anyway. Segregation in the southern United States and *apartheid* in South Africa provide two examples of de jure discrimination, which no longer are in existence. In both systems, by law, blacks and whites had different rights and privileges. Their social interaction ("mixing") was legally curtailed.

Anthropology Works

Law enforcement agents benefit from anthropological understandings of race and ethnicity. Being aware of the human tendency to hold stereotypes and prejudices, agents can work to combat discrimination, both in their own organization and within the community.

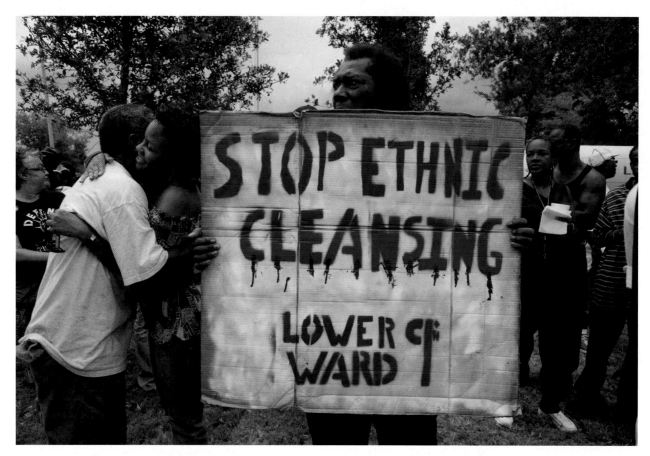

Discrimination *refers to policies and practices that harm a group and its members. This protest sign, hoisted in New Orleans' lower 9th ward, shows that at least some community residents see ethnic and racial bias.*

CHIPS IN THE MOSAIC

Although the multicultural model is increasingly prominent in North America, ethnic competition and conflict also are evident. There is conflict between newer arrivals—for instance, Central Americans and Koreans—and longer-established ethnic groups, such as African Americans. Ethnic antagonism flared in South-Central Los Angeles in spring 1992 in rioting that followed the acquittal of four white police officers who were tried for the videotaped beating of Rodney King (see Abelmann and Lie 1995).

Angry blacks attacked whites, Koreans, and Latinos. This violence expressed frustration by African Americans about their prospects in an increasingly multicultural society. A *New York Times* CBS News poll conducted just after the Los Angeles riots found that blacks had a bleaker outlook than whites about the effects of immigration on their lives. Only 23 percent of the blacks felt they had more opportunities than recent immigrants, compared with twice that many whites (Toner 1992).

Korean stores were hard hit during the 1992 riots, and more than a third of the businesses destroyed were Latino-owned. A third of those who died in the riots were Latinos. These mainly recent migrants lacked deep roots to the neighborhood and, as Spanish speakers, faced language barriers (Newman 1992). Many Koreans also had trouble with English.

Koreans interviewed on ABC's *Nightline* on May 6, 1992, recognized that blacks resented them and considered them unfriendly. One man explained, "It's not part of our culture to smile." African Americans interviewed on the same program did complain about Korean unfriendliness. "They come into our neighborhoods and treat us like dirt." These comments suggest a shortcoming of the multicultural perspective: Ethnic groups (blacks here) expect other ethnic groups in the same nation-state to assimilate to some extent to a shared (national) culture. The African Americans' comments invoked a general American value system that includes friendliness, openness, mutual respect, community participation, and "fair play." Los Angeles blacks wanted their Korean neighbors to act more like generalized Americans—and good neighbors.

> **genocide** Policies aimed at, and/or resulting in, the physical extinction (through mass murder) of a people perceived as a racial group, that is, as sharing defining physical, genetic, or other biological characteristics.

AFTERMATHS OF OPPRESSION

Fueling ethnic conflict are such forms of discrimination as genocide, forced assimilation, ethnocide, and cultural colonialism. The most extreme form of ethnic discrimination is **genocide,** the deliberate elimination of a group (such as Jews in Nazi Germany, Muslims in Bosnia, or Tutsi in Rwanda) through mass murder. A dominant group may try to destroy the cultures of certain ethnic

Did You Know?

An example of cultural colonialism would be Tibet, which was taken over by the Chinese Communists in 1949. The Chinese eventually broke up the authority of the Buddhist monasteries in Tibet and called for Tibet's assimilation into the larger Chinese state.

groups (**ethnocide**) or force them to adopt the dominant culture (*forced assimilation*). Many countries have penalized or banned the language and customs of an ethnic group (including its religious observances). One example of forced assimilation is the anti-Basque campaign that the dictator Francisco Franco (who ruled between 1939 and 1975) waged in Spain. Franco banned Basque books, journals, newspapers, signs, sermons, and tombstones and imposed fines for using the Basque language in schools (Ryan 1990). His policies led to the formation of a Basque terrorist group and spurred strong nationalist sentiment in the Basque region.

A policy of *ethnic expulsion* aims at removing culturally different groups from a country. There are many examples, including Bosnia-Herzegovina in the 1990s. Uganda expelled 74,000 Asians in 1972. The neofascist parties of contemporary Western Europe advocate repatriation (expulsion) of immigrant workers (West Indians in England, Algerians in France, and Turks in Germany) (see Friedman 2003; Ryan 1990, p. 9). A policy of expulsion may create **refugees**—people who have been forced (involuntary refugees) or who have chosen (voluntary refugees) to flee a country, to escape persecution or war.

ethnocide Destruction by a dominant group of the culture of an ethnic group.

refugees People who have been forced (involuntary refugees) or who have chosen (voluntary refugees) to flee a country, to escape persecution or war.

cultural colonialism Within a nation or empire, domination by one ethnic group or nationality and its culture/ ideology over others—e.g., the dominance of Russian people, language, and culture in the former Soviet Union.

In many countries, colonial nation-building left ethnic strife in its wake. Thus, over a million Hindus and Muslims were killed in the violence that accompanied the division of the Indian subcontinent into India and Pakistan. Problems between Arabs and Jews in Palestine began during the British mandate period.

Multiculturalism may be growing in the United States and Canada, but the opposite is happening in the former Soviet Union, where ethnic groups (nationalities) want their own nation-states. The flowering of ethnic feeling and conflict as the Soviet empire disintegrated illustrates that years of political repression and ideology provide insufficient common ground for lasting unity. **Cultural colonialism** refers to internal domination—by one group and its culture or ideology over others. One example is the domination over the former Soviet empire by Russian people, language, and culture, and by communist ideology. The dominant culture makes itself the official culture. This is reflected in schools, the media, and public interaction. Under Soviet rule ethnic minorities had very limited self-rule in republics and regions controlled by Moscow. All the republics and their peoples were to be united by the oneness of "socialist internationalism." One common technique in cultural colonialism is to flood ethnic areas with members of the dominant ethnic group. Thus, in the former Soviet Union, ethnic Russian colonists were sent to many areas, to diminish the cohesion and clout of the local people.

The Commonwealth of Independent States (CIS), founded in 1991 and headquartered in Minsk, Belarus, is what remains of the once-powerful Soviet Union (see Yurchak 2005). In Russia and other formerly Soviet na-

Two faces of ethnic difference in the former Soviet empire. A propaganda poster depicts a happy mix of nationalities that make up the population of Kyrgyzstan, Central Asia (left); ethnic Georgians in a refugee camp near Tblisi, Georgia, in August 2008 (right). They fled Georgia's breakaway province, the self-proclaimed new republic of South Ossetia, where Russians were fighting the Georgian army. A cease-fire did not end the tension; Georgia still views South Ossetia as a Russian-occupied territory.

tions, ethnic groups (nationalities) have sought, and continue to seek, to forge separate and viable nation-states based on cultural boundaries. This celebration of ethnic autonomy is part of an ethnic flowering that—as surely as globalization and transnationalism—is a trend of the late twentieth and early twenty-first centuries.

get involved!

Test your stereotypes about ethnicity and "race" in sports. What ethnicity do you assume to be especially common among players in each of the following: hockey, baseball, football, and basketball? Pick a city near you with a professional sports team or a college or university sports program you know well. Find rosters of players, then use photos of the players and their family names to help you ascertain ethnic backgrounds. Watch a game in each sport and see who plays the most. How do your stereotypes accord with the rosters and the players you see in the games? Might players of a particular ethnic background excel in or even dominate certain sports? If so, what roles do you think society's ethnic stereotypes, players' early enculturation, and their family's regional and social class background might play in this dominance?

For REVIEW

I. How are race and ethnicity socially constructed?

- Both ethnic groups and "races" derive from contrasts perceived and perpetuated in particular societies. Members of an ethnic group define themselves through a common language, religion, historical experience, geographic placement, kinship, and/or "race." Other people regard the group as having the ethnic identity it claims. Ethnic group markers include a collective name, belief in common descent, sense of solidarity, and association with a territory, real or imagined. Race is an ethnic group that is assumed to have a biological basis. Racial labels really designate *culturally* perceived groups. American culture assigns racial status arbitrarily. Children of a union between members of different groups are assigned the status of the minority group.

II. How does contemporary racial classification differ in three contemporary nations: the United States, Japan, and Brazil?

- In the United States, race is assumed to have a biological basis and racial status is ascribed. Traditional American racial categories are changing as biracial and multiracial children begin to resist having the hypodescent rule dictate their identity. In Japan, a perceived racial difference is sufficient reason to value one person less than another. Offspring of marriages between "pure" majority Japanese and members of a minority are stigmatized. In Brazil, classification is more flexible and racial identity is more of an achieved status. If a Brazilian's phenotype changes because of environmental factors, racial labels change accordingly.

III. What are the negative and positive aspects of ethnicity?

- Ethnic diversity may be associated both with conflict and with positive group interaction and coexistence. The assimilation of an ethnic minority group may be expected or even forced. Although multiculturalism seeks ways for different groups to interact with and learn from one other, it does not necessarily end conflict. Unequal access to resources, economic or political competition, prejudice, and discrimination may lead to conflict and violence. Genocide is the deliberate elimination of a group. Ethnocide, forced expulsion, and cultural colonialism also endanger ethnic groups and fuel conflict. Ethnicity may be the basis for mobilizing group members to self-help and dealing with discrimination. It also may be the basis for seeking to forge separate nation-states.

Pop Quiz

1. What is the term for identifying with, and feeling part of, an ethnic group, and excluded from other ethnic traditions?
   a. Cultural relativism
   b. Ethnicity
   c. Assimilation
   d. Ethnocentrism

2. When a person's identities are not mutually exclusive, but one identity is used in a certain setting while another identity is used in another setting, we say that:
   a. The person is having an identity crisis.
   b. The identities are situationally nonnegotiable.
   c. Affiliation shifts as identity is negotiated.
   d. Shifting identities is unlikely, because people always have one overwhelming primary identity.

3. Which of the following statements would apply to both ethnicity and race?
   a. Both terms describe a minority group.
   b. Both terms are cultural rather than biological categories.
   c. American culture defines these terms in a way that sharply distinguishes one from the other.
   d. The basis of both of these terms is biological.

4. The rule or principle that automatically places the children of a union between members of different socioeconomic groups in the minority group is called:
   a. Hypodescent
   b. Natural descent
   c. Racial mixing
   d. Achieved status

5. What distinguishes racial classification in Brazil from that in the United States?
   a. Race in Brazil is ascribed.
   b. Brazilians have created a profusion of racial labels that often leads to mislabeling a person's race.
   c. Brazilian racial identity is flexible, more of an achieved status.
   d. A Brazilian's phenotype remains fixed.

6. A nationality is considered:
   a. One nation-state.
   b. One ethnic community that is politically united.
   c. A minority within a single state.
   d. An imagined community.

7. Which of the following is *not* true about minority groups that move to a country where another culture dominates?
   a. They usually assimilate by the second or, at latest, the third generation.
   b. Their members may continue to speak their own languages and practice their ways yet still live in ethnic harmony with the dominant culture.
   c. If they maintain their ethnicity and use environmental resources different from those used by other groups, they may live in a state of ecological interdependence with those groups.
   d. The boundaries between ethnic groups are most stable and enduring when the groups occupy different ecological niches.

8. Which of the following statements is *not* true about multiculturalism?
   a. It contrasts with assimilation, the process by which a minority abandons its traditions and adopts the patterns of the majority culture.
   b. Living together in a multicultural society with little interaction among them, ethnic groups have little to teach or offer one another.
   c. The number and size of ethnic groups in the United States have grown dramatically in recent years.
   d. Multiculturalism is related to globalization.

9. Which one of the following is *not* generally one of the roots of ethnic conflict?
   a. Differential access to resources and prospects for the future.
   b. Political conflict.
   c. Reaction to prejudice and discrimination.
   d. People's understanding that many ethnic groups cannot assimilate readily to a shared national culture.

10. What is the term for a dominant group's attempt to destroy the cultures of certain ethnic groups or attempt to force them to adopt the dominant culture?
    a. Colonialism
    b. Genocide
    c. Ethnocide
    d. Ethnic expulsion

1. (b), 2. (c), 3. (b), 4. (a), 5. (c), 6. (d), 7. (d), 8. (a), 9. (d), 10. (c)

13

ANTHROPOLOGY'S ROLE IN A GLOBALIZING WORLD

UNDERSTANDING OURSELVES

Modern technology makes it easier than ever for us to perceive the Earth as both a planet and our world. Images of Earth taken from space have become commonplace. Anthropologists have even used such images to choose communities to study on Earth. Interested in the causes of deforestation in Madagascar, for example, Lisa Gezon, Conrad Kottak, and their colleagues examined a series of satellite images taken in successive years to determine areas where the forest cover had diminished significantly. Then they traveled to Madagascar to study those areas on the ground.

Intensifying global trends include reliance on fossil fuels and increased fossil-fuel emissions, human population increase, and the shift from subsistence to cash economies. These trends promote agricultural intensification, resource depletion (from deforestation to oil spills), and emigration.

Worldwide, young people are abandoning traditional subsistence pursuits. An old popular song asked, "How ya' gonna keep 'em down on the farm after they've seen Paree." Nowadays most people *have* seen Paree—Paris, that is—along with other world capitals, maybe not in person, but in print or on-screen images. Young people today are better educated and wiser in the ways of the world than ever before. They are increasingly exposed to the promises of a better life away from the farm. They seek paying jobs, but work is scarce, spurring migration within and across national boundaries. In turn, transnational migration increases cultural diversity in the United States, Canada, and western European countries.

Small towns throughout America now have Chinese restaurants. Pizza and tacos are as American as apple pie. Your McDonald's outlet sells burritos, lattes, and cappuccino. Every day you encounter not just products, but people whose ancestral countries and cultures have been studied by anthropologists for generations—making cultural anthropology all the more relevant to our daily lives in an increasingly interconnected world.

As You READ

- What is global climate change, and how can anthropologists study it, along with other environmental threats?

- What is cultural imperialism, and what forces work to favor and oppose it?

- What are indigenous peoples, and how and why has their importance increased in recent years?

>> Global Climate Change

The Earth's surface temperatures have risen about 1.48 degrees Fahrenheit (0.78 degrees Centigrade) since the early twentieth century. About two-thirds of this increase has been since 1978 (see "Global Temperature Change").

Along with rising temperatures, shrinking glaciers and melting polar ice provide additional evidence for global warming. Scientific measurements confirm that global warming is not due to increased solar radiation. The causes are mainly anthropogenic—caused by humans and their activities.

Because our planet's climate is always changing, the key question becomes this: How much global warming is

Global Temperature Change

Annual global mean surface air temperature (°Celsius)   (°Farenheit)

— Annual mean
— 5-year mean

14.6°		58.3°
14.4°		58.0°
14.2°		57.6°
14.0°		57.2°
13.8°		56.8°
13.6°		56.5°

1880   1900   1920   1940   1960   1980   2000

Year

Global annual-mean surface air temperature derived from measurements at meteorological stations has increased by 1.4°F (0.7°C) since the early twentieth century, with about 0.9°F (0.5°C) of the increase occurring since 1978.

Source: Goddard Institute for Space Studies, from "Understanding and Responding to Climate Change: Highlights of National Academies Reports," http://dels.nas.edu/basc/Climate-HIGH.pdf.

Is the future depicted in the movie Wall-E a likely one, and how does it relate, if at all, to global climate change?

due to human activities versus natural climate variability? Most scientists agree that human activities play a major role in global climate change. How can the human factor not be significant given population growth and rapidly increasing use of fossil fuels, which produce greenhouse gases in the atmosphere?

The role of one such gas—carbon dioxide (CO_2)—in warming the Earth's surface has been known for over a century. For hundreds of thousands of years, world temperatures have varied depending on the amount of CO_2 in the atmosphere. The burning of fossil fuels (oil, natural gas, and coal) releases substantial amounts of carbon dioxide. The recent rapid rise in both CO_2 and the Earth's surface temperature is one proof that humans are fueling global warming.

The **greenhouse effect** is a natural phenomenon that keeps the Earth's surface warm. Without greenhouse gases—water vapor (H_2O), carbon dioxide (CO_2), methane (CH_4), nitrous oxide (N_2O), halocarbons, and ozone (O_3)—life as we know it wouldn't exist. Like a greenhouse window, such gases allow sunlight to enter and then prevent heat from escaping the atmosphere. All those gases have increased since the Industrial Revolution. Today, the atmospheric concentration of greenhouse gases has reached its highest level in four hundred thousand years. It will continue to rise—as will global temperatures—without actions to slow it down (National Academies 2006).

Scientists prefer the term **climate change** to *global warming*. The former term points out that, beyond rising temperatures, there have been changes in sea levels, precipitation, storms, and ecosystem effects. (Table 13.1 summarizes forces that work to warm and cool the earth.) Along with many ordinary people, some scientists see recent weather events as reflecting climate change. Such events include Pakistan's floods of 2010, Florida's 2007 worst-in-a-century drought, the 2005 hurricane season

featuring Katrina, the first-ever hurricane in the South Atlantic in 2004, and the severe European heat wave of 2003. Although linking any one event to climate change is difficult, the conjunction of several events may indicate climate change is playing a role.

The precise effects of climate change on regional weather patterns have yet to be determined. Land areas are expected to warm more than oceans, with the greatest warming in higher latitudes, such as Canada, the northern United States, and northern Europe. Global warming may benefit these areas, offering milder winters and extended growing seasons. However, many more people worldwide probably will be harmed. Already we know that in the Arctic, temperatures have risen almost twice as much as the global average. Arctic landscapes and ecosystems are changing rapidly and perceptibly.

The Intergovernmental Panel on Climate Change (IPCC) is composed of hundreds of scientists from the United States and other countries. In 2001 the IPCC predicted that by 2100 average global surface temperatures will rise 2.5 to 10.4 degrees Fahrenheit (1.4 to 5.8 degrees Centigrade) above 1990 levels. The IPCC also forecast ocean warming trends—the combined effects of melting glaciers, melting ice caps, and seawater expansion. The global average sea level is projected to rise 4 to 35 inches (0.1 to 0.9 meters) between 1990 and 2100.

> **greenhouse effect** Warming from trapped atmospheric gases.
>
> **climate change** Global warming, plus changing sea levels, precipitation, storms, and ecosystem effects.

Coastal communities can anticipate increased flooding and more severe storms and surges. At risk are people, animals, plants, freshwater supplies, and such industries as tourism and farming. Along with many island nations, Bangladesh, one of the world's poorest countries, is projected to lose a significant portion (17.5 percent) of its land, displacing millions of people (National Academies 2006). Given the political will, developed countries might use sci-

TABLE 13.1

What Heats, What Cools, the Earth?

Warming	
Carbon dioxide (CO_2)	Has natural and human sources; levels increasing due to burning of fossil fuels.
Methane (CH_4)	Has risen due to an increase in human activities, including livestock raising, rice growing, landfill use, and the extraction, handling, and transport of natural gas.
Ozone (O_3)	Has natural sources, especially in the stratosphere, where chemicals have depleted the ozone layer; ozone also produced in the troposphere (lower part of the atmosphere) when hydrocarbons and nitrogen oxide pollutants react.
Nitrous oxide (N_2O)	Has been rising from agricultural and industrial sources.
Halocarbons	Include chlorofluorocarbons (CFCs), which remain from refrigerants in appliances made before CFC ban.
Aerosols	Some airborne particles and droplets warm the planet; black carbon particles (soot) produced when fossil fuels or vegetation are burned; generally have a warming effect by absorbing solar radiation.
Cooling	
Sea ice	Reflects sunlight back to space.
Tundra	Reflects sunlight back to space.
Aerosols	Some cool the planet; (SO_4) aerosols from burning fossil fuels reflect sunlight back to space.
Volcanic eruptions	Emit gaseous SO_2 which, once in the atmosphere, forms sulfate aerosol; and ash. Both reflect sunlight back to space.
Warming/Cooling	
Forests	Deforestation creates land areas that reflect more sunlight back to space (cooling); it also removes trees that absorb CO_2 (warming).

ence and technology to anticipate and deal with climate impacts and to help less developed countries adapt to climate change.

The U.S. National Academy of Sciences and other national academies have issued several reports on climate change. Citations and highlights of these reports can be found in a brochure titled "Understanding and Responding to Climate Change: Highlights of National Academies Reports" (http://dels.nas.edu/basc/Climate-HIGH.pdf), on which some of this discussion is based (see also Crate and Nuttall 2008).

Meeting energy needs is the single greatest obstacle to slowing climate change. In the United States, about 80 percent of all energy used comes from fossil fuels. Worldwide, energy use continues to grow with economic and popula-

tion expansion. China and India in particular are rapidly increasing their use of energy, mainly from fossil fuels, and consequently their emissions of CO_2 (see "Projected Emission of Greenhouse Gases"). These emissions could be reduced by using energy more efficiently or by using renewable sources. One alternative is ethanol, of which the United States is a limited producer. American policy makers give lip service to the value of ethanol, while restricting its inflow from nations, such as Brazil, that produce it most effectively.

Among the alternatives to fossil fuels are nuclear power and such renewable energy technologies as solar, wind, and biomass generators. Replacing coal-fired electric power plants with more efficient natural-gas-fired turbines would reduce carbon emissions. In the United States, these

Many scientists see recent weather catastrophes as reflecting climate change. Such events include the 2005 hurricane season featuring Katrina and fires that devastated Southern California in late October 2007. The map above shows Hurricane Katrina, which sustained winds of 140 m.p.h., in the Gulf of Mexico. The photo (right) shows one of dozens of epic fires that swept Southern California. Shown here, firefighters watch as a San Diego Fire Department helicopter drops water on a fire in Via Conejo, between Lake Hodges and Escondido.

Projected Emission of Greenhouse Gases, 2025

Trillions of tons of carbon equivalent

World	57%
Developed	35%
Developing	84%

U.S.	39%
China	118%
EU	19%
Former Soviet Union	42%
India	70%
Africa	80%
Brazil	68%
Japan	26%
Mexico	124%

■ 2000 emissions

● Projected emissions, 2025

50% Projected increase from 2000 levels

Greenhouse gasses do not include CO_2 from land use change.

In 2000, the United States was the largest emitter of CO_2 from fossil fuels. China is expected to take the lead by 2025.

Source: Baumert 2005.

CULTURE THINK

Ethanol, made from corn, has been criticized as an alternative source of fuel. Some analysts claim that it raises the price of food and that producing ethanol uses more energy than it yields. Others maintain that it has significant environmental benefits. Do an online search. What is the current status of this debate?

technologies currently are too expensive, or, in the case of nuclear power, they raise environmental or other concerns. This could change with the development and increasing use of new technologies and as the cost of fossil fuels rises.

>> Environmental Anthropology

Anthropology always has been concerned with how environmental forces influence humans and how human activities affect the biosphere and the Earth itself. The 1950s–1970s witnessed the emergence of an area of study

Traditional ecological knowledge often provides solutions to contemporary problems. One development project in southern Peru revived an ancient irrigation and drainage system that had been abandoned a thousand years ago. This permitted food production in low-lying, flood-prone, poorly drained lands.

known as *cultural ecology* or **ecological anthropology.** That field focused on how cultural beliefs and practices helped human populations adapt to their environments, and how people used elements of their culture to maintain their ecosystems.

Early ecological anthropologists showed that many indigenous groups did a reasonable job of managing their resources and preserving their ecosystems. Such groups had traditional ways of categorizing resources, regulating their use, and preserving the environment. An **ethnoecology** is any society's set of environmental practices and perceptions—that is, the society's cultural model of the environment and its relation to people and society. Indigenous ethnoecologies increasingly are being challenged, as migration, media, and commerce spread people, institutions, information, and technology. In the face of national and international incentives to exploit and degrade, ethnoecological systems that once preserved local and regional environments increasingly are ineffective or irrelevant.

ecological anthropology
Study of cultural adaptations to environments.

ethnoecology A culture's set of environmental practices and perceptions.

Anthropologists routinely witness threats to the people they study and their environments. Among such threats are commercial logging, industrial pollution, and the imposition of external management systems on local ecosystems (see Johnston 2009). Today's ecological anthropology, aka *environmental anthropology,* attempts not only to understand but also to find solutions to environmental problems. Such problems must be tackled at the national and international levels (e.g., global warming). Even in remote places, ecosystem management now involves multiple levels. For example, author Lisa Gezon found that among the Antankarana of northern Madagascar (Gezon 2006), several levels of authority claim the right to use and regulate natural resources and local ecosystems. Actual or would-be regulators there include local communities, traditional leaders (the regional king or chief), provincial and national governments, and the WWF, the Worldwide Fund for Nature (formerly the World Wildlife Fund), an international nongovernmental organization (NGO). Local people, their landscapes, their ideas, their values, and their traditional management systems face attacks from all sides. Outsiders attempt to remake native landscapes and cultures in their own image. The aim of many agricultural development projects, for example, seems to be to make the world as much like a midwestern American agricultural state as possible. Often there is an attempt to impose mechanized farming and nuclear family ownership, even though these institutions may be inappropriate in areas far removed from the midwestern United States. Development projects usually fail when they try to replace indigenous institutions with culturally alien concepts (Kottak 1990b).

The world's most populous nations, China and India, are rapidly increasing their use of energy, mainly from fossil fuels, and consequently their emissions of CO_2. Pictured here are crowds of cars and busses moving slowly during a serious Beijing traffic jam.

GLOBAL ASSAULTS ON LOCAL AUTONOMY

A clash of cultures related to environmental change may occur when development threatens indigenous peoples and their environments. A second clash of cultures related to environmental change may occur when external regulation aimed at conservation confronts indigenous peoples and their ethnoecologies. Like development projects, conservation schemes may ask people to change their ways in order to satisfy planners' goals rather than local goals. In places as different as Madagascar, Brazil, and the Pacific Northwest of the United States, people have been asked, told, or forced to abandon basic economic activities because to do so is good for "nature" or "the globe." "Good for the globe" doesn't play very well in Brazil, whose Amazon is a focus of international environmentalist attention. Brazilians complain that outsiders (e.g., Europeans and North Americans) promote "global needs" and "saving the Amazon" after having destroyed their own forests for economic growth. Well-intentioned conservation plans can be as insensitive as development schemes that promote radical changes without involving local people in planning and carrying out the policies that affect them. When people are asked to give up the basis of their livelihood, they usually resist.

The spread of environmentalism may expose radically different notions about the "rights" and value of plants and animals versus humans. In Madagascar, many intellectuals and officials complain that foreigners seem more concerned about lemurs and other endangered species than about the people of Madagascar (the Malagasy). As a geographer there remarked to Conrad Kottak, "The next time you come to Madagascar, there'll be no more Malagasy. All the people will have starved to death, and a lemur will have to meet you at the airport." Most Malagasy perceive human poverty as a more pressing problem than animal and plant survival.

Still, who can doubt that conservation, including the preservation of biodiversity, is a worthy goal? The challenge for applied ecological anthropology is to devise culturally appropriate strategies for achieving biodiversity conservation in the face of unrelenting population growth and commercial expansion. How does one get people to support conservation measures that may, in the short run at least, diminish their access to resources? Like development plans in general, the most effective conservation strategies pay attention to the needs and wishes of the local people.

STUDY **TIP**

A clash of cultures over environmental issues occurs (1) when development projects degrade local resources; (2) when external authorities impose conservation measures on local people.

A scene from the "great red island" of Madagascar. On that island, the effects of deforestation, water runoff, and soil erosion are visible to the naked eye.

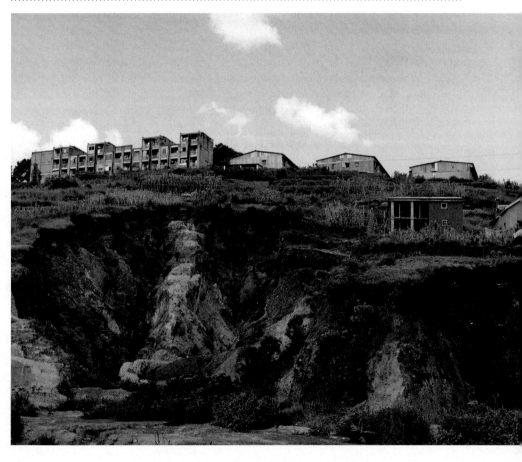

DEFORESTATION

Forest loss—a global concern—can lead to increased greenhouse gas (CO_2) production, which contributes to global warming. The destruction of tropical forests also is a major factor in the loss of global biodiversity, since many species, often of limited distribution and including many primates, live in forests. Tropical forests contain at least half of Earth's species while covering just 6 percent of the planet's land surface. Yet tropical forests are disappearing at the rate of ten million to twenty million hectares per year (the size of New York State).

Generations of anthropologists have studied how human economic activities (ancient and modern) affect the environment. Anthropologists know that food producers (farmers and herders) typically do more to degrade the environment than foragers do. Population increase and the need to expand farming caused deforestation in many parts of the ancient Middle East and Mesoamerica (see Hornborg and Crumley 2007). Even today, many farmers think of trees as giant weeds to be removed and replaced with productive fields.

Often, deforestation is demographically driven—caused by population pressure. For example, Madagascar's population is growing at a rate of 3 percent annually, doubling every generation. Population pressure leads to migration, including rural–urban migration. Madagascar's capital, Antananarivo, had one hundred thousand people in 1967. The population grew to about two million by 2007.

Urban growth promotes deforestation if city dwellers rely on fuel wood from the countryside, as is true in Madagascar. As forested watersheds disappear, crop productivity declines. Madagascar is known as the "great red island," after the color of its soil. On that island, the effects of soil erosion and water runoff are visible to the naked eye. From the look of its rivers, Madagascar appears to be bleeding to death. Increasing runoff of water no longer trapped by trees causes erosion of low-lying rice fields near swollen rivers as well as siltation in irrigation canals (Kottak 2007).

The global scenarios of deforestation include demographic pressure (from births or immigration) on subsistence economies, commercial logging, road building, cash cropping, fuel wood needs associated with urban expansion, and clearing and burning associated with livestock and grazing. The fact that forest loss has several causes has a policy implication: Different deforestation scenarios require different conservation strategies.

Applied anthropology uses anthropological perspectives to identify and solve contemporary problems that affect humans. Deforestation is one such problem. Here women take part in a reforestation project in coastal Tanzania near Dar es Salaam.

What can be done? On this question applied anthropology weighs in (see Chapter 4), spurring policy makers to think about new conservation strategies. The traditional approach has been to restrict access to forested areas designated as parks, then employ park guards and punish violators. Modern strategies are more likely to consider the needs, wishes, and abilities of the people (often impoverished) living in and near the forest. Since effective conservation depends on the cooperation of the local people, their concerns must be addressed in devising conservation strategies.

Reasons to change behavior must make sense to local people (see Sillitoe 2007). In Madagascar, the economic value of the forest for agriculture (as an antierosion mechanism and reservoir of potential irrigation water) provides a much more powerful incentive against forest degradation than do such global goals as "preserving biodiversity." Most Malagasy have no idea that lemurs and other endemic species exist only in Madagascar. Nor would such knowledge provide much of an incentive for them to conserve the forests if doing so jeopardized their livelihoods.

To curb the global deforestation threat, we need conservation strategies that work. Laws and enforcement may

CULTURETHINK

People concerned with conservation debate which is more effective: putting up fences and hiring guards to keep people out of areas to be preserved, or engaging local people as partners and allowing limited use of endangered resources. What do you think would be the strengths and weaknesses of each approach?

help reduce commercially driven deforestation caused by burning and clear-cutting. But local people also use and abuse forested lands. A challenge for the environmentally oriented applied anthropologist is to find ways to make forest preservation attractive to local people and ensure their cooperation. Applied anthropologists must work to make "good for the globe" good for the people.

>> Interethnic Contact

Since at least the 1920s anthropologists have investigated the changes—on both sides—that arise from contact between industrial and nonindustrial societies. Studies of "social change" and "acculturation" are abundant. British and American ethnographers, respectively, have used these terms to describe the same process. *Acculturation* refers to changes that result when groups come into continuous firsthand contact—changes in the cultural patterns of either or both groups (Redfield, Linton, and Herskovits 1936, p. 149).

Acculturation differs from diffusion, or cultural borrowing, which can occur without firsthand contact. For example, most North Americans who eat hot dogs ("frankfurters") have never been to Frankfurt, Germany, nor have most North American Toyota owners or sushi eaters ever visited Japan. Although *acculturation* can be applied to any case of cultural contact and change, the term most often has described *Westernization*—the influence of Western expansion on indigenous peoples and their cultures. Thus, local people who wear store-bought clothes, learn Indo-European languages, and otherwise adopt Western customs are called acculturated. Acculturation may be voluntary or forced, and there may be considerable resistance to the process.

Different degrees of destruction, domination, resistance, survival, adaptation, and modification of native cultures may follow interethnic contact. In the most destructive encounters, native and subordinate cultures face obliteration. In cases where contact between the indigenous societies and more powerful outsiders leads to destruction—a situation that is particularly characteristic of colonialist and expansionist eras—a "shock phase" often follows the initial encounter (Bodley 2008). Outsiders may attack or exploit the native people. Such exploitation may increase mortality, disrupt subsistence, fragment kin groups, damage social support systems, and inspire new religious movements, such as the cargo cults examined in the chapter "Religion" (Bodley 2008). During the shock

STUDY **TIP**

Diffusion is a form of cultural borrowing that can occur without firsthand contact, while *acculturation,* which may be voluntary or forced, refers to changes that occur with firsthand contact.

phase, there may be civil repression backed by military force. Such factors may lead to the group's cultural collapse (*ethnocide*) or physical extinction (*genocide*).

RELIGIOUS CHANGE

Religious proselytizing can promote ethnocide, as native beliefs and practices are replaced by Western ones. Sometimes a religion and associated customs are replaced by ideology and behavior more compatible with Western culture. One example is the Handsome Lake religion (as described in the chapter on religion), which led the Iroquois to copy European farming techniques, stressing male rather than female labor. The Iroquois also gave up their communal longhouses and matrilineal descent groups for nuclear family households. The teachings of Handsome Lake led to a new church and religion. This revitalization movement helped the Iroquois survive in a drastically modified environment, but much ethnocide was involved.

Handsome Lake was a native who created a new religion, drawing on Western models. More commonly, missionaries and proselytizers representing the major world religions, especially Christianity and Islam, are the proponents of religious change. Protestant and Catholic missionization continues even in remote corners of the world. Evangelical Protestantism, for example, is advancing today in Peru, Brazil, and other parts of Latin America. It challenges an often jaded Catholicism that has too few priests and that is sometimes seen mainly as women's religion.

Sometimes the political ideology of a nation-state is pitted against traditional religion. Officials of the former Soviet empire discouraged Catholicism, Judaism, and Islam. In Central Asia, Soviet dominators destroyed Muslim mosques and discouraged religious practice. On the other hand, governments often use their power to advance a religion, such as Islam in Iran or Sudan.

A military government seized power in Sudan in 1989. It immediately launched a campaign to change that country of more than thirty-five million people, where one-quarter were not Muslims, into an Islamic nation. Sudan adopted a policy of religious, linguistic, and cultural imperialism. The government sought to extend Islam and the Arabic language to the non-Muslim south. This was an area of Christianity and tribal religions that had resisted the central government for a decade (Hedges 1992).

Arab militias have forced black Africans off their land in the Darfur region of western Sudan through a campaign of killing, rape, and pillage. Since the violence began in March 2003, more than two million people have fled to refugee camps in Sudan and Chad. In this photo, children play among thousands of makeshift huts in the El-Geneina camp.

This resistance continues and has spilled over into Sudan's drought-stricken and impoverished western province of Darfur. As of this writing, more than two million Sudanese are living in camps, having fled years of fighting in the region. Sudan's government and pro-government Arab militias have been accused of war crimes against the region's black African population. The Darfur conflict began early in 2003 as non-Islamic rebels waged attacks against government targets, claiming the government was oppressing black Africans in favor of Arabs. Darfur has faced many years of tension over land and grazing rights between nomadic Arabs and black African farmers. One of the two main rebel groups, the Sudan Liberation Army (SLA), includes Nuer and other Nilotic populations.

cultural imperialism The rapid spread or advance of one culture at the expense of others, or its imposition on other cultures, which it modifies, replaces, or destroys—usually because of differential economic or political influence.

CULTURAL IMPERIALISM

Children in the French colonial empire learned French history, language, and culture from standard textbooks also used in France. Tahitians, Malagasy, Vietnamese, and Senegalese learned the French language by reciting from books about "our ancestors the Gauls." This is an example of **cultural imperialism**—the spread or advance of one culture at the expense of others, or its imposition on other cultures, which it modifies, replaces, or destroys, usually because of differential economic or political influence.

To what extent is modern technology, especially the mass media, an agent of cultural imperialism? Some commentators see modern technology as erasing cultural differences, as homogeneous products reach more people worldwide. But others see a role for modern technology in allowing social groups (local cultures) to express themselves and to survive (Marcus and Fischer 1999). Modern radio and TV, for example, constantly bring local happenings (for example, a "chicken festival" in Iowa) to the

Native children throughout the French colonial empire learned the French language by reciting from books about "our ancestors the Gauls." More recently, French citizens have criticized or resisted what they see as American "cultural imperialism"—one prominent symbol of which has been Euro Disneyland. Has there also been resistance to the expansion of Disney enterprises in the United States?

In San Gimignano, Italy, boys and young men don medieval costumes and beat drums in a parade through the streets during one of the town's many pageants. Increasingly, local communities perform "traditional" ceremonies for TV and tourists.

attention of a larger public. The North American media play a role in stimulating local activities of many sorts. Similarly, in Brazil, local practices, celebrations, and performances are changing in the context of outside forces, including the mass media and tourism.

In the town of Arembepe, Brazil (Kottak 2006), TV coverage has stimulated participation in a traditional annual performance, the *Chegança.* This is a fishermen's danceplay that reenacts the Portuguese discovery of Brazil. Arembepeiros have traveled to the state capital to perform the *Chegança* before television cameras, for a TV program featuring traditional performances from many rural communities.

One national Brazilian Sunday-night variety program (*Fantástico*) is especially popular in rural areas because it shows such local events. In several towns along the Amazon River, annual folk ceremonies are now staged more lavishly for TV cameras. In the Amazon town of Parantíns, for example, boatloads of tourists arriving any time of year are shown a videotape of the town's annual Bumba Meu Boi festival. This is a costumed performance mimicking bullfighting, parts of which have been shown on *Fantástico.* This pattern, in which local communities preserve, revive, and intensify the scale of traditional ceremonies to perform for TV and tourists, is expanding.

Brazilian television also has played a "top-down" role, by spreading the popularity of holidays like Carnaval and Christmas (Kottak 1990a). TV has aided the national spread of Carnaval beyond its traditional urban centers. Still, local reactions to the nationwide broadcasting of Car-

naval and its trappings (elaborate parades, costumes, and frenzied dancing) are not simple or uniform responses to external stimuli.

Rather than direct adoption of Carnaval, local Brazilians respond in various ways. Often they don't take up Carnaval itself but modify their local festivities to fit Carnaval images. Others actively spurn Carnaval. One example is Arembepe, where Carnaval has never been important, probably because it occurs around the same time as the main local festival, which is held in February to honor Saint Francis of Assisi. In the past, villagers couldn't afford to celebrate both occasions. Now, not only do the people of Arembepe reject Carnaval; they are also increasingly hostile to their own main festival. Arembepeiros resent the fact that the Saint Francis festival has become "an outsiders' event," because it draws thousands of tourists to Arembepe each February. The villagers think that commercial interests and outsiders have appropriated Saint Francis.

In opposition to these trends, many Arembepeiros now say they like and participate more in the traditional June festivals honoring Saint John, Saint Peter, and Saint Anthony. In the past, these were observed on a much smaller scale than was the festival honoring Saint Francis. Arembepeiros celebrate them now with a new vigor and enthusiasm, as they react to outsiders and their celebrations, real and televised.

CULTURETHINK

To what extent do you think modern technology, especially the mass media, is an agent of cultural imperialism?

>> Making and Remaking Culture

To understand culture change, we must recognize that meaning may be locally manufactured. People assign their own meanings and value to the texts, messages, and products they receive. Those meanings reflect their cultural backgrounds and experiences.

INDIGENIZING POPULAR CULTURE

When forces from world centers enter new societies, they are **indigenized**—modified to fit the local culture. This is true of cultural forces as different as fast food, music, housing styles, science, terrorism, celebrations, and political ideas and institutions (Appadurai 1990). Consider the reception of the movie *Rambo* in Australia as an example of how popular culture may be indigenized. One researcher (Michaels 1986) found that the character Rambo was very popular among aborigines in the deserts of central Australia, who had manufactured their own meanings from the film. Their "reading" was different from the one imagined by the movie's creators and by most North Americans. The

indigenized Modified to fit the local culture.

Native Australians saw Rambo as a representative of the Third World who was engaged in a battle with the white officer class. This reading expressed their negative feelings about white paternalism and about existing race relations. The Native Australians also imagined that there were tribal ties and kin links between Rambo and the prisoners he was rescuing. All this made sense, based on their experience. Native Australians are disproportionately represented in Australian jails. Their most likely liberator would be someone with a personal link to them. These readings of *Rambo* were relevant meanings produced *from* the text, not by it (Fiske 1989).

A GLOBAL SYSTEM OF IMAGES

All cultures express imagination—in dreams, fantasies, songs, myths, and stories. Today, however, more people in many more places imagine "a wider set of 'possible' lives than they ever did before. One important source of this change is the mass media [radio, TV, movies, video games, and the Internet], which present a rich, ever-changing store of possible lives" (Appadurai 1991, p. 197). The United States as a media center has been joined by Canada, Japan, Western Europe, Brazil, Mexico, Nigeria, Egypt, India, and Hong Kong.

As print has done for centuries (Anderson 1991), the electronic mass media also can spread, even help create, national and ethnic identities. Like print, television, radio, and the Internet can diffuse the cultures of different countries within their own boundaries, thus enhancing national cul-

Illustrating a process of indigenizing offerings of the modern world system, children dress as Colonel Sanders to promote egg tarts (a local dish now offered by an international restaurant chain) at a KFC store in Shanghai, China.

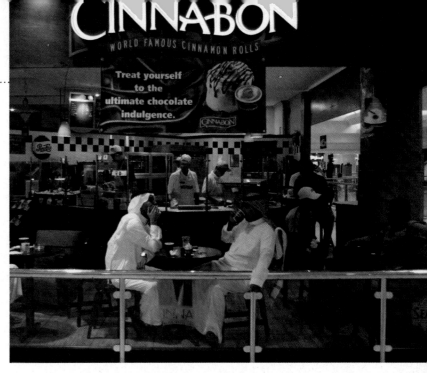

Foods offered in such chains as McDonald's, KFC, and Cinnabon (shown here) are now consumed internationally, though always indigenized somewhat to meet local expectations.

tural identity. For example, millions of Brazilians who were formerly cut off (by geographic isolation or illiteracy) from urban and national events and information now participate in a national—even international—communication system, through TV and the Internet (Kottak 2009). Social networking media such as Facebook permit regular communication among Brazilians in their own country and throughout Brazil's global diaspora.

Cross-cultural studies of television contradict a belief Americans ethnocentrically hold about televiewing in other countries. This misconception is that American programs inevitably triumph over local products. This doesn't happen when there is appealing local competition. In Brazil, for example, the most popular network (TV Globo) relies heavily on native productions, especially *telenovelas*. Globo plays each night to one of the world's largest and most devoted audiences (perhaps eighty million viewers throughout the nation and beyond—via satellite TV). The programs that attract this horde are made by Brazilians, for Brazilians. Thus, it is not North American culture but a new pan-Brazilian national culture that Brazilian TV is propagating. Brazilian productions also compete internationally. They are exported to over a hundred countries, spanning Latin America, Europe, Asia, and Africa.

We may generalize that culturally alien programming won't do very well anywhere when a quality local choice is available. Confirmation comes from many countries. National productions are highly popular in Japan, Mexico, India, Egypt, and Nigeria. In a survey during the mid-1980s, 75 percent of Nigerian viewers preferred local productions. Only 10 percent favored imports, and the remaining 15 percent liked the two options equally. Local productions are successful in Nigeria because "they are filled with everyday moments that audiences can identify with. These shows are locally produced by Nigerians" (Gray 1986). Thirty million people watched one of the most popular series, *The Village Headmaster,* each week. That program brought rural values to the screens of urbanites who had lost touch with their rural roots (Gray 1986).

CULTURETHINK

One way that media help establish a national identity is to create the sense that those who are not citizens of that nation are different. What images of non-Western peoples do television and other media provide? Do you think these images represent those people fairly?

The mass media also can play a role in maintaining ethnic and national identities among people who lead transnational lives. Arabic-speaking Muslims, including migrants, in several countries follow the TV network Al Jazeera, based in Qatar, which helps reinforce ethnic and religious identities. As groups move, they can stay linked to each other and to their homeland through the media. **Diasporas**—people who have spread out from an original, ancestral homeland—have enlarged the markets for media, communication, and travel services targeted at specific ethnic, national, or religious audiences. For a fee, a PBS station in Fairfax, Virginia, offers more than thirty hours a week to immigrant groups in the D.C. area, to make programs in their own languages.

> **diaspora** people who have spread out from an original, ancestral homeland.

A GLOBAL CULTURE OF CONSUMPTION

Besides the electronic media, another key transnational force is finance. Multinational corporations and other business interests look beyond national boundaries for places to invest and draw profits. As Arjun Appadurai (1991, p. 194) puts it, "money, commodities, and persons unendingly chase each other around the world." Residents of many Latin American communities now depend on outside cash, remitted from international labor migration. Also, the U.S. economy is increasingly influenced by foreign investment, especially from Britain, China, Canada, Germany, the Netherlands, and Japan (Rouse 1991). The American economy also has increased its dependence on foreign labor—through both the immigration of laborers and the export of jobs.

What's your favorite science fiction movie or TV show? What images of other planets stand out in your memory? Can you easily visualize *Star Wars'* Death Star, poor old Alderan, Yoda's misty world in the Dagoba system, the two suns of Tatooine? How about *Avatar's* Pandora? Such movie images may be as familiar to you as those of real planets. Think, too, about how extraterrestrials have been portrayed in movies. On the one hand are *ET's* harmless plant collectors and *Avatar's* endangered Na'vi. On the other hand—and more typical—are Earth's would-be conquerors, as shown in *Independence Day, Starship Troopers, V,* and a hundred others. Still other films, most notably *The Day the Earth Stood Still* (either the 1951 or the 2008 version), feature omnipotent, omniscient guardians of interplanetary affairs. How, if at all, do the issues portrayed in such science fiction movies relate to the global issues examined in this chapter?

The flow of people, technology, finance, information, images, and ideology drive contemporary global culture (Appadurai 1990, 2001). Business, technology, and the media have increased the craving for commodities and images throughout the world (Gottdiener 2000). This has forced nation-states to open to a global culture of consumption. Almost everyone today participates in this culture. Few people have never seen a T-shirt advertising a Western product. American and English rock stars' recordings blast through the streets of Rio de Janeiro, while taxi drivers from Toronto to Madagascar play Brazilian music tapes. Peasants and tribal people participate in the modern world system not only because they have been hooked on cash, but also because their products and images are appropriated by world capitalism (Root 1996). They are commercialized by others (like the San in the movie *The Gods Must Be Crazy*). Furthermore, indigenous peoples also market their own images and products, through outlets like Cultural Survival (see Mathews 2000).

postmodernity Condition of a world in flux, with people on the move, in which established groups, boundaries, identities, contrasts, and standards are reaching out and breaking down.

elytizers, laborers, businesspeople, development workers, employees of nongovernmental organizations, politicians, terrorists, soldiers, sports figures, or media-borne images, people appear to travel more than ever.

In previous chapters, we saw that foragers and herders are typically seminomadic or nomadic. Today, the scale of human movement has expanded dramatically. So important is transnational migration that many Mexican villagers find "their most important kin and friends are as likely to be living hundreds or thousands of miles away as immediately around them" (Rouse 1991). Most migrants maintain their ties with their native land (phoning, emailing, visiting, sending money, watching "ethnic TV"). In a sense, they live multilocally—in different places at once. Dominicans in New York City, for example, have been characterized as living "between two islands": Manhattan and the Dominican Republic (Grasmuck and Pessar 1991). Many Dominicans—like migrants from other countries—migrate to the United States temporarily, seeking cash to transform their lifestyles when they return to the Caribbean.

>> People in Motion

The linkages in the modern world system have both enlarged and erased old boundaries and distinctions. Arjun Appadurai (1990, p. 1) characterizes today's world as a "translocal" "interactive system" that is "strikingly new." Whether as refugees, migrants, tourists, pilgrims, pros-

CULTURETHINK

With so many people having ties across the globe, anthropologists face new challenges in fieldwork. What methods and techniques do you think ethnographers could use to learn about phenomena that span geographical zones, such as migration?

With so many people "in motion," the unit of anthropological study expands from the local community to the diaspora. As anthropologists, we increasingly follow descendants of the villages we have studied as they move from rural to urban areas and across national boundaries.

Postmodernity describes our time and situation: today's world in flux, these people on the move who have learned to manage multiple identities depending on place and context. In its most general sense, **postmodern** refers to the blurring and breakdown of established canons (rules or standards), categories, distinctions, and boundaries. The word is taken from **postmodernism**—a style and movement in architecture that began in the 1970s and followed modernism. Postmodern architecture rejected the rules, geometric order, and austerity of modernism. Modernist buildings were expected to have a clear and functional design. Postmodern design is "messier" and more playful. It draws on a diversity of styles from different times and places—including popular, ethnic, and non-Western cultures. Postmodernism extends "value" well beyond classic, elite, and Western cultural forms. *Postmodern* is now used to describe comparable developments in music, literature, and visual art. From this origin, *postmodernity* describes a world in which traditional standards, contrasts, groups, boundaries, and identities are opening up, reaching out, and breaking down.

New kinds of political and ethnic units are emerging. In some cases, cultures and ethnic groups have banded together in larger associations. There is a growing pan-Indian identity (Nagel 1996) and an international pantribal movement as well. Thus, in June 1992, the World Conference of Indigenous Peoples met in Rio de Janeiro concurrently with UNCED (the United Nations Conference on the Environment and Development). Along with diplomats, journalists, and environmentalists came 300 representatives of the tribal diversity that survives in the modern world—from Lapland to Mali (Brooke 1992; see also Maybury-Lewis 2002).

>> Indigenous Peoples

The term *indigenous people* entered international law with the creation in 1982 of the United Nations Working Group on Indigenous Populations (WGIP). This group, which meets annually, has members from six continents. The draft of the Declaration of Indigenous Rights, produced by the WGIP in 1989, was accepted by the UN for discussion in 1993. Convention 169, an ILO (International Labor Organization) document that supports cultural diversity and indigenous empowerment, was approved in 1989. Such documents, along with the work of the WGIP, have influenced governments, NGOs, and international agencies to adopt policies aimed at benefiting indigenous peoples. Social movements worldwide now use the term "indigenous people" as

a self-identifying label in their quests for social, cultural, and political rights (Brower and Johnston 2007; de la Peña 2005).

In Spanish-speaking Latin America, social scientists and politicians now favor the term *indígena* (indigenous person) over *indio* (Indian). The latter is a colonial term that European conquerors used for Native Americans, whose situation did not necessarily improve after Latin American nations gained independence from Spain and Portugal, mostly by the 1820s. For the white and *mestizo* (mixed) elites of the new nations, *indios* and their lifestyle seemed alien to (European) civilization (de la Peña 2005).

Until the mid- to late 1980s, Latin American public policy emphasized assimilation. Indians were associated with a romanticized past, but marginalized in the present, except for museums, tourism, and folkloric events. Indigenous Bolivians and Peruvians were encouraged to self-identify as *campesinos* (peasants). The last thirty years have

postmodern In its most general sense, describes the blurring and breakdown of established canons (rules, standards), categories, distinctions, and boundaries.

postmodernism A style and movement in architecture that followed modernism. Compared with modernism, it is less geometric, less functional, less austere, more playful, and more willing to include elements from diverse times and cultures; *postmodern* now describes comparable developments in music, literature, and visual art.

Working to promote cultural survival is a growing international pantribal movement. In June 1992, the World Conference of Indigenous Peoples met in Rio de Janeiro. Along with diplomats, journalists, and environmentalists came 300 representatives of the tribal diversity that survives in the modern world.

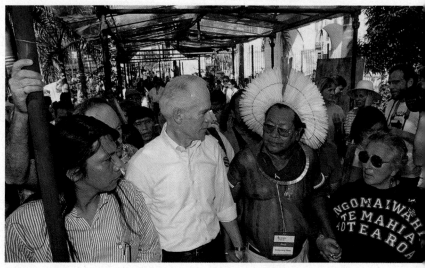

witnessed a dramatic shift from assimilation—*mestizaje*—to cultural difference. In Ecuador, groups seen previously as Quichua-speaking peasants are classified now as indigenous communities with their own territories. Brazil has recognized thirty new indigenous communities in the northeast, a region previously seen as having lost its native population. Guatemala, Nicaragua, Brazil, Colombia, Mexico, Paraguay, Ecuador, Argentina, Bolivia, Peru, and Venezuela now are officially multicultural (Jackson and Warren 2005). Several national constitutions recognize the rights of indigenous peoples to cultural distinctiveness and political representation. In Colombia, indigenous territories have the same benefits as any local government (de la Peña 2005).

essentialism The process of viewing an identity as established, real, and frozen, so as to hide the historical processes and politics within which that identity developed.

The indigenous rights movement exists in the context of globalization, including transnational movements focusing on human rights, women's rights, and environmentalism. Transnational organizations have helped indigenous peoples to influence legislation. Since the 1980s there has been a general shift in Latin America from authoritarian to democratic rule. Still, inequality and discrimination persist, and there has been resistance to indigenous mobilization, including assassinations of leaders and their supporters. Guatemala, Peru, and Colombia have witnessed severe repression. There have been thousands of indigenous deaths, refugees, and internally displaced persons (Jackson and Warren 2005).

Ceuppens and Geschiere (2005) explore a recent upsurge, in multiple world areas, of the notion of *autochthony* (being native to, or formed, in the place where found), with an implicit call for excluding strangers. The terms *autochthony* and *indigenous* both go back to classical Greek history, with similar implications. Autochthony refers to self and soil. Indigenous literally means born inside, with the connotation in classical Greek of being born "inside the house." Both notions stress the need to safeguard ancestral lands (patrimony) from strangers, along with the rights of first-comers to special rights and protection versus later immigrants—legal or illegal (Ceuppens and Geschiere 2005).

During the 1990s, autochthony became an issue in many parts of Africa, inspiring violent efforts to exclude (European and Asian) "strangers." Simultaneously, autochthony became a key notion in debates about immigration and multiculturalism in Europe. European majority groups have claimed the label *autochthon*. This term highlights the prominence that the exclusion of strangers has assumed in day-to-day politics worldwide (Ceuppens and Geschiere 2005). One familiar example is the United States, as represented in the congressional debate in 2006–2007, over illegal immigration.

Bolivians claiming an Indian (indigenous) identity rally for indigenous rights and the nationalization of that country's natural gas resources. In December 2005, Bolivians elected as their president Evo Morales, the candidate of the Indigenous Movement toward Socialism party. The party made further gains in 2006 parliamentary elections.

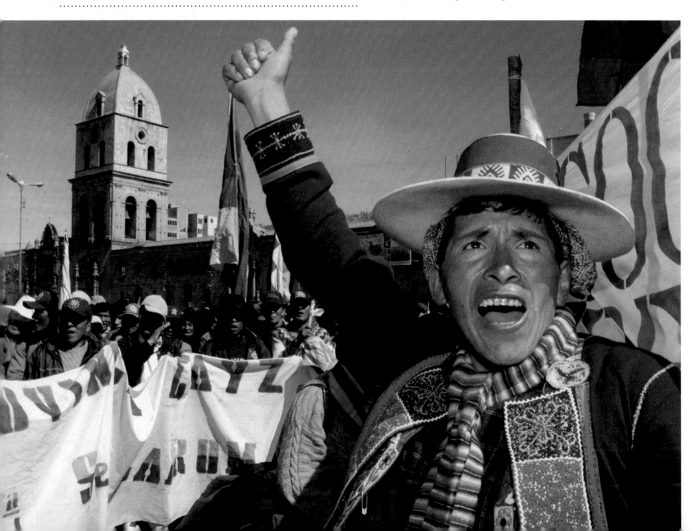

IDENTITY IN INDIGENOUS POLITICS

Essentialism describes the process of viewing an identity as established, real, and frozen, so as to hide the historical processes and politics within which that identity developed. Identities, emphatically, are not fixed. We saw in the chapter "Ethnicity and Race" that identities can be fluid and multiple. People seize on particular, sometimes competing, self-labels and identities. Some Peruvian groups, for instance, self-identify as mestizos but still see themselves as indigenous. Identity is a fluid, dynamic process, and there are multiple ways of being indigenous. Neither speaking an indigenous language nor wearing "native" clothing is required. Identities are asserted at particular times and places by particular individuals and groups and after various kinds of negotiations. Indigenous identity co-exists with, and must be managed in the context of, other identity components, including religion, race, and gender. Identities always must be seen as (1) potentially plural, (2) emerging through a specific process, (3) ways of being someone or something in particular times and places (Jackson and Warren 2005).

>> The Continuance of Diversity

Anthropology has a crucial role to play in promoting a more humanistic vision of social change, one that respects the value of human biological and cultural diversity. The existence of anthropology is itself a tribute to the continuing need to understand similarities and differences among human beings throughout the world. Anthropology teaches us that the adaptive responses of humans can be more flexible than those of other species because our main adaptive means are sociocultural. However, the cultural forms, institutions, values, and customs of the past always influence subsequent adaptation, producing continued diversity and giving a certain uniqueness to the actions and reactions of different groups. With our knowledge and our awareness of our professional responsibilities, let us work to keep anthropology, the study of humankind, the most humanistic of all the sciences.

Pay attention to the behavior of members of ethnic dance or music groups who perform on your campus or in your town or city. What do they wear when performing that expresses their traditional or indigenous culture? Does any other part of their dress or performance seem to conflict or compete with this traditional element? Observe or inquire about these people's behavior in various places and contexts. For example, do they speak English at certain times but not others? How often do they use their own language when talking among themselves? How would you evaluate whether their traditional ethnic identities are being lost or reinforced? Give a few examples of how their ethnic identity seems to be a matter of time, place, and negotiation.

get involved!

For REVIEW

CULTURE CLIPS

TO ACCESS THESE VIDEOS ON
YOUR COMPUTER, VISIT

www.mhhe.com/gezonqr

13-1

13-2

13-3

I. What is global climate change, and how can anthropologists study it, along with other environmental threats?

- Earlier ecological anthropology studied how culture helps
  human populations adapt to their environments. Today this
  field focuses on understanding and finding solutions to
  environmental threats that must be tackled at the national
  and international as well as local levels. Global climate
  change includes rising temperatures and changes in sea
  levels, precipitation, storms, and ecosystems. Human population growth and the increasing use of fossil fuels contribute to these changes. Global forces challenge indigenous
  peoples; outside environmental regulation confronts their
  ethnoecologies. Anthropologists believe that the most
  effective conservation strategies are those that pay attention to the needs and wishes of local people.

II. What is cultural imperialism, and what forces work to favor
and oppose it?

- Cultural imperialism is the spread or advance of one culture at the expense of others, or its imposition on other
  cultures, which it modifies, replaces, or destroys. Modern
  mass media are alternately viewed as agents of cultural
  imperialism and means for allowing local cultures to
  express themselves. Electronic mass media can reinforce
  national and ethnic identities. Cultural forces entering new
  societies from world centers are often modified to fit the
  local culture. Business, technology, and mass media have
  increased the craving for commodities and images worldwide. Peasants and tribal peoples participate in the world
  system in part because world capitalism appropriates their
  products and images, but indigenous peoples may market
  their own images and products to the world.

III. What are indigenous peoples, and how and why has their
importance increased in recent years?

- Social movements worldwide use the term *indigenous
  people* as a self-identifying political label that is
  based on past oppression but now signals a quest
  for social, cultural, and political rights. International
  law and the work of the UN's Working Group
  on Indigenous Populations have influenced governments,
  nongovernmental organizations, and international agencies
  to adopt policies aimed at recognizing and benefiting indigenous peoples. The indigenous rights movement exists in
  the global context of transnational movements that focus
  on human rights, women's rights, and environmentalism.
  Various world areas have seen an upsurge in the notion
  of *autochthony*, with an implicit call from native peoples to
  exclude strangers. Indigenous identities are fluid, multiple,
  and sometimes competing, asserted at particular times and
  places.

Pop Quiz

1. Scientific measurements confirm that global warming isn't caused by increased solar radiation. Rather, the causes are mainly anthropogenic. This means that:
   a. Humans and their activities cause global warming.
   b. The causes are indigenized.
   c. Global warming caused by normal climate fluctuations affects humans.
   d. The causes are social constructions used for political purposes.

2. All the following are true about global climate change *except:*
   a. The atmospheric concentration of greenhouse gases has reached its highest level in four hundred thousand years.
   b. The recent rise in CO_2 and the Earth's surface temperature is one proof that humans are fueling global warming.
   c. Worldwide, energy use has been falling, thanks to increased energy efficiency.
   d. Scientists prefer the term *climate change* to *global warming.*

3. Ecological anthropology:
   a. Is concerned with ethnoecology—how indigenous societies' environmental practices become irrelevant as national policies replace them.
   b. Focuses on the local community, because other levels of authority lack the right to use and regulate local ecosystems.
   c. Attempts to understand and solve environmental problems.
   d. Favors top-down agricultural development projects.

4. Which of the following statements about concern for environmental change and conservation is *false?*
   a. Some indigenous peoples have been forced to abandon basic economic activities because to do so is "good for nature" or for "the globe."
   b. Environmentalism began in Brazil in response to local and international attention given to the destruction of tropical Amazonian forests.
   c. Conservation plans should involve local people in planning and implementing policies that affect them.
   d. Applied anthropologists must make forest preservation attractive to local people to ensure their cooperation.

5. Which of the following is *not* true of changes arising from contact between native cultures and more powerful outsiders?
   a. Such changes typically occur on just one side of the contact.
   b. Westernization is a form of acculturation involving the influence of Western expansion on indigenous peoples and their cultures.
   c. Interethnic contact may cause destruction, domination, resistance, adaptation, and modification of native cultures.
   d. Religious proselytizing can promote ethnocide.

6. The spread or advance of one culture at the expense of others, or its imposition on other cultures, which it modifies, replaces, or destroys, is most accurately called:
   a. Cultural relativism
   b. Westernization
   c. Cultural imperialism
   d. Acculturation

7. When forces from world centers are modified to fit the local culture, this process is called:
   a. Religious proselytizing
   b. Indigenization
   c. Acculturation
   d. Assimilation

8. Which of the following statements about mass media is true?
   a. The United States is unique among media centers in offering varied images of possible lives.
   b. Media images and ideas are too general to help create or spread national and ethnic identities.
   c. American television programs don't necessarily triumph over local competition.
   d. Mass media can only work to maintain ethnic identities when people live inside their nation of origin.

9. What term does Arjun Appadurai use to refer to both the enlargening and the erasing of old boundaries and distinctions in the modern world?
   a. "Translocal" interactive system
   b. Postmodernism
   c. Essentialism
   d. Diaspora

10. In Latin America, which of the following would be an exception to the drive by indigenous peoples for indigenous identity and empowerment?
    a. Favoring of the term *indígena* over *indio* (Indian).
    b. A shift in policy from cultural difference to assimilation.
    c. National constitutions recognizing rights of indigenous peoples to political representation.
    d. Participation in transnational indigenous rights movements.

1. (a), 2. (c), 3. (c), 4. (b), 5. (a), 6. (c), 7. (b), 8. (c), 9. (a), 10. (b)

A

acculturation   The exchange of cultural features that results when groups come into continuous firsthand contact; the original cultural patterns of either or both groups may be altered, but the groups remain distinct.

achieved status   Social status that comes through talents, actions, efforts, activities, and accomplishments (e.g., big man, convicted felon).

adaptation   The process by which organisms cope with environmental stresses.

age set   Group uniting all men or women (usually men) born during a certain time span; this group controls property and often has ritual, political, and military functions.

agriculture   Nonindustrial system of plant cultivation characterized by continuous and intensive use of land and labor.

animism   Belief in souls or doubles.

anthropology   The study of the human species and its immediate ancestors

anthropology and education   Anthropological research in classrooms, homes, and neighborhoods, viewing students as total cultural creatures whose enculturation and attitudes toward education belong to a larger context that includes family, peers, and society.

applied anthropology   The application of anthropological data, perspectives, theory, and methods to identify, assess, and solve contemporary social problems.

archaeological anthropology   The branch of anthropology, commonly known as "archaeology," that reconstructs, describes, and interprets human behavior and cultural patterns through material remains; best known for the study of prehistory.

ascribed status   Social status that people have little or no choice about occupying (e.g., race, gender).

assimilation   The process of change that a minority group may experience when it moves to a country where another culture dominates; the minority is incorporated into the dominant culture to the point that it no longer exists as a separate cultural unit.

B

band   Basic unit of social organization among foragers. A band includes fewer than 100 people; it often splits up seasonally.

big man   Figure often found among tribal horticulturalists and pastoralists. The big man occupies no office but creates his reputation through entrepreneurship and generosity to others. Neither his wealth nor his position passes to his heirs.

biocultural   Referring to the inclusion and combination (to solve a common problem) of both biological and cultural approaches—one of anthropology's hallmarks.

biological anthropology   Also called *physical anthropology,* the branch of anthropology that studies human biological diversity in time and space—for instance, hominid evolution, human genetics, human biological adaptation; also includes primatology (behavior and evolution of monkeys and apes).

Black English Vernacular (BEV)   A rule-governed dialect of American English (sometimes called "ebonics") with roots in southern English. Many African American youth and adults speak BEV in their casual, intimate speech.

bourgeoisie   One of Karl Marx's opposed classes; owners of the means of production (factories, mines, large farms, and other sources of subsistence).

bridewealth   A customary gift before, at, or after marriage from the husband and his kin to the wife and her kin; see also *progeny price.*

C

call systems   Systems of communication among nonhuman primates, composed of a limited number of sounds that vary in intensity and duration; tied to environmental stimuli.

capital   Wealth or resources invested in business, with the intent of producing a profit.

capitalist world economy   The single world system, which emerged in the sixteenth century, committed to production for sale, with the object of maximizing profits rather than supplying domestic needs.

cargo cults   Postcolonial, acculturative, religious movements common in Melanesia that attempt to explain European domination and wealth and to achieve similar success magically by mimicking European behavior.

caste system   Closed, hereditary system of stratification, often dictated by religion; hierarchical social status is ascribed at birth, so that people are locked into their parents' social position.

chiefdom   Form of sociopolitical organization intermediate between the tribe and the state; kin-based with differential access to resources and a permanent political structure.

clan   Unilineal descent group based on stipulated descent.

climate change   Global warming, plus changing sea levels, precipitation, storms, and ecosystem effects.

colonialism   The political, social, economic, and cultural domination of a territory and its people by a foreign power for an extended time.

communal religions   In Wallace's typology, these religions have—in addition to shamanic cults—communal cults in which people organize community rituals such as harvest ceremonies and rites of passage.

communism   Spelled with a lowercase *c,* describes a social system in which the community owns property and people work for the common good.

Communism   Spelled with an uppercase *C,* describes a political movement and doctrine seeking to overthrow capitalism and to establish a form of communism such as that which prevailed in the Soviet Union (USSR) from 1917 to 1991.

communitas   Intense community spirit, a feeling of great social solidarity, equality, and togetherness; characteristic of people experiencing liminality together.

complex societies   Nations; large and populous, with social stratification and central governments.

conflict resolution   The means by which disputes are socially regulated and settled; found in all societies, but the resolution methods tend to be more formal and effective in states than in nonstates.

core   Dominant structural position in the world system; consists of the strongest and most powerful states with advanced systems of production.

core values   Key, basic, or central values that integrate a culture and help distinguish it from others.

correlation   An association between two or more variables such that when one changes (varies), the other(s) also change(s) (covaries); for example, temperature and sweating.

cultural anthropology   The study of human society and culture; describes, analyzes, interprets, and explains social and cultural similarities and differences.

cultural colonialism   Within a nation or empire, domination by one ethnic group or nationality and its culture/ ideology over others—e.g., the dominance of Russian people, language, and culture in the former Soviet Union.

cultural consultant   Someone the ethnographer gets to know in the field, who teaches him or her about their society and culture (also called "informant").

cultural imperialism   The rapid spread or advance of one culture at the expense of others, or its imposition on other cultures, which it modifies, replaces, or destroys—usually because of differential economic or political influence.

cultural relativism   The position that the values and standards of cultures differ and deserve respect. Anthropology is characterized by methodological rather than moral relativism: In order to understand another culture fully, anthropologists try to understand its members' beliefs and motivations. Methodological relativism does not preclude making moral judgments or taking action.

cultural resource management (CRM)   The branch of applied archaeology aimed at preserving sites threatened by dams, highways, and other projects.

cultural rights   Doctrine that certain rights are vested not in individuals but in identifiable groups, such as religious and ethnic minorities and indigenous societies.

cultural transmission   A basic feature of language; transmission through learning.

culture   Traditions and customs that govern behavior and beliefs; distinctly human; transmitted through learning.

curer   Specialized role acquired through a culturally appropriate process of selection, training, certification, and acquisition of a professional image; the curer is consulted by patients, who believe in his or her special powers, and receives some form of special consideration; a cultural universal.

D

daughter languages   Languages developing out of the same parent language; for example, French and Spanish are daughter languages of Latin.

descent   Rule assigning social identity on the basis of some aspect of one's ancestry.

descent group   A permanent social unit whose members claim common ancestry; fundamental to tribal society.

descriptive linguistics   The scientific study of a spoken language, including its phonology, morphology, lexicon, and syntax.

development anthropology   The branch of applied anthropology that focuses on social issues in, and the cultural dimension of, economic development.

diaspora   people who have spread out from an original, ancestral homeland.

differential access   Unequal access to resources; basic attribute of chiefdoms and states. *Superordinates* have favored access to such resources, while the access of *subordinates* is limited by superordinates.

diffusion   Borrowing between cultures either directly or through intermediaries.

diglossia   The existence of "high" (formal) and "low" (familial) dialects of a single language, such as German.

discrimination   Policies and practices that harm a group and its members.

disease   An *etic,* or scientifically identified, health threat caused by a bacterium, virus, fungus, parasite, or other pathogen.

displacement   A linguistic capacity that allows humans to talk about things and events that are not present.

domestic–public dichotomy   Contrast between women's role in the home and men's role in public life, with a corresponding social devaluation of women's work and worth.

dowry   A marital exchange in which the wife's group provides substantial gifts to the husband's family.

E

ecological anthropology   Study of cultural adaptations to environments.

economy   A population's system of production, distribution, and consumption of resources.

emic   The research strategy that focuses on native explanations and criteria of significance.

enculturation   The social process by which culture is learned and transmitted across the generations.

endogamy   Marriage between people of the same social group.

equity, increased   A reduction in absolute poverty and a fairer (more even) distribution of wealth.

essentialism   The process of viewing an identity as established, real, and frozen, so as to hide the historical processes and politics within which that identity developed.

ethnic group   Group distinguished by cultural similarities (shared among members of that group) and differences (between that group and others); ethnic group members are thought to share beliefs, values, habits, customs, and norms, and a common language, religion, history, geography, kinship, and/or race.

ethnicity   Identification with, and feeling part of, an ethnic group, and exclusion from certain other groups because of this affiliation.

ethnocentrism   The tendency to view one's own culture as best and to judge the behavior and beliefs of culturally different people by one's own standards.

ethnocide   Destruction by a dominant group of the culture of an ethnic group.

ethnoecology   A culture's set of environmental practices and perceptions.

ethnography   Fieldwork in a particular culture.

ethnology   The theoretical, comparative study of society and culture; compares cultures in time and space.

etic   The research strategy that emphasizes the observer's rather than the natives' explanations, categories, and criteria of significance.

exogamy   Mating or marriage outside one's kin group; a cultural universal.

extended family household   Expanded household including three or more generations.

extradomestic   Outside the home; within or pertaining to the public domain.

F

family   A group of people (e.g., parents, children, siblings, grandparents, grandchildren, uncles, aunts, nephews, nieces, cousins, spouses, siblings-in-law, parents-in-law, children-in-law) who are considered to be related in some way, such as by "blood" (common ancestry or descent) or marriage.

family of orientation   Nuclear family in which one is born and grows up.

family of procreation   Nuclear family established when one marries and has children.

fiscal   Pertaining to finances and taxation.

focal vocabulary   A set of words and distinctions that are particularly important to certain groups (those with particular foci of experience or activity), such as types of snow to Eskimos or skiers.

food production   Plant cultivation and animal domestication.

G

gender roles   The tasks and activities that a culture assigns to each sex.

gender stereotypes   Oversimplified but strongly held ideas about the characteristics of males and females.

gender stratification   Unequal distribution of rewards (socially valued resources, power, prestige, and personal freedom) between men and women, reflecting their different positions in a social hierarchy.

genealogical method   Procedures by which ethnographers discover and record connections of kinship, descent, and marriage, using diagrams and symbols.

general anthropology   The field of anthropology as a whole, consisting of cultural, archaeological, biological, and linguistic anthropology.

generality   Culture pattern or trait that exists in some but not all societies.

genocide   Policies aimed at, and/or resulting in, the physical extinction (through mass murder) of a people perceived as a racial group, that is, as sharing defining physical, genetic, or other biological characteristics.

globalization   A set of processes, including *diffusion,* migration, and *acculturation,* that promote change in today's interlinked world.

greenhouse effect   Warming from trapped atmospheric gases.

H

head, village   See *village head.*

health care systems   Beliefs, customs, and specialists concerned with ensuring health and preventing and curing illness; a cultural universal.

historical linguistics   Subdivision of linguistics that studies languages over time.

holistic   Interested in the whole of the human condition past, present, and future; biology, society, language, and culture.

hominids   Members of the zoological family that includes fossil and living humans, chimps, and gorillas.

hominins   Members of the evolutionary line leading to and including modern humans, as distinct from chimps and gorillas.

horticulture   Nonindustrial system of plant cultivation in which plots lie fallow for varying lengths of time.

human rights   Doctrine that invokes a realm of justice and morality beyond and superior to particular countries, cultures, and religions. Human rights, usually seen as vested in individuals, include the right to speak freely, to hold religious beliefs without persecution, and not to be enslaved.

hypodescent   A rule that automatically places the children of a union or mating between members of different socioeconomic groups in the less privileged group.

I

illness An *emic* condition of poor health felt by the individual.

imperialism A policy of extending the rule of a nation or empire over foreign nations and of taking and holding foreign colonies.

incest Sexual relations with a close relative.

independent invention Development of the same culture trait or pattern in separate cultures as a result of comparable needs and circumstances.

indigenized Modified to fit the local culture.

indigenous peoples The original inhabitants of particular territories; often descendants of tribespeople, they live on as culturally distinct colonized peoples, many of whom aspire to autonomy.

Industrial Revolution The historical transformation (in Europe, after 1750) of "traditional" into "modern" societies through industrialization of the economy.

informed consent An agreement sought by ethnographers from community members to take part in research.

intellectual property rights (IPR) Each society's cultural base—its core beliefs and principles. IPR is claimed as a group right—a cultural right, allowing indigenous groups to control who may know and use their collective knowledge and its applications.

international culture Cultural traditions that extend beyond national boundaries.

intervention philosophy Guiding principle of colonialism, conquest, missionization, or development; an ideological justification for outsiders to guide native peoples in specific directions.

interview schedule Ethnographic tool for structuring a formal interview. A prepared form that guides interviews with households or individuals being compared systematically. This contrasts with a questionnaire because the researcher has personal contact and records people's answers.

K

key cultural consultant An expert on a particular aspect of local life who helps the ethnographer understand that aspect.

kinesics The study of communication through body movements, stances, gestures, and facial expressions.

L

language subgroups Languages within a taxonomy of related languages that are most closely related.

law A legal code, including trial and enforcement; characteristic of state-organized societies.

leveling mechanisms Customs and social actions that operate to reduce differences in wealth and thus to bring standouts in line with community norms.

levirate Custom by which a widow marries the brother of her deceased husband.

lexicon Vocabulary; a dictionary containing all the morphemes in a language and their meaning.

life history Of a cultural consultant; provides a personal cultural portrait of existence or change in a culture.

liminality The critically important marginal or in-between phase of a rite of passage.

lineage Unilineal descent group based on demonstrated descent.

linguistic anthropology The branch of anthropology that studies linguistic variation in time and space, including interrelations between language and culture; includes historical linguistics and sociolinguistics.

longitudinal research Long-term study of a community, society, culture, or other unit, usually based on repeated visits.

M

magic Use of supernatural techniques to accomplish specific aims.

majority groups Superordinate, dominant, or controlling groups in a social–political hierarchy.

mana Sacred impersonal force in Melanesian and Polynesian religions.

market principle Profit-oriented principle of exchange that dominates in states, particularly industrial states. Goods and services are bought and sold, and values are determined by supply and demand.

matriarchy A political system in which women play a much more prominent role than men do in social and political organization.

matrilineal descent Unilineal descent rule in which people join the mother's group automatically at birth and stay members throughout life.

matrilocality Customary residence with the wife's relatives after marriage, so that children grow up in their mother's community.

means (or factors) of production Land, labor, technology, and capital—major productive resources.

medical anthropology Unites biological and cultural anthropologists in the study of disease, health problems, health care systems, and theories about illness in different cultures and ethnic groups.

minority groups Subordinate groups in a social–political hierarchy, with inferior power and less secure access to resources than majority groups have.

mode of production Way of organizing production—a set of social relations through which labor is deployed to wrest energy from nature by means of tools, skills, and knowledge.

monotheism Worship of an eternal, omniscient, omnipotent, and omnipresent supreme being.

morphology The study of form; used in linguistics (the study of morphemes and word construction) and for form in general—for example, biomorphology relates to physical form.

multiculturalism The view of cultural diversity in a country as something good and desirable; a multicultural society socializes individuals not only into the dominant (national) culture, but also into an ethnic culture.

N

national culture Cultural experiences, beliefs, learned behavior patterns, and values shared by citizens of the same nation.

nationalities Ethnic groups that once had, or wish to have or regain, autonomous political status (their own country).

nation-state An autonomous political entity, a country like the United States or Canada. See also *state*.

natural selection Originally formulated by Charles Darwin and Alfred Russel Wallace; the process by which nature selects the forms most fit to survive and reproduce in a given environment, such as the tropics.

neoliberalism Revival of Adam Smith's classic economic liberalism, the idea that governments should not regulate private enterprise and that free market forces should rule; a currently dominant intervention philosophy.

neolocality Postmarital residence pattern in which a couple establishes a new place of residence rather than living with or near either set of parents.

nomadism, pastoral Movement throughout the year by the whole pastoral group (men, women, and children) with their animals. More generally, such constant movement in pursuit of strategic resources.

O

office Permanent political position.

Olympian religions In Wallace's typology, religions that develop with state organization; have full-time religious specialists—professional priesthoods.

open-class system Stratification system that facilitates social mobility, with individual achievement and personal merit determining social rank.

overinnovation Characteristic of development projects that require major changes in people's daily lives, especially ones that interfere with customary subsistence pursuits.

P

pantribal sodality A nonkin-based group that exists throughout a tribe, spanning several villages.

participant observation A characteristic ethnographic technique; taking part in the events one is observing, describing, and analyzing.

particularity Distinctive or unique culture trait, pattern, or integration.

pastoralists People who use a food-producing strategy of adaptation based on caring for herds of domesticated animals.

patriarchy Political system ruled by men in which women have inferior social and political status, including fewer basic human rights.

patrilineal descent Unilineal descent rule in which people join the father's group automatically at birth and stay members throughout life.

patrilineal–patrilocal complex An interrelated constellation of patrilineality, patrilocality, warfare, and male supremacy.

patrilocality Customary residence with the husband's relatives after marriage, so that children grow up in their father's community.

peasant Small-scale agriculturist living in a state, with rent fund obligations.

periphery Weakest structural position in the world system; less mechanized producers of raw materials, agricultural commodities, and human labor.

phenotype An organism's evident traits, its "manifest biology"—anatomy and physiology.

phoneme Significant sound contrast in a language that serves to distinguish meaning, as in minimal pairs.

phonemics The study of the sound contrasts (phonemes) of a particular language.

phonetics The study of speech sounds in general; what people actually say in various languages.

phonology The study of sounds used in speech.

physical anthropology See *biological anthropology*.

plural marriage Marriage of a man to two or more women (polygyny) or marriage of a woman to two or more men (polyandry)—at the same time; see also *polygamy*.

plural society A society that combines ethnic contrasts, ecological specialization (i.e., use of different environmental resources by each ethnic group), and the economic interdependence of those groups.

polyandry Variety of plural marriage in which a woman has more than one husband.

polygamy Marriage with three or more spouses, at the same time; see also *plural marriage*.

polygyny Variety of plural marriage in which a man has more than one wife.

polytheism Belief in several deities who control aspects of nature.

postcolonial Referring to interactions between European nations and the societies they colonized (mainly after 1800); more generally, it may be used to signify a position against imperialism and Eurocentrism.

postmodern In its most general sense, describes the blurring and breakdown of established canons (rules, standards), categories, distinctions, and boundaries.

postmodernism A style and movement in architecture that followed modernism. Compared with modernism, it is less geometric, less functional, less austere, more playful, and more willing to include elements from diverse times and cultures; *postmodern* now describes comparable developments in music, literature, and visual art.

postmodernity Condition of a world in flux, with people on the move, in which established groups, boundaries, identities, contrasts, and standards are reaching out and breaking down.

potlatch Competitive feast among Indians on the North Pacific Coast of North America.

power The ability to exercise one's will over others—to do what one wants; the basis of political status.

prejudice Devaluing (looking down on) a group because of its assumed behavior, values, capabilities, or attributes.

prestige Esteem, respect, or approval for acts, deeds, or qualities considered exemplary.

primates Members of the zoological order that includes humans, apes, monkeys, and prosimians (e.g., lemurs).

productivity The ability to use the rules of one's language to create new expressions comprehensible to other speakers; a basic feature of language.

proletariat See *working class.*

progeny price A gift from the husband and his kin to the wife and her kin before, at, or after marriage; legitimizes children born to the woman as members of the husband's descent group.

protolanguage Language ancestral to several daughter languages.

R

race An ethnic group assumed to have a biological basis.

racial classification The attempt to assign humans to discrete categories (purportedly) based on common ancestry.

racism Discrimination against an ethnic group assumed to have a biological basis.

random sample A sample in which all members of the population have an equal statistical chance of being included.

reciprocity One of the three principles of exchange. Governs exchange between social equals; major exchange mode in band and tribal societies.

reciprocity continuum Regarding exchanges, a range running from generalized reciprocity (closely related/deferred return) through balanced reciprocity, to negative reciprocity (strangers/immediate return).

redistribution Flow of goods into the center, then back out; characteristic of chiefdoms, many archaic states, and some states with managed economies.

refugees People who have been forced (involuntary refugees) or who have chosen (voluntary refugees) to flee a country, to escape persecution or war.

religion Beliefs and rituals concerned with supernatural beings, powers, and forces.

revitalization movements Movements that occur in times of change, in which religious leaders emerge and undertake to alter or revitalize a society.

rites of passage Culturally defined activities associated with the transition from one place or stage of life to another.

ritual Behavior that is formal, stylized, repetitive, and stereotyped, performed earnestly as a social act; rituals are held at set times and places and have liturgical orders.

S

sample A smaller study group chosen to represent a larger population.

Sapir-Whorf hypothesis Theory that different languages produce different ways of thinking.

science A systematic field of study or body of knowledge that aims, through experiment, observation, and deduction, to produce reliable explanations of phenomena, with reference to the material and physical world.

scientific medicine A health care system based on scientific knowledge and procedures, encompassing such fields as pathology, microbiology, biochemistry, surgery, diagnostic technology, and applications.

semantics A language's meaning system.

semiperiphery Structural position in the world system intermediate between core and periphery; exporters of goods and commodities, but lacking the power of core nations.

sexual dimorphism Marked differences, such as in height and weight, in male and female biology besides the contrasts in breasts and genitals.

sexual orientation A person's habitual sexual attraction to, and activities with, persons of the opposite sex (heterosexuality), the same sex (homosexuality), or both sexes (bisexuality); also, the lack of sexual attraction (asexuality).

shaman A part-time religious practitioner who mediates between ordinary people and supernatural beings and forces.

slavery The most extreme, coercive, abusive, and inhumane form of legalized inequality; people are treated as property.

sociolinguistics Study of relationships between social and linguistic variation; study of language in its social context.

sociopolitical typology Classification scheme based on the scale and complexity of social organization and the effectiveness of political regulation; includes band, tribe, chiefdom, and state.

sodality See *pantribal sodality.*

sororate Custom by which a widower marries the sister of the deceased wife.

state (nation-state) Complex sociopolitical system that administers a territory and populace with substantial contrasts in occupation, wealth, prestige, and power. An independent, centrally organized political unit, a government.

status Any position that determines where someone fits in society; may be ascribed or achieved.

stereotypes Fixed ideas—often unfavorable—about what members of a group are like.

stratification Characteristic of a system with socioeconomic strata.

style shifts Variations in speech in different contexts.

subcultures Different cultural symbol-based traditions associated with subgroups in the same complex society.

subordinate The lower, or underprivileged, group in a stratified system.

superordinate The higher, or privileged, group in a stratified system.

survey research Characteristic research procedure among social scientists other than anthropologists, which studies society through sampling, statistical analysis, and impersonal data collection.

symbol Something, verbal or nonverbal, that arbitrarily and by convention stands for something else, with which it has no necessary or natural connection.

syntax The arrangement and order of words in phrases and sentences.

T

taboo Prohibition backed by supernatural sanctions.

transhumance One of two variants of pastoralism; part of the population moves seasonally with the herds while the other part remains in home villages.

tribe Form of sociopolitical organization usually based on horticulture or pastoralism. Socioeconomic stratification and centralized rule are absent in tribes, and there is no means of enforcing political decisions.

tropics Geographic belt extending about 23 degrees north and south of the equator, between the Tropic of Cancer (north) and the Tropic of Capricorn (south).

typology, sociopolitical See *sociopolitical typology.*

U

underdifferentiation Planning fallacy of viewing less-developed countries as an undifferentiated group; ignoring cultural diversity and adopting a uniform approach (often ethnocentric) for very different types of project beneficiaries.

unilineal descent Matrilineal or patrilineal descent.

universal Something that exists in every culture.

urban anthropology The anthropological study of life in and around world cities, including the study of urban social problems, differences between urban and other environments, and adaptation to city life.

V

variables Attributes (e.g., sex, age, height, weight) that differ from one person or case to the next.

vertical mobility Upward or downward change in a person's social status.

village head Leadership position in a village (as among the Yanomami, where the head is always a man); has limited authority; leads by example and persuasion.

W

wealth All of a person's material assets, including income, land, and other types of property; the basis of economic status.

Westernization The acculturation influence of European cultures on tribal societies.

working class (proletariat) Those who must sell their labor to survive; the antithesis of the bourgeoisie in Marx's class analysis.

world-system theory Argument for the historic and contemporary social, political, and economic significance of an identifiable global system, based on wealth and power differentials, that extends beyond individual countries.

Abelmann, N., and J. Lie. 1995. *Blue Dreams: Korean Americans and the Los Angeles Riots.* Cambridge, MA: Harvard University Press.

Adams, Beatrice. 2007. McDonald's Strange Menu Around the World. http://thrifter.com/practical-travel/budget-travel/mcdonald%E2%80%99s-strange-menu-around-the-world/.

Adherents.com. 2002. Major Religions of the World Ranked by Number of Adherents. http://www.adherents.com/Religions_By_Adherents.html.

Ahmed, A. S. 1992. *Postmodernism and Islam: Predicament and Promise.* New York: Routledge.

———. 2004. *Postmodernism and Islam: Predicament and Promise.* Rev. ed. New York: Routledge.

Amadiume, I. 1987. *Male Daughters, Female Husbands.* Atlantic Highlands, NJ: Zed.

American Anthropological Association. *Anthropology Newsletter.* Published nine times annually by the American Anthropological Association, Washington, DC.

———. 2010. Anthropologists Challenge New Arizona Immigration Law. http://aaanet.org/issues/press/Arizona-Immigration.cfm.

Anderson, B. 1991. *Imagined Communities: Reflections on the Origin and Spread of Nationalism.* Rev. ed. London: Verso.

Anderson, R. 1996. *Magic, Science, and Health: The Aims and Achievements of Medical Anthropology.* Fort Worth, TX: Harcourt Brace.

Antoun, R. T. 2008. *Understanding Fundamentalism: Christian, Islamic, and Jewish Movements.* 2nd ed. Lanham, MD: AltaMira.

Aoki, M. Y., and M. B. Dardess, eds. 1981. *As the Japanese See It: Past and Present.* Honolulu: University Press of Hawaii.

Aoyagi, K., P. J. M. Nas, and J. Traphagan, eds. 1998. *Toward Sustainable Cities: Readings in the Anthropology of Urban Environments.* Leiden: Leiden Development Studies, Institute of Cultural and Social Studies, University of Leiden.

Appadurai, A. 1990. Disjuncture and Difference in the Global Cultural Economy. *Public Culture* 2(2):1–24.

———. 1991. Global Ethnoscapes: Notes and Queries for a Transnational Anthropology. In *Recapturing Anthropology: Working in the Present,* R. G. Fox, ed., pp. 191–210. Santa Fe, NM: School of American Research Advanced Seminar Series.

———. 1996. *Modernity at Large. Cultural Dimensions of Globalization.* Minneapolis: University of Minnesota Press.

———. 2001. *Globalization.* Durham, NC: Duke University Press.

Appiah, K. A. 1990. Racisms. In *Anatomy of Racism,* David Theo Goldberg, ed., pp. 3–17. Minneapolis: University of Minnesota Press.

Applebome, P. 1996. English Unique to Blacks Is Officially Recognized. *New York Times,* December 20. http://www.nytimes.com.

Arensberg, C. 1987. Theoretical Contributions of Industrial and Development Studies. In *Applied Anthropology in America,* 2nd ed., E. M. Eddy and W. L. Partridge, eds. New York: Columbia University Press.

Arrighi, G. 1994. *The Long Twentieth Century; Money, Power, and the Origins of Our Times.* New York: Verso.

Ashcroft, B., G. Griffiths, and H. Tiffin. 1989. *The Empire Writes Back: Theory and Practice in Post-colonial Literatures.* New York: Routledge.

Baer, H., and M. Singer. 2008. *Global Warming and the Political Ecology of Health.* Walnut Creek, CA: Left Coast Press.

Baer, H. A., M. Singer, and I. Susser. 2003. *Medical Anthropology and the World System.* Westport, CT: Praeger.

Bailey, E. J. 2000. *Medical Anthropology and African American Health.* Westport, CT: Bergin and Garvey.

Bailey, R. C. 1990. *The Behavioral Ecology of Efe Pygmy Men in the Ituri Forest, Zaire.* Ann Arbor: Anthropological Papers, Museum of Anthropology, University of Michigan, no. 86.

Bailey, R. C., G. Head, M. Jenike, B. Owen, R. Rechtman, and E. Zechenter. 1989. Hunting and Gathering in Tropical Rain Forests: Is It Possible? *American Anthropologist* 91:59–82.

Banton, M. 1957. *West African City. A Study in Tribal Life in Freetown.* London: Oxford University Press.

Barber, B. R. 1992. Jihad vs. McWorld. *Atlantic Monthly* 269(3):53–65, March 1992.

———. 1995. *Jihad vs. McWorld.* New York: Times Books.

Barker, C. 1997. *Global Television: An Introduction.* Malden, MA: Blackwell.

———. 2003. *Cultural Studies: Theory and Practice.* Thousand Oaks, CA: Sage.

Barnaby, F., ed. 1984. *Future War: Armed Conflict in the Next Decade.* London: M. Joseph.

Barnes, E. 2005. *Diseases and Human Evolution.* Albuquerque: University of New Mexico Press.

Baro, M., and T. F. Deubel. 2006. Persistent Hunger: Perspectives on Vulnerability, Famine, and Food Security in Sub-Saharan Africa. *Annual Review of Anthropology* 35:521–538.

Barringer, F. 1992. New Census Data Show More Children Living in Poverty. *New York Times,* May 29, pp. A1, A12–A13.

Barth, F. 1968. (orig. 1958). Ecologic Relations of Ethnic Groups in Swat, North Pakistan. In *Man in Adaptation: The Cultural Present,* Yehudi Cohen, ed., pp. 324–331. Chicago: Aldine.

———. 1969. *Ethnic Groups and Boundaries: The Social Organization of Cultural Difference.* London: Allen & Unwin.

Bearak, B. 2010. Shaky Rule in Madagascar Threatens Trees. *New York Times,* May 24. http://www.nytimes.com.

Beeman, W. 1986. *Language, Status, and Power in Iran.* Bloomington: Indiana University Press.

Behar, R. 1993. *Translated Woman: Crossing the Border with Esperanza's Story.* Boston: Beacon Press.

Bell, W. 1981. Neocolonialism. In *Encyclopedia of Sociology,* p. 193. Guilford, CT: DPG Publishing.

Bellah, R. N. 1978. Religious Evolution. In *Reader in Comparative Religion: An Anthropological Approach,* 4th ed., W. A. Lessa and E. Z. Vogt, eds., pp. 36–50. New York: Harper and Row.

Benedict, R. 1940. *Race, Science and Politics.* New York: Modern Age Books.

Berlin, B., and P. Kay. 1992. *Basic Color Terms: Their Universality and Evolution.* 2nd ed. Berkeley: University of California Press.

Bernard, H. R. 2002. *Research Methods in Anthropology: Qualitative and Quantitative Methods.* 3rd ed. Walnut Creek, CA: AltaMira.

———. 2006. *Research Methods in Anthropology: Qualitative and Quantitative Approaches.* 4th ed. Lanham, MD: AltaMira.

Bernard, H. R., ed. 1998. *Handbook of Methods in Cultural Anthropology,* Walnut Creek, CA: AltaMira.

Bicker, A., P. Sillitoe, and J. Pottier. 2004. *Investigating Local Knowledge: New Directions, New Approaches.* Burlington, VT: Ashgate.

Bird-David, N. 1992. Beyond "The Original Affluent Society": A Culturalist Reformulation. *Current Anthropology* 33(1):25–47.

Bjuremalm, H. 1997. Rattvisa kan skippas i Rwanda: Folkmordet 1994 gar attt forklara och analysera pa samma satt som forintelsen av judarna. *Dagens Nyheter* [06–03–1997, p. B3].

Blackwood, E., and S. Wieringa, eds. 1999. *Female Desires: Same-Sex Relations and Transgender Practices across Cultures.* New York: Columbia University Press.

Bloch, M., ed. 1975. *Political Language and Oratory in Traditional Societies.* London: Academic Press.

Boas, F. 1966 (orig. 1940). *Race, Language, and Culture.* New York: Free Press.

Bodley, J. H. 2003. *The Power of Scale: A Global History Approach.* Armonk, NY: M. E. Sharpe.

———. 2007. *Anthropology and Contemporary Human Problems.* 5th ed. Lanham, MD: AltaMira.

———. 2008. *Victims of Progress.* 5th ed. Lanham, MD: AltaMira.

Bodley, J. H., ed. 1988. *Tribal Peoples and Development Issues: A Global Overview.* Mountain View, CA: Mayfield.

Boellstorff, T. 2007. Queer Studies in the House of Anthropology. *Annual Review of Anthropology* 36:375–389.

Bogoras, W. 1904. The Chukchee. In *The Jesup North Pacific Expedition,* F. Boas, ed. New York: Memoir of the American Museum of Natural History.

Bolinger, D., and D. Sears. 1981. *Aspects of Language.* 3rd ed. New York: Harcourt Brace Jovanovich.

Bolton, R. 1981. Susto, Hostility, and Hypoglycemia. *Ethnology* 20(4): 227–258.

Bonvillain, N. 2001. *Women and Men: Cultural Constructions of Gender.* 3rd ed. Upper Saddle River, NJ: Prentice Hall.

———. 2008. *Language, Culture, and Communication: The Meaning of Messages.* 5th ed. Upper Saddle River, NJ: Prentice Hall.

Boserup, E. 1970. *Women's Role in Economic Development.* London: Allen and Unwin.

Bourdieu, P. 1977. *Outline of a Theory of Practice.* R. Nice (trans.). Cambridge: Cambridge University Press.

———. 1982. *Ce Que Parler Veut Dire.* Paris: Fayard.

———. 1984. *Distinction: A Social Critique of the Judgment of Taste.* R. Nice (trans.). Cambridge, MA: Harvard University Press.

Bourque, S. C., and K. B. Warren. 1987. Technology, Gender and Development. *Daedalus* 116(4):173–197.

Bowen, J. R. 2008. *Religion in Practice: An Approach to Anthropology of Religion.* 4th ed. Boston: Pearson/Allyn and Bacon.

Bowie, F. 2006. *The Anthropology of Religion: An Introduction.* Malden, MA: Blackwell.

Braudel, F. 1981. *Civilization and Capitalism, 15th–18th Century,* Vol. I, *The Structure of Everyday Life: The Limits.* S. Reynolds (trans.). New York: Harper and Row.

———. 1982. *Civilization and Capitalism, 15th–18th Century,* Vol. II, *The Wheels of Commerce.* New York: Harper and Row.

———. 1992. *Civilization and Capitalism, 15th–18th Century,* Vol. III, *The Perspective of the World.* Berkeley: University of California Press.

Bremen, J. V., and A. Shimizu, eds. 1999. *Anthropology and Colonialism in Asia and Oceania.* London: Curzon.

Brenneis, D. 1988. Language and Disputing. *Annual Review of Anthropology* 17:221–237.

Brettell, C. B., and C. F. Sargent, eds. 2005. *Gender in Cross-Cultural Perspective.* Upper Saddle River, NJ: Pearson/Prentice Hall.

Briggs, C. L. 2005. Communicability, Racial Discourse, and Disease. *Annual Review of Anthropology* 34:269–291.

Brooke, J. 1992. Rio's New Day in Sun Leaves Laplander Limp. *New York Times,* June 1, p. A7.

Brower, B., and B. R. Johnston 2007. *Disappearing Peoples?: Indigenous Groups and Ethnic Minorities in South and Central Asia.* Walnut Creek, CA: Left Coast Press.

Brown, A. 2001. Communism. *International Encyclopedia of the Social & Behavioral Sciences,* pp. 2323–2326. New York: Elsevier.

Brown, D. 1991. *Human Universals.* New York: McGraw-Hill.

Brown, P. J. 1998. *Understanding and Applying Medical Anthropology.* Mountain View, CA: Mayfield.

Brown, R. W. 1958. *Words and Things.* Glencoe, IL: Free Press.

Burns, J. F. 1992a. Bosnian Strife Cuts Old Bridges of Trust. *New York Times,* May 22, pp. A1, A6.

———. 1992b. A Serb, Fighting Serbs, Defends Sarajevo. *New York Times,* July 12, sec. 4, p. E3.

———. 1997. A Year of Harsh Islamic Rule Weighs Heavily for Afghans. September 24. www.nytimes.com.

Butler, R. 2005. World's Largest Cities: [Ranked by City Population]. http://www.mongabay.com/cities_pop_01.htm.

Buvinic, M. 1995. The Feminization of Poverty? Research and Policy Needs. In *Reducing Poverty through Labour Market Policies.* Geneva: International Institute for Labour Studies.

Carey, B. 2007. Washoe, a Chimp of Many Words Dies at 42. *New York Times,* November 1. http://www.nytimes.com.

Carneiro, R. L. 1956. Slash-and-Burn Agriculture: A Closer Look at Its Implications for Settlement Patterns. In *Men and Cultures,* Selected Papers of the Fifth International Congress of Anthropological and Ethnological Sciences, pp. 229–234. Philadelphia: University of Pennsylvania Press.

———. 1968 (orig. 1961). Slash-and-Burn Cultivation among the Kuikuru and Its Implications for Cultural Development in the Amazon Basin. In *Man in Adaptation: The Cultural Present,* Y. A. Cohen, ed., pp. 131–145. Chicago: Aldine.

———. 1970. A Theory of the Origin of the State. *Science* 69: 733–738.

Carsten, J. 2004. *After Kinship.* New York: Cambridge University Press.

Carter, J. 1988. Freed from Keepers and Cages, Chimps Come of Age on Baboon Island. *Smithsonian,* June, pp. 36–48.

Cernea, M., ed. 1991. *Putting People First: Sociological Variables in Rural Development.* 2nd ed. New York: Oxford University Press (published for the World Bank).

Ceuppens, B., and P. Geschiere. 2005. Autochthony: Local or Global? New Modes in the Struggle over Citizenship and Belonging in Africa and Europe. *Annual Review of Anthropology* 34:385–407.

Chagnon, N. A. 1967. *Yanomamo Warfare: Social Organization and Marriage Alliances.* Ann Arbor, MI: University Microfilms.

———. 1992 (orig. 1983). *Yanomamo: The Fierce People.* 4th ed. New York: Harcourt Brace.

———. 1997. *Yanomamo.* 5th ed. Fort Worth, TX: Harcourt Brace.

Chambers, E. 1987. Applied Anthropology in the Post-Vietnam Era: Anticipations and Ironies. *Annual Review of Anthropology* 16:309–337.

Chatterjee, P. 2004. *The Politics of the Governed: Reflections on Popular Politics in Most of the World.* New York: Columbia University Press.

Chiseri-Strater, E., and B. S. Sunstein. 2001. *Fieldworking: Reading and Writing Research.* 2nd ed. Upper Saddle River, NJ: Prentice Hall.

Chomsky, N. 1957. *Syntactic Structures.* The Hague: Mouton.

Christensen, L. 2003. The Politics of Correction. *Rethinking Schools Online.* Fall. http://www.rethinkingschools.org/archive/18_01/corr181.html.

Clifford, J. 1982. *Person and Myth: Maurice Leenhardt in the Melanesian World.* Berkeley: University of California Press.

———. 1988. *The Predicament of Culture: Twentieth-Century Ethnography, Literature and Art.* Cambridge, MA: Harvard University Press.

Coates, J. 1986. *Women, Men, and Language.* London: Longman.

Cody, D. 1998. British Empire. http://www.stg.brown.edu/projects/hypertext/landow/victorian/history/Empire.html, May 18.

Cohen, M. 1998. *Culture of Intolerance: Chauvinism, Class, and Racism.* New Haven, CT: Yale University Press.

Cohen, M. N., and Armelagos, G., eds. 1984. *Paleopathology at the Origins of Agriculture.* New York: Academic Press.

Cohen, R. 1967. *The Kanuri of Bornu.* New York: Holt, Rinehart & Winston.

Cohen, Y. 1974. Culture as Adaptation. In *Man in Adaptation: The Cultural Present,* 2nd ed., Y. A. Cohen, ed., pp. 45–68. Chicago: Aldine.

Colson, E., and T. Scudder. 1975. New Economic Relationships between the Gwembe Valley and the Line of Rail. In *Town and Country in Central and Eastern Africa,* David Parkin, ed., pp. 190–210. London: Oxford University Press.

———. 1988. *For Prayer and Profit: The Ritual, Economic, and Social Importance of Beer in Gwembe District, Zambia, 1950–1982.* Stanford, CA: Stanford University Press.

Connor, W. 1972. Nation-Building or Nation-Destroying. *World Politics* 24(3).

Cooper, F., and A. L. Stoler, eds. 1997. *Tensions of Empire: Colonial Cultures in a Bourgeois World.* Berkeley: University of California Press.

Council on International and Public Affairs. 2006. How Many Dollars at the Top? *Too Much: A Commentary on Excess and Inequality.* New York, April 24. http://www.toomuchonline.org/articlenew2006/April24a.html.

Crapo, R. H. 2006. *Anthropology of Religion: The Unity and Diversity of Religions.* Boston: McGraw-Hill.

Crate, S. A., and M. Nuttall 2008. *Anthropology and Climate Change: From Encounters to Actions.* Walnut Creek, CA: Left Coast Press.

Cresswell, T. 2006. *On the Move: Mobility in the Modern West.* New York: Routledge.

Crosby, A. W., Jr. 1986. *Ecological Imperialism: The Biological Expansion of Europe 900–1900.* Cambridge: Cambridge University Press.

———. 2003. *The Columbian Exchange: Biological and Cultural Consequences of 1492.* Westport, CT: Praeger.

Cultural Survival Quarterly. Quarterly Journal. Cambridge, MA: Cultural Survival, Inc.

———. 2009. A Closer Look: Sudan—The Peoples of Darfur. http://www.culturalsurvival.org/publications/cultural-survival-quarterly/sudan/closer-look-sudanbrthe-peoples-darfur.

Cunningham, G. 1999. *Religion and Magic: Approaches and Theories.* New York: New York University Press.

DaMatta, R. 1991. *Carnivals, Rogues, and Heroes: An Interpretation of the Brazilian Dilemma.* John Drury (trans.). Notre Dame, IN: University of Notre Dame Press.

D'Andrade, R. 1984. Cultural Meaning Systems. In *Culture Theory: Essays on Mind, Self, and Emotion,* R. A. Shweder and R. A. Levine, eds., pp. 88–119. Cambridge: Cambridge University Press.

Das, V., and D. Poole, eds. 2004. *Anthropology in the Margins of the State.* Santa Fe, NM: School of American Research Press.

Degler, C. 1970. *Neither Black nor White: Slavery and Race Relations in Brazil and the United States.* New York: Macmillan.

de la Peña, G. 2005. Social and Cultural Policies toward Indigenous Peoples: Perspectives from Latin America. *Annual Review of Anthropology* 34:717–739.

DeNavas-Walt, C., B. D. Proctor, and C. H. Lee. 2006. Income, Poverty, and Health Insurance Coverage in the United States: 2005, U.S. Census Bureau. Current Population Reports, Consumer Income. http://www.census.gov/rpod/2006pubs/p60–231.pdf.

Dentan, R. K. 1979. *The Semai: A Nonviolent People of Malaya,* Fieldwork ed. New York: Harcourt Brace.

De Vos, G. A., and H. Wagatsuma. 1966. *Japan's Invisible Race: Caste in Culture and Personality.* Berkeley: University of California Press.

De Vos, G. A., W. O. Wetherall, and K. Stearman. 1983. *Japan's Minorities: Burakumin, Koreans, Ainu and Okinawans.* Report no. 3. London: Minority Rights Group.

De Waal, F. B. M. 1997. *Bonobo: The Forgotten Ape.* Berkeley: University of California Press.

Di Leonardo, M., ed. 1991. *Toward a New Anthropology of Gender.* Berkeley: University of California Press.

Diamond, J. M. 1997. *Guns, Germs, and Steel: The Fates of Human Societies.* New York: Norton.

Dillon, S. 2006. In Schools Across U.S., the Melting Pot Overflows. *New York Times,* August 27. http://www.nytimes.com.

Divale, W. T., and M. Harris. 1976. Population, Warfare, and the Male Supremacist Complex. *American Anthropologist* 78: 521–538.

Douglass, W. A. 1969. *Death in Murelaga: Funerary Ritual in a Spanish Basque Village.* Seattle: University of Washington Press.

———. 1975. *Echalar and Murelaga: Opportunity and Rural Exodus in Two Spanish Basque Villages.* London: C. Hurst.

———. 1992. Basques. *Encyclopedia of World Cultures,* Vol. 4. Boston: G. K. Hall.

Draper, P. 1975. !Kung Women: Contrasts in Sexual Egalitarianism in Foraging and Sedentary Contexts. In *Toward an Anthropology of Women,* R. Reiter, ed., pp. 77–109. New York: Monthly Review Press.

Dressler, W. W., K. S. Oths, and C. C. Gravlee. 2005. Race and Ethnicity in Public Health Research. *Annual Review of Anthropology* 34:231–252.

Durkheim, E. 1951 (orig. 1897). *Suicide: A Study in Sociology.* Glencoe, IL: Free Press.

———. 1961 (orig. 1912). *The Elementary Forms of the Religious Life.* New York: Collier Books.

———. 2001 (orig. 1912). *The Elementary Forms of the Religious Life.* Carol Cosman (trans.). Abridged with an introduction and notes by Mark S. Cladis. New York: Oxford University Press.

Durrenberger, E. P., and T. D. King, eds. 2000. *State and Community in Fisheries Management: Power, Policy, and Practice.* Westport, CT: Bergin and Garvey.

Dwyer, K. 1982. *Moroccan Dialogues: Anthropology in Question.* Baltimore: Johns Hopkins University Press.

Earle, T. K. 1987. Chiefdoms in Archaeological and Ethnohistorical Perspective. *Annual Review of Anthropology* 16:279–308.

———. 1997. *How Chiefs Come to Power: The Political Economy in Prehistory.* Stanford, CA: Stanford University Press.

Eastman, C. M. 1975. *Aspects of Language and Culture.* San Francisco: Chandler and Sharp.

Echeverria, J. 1999. *Home Away from Home: A History of Basque Boardinghouses.* Reno: University of Nevada Press.

Eckert, P. 1989. *Jocks and Burnouts: Social Categories and Identity in the High School.* New York: Teachers College Press, Columbia University.

———. 2000. *Linguistic Variation as Social Practice: The Linguistic Construction of Identity in Belten High.* Malden, MA: Blackwell.

Eckert, P., and S. McConnell-Ginet. 2003. *Language and Gender.* New York: Cambridge University Press.

Edelman, M., and A. Haugerud. 2004. *The Anthropology of Development and Globalization: From Classical Political Economy to Contemporary Neoliberalism.* Malden, MA: Blackwell.

Escobar, A. 1991. Anthropology and the Development Encounter: The Making and Marketing of Development Anthropology. *American Ethnologist* 18:658–682.

———. 1994. Welcome to Cyberia: Notes on the Anthropology of Cyberculture. *Current Anthropology* 35(3):211–231.

———. 1995. *Encountering Development: The Making and Unmaking of the Third World.* Princeton, NJ: Princeton University Press.

Eskridge, W. N., Jr. 1996. *The Case for Same-Sex Marriage: From Sexual Liberty to Civilized Commitment.* New York: Free Press.

Evans-Pritchard, E. E. 1970. Sexual Inversion among the Azande. *American Anthropologist* 72:1428–1433.

Fagan, B. M. 1998. *World Prehistory: A Brief Introduction.* 4th ed. New York: Longman.

———. 2002. *World Prehistory: A Brief Introduction.* 5th ed. Upper Saddle River, NJ: Prentice Hall.

Farner, R. F., ed. 2004. *Nationalism, Ethnicity, and Identity: Cross-National and Comparative Perspectives.* New Brunswick, NJ: Transaction Publishers.

Farooq, M. 1966. Importance of Determining Transmission Sites in Planning Bilharziasis Control: Field Observations from the Egypt-49 Project Area. *American Journal of Epidemiology* 83:603–612.

Farr, D. M. L. 1980. British Empire. *Academic American Encyclopedia,* Vol. 3, pp. 495–496. Princeton, NJ: Arete.

Fasold, R. W. 1990. *The Sociolinguistics of Language.* Oxford: Blackwell.

Fearson, J. 2003. Ethnic Structure and Cultural Diversity around the World: A Cross-National Data Set on Ethnic Groups. *Stanford Education Working Papers.* http://stanford.edu/group/ethnic/workingpapers/egroups.pdf.

Ferguson, R. B. 1995. *Yanomami Warfare: A Political History.* Santa Fe, NM: School of American Research.

———. 2002. *The State, Identity, and Violence: Political Disintegration in the Post-Cold War Era.* New York: Routledge.

Ferraro, G. 2006. *The Cultural Dimension of International Business.* 5th ed. Upper Saddle River, NJ: Prentice Hall.

Fields, J. M. 2004. America's Families and Living Arrangements: 2003. U.S. Census Bureau. *Current Population Reports,* P20–553, November. http://www.census.gov.

Fields, J. M., and L. M. Casper. 2001. America's Families and Living Arrangements: Population Characteristics, 2000. U.S. Census

Bureau. *Current Population Reports,* P20–537, June. http://www
.census.gov/prod/2001pubs/p20–537.pdf.

Files, J. 2005. Report Describes Immigrants as Younger and More
Diverse. *New York Times,* National ed., June 10, p. A11.

Finkler, K. 1985. *Spiritualist Healers in Mexico: Successes and Fail-
ures of Alternative Therapeutics.* South Hadley, MA: Bergin and
Garvey.

Finnstrom, S. 1997. Postcoloniality and the Postcolony: Theories of the
Global and the Local. http://www.stg.brown.edu/projects/hypertext/
landow/post/poldiscourse/finnstrom/finnstrom1.html.

Fischer, Steven Roger. 2001. *A History of Writing.* London: Reaktion
Books.

Fiske, J. 1989. *Understanding Popular Culture.* Boston: Unwin
Hyman.

Fiske, J., and J. Hartley. 2003. *Reading Television.* New York:
Routledge.

Fleisher, M. L. 2000. *Kuria Cattle Raiders: Violence and Vigilantism
on the Tanzania/Kenya Frontier.* Ann Arbor: University of Michigan Press.

Food, Inc. promotional website. About the Issues. http://www
.foodincmovie.com/about-the-issues.php.

Ford, C. S., and F. A. Beach. 1951. *Patterns of Sexual Behavior.* New
York: Harper Torchbooks.

Fortes, M. 1950. Kinship and Marriage among the Ashanti. In *African
Systems of Kinship and Marriage,* A. R. Radcliffe-Brown and
D. Forde, eds., pp. 252–284. London: Oxford University Press.

Fortmann, Louise, Camille Antinori, and Nontokozo Nabane. 1997.
Fruits of Their Labors: Gender, Property Rights, and Tree Planting
in Two Zimbabwe Villages. *Rural Sociology* 62(3): 295–314.

Foster, G. M. 1965. Peasant Society and the Image of Limited Good.
American Anthropologist 67:293–315.

Foster, G. M., and B. G. Anderson. 1978. *Medical Anthropology.* New
York: McGraw-Hill.

Foucault, M. 1979. *Discipline and Punish: The Birth of the Prison.*
A. Sheridan (trans.). New York: Vintage Books.

———. 1990. *The History of Sexuality,* Vol. 2, *The Use of Pleasure.*
R. Hurley (trans.). New York: Vintage.

Fouts, R. S. 1997. *Next of Kin: What Chimpanzees Have Taught Me
about Who We Are.* New York: William Morrow.

Fouts, R. S., D. H. Fouts, and T. E. Van Cantfort. 1989. The Infant
Loulis Learns Signs from Cross-Fostered Chimpanzees. In *Teaching Sign Language to Chimpanzees,* R. A. Gardner, B. T. Gardner,
and T. E. Van Cantfort, eds., pp. 280–292. Albany: State University
of New York Press.

Frake, C. O. 1961. The Diagnosis of Disease among the Subanun of
Mindanao. *American Anthropologist* 63:113–132.

Franke, R. 1977. Miracle Seeds and Shattered Dreams in Java. In
Readings in Anthropology, pp. 197–201. Guilford, CT: Dushkin.

French, H. W. 2002. Whistling Past the Global Graveyard. *New
York Times,* July 14. http://www./nytimes.com/2002/01/14
.weekinreview/14FREN.html.

Fricke, T. 1994. *Himalayan Households: Tamang Demography and
Domestic Processes.* 2nd ed. New York: Columbia University Press.

Fried, M. H. 1960. On the Evolution of Social Stratification and the
State. In *Culture in History,* S. Diamond, ed., pp. 713–731. New
York: Columbia University Press.

———. 1967. *The Evolution of Political Society: An Essay in Political
Anthropology.* New York: McGraw-Hill.

Friedl, E. 1975. *Women and Men: An Anthropologist's View.* New York:
Holt, Rinehart & Winston.

Friedman, J., ed. 2003. *Globalization, the State, and Violence.* Walnut
Creek, CA: AltaMira.

Friedman, K. E., and J. Friedman. 2008. *The Anthropology of Global
Systems.* Lanham, MD: AltaMira.

Gal, S. 1989. Language and Political Economy. *Annual Review of
Anthropology* 18:345–367.

Gardner, R. A., B. T. Gardner, and T. E. Van Cantfort, eds. 1989. *Teaching Sign Language to Chimpanzees.* Albany: State University of
New York Press.

Geertz, C. 1973. *The Interpretation of Cultures.* New York: Basic
Books.

Geis, M. L. 1987. *The Language of Politics.* New York:
Springer-Verlag.

Gellner, E. 1997. *Nationalism.* New York: New York University Press.

Gezon, L. L. 2006. *Global Visions, Local Landscapes: A Political Ecology of Conservation, Conflict, and Control in Northern Madagascar.* Lanham, MD: AltaMira.

Giddens, A. 1973. *The Class Structure of the Advanced Societies.* New
York: Cambridge University Press.

———. 2000. *Runaway World: How Globalization Is Reshaping Our
Lives.* New York: Routledge.

Gilmore, D. D. 1987. *Aggression and Community: Paradoxes of Anda-
lusian Culture.* New Haven, CT: Yale University Press.

———. 1991. *Manhood in the Making: Cultural Concepts of Masculinity.* New Haven, CT: Yale University Press.

———. 2001. *Misogyny: The Male Malady.* Philadelphia: University
of Pennsylvania Press.

Gledhill, J. 2000. *Power and Its Disguises: Anthropological Perspectives on Politics.* Sterling, VA: Pluto Press.

Gmelch, G. 1978. Baseball Magic. *Human Nature* 1(8):32–40.

———. 2001. *Inside Pitch: Life in Professional Baseball.* Washington,
DC: Smithsonian Institution Press.

Gmelch, G., and W. Zenner, eds. 2002. *Urban Life: Readings in the
Anthropology of the City.* Prospect Heights, IL: Waveland.

Gogoi, Pallavi. 2005. Wal-Mart's China Card. *Bloomberg Business
Week,* July 26. http://www.businessweek.com.

Goldberg, D. T. 2002. *The Racial State.* Malden, MA: Blackwell.

Golden, T. 1997. Oakland Revamps Plan to Teach Black English. *New
York Times,* January 14. http://www.nytimes.com.

Goleman, D. 1992. Anthropology Goes Looking for Love in All the
Old Places. *New York Times,* November 24, 1992, p. B1.

Goode, Erich. 2008. Drugs in American Society. 7th ed. New York:
McGraw-Hill.

Gottdiener, M., ed. 2000. *New Forms of Consumption: Consumers, Culture, and Commodification.* Lanham, MD: Rowman & Littlefield.

Gough, E. K. 1959. The Nayars and the Definition of Marriage. *Journal of the Royal Anthropological Institute* 89:23–34.

Gramsci, A. 1971. *Selections from the Prison Notebooks.* Q. Hoare and
G. N. Smith, ed. and trans. London: Wishart.

Grasmuck, S., and P. Pessar. 1991. *Between Two Islands: Dominican
International Migration.* Berkeley: University of California Press.

Gray, J. 1986. With a Few Exceptions, Television in Africa Fails to
Educate and Enlighten. *Ann Arbor News,* December 8.

Greaves, T. C. 1995. Problems Facing Anthropologists: Cultural Rights
and Ethnography. *General Anthropology* 1(2):1, 3–6.

Green, E. C. 1992 (orig. 1987). The Integration of Modern and Tra-
ditional Health Sectors in Swaziland. In *Applying Anthropology,*
A. Podolefsky and P. J. Brown, eds., pp. 246–251. Mountain View,
CA: Mayfield.

Greenwood, D. J. 1976. *Unrewarding Wealth: The Commercialization
and Collapse of Agriculture in a Spanish Basque Town.* Cambridge:
Cambridge University Press.

Grekova, M. 2001. Postsocialist Societies. *International Encyclopedia
of the Social & Behavioral Sciences,* pp. 11877–11881. New York:
Elsevier.

Griffin, P. B., and A. Estioko-Griffin, eds. 1985. *The Agta of Northern
Luzon: Recent Studies.* Cebu City, Philippines: University of San
Carlos.

Gudeman, S., ed. 1999. *Economic Anthropology.* Northhampton, MA:
E. Elgar.

Gumperz, J. J., and S. C. Levinson, eds. 1996. *Rethinking Linguistic
Relativity.* New York: Cambridge University Press.

Gupta, A., and J. Ferguson. 1997a. Culture, Power, Place: Ethnography
at the End of an Era. In *Culture, Power, Place: Explorations in
Critical Anthropology,* A. Gupta and J. Ferguson, eds., pp. 1–29.
Durham, NC: Duke University Press.

———. 1997b. Beyond "Culture": Space, Identity, and the Politics
of Difference. In *Culture, Power, Place: Explorations in Critical*

Anthropology, A. Gupta and J. Ferguson, eds., pp. 33–51. Durham, NC: Duke University Press.

Gupta, A., and J. Ferguson, eds. 1997c. *Anthropological Locations: Boundaries and Grounds of a Field Science.* Berkeley: University of California Press.

———. 1997d. *Culture, Power, Place: Explorations in Critical Anthropology.* Durham, NC: Duke University Press.

Guyot, J., and C. Hughes. 2007. Researchers Find Earliest Evidence for Modern Human Behavior. *Arizona State University Research Magazine.* http://researchmag.asu.edu/2008/02researchers_find _earliest_evid.html.

Hall, Edward T. 1990 (orig. 1966). *The Hidden Dimension.* New York: Anchor.

Hallowell, A. I. 1955. *Culture and Experience.* Philadelphia: University of Pennsylvania Press.

Hansen, K. V. 2004. *Not-So-Nuclear Families: Class, Gender, and Networks of Care.* New Brunswick, NJ: Rutgers University Press.

Hansen, K. V., and A. I. Garey, eds. 1998. *Families in the U.S.: Kinship and Domestic Politics.* Philadelphia: Temple University Press.

Harding, S. 1975. Women and Words in a Spanish Village. In *Toward an Anthropology of Women,* R. Reiter, ed., pp. 283–308. New York: Monthly Review Press.

Harper, J. 2002. *Endangered Species: Health, Illness, and Death among Madagascar's People of the Forest.* Durham, NC: Carolina Academic Press.

Harris, M. 1964. *Patterns of Race in the Americas.* New York: Walker.

———. 1970. Referential Ambiguity in the Calculus of Brazilian Racial Identity. *Southwestern Journal of Anthropology* 26(1):1–14.

———. 1974. *Cows, Pigs, Wars, and Witches: The Riddles of Culture.* New York: Random House.

———. 1978. *Cannibals and Kings.* New York: Vintage Books.

———. 2001 (orig. 1968). *The Rise of Anthropological Theory.* Walnut Creek, CA: AltaMira.

Harris, M., and C. P. Kottak. 1963. The Structural Significance of Brazilian Racial Categories. *Sociologia* 25:203–209.

Harrison, G. G., W. L. Rathje, and W. W. Hughes. 1994. Food Waste Behavior in an Urban Population. In *Applying Anthropology: An Introductory Reader,* 3rd ed., A. Podolefsky and P. J. Brown, eds., pp. 107–112. Mountain View, CA: Mayfield.

Harrison, K. D. 2007. *When Languages Die: The Extinction of the World's Languages and the Erosion of Human Knowledge.* New York: Oxford University Press.

Hart, C. W. M., A. R. Pilling, and J. C. Goodale. 1988. *The Tiwi of North Australia.* 3rd ed. Fort Worth, TX: Harcourt Brace.

Harvey, D. J. 1980. French Empire. *Academic American Encyclopedia,* Vol. 8, pp. 309–310. Princeton, NJ: Arete.

Hastings, A. 1997. *The Construction of Nationhood: Ethnicity, Religion, and Nationalism.* New York: Cambridge University Press.

Hawkes, K., J. O'Connell, and K. Hill. 1982. Why Hunters Gather: Optimal Foraging and the Aché of Eastern Paraguay. *American Ethnologist* 9:379–398.

Hedges, C. 1992. Sudan Presses Its Campaign to Impose Islamic Law on Non-Muslims. *New York Times,* June 1, p. A7.

Helman, C. 2001. *Culture, Health, and Illness: An Introduction for Health Professionals.* 4th ed. Boston: Butterworth-Heinemann.

Henry, J. 1955. Docility, or Giving Teacher What She Wants. *Journal of Social Issues* 2:33–41.

Herdt, G. H. 1981. *Guardians of the Flutes.* New York: McGraw-Hill.

Herdt, G. H., ed. 1984. *Ritualized Homosexuality in Melanesia.* Berkeley: University of California Press.

Hill, J. H. 1978. Apes and Language. *Annual Review of Anthropology* 7:89–112.

Hill, K., H. Kaplan, K. Hawkes, and A. Hurtado. 1987. Foraging Decisions among Aché Hunter-gatherers: New Data and Implications for Optimal Foraging Models. *Ethology and Sociobiology* 8:1–36.

Hill-Burnett, J. 1978. Developing Anthropological Knowledge through Application. In *Applied Anthropology in America,* E. M. Eddy and W. L. Partridge, eds., pp. 112–128. New York: Columbia University Press.

Hobhouse, L. T. 1915. *Morals in Evolution.* Rev. ed. New York: Holt.

Hoebel, E. A. 1954. *The Law of Primitive Man.* Cambridge, MA: Harvard University Press.

———. 1968 (orig. 1954). The Eskimo: Rudimentary Law in a Primitive Anarchy. In *Studies in Social and Cultural Anthropology,* J. Middleton, ed., pp. 93–127. New York: Crowell.

Hoenisch, Steve. 2004. Identifying and Resolving Ambiguity. http:// www.criticism.com/linguistics/types-of-ambiguity.php.

Hoge, W. 2001. Kautokeino Journal; Reindeer Herders, at Home on a (Very Cold) Range. *New York Times,* March 26, late ed.—final, sec. A, p. 4.

Holden, A. 2005. *Tourism Studies and the Social Sciences.* New York: Routledge.

Hopkins, T., and I. Wallerstein. 1982. Patterns of Development of the Modern World System. In *World System Analysis: Theory and Methodology,* by T. Hopkins, I. Wallerstein, R. Bach, C. Chase-Dunn, and R. Mukherjee, eds., pp. 121–141. Thousand Oaks, CA: Sage.

Hornborg, A., J. R. McNeill, and J. Martinez-Alier. 2007. *Rethinking Environmental History: World-System History and Global Environmental Change.* Lanham, MD: AltaMira.

Hornborg, A., and C. L. Crumley, eds. 2007. *The World System and the Earth System: Global Socioenvironmental Change and Sustainability since the Neolithic.* Walnut Creek, CA: Left Coast Press.

Hunt, R. C. 2007. *Beyond Relativism: Comparability in Cultural Anthropology.* Lanham, MD: AltaMira.

Hunter, M. L. 2005. *Race, Gender, and the Politics of Skin Tone.* New York: Routledge.

Hurtado, A. M., C. A. Lambourne, P. James, K. Hill, K. Cheman, and K. Baca. 2005. Human Rights, Biomedical Science, and Infectious Diseases among South American Indigenous Groups. *Annual Review of Anthropology* 34:639–665.

Inda, J. X., and R. Rosaldo, eds. 2008. *The Anthropology of Globalization: A Reader.* Malden, MA: Blackwell.

Ingraham, C. 2008. *White Weddings: Romancing Heterosexuality in Popular Culture.* 2nd ed. New York: Routledge.

Inhorn, M. C., and P. J. Brown. 1990. The Anthropology of Infectious Disease. *Annual Review of Anthropology* 19:89–117.

International Labor Rights Forum. 2009. About ILRF. http://www .laborrights.org/about-ilrf.

Iqbal, S. 2002. A New Light on Skin Color. *National Geographic Online Extra.* http://magma.nationalgeographic.com/ngm/0211/ feature2/online_extra.html.

Jablonski, N. G., and G. Chaplin. 2000. The Evolution of Human Skin Coloration. *Journal of Human Evolution* (39):57–106.

Jackson, J., and K. B. Warren. 2005. Indigenous Movements in Latin America, 1992–2004: Controversies, Ironies, New Directions. *Annual Review of Anthropology* 34:549–573.

Jayson, Sharon. 2009. Federally Funded Ad Campaign Holds Up Value of Marriage. *USA Today,* Feb. 17. http://www.usatoday.com.

Jenks, C. 2003. *Culture.* 2nd ed. New York: Routledge.

Johansen, B. E. 2003. *Indigenous Peoples and Environmental Issues: An Encyclopedia.* Westport, CT: Greenwood.

Johnson, A. W. 1978. *Quantification in Cultural Anthropology: An Introduction to Research Design.* Stanford, CA: Stanford University Press.

Johnson, A. W., and T. K. Earle. 2000. *The Evolution of Human Societies: From Foraging Group to Agrarian State.* 2nd ed. Stanford, CA: Stanford University Press.

Johnston, B. R. 2009. *Life and Death Matters: Human Rights, Environment, and Social Justice.* 2nd ed. Walnut Creek, CA: Left Coast Press.

Jones, D. 1999. Hot Asset in Corporate: Anthropology Degrees. *USA Today,* February 18, p. B1.

Joralemon, D. 2006. *Exploring Medical Anthropology.* 2nd ed. Boston: Pearson.

Jordan, A. 2003. *Business Anthropology.* Prospect Heights, IL: Waveland.

Kan, S. 1986. The 19th-Century Tlingit Potlatch: A New Perspective. *American Ethnologist* 13:191–212.

———. 1989. *Symbolic Immortality: The Tlingit Potlatch of the Nineteenth Century.* Washington, DC: Smithsonian Institution Press.

Kantor, P. 1996. Domestic Violence against Women: A Global Issue. http://metalab.unc.edu/ucis/pubs/Carolina_Papers/Abuse/figure1.html.

Kaufman, S. R., and L. M. Morgan. 2005. The Anthropology of the Beginnings and Ends of Life. *Annual Review of Anthropology* 34:317–341.

Kearney, M. 1996. *Reconceptualizing the Peasantry: Anthropology in Global Perspective.* Boulder, CO: Westview Press.

———. 2004. *Changing Fields of Anthropology: From Local to Global.* Lanham, MD: Rowman & Littlefield.

Kelly, R. C. 1976. Witchcraft and Sexual Relations: An Exploration in the Social and Semantic Implications of the Structure of Belief. In *Man and Woman in the New Guinea Highlands,* P. Brown and G. Buchbinder, eds., pp. 36–53. Special Publication no. 8. Washington, DC: American Anthropological Association.

Kelly, R. L. 1995. *The Foraging Spectrum: Diversity in Hunter-Gatherer Lifeways.* Washington, DC: Smithsonian Institution Press.

Kent, S. 1992. The Current Forager Controversy: Real versus Ideal Views of Hunter-gatherers. *Man* 27:45–70.

———. 1996. *Cultural Diversity among Twentieth-Century Foragers: An African Perspective.* New York: Cambridge University Press.

Kent, S., and H. Vierich. 1989. The Myth of Ecological Determinism: Anticipated Mobility and Site Organization of Space. In *Farmers as Hunters: The Implications of Sedentism,* S. Kent, ed., pp. 96–130. New York: Cambridge University Press.

Keppel, K. G., J. N. Pearch, and D. K. Wagener. 2002. Trends in Racial and Ethnic-Specific Rates for the Health Status Indicators: United States, 1990–98. *Healthy People Statistical Notes* No. 23. Hyattsville, MD: National Center for Health Statistics.

Kerbo, H. R. 2006. World Poverty: *Global Inequality and the Modern World System.* Boston: McGraw-Hill.

Keynes, J. M. 1927. *The End of Laissez-Faire.* London: L and Virginia Woolf.

———. 1936. *General Theory of Employment, Interest, and Money.* New York: Harcourt Brace.

Kimmel, M. S. 2007. *The Gendered Society.* 3rd ed. New York: Oxford University Press.

Kimmel, M. S., and M. A. Messner, eds. 2007. *Men's Lives.* 7th ed. Boston: Pearson.

Kimmel, M. S., and R. Plante. 2004. *Sexualities: Identities, Behaviors, and Society.* New York: Oxford University Press.

Kimmel, M. S., J. Hearn, and R. W. Connell. 2004. *Handbook of Studies on Men and Masculinities.* Thousand Oaks, CA: Sage.

Kinsey, A. C., W. B. Pomeroy, and C. E. Martin. 1948. *Sexual Behavior in the Human Male.* Philadelphia: W. B. Saunders.

Klass, M. 2003. *Mind over Mind: The Anthropology and Psychology of Spirit Possession.* Lanham, MA: Rowman & Littlefield.

Klein, R. G., with B. Edgar. 2002. *The Dawn of Human Culture.* New York: Wiley.

Kleinfeld, J. 1975. Positive Stereotyping: The Cultural Relativist in the Classroom. *Human Organization* 34:269–274.

Kluckhohn, C. 1944. *Mirror for Man: A Survey of Human Behavior and Social Attitudes.* Greenwich, CT: Fawcett.

Kottak, C. P. 1980. *The Past in the Present: History, Ecology, and Social Organization in Highland Madagascar.* Ann Arbor: University of Michigan Press.

———. 1990a. Culture and "Economic Development." *American Anthropologist* 93(3):723–731.

———. 1990b. *Prime-Time Society: An Anthropological Analysis of Television and Culture.* Belmont, CA: Wadsworth.

———. 1991. When People Don't Come First: Some Lessons from Completed Projects. In *Putting People First: Sociological Variables in Rural Development,* 2nd ed., M. Cernea, ed., pp. 429–464. New York: Oxford University Press.

———. 2004. An Anthropological Take on Sustainable Development: A Comparative Study of Change. *Human Organization* 63(4): 501–510.

———. 2006. *Assault on Paradise: The Globalization of a Little Community in Brazil.* 4th ed. New York: McGraw-Hill.

———. 2007. Return to Madagascar: A Forty Year Retrospective. *General Anthropology: Bulletin of the General Anthropology Division of the American Anthropological Association* 14(2):1–10.

Kottak, C. P., and K. A. Kozaitis. 2008. *On Being Different: Diversity and Multiculturalism in the North American Mainstream.* 3rd ed. Boston: McGraw-Hill.

Kottak, N. C. 2002. *Stealing the Neighbor's Chicken: Social Control in Northern Mozambique.* Ph.D. dissertation. Department of Anthropology, Emory University, Atlanta, GA.

Kreider, R. M., and J. M. Fields. 2002. Number, Timing and Duration of Marriages and Divorces: 1996. U.S. Census Bureau. *Current Population Reports,* P70–80, February. http://www.census.gov/prod/2002pubs/p70–80.pdf.

Kuhn, S. L., M. C. Stiner, and D. S. Reese. 2001. Ornaments of the Earliest Upper Paleolithic: New Insights from the Levant. *Proceedings of the National Academy of Sciences of the United States of America* 98(13):7641–7646.

Kulick, D. 1998. *Travesti: Sex, Gender, and Culture among Brazilian Transgendered Prostitutes.* Chicago: University of Chicago Press.

Kuper, L. 2006. *Race, Class, and Power: Ideology and Revolutionary Change in Plural Societies.* New Brunswick, NJ: Transaction Publishers.

Kurtz, D. V. 2001. *Political Anthropology: Power and Paradigms.* Boulder, CO: Westview Press.

Kutsche, P. 1998. *Field Ethnography: A Manual for Doing Cultural Anthropology.* Upper Saddle River, NJ: Prentice Hall.

Labov, W. 1972a. *Language in the Inner City: Studies in the Black English Vernacular.* Philadelphia: University of Pennsylvania Press.

———. 1972b. *Sociolinguistic Patterns.* Philadelphia: University of Pennsylvania Press.

La Fraugh, R. J. n.d. Euskara: The History, a True Mystery. The La Fraugh Name History. http://planetrjl.tripod.com/LaFraughName/id5.html.

Laguerre, M. 1984. *American Odyssey: Haitians in New York.* Ithaca, NY: Cornell University Press.

———. 1998. *Diasporic Citizenship: Haitian Americans in Transnational America.* New York: St. Martin's Press.

———. 1999. *The Global Ethnopolis: Chinatown, Japantown, and Manilatown in American Society.* New York: St. Martin's Press.

———. 2001. *Urban Multiculturalism and Globalization in New York City.* New York: Palgrave Macmillan.

Laird, S. A. 2002. *Biodiversity and Traditional Knowledge: Equitable Partnerships in Practice.* Sterling, VA: Earthscan.

Lakoff, R. T. 2000. *The Language War.* Berkeley: University of California Press.

———. 2004. *Language and Woman's Place.* Rev. ed. New York: Oxford University Press.

Lambek, M. 2008. *A Reader in the Anthropology of Religion.* Malden, MA: Blackwell.

Lancaster, R. N., and M. Di Leonardo, eds. 1997. *The Gender/Sexuality Reader: Culture, History, Political Economy.* New York: Routledge.

Lance, L. M., and E. E. Mckenna. 1975. Analysis of Cases Pertaining to the Impact of Western Technology on the Non-Western World. *Human Organization* 34:87–94.

Larson, A. 1989. Social Context of Human Immunodeficiency Virus Transmission in Africa: Historical and Cultural Bases of East and Central African Sexual Relations. *Review of Infectious Diseases* 11:716–731.

Lassiter, L. E. 1998. *The Power of Kiowa Song: A Collaborative Ethnography.* Tucson: University of Arizona Press.

Leach, E. R. 1955. Polyandry, Inheritance and the Definition of Marriage. *Man* 55:182–186.

———. 1961. *Rethinking Anthropology.* London: Athlone Press.

Lee, R. B. 1979. *The !Kung San: Men, Women, and Work in a Foraging Society.* New York: Cambridge University Press.

———. 1984. *The Dobe !Kung.* New York: Harcourt Brace.

———. 1993. *The Dobe Ju/'hoansi.* 2nd ed. Fort Worth, TX: Harcourt Brace.

———. 2003. *The Dobe Ju/'hoansi.* 3rd ed. Belmont, CA: Wadsworth.

Lee, R. B., and R. H. Daly. 1999. *The Cambridge Encyclopedia of Hunters and Gatherers.* New York: Cambridge University Press.

Lehmann, A. C., J. E. Meyers, and P. A. Moro, eds. 2005. *Magic, Witchcraft, and Religion: An Anthropological Study of the Supernatural.* 6th ed. Boston: McGraw-Hill.

Leman, J. 2001. *The Dynamics of Emerging Ethnicities: Immigrant and Indigenous Ethnogenesis in Confrontation.* New York: Peter Lang.

Lenski, G. 1966. *Power and Privilege: A Theory of Social Stratification.* New York: McGraw-Hill.

Levine, N. E. 2008. Alternative Kinship, Marriage, and Reproduction. *Annual Review of Anthropology* 37:17–35.

Lèvi-Strauss, C. 1963. *Totemism.* R. Needham (trans.). Boston: Beacon Press.

———. 1967. *Structural Anthropology.* New York: Doubleday.

Levy, J. E., with B. Pepper. 1992. *Orayvi Revisited: Social Stratification in an "Egalitarian" Society.* Santa Fe, NM: School of American Research Press, and Seattle: University of Washington Press.

Lewellen, T. C. 2003. *Political Anthropology: An Introduction.* 3rd ed. Westport, CT: Praeger.

Lewis, M. Paul, ed. 2009. *Ethnologue: Languages of the World.* 16th ed. Dallas: SIL International.

Lewis, P. 1992. U.N. Sees a Crisis in Overpopulation. *New York Times,* p. A6.

Lie, J. 2001. *Multiethnic Japan.* Cambridge, MA: Harvard University Press.

Lieban, R. W. 1977. The Field of Medical Anthropology. In *Culture, Disease, and Healing: Studies in Medical Anthropology,* D. Landy, ed., pp. 13–31. New York: Macmillan.

Lindenbaum, S. 1972. Sorcerers, Ghosts, and Polluting Women: An Analysis of Religious Belief and Population Control. *Ethnology* 11:241–253.

Linton, R. 1943. Nativistic Movements. *American Anthropologist* 45:230–240.

Little, K. 1965. *West African Urbanization: A Study of Voluntary Associations in Social Change.* Cambridge: Cambridge University Press.

———. 1971. *Some Aspects of African Urbanization South of the Sahara.* Reading, MA: Addison-Wesley, McCaleb Modules in Anthropology.

Lockwood, W. G. 1975. *European Moslems: Economy and Ethnicity in Western Bosnia.* New York: Academic Press.

Lohr, S. 2005. Cutting Here, but Hiring Over There. *New York Times,* June 24. http://www.nytimes.com.

Lowie, R. H. 1961 (orig. 1920). *Primitive Society.* New York: Harper & Brothers.

Lucentini, J. 2002. Bones Reveal Some Truth in "Noble Savage Myth." *Washington Post,* April 15, p. A09.

Lugaila, T. 1999. Married Adults Still in the Majority, Census Bureau Reports. http://www.census.gov/Press-Release/www/1999/cb99 –03.html.

Madra, Y. M. 2004. Karl Polanyi: Freedom in a Complex Society. *Econ-Atrocity Bulletin: In the History of Thought.* http://www .fguide.org/Bulletin/polanyi.htm.

Malinowski, B. 1929. Practical Anthropology. *Africa* 2:23–38.

———. 1961 (orig. 1922). *Argonauts of the Western Pacific.* New York: Dutton.

———. 1978 (orig. 1931). The Role of Magic and Religion. In *Reader in Comparative Religion: An Anthropological Approach,* 4th ed., W. A. Lessa and E. Z. Vogt, eds., pp. 37–46. New York: Harper and Row.

Malkki, Liisa H. 1995. *Purity and Exile: Violence, Memory, and National Cosmology among Hutu Refugees in Tanzania.* Chicago: University of Chicago Press.

Maquet, J. 1964. Objectivity in Anthropology. *Current Anthropology* 5:47–55.

Mar, M. E. 1997. Secondary Colors: The Multiracial Option. *Harvard Magazine,* May–June, pp. 19–20.

Marcus, G. E., and D. Cushman. 1982. Ethnographies as Texts. *Annual Review of Anthropology* 11:25–69.

Marcus, G. E., and M. M. J. Fischer. 1986. *Anthropology as Cultural Critique: An Experimental Moment in the Human Sciences.* Chicago: University of Chicago Press.

———. 1999. *Anthropology as Cultural Critique: An Experimental Moment in the Human Sciences.* 2nd ed. Chicago: University of Chicago Press.

Marcus, G. E., and F. R. Myers, eds. 1995. *The Traffic in Culture: Refiguring Art and Anthropology.* Berkeley: University of California Press.

Margolis, M. L. 1984. *Mothers and Such: American Views of Women and How They Changed.* Berkeley: University of California Press.

———. 2000. *True to Her Nature: Changing Advice to American Women.* Prospect Heights, IL: Waveland.

———. 2003. The Relative Status of Men and Women. In *Encyclopedia of Sex and Gender: Men and Women in the World's Cultures,* C. Ember and M. Ember, eds., pp. 137–145. New York: Kluwer Academic/Plenum.

Martin, E. 1992. The End of the Body? *American Ethnologist* 19:121–140.

Martin, K., and B. Voorhies. 1975. *Female of the Species.* New York: Columbia University Press.

Martin, Steven P. 2005. Growing Evidence for a "Divorce Divide"? Education and Marital Dissolution Rates in the U.S. Since the 1970s. *Russell Sage Foundation Working Papers.*

Martinez, E., and A. Garcia. 2000. What Is "Neo-Liberalism"? A Brief Definition. http://www. globalexchange.org/campaigns/econ101/ neoliberalDefined.html.pdf.

Marx, K., and F. Engels. 1976 (orig. 1948). *Communist Manifesto.* New York: Pantheon.

Mascia-Lees, F., and N. J. Black. 2000. *Gender and Anthropology.* Prospect Heights, IL: Waveland.

Mathews, G. 2000. *Global Culture/Individual Identity: Searching for Home in the Cultural Supermarket.* New York: Routledge.

Maugh, T. H., III. 2007. One Language Disappears Every 14 Days; about Half of the World's Distinct Tongues Could Vanish This Century, Researchers Say. *Los Angeles Times,* September 19.

Maybury-Lewis, D. 2002. *Indigenous Peoples, Ethnic Groups, and the State.* 2nd ed. Boston: Allyn & Bacon.

Mayell, H. 2004. Is Bead Find Proof Modern Thought Began in Africa? *National Geographic News,* March 31. http://news .nationalgeographic.com/news/2004/03/0331_040331_ostrichman .html.

McBrearty, S., and A. S. Brooks. 2000. The Revolution That Wasn't: A New Interpretation of the Origin of Modern Human Behavior. *Journal of Human Evolution* 39:453–563.

McElroy, A., and P. K. Townsend. 2003. *Medical Anthropology in Ecological Perspective.* 4th ed. Boulder, CO: Westview Press.

McKinnon, S. 2005. On Kinship and Marriage: A Critique of the Genetic and Gender Calculus of Evolutionary Psychology. In *Complexities: Beyond Nature and Nurture,* S. McKinnon and S. Silverman, eds., pp. 106–131. Chicago: The University of Chicago Press.

Meigs, A., and K. Barlow. 2002. Beyond the Taboo: Imagining Incest. *American Anthropologist* 104(1):38–49.

Merry, S. E. 2006. Anthropology and International Law. *Annual Review of Anthropology* 35:99–116.

Michaels, E. 1986. Aboriginal Content. Paper presented at the meeting of the Australian Screen Studies Association, December, Sydney.

Miles, H. L. 1983. Apes and Language: The Search for Communicative Competence. In *Language in Primates,* J. de Luce and H. T. Wilder, eds., pp. 43–62. New York: Springer Verlag.

Miller, B. D. 1997. *The Endangered Sex: Neglect of Female Children in Rural North India.* New York: Oxford University Press.

Miller, J. n.d. Alaskan Tlingit and Tsimtsian. Seattle: University of Washington Libraries, Digital Collections. http://content.lib .washington.edu/aipnw/miller1.html.

Miller, N., and R. C. Rockwell, eds. 1988. *AIDS in Africa: The Social and Policy Impact.* Lewiston, NY: Edwin Mellen.

Mintz, S. 1985. *Sweetness and Power: The Place of Sugar in Modern History.* New York: Viking Penguin.

Mitchell, J. C. 1966. Theoretical Orientations in African Urban Studies. In *The Social Anthropology of Complex Societies,* M. Banton, ed., pp. 37–68. London: Tavistock.

Moerman, M. 1965. Ethnic Identification in a Complex Civilization: Who Are the Lue? *American Anthropologist* 67(5, Part I):1215–1230.

Montagu, A., ed. 1997. *Man's Most Dangerous Myth: The Fallacy of Race.* Walnut Creek, CA: AltaMira.

Morgen, S., ed. 1989. *Gender and Anthropology: Critical Reviews for Research and Teaching.* Washington, DC: American Anthropological Association.

Motseta, S. 2006. Botswana Gives Bushmen Tough Conditions. *Tulsa World,* December 14.

Mukhopadhyay, C., and P. Higgins. 1988. Anthropological Studies of Women's Status Revisited: 1977–1987. *Annual Review of Anthropology* 17:461–495.

Mukhopadhyay, C., R. Henze, and Y. T. Moses. 2007. *How Real Is Race? A Sourcebook on Race, Culture, and Biology.* Lanham, MD: AltaMira.

Mullings, L., ed. 1987. *Cities of the United States: Studies in Urban Anthropology.* New York: Columbia University Press.

Murdock, G. P. 1934. *Our Primitive Contemporaries.* New York: Macmillan.

———. 1949. *Social Structure.* New York: Macmillan.

———. 1957. World Ethnographic Sample. *American Anthropologist* 59:664–687.

Murdock, G. P., and C. Provost. 1973. Factors in the Division of Labor by Sex: A Cross-Cultural Analysis. *Ethnology* XII(2):203–225.

Murphy, R. F., and L. Kasdan. 1959. The Structure of Parallel Cousin Marriage. *American Anthropologist* 61:17–29.

Murray, S. O., and W. Roscoe, eds. 1998. *Boy-wives and Female Husbands: Studies in African Homosexualities.* New York: St. Martin's Press.

Mydans, S. 1992a. Criticism Grows over Aliens Seized during Riots. *New York Times,* May 29, p. A8.

———. 1992b. Judge Dismisses Case in Shooting by Officer. *New York Times,* June 4, p. A8.

Nagel, J. 1996. *American Indian Ethnic Renewal: Red Power and the Resurgence of Identity and Culture.* New York: Oxford University Press.

Nanda, S. 2000. *Gender Diversity: Crosscultural Variations.* Prospect Heights, IL: Waveland.

National Academies. 2007. Understanding and Responding to Climate Change: Highlights of National Academies Reports. http://dels.nas .edu/basc/Climate-HIGH.pdf.

Naylor, L. L. 1996. *Culture and Change: An Introduction.* Westport, CT: Bergin and Garvey.

Nazarea, V. D. 2006. Local Knowledge and Memory in Biodiversity Conservation. *Annual Review of Anthropology* 35:317–335.

Newman, M. 1992. Riots Bring Attention to Growing Hispanic Presence in South-Central Area. *New York Times,* May 11, p. A10.

Nielsson, G. P. 1985. States and Nation-Groups: A Global Taxonomy. In *New Nationalisms of the Developed World,* E.A. Tiryakian and R. Rogowski, eds., pp. 27–56. Boston: Allen and Unwin.

Nolan, R. W. 2002. *Development Anthropology: Encounters in the Real World.* Boulder, CO: Westview Press.

———. 2003. *Anthropology in Practice.* Boulder, CO: Lynne Rienner.

Nordstrom, C. 2004. *Shadows of War: Violence, Power, and International Profiteering in the Twenty-First Century.* Berkeley: University of California Press.

Nugent, D., and J. Vincent, eds. 2004. *A Companion to the Anthropology of Politics.* Malden, MA: Blackwell.

Ohlemacher, S. 2006. 2006: The Year of the 300M Mark: Face of America Changes as Country Grows. *Charleston Post and Courier,* June 26, pp. 1A, 11A.

O'Leary, C. 2002. *Class Formation, Diet and Economic Transformation in Two Brazilian Fishing Communities.* Unpublished Ph.D. dissertation, University of Michigan, Ann Arbor.

Omohundro, J. T. 2001. *Careers in Anthropology.* 2nd ed. Boston: McGraw-Hill.

Ong, A. 1987. *Spirits of Resistance and Capitalist Discipline: Factory Women in Malaysia.* Albany: State University of New York Press.

———. 1989. Center, Periphery, and Hierarchy: Gender in Southeast Asia. In *Gender and Anthropology: Critical Reviews for Research and Teaching,* S. Morgen, ed., pp. 294–312. Washington, DC: American Anthropological Association.

Ong, A., and S. J. Collier, eds. 2005. *Global Assemblages: Technology, Politics, and Ethics as Anthropological Problems.* Malden, MA: Blackwell.

Ontario Consultants on Religious Tolerance. 1996. Religious Access Dispute Resolved. Internet Mailing List, April 12, http://www .religious tolerance.org/news_694.htm.

———. 2001. Religions of the World: Number of Adherents; Rates of Growth. http://www.religioustolerance.org/worldrel.htm.

Ortner, S. B. 1984. Theory in Anthropology Since the Sixties. *Comparative Studies in Society and History* 126(1):126–166.

Ott, S. 1981. *The Circle of Mountains: A Basque Shepherding Community.* Oxford: Clarendon Press.

Parkin, R., and L. Stone, eds. 2004. *Kinship and Family: An Anthropological Reader.* Malden, MA: Blackwell.

Patterson, F. 1978. Conversations with a Gorilla. *National Geographic,* October, pp. 438–465.

Paulson, T. E. 2005. Chimp, Human DNA Comparison Finds Vast Similarities, Key Differences. *Seattle Post-Intelligencer Reporter,* September 1. http:// seattlepi.nwsource.com/local/238852 _chimp01.html.

Peletz, M. 1988. *A Share of the Harvest: Kinship, Property, and Social History among the Malays of Rembau.* Berkeley: University of California Press.

Pelto, P. 1973. *The Snowmobile Revolution: Technology and Social Change in the Arctic.* Menlo Park, CA: Cummings.

Peplau, L. A., ed. 1999. *Gender, Culture, and Ethnicity: Current Research about Women and Men.* Mountain View, CA: Mayfield.

Peters, J. D. 1997. Seeing Bifocally: Media, Place, Culture. In *Culture, Power, Place: Explorations in Critical Anthropology,* A. Gupta and J. Ferguson, eds., pp. 75–92. Durham, NC: Duke University Press.

Peters-Golden, H. 2006. *Culture Sketches: Case Studies in Anthropology.* 4th ed. New York: McGraw-Hill.

Petraglia-Bahri, D. 1996. Introduction to Postcolonial Studies. http:// www.emory.edu/ENGLISH/Bahri/.

Piddington, R. 1960. Action Anthropology. *Journal of the Polynesian Society* 69:199–213.

Piddocke, S. 1969. The Potlatch System of the Southern Kwakiutl: A New Perspective. In *Environment and Cultural Behavior,* A. P. Vayda, ed., pp. 130–156. Garden City, NY: Natural History Press.

Plattner, S., ed. 1989. *Economic Anthropology.* Stanford, CA: Stanford University Press.

Podolefsky, A., and P. J. Brown, eds. 1992. *Applying Anthropology: An Introductory Reader.* 2nd ed. Mountain View, CA: Mayfield.

Polanyi, K. 1968. *Primitive, Archaic and Modern Economies: Essays of Karl Polanyi,* G. Dalton, ed., Garden City, NY: Anchor Books.

Pospisil, L. 1963. *The Kapauku Papuans of West New Guinea.* New York: Holt, Rinehart & Winston.

Potash, B., ed. 1986. *Widows in African Societies: Choices and Constraints.* Stanford, CA: Stanford University Press.

Price, R., ed. 1973. *Maroon Societies.* New York: Anchor Press/ Doubleday.

Race, Ethnicity, and Genetics Working Group. 2005. The Use of Racial, Ethnic, and Ancestral Categories in Human Genetics Research. *American Journal of Human Genetics* 77(4):519–532.

Radcliffe-Brown, A. R. 1965 (orig. 1962). *Structure and Function in Primitive Society.* New York: Free Press.

Ramirez, R. R., and G. P. de la Cruz. 2003. The Hispanic Population in the United States. U.S. Census Bureau. *Current Population Reports,* P20–545, March. http://www.census.gov/prod/2003pubs/p20–545.pdf.

Ranger, T. O. 1996. Postscript. In *Postcolonial Identities,* R. Werbner and T. O. Ranger, eds. London: Zed.

Rappaport, R. A. 1974. Obvious Aspects of Ritual. *Cambridge Anthropology* 2:2–60.

———. 1999. *Holiness and Humanity: Ritual in the Making of Religious Life.* New York: Cambridge University Press.

Rathje, W. L., and C. Murphy. 2001. *Rubbish!: The Archaeology of Garbage.* Tucson: University of Arizona Press.

Rathus, S. A., J. S. Nevid, and J. Fichner-Rathus. 2008. *Human Sexuality in a World of Diversity.* 7th ed. Boston: Allyn & Bacon.

Redfield, R. 1941. *The Folk Culture of Yucatan.* Chicago: University of Chicago Press.

Redfield, R., R. Linton, and M. Herskovits. 1936. Memorandum on the Study of Acculturation. *American Anthropologist* 38:149–152.

Reese, W. L. 1999. *Dictionary of Philosophy and Religion: Eastern and Western Thought.* Amherst, NY: Humanities Books.

Reiter, R. 1975. Men and Women in the South of France: Public and Private Domains. In *Toward an Anthropology of Women,* R. Reiter, ed., pp. 252–282. New York: Monthly Review Press.

Rickford, J. R. 1997. Suite for Ebony and Phonics, Discover, December. http://www.stanford.edu/~rickford/papers/SuiteForEbonyAndPhonics.html.

———. 1999. *African American Vernacular English: Features, Evolution, Educational Implications.* Malden, MA: Blackwell.

Rickford, J. R., and R. J. Rickford. 2000. *Spoken Soul: The Story of Black English.* New York: Wiley.

Roberts, S. 2010. More Men Marrying Wealthier Women. *New York Times,* January 18. http://www.nytimes.com.

Roberts, S., A. Sabar, B. Goodman, and M. Balleza. 2007. 51% of Women Are Now Living without Spouse. *New York Times,* January 16. http://www.nytimes.com.

Robertson, A. F. 1995. *The Big Catch: A Practical Introduction to Development.* Boulder, CO: Westview Press.

Robertson, J. 1992. *Koreans in Japan.* Paper presented at the University of Michigan Department of Anthropology, Martin Luther King Jr. Day Panel, January. Ann Arbor: University of Michigan Department of Anthropology (unpublished).

Rodseth, L., R. W. Wrangham, A. M. Harrigan, and B. Smuts. 1991. The Human Community as a Primate Society. *Current Anthropology* 32:221–254.

Rogers, S. More Criticism for Ethanol: Now it's Affecting Food Prices. *Earth First.* http://earthfirst.com.

Romaine, S. 1999. *Communicating Gender.* Mahwah, NJ: Erlbaum.

———. 2000. *Language in Society: An Introduction to Sociolinguistics.* 2nd ed. New York: Oxford University Press.

Root, D. 1996. *Cannibal Culture: Art, Appropriation, and the Commodification of Difference.* Boulder, CO: Westview Press.

Rosaldo, M. Z. 1980a. *Knowledge and Passion: Notions of Self and Social Life.* Stanford, CA: Stanford University Press.

———. 1980b. The Use and Abuse of Anthropology: Reflections on Feminism and Cross-Cultural Understanding. *Signs* 5(3):389–417.

Rouse, R. 1991. Mexican Migration and the Social Space of Postmodernism. *Diaspora* 1(1):8–23.

Royal Anthropological Institute. 1951. *Notes and Queries on Anthropology.* 6th ed. London: Routledge and Kegan Paul.

Ryan, Barbara E., Tom Colthurst, and Lance Segars. 2009. *College Alcohol Risk Assessment Guide: Environmental Approaches to Prevention.* A publication of the Higher Education Center for Alcohol and Other Drug Abuse and Violence Prevention Funded by the U.S. Department of Education. http://www.higheredcenter.org/files/product/cara.txt.

Ryan, S. 1990. *Ethnic Conflict and International Relations.* Brookfield, MA: Dartmouth.

Sahlins, M. D. 1968. *Tribesmen.* Englewood Cliffs, NJ: Prentice Hall.

———. 2004. *Stone Age Economics.* New York: Routledge.

Salzman, P. C. 1974. Political Organization among Nomadic Peoples. In *Man in Adaptation: The Cultural Present,* 2nd ed., Y. A. Cohen, ed., pp. 267–284. Chicago: Aldine.

———. 2004. *Pastoralists: Equality, Hierarchy, and the State.* Boulder, CO: Westview Press.

Salzmann, Z. 2007. *Language, Culture, and Society: An Introduction to Linguistic Anthropology.* 4th ed. Boulder, CO: Westview.

Sanday, P. R. 1974. Female Status in the Public Domain. In *Woman, Culture, and Society,* M. Z. Rosaldo and L. Lamphere, eds., pp. 189–206. Stanford, CA: Stanford University Press.

———. 2002. *Women at the Center: Life in a Modern Matriarchy.* Ithaca, NY: Cornell University Press.

Sapir, E. 1931. Conceptual Categories in Primitive Languages. *Science* 74:578–584.

Savage-Rumbaugh, E. Sue, Jeannine Murphy, Rose A. Sevcik, Karen E. Brakke, Shelly L. Williams, Duane M. Rumbaugh and Elizabeth Bates. 1993. Language Comprehension in Ape and Child. *Monographs of the Society for Research in Child Development* 58(3/4):i, iii, v–vi, 1–252.

Scheidel, W. 1997. Brother-Sister Marriage in Roman Egypt. *Journal of Biosocial Science* 29(3):361–371.

Scheinman, M. 1980. Imperialism. *Academic American Encyclopedia,* Vol. 11, pp. 61–62. Princeton, NJ: Arete.

Scheper-Hughes, Nancy. 1993. *Death Without Weeping: The Violence of Everyday Life in Brazil.* Berkeley: University of California Press.

Schneider, D. M. 1967. Kinship and Culture: Descent and Filiation as Cultural Constructs. *Southwestern Journal of Anthropology* 23:65–73.

Scholte, J. A. 2000. *Globalization: A Critical Introduction.* New York: St. Martin's Press.

Scott, J. C. 1985. *Weapons of the Weak.* New Haven, CT: Yale University Press.

———. 1990. *Domination and the Arts of Resistance.* New Haven, CT: Yale University Press.

Scudder, T., and E. Colson. 1980. *Secondary Education and the Formation of an Elite: The Impact of Education on Gwembe District, Zambia.* London: Academic Press.

Scupin, R. 2003. *Race and Ethnicity: An Anthropological Focus on the United States and the World.* Upper Saddle River, NJ: Prentice Hall.

Sebeok, T. A., and J. Umiker-Sebeok, eds. 1980. *Speaking of Apes: A Critical Anthropology of Two-Way Communication with Man.* New York: Plenum.

Service, E. R. 1962. *Primitive Social Organization: An Evolutionary Perspective.* New York: McGraw-Hill.

———. 1966. *The Hunters.* Englewood Cliffs, NJ: Prentice Hall.

Shanklin, E. 1995. *Anthropology and Race.* Belmont, CA: Wadsworth.

Shannon, T. R. 1996. *An Introduction to the World-System Perspective.* 2nd ed. Boulder, CO: Westview Press.

Sharma, A., and A. Gupta, eds. 2006. *The Anthropology of the State: A Reader.* Malden, MA: Blackwell.

Shivaram, C. 1996. Where Women Wore the Crown: Kerala's Dissolving Matriarchies Leave a Rich Legacy of Compassionate Family Culture. *Hinduism Today.* http://www.spiritweb.org/HinduismToday/96_02_Women_Wore_Crown.html.

Shostak, M. 1981. *Nisa: The Life and Words of a !Kung Woman.* Cambridge, MA: Harvard University Press.

Silberbauer, G. 1981. *Hunter and Habitat in the Central Kalahari Desert.* New York: Cambridge University Press.

Sillitoe, P., ed. 2007. *Local Science versus Global Science: Approaches to Indigenous Knowledge in International Development.* New York: Berghahn Books.

Singer, M., and H. Bauer. 2007. *Introducing Medical Anthropology: A Discipline in Action.* Lanham, MD: AltaMira.

Sinnott, M. J. 2004. *Toms and Dees: Transgender Identity and Female Same-Sex Relationships in Thailand.* Honolulu: University of Hawaii Press.

Slade, M. 1984. Displaying Affection in Public. *New York Times,* December 17.

Smart, A., and J. Smart. 2003. Urbanization and the Global Perspective. *Annual Review of Anthropology* 32:263–285.

Smith, A. T. 2003. *The Political Landscape: Constellations of Authority in Early Complex Polities.* Westport, CT: Praeger.

Smitherman, G. 1986 (orig. 1977). *Talkin and Testifyin: The Language of Black America.* Detroit: Wayne State University Press.

Sneath, Julie Z., Megehee, Carol M., and Deborah F. Spake. 2008. Social Identity in the American South: Mardi Gras Societies in Coastal Mississippi and Alabama. *International Journal of Culture, Tourism and Hospitality Research* 2(2):170–186.

Solway, J., and R. Lee. 1990. Foragers, Genuine and Spurious: Situating the Kalahari San in History (with CA treatment). *Current Anthropology* 31(2):109–146.

Spickard, P., ed. 2004. *Race and Nation: Ethnic Systems in the Modern World.* New York: Routledge.

Spindler, G. D. 2005. *New Horizons in the Anthropology of Education.* Mahwah, NJ: Erlbaum.

Spindler, G. D., ed. 2000. *Fifty Years of Anthropology and Education, 1950–2000: A Spindler Anthology.* Mahwah, NJ: Erlbaum.

Srivastava, J., N. J. H. Smith, and D. A. Forno. 1998. *Integrating Biodiversity in Agricultural Intensification: Toward Sound Practices.* Washington, DC: World Bank.

Stack, C. B. 1975. *All Our Kin: Strategies for Survival in a Black Community.* New York: Harper Torchbooks.

Statistical Abstract of the United States. 1991. 111th ed. Washington, DC: U.S. Bureau of the Census, U.S. Government Printing Office.

———. 1996. 116th ed. Washington, DC: U.S. Bureau of the Census, U.S. Government Printing Office.

———. 1999. 119th ed. Washington, DC: U.S. Bureau of the Census, U.S. Government Printing Office.

———. 2001. http://www.census.gov/prod/www/statistical-abstract-us .html.

———. 2002. http://www.census.gov/prod/www/statistical-abstract-us .html.

———. 2007. http://www.census.gov/prod/www/statistical-abstract .html.

———.2008. http://www.census.gov/prod/www/statistical-abstract .html.

Statistics Canada. 2001. *1996 Census.* National Tables. http://www .statcan.ca/english/census96/nation.htm.

———. 2003. Religions in Canada. *2001 Census*—Release 8, May 13. http://www12.statcan.ca/english/census01/release/index.cfm.

Stein, R. L., and P. L. Stein. 2008. *The Anthropology of Religion, Magic, and Witchcraft.* Boston: Pearson.

Stevens, W. K. 1992. Humanity Confronts Its Handiwork: An Altered Planet. *New York Times,* May 5, pp. B5–B7.

Stevenson, D. 2003. *Cities and Urban Cultures.* Philadelphia: Open University Press.

Stoler, A. 1977. Class Structure and Female Autonomy in Rural Java. *Signs* 3:74–89.

Stone, L. S. 2004. Gay Marriage and Anthropology. *Anthropology News* 45(5). http://www.aaanet.org/press/an/0405if-comm4.htm.

Strathern, A., and P. J. Stewart. 1999. *Curing and Healing: Medical Anthropology in Global Perspective.* Durham, NC: Carolina Academic Press.

Sunderland, P. L., and R. M. Denny. 2007. *Doing Anthropology in Consumer Research.* Walnut Creek, CA: Left Coast Press.

Suttles, W. 1960. Affinal Ties, Subsistence, and Prestige among the Coast Salish. *American Anthropologist* 62:296–305.

Svoboda, E. 2005. UC Scientist Says Ethanol Uses More Energy Than It Makes / A Lot of Fossil Fuels Go into Producing the Gas Substitute. *San Francisco Chronicle,* June 27.

Swift, M. 1963. Men and Women in Malay Society. In *Women in the New Asia,* B. Ward, ed., pp. 268–286. Paris: UNESCO.

Tanaka, J. 1980. *The San Hunter-Gatherers of the Kalahari.* Tokyo: University of Tokyo Press.

Tannen, D. 1990. *You Just Don't Understand: Women and Men in Conversation.* New York: Ballantine Books.

Tannen, D., ed. 1993. *Gender and Conversational Interaction.* New York: Oxford University Press.

Taylor, C. 1987. Anthropologist-in-Residence. In *Applied Anthropology in America,* 2nd ed., E. M. Eddy and W. L. Partridge, eds. New York: Columbia University Press.

Terrace, H. S. 1979. *Nim.* New York: Knopf.

Thomas, L. 1999. *Language, Society and Power.* New York: Routledge.

Thomas, L., and S. Wareing, eds. 2004. *Language, Society, and Power: An Introduction.* New York: Routledge.

Thompson, W. 1983. Introduction: World System with and without the Hyphen. In *Contending Approaches to World System Analysis,* W. Thompson, ed., pp. 7–26. Thousand Oaks, CA: Sage.

Tice, K. 1997. Reflections on Teaching Anthropology for Use in the Public and Private Sector. In *The Teaching of Anthropology: Problems, Issues, and Decisions,* C. P. Kottak, J. J. White, R. H. Furlow, and P. C. Rice, eds., pp. 273–284. Mountain View, CA: Mayfield.

Tishkov, V. A. 2004. *Chechnya: Life in a War-Torn Society.* Berkeley: University of California Press.

Titiev, M. 1992. *Old Oraibi: A Study of the Hopi Indians of Third Mesa.* Albuquerque: University of New Mexico Press.

Toma, Catalina L., and Jeffrey T. Hancock. 2008. Separating Fact from Fiction: An Examination of Deceptive Self-Presentation in Online Dating Profiles. *Personality and Social Psychology Bulletin* 34(8):1023–1036.

Tomlinson, J. 1991. *Cultural Imperialism: A Critical Introduction.* Baltimore: Johns Hopkins University Press.

———. 1999. *Globalization and Culture.* Chicago: University of Chicago Press.

Toner, R. 1992. Los Angeles Riots Are a Warning, Americans Fear. *New York Times,* May 11, pp. A1, A11.

Trask, L. 1996. FAQs about Basque and the Basques. http://www.cogs .susx.ac.uk/users/larryt/basque.faqs.html.

Trevathan, W. R., Smith, E. O., and McKenna, J., eds. 2007. *Evolutionary Medicine and Health.* New York: Oxford University Press.

Trivedi, B. P. 2001. Scientists Identify a Language Gene. *National Geographic News,* October 4. http://news.nationalgeographic.com/ news/2001/10/1004_Tvlanguagegene.html.

Trudgill, P. 2000. *Sociolinguistics: An Introduction to Language and Society.* 4th ed. New York: Penguin Books.

Turnbull, C. 1965. *Wayward Servants: The Two Worlds of the African Pygmies.* Garden City, NY: Natural History Press.

Turner, V. W. 1974 (orig. 1967). *The Ritual Process.* Harmondsworth, England: Penguin Books.

———. 1995 (orig. 1969). *The Ritual Process.* Hawthorne, NY: Aldine de Gruyter.

Tylor, E. B. 1958 (orig. 1871). *Primitive Culture.* New York: Harper Torchbooks.

U.S. Census Bureau. 2000. http://www.census.gov.

———. 2004. *Statistical Abstract of the United States, 2003.* Table 688, p. 459. http://www.census.gov/prod/2004pubs/03statab/ income.pdf.

———. 2005. *Statistical Abstract of the United States, 2004.* http:// www.census.gov/prod/2004pubs/04statab/labor.pdf.

———. 2006. http://quickfacts.census.gov/qfd/index.html.

———. 2009. Trade with China: 2009. http://www.census.gov/foreign-trade/balance/c5700.html#2009.

Ulijaszek, S. J., and H. Lofink. 2006. Obesity in Biocultural Perspective. *Annual Review of Anthropology* 35:337–360.

Van Cantfort, T. E., and J. B. Rimpau. 1982. Sign Language Studies with Children and Chimpanzees. *Sign Language Studies* 34:15–72.

Van der Elst, D., and P. Bohannan. 2003. *Culture as Given, Culture as Choice.* 2nd ed. Prospect Heights, IL: Waveland.

Van Willigen, J. 2002. *Applied Anthropology: An Introduction.* 3rd ed. Westport, CT: Bergin and Garvey.

Vayda, A. P. 1968 (orig. 1961). Economic Systems in Ecological Perspective: The Case of the Northwest Coast. In *Readings in Anthropology,* 2nd ed., Vol. 2, M. H. Fried, ed., pp. 172–178. New York: Crowell.

Veblen, T. 1934. *The Theory of the Leisure Class: An Economic Study of Institutions.* New York: Modern Library.

Verdery, K. 2001. Socialist Societies: Anthropological Aspects. *International Encyclopedia of the Social & Behavioral Sciences,* pp. 14496–14500. New York: Elsevier.

Vidal, J. 2003. Every Third Person Will Be a Slum Dweller within 30 Years, UN Agency Warns: Biggest Study of World's Cities Finds 940 Million Already Living in Squalor. *The Guardian,* October 4. http://www.guardian.co.uk/international/story/0,3604,1055785,00.html.

Vigil, J. D. 2003. Urban Violence and Street Gangs. *Annual Review of Anthropology* 32: 225–242.

Viola, H. J., and C. Margolis. 1991. *Seeds of Change: Five Hundred Years since Columbus, a Quincentennial Commemoration.* Washington, DC: Smithsonian Institution Press.

Wade, N. 2005. For Gay Men, Different Scent of Attraction. *New York Times,* May 10, late ed.—final, p. A1.

Wade, P. 2002. *Race, Nature, and Culture: An Anthropological Perspective.* Sterling, VA: Pluto Press.

Wagley, C. W. 1968 (orig. 1959). The Concept of Social Race in the Americas. In *The Latin American Tradition,* C. Wagley, ed., pp. 155–174. New York: Columbia University Press.

Wallace, A. F. C. 1956. Revitalization Movements. *American Anthropologist* 58:264–281.

———. 1966. *Religion: An Anthropological View.* New York: McGraw-Hill.

———. 1969. *The Death and Rebirth of the Seneca.* New York: Knopf.

Wallerstein, I. M. 1982. The Rise and Future Demise of the World Capitalist System: Concepts for Comparative Analysis. In *Introduction to the Sociology of "Developing Societies,"* H. Alavi and T. Shanin, eds., pp. 29–53. New York: Monthly Review Press.

———. 2000. *The Essential Wallerstein.* New York: New Press, Norton.

———. 2004a. *The Decline of American Power: The U.S. in a Chaotic World.* New York: New Press.

———. 2004b. *World-Systems Analysis: An Introduction.* Durham, NC: Duke University Press.

Walmart Watch. 2009. Issues: Supplier Relathionships. http://walmartwatch.com/issues/supplier_relationships/.

Ward, M. C. 2003. *A World Full of Women.* 3rd ed. Needham Heights, MA: Allyn & Bacon.

Ward, M. C., and M. Edelstein. 2008. *A World Full of Women.* 5th ed. Needham Heights, MA: Allyn & Bacon.

Warms, R., J. Garber, and R. J. McGee, eds. 2009. *Sacred Realms: Readings in the Anthropology of Religion.* 2nd ed. New York: Oxford University Press.

Weber, M. 1958 (orig. 1904). *The Protestant Ethic and the Spirit of Capitalism.* New York: Scribner.

———. 1968 (orig. 1922). *Economy and Society.* E. Fischoff et al. (trans.). New York: Bedminster Press.

Webster's New World Encyclopedia. 1993. College Edition. Englewood Cliffs, NJ: Prentice Hall.

Wedel, J. 2002. *Blurring the Boundaries of the State-Private Divide: Implications for Corruption.* Paper presented at the European Association of Social Anthropologists (EASA) Conference in Copenhagen, August 14–17. http://www.anthrobase.com/Txt/W/Wedel_J_01.htm.

Weinberg, D. 1996. Press Briefing on 1995 Income, Poverty, and Health Insurance Estimates. Housing and Household Economic Statistics Division, U.S. Bureau of the Census. Washington, DC, September 26. http://www.census.gov/Press-Release/speech1.html.

Weise, E. 1999. Anthropologists Adapt Technology to World's Cultures. *USA Today,* May 26. http://www. usatoday.com/life/cyber/tech/ctf256.htm.

Weston, K. 1991. *Families We Choose: Lesbians, Gays, Kinship.* New York: Columbia University Press.

White, L. A. 1959. *The Evolution of Culture: The Development of Civilization to the Fall of Rome.* New York: McGraw-Hill.

Whorf, B. L. 1956. A Linguistic Consideration of Thinking in Primitive Communities. In *Language, Thought, and Reality: Selected Writings of Benjamin Lee Whorf,* J. B. Carroll, ed., pp. 65–86. Cambridge, MA: MIT Press.

Whyte, M. F. 1978. Cross-Cultural Codes Dealing with the Relative Status of Women. *Ethnology* XII(2):203–225.

Wilford, J. N. 2002. When Humans Became Human. *New York Times,* February 26, late ed.—final, sec. F, p. 1, col. 1. http://www.nytimes.com.

Wilk, R. R. 1996. *Economies and Cultures: An Introduction to Economic Anthropology.* Boulder, CO: Westview Press.

Williams, B. 1989. A Class Act: Anthropology and the Race to Nation across Ethnic Terrain. *Annual Review of Anthropology* 18:401–444.

Williams, L. M., and D. Finkelhor. 1995. Paternal Caregiving and Incest: Test of a Biosocial Model. *American Journal of Orthopsychiatry* 65(1):101–113.

Willie, C. V. 2003. *A New Look at Black Families.* Walnut Creek, CA: AltaMira.

Wilmsen, E. N. 1989. *Land Filled with Flies: A Political Economy of the Kalahari.* Chicago: University of Chicago Press.

Wilson, R., ed. 1996. *Human Rights: Culture and Context: Anthropological Perspectives.* Chicago: Pluto Press.

Winter, R. 2001. Religions of the World: Number of Adherents; Names of Houses of Worship; Names of Leaders; Rates of Growth. http://www.religioustolerance.org/worldrel.htm.

Winzeler, R. L. 2007. *Anthropology and Religion.* Lanham, MD: AltaMira.

Wittstock, L. W., and E. J. Salinas. 2010. *A Brief History of the American Indian Movement.* http://www.aimovement.org/ggc/history.html.

Wolcott, H. F. 2008. *Ethnography: A Way of Seeing.* 2nd ed. Lanham, MD: AltaMira.

Wolf, E. R. 1966. *Peasants.* Englewood Cliffs, NJ: Prentice Hall.

———. 1982. *Europe and the People without History.* Berkeley: University of California Press.

Wolf, E. R., with S. Silverman. 2001. *Pathways of Power: Building an Anthropology of the Modern World.* Berkeley: University of California Press.

Worsley, P. 1985 (orig. 1959). Cargo Cults. In *Readings in Anthropology 85/86.* Guilford, CT: Dushkin.

Yetman, N., ed. 1991. *Majority and Minority: The Dynamics of Race and Ethnicity in American Life.* 5th ed. Boston: Allyn & Bacon.

Yurchak, A. 2002. Entrepreneurial Governmentality in Postsocialist Russia. In *The New Entrepreneurs of Europe and Asia,* V. Bonnell and T. Gold, eds., p. 301. Armonk, NY: M. E. Sharpe.

———. 2005. *Everything Was Forever until It Was No More: The Last Soviet Generation.* Princeton, NJ: Princeton University Press.

Zimmer-Tamakoshi, L. 1997. The Last Big Man: Development and Men's Discontents in the Papua New Guinea Highlands. *Oceania* 68(2):107–122

Zou, Y., and E. T. Trueba. 2002. *Ethnography and Schools: Qualitative Approaches to the Study of Education.* Lanham, MD: Rowman & Littlefield.

Zulaika, J. 1988. *Basque Violence: Metaphor and Sacrament.* Reno: University of Nevada Press.

Chapter 1

p. xxxvi: Friedrich Stark/Alamy; p. 2B: Ron Gilling/Peter Arnold Inc.; p. 3: © Michael S. Yamashita/Corbis; p. 4L: © iStockphoto.com/ Bartosz Hadyniak; p. 4R: BananaStock/Jupiterimages; p. 5T: David Samuel Robbins/Getty Images; p. 5B: Michael Dunning/Getty Images; p. 6: © National Anthropological Archives. Neg.#906-B; p. 7TL: © Hubert Stadler/Corbis; p. 7BL: © Nigel Pavitt/JAI/ Corbis; p. 7TR: © Danita Delimont/Alamy; p. 7BR: © Ed George/ National Geographic Image Collection; p. 8L: © Blickwinkel/ Alamy; p. 8ML: dbimages/Alamy; p. 8MR: David Levenson/ Alamy; p. 8R: © Ariadne Van Zandbergen/africanpictures.net/The Image Works; p. 11: SSPL/The Image Works; p. 12: © AP Images/ Obama Presidential Campaign; p. 13TL: iStockphoto.com/ ollo; p. 13TR: © iStockphoto.com/malerapaso; p. 13B: The Kobal Collection/Lucasfilm/Paramount Pictures; p. 14: © Randy Olson/ Aurora Photos; p. 15TL: Digital Vision/Getty Images; p. 15TM: © Eric Martin/Iconotec.com; p. 15TR: © Photodisc/Gettty Images; p. 15B: Emma Wood/Alamy; p. 17T: © C Squared Studios/Getty Images; p. 17M: © Bruce Avera Hunter/National Geographic Image Collection; p. 17B: Glow Images/Getty Images

Chapter 2

p. 20: James L. Stanfield/National Geographic Stock; p. 22: © Ferdinando Scianna/Magnum Photos; p. 23: Royalty-Free/Corbis; p. 24TL: Jenny Matthews/Alamy; p. 24TR: © Neil Emmerson/ Robert Harding World Imagery/Corbis; p. 24MR: © Mary Evans Picture Library/The Image Works; p. 24BR: Frederick M. Brown/ Getty Images; p. 25T: Michael Loccisano/Getty Images; p. 25B: © Tim Pannell/Corbis; p. 26T © William Gottlieb/Corbis; p. 26B: © 2009 Jupiterimages Corporation; p. 27T: Siede Preis/Getty Images; p. 27B: © OSF/Clive Bromhall/Animals Animals; p. 28M: © iStockphoto.com/Eric Isselée; p. 28B: DAJ/Getty Images; p. 30T: © Stockbyte/PunchStock; p. 30L: © Hideo Haga/The Image Works; p. 30R: © Carl D. Walsh/Aurora Photos; p. 31L: Bob Rowan/Corbis; p. 31R: © Robert Holmes/Corbis; p. 32: © iStockphoto.com/Vasko Miokovic; p. 33T: © Frans Lemmens/ Getty Images; p. 33B: © Mandel Ngan/AFP/Getty Images; p. 34: Monica Stevenson Photography/Getty Images; p. 35: Anders Ryman/Corbis; p. 36: © Bill Bachmann/Alamy; p. 37: © SuperStock

Chapter 3

p. 40: Melvin Konner/Anthro-Photo; p. 43T: © Peggy & Yoran Kahana/Peter Arnold/Photolibrary; p. 43B: Courtesy of Nancy Scheper-Hughes; p. 44: © AP Images; p. 45: Neil McAllister/ Alamy; p. 46T: The McGraw-Hill Companies Inc./Ken Cavanagh Photographer; p. 46B: © Richard Lord/PhotoEdit; p. 47T: Asia Images/Getty Images; p. 48: © Historical Picture Archive/Corbis; p. 49T: © 20th Century Fox. All rights reserved/Courtesy Everett Collection; p. 49M: © Beawiharta/Reuters/Corbis; p. 49B: © Athar Hussain/Reuters/Corbis; p. 50: © Mary Evans Picture Library/The Image Works; p. 51: Courtesy of Conrad Kottak; p. 52: Courtesy of Lisa Gezon; p. 53: © Chris Fitzgerald/CandidatePhotos/The Image Works; p. 54L: Peggy & Yoran Kahana/Peter Arnold Inc.; p. 54R: © iStockphoto.com/Silvia Jansen; p. 55: © Bob Daemmrich/The Image Works

Chapter 4

p. 58: © Ian Berry/Magnum Photos; p. 60BL: © iStockphoto.com/JasonRWarren; p. 60BML: Getty Images/Photographer's Choice RF; p. 60BMR: Adam Gault/Getty Images; p. 60BR: Digital Vision/ Getty Images; p. 62T: © Charles Harbutt/Actuality, Inc. ; p. 62B: © Mike Yamashita/Woodfin Camp & Associates; p. 63: Chris Maddaloni/Getty Images; p. 64: © J.L. Dugast/Lineair/Peter Arnold; p. 65T: Alexander Joe/AFP/Getty Images; p. 65B: © Betty Press/ Woodfin Camp & Associates; p. 66: © Oleg Popov/Reuters/Cor-

bis; p. 67T: Gideon Mendel/ActionAid/Corbis; p. 67B: © Antonio Scorza/AFP/Getty Images; p. 68: The Kobal Collection/20th Century Fox Television; p. 69: © Photodisc/Getty Images; p. 71T: © Punchstock/Creatas; p. 71B: © UNEP/Peter Arnold/Photolibrary; p. 73: Corbis Super RF/Alamy; p. 74: © Najlah Feanny/Corbis; p. 75: Image Source/Getty Images

Chapter 5

p. 78: © Olivier Martel/Corbis; p. 80B: Donald Pye/Alamy; p. 81T: © Jason Lee/Reuters/Corbis; p. 81B: © Michael Nichols/National Geographic Image Collection; p. 82T: h.e.r./Getty Images; p. 83TL: Corbis; p. 83TR: © Digital Vision/Punchstock; p. 83B: © Sandro Vannini/Corbis; p. 84T: Per-Anders Pettersson/Getty Images; p. 84BL: The McGraw-Hill Companies, Inc./Andrew Resek, photographer; p. 84BR: Bloom Productions/Getty Images; p. 85T: Martin Thomas Photography/Alamy; p. 85B: Noel Hendrickson/ Getty Images; p. 86: iStockphoto.com/Mark Strozier; p. 87T: © David Brabyn/Corbis; p. 87B: © Lonny Shavelson; p. 88T: Keijiro Komine/Getty Images; p. 88B: © Steven Kazlowski/Alaska Stock LLC/National Geographic Stock; p. 89T: Ryan McVay/Getty Images; p. 89B: Steve Smith/Getty Images; p. 90T: Bob Daemmrich/ The Image Works; p. 90B: Blend Images/Hill Street Studios/Getty Images; p. 91T: © iStockphoto.com/Alexander Drack; p. 92T: Michael Siluk/The Image Works; p. 92B: © Lawrence Jackson, White House Photo; p. 93: Ben Rose/WireImage/Getty Images; p. 95B: © Brand X/JupiterImages/Getty Images; p. 95TL: Barbara Penoyar/ Getty Images; p. 95TR: Barbara Penoyar/Getty Images; p. 95TML: Barbara Penoyar/Getty Images; p. 95TMR: Amos Morgan/Getty Images; p. 95TBL: Kevin Peterson/Getty Images; p. 95TBR: Barbara Penoyar/Getty Images; p. 95B: Brand X/JupiterImages/ Getty Images

Chapter 6

p. 98: © Author's Image/PunchStock; p. 100B: Steve Raymer/Getty Images; p. 103T: Danita Delimont/Getty Images; p. 103B: © D. Halleux/BIOS/Peter Arnold/D. Halleux/BIOS/Photolibrary; p. 104: © Earl & Nazima Kowall/Corbis; p. 105B: Santokh Kochar/Getty Images; p. 107TL: MedioImages/Getty Images; p. 107TML: © iStockphoto.com/Morley Read; p. 107TM: Kent Knudson/ PhotoLink/Getty Images; p. 107TMR: Getty Images; p. 107TR: Steve Allen/Brand X Pictures; p. 108T: © Carl D. Walsh/Aurora Photos; p. 109: © BananaStock/PunchStock; p. 110: Guang Niu/ Getty Images; p. 111T: Steve Mason/Getty Images ; p. 111B: Jupiter Images; p. 112T: Burke/Triolo Productions/Getty Images; p. 113T: © Blend Images/Alamy; p. 113B: © John Eastcott/Yva Momatiuk/Woodfin Camp & Associates; p. 114: Frank Micelotta/ Getty Images; p. 115T: Elbridge W. Merrill Collection Photograph Collection/Alaska State Library and Archives [P57–028]; p. 115B: Jesse Grant/WireImage/Getty Images

Chapter 7

p. 118: © Owen Franken/Corbis; p. 120B: © Alessandro Di Meo/ epa/Corbis; p. 122T: Eduard Korniyenko/Reuters/Corbis; p. 122B © Joy Tessman/National Geographic Image Collection; p. 124: Photolibrary.com; p. 125: © Peer Grimm/epa/Corbis; p. 126: © Burt Glinn/Magnum Photos; p. 127T: Amos Morgan/Getty Images; p. 127BL: AKG Images/The Image Works; p. 127BR: The Kobal Collection/Marvel Enterprises; p. 129: © Douglas Kirkland; p. 131: © Peter Adams/Getty Images; p. 132: © Anders Ryman/ Corbis; p. 134T: © Pawan Kumar/Reuters/Corbis; p. 134B: © Tim Mosenfelder/Corbis; p. 135B: David W. Hamilton/Getty Images; p. 135TL: Library of Congress Prints and Photographs Division [LC-USZ62–13912]; p. 135TML: Brand X Pictures/Punch-Stock; p. 135TMR: © Bruno Morandi/Hemis/Corbis; p. 135TR: Royalty-Free/Corbis; p. 136: Hans Deryk/Reuters/Corbis; p. 137T: The Image Works; p. 137B: Ariel Skelley/Getty Images

Page references in **bold** refer to glossary definitions.

social networking, 87*f*
Communism, 216–217, 216*f*
communism, 216
communitas, 186, 190*f*, **191**
complex societies, **54**–55
conflict resolution, **123**, 125
consumption, global culture of, 257–258, 257*f*
contagious magic, 188
Convention 169, 259
conversation, in field work, 46–47
cooperatives, 65
Copsa Mica, Romania, 220*f*
core nations, 204, **205**, 217, 217*t*
core values, **26**
correlations, **102**
corruption, 217
The Cosby Show, 145*f*
cremation, 30
creole languages, 87
crimes, 135
CRM (cultural resource management), **17**, 62
Cuban Americans, 227, 227*f*
cults, 191–192, 197–199, 198*f*
cultural adaptation, 4–5, 4*t*
cultural anthropology, 5–6, **12**, 13*t*
cultural change mechanisms, 34–36
cultural colonialism, **240**
cultural consultants, 48, **49**
cultural ecology, 115, 250. *See also* environmental anthropology
cultural imperialism, **254**–255, 254*f*
cultural learning, 23
cultural relativism, **33**–34
cultural resource management (CRM), **17**, 62
cultural rights, **34**
cultural sensitivity, 42–43
cultural transmission, **82**
culture(s), **3**, 21–37
    adaptive or maladaptive, 26
    agency and practice in, 31
    definitions of, 3, 22–23
    ethnocentrism and cultural relativism, 32–34
    evolutionary basis of, 26–29, 28*t*
    global culture of consumption, 257–258, 257*f*
    globalization and, 36–37
    ideal *vs.* real, 31
    indigenizing popular culture, 256
    influence on development, 1

interactions between, 12
language and thought in, 86–89, 87*f*, 88*f*, 89*f*
levels of, 31–32, 32*t*
mechanisms of change in, 34–36
nature and, 24–25
particularities in, 29, 30–31
qualities of, 22–26
symbols in, 23–24
transmission of, 3–4, 23
universals and generalities in, 29–30
curers, **71**–72, 71*f*

D

Dalits, 134*f*
Darfur, Sudan, 253–254, 254*f*
Darwin, Charles, 9, 15
daughter languages, **93**–94, 94*f*
Declaration of Indigenous Rights, 259
defecation, 25
deforestation, 252–253
demonstrated descent, 150
Descartes, Lara, 145*f*
descent, **229**–230
descent groups, **149**
    innovation and, 66
    patrilineal and matrilineal, 149–150, 149*f*, 150*f*
    status and, 132
    in tribal societies, 124
descriptive linguistics, **85**
development anthropology, **63**–64
dialects, 90, 92, 93
dialogic ethnography, 50
diaries, personal, 45
diasporas, **257**
Dickens, Charles, 208
differential access, **132**
diffusion, 30, **34**–35
diglossia, **90**
discrimination, **238**
disease, 49, **70**
displacement, linguistic, 82–**83**
Disraeli, Benjamin, 212
distribution and exchange
    coexistence of exchange principles, 114
    differential access and, 132
    market principle, 112
    potlatching, 114–115, 114*f*, 115*f*
    reciprocity, 112–113, 113*f*
    redistribution, 112, 131

diversity. *See also* ethnicity and race
    biological, 6–12, 7*f*, 10*f*, 11*f*
    human, 225
    multiculturalism, 236–238, 236*f*, 239
division of labor, 103, 107–109, 166–167, 166*t*, 167*f*
divorce, 147, 147*f*, 157–158, 158*f*
divorce divide, 158
domestic–public dichotomy, **168**, 175, 178
domestic violence shelters, 181*f*
dowry, **156**–157, 175
dowry murders, 175
drug use and abuse, 70, 72
Dunn, Janet, 52
Durkheim, Émile, 44, 186

E

Earle, Timothy, 132
ecological anthropology, 115, **250**. *See also* environmental anthropology
ecology, 13
economic production. *See* making a living
economic systems. *See also* making a living
    alienation and, 109–110, 110*f*
    distribution and exchange in, 112–115, 113*f*, 114*f*, 115*f*
    division of labor in, 103, 107–109, 166–167, 166*t*, 167*f*
    economizing and maximization in, 110–111
    means of production, 108–109
economy, **107**
ecosystems, 13
education
    applied anthropology in, 63, 66–67, 66*f*
    gender gap in, 178
Efe, 101
effervescence, religious, 186
egalitarian bands, 103
emic approach, **48**–49, 70
emotionalistic disease theories, 71
employment. *See* making a living
enculturation, 3, **23**
endogamy, **153**–154
Enduring Voices Project, 94
energy consumption, 218–219, 218*f*, 219*f*
enforcement systems, 136

MAP ATLAS

CONTENTS

MAP I

Annual Percent
of World Forest Loss,
1990–2000

Deforestation is a major environmental problem. In the tropics, large corporations clear forests seeking hardwoods for the global market in furniture and fine woods. As well, the agriculturally driven clearing of the great rain forests of the Amazon Basin, west and central Africa, Middle America, and Southeast Asia has drawn public attention. Reduced forest cover means the world's vegetation system will absorb less carbon dioxide, resulting in global warming. Of concern, too, is the loss of biodiversity (large numbers of plants and animals), the destruction of soil systems, and disruptions in water supply that accompany clearing.

QUESTIONS

Look at Map 1, "Annual Percent of World Forest Loss, 1990–2000."

1. On what continents do you find stable or increased forest cover?

2. Are there areas of Africa with stable or increased forest cover? Where are they? What might the reasons be for this lack of deforestation?

3. How does deforestation in India compare with the area to its east, which includes mainland and insular Southeast Asia?

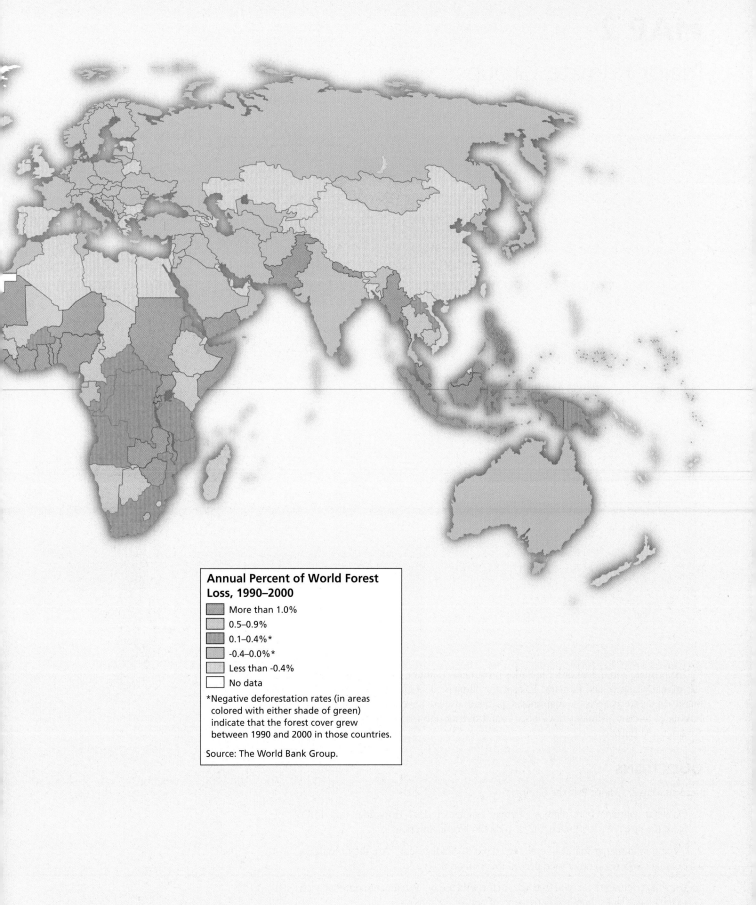

**Annual Percent of World Forest
Loss, 1990–2000**

More than 1.0%

0.5–0.9%

0.1–0.4%*

-0.4–0.0%*

Less than -0.4%

No data

*Negative deforestation rates (in areas
 colored with either shade of green)
 indicate that the forest cover grew
 between 1990 and 2000 in those countries.

Source: The World Bank Group.

MAP 2
Major Primate Groups

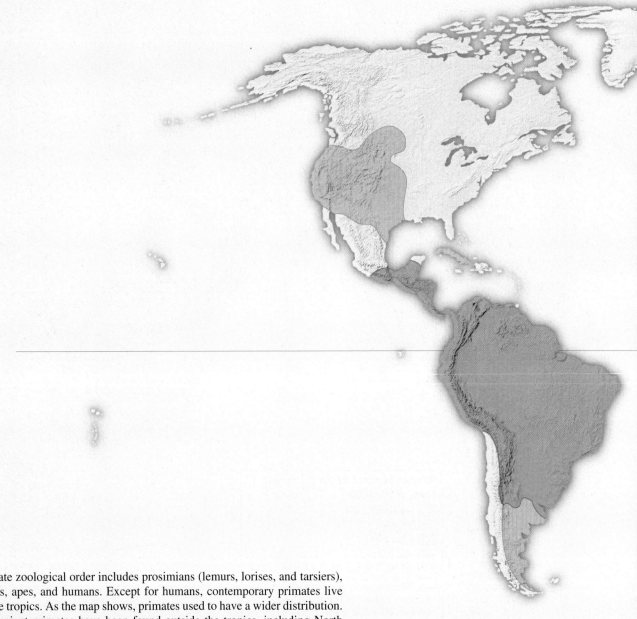

The primate zoological order includes prosimians (lemurs, lorises, and tarsiers), monkeys, apes, and humans. Except for humans, contemporary primates live mainly in the tropics. As the map shows, primates used to have a wider distribution. Fossils of ancient primates have been found outside the tropics, including North America and Europe.

QUESTIONS

Look at Map 2, "Major Primate Groups."

1. On what continents are there nonhuman primates today? How does this differ from the past? What primate thrives today in North America?

2. What nonhuman primates live on the island of Madagascar? Are they monkeys or what? Where do other members of their suborder live?

3. On what continents can you find apes in the wild today? What continent that used to have apes lacks them today (except, of course, in zoos).

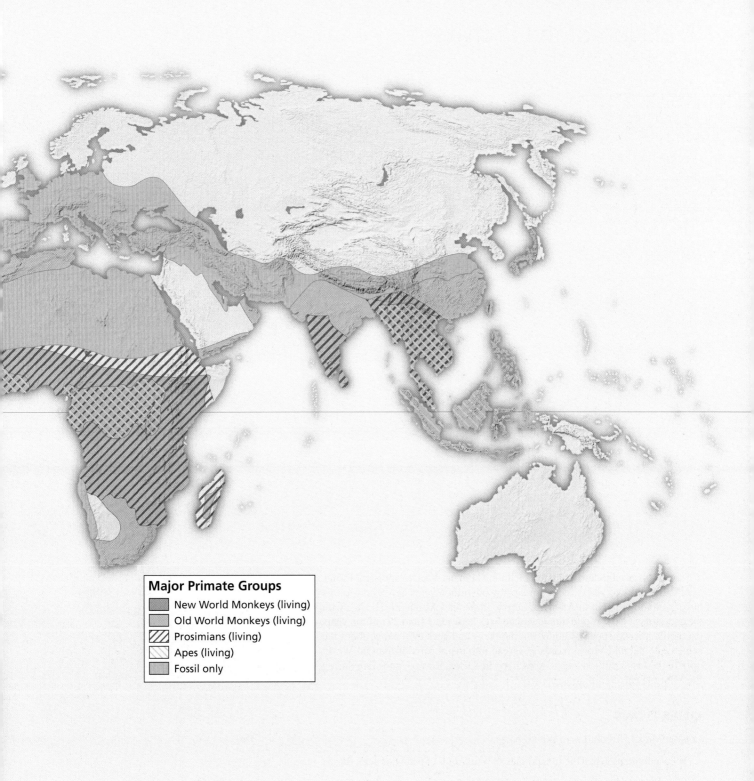

Major Primate Groups

- New World Monkeys (living)
- Old World Monkeys (living)
- Prosimians (living)
- Apes (living)
- Fossil only

MAP 3
Evolution of the Primates

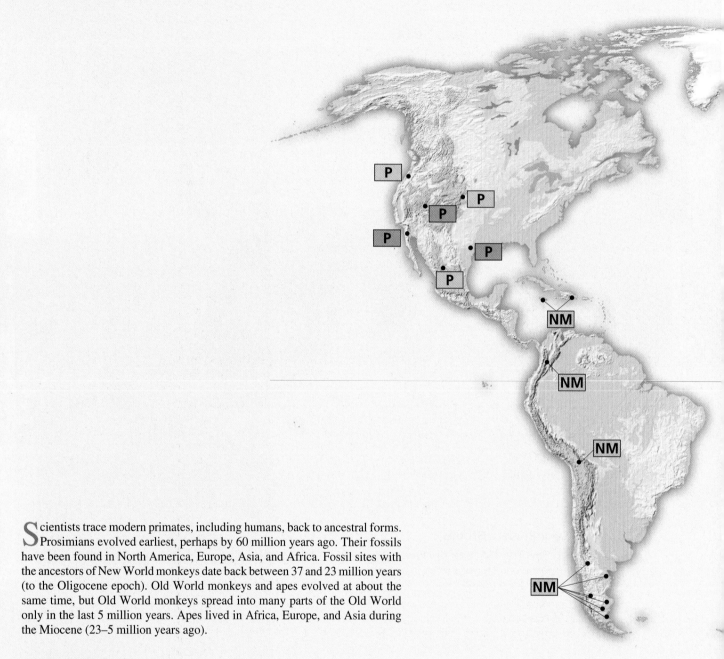

Scientists trace modern primates, including humans, back to ancestral forms. Prosimians evolved earliest, perhaps by 60 million years ago. Their fossils have been found in North America, Europe, Asia, and Africa. Fossil sites with the ancestors of New World monkeys date back between 37 and 23 million years (to the Oligocene epoch). Old World monkeys and apes evolved at about the same time, but Old World monkeys spread into many parts of the Old World only in the last 5 million years. Apes lived in Africa, Europe, and Asia during the Miocene (23–5 million years ago).

QUESTIONS

Look at Map 3, "Evolution of the Primates."

1. What continent(s) had the first primates? What kinds of primates were those?

2. On what continent has the evolution of primates been most continuous? Does this have implications for human evolution?

3. Which continent with several of the earliest primates has the fewest non-human primates today?

Evolution of the Primates

Eocene: 57–37 million years ago
Oligocene: 37–23 million years ago
Miocene: 23–5 million years ago

OM Old World monkeys
NM New World monkeys
 P Prosimians
 A Apes

MAP 4
Early Hominins (and Hominids): Origins and Diffusion

The earliest hominins, including the ancestors of modern humans, evolved in Africa around 6 million years ago. Many sites date to the late Miocene (8–5 million years ago) when the lines leading to modern humans, chimps, and gorillas may have separated. Some sites dating to the end of the Pliocene epoch (5–1.8 million years ago) contain fossil remains of human ancestors, *Homo*. During the Pleistocene Era (1.8 million–11,000 years ago), humans spread all over the world. Scholars don't always agree on the evolutionary connections between the different fossils, as indicated in the question marks and broken lines on the time line.

QUESTIONS

Look at Map 4, "Early Hominins (and Hominids): Origins and Diffusion."

1. How many African countries have early hominin or hominid sites? Which countries contain sites of hominids that may not have been hominins? Name those two sites. How many African countries have sites from the Miocene? From the Pliocene? And from the Pleistocene?

2. Compare the African distribution of nonhuman primate fossils in Map 3 with the distribution of early hominins in Map 4. Which fossil record is better—the one for nonhuman primates or the one for hominins?

3. Compare the distribution of contemporary African apes, as shown in Map 2, with the distribution of early hominin sites in Map 4. Also look at the distribution of extinct African apes in Map 3. What patterns do you notice? Where did early hominins overlap with the African apes (extinct and contemporary)? Where were there apes but no known early hominins, and vice versa?

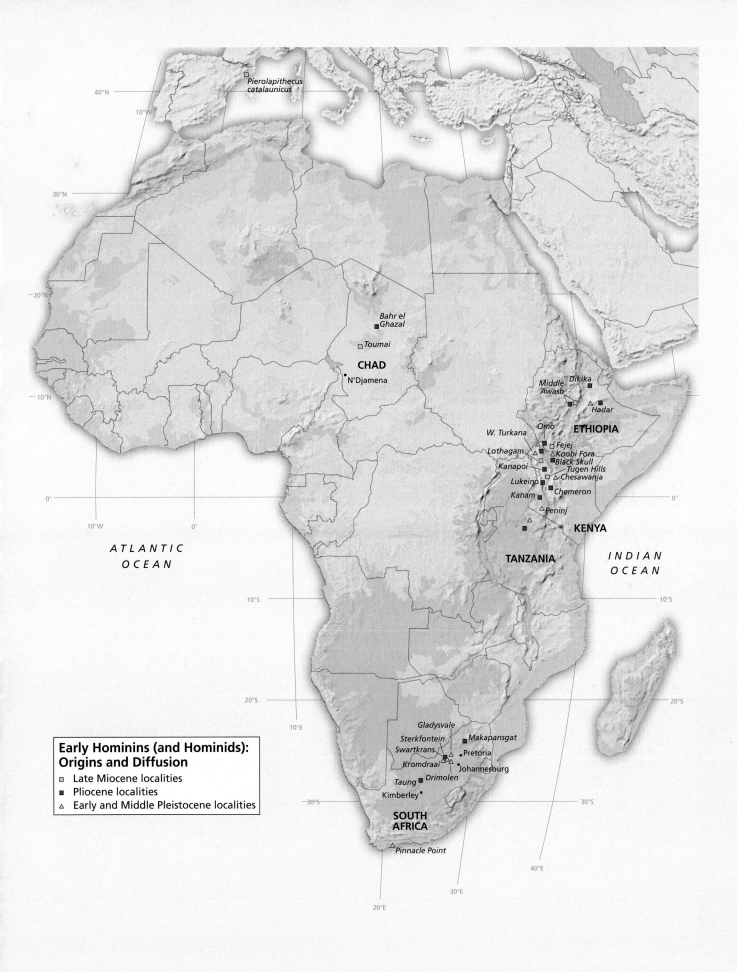

Early Hominins (and Hominids): Origins and Diffusion

□ Late Miocene localities
■ Pliocene localities
△ Early and Middle Pleistocene localities

Pierolapithecus catalaunicus

Bahr el Ghazal

□ *Toumai*

CHAD

• N'Djamena

Middle Awash

Dikika

Hadar

W. Turkana

Omo

ETHIOPIA

Fejej

Lothagam

△ *Koobi Fora*

Black Skull

Kanapoi

Tugen Hills

△ *Chesawanja*

Lukeino

Chemeron

Kanam

△ *Peninj*

KENYA

TANZANIA

Gladysvale

Sterkfontein

Makapansgat

Swartkrans

• *Pretoria*

Kromdraai

• *Johannesburg*

Taung

Drimolen

Kimberley •

SOUTH AFRICA

△ *Pinnacle Point*

ATLANTIC OCEAN

INDIAN OCEAN

40°N

30°N

20°N

10°N

0°

10°S

20°S

30°S

10°W

0°

10°E

20°E

30°E

40°E

40°W

10°W

0°

MAP 5

The Emergence of Modern Humans

Early forms of *Homo (H.) erectus*, sometimes called *H. ergaster,* have been found in East Africa and the former Soviet Georgia. By 1.7 million years ago, *H. erectus* had spread from Africa into Asia, including Indonesia, and eventually Europe. The *H. erectus* period may have lasted until 300,000 years ago. Other archaic forms of *Homo,* including fossils sometimes called *H. antecessor* and *H. heidelbergensis,* have been found in various parts of the Old World.

QUESTIONS

Look at Map 5, "The Emergence of Modern Humans."

1. Locate the site of Dmanisi (Georgia). Locate the site of Nariokotome (East Turkana, Kenya). These are sites where similarly dated early remains of *Homo erectus* (or *Homo ergaster*) have been found. Find two additional sites where hominins with similar dates (1.8–1.6 m.y.a.) have been found.

2. Considering Africa and Asia, name five sites (other than Dmanisi and Nariokotome) where *Homo erectus* fossils have been found.

3. Locate Heidelberg (Mauer) and Ceprano. What kinds of hominin fossils have been found there?

Okladnikov
Cave

Dmanisi (1.7–1.8 m.y.a.)

CAUCASUS MTS.

Black Sea

Caspian Sea

ASIA

Teshik Tash

Zhoukoudian, "Peking man"
(450,000 years ago)

Shanidar

Lantian

Langtandong

Skhul   Amud
Tabun
ebara Cave   Zuttiyen
Qafzeh

Yunxian

Hominid
migration

Yuanmou
(Earliest evidence of
hominids in East Asia,
1.7 million years ago)

Maba

Nazlet Khatir

Tham Khuyen

Red Sea

Buia

Herto

Hadar

Bouri

FRICA

Omo
Nariokotome   Konso-Gardula

Koobi Fora
Ileret

Lake Turkana,
"Nariokotome boy" (1.6 m.y.a.)

INDIAN OCEAN

Olduvai Gorge

Sangiran, Java (1.6–1.8 m.y.a.)

Kedungbrubus

Trinil, "Java man"
(700,000 years ago)

Flores

ve of Hearths

rkfontein (2 m.y.a.)

Border Cave

Swartkrans (1.5 m.y.a.)

AUSTRALIA

iver Mouth
ome of the earliest
natomically modern
c. 100,000 years ago)

ARCHAEOLOGICAL SITE

- *Homo habilis*
- *Homo erectus*
- Archaic *Homo sapiens*
- Neandertals
- *Homo sapiens*
- *Homo floresiensis*

MAP 6

Origins and Distribution of Modern Humans

Anatomically modern humans (AMHs), appeared earliest in Africa (at Herto?) and migrated into the rest of the Old World, perhaps around 130,000 years ago. Whether these early modern humans interbred with archaic humans, such as Neandertals, outside of Africa is still debated. Sometime between 25,000 and 9,000 years ago, humans colonized the New World.

QUESTIONS

Look at Map 6, "Origins and Distribution of Modern Humans."

1. When and from where was Australia first settled?

2. When and from where was North America first settled? How many migrations are shown as figuring in the settlement of North America? How were these migrations related to the glacial ice cover? Did they all follow the same route?

3. Locate three sites providing early evidence of AMHs in Africa. How do their dates compare with those of AMHs in Europe?

LAURENTIDE ICE SHEET

St. Lawrence R.

Great Lakes

NORTH AMERICA

Meadowcroft

Corridor
opened
from
11,300 B.P.

ROCKY MTS.

GREAT PLAINS

APPALACHIAN MTS.

ATLANTIC OCEAN

BERINGIA
(c. 80,000 to 7,000 B.P.)

Clovis

Rio Grande

Mississippi R.

West Indies

EAN

Orinoco R.

GUIANA HIGHLANDS

Nanchoc Valley

A
N
D
E
S

AMAZON BASIN

Pedra
Furada

ealand

Monte
Verde

PATAGONIA

**Origins and Distribution
of Modern Humans**

↖ Possible settlement direction

▲ Archaic *Homo sapiens* (c. 650,000–28,000 B.P.)

△ Neandertals (c. 130,000–28,000? B.P.)

■ Modern *Homo sapiens* (c. 130,000 B.P.–present)

☐ Areas covered by ice in late
   Pleistocene era (18,000 B.P.)

▨ Beringia

MAP 7

The Distribution of Human Skin Color (Before C.E. 1400)

H uman skin color varies. The pigmentation is caused by the presence of melanin in the skin, which protects the skin from damage due to ultraviolet radiation. In areas with much UV radiation, people biologically adapted to their environments by increased melanin production.

QUESTIONS

Look at Map 7, "The Distribution of Human Skin Color (Before C.E. 1400)."

1. Where are the Native Americans with the darkest skin color located? What factors help explain this distribution?

2. In both western and eastern hemispheres, is the lightest skin color found in the north or the south? Outside Asia, where do you find skin color closest to northern Asian skin color? Is this surprising given what you have read about migrations and settlement history?

3. Where are skin colors darkest? How might you explain this distribution?

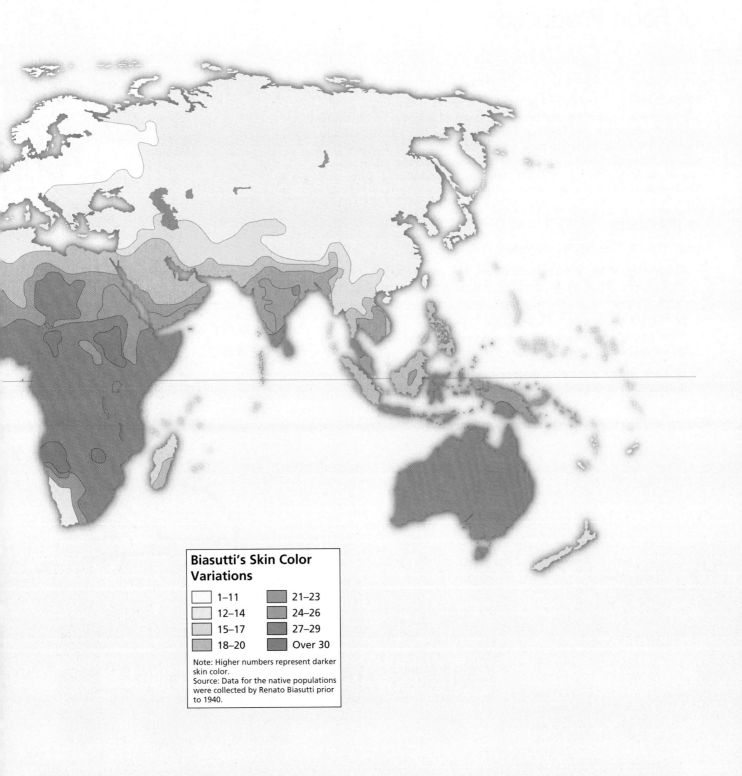

Biasutti's Skin Color Variations

- 1–11
- 12–14
- 15–17
- 18–20
- 21–23
- 24–26
- 27–29
- Over 30

Note: Higher numbers represent darker skin color.

Source: Data for the native populations were collected by Renato Biasutti prior to 1940.

MAP 8

The Origin and Spread of Food Production

The Neolithic, or New Stone Age, refers to the period of early farming settlements when people who had been foragers shifted to food production. This pattern of subsistence was based on the domestication of plants and animals. Through domestication, people transformed plants and animals from their wild state to a form more useful to humans. The Neolithic began in the fertile crescent area of the Middle East over 10,000 years ago. It spread to the Levant and Mediterranean, finally reaching Britain and Scandinavia around 5,000 years ago.

QUESTIONS

Look at Map 8, "The Origin and Spread of Food Production."

1. Considering the map and the timeline, name three regions where cattle were domesticated. Based on the timeline, what animals were domesticated in North America?

2. Did Ireland receive Middle Eastern domesticates? What is the origin of the "Irish potato," or white potato (see the timeline), which became, much later, the caloric basis of Irish subsistence?

3. Besides cattle, what animals were domesticated more than once? Where were those areas of domestication?

ATLANTIC OCEAN

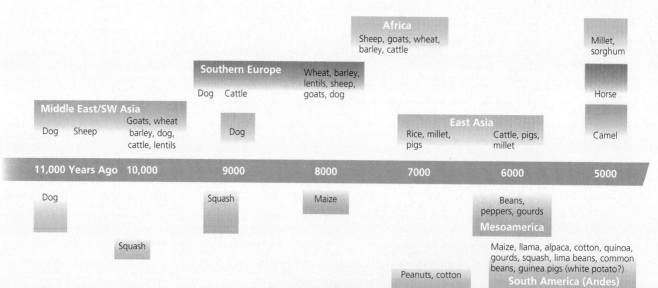

				Africa Sheep, goats, wheat, barley, cattle		Millet, sorghum
		Southern Europe Dog Cattle	Wheat, barley, lentils, sheep, goats, dog			
						Horse
Middle East/SW Asia Dog Sheep	Goats, wheat barley, dog, cattle, lentils	Dog		**East Asia** Rice, millet, pigs	Cattle, pigs, millet	Camel
11,000 Years Ago 10,000		**9000**	**8000**	**7000**	**6000**	**5000**
Dog		Squash	Maize		Beans, peppers, gourds	
	Squash				**Mesoamerica**	
					Maize, llama, alpaca, cotton, quinoa, gourds, squash, lima beans, common beans, guinea pigs (white potato?)	
				Peanuts, cotton	**South America (Andes)**	

Early Neolithic Sites of the Middle East and Europe

Settlement region and date

• Settlement sites

← Possible migration routes

Areas of domestication

Lake Ladoga

Lake Peipus

Baltic Sea

Aral Sea

Caspian Sea

Elbe R.

Goose

Oder R.

Bug R.

Vistula R.

Dniester R.

Dnieper R.

Ural R.

Volga R.

Horse

Danube R.

Sea of Azov

Black Sea

7,500

Sava R.

7,700

7,700

Danube R.

7,800

Po R.

Adriatic Sea

7,800

9,000

Cattle

8,000

Cattle

8,400

9,000

8,900

9,000

9,600

9,800

10,300

Cattle

Pig

Sheep

Goat

Tigris R.

Euphrates R.

Goat

9,400?

10,300

Dromedary

Persian Gulf

M e d i t e r r a n e a n   S e a

Ass
Honey Bee
Cat

Mediterranean Domestication

Barley	Dates	Grapes
Cattle	Garlic	Lentils
Celery	Goat	Lettuce
		Olives

Southwest Asia Domestication

Barley	Duck	Melons
Beans	Fruits (seed	Oats
Beets	and stone)	Oil seeds
Camel (Bactrian)	Goat	Onions
Carrots	Grapes	Rye
Cattle	Hemp	Sheep
Dog	Horse	Wheat

Yam, oil palm

Cat (Egypt)

Chickens (south-central Asia)

4000	3000	2000	1000 Years Ago

Marsh elder
Sunflower
Squash

Lamb's quarters

Maize

North America

White potato

MAP 9

Ancient Civilizations of the Old World

North
Sea

Kumbi Saleh

Ghana
A.D. 800–1076

Songhay/Songhai
A.D. 1325–1550

Mali
A.D. 1230–1500

Jenne-jeno
2200 B.P.–
1000 B.P. (A.D. 1000)

*ATLANTIC
OCEAN*

Archaic states developed in many parts of the Old World at different periods. The earliest civilizations, such as Mesopotamia, Egypt, and the Indus Valley, are generally placed at about 5500 B.P. States developed later in Asia, Africa, and the Americas (see Map 13).

QUESTIONS

Look at Map 9, "Ancient Civilizations of the Old World."

1. What contemporary nations would you have to visit if you wanted to see all the places where ancient civilizations developed in the Old World? Would some countries be off limits for political reasons? How do you think such limitations have affected the archaeological record?

2. Of the ancient states shown on Map 9, which developed latest? Why do you think the first states developed when and where they did?

3. In which of the ancient states shown on Map 9 were Middle Eastern domesticates basic to the economy? In which states shown on Map 9 were other domesticates basic to the economy?

Tigris-Euphrates (Mesopotamia and Babylonia)

Nile (Ancient Egypt)

Minoan-Mycenaean

Yellow River (Shang)

Indus-Ganges (Harappan and Vedic Civilizations)

| 5500 | 5000 | 4500 | 4000 | 3500 | 3 |

Years (B.P.)

a-Mycenaean
050 B.P.
Çatal Hüyük

Jericho

**Tigris-Euphrates
(Mesopotamia and
Babylonia)**
5500 B.P.–4000 B.P.

Tell el-Ubaid

**Nile
(Ancient Egypt)**
4920 B.P.–3100 B.P..

Harappa

Mohenjo-daro

**Indus-Ganges
(Harappan and Vedic Civilizations)**
5000 B.P.–2150 B.P.

Caspian Sea

Red Sea

*Arabian
Sea*

Bay of Bengal

Aksum/Axum
?2200 B.P.–1300 B.P. (A.D. 700)

eroe (Nubia)
2591 B.P.–
B.P. (A.D. 325)

imbabwe
.D. 1000–1450

Yellow River (Shang)
4000 B.P.–3027 B.P.

Nok Nok Tha

Khmer
A.D. 802–1218

Funan
A.D. 100–546

Chenla
A.D. 611–802

*Lake
Baikal*

*Sea
of
Okhotsk*

*Sea
of
Japan*

*East
China
Sea*

PACIFIC
OCEAN

*South
China
Sea*

INDIAN OCEAN

**Ancient Civilizations of
the Old World**

- Before 5500 B.P.
- 5500–3000 B.P.
- 4100–3000 B.P.
- After 2600 B.P.

Funan

Meroe (Nubia)

Aksum/Axum

Chenia

Jenne-jeno

Ghana

Khmer

Rome

Zimbabwe

Mali

Songhay/Songhai

| 2500 | 2000 | 1500
(500 A.D) | 1000
(1000 A.D) | 500
(1500 A.D) |

Years (B.P.)

MAP 10
Ethnographic Study Sites Prior to 1950

The development of anthropology as a scientific discipline can be traced to the middle to late part of the 19th century. In cultural anthropology, ethnographic field work became usual and common during the early 20th century. American ethnographers turned to the study of Native Americans, while European anthropologists often studied people living in world areas, such as Africa, which had been conquered and/or colonized by the anthropologist's nation of origin.

QUESTIONS

Look at Map 10, "Ethnographic Study Sites Prior to 1950."

1. Anthropology originated as the scientific study of nonwestern peoples and cultures. Yet Map 10 shows that many anthropological studies conducted prior to 1950 were done in North America. What societies were being studied in North America? Were they considered western or nonwestern? What does this tell us about the concept of "western"?

2. How would you describe the range of ethnographic sites prior to 1950? Were some world areas being neglected, such as the Middle East or mainland Asia? What might be the reasons for such omissions?

3. Think about how changes in transportation and communication have affected the way anthropologists do their research. How might a list of contemporary ethnographic sites contrast with the distribution shown in Map 10. How has longitudinal research been affected by changes in transportation and communication?

Ethnographic Study Sites Prior to 1950

North America

1. Eastern Eskimo
2. Central Eskimo
3. Naskapi
4. Iroquois
5. Delaware
6. Natchez
7. Shawnee
8. Kickapoo
9. Sioux
10. Crow
11. Nez Percé
12. Shoshone
13. Paviotso
14. Kwakiutl
15. Tsimshian
16. Haida
17. Tlingit
18. Navajo
19. Hopi
20. Zuñi
21. Aztec
22. Tzintzuntzan and Cuanajo
23. Maya
24. Cherokee
25. San Pedro

South America

Ecuador
26. Jívaro

Peru
27. Inca
28. Machiguenga
29. Achuara
30. Campa

Bolivia
31. Aymara

Chile
32. Yahgan

Venezuela
33. Yanomamö

Brazil
34. Tapirapé
35. Mundurucu
36. Mehinacu
37. Kuikuru
38. Caingang

Africa

Ghana
39. Ashanti

Nigeria
40. Kadar

Sudan
41. Fur
42. Dinka
43. Nuer
44. Azande

Uganda
45. Bunyoro
46. Ganda

Dem. Rep. of Congo
47. Mbuti

Rwanda
48. Watusi

Kenya
49. Masai

Tanzania
50. Nyakyusa
51. Lovedu

Zambia
52. Ndembu
53. Barotse

Mozambique
54. Bathonga

South Africa
55. !Kung Bushmen
56. Zulu

Asia

Sri Lanka
57. Vedda
58. Sinhalese

India
59. Andaman
60. Nayar
61. Tamil
62. Rajput

Siberia
63. Tungus

Japan
64. Ainu

China
65. Luts'un village

Taiwan
66. Taiwan Chinese

Vietnam
67. Mnong-Gar

Malaya
68. Semai

Pacific

Philippines
69. Tasaday

Indonesia Area
70. Dyaks
71. Alorese
72. Tetum

Australia
73. Tiwi
74. Arunta
75. Murngin
76. Saibai Islanders

New Guinea
77. Arapesh
78. Dani
79. Gururumba
80. Kai
81. Kapauku
82. Mae Enga
83. Kuma
84. Mundugumor
85. Tchambuli
86. Tsembaga Maring
87. Tavade
88. Foré
89. Etoro

Melanesian Islands

90. Manus Islanders
91. New Hanover Islanders
92. Trobriand Islanders
93. Dobuans
94. Rossel Islanders
95. Kaoka
96. Malaita Islanders
97. Espiritu Santo Islanders
98. Tana Islanders
99. Tikopia
100. Sivai

Polynesian Islands

101. Maori
102. Tongans
103. Samoans
104. Mangians
105. Tahitians
106. Hawaiians

Micronesian Islands

107. Truk

MAP 11
Major Families
of World Languages

Language, like religion, is an important identifying and distinguishing characteristic of culture. Knowing the distribution of the major world languages and language families helps us understand some of the reasons behind important current events. In areas that have emerged from recent colonial rule, for example, the participants in conflicts over territory and power are often defined in terms of linguistic groups. Language distributions also help us understand our past by providing clues that enable us to chart the course of human migrations, as is suggested by the distribution of Indo-European, Austronesian, and Hamito-Semitic languages.

QUESTIONS

Look at Map 11, "Major Families of World Languages."

1. Name three language families or subfamilies that are spoken on more than one continent. How do you explain this distribution?

2. Where are the Austronesian languages spoken? How might one explain this distribution?

3. What language families are spoken on the African continent? Locate the Niger-Congo language family, of which the Bantu languages comprise a subfamily.

Major Families of World Languages

Indo-European
1 Germanic	6 Indo-Aryan
2 Romance	7 Celtic
3 Slavic	8 Greek
4 Baltic	9 Armenian
5 Iranian	

Eskimo-Aleut
Native American
Hamito-Semitic
Niger-Congo
Nilo-Saharan
Austronesian
Australian
Samoyed
Finno-Ugric
Basque
Khoisan
Ural-Altaic

Caucasian
Sino-Tibetan
Paleo-Siberian
Korean
Japanese
Burushaski
Austro-Asiatic
Vietnamese
Thai-Kadai
Papuan
Dravidian
Unpopulated Regions

MAP 12
World Land Use,
C.E. 1500

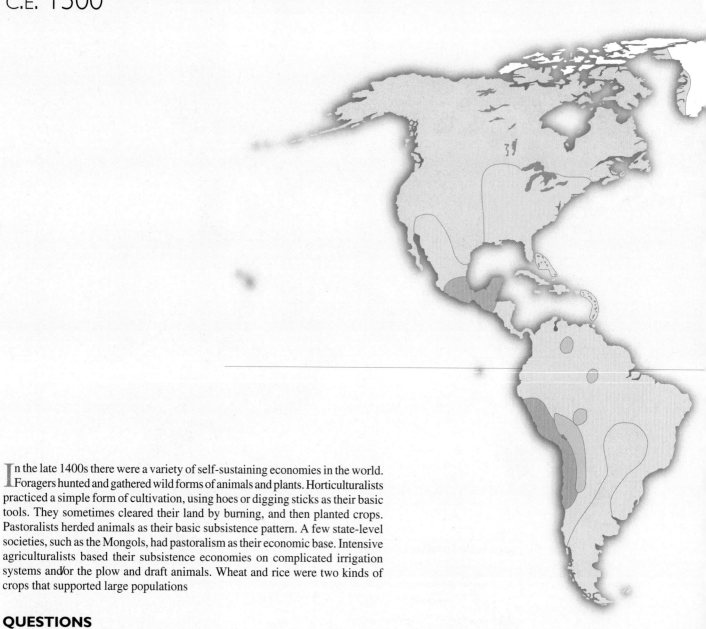

In the late 1400s there were a variety of self-sustaining economies in the world. Foragers hunted and gathered wild forms of animals and plants. Horticulturalists practiced a simple form of cultivation, using hoes or digging sticks as their basic tools. They sometimes cleared their land by burning, and then planted crops. Pastoralists herded animals as their basic subsistence pattern. A few state-level societies, such as the Mongols, had pastoralism as their economic base. Intensive agriculturalists based their subsistence economies on complicated irrigation systems and/or the plow and draft animals. Wheat and rice were two kinds of crops that supported large populations

QUESTIONS

Look at Map 12, "World Land Use, C.E. 1500."

1. Name three continents with significant herding economies. On which continents was pastoralism absent?

2. How do the various types of agriculture vary among the continents? Which continent had the largest area under intensive cultivation? Which continent or continents had the least amount of intensive cultivation?

3. What were the main uses of land in Europe when the European age of discovery and conquest began?

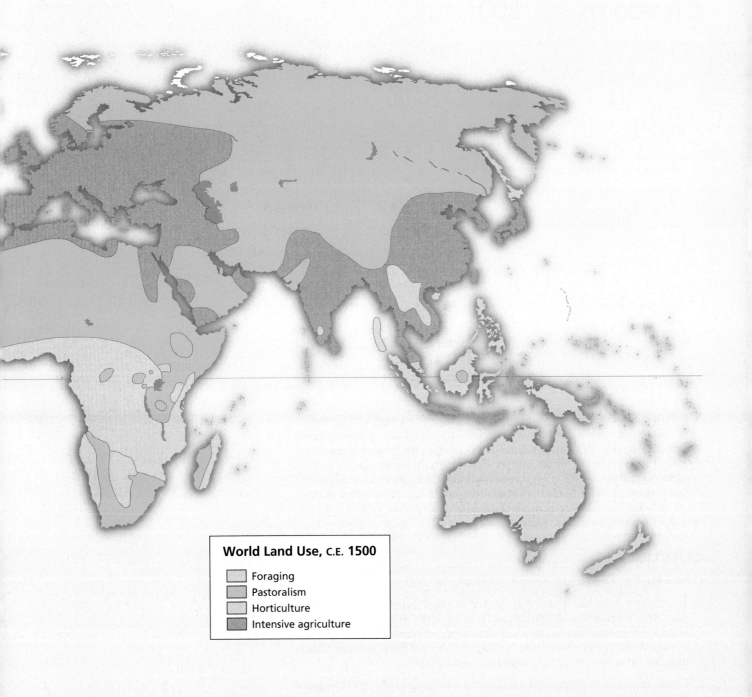

World Land Use, C.E. 1500

- Foraging
- Pastoralism
- Horticulture
- Intensive agriculture

MAP 13
Organized States and Chiefdoms, C.E. 1500

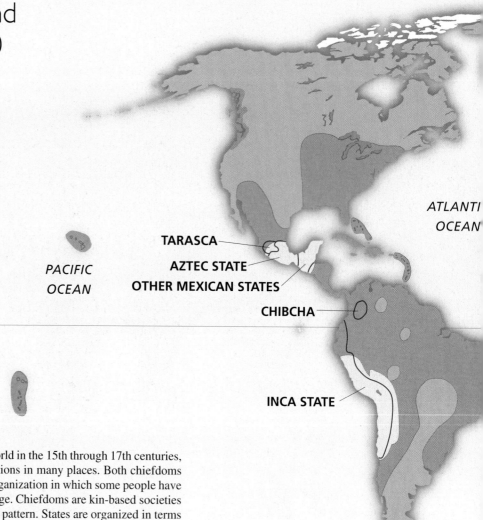

When Europeans started exploring the world in the 15th through 17th centuries, they found complex political organizations in many places. Both chiefdoms and states are large-scale forms of political organization in which some people have privileged access to power, wealth, and prestige. Chiefdoms are kin-based societies in which redistribution is the major economic pattern. States are organized in terms of socioeconomic classes, headed by a centralized government that is led by an elite. States include a full-time bureaucracy and specialized subsystems for such activities as military action, taxation, and social control.

QUESTIONS

Look at Map 13, "Organized States and Chiefdoms, C.E. 1500."

1. Locate and name the states that existed in the Western Hemisphere in C.E. 1500. Compare Map 12, "World Land Use: C.E. 1500," with Map 13. Looking at the Western Hemisphere, can you detect a correlation between land use (and economy) and the existence of states? What's the nature of that correlation? Does that correlation also characterize other parts of the world?

2. Locate three regions of the world where chiefdoms existed in C.E. 1500. Compare Map 12, "World Land Use: C.E. 1500," with Map 13. Can you detect a correlation between land use (and economy) and the existence of chiefdoms? What's the nature of that correlation?

3. Some parts of the world lacked either chiefdoms or states in C.E. 1500. What are some of those areas? What kinds of political systems did they probably have?

EUROPEAN STATES

SEMI NOMADIC STATES

JAPAN

PACIFIC OCEAN

ISLAMIC STATES

CHINA

INDIAN STATES

SONGHAI

KANEM-BORNU

ETHIOPIA

PHILIPPINES

HINDU/ MUSLIM STATES

NEW GUINEA

Ceylon

Malaya

Strait of Malacca

Moluccas

OYO BENIN

Sumatra

KONGO

Zanzibar

LUBA

Kilwa

Java

THE EAST INDIES

INDIAN OCEAN

AUSTRALIA

Sofala

MONOMATAPA

Organized States and Chiefdoms, C.E. **1500**

No chiefdoms or states

Chiefdoms

States

MAP 14

Female/Male Inequality in Education and Employment

Inuit

Hidatsa

Iroquois

Pawnee

Aremb

Women in developed countries have made significant advances in socioeconomic status in recent years. In most of the world, however, females suffer from significant inequality when compared with their male counterparts. Although women can vote in most countries, in over 90 percent of those countries that right was granted only during the last 50 years. In most regions, literacy rates for women still fall far short of those for men. In Africa and Asia, for example, only about half as many women are as literate as men. Inequalities in education and employment are perhaps the most telling indicators of the unequal status of women in most of the world. Even where women are employed in positions similar to those held by men, they tend to receive less compensation. The gap between rich and poor involves not only a clear geographic differentiation, but a clear gender differentiation as well.

QUESTIONS

Look at Map 14 "Female/Male Inequality in Education and Employment."

1. Locate and name three Third World countries with the same degree of gender-based inequality as the United States and Canada.

2. Two of the world's largest developing nations are coded as having "less inequality." What are they?

3. Most European countries are coded as having "least inequality." Which western European countries are exceptions?

Female/Male Inequality in Education and Employment

- Least inequality
- Less inequality
- Average inequality
- More inequality
- Most inequality
- No data

Wadaabe

Igbo

Azande

Mbuti 'pygmies'

Ju/'hoansi San

Betsileo

Bangalore
(Bengaluru)

Ilongots

Agta

Negeri Sembilan

Minangkabau

Etoro, Kaluli, and Sambia

MAP 15
World Religions

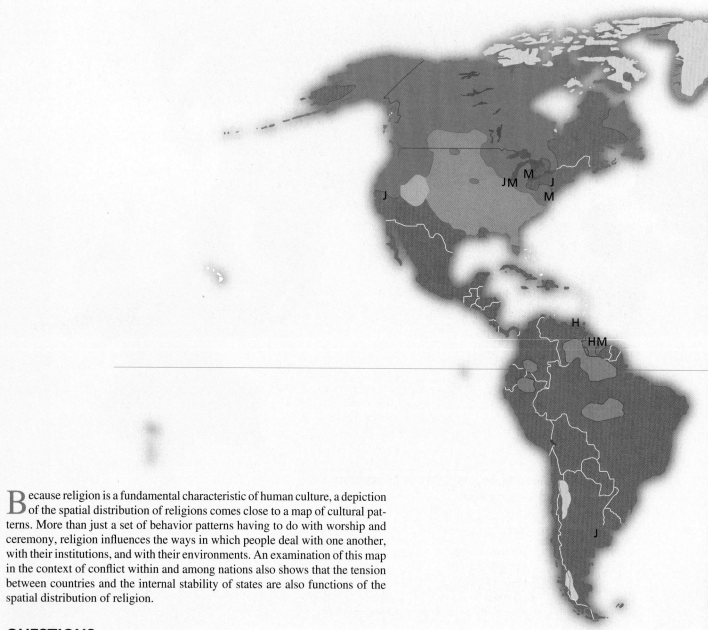

Because religion is a fundamental characteristic of human culture, a depiction of the spatial distribution of religions comes close to a map of cultural patterns. More than just a set of behavior patterns having to do with worship and ceremony, religion influences the ways in which people deal with one another, with their institutions, and with their environments. An examination of this map in the context of conflict within and among nations also shows that the tension between countries and the internal stability of states are also functions of the spatial distribution of religion.

QUESTIONS

Look at Map 15, "World Religions."

1. Which continent has the most diversity with respect to the major religions?

2. Which continent is most Protestant? Why do you think that is the case?

3. Where in the world are "tribal" religions still practiced?

Predominant Religions

Christianity (C)*
- Roman Catholic
- Protestant
- Mormon (LDS)
- Eastern Churches
- Mixed

Islam (M)
- Sunni
- Shi'a

Buddhism (B)
- Hinayanistic
- Lamaistic

Hinduism (H)

Judaism (J)

Sikhism

Animism (Tribal)

Chinese Complex
(Confucianism, Taoism, and Buddhism)

Korean Complex
(Buddhism, Confucianism, Christianity, and Chondogyo)

Japanese Complex
(Shinto and Buddhism)

Vietnamese Complex
(Buddhism, Taoism, Confucianism, and Cao Dai)

Unpopulated Regions

*Capital letters indicate the presence of locally important minority adherents of nonpredominant faiths.

MAP 16

Total Annual Energy Consumption by Country

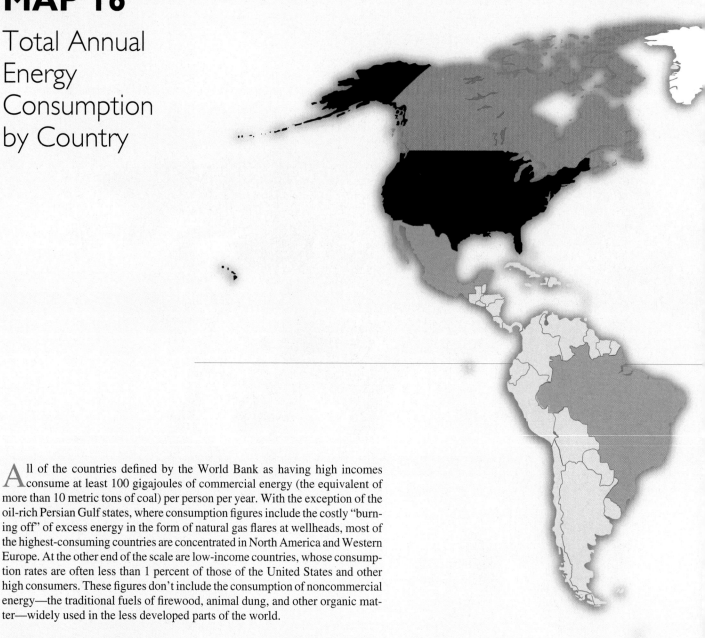

All of the countries defined by the World Bank as having high incomes consume at least 100 gigajoules of commercial energy (the equivalent of more than 10 metric tons of coal) per person per year. With the exception of the oil-rich Persian Gulf states, where consumption figures include the costly "burning off" of excess energy in the form of natural gas flares at wellheads, most of the highest-consuming countries are concentrated in North America and Western Europe. At the other end of the scale are low-income countries, whose consumption rates are often less than 1 percent of those of the United States and other high consumers. These figures don't include the consumption of noncommercial energy—the traditional fuels of firewood, animal dung, and other organic matter—widely used in the less developed parts of the world.

QUESTIONS

Look at Map 16, " Total Annual Energy Consumption by Country." What five countries are the world's foremost energy consumers? Does this mean that the average person in each of these countries consumes more energy than the average European? Why or why not?

1. Compare energy consumption in Europe and North America. Do all European countries consume energy at the same rate as the United States and Canada?

2. What are some exceptions to the generalization that the highest rates of energy consumption are in core countries, with the lowest rates on the periphery?

3. How is energy consumption related to measures of the quality of life, as shown in Map 17?

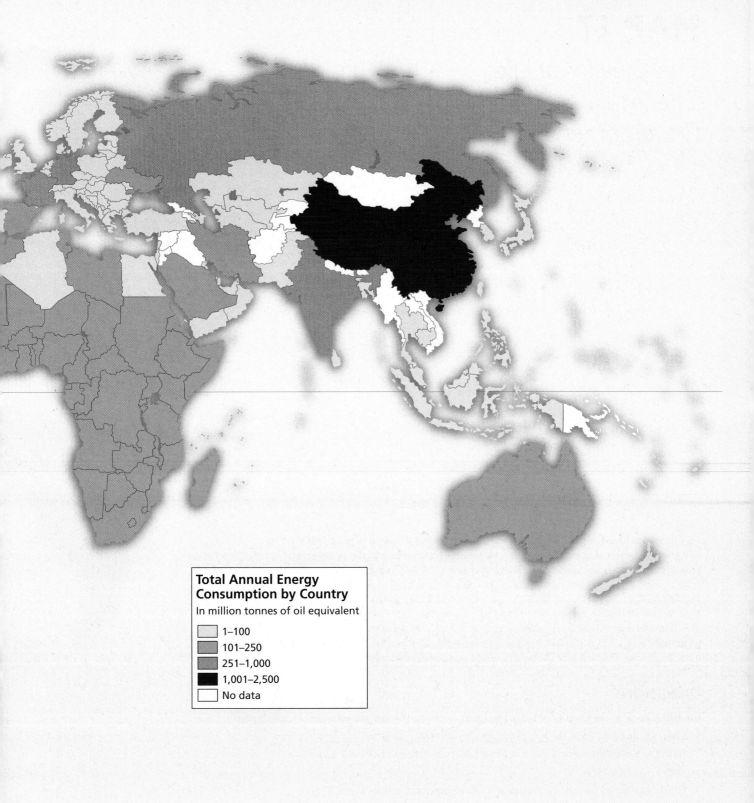

Total Annual Energy Consumption by Country

In million tonnes of oil equivalent

- 1–100
- 101–250
- 251–1,000
- 1,001–2,500
- No data

MAP 17

The Quality of Life: The Index of Human Development, 2007

This map is based on a development index that considers a wide variety of demographic, health, and educational data, including population growth, per capita gross domestic income, longevity, literacy, and years of schooling. Compared with earlier years, there has been substantial improvement in the quality of life in Middle and South America. Africa and South Asia, however, face the challenge of providing basic access to health care, education, and jobs for rapidly increasing populations. This map illustrates an enduring difference in quality of life between those who inhabit the world's equatorial and tropical regions and those fortunate enough to live in the temperate zones, where the quality of life is significantly higher.

QUESTIONS

Look at Map 17, "The Quality of Life: The Index of Human Development, 2007."

1. What countries in central and South America have Human Development Index (HDI) scores comparable to those of some European nations? Does this surprise you?

2. Given that Brazil has one of the world's top 10 economies, does its HDI score surprise you? How do Brazil, Mexico, and Venezuela compare in terms of the HDI?

3. Do you notice a correlation between deforestation (Map 1) and quality of life? Does India fit this correlation?

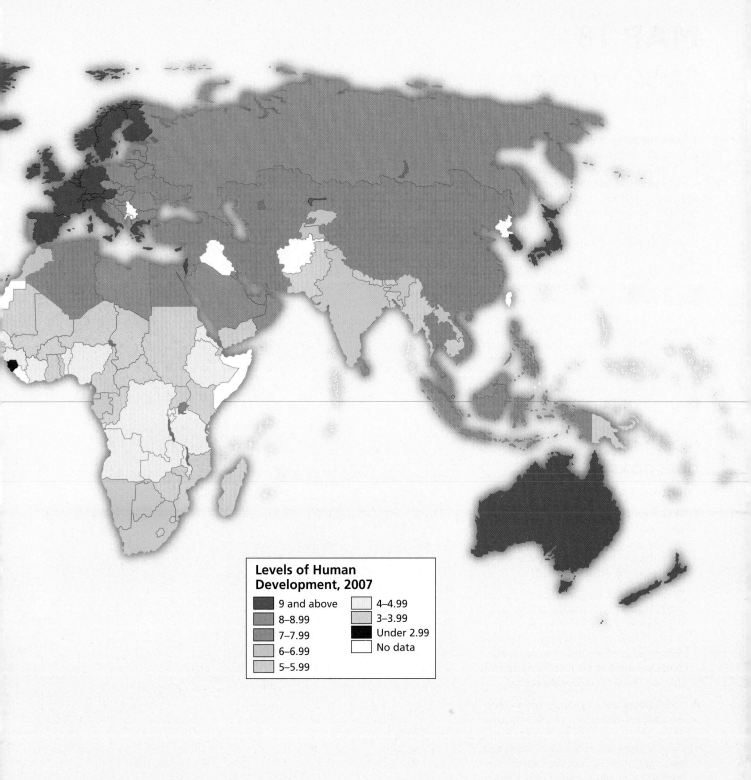

Levels of Human Development, 2007

■ 9 and above		▢ 4–4.99	
■ 8–8.99		▢ 3–3.99	
■ 7–7.99		■ Under 2.99	
▢ 6–6.99		▢ No data	
▢ 5–5.99			

MAP 18
Global Warming

Since the early 20th century, the Earth's surface temperatures have risen about 1.4° F (0.7° C). Rising temperatures, shrinking glaciers, and melting polar ice provide additional evidence for global warming. Scientists prefer the term climate change to *global warming*. Scientific measurements confirm that global warming is not due to increased solar radiation, but rather are mainly *anthropogenic*—caused by humans and their activities. Because our planet's climate is always changing, the key question becomes: How much global warming is due to human activities versus natural climate variability. Most scientists agree that human activities play a major role in global climate change. Given population growth and rapidly increasing use of fossil fuels, the human factor is significant. The map represents the relative impact of global warming in different regions of the world.

QUESTIONS

Look at Map 18, "Global Warming."

1. Which geographical regions of the world show noticeable effects of global warming? Which show the least? What about the polar regions? Why are certain major sections of the oceans affected?

2. Widespread and long-term trends toward warmer global temperatures and a changing climate are referred to as "fingerprints." Researchers look for them to detect and confirm that climate change. What are some of the recent fingerprints that have been covered in the media?

3. "Harbingers" refer to such events as fires, exceptional droughts, and downpours. They can also include the spread of disease-bearing insects and widespread bleaching of coral reefs. Any and all may be directly or partly caused by a warmer climate. Have you noticed any recent harbingers in the U.S. in the past year? Have they been confined to any specific geographical regions?

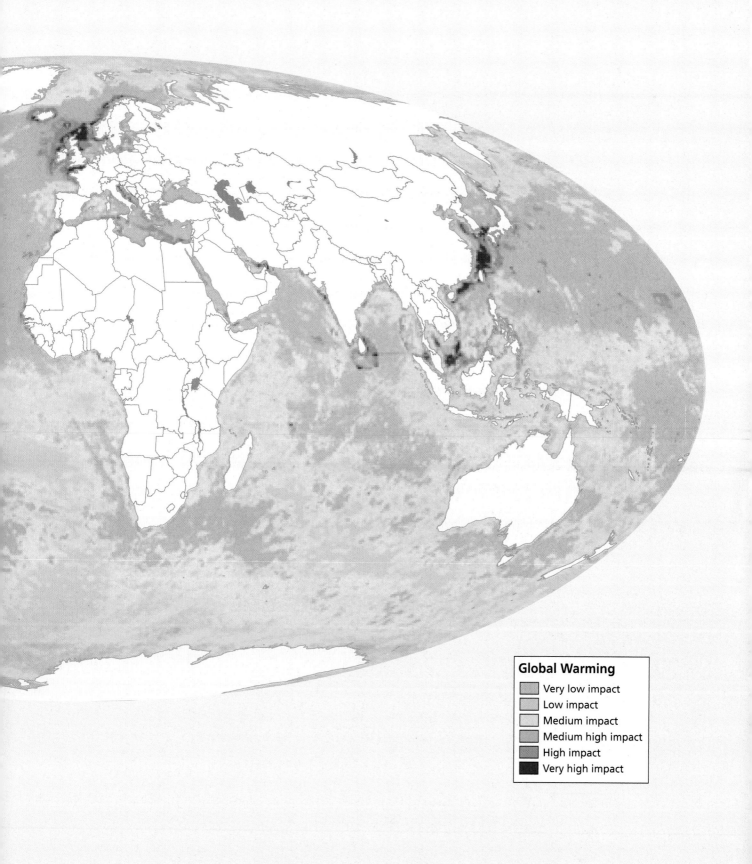

Global Warming

- Very low impact
- Low impact
- Medium impact
- Medium high impact
- High impact
- Very high impact